PORT OF SPAIN

PORT OF SPAIN

The Construction of a Caribbean City, 1888–1962

STEPHEN STUEMPFLE

The University of the West Indies Press
Jamaica • Barbados • Trinidad and Tobago

The University of the West Indies Press
7A Gibraltar Hall Road, Mona
Kingston 7, Jamaica
www.uwipress.com

© 2018 by Stephen Stuempfle
All rights reserved. Published 2018

A catalogue record of this book is available from the National Library of Jamaica.

ISBN: 978-976-640-663-9 (print)
978-976-640-664-6 (Kindle)
978-976-640-665-3 (ePub)

Cover photograph: Frederick Street at Marine Square, Port of Spain, 1930s.
Courtesy Allen Morrison.
Cover design by The Invisible Creative, theinvisibleisland.com.
Book design by Robert Harris.
Set in Adobe Garamond Pro 11/14.5 x 24.

Printed in the United States of America.

The University of the West Indies Press has no responsibility for the persistence or accuracy of URLs for external or third-party Internet websites referred to in this publication and does not guarantee that any content on such websites is, or will remain, accurate or appropriate.

FOR DENISE,
AND IN MEMORY OF HERMAN G. STUEMPFLE JR

CONTENTS

List of Illustrations | viii

Acknowledgements | xi

List of Abbreviations | xiii

Introduction | 1

PART 1. THE COCOA BOOM ERA, 1888–1920

1. The Components of the City | 34

2. The City as a Whole | 78

PART 2. THE INTERWAR ERA, 1920–1940

3. The Enhancement of the City | 117

4. The Housing and Lives of Working People | 153

5. The Spatiality of Carnival | 188

PART 3. WORLD WAR II AND THE POSTWAR YEARS, 1940–1962

6. The City at War | 229

7. The Landscape of Independence | 273

8. Modern Architecture for an Emerging Nation | 311

Conclusion | 354

Notes | 373

Bibliography | 439

Index | 457

ILLUSTRATIONS

MAPS

1. The Caribbean | xiv
2. Trinidad and Tobago | xv
3. Port of Spain and suburbs to the north and west, 1912 | xvi
4. Downtown Port of Spain, 1912 | xvii
5. Port of Spain and suburbs, 1962 | xviii

FIGURES

Part 1. The Cocoa Boom Era, 1888–1920

1. Harbour and Queen's Wharf | 22
2. Marine Square at Frederick Street | 23
3. Frederick Street at Marine Square | 24
4. Brunswick Square | 25
5. The Red House | 26
6. Eastern downtown Port of Spain from the Laventille Hills | 27
7. The Queen's Park Savannah | 28
8. Government House and a portion of the Botanic Gardens | 29
9. Piccadilly Street at the bottom of Calvary Hill | 30
10. 95 Woodford Street at Marli Street, New Town | 31
11. Boissière House, 12 Queen's Park West | 32
12. Water protest at Brunswick Square and the Red House, 1903 | 33

Part 2. The Interwar Era, 1920–1940

13. Trinidad War Memorial | 108
14. New Railway Headquarters | 109

15. Treasury Building | 110
16. Queen's Park Hotel, with central addition | 111
17. Metro Cinema | 112
18. De Luxe Theatre | 113
19. Plan of barrack yards | 114
20. Barrack yard | 115
21. Carnival, Marine Square at Frederick Street, 1920s | 116

Part 3. World War II and the Postwar Years, 1940–1962

22. Docksite, US Army | 218
23. Barracks, St Clair Cantonment, US Army | 219
24. USO No. 2, Mucurapo | 220
25. Gonzales Rhythm Makers, Leotaud Street, Gonzales | 221
26. PNM March for Chaguaramas, 1960 | 221
27. Government flats on Duncan Street | 222
28. Perspective drawing of house in Diamond Vale | 223
29. New Town Hall | 224
30. Queen's Hall | 225
31. Trinidad Hilton Hotel | 226
32. Paschim Kaashi Hindu Mandir | 227
33. Aerial view of Port of Spain and harbour | 228

ACKNOWLEDGEMENTS

I TRAVELLED FROM THE UNITED STATES to Trinidad for the first time in 1987, in order to carry out a study of the history and contemporary manifestation of steelbands. A year and a half's residence in Port of Spain enabled me to learn much about these musical ensembles and to gain familiarity with the whole way of life in this complex locale. During this period and subsequent visits on a roughly annual basis, I became increasingly fascinated by the spatial organization of the city, its architectural traditions, and its inhabitants' detailed knowledge of their environment. By the mid-2000s, I had decided to write a book about the cultural history of the city, which was changing rapidly as the result of a building boom. I began conducting extensive research in local archives, while also photographing the contemporary landscape. Through these investigations, I gradually discerned patterns in the development of the city, which are suggested in the following pages.

My work on this project has been greatly facilitated by many people. First, thanks are due to the National Archives of Trinidad and Tobago staff, who cordially accommodated me for over a decade in their St Vincent Street premises in the heart of Port of Spain. I am also grateful for assistance from staff at various other institutions: the Heritage Library of the National Library of Trinidad and Tobago; the West Indiana and Special Collections Division of the Alma Jordan Library, University of the West Indies, St Augustine; Herman B Wells Library, Indiana University, Bloomington; Richter Library, University of Miami; George A. Smathers Libraries, University of Florida; New York Public Library; and the National Archives of the United States.

Many other individuals offered information, assistance or general encouragement in the course of my research. In Trinidad, I am particularly grateful to Joanne Beckles, David Benjamin, Gérard and Alice Besson, Bridget Brereton, Adrian Camps-Campins, Christopher Cozier, Patricia Dardaine-Ragguet, Carol De Merieux, Sonja Dumas, Patrice Kareem, Kim Johnson, Christopher Laird, Annelize Lemessy, Brian Lewis, Kendall Lewis, Geoffrey MacLean, Antoinette Maund, Eric McAllister, Lystra Parke, Judy Raymond, Rudylynn Roberts, Yvonne Roberts-White, Irénée Shaw, Grace Steele, Gordon and Betty

Rohlehr, Jeanne Roseman, Margaret Thompson and Dion Wilson. I also thank Ray Allen, Pam Everett, Michael Foster, Ray Funk, Henry Glassie, Aisha Khan, Allen Morrison, Ivar Oxaal, Elton Perot, Laurie Russell, Pravina Shukla and Michiko Suzuki. Between 1995 and 2007, I was employed as a curator at the Historical Museum of Southern Florida (HistoryMiami Museum) and benefited much from working with colleagues (especially archivists Dawn Hugh and Rebecca Smith) and guest curators (especially Jean-François Lejeune and Allan Shulman).

As this study moved towards publication, I had the pleasure of working with Joseph Powell and the other excellent staff at the University of the West Indies Press. Special thanks also to Erin Greb for drawing the maps of Port of Spain and to Robert Harris for designing the book.

Finally, I have received much support over the years from my family in the United States and from an extended circle of Trinidadian in-laws (encompassing Stephensons and Tobys). This book is dedicated to my late father, Herman G. Stuempfle Jr, whose interest in cities was boundless, and to Denise Stephenson Stuempfle – a child of Belmont, dutiful daughter of Cascade, and my consort in the city and beyond. Denise helped me discover Port of Spain in the late 1980s and was the first to assess my story of the place thirty years later.

ABBREVIATIONS

ICC	Independence Celebrations Committee
IDC	Industrial Development Corporation
MGM	Metro-Goldwyn-Mayer
NWCSA	Negro Welfare Cultural and Social Association
PNM	People's National Movement
POSG	*Port-of-Spain Gazette*
TECA	Teachers' Economic and Cultural Association
TG	*Trinidad Guardian*
TLP	Trinidad Labour Party
TNT	*Trinidad News Tips*
TWA	Trinidad Workingmen's Association
USED	US Engineer Department
USO	United Services Organization

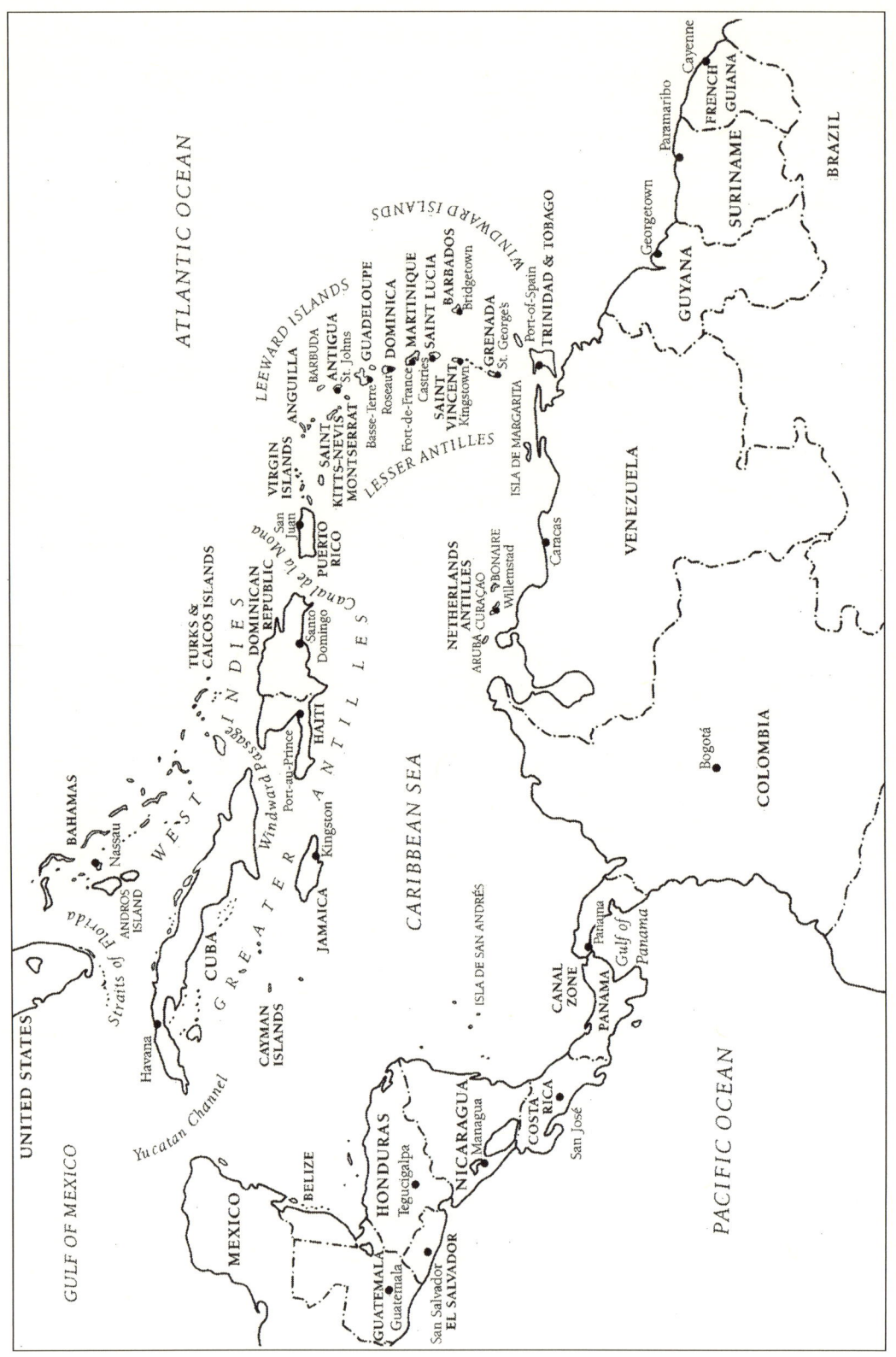

Map 1. The Caribbean. Reprinted from *The Modern Caribbean*, edited by Franklin W. Knight and Colin A. Palmer. Copyright © 1989 by the University of North Carolina Press. Used by permission of the publisher.

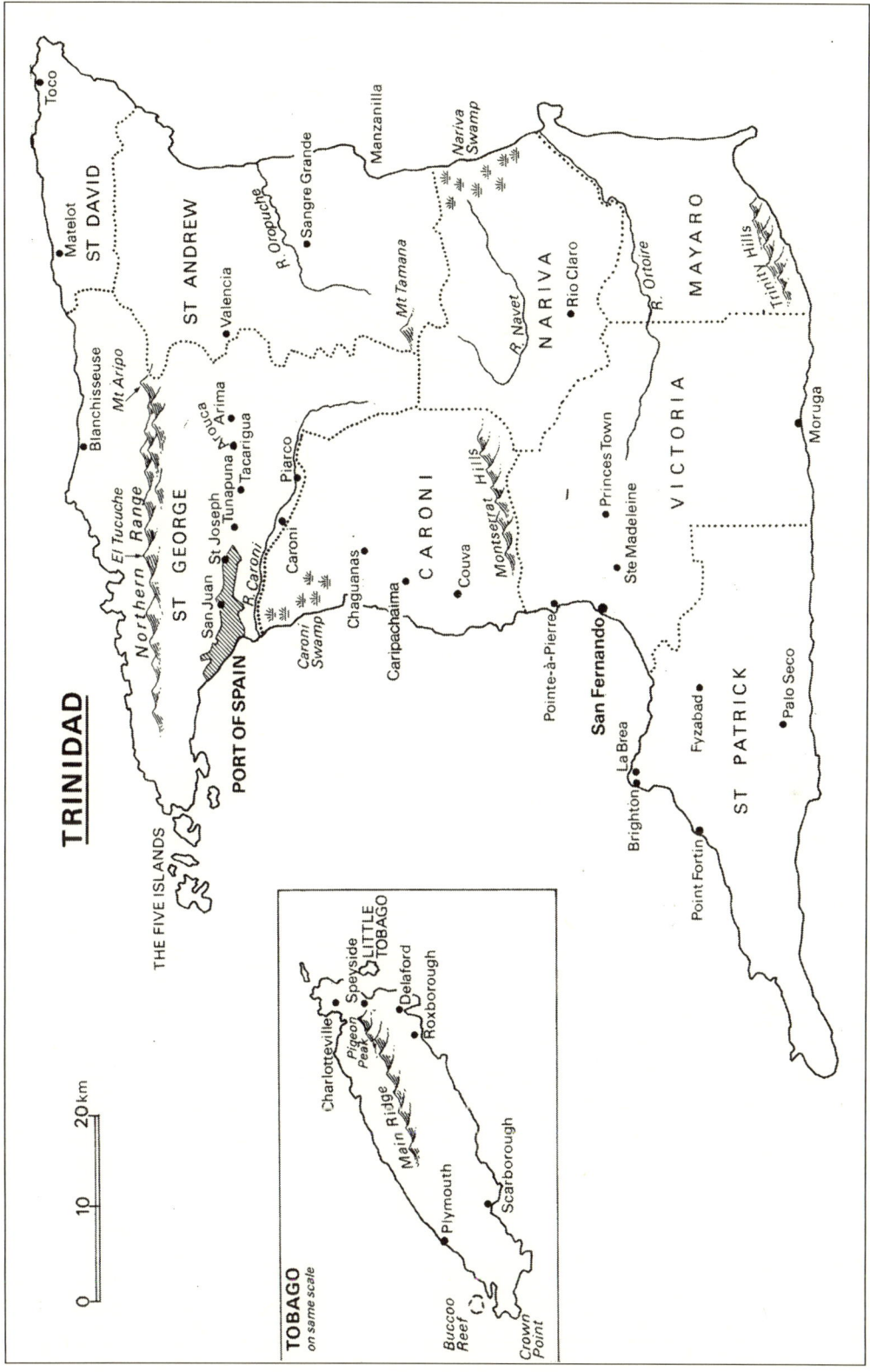

Map 2. Trinidad and Tobago. Reprinted from *A History of Modern Trinidad, 1783–1962*, by Bridget Brereton (Kingston: Heinemann, 1981). Shaded area shows the main portion of the Port of Spain metropolitan area, circa 1980. Courtesy Bridget Brereton.

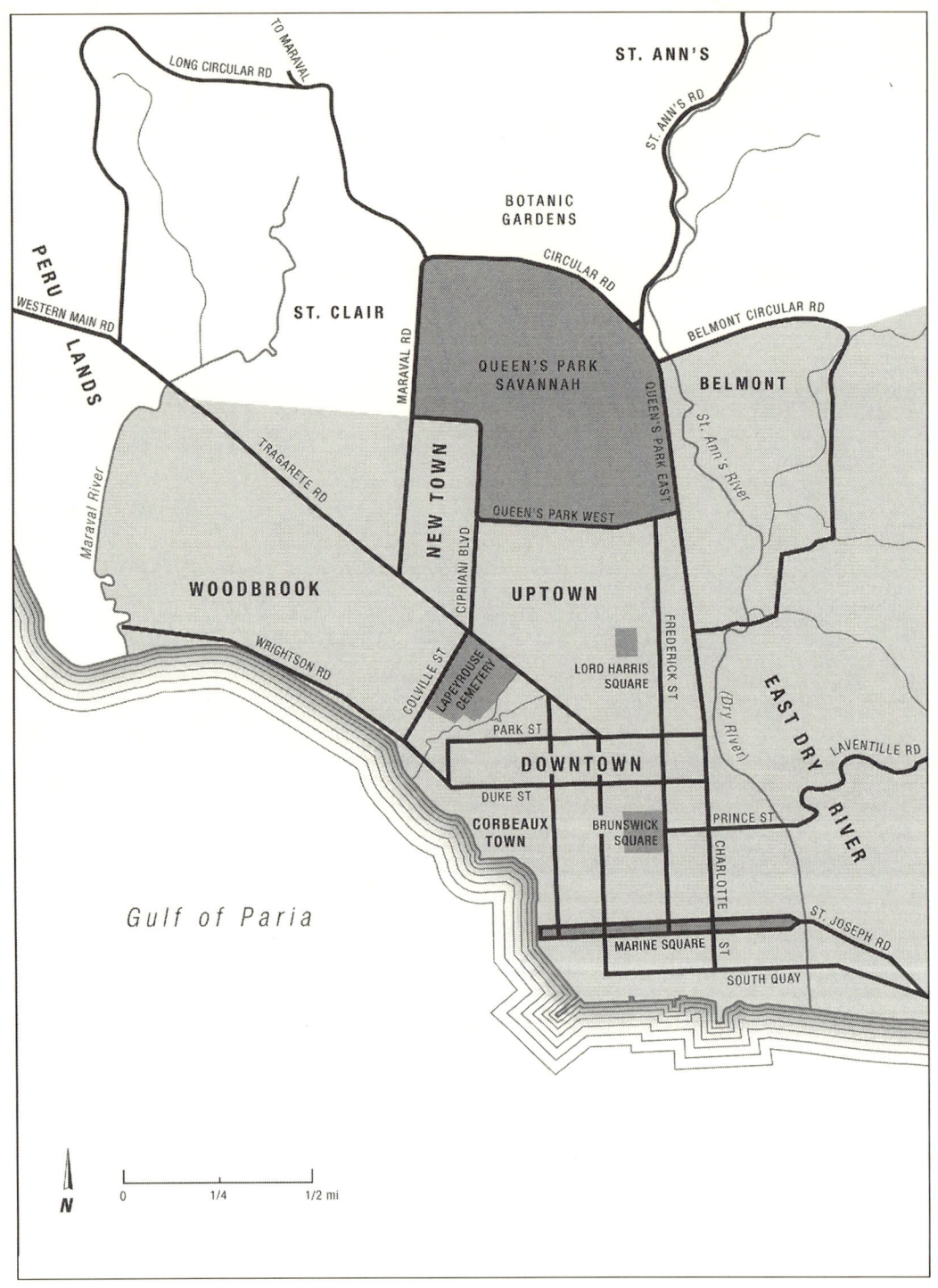

Map 3. Port of Spain and suburbs to the north and west, 1912. Based on *Plan of Port of Spain and Suburbs*, by J. Girod (Port of Spain: Muir, Marshall and Company, 1912). Map drawn by Erin Greb.

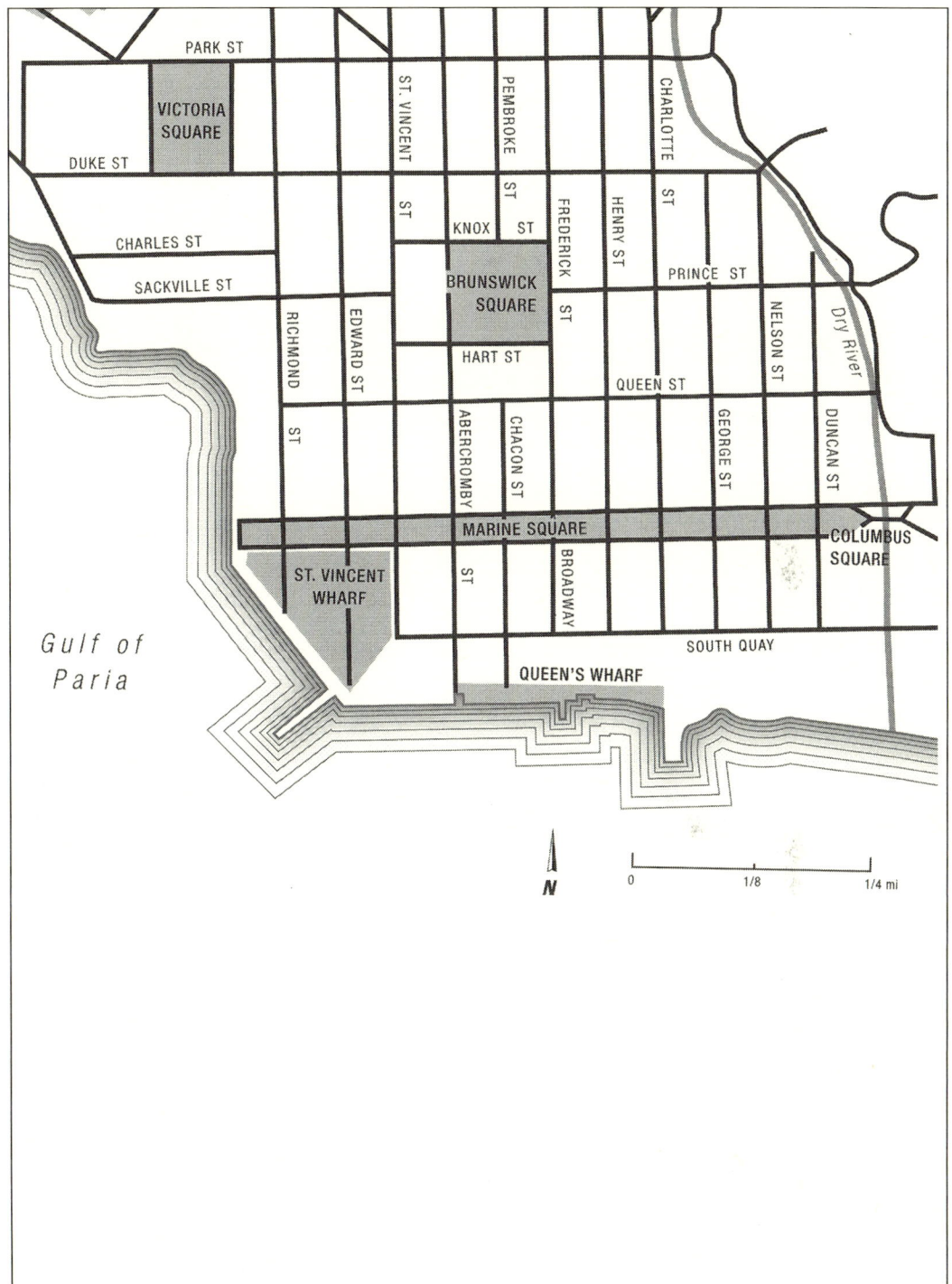

Map 4. Downtown Port of Spain, 1912. Based on *Plan of Port of Spain and Suburbs*, by J. Girod (Port of Spain: Muir, Marshall and Company, 1912). Map drawn by Erin Greb.

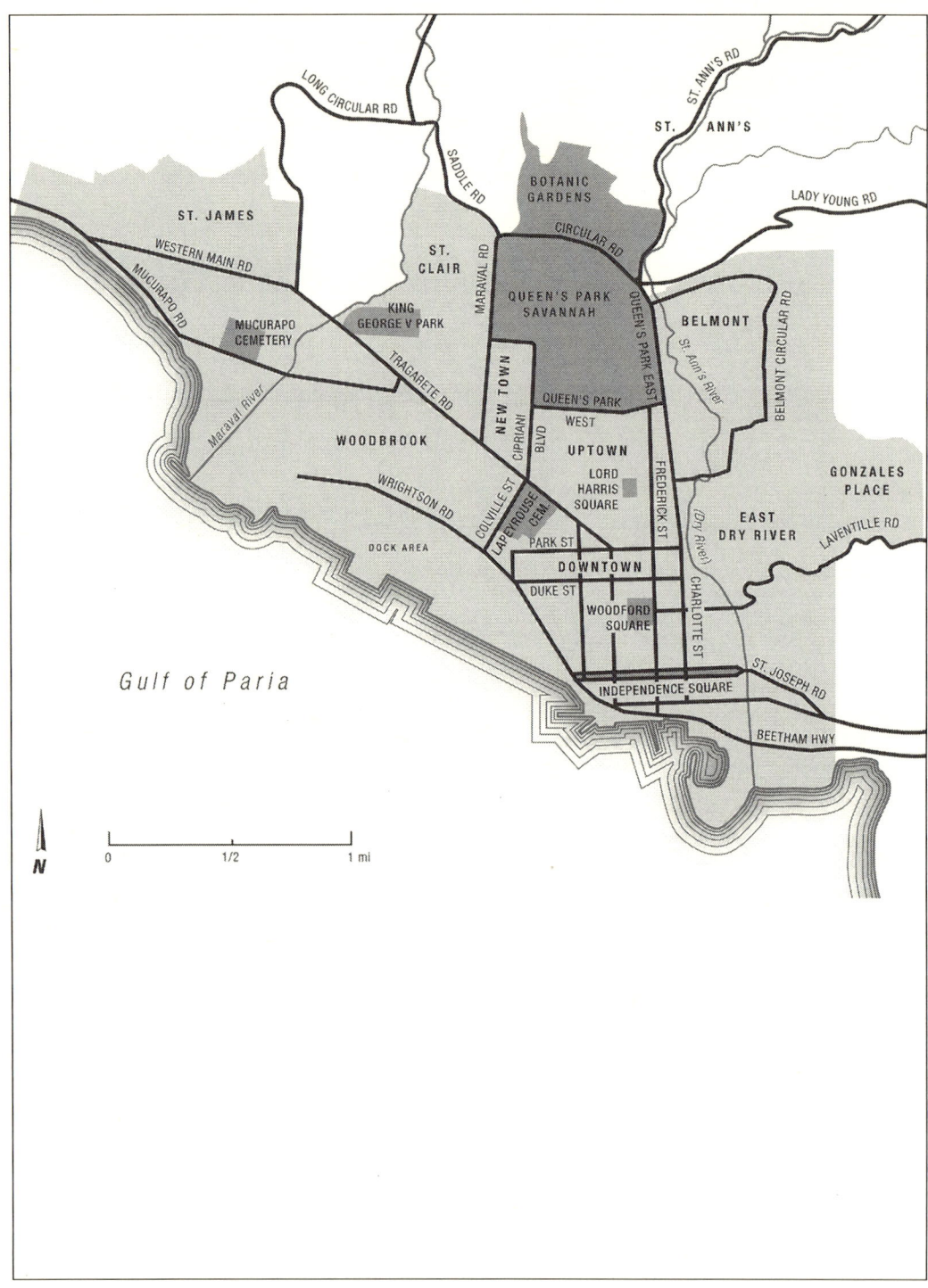

Map 5. Port of Spain and suburbs, 1962. Based on *Sketch Map of Port of Spain*, by Trinidad and Tobago Lands and Surveys Department (Trinidad: Lands and Surveys Litho., 1962). Map drawn by Erin Greb.

INTRODUCTION

POSITIONED ON THE GULF OF PARIA at the southern end of the Caribbean, Port of Spain, Trinidad, has long enthralled its diverse residents and visitors from many lands. It is a city of modest size that extends for a few square miles across a relatively flat plain on Trinidad's northwest coast, surrounded by the sea on the south and steep hills on the north and east. Across the gulf to the west is Venezuela and, farther south, the mouth of the Orinoco River. Lush tropical foliage covers much of the hills and lower-lying area, providing a degree of shade to yards, squares and a dense network of narrow streets. Throughout the day and into the night, these spaces are filled with the city's inhabitants – a people that traces its ancestry to western and central Africa, India, China, Britain, France, Spain, Portugal, Syria and Lebanon, as well as to many places around the Caribbean. Life within the city is generally noisy and often contentious, but, while much seems difficult, much more seems possible. There is ongoing construction of new buildings, commerce ranging from street vending to the transactions of business conglomerates, and instruction within prestigious schools that have offered advancement for generations of youths. Though the city is notably famous for its pre-Lenten Carnival with its masqueraders, calypsonians and steelbands, there are many other visual artists, musicians, dancers, actors and writers at work throughout the year. After all, this is a place that nurtured the careers of C.L.R. James, man of letters and world revolutionary; Eric Williams, Caribbean historian and first prime minister of the twin-island nation-state of Trinidad and Tobago; V.S. Naipaul, winner of the Nobel Prize in Literature in 2001; and St Lucian-born Derek Walcott, winner of the Nobel Prize in Literature in 1992. In reading the books of these and other writers, one can discover a city of brutality and beauty, of confinement and openness, of frustration and pleasure.

A city of this sort can be examined from many perspectives and described in many ways. My objective in this book is to offer a history of the design, use and representation of Port of Spain's landscape from the height of British colonialism during the late nineteenth and early twentieth centuries through the independence of Trinidad and Tobago in 1962. By "landscape" I mean the total material environment of the city – its streets, squares, parks, yards, buildings, monuments and other features. Since an urban landscape offers tangible, multifaceted evidence of how people conceptualize their world and of how this world changes over time, it is an immensely rich subject for investigation. My argument is that the landscape of Port of Spain served as a central site for the display and negotiation of Trinidad's social order during its gradual transition from colonial rule to self-government. In other words, the city's material environment manifested systems of social differentiation and association (along with related configurations of wealth and power) that were fundamental to both colonialism and decolonization. While such patterns were embodied in landscapes throughout Trinidad, they assumed a heightened visibility in Port of Spain, which, as a transportation node and capital, was a focal point of interaction and attention for the territory's populace and visitors. Here people viewed, within a densely built zone, the primary institutions of colonial governance, the leading facilities of commerce, the housing of a range of social classes and a variety of outdoor public spaces employed for leisure, celebration and political expression. Moreover, they constantly recreated this landscape as they envisioned diverse possibilities for the future. Thus the city was experienced as a particularly dynamic locale – a vanguard space of potentiality and innovation within the wider realm of colonial Trinidad.

I begin this study during Trinidad's cocoa boom of the late nineteenth and early twentieth centuries, move through the more challenging era between the world wars and conclude with the general prosperity of the postwar years. An appropriate starting point is 1888, since this was the year that Trinidad observed the fiftieth anniversary of the end of slavery – a multiyear process in the British Caribbean that began in 1834 and concluded in 1838. The seventy-four-year period from this moment of commemoration to independence in 1962 was one of wide-ranging change for Trinidad and for Port of Spain in particular. There was a large increase in the city's population, an extension of its geographic boundaries, economic diversification, construction of an array of new buildings and outdoor spaces, modernization of transportation and utilities, development of a labour movement, expansion of educational opportunities and a middle class, major political reforms and exceptional creativity in literature, music and visual arts.

Throughout this period, British colonialism remained a pervasive force. After Britain captured Trinidad from Spain in 1797, Port of Spain gradually evolved during the nineteenth century from a Spanish colonial city (with a large francophone population) into a city of the British empire. Like other colonial capitals, it served as Trinidad's main point of linkage with London and was the centre of British power and influence. Located here were the headquarters of government agencies, courts and the police; the largest medical, social welfare and educational institutions; and the Catholic and Anglican cathedrals. As a colonial capital, the city's main function was to facilitate the economic exploitation of the territory's landscape, which involved the production (by labourers of mainly African and East Indian descent) of sugar, cocoa and other tropical agricultural commodities, as well as the extraction of asphalt and oil. The city was the principal location for the export of agricultural products, while asphalt and oil were shipped from ports in southern Trinidad. In addition, it was the centre for the import and sale of manufactured goods from Britain and other countries. Thus, the maintenance of Port of Spain as an orderly capital was critical to the ongoing flow of British commerce in Trinidad and the wider Caribbean. It was not until the 1950s that Britain seriously contemplated relinquishing Trinidad as a colony. Its concern then focused on a constitutional transition to independence and continued political influence and economic activity within the framework of the British Commonwealth.

Though British colonialism shaped all aspects of life in Trinidad from the late nineteenth through mid-twentieth century, this was also a period of increasing local empowerment in Port of Spain and the territory. The Port of Spain Borough Council (elected with a limited franchise) served as a centre for political expression during the late nineteenth century, was abolished by the colonial governor in 1898, re-emerged as an elected city council in 1914, and continued to evolve as an arena for the debate and management of municipal affairs. Throughout this period, there were also challenges to Trinidad's crown colony form of government, administered by a governor and a legislative council with no elected representatives. Popular movements and reform initiatives resulted in the introduction of a limited franchise in 1925, elections with universal adult suffrage in 1946, and a gradually increasing number of elected representatives within the legislative council during the transition to self-government. Local empowerment during this period also involved the growth of a vibrant press, the founding of political and labour associations and the development of diverse fraternal and charitable organizations, sports clubs, Carnival bands and other artistic groups. All these organizations were integral to the formation of a more inclusive and resourceful civic community. However, processes of local empowerment and colonialism intersected in complex ways. While colonial officials worked to suppress political reform initiatives and grassroots forms of collective action and expression, they at times facilitated and incorporated such activities as ways of expanding and perpetuating colonial rule. In addition, both officials and local community leaders often employed a common rhetoric of city-building and civic pride.

The imbrication of British colonialism and local empowerment during this era was further complicated by American expansionism. By the latter nineteenth century, the United States increasingly viewed the nearby Caribbean as a realm of economic and strategic value, as well as a destination for elite tourism. While the impact of the United States was greatest in the northern Caribbean, the whole region gradually experienced more American interaction and influence. By the turn of the century, a small but growing number of well-to-do Americans were visiting Port of Spain for both leisure and business opportunities, and in the following decades, trade between the United States and Trinidad increased substantially. During World War II, the American presence expanded dramatically with the establishment of major army and navy bases on the island and a command headquarters in Port of Spain. This military enterprise had a wide-ranging impact on the city's infrastructure, social relations and entertainment industry. During the postwar era, the bases gradually closed down, but American economic activity and tourism increased. Throughout this period, the United States figured as both an ostensibly democratic alternative to British colonialism and a new force of external control.

INTERPRETING THE LANDSCAPE OF PORT OF SPAIN

In tracing the history of the construction and significance of Port of Spain's landscape, I employ a methodology derived principally from cultural geography. A classic compilation of perspectives from this field is *The Interpretation of Ordinary Landscapes* (1979), edited by D.W. Meinig. Here Meinig asserted that landscapes are symbolic in the sense that they are "expressions of cultural values, social behavior, and individual actions worked upon particular localities over a span of time". In other essays in this volume, Peirce Lewis suggested that "our human landscape is our unwitting autobiography, reflecting our tastes, our values, our aspirations, and even our fears, in tangible, visible form", while Yi-Fu Tuan discussed culturally conditioned mental constructs of environments and stressed that "landscape appears to us through an effort of the imagination exercised over a highly selected array of sense data". A subsequent generation of geographers critiqued analyses of landscapes as general reflections of cultural values and developed interpretive methods that focused on the processes by which people actively construct landscapes and their meanings in the context of socioeconomic and political differences and conflicts. For example, Denis Cosgrove, in *Social Formation and Symbolic Landscape* (1984), examined modern European ways of seeing and organizing landscapes in relation to capitalist social relations, while James Duncan, in *The City as Text* (1990), discussed how the production of an urban landscape in nineteenth-century Sri Lanka was interrelated with written and oral texts and served as a site of conflicting discourses and political struggle.[1] In more recent years, geographers have continued to explore landscapes from a variety of perspectives, with attention to issues ranging from social domination, inequality and justice to multisensory experience, inhabitation and forms of mobility. Meanwhile, debate continues concerning the concept of landscape and its relation to such terms as "place" and "environment". For many researchers, "landscape" remains useful since it suggests both a humanly shaped portion of land and the perception or experience of that land.[2]

In drawing on this rich body of landscape study, I examine the environment of Port of Spain as a heterogeneous material phenomenon that was designed, used and represented over time by social groups and individuals with diverse worldviews, values and interests. From the late nineteenth century through independence, there was a wide range of construction activity in and around the city and, with limited space, ongoing competition for building sites. Additions to the landscape during this period included the expansion of the port, layout of new streets, improvements in water supply and drainage, introduction of electricity, development of new squares and parks, and erection of myriad public buildings, stores, offices, warehouses, factories, movie theatres, hotels and housing. This construction was carried out by a variety of engineers, architects, planners, building companies, craftsmen and labourers, with increasing participation by trained architects and planners from the 1930s onward. Designers pursued their work in terms of three major architectural orientations: European/Euro-American city-planning concepts and historical revival styles; Trinidadian vernacular practices that incorporated the island's Spanish, French, British, western/central African, Indian and indigenous heritage; and, by the 1930s, emerging forms of modernism. Two other architectural traditions employed in the city were Indian design principles for mosques and temples, and American military-base design during World War II.[3]

This complex landscape served the range of functions typical of a capital/port city, from governance, commerce and shipping to domestic activity, education, casual and organized leisure, and religious worship. Throughout this study, I examine such quotidian uses of the landscape, the interrelatedness of spatial design and practices and the ways in which different social groups viewed spaces and negotiated their employment. However, I give special attention to the use of streets and other outdoor public spaces for the staging of large-scale performances, including British imperial celebrations, political rallies and protests and the pre-Lenten Carnival. Such public performances were systematic appropriations of the urban landscape for the purpose of collective expression. Through conventions in spatial positioning and movement, along with traditional forms of visual, verbal and musical communication, segments of the city's diverse population created compelling displays of their various values and concerns. Analysis of these civic theatrics offers insights into how people comprehended spatial distinctions within their environment and utilized this knowledge to achieve social goals.[4]

Along with facilitating various forms of activity, the evolving landscape of Port of Spain inspired a wide array of verbal and visual representations, produced by both residents and visitors. The most common form of representing the landscape was daily conversation with references to particular places. Though most of this past talk is not recoverable in a historical study, traces of quoted speech are recorded in various written sources and provide some sense of how diverse sectors of the population spoke about the city. Meanwhile, literate individuals expressed their perceptions in a range of genres, including government documents, newspapers, local histories, autobiographies, travel guides and reports, ethnographic studies and fiction (which included descriptions of places in both narration and dialogue). Some of these genres also contained photographs of the city, though many more images were published as postcards or in portfolios. In addition, colonial authorities periodically produced and published maps of the city. This range of literature, photographs and maps offered a variety of perspectives on the urban landscape as a whole and on particular kinds of buildings and outdoor spaces. Some depictions emphasized order, beauty and achievement, while others accentuated degradation and failure. As Port of Spain developed, an increasing body of written and visual representations circulated both locally and abroad and influenced how people perceived and understood the city's landscape.

Through diverse processes of design, use and representation, Port of Spain's inhabitants and visitors invested the landscape with a complex and ever-changing significance. Meanings of places were constructed on different scales, ranging from individual buildings and outdoor spaces through neighbourhoods or districts to the entire city in relation to the rest of Trinidad or other territories. Each element of the landscape carried significance in terms of its design and positioning in relation to other landscape components, its uses in the context of the variety of social practices within the city and its representation in oral conversation and diverse literary and visual media. There was considerable variation in how different social groups and individuals interpreted the landscape, and their interpretations evolved over time. However, there was also a generally shared body of understandings of individual spaces, districts and the larger city that enabled people to interact within this terrain in mutually intelligible ways.[5]

It was through these multifaceted processes of constructing places and their significance that the landscape of Port of Spain served as a central site for the display and negotiation of Trinidad's social order. Social distinctions and relationships were manifested in spatial distinctions and relationships, which in turn shaped social systems. In essence, people created the city's landscape as a socio-spatial order – as a realm with interacting social and spatial dimensions. Profound inequalities in wealth and power existed within the society, which comprised, in broadest terms, colonial authorities allied with a small agricultural and commercial elite, a growing middle class and a large mass of working and chronically underemployed people. Though this social order was well established, it was also intrinsically unstable, with the middle and working classes increasingly seeking greater opportunities and rights. By designing, using and representing the landscape in disparate ways, social groups expressed themselves and both competed and collaborated with each other. As noted, such processes occurred throughout Trinidad, but had a particularly dramatic manifestation within Port of Spain, due to its concentration of people, its centrality to governance and commerce and its vivid presence in media representations and promotions. Moreover, the city was the main site for the arrival of newcomers, including a variety of workers, businesspeople, government officials, military personnel, tourists, architects and builders. All these people played roles in the construction of the city's landscape and its significance for Trinidad and the wider world.

From the late nineteenth century through independence, a fundamental dynamic in the creation of Port of Spain's landscape was the interplay between British colonialism and local empowerment. Much of the design, use and representation of the landscape perpetuated the colonial order. Prominent public buildings and commercial facilities, as well as the spectrum of housing, were emblematic of colonial authority, elite control and social hierarchy; prevailing activities included the extraction of the territory's wealth, regulation of its population and celebratory displays of imperialism; and dominant literary and visual representations promoted the city as an orderly colonial capital and port. However, the maintenance of colonialism was not a unilateral, top-down process but one that involved constant accommodation with the city's varied inhabitants. The local population acted in a multitude of ways to construct a city in which it could pursue its own economic interests, develop its own forms of social organization and expression, participate in its own governance and generally chart its own future. Communal yards, the buildings of grassroots associations and the town hall were centres of local collaboration and organizing; streets and other public spaces served as stages for community expression; architects eventually employed modern design principles in projects that moved beyond the colonial legacy; and various fiction writers and visual artists examined and affirmed the local landscape and its traditions. The growing American influence in the city and throughout the territory also challenged the perpetuation of existing systems by introducing new economic opportunities, consumer goods, cultural styles and displays of military power. Ultimately, these multifaceted negotiations of the colonial order brought about its demise and the emergence of an independent nation-state, though one that continued to be shaped by socioeconomic inequality and external dominance.[6]

Within this complex dynamic, many of Port of Spain's inhabitants, regardless of socioeconomic background, viewed the city in terms of concepts of progress. People generally believed they could improve themselves in the city and perhaps also improve the city itself. In essence, the city was a site for contemplating and pursuing a more promising future. Migrants arrived in search of economic and educational opportunities and new forms of excitement. Government officials and business leaders typically described the city's infrastructure and amenities in terms of modernization that would facilitate economic growth. Members of political and labour movements all assumed the possibility of democratization and greater socioeconomic justice. Finally, architects and urban planners envisioned perfected landscapes and attempted to implement these visions within the limits of existing conditions. Thus a rhetoric of progress permeated representations of the landscape and contributed to a sense of forward momentum in the city. In general, there was a belief that ingenuity, entrepreneurship and determination in Port of Spain could lead Trinidad to secure a more prominent position in the wider world.

From the late nineteenth century to independence, Port of Spain was, in short, a landscape of aspiration as well as subjugation. It was a place of racism, economic exploitation, political oppression and, for many, deplorable living conditions. However, it was also a locale in which change seemed feasible, in spite of barriers and hardship. In the following chapters, I explore some of the ways in which the creation of this particular urban environment both constrained and expanded the lives of its inhabitants.

While Port of Spain's material and social character was unique, the city's dynamic development from the late nineteenth to mid-twentieth century was part of a broader process of urban growth across much of the Caribbean. During this period, cities and towns gained prominence in relation to plantations and villages as fundamental spaces of residence and experience. Increasing numbers of people, in search of economic and other opportunities, migrated from the countryside to urban areas, which expanded in both population and territorial size. In urban cores, there was often substantial construction of new public and commercial buildings, as well as improvements in infrastructure and outdoor spaces. These cores were typically surrounded by the self-built housing of low-income populations, though new middle-class and elite residential districts also developed. As cities grew in size, their territorial dominance in governance, transportation, trade and services increased. In addition, urban dwellers formed numerous occupational, benevolent, political, artistic and recreational organizations (offering a range of vehicles for association and expression), while artistic and entertainment venues (catering to both residents and growing numbers of tourists) flourished in several of the region's larger cities. This was an era during which Caribbean cities manifested what Derek Walcott describes as ideal proportions as measured by their own citizenries: streets suited for walking, leafy parks, accessible docks, vibrant commercial areas, buildings with baroque woodwork, and heterogeneous populations that would "find it increasingly futile to trace their genealogy". However, Caribbean cities of this period were also deeply conflicted places, with authoritarian political systems, economic dependence on external markets, extensive socioeconomic inequality and major internal disparities in public services and environmental conditions.[7]

Port of Spain, as a capital and chief port, was a focal point for Trinidad, but its landscape was *not* representative of the territory as a whole. Like other Caribbean colonies, the primary sectors of the island's economy remained based in rural areas: cocoa was cultivated mainly in hilly or mountainous terrain, sugar plantations were concentrated in the western central plains, and oil was extracted from southern districts. Each of these industries (along with other agricultural pursuits) generated its own forms of land organization, technology, buildings and social relations. Thus there was a range of settlement types across the island, including housing on plantations for owners, managers and workers; rustic accommodation for oilfield employees; small villages in both uplands and plains; several major market towns (such as Arima, Chaguanas and Princes Town); and the smaller city of San Fernando, located at the geographic intersection of the sugar and oil industries. Diverse regions and industries also varied in their ethnic composition. As the largest population centre, Port of Spain included residents of all ethnic backgrounds, but not in the same proportions that existed in the territory overall. Within the city there were relatively higher percentages of people of European and Chinese descent (though these were still small minorities compared to Afro-Trinidadians) and a much lower percentage of those of Indian descent.[8] The largest population of Indo-Trinidadians was in the western central sugar region, where they developed a particularly vibrant configuration of cultural traditions that differed from the dominant European/African-derived cultural patterns of Port of Spain. During the post–World War II era, Trinidadians' constructions of African and Indian ethnic distinctions carried increasing salience in electoral politics and, to a significant degree, were associated with urban/rural distinctions. So, while Port of Spain was a central site for the display and negotiation of Trinidad's social order, these processes unfolded within an environment shaped by specific economic and demographic circumstances. Here the city's residents articulated a version of Trinidadian society that highlighted their particular values and concerns.

THE DEVELOPMENT OF PORT OF SPAIN

When Christopher Columbus arrived at Trinidad in 1498, on his third voyage to the Caribbean, the island was inhabited by various indigenous peoples. Among their many settlements was Cumucurapo ("the place of the silk cotton trees") in the area of present-day Mucurapo in western Port of Spain. Spanish explorer Antonio Sedeño, the first governor of Trinidad, attempted to establish a settlement here in the early 1530s but abandoned it in 1534. However, the Spanish remained interested in Trinidad in the course of the sixteenth century as a base for exploring the nearby South American mainland. In 1592 Antonio de Berrío, the newly appointed governor of Trinidad, dispatched his lieutenant Domingo de Vera to take formal possession of the island, in a ceremony that appears to have occurred at Cumucurapo. Afterwards, Vera headed some eight miles east to another indigenous village, where he founded San José de Oruña (St Joseph) as the capital city of Trinidad – in keeping with the Spanish preference for inland capitals as a protection against sea assaults by rival powers. Three years later, Sir Walter Raleigh attacked and burned St Joseph, took Berrío prisoner, and pried him for knowledge of Guiana in preparation for a journey up the Orinoco River in search of El Dorado. Before sacking St Joseph, however, Raleigh landed at a place that, in his words, the inhabitants called "Conquerabia" and the Spaniards referred to as "Puerto de los Hispanioles". It is unclear whether this location was Cumucurapo or a site farther east, near what is now Independence Square in present-day Port of Spain. In any case, Puerto de España (as it was better known) remained a very small settlement during the seventeenth century and suffered multiple attacks. By the latter part of the century, however, the settlement was permanently situated at the easterly site and would eventually expand from here.[9]

From 1592 until the 1770s, the Spanish did little to develop Port of Spain, St Joseph or the surrounding territory. In 1757 Governor Pedro de Moneda described St Joseph as consisting of not more than twenty houses (some in ruins) and took up residence in Port of Spain, a practice followed by subsequent governors. In 1762 Governor José Antonio Gil recorded approximately sixteen houses in each settlement and said they were inhabited more by snakes than by men. He proceeded to construct thirty houses at Port of Spain and another thirty at St Joseph. Though St Joseph remained the official capital, Port of Spain was proving more attractive, owing to its seaside location and opportunities for maritime transportation and trade. Initially, the town consisted of two parallel streets, Calle del Príncipe and Calle del Infante (later named Nelson and Duncan Streets); additional streets were eventually added to the west and north. Early residents constructed houses with earth-and-grass walls and thatched roofs, while sustaining themselves by growing crops and hunting in the immediate environs of the town.[10]

In an effort to bring new economic enterprise to Trinidad, Spain issued decrees in 1776 and 1783 that opened the territory to settlement by foreign Catholics. The 1783 proclamation was particularly effective: in the following fourteen years, hundreds of French planters and enslaved Africans arrived in Trinidad, in flight from turmoil across the Caribbean generated by French-British rivalry, the French Revolution and the Haitian Revolution. It was during this period that Trinidad developed as a slavery-based sugar-plantation colony, and Port of Spain grew as a predominantly francophone town. Moreover, the move of the cabildo (municipal administration) here from St Joseph in 1783 and the governor's earlier relocation established Port of Spain as the capital of the territory. In order to accommodate the increasing population and new functions of the town, the Spanish authorities implemented several improvements: streets were realigned, houses were cleared from the shore to allow for commercial and governmental use and in 1787 Governor José María Chacón appointed an engineer (José del Pozo y Sucre) to divert the Río Santa Ana from its course through present-day Woodford Square and Chacon Street to the east side of the town, at the foot of the Laventille Hills. This rerouting of the river, carried out by 638 enslaved and 405 "free coloured" workers, enabled the expansion of the city in an orderly grid of seven north-south and four east-west streets by the end of the century. Between the grid and the shore was the town plaza, with the Catholic church (one block east of its present location) and military barracks. Extending from the shore was a mole with a quay at the end and a connecting battery (Fort San Andrés). Other features of the town were the governor's residence, town hall, customs house, treasury, hospital, jail, warehouses, dance halls and an outdoor market on the west side of Calle del Príncipe, a block and a half north of the plaza. Public and commercial buildings, as well as the large number of new houses, were constructed from wood. While the town's population was 632 in 1777, by 1797 it had reached 4,525, including 938 whites, 1,671 free coloureds, and 1,916 enslaved blacks.[11]

In 1797 Britain captured Trinidad, with minimal resistance from Spanish forces, and formally acquired the colony by treaty in 1802. During the early nineteenth century, British planters and their enslaved Africans expanded the island's plantation economy, while colonial officials tried to control what remained a mainly francophone populace. Port of Spain continued to develop with the overall growth of the territory's economy and population. British authorities assigned English names to streets, and by around 1808 had enlarged the street grid and laid out building lots as far as Richmond Street to the west and Oxford Street (above Park Street) to the north. In 1808 a massive fire devastated much of the city, destroying over four hundred houses and all government buildings. While the residents suffered staggering financial losses, they had an opportunity to rebuild their city with more durable materials. Though there was limited compliance with a new law prohibiting wood construction, many downtown commercial and residential buildings were erected from stone during this period. In 1813 Governor Ralph Woodford arrived and, in the course of his fifteen-year administration, had a major impact on the composition and character of the city. In addition to directing the repaving of streets, installation of street signs and improvement of pavements, he enlisted the town engineer to lay out Marine Square and Brunswick Square and beautify these spaces with trees. Marine Square was an enhancement of the old Spanish plaza towards the southern end of the city, while Brunswick Square was the development of an open site at the city's centre. Woodford also supervised the continued reclamation of land from the sea and laying out lots from Marine Square south to present-day South Quay. This became a vital commercial district, with the main docks along South Quay and a new St Vincent Wharf at the west end. Finally, Woodford laid cornerstones for a new Catholic church at Marine Square and an Anglican church adjacent to Brunswick Square, and guided the acquisition of lands to the north of the city that would become the Queen's Park Savannah.[12]

Emancipation in 1838 and the general expansion of Trinidad's sugar industry from 1850 to the early 1880s shaped the further growth of Port of Spain. While the city's population was roughly 12,000 at the time of emancipation, it reached 31,858 by 1881. During this era, many formerly enslaved Africans left plantations and migrated to towns, especially to Port of Spain. Here they settled in the Laventille Hills to the east of the city, as well as in the downtown area and in the new districts of Belmont (east of the Savannah) and Corbeaux Town (west of downtown). This population was soon joined by migrants from other British Caribbean islands. In addition, British officials and other colonists settled in Port of Spain. Upper- and middle-class families tended to live on the western side of the city and in northwestern New Town, areas that also attracted wealthier families who had formerly lived in the central city. Meanwhile, a variety of institutions developed during the post-emancipation decades: new government office and court buildings at Brunswick Square, a new hospital at the northeast end of the city, a public library, a chamber of commerce, several churches, and secondary schools, including St Joseph's Convent for girls and the Queen's Collegiate School and St Mary's College for boys. During this period, the British colonial government intensified its efforts to anglicize the society and, as part of this initiative, replaced the old Spanish cabildo in 1840 with a town council. Though this new body had lesser powers, it was elected through a limited franchise.[13]

The growing city of Port of Spain also attracted commentary by prominent British writers. In 1859, for example, Anthony Trollope described the place as "a large town, excellently well laid out, with streets running all at right angles to each other" and added that it had "a degree of commercial enterprise quite unlike the sleepiness of Jamaica or the apathy of the smaller islands". However, he went on to condemn the Trinidadian population's prospects for self-government. In 1871 Charles Kingsley offered a generally favourable assessment of Port of Spain. He noted "pretty 'Marine Square,' with its fountain and flowering trees" and the Catholic cathedral, "a stately building, with Palmistes standing as tall sentries round". On commercial streets, he observed, "Under cool porticoes and through tall doorways are seen dark 'stores,' filled with all manner of good things, from Britain or from the United States." In the newer part of the city (presumably north towards the Savannah), he saw houses ranging from "mere wooden sheds of one or two rooms" to the wooden homes of the well-to-do – "Over high walls you catch sight of jalousies and verandahs, inside which must be most delightful darkness and coolness." Moreover, houses were "embowered in trees and flowers". Kingsley was similarly impressed with the variety of the city's residents that he observed on the streets: Africans, Indians, Chinese, "coloured young ladies . . . well-dressed according to the fashions of Paris or New York", an "unmistakeable Englishman", and a "Frenchman or Spaniard of old family".[14]

Indeed, by the latter nineteenth century, Port of Spain was inhabited by an exceptionally diverse population, organized in a hierarchy of social classes and ethnic categories. People classified themselves and others in terms of perceptions of social status, cultural practices, ancestry and physical characteristics. Individuals negotiated their positions within this social order on an ongoing basis and in some cases were able to change their locations over time.

A very small upper class of European descent included high-ranking colonial officials; planters who maintained homes in town as well as on their country estates; merchants who ran import-export businesses, large stores and other enterprises; and a few of the city's doctors and other professionals. Along with Britons who lived in the city for limited periods of time, this class encompassed French creoles (the descendants of old families of French, Spanish and other European backgrounds) and English creoles (descendants of British families who had settled in Trinidad during the nineteenth century). Sometimes referred to as the "French party" and the "English party", the former was traditionally francophone and Catholic, while the latter was anglophone and Protestant. By the end of the nineteenth century, the French creoles were increasingly speaking English and tensions with the English creoles were becoming less pronounced. Both groups maintained an ideology of superiority to everyone else in the society.

At the other end of Port of Spain's social hierarchy was a large class of labourers, domestic workers and craftsmen, a substantial portion of whom were marginally employed or chronically unemployed. Mainly of African descent, this population included individuals born in Trinidad, migrants from other Caribbean territories and a small number born in Africa. Many working people spoke a French Creole language but were increasingly conversing in an English Creole by the turn of the century. Migrants from several other British islands spoke varieties of English or English Creole. The city's working class belonged to the Catholic Church, various Protestant denominations or African-derived and creolized religions. In general, the African-derived and creole cultural practices of the working class were strongly condemned by the upper and middle classes.

Port of Spain's growing middle class included attorneys, doctors, teachers, journalists, other professionals, civil servants and office workers. This group consisted of individuals of both African and mixed African/European descent, francophones and anglophones (with a shift towards the latter), and Catholics and Protestants. The middle class had its roots in the free people of colour of the pre-emancipation era and expanded during the second half of the nineteenth century with increasing access to primary and secondary schools and the diversification of the economy. Individuals generally valued European cultural traditions, but also strongly resisted racist discrimination by the elite, and worked assiduously to expand their occupational opportunities and political rights. To this end, they were active in many of the city's social organizations.

The social hierarchy of Port of Spain also included people of various other ethnic backgrounds. Between 1845 and 1917, the colonial government brought approximately 147,000 indentured labourers from India to Trinidad to work on sugar plantations. By 1901 Indians constituted a third of Trinidad's population, though a very small number lived in Port of Spain proper. On the western outskirts of the city, however, there was an Indian community known as Peru Village, which would later be annexed as part of the district of St James. Indians perpetuated many of their cultural traditions in Trinidad; the majority was Hindu, though there were also Muslims and Christian converts. Increasing urban migration during the twentieth century facilitated more interaction with other segments of the population, as well as the growth of a middle class.

Other population groups in Port of Spain were the Portuguese (Madeira Islanders) and Chinese whose ancestors had arrived in Trinidad as indentured labourers, mainly during the mid-nineteenth century. In the city, they became active as shopkeepers and eventually entered a variety of other occupations. Migrants from Syria and Lebanon began arriving in the 1890s. Initially, they were pedlars, but in time opened shops and other businesses. Finally, Venezuelans had been settling in Trinidad since the early nineteenth century. Though most lived in rural districts as small farmers or labourers, there was a significant population in Port of Spain. Some of these urban dwellers were political refugees who remained actively involved in the affairs of Venezuela.[15]

In 1888 tensions inherent to the above social order were manifested in the debate and newspaper commentary that accompanied the fiftieth anniversary of emancipation in Trinidad. Historian Bridget Brereton notes that while there had been occasional observations of 1 August anniversaries after 1838, these largely disappeared after 1860. By the late 1880s, however, there was growing political consciousness among Port of Spain's black and mixed-descent middle class, a group of whom planned a public dinner and other celebrations for the emancipation jubilee. They envisioned this anniversary as an occasion for expressing unity among African-descended Trinidadians, affirming their accomplishments to date, and generating pride in Africa and African ancestry. On the other hand, some French creoles and individuals of other backgrounds argued that slavery was best forgotten and advocated a low-key observance of the anniversary, fearing that heightened attention would intensify social animosities. Meanwhile, the governor refused to declare a public holiday on the ground that the event would not be relevant to various segments of the population, such as Indians, Venezuelans and Africans who arrived after 1838 as indentured labourers. In the end, it appears that there was minimal participation in the event by the city's large African-descended working class. However, Brereton argues that the jubilee "helped to sharpen race consciousness among the educated mixed-race and black middle stratum, and to generate an ideology with which to confront racism at home and abroad". In addition, many of the organizers of the jubilee would become leaders of a political reform movement in Port of Spain over the next fifteen years.[16]

THE STUDY OF PORT OF SPAIN

As the capital of Trinidad and Tobago and a city of extraordinary cultural vitality, Port of Spain has been the subject of substantial historical research over the past several decades. The first book-length study of the city's history is Carlton Ottley's *The Story of Port of Spain* (1962), published in conjunction with the growing interest in Trinidad's past at the time of independence. More extensive chronicles of events in the city are Michael Anthony's *The Making of Port-of-Spain* (1978) and *Port-of-Spain in a World at War, 1939–1945* (n.d.). Several studies have focused on well-known buildings and sites and have featured copious photographs along with historical information. Examples are Olga Mavrogordato's *Voices in the Street* (1977), Michael Anthony's *Historic Landmarks of Port of Spain* (2008), the National Trust's *The Built Heritage of Trinidad and Tobago* (2012) and Anthony de Verteuil's and Adrian Camps-Campins's *The Great Eight* (2015), which explores prominent homes around the Queen's Park Savannah. Numerous photographs and texts pertaining to the city are also contained in *The Book of Trinidad* (1992), edited by Gérard Besson and Bridget Brereton. Examples of architectural studies are John Newel Lewis's *Ajoupa* (1983), a general examination of Trinidad with extensive material on Port of Spain; an article by Mark Raymond on modernists Colin Laird and Anthony Lewis (2005); and Geoffrey MacLean's and Brian Lewis's *Manikin: The Art and Architecture of Anthony C. Lewis* (2009). Other specialized studies of the city include works by Suzanne Goodenough (1976, 1978) and Dennis Conway (1989) on demography and residence patterns; Alvin Magid's *Urban Nationalism: A Study of Political Development in Trinidad* (1988), which examines anti-colonialism in the city from 1895 to 1914; James Cummings's *Barrack-Yard Dwellers* (2004), a description of a major form of housing until the 1950s; and an article by David Trotman on the postcolonial significance of public monuments in the city (2006). Finally, as the bibliography for this present book suggests, there is much discussion of Port of Spain in general studies of the history of Trinidad, as well as in works focused on politics, Carnival, literature and other topics.[17]

My objective is to build on the above research to develop a more comprehensive understanding of the construction and significance of the landscape of Port of Spain from the era of high colonialism through decolonization. To this end, I compile a wide range of visual and literary documents of the city and assemble a nuanced account of what the landscape looked like as it developed over time. In addition, I offer an analysis of a variety of individual buildings, outdoor spaces and other elements of the environment and examine their relationships within the broader composition of the city. In pursuing this analysis, I consider landscape elements in the context of larger cultural patterns and social processes in Trinidad. As a medium of thought, the landscape reveals how diverse social groups and individuals conceptualized the organization of Trinidadian society. As a medium of action, it discloses how groups and individuals interacted both to perpetuate and to change this social order. An exploration of these patterns and processes thus enables an understanding of how colonialism and local empowerment were lived at the ground level, as part of day-to-day spatial orientations, practices and experiences. Moreover, it demonstrates that the perpetuation and dismantling of the colonial system involved not only political institutions and discourses but also the material environment. My hope is that the perspective developed here will broaden the scrutiny of Caribbean urban landscapes and thereby enrich the historiography of social relations and politics in the region during the late nineteenth and twentieth centuries.

As outlined earlier, my examination of the landscape of Port of Spain encompasses its design, customary use and representation. In considering design, I suggest that this landscape (like that of other cities) is an immensely complex creative work – one that has been collectively produced over time by a variety of architects, engineers, city planners, construction companies and individual builders. Indeed, it is a major cultural achievement, shaped by diverse visions, aesthetic principles, functional goals, technologies, material resources and environmental/climatic considerations. However, the city's landscape has been the subject of far less research than Trinidad's other visual arts or its creative literature and music. The discussion offered here encourages appreciation of a wider range of creative workers in the city and their artistic and social objectives. Similarly, there is a need for expanded research on large-scale public performances in Port of Spain. The present study provides an analysis not only of Carnival but also of imperial celebrations and the expressive aspects of political rallies and protests. By comparing this variety of performances and their spatial dimensions, it suggests a fuller understanding of their shared symbolic vocabulary and impact within Trinidadian society. Finally, the large body of literary and visual representations of Port of Spain warrants more systematic exploration in order to discover how diverse residents and visitors have perceived and interpreted the city over time. These works have played a major role in shaping images of the city disseminated across Trinidad, the Caribbean and the wider world.

In pursuing this historical study, I have faced several challenges and limitations. One fundamental interpretive challenge is that most of my evidence of the design and use of the past landscape is obtained from representations. In other words, I examine literary and pictorial materials both as sources of information on other phenomena and as a topic in themselves. In treating representations as evidence, I have gathered a wide range of material and, through comparative analysis, attempt to account for the subjective perspectives of authors in developing my descriptions of the appearance and use of the landscape. In considering representations as a topic, I explicitly discuss subjective positions and goals in depictions of the landscape. My intent, however, is not to engage in aesthetic criticism but simply to outline how such works portray diverse spaces within Port of Spain and the city as a whole.

Other research challenges are posed by the particular sources that are available in archives. First, far more material exists on the central city and the Queen's Park Savannah area to its north than on other districts, and there is a particular scarcity of evidence concerning the city's low-income eastern neighbourhoods. My focus in this study on the central city and Savannah area is guided by this availability of source material but also by the importance of these two districts to my overall argument concerning the city's socio-spatial order. From the late nineteenth century to independence, the central city contained a large percentage of the urban population and, along with the Savannah, included the municipality's primary public spaces and institutions.

A second research challenge is that available literary sources represent the views primarily of the territory's middle and upper classes. While some working-class voices are recorded in newspapers and other documents, I devote substantial attention to the expressive qualities of public performances in an effort to comprehend how working people perceived their landscape and society. A third problem is that most available sources were produced by men. During the period under investigation, the great majority of public officials, civic leaders, architects, builders, writers and photographers in Port of Spain were men, and it is mainly their views that appear here. However, I also include the observations of several female journalists and discuss various women who were prominent in social work, labour and political organizing and the arts.

Two conceivable ways of addressing the above limitations of archival sources are oral history and examination of the landscape of Port of Spain today. It would certainly be possible to interview a range of people (including women and individuals of various socioeconomic backgrounds) about their recollections of the city's environment before 1962. However, I decided against this approach, since only the latter portion of my research period would be accessible through remembered observations, and these memories would be filtered by current concerns. My objective is to examine perceptions contemporaneous with the built forms and events described, not memories of the past. On the other hand, I have studied Port of Spain's landscape in recent times. Between 2008 and 2014, I photographed the city extensively and have used these images as a source in conjunction with archival photographs, maps and literary documents. Though much of its street plan remains intact, the city has undergone massive change since 1962, particularly during the petrochemical booms of the mid-1970s to early 1980s and late 1990s to late 2000s. A large number of the buildings that existed in 1962 are gone and many have been substantially modified. Thus recent observations and photographs must be used with much caution in attempting to determine what the city looked like in the past.

Given my research objectives and the limitations of the archive, the portrait of Port of Spain offered here is highly selective in terms of the locales, buildings, individuals and events included or emphasized. Many elements of the city's landscape are not discussed at all. This study offers a particular trajectory through the city over a seventy-four-year period, with a focus on the major expressions of its socio-spatial order. Another researcher setting out on this project would likely follow a somewhat different path and depict a somewhat different city. Nonetheless, I believe that the city represented here is one that its inhabitants will recognize, whether they have memories of the pre-1962 landscape or arrived more recently.

The following chapters are divided into three parts and a conclusion. Part 1 concerns the cocoa boom era of the late nineteenth and early twentieth centuries and includes two chapters. Chapter 1 offers an overview of the components of the city, including diverse districts, public spaces, types of buildings and other landscape features in order to outline the basic socio-spatial characteristics of the place. In addition, it considers the increasing quantity of literary representations, photographs and maps of the city during this period. Chapter 2 then examines infrastructural projects, such as water management and electrification, and analyses the major types of housing in the city. This investigation of fundamental elements of the landscape is followed by a discussion of public performances (imperial celebrations and popular protests) in outdoor spaces. Part 2 of the study addresses the twenty-year period between the world wars. Chapter 3 explores a variety of efforts to enhance the urban landscape, including the initiation of formal town planning, improvements of the port and other components of the infrastructure, the erection of a memorial to World War I deceased servicemen, the construction of various public and commercial buildings and the particular popularity of movie theatres. Chapter 4 focuses on the housing and lives of working people, including government efforts to address the city's housing crisis and the people's protests against socioeconomic conditions. The perspectives of both local and foreign writers on the urban environment are also considered. Chapter 5 offers an analysis of pre-Lenten Carnival traditions, the characteristics of masquerades and calypso during the interwar years, the population's festive play with the city's socio-spatial order and the event's attraction of a growing number of tourists.

Part 3 of the study is devoted to the period 1940 to 1962. Chapter 6 examines the construction of US military bases in Port of Spain and elsewhere in Trinidad during World War II, the arrival of thousands of American military troops and civilian contractors, interactions between Trinidadians and Americans and the general disruption of the British colonial order during these years. Three novels about the wartime city are also reviewed. Chapter 7 investigates the flourishing of both artistic expression and political organizing in the postwar city, with special attention to steelbands and their yards and to the employment of Woodford Square as a public stage by the People's National Movement (PNM). Also included are an account of independence celebrations in 1962 and a discussion of diverse writers' perspectives on the city at the end of colonialism. In addition to investigating some of the urban planning and housing projects of the PNM, chapter 8 explores the development of creole modernism in residential, commercial and public buildings, with attention to several of the leading architects of this period. Finally, the conclusion examines the construction of Port of Spain from the late nineteenth to mid-twentieth century in the context of parallel developments in several other British Caribbean cities during this same period. Also offered are some general reflections on the significance of Port of Spain's landscape and the value of historical knowledge for comprehending the city's conditions at present.

PART 1

THE COCOA BOOM ERA, 1888–1920

Figure 1. Harbour and Queen's Wharf, with Custom House and railway tracks, cocoa boom era. Postcard published by Muir, Marshall and Company. The Michael Goldberg Postcard Collection, Alma Jordan Library, University of the West Indies, St Augustine, Trinidad and Tobago.

Figure 2. Marine Square at Frederick Street, before 1895. Note commercial buildings and central fountain. Postcard published by Muir, Marshall and Company. The Michael Goldberg Postcard Collection, Alma Jordan Library, University of the West Indies, St Augustine, Trinidad and Tobago.

Figure 3. Frederick Street at Marine Square, cocoa boom era. Photograph by Strong. Postcard published by Davidson and Todd.

Figure 4. Brunswick Square with central fountain, late nineteenth century. Paria Publishing Co. Ltd.

Figure 5. The Red House. Designed by Daniel Meinerts Hahn, completed 1907. Postcard published by Maillard's. HistoryMiami Museum.

Figure 6. Eastern downtown Port of Spain from the Laventille Hills, cocoa boom era. Note Prince Street leading to Brunswick (Woodford) Square, with Trinity Cathedral to the left. Postcard published by G.G. Belgrave. HistoryMiami Museum.

Figure 7. The Queen's Park Savannah, facing southeast, early twentieth century. Postcard.

Figure 8. Government House (erected circa 1875) and a portion of the Botanic Gardens, early twentieth century. Postcard published by Muir, Marshall and Company. HistoryMiami Museum.

Figure 9. Piccadilly Street at the bottom of Calvary Hill, East Dry River, cocoa boom era. Note brick Stations of the Cross. Paria Publishing Co. Ltd.

Figure 10. 95 Woodford Street at Marli Street, New Town. An example of a mid-size Trinidadian-creole house of the cocoa boom era. Photographed by the author in 2008.

Figure 11. Boissière House, 12 Queen's Park West. Designed by Edward Bowen, completed 1904. Photographed by the author in 2008.

Figure 12. Water protest at Brunswick Square (*left*) and the Red House (*right*), 23 March 1903, between 12:00 and 1:00 p.m. Riot began around 1:30 p.m. Paria Publishing Co. Ltd.

1. THE COMPONENTS OF THE CITY

BY 1888 THE LANDSCAPE OF PORT OF SPAIN was changing rapidly and generating considerable debate about the future of the city and Trinidad as a whole. Among the occurrences of the next three decades were a substantial increase in the city's population; extension of its boundaries to include districts to the east and west; construction of a wide array of new residential, commercial, and public buildings; development of several squares and parks; and various improvements in utilities and transportation. It was an era of much excitement. The city's residents and visitors could observe a harbour frequented by ships from many parts of the Atlantic world, trains arriving at the port from across the island, electric tramcars circulating through main streets, downtown stores filled with foreign goods and outdoor markets with local products, prominent buildings designed in a range of local and European styles, and diverse open spaces, such as Brunswick Square (with its enhanced layout and new bandstand) and the Queen's Park Savannah (with vast lawns for horse racing, cricket and other recreation). New construction in the city was fuelled by a relatively strong economy, particularly the expansion of the island's cocoa industry. With increasing financial resources, novel technologies and concepts of civic order, the inhabitants of Port of Spain believed they could create a city that was modern, efficient and attractive – a city that could serve as a vanguard setting for the further development of Trinidad during the twentieth century. In fact, many of the buildings and other landscape features constructed between the late 1880s and 1920 remained in place through independence in 1962 and beyond.

The florescence of Port of Spain during the late nineteenth and early twentieth centuries coincided with the apex of Britain's imperial power. With the expansion of its possessions across Africa and Asia, Britain and its colonial governments controlled a global system of agriculture, mining, industry and commerce. Though the overall economic significance of Britain's Caribbean colonies had declined in the course of the nineteenth century, these possessions continued to be tightly administered in efforts to renew their value. Trinidad remained a particularly promising colony, and Port of Spain served as its nucleus for shipping, banking, commerce, governance and British cultural hegemony. However, the cocoa boom era was also a time of increasing discontent among Trinidad's middle and working classes, who demanded further economic opportunities and greater participation in the political affairs of the colony and capital city. Thus Port of Spain was also the setting for an array of reform movements, new social organizations and the publication of political critique.

For most of the nineteenth century, sugar was Trinidad's principal export. During the second half of the century, large British-owned firms increasingly controlled this industry and employed improved technologies for expanding production. However, the industry fell into a deep depression during the 1880s and 1890s, due largely to competition from beet sugar grown in Europe and North America. These difficult years were followed by a recovery during the 1900s and 1910s, facilitated by the termination of government subsidies for beet-sugar exports and a decline in production in Europe during World War I. While sugar revenues fluctuated, Trinidad's cocoa industry experienced a major boom from the 1870s through the 1910s, especially after 1890. By the close of the nineteenth century, cocoa was the island's leading export. This product was transported primarily to Britain and the United States for manufacturing chocolate and cocoa beverages. While sugar was dominated by British interests, the cocoa industry was mainly controlled by French creoles, who owned estates in upland areas of the island and operated as dealers in Port of Spain. The growth of the industry was propelled not only by market demand but also through increased access to crown lands and the development of an elaborate local system of credit and production involving dealers, landowners, contract growers and wage labourers.

Though cocoa and sugar were the main elements of Trinidad's economy from the 1880s to the 1910s, the island also produced coconuts, rice, fruits and other agricultural goods. Meanwhile, Port of Spain, in addition to functioning as a service centre for this agricultural economy, was the site of Siegert's Angostura Bitters factory and small-scale manufacturing of such products as rum, ice, coconut oil, leather, matches, soap and cigars. Other components of the economy were based in the southern part of the island: asphalt (mined at the Pitch Lake) and oil. The oil industry developed rapidly during the first decades of the twentieth century and petrochemicals would eventually become the highest-value component of the territory's economic fortunes, generating new wealth for the capital city.[1]

Trinidad's economy was directed through a crown colony form of government, which consisted of a governor and a legislative council with no elected members. In other words, it was a government that was entirely undemocratic and unrepresentative. Power flowed from the British Parliament and cabinet through the secretary of state for the colonies to the governor and his colleagues on the council. In addition to the governor, the council included such high-level officials as the colonial secretary and attorney general, as well as a group of "Unofficials" – citizens who were nominated by the governor to represent different interest groups in the society. Generally, the Unofficials advocated the interests of the elite, especially those involved in the sugar industry. The primary objectives of crown colony governance were to maintain law and order and to facilitate the profits of the plantation economy and the emerging oil industry. Thus the system maximized benefits for the British metropole and the local elite at the expense of the masses of primarily African and Indian working people.

During the 1880s and 1890s, local reform movements developed in reaction to the crown colony system. These movements were spearheaded by Trinidad's urban middle class, especially residents of Port of Spain. Reformers called for the addition of elected members to the legislative council – representatives who would be selected through a franchise limited by wealth and literacy requirements. They also demanded employment opportunities in the higher levels of the civil service, where such posts were generally reserved for Britons. These reform initiatives were accompanied by debate about whether Trinidadians were capable of democratic self-government. Employing colonial assumptions of European superiority, supporters of the status quo asserted that it was doubtful that African and Asian peoples would be able to govern themselves for many years, if ever, and argued that the challenges were even greater in Trinidad owing to the diversity of its population.[2]

Such was the position of the prominent English writer James Anthony Froude, who visited Trinidad and other Caribbean islands in 1887 and published *The English in the West Indies* (1888). In reference to Afro-Trinidadians, Froude proclaimed that if "we force them to govern themselves, the state of Hayti stands as a ghastly example of the condition into which they will then inevitably fall". He added: "The blacks depend for the progress which they may be capable of making on the presence of the white community." The most trenchant response to Froude was delivered by the Trinidadian linguist and educator J.J. Thomas, who published a book titled *Froudacity* in London in 1889, a few months before he died at age forty-nine. Thomas criticized Froude for his deep prejudices, slipshod research in the West Indies and misunderstanding of much of what he observed. He wrote: "Crown Colony Government – denying, as it does, to even the wisest and most interested in a community cursed with it all participation in the conduct of their own affairs, while investing irresponsible and uninterested 'birds of passage' . . . with the right of making ducks and drakes of its resources wrung from the inhabitants – *is* a degrading tyranny, which the sneers of Mr Froude cannot make otherwise." In the following decades, reformers generally advocated democratization in Trinidad within the context of the British empire and ideals of the parliamentary system. For example, journalist and advertisement writer Algernon Albert Burkett published a small book in 1914 titled *Trinidad: "A Jewel of the West"*, a paean to the island and its inhabitants. In discussing such topics as civic responsibility and reform, Burkett affirmed that "the Island's advancement stands forth in strong vindication of representative government" and "the people of Trinidad are becoming more and more alive to their responsibilities as citizens and subjects of a mighty Empire; and side by side with these aspirations grow the very necessary sentiments for equal treatment at the hands of those placed over them".[3]

Given the limits on local participation in Trinidad's crown colony government, the municipal government of Port of Spain assumed special significance for the populace (especially the middle class) as a vehicle for political expression. Though the franchise for the election of the mayor and borough councillors was limited to adult men who met a property requirement, municipal politics attracted many active opponents of the crown colony system, such as attorneys Henry Alcazar, Vincent Brown, C.P. David and Edgar Maresse-Smith. By the latter 1890s, tensions between the municipal and colonial governments had escalated over the distribution of financial resources and responsibilities between the two bodies. In 1898 Joseph Chamberlain, the secretary of state for the colonies and a major proponent of crown colony government, called for the abolition of the Port of Spain Borough Council unless it met certain financial and managerial conditions. When the council refused, Governor Hubert Jerningham abolished the body at the end of the year, an act that generated even greater antipathy between the colonial government and the citizens of Port of Spain. The governor then appointed a group of commissioners to run the municipal government and in 1907 reorganized this group as the town board. During the early years of the twentieth century, the Trinidad Workingmen's Association (TWA, formed in the mid-1890s) and the Ratepayers' Association (formed in 1901) promoted the restoration of elected municipal government, while also opposing crown colony rule. In 1914 an elected city council was re-established, with a franchise that now included women but retained a substantial property/income requirement. As the century progressed, municipal, labour and other community leaders continued to work in various ways to challenge the authoritarian character of the colonial regime.[4]

DOCUMENTS OF THE CITY

The multifaceted growth of Port of Spain during the cocoa boom era was paralleled by increasing representation of the city in literature, photographs and maps. Numerous individuals, from diverse backgrounds, attempted to record and more fully understand the many facets of this thriving locale. Much of this documentation was promotional in tone, with an emphasis on the variety, dynamism and sophistication of the urban landscape, as well as its natural beauty. As published images and written accounts circulated both locally and abroad, they increasingly affected residents' and visitors' perceptions of the city, thus augmenting direct experiences of the place.

A major advance in the cartography of the city was the *Insurance Plan of Port of Spain, Trinidad*, published by Chas. E. Goad in London in 1895. Goad was an English civil engineer who had emigrated to Canada and, in the 1870s, established a business for producing fire-insurance plans of urban areas, similar to those of the Sanborn Company in the United States. He later opened an additional office in London and published plans of various places in Europe, Africa, Latin America and the Caribbean.[5] His map of Port of Spain included highly detailed information on the urban landscape, including the dimensions of streets, blocks and buildings; the material composition of buildings; the characteristics of the municipal water supply; and the use of buildings, with some designations of particular governmental and commercial occupants. A general plan of the city was accompanied by eleven sheets at a higher scale of sections of the downtown area. Intended for use by insurance companies in assessing risks and claims, the set offered an exceptionally precise record of the composition of Port of Spain at the time of the survey in January 1895.

A second important map from this era was a *Plan of Port of Spain and Suburbs*, prepared by J. Girod and published by Muir, Marshall and Company (stationers) in Port of Spain in 1912. Though not nearly as detailed as Goad's fire-insurance plan, this map showed the expansion of the city towards the end of the cocoa boom years. The newer neighbourhoods of Victoria Square, Tranquillity, Woodbrook and St Clair are all included, while a variety of public buildings, churches, schools and hotels are also indicated. As a locally published document for general use, Girod's plan presumably had much wider circulation in Port of Spain than Goad's set.

While relatively few maps of Port of Spain were created during the late nineteenth and early twentieth centuries, photographs were extensively produced and published. By the 1890s, technological advancements in portable cameras facilitated a large increase in onsite photography around the city. Among the leading local photographers of this era were Felix Morin, L.F. Sellier and W.A. Dunn, all of whom had studios on Frederick Street – the city's premier commercial area. In an 1895 advertisement, Sellier said he was a "High Class Photographer Diplomatist & Medalist", with several awards for artistic excellence received in London, Brussels and Paris. Morin advertised in 1897 that he produced portraits, views, types and stereographic views, including "special views taken to order". He noted that he was also a sworn land surveyor.[6] Along with such local figures, various foreign photographers carried out shoots in Trinidad. Photographs during this period were commonly published in local portfolios, travel books and postcards; the latter were often manufactured in Europe for publication or distribution by local shops. The array of photographs appearing in these works demonstrates a fascination with the booming city and its scenic spots. Certain images appear repeatedly, such as views of Frederick Street from Marine Square, palm trees in the Botanic Gardens and the Queen's Park Savannah and stately buildings such as the Red House (seat of the colonial government), Colonial Hospital and Custom House. Generally, the photographs depict and promote Port of Spain as a modern, orderly city. Photographs of poorer sections of the city were rarely published.

Along with photographs and maps, a wide range of written material about Port of Spain appeared during the cocoa boom era. The colonial government released much statistical information and other records, while a growing number of individuals recorded their observations of the city in local newspapers and books, travel literature and occasionally fiction. These literary representations offered a variety of perspectives, while also establishing certain tropes concerning the vibrancy of the city's streets, the abundance of its vegetation and the dress, speech and general habits of its population. In addition, writers frequently commented on the qualities of Port of Spain in comparison with other cities in the Caribbean. In much of this literature, writers (both local and foreign) aimed more fully to familiarize readers with a locale believed to be insufficiently known and appreciated.

A seminal publication of this era was J.H. Collens's expanded second edition of *A Guide to Trinidad: A Handbook for the Use of Tourists and Visitors* (1888). With several chapters devoted to Port of Spain, Collens (a resident English schoolteacher and administrator) offered the most comprehensive portrait of the city yet published. He had a keen interest in all aspects of life in Port of Spain and carried out wide-ranging research. Among his many topics were the city's squares, parks, churches, public institutions and a variety of associations, such as the Agricultural Society, Chamber of Commerce, Trinidad Volunteer Corps, Scientific Association of Trinidad, Philharmonic Union, Trinidad Rifle Association, Trinidad Auxiliary Bible Society, Trinidad Purity Alliance and Freemasons. In addition, Collens examined the customs of working people, albeit from an elitist perspective. He commented on spiritual beliefs, attitudes towards marriage, pastimes, celebrations and language use, with examples of verbal exchanges in English Creole and vendors' street cries in French. In short, Collens prepared visitors for an initial encounter with the scenic and cultural variety of Port of Spain and Trinidad as a whole. He said his aim was "to make this fair island 'the pearl of the Antilles', as [former governor] Lord Harris used to term it, better known". He also noted that the British *Whitaker's Almanack* described Port of Spain as "one of the finest towns in the West Indies", a reference frequently repeated by subsequent travel writers.[7]

During the following decades, numerous local and foreign writers offered accounts of the landscape and community life of Port of Spain, generally as part of broader descriptions of Trinidad. The majority viewed the city as appealing and progressive, or at least accentuated its positive qualities in an effort to attract visitors and investors. In 1893, for example, the Government Printing Office published *"Iere": Land of the Humming Bird, Being a Sketch of the Island of Trinidad Specially Written for the Trinidad Court of the World's Fair, Chicago*. The book was written by Henry James Clark, superintendent of the Printing Office and a former publisher of the *Port-of-Spain Gazette*, while its photographs were provided by Felix Morin. Concerning Port of Spain, Clark said: "It is admittedly one of the finest cities in the West Indies, but the level nature of its site prevents it being seen to advantage from the harbour, while, owing to the large number of trees in the various squares and around the houses, the view from the neighbouring hills shows more of the foliage by which it is everywhere shaded than of the city itself." Clark goes on to describe various scenes and institutions in the city, with some of his material apparently derived from Collens's *Guide*.[8]

In 1901 J. Paget, another staff member at the Government Printing Office, wrote the *New Illustrated Guide to Trinidad*. He asserted that Trinidad's attractions were insufficiently appreciated and observed: "We have good reason to believe that the outlook is becoming brighter and brighter year by year, and if this Souvenir Album will help to make Trinidad better known beyond the seas, and bring strangers to our shores, the writer will have accomplished a pleasing task." In reference to the colony's capital, he said:

> Port-of-Spain is the finest City in the West Indies. In recent years it has undergone quite a transformation – new buildings have been erected, street, railway, and wharf improvements and extensions carried out, tram lines constructed, the electric light installed, and improved sanitary methods adopted, the latter measure having swept away the prevailing epidemics of a decade ago. Viewed from the surrounding hills, the City presents a most picturesque sight. A kaleidoscopic view of land and marine scenery greets the eye in every direction. In the distant harbour may be seen the merchant vessels of many nations, pretty villas of Government officials and City merchants, dotted here and there, adorn the suburbs, and in every direction a superabundance of floral beauty and tropical scenery meets the eye, which can

only be witnessed in a land of perpetual sunshine. The entrance to the harbour is enchanting.[9]

Most visiting writers also had favourable impressions of Port of Spain. In 1903, for example, prominent American geologist Robert T. Hill described it as "a pretty, hilly town" with a "curious combination of English, French, and Spanish buildings, arranged on broad streets and with many squares or plazas". He added, "owing to its exposure to the combined breezes of the sea and mountain, with a most delicious climate, Port of Spain is a very healthful place, while its situation in a rich and fertile country, its extended views, the beauty of its women, and the hospitality of its inhabitants, make it a most attractive town". In 1904 American naturalist and popular writer Frederick A. Ober observed: "Hot, but not notoriously unhealthy, Port of Spain simmers calmly in the tropical sun without complaint, takes its siesta at the noon hours, wakes up toward evening . . . and settles down to silence only after the midnight hour. Its people are famous for their gambling propensities, horseracing, and even athletic games, like cricket and base-ball. They like to picnic and pleasure-seek." In a second guidebook published four years later, Ober says Port of Spain is one of the busiest cities in the West Indies and notes that the city's "merchants were, and are, of the princely kind, whose trading with distant ports gave them broad views and elevated sentiments".[10]

There were dissenting views to these generally positive accounts of Port of Spain. In 1903, for example, American travel writer and novelist Ida M.H. Starr asserted:

> The city is neither beautiful nor clean. Its architecture, dominated by the taste of the Englishman, is about as unattractive as that of our own country. The business streets are dusty, shadeless, and devoid of cleaners, except for the vulture. . . .
>
> You come to a country which has been under beneficent English rule for over one hundred years, and you find the natives . . . all speaking an almost unintelligible jargon of French, Spanish, Portuguese, English, with a little Hindustani and Chinese thrown in.

Starr had a more favourable opinion of the Queen's Park Savannah area of the city: "Fine residences skirt the savannah, each garden a marvel of beauty, in palms and trees whose names we do not know. Each little villa has its English name plastered upon the gateway. This part of the city is clean, and the road is fine, so we will try to forgive and forget the shabby appearance of the lower town."[11]

Sir Frederick Treves, a prominent British physician and travel writer, offered a similarly divided opinion of Port of Spain's downtown and Savannah area in 1908. He judged the town to be "not noteworthy", but nonetheless offered various observations:

> The main thoroughfares are made up largely of wooden shops of two stories, scorched and warped out of shape by the sun, tinted with more or less decolorised paint and richly endowed with corrugated iron. The space of the street is encroached upon by arcades, latticed balconies, by sloping sun-shutters, shop signs, palms and telegraph poles. . . . The streets are glaring and steamy as well as a-rattle with electric trams. . . .
>
> The town folk of Trinidad appear to live mainly in the streets and to spend their days leaning out of windows or over balconies, for the climate is unfavourable to movement. So many nationalities are represented in the highways and byways of Port of Spain that it might have been on this island that the Tower of Babel was erected.

On the other hand, Treves found the Savannah area "most delightful" and noted that in "a circle round the Savannah are brilliant villas standing in more brilliant gardens". He concluded his account of the city by suggesting, "So prodigal in the tropics is the growth of all things green that if the good folk of Port of Spain were to march out of their town on a certain day and not come back until five years had passed they would find the place lost in jungle."[12]

While observers such as Starr and Treves questioned the beauty and cleanliness of central Port of Spain, most visiting writers during the cocoa boom years were favourably impressed. In 1917, near the end of this era, American popular writer A. Hyatt Verrill delivered one of the most effusive accounts of the city:

> Beneath the shadow of the mountains, upon a gently sloping plain, lies Port-of-Spain, its buildings stretching for miles along the shore, but with little of the city itself visible amid the waving palms and clustering verdure, and, seeing it from a distance, no one would dream that here is a town of seventy thousand inhabitants, the largest, busiest port in the British West Indies. . . .
>
> When the visitor steps ashore at Port-of-Spain he steps into a big, modern, bustling town. At the large, commodious, well-built docks which line the water-front are scores of sailing vessels. . . .
>
> The broad, smooth thoroughfares are crowded with moving vehicles of every description. . . . All the streets are beautifully paved with asphalt . . . all are wide, straight, well kept, and so clean they would put the best of New York's avenues to shame.
>
> The city is well laid out, nearly all the streets running at right angles, there are numerous shaded parks and breathing spaces, trolley cars run everywhere, and the whole aspect of the town is one of progress, modernity, prosperity, and neatness.[13]

Finally, Port of Spain's modern and prosperous character during the cocoa boom years was highlighted in a novel written by Stephen Cobham: *Rupert Gray: A Tale in Black and White* (1907). A teacher and legal clerk by profession, Cobham participated not only in Trinidad's literary circles but in the black consciousness and political reform movements of the era. He opens his story of the colony's colour and class relations with an English-creole heroine, Gwendoline Serle, at the railway station near the city's wharf:

> The Port-of-Spain Railway Station was a scene of hurrying and hustling. Cabs kept arriving in an endless procession. Coolies staggered in under heavy burdens which they deposited with great relief. Country belles, in the latest style, sent their young men – flannel and white boots wearers, in white tunics and sporting hooked walking-sticks – to purchase tickets. Men with umbrellas and hand-bags crossing from the restaurant opposite hastily consulted their watches. The gong clanged everlastingly of each tramcar as it circled past. Newsboys, stumbling after reluctant buyers, hawked the daily papers.

Gwen's father owns a prominent city business, where the Afro-Trinidadian Rupert Gray, her future love, is employed as an accountant. The firm is introduced in the second chapter, when Rupert arrives for work: "He looked in, everywhere. The saw mill, the lumber yard with its busy labourers lifting while they sang, the rattling ice-machinery, the ship chandlery branch with its dozen or so requisitions, the cocoa store whence were being carted load after load, the wholesale provision store, ironmongery, patent fuel department, all came in for a share of attention."

In contrast to the commercial bustle of downtown is the tranquil Queen's Park Savannah area, including the Botanic Gardens on its north side. Rupert visits this setting midway through the novel:

> The band discoursed sweet music at the Botanic Gardens. Beauty and fashion filled Trinidad's Eden. Little children with chubby limbs and faces gambolled round the fountain. A long row of carriages, wherein reclined the rich, was drawn up before the Governor's palace. Opposite, on the savannah which stretched away like a miniature prairie, there was a parade of the Local Forces. These comprised a motley group of fighting units representing every shade of colour.

In the gardens, Rupert meets the Countess of Rothberry, a Kodak-carrying British naturalist who is staying at the Queen's Park Hotel and conducting incognito research in association with the Linnaean Society. He promptly begins to identify some of the many species of trees on the grounds by both their local and scientific names. Surprised by his botanical knowledge, the countess asks: "Are there many more natives like you?" Rupert replies: "There are hundreds in this city alone. My people, Lady Rothberry, are striving to advance."[14]

Throughout the novel, Cobham portrays Port of Spain as a colonial capital that, while hampered by colour prejudice, offers diverse opportunities for its aspiring inhabitants. It is a locale of prosperous businesses, luxurious gardens, genteel theatrical productions and successful professionals contributing to civic life. Decay, poverty and oppression do not figure in this idealized city.

THE CENTRAL CITY

The myriad texts, photographs and maps published during the cocoa boom era collectively constitute a rich archive of the landscape of central Port of Spain and the Queen's Park Savannah area, while also offering some impressions of surrounding districts. Through close scrutiny of these documents in relation to each other, it is possible to assemble a portrait of numerous spaces in the city and to delineate patterns in how they were used by residents and visitors. A city of immense variety appears – one that manifests the imagination and enterprise of a constantly expanding populace.

Central Port of Spain, where much of the population lived and worked, consisted of an orderly grid of north-south and east-west streets, stretching from the harbour in the south to the Savannah in the north, and from Colville Street and Cipriani Boulevard on the west to the Dry River on the east. Though there was variation in the dimensions of blocks, many of those constituting the downtown area extended roughly 500 feet north-to-south and 220 feet east-to-west. Frederick and other major streets were approximately 38 feet wide. By the turn of the century, central streets were generally paved with asphalt (from the Pitch Lake) and included side drains and concrete pavements. During the nineteenth century, the main north-south streets carried different names on the south and north sides of Park Street, with additional variations pertaining to the streets bordering Brunswick Square. In 1901 these streets' southern names were extended to the north, although Chacon Street remained below the square and Pembroke Street above. Districts on the flat land to the west and northwest of the central city were also laid out on grid plans. In the western district of Woodbrook, this grid was shifted as a result of the generally northwestern direction of the main artery of Tragarete Road and the corresponding shoreline. In the hilly terrain to the east of the central city, a network of streets and paths followed circuitous routes up and around steep slopes. The relatively level terrain of lower Belmont to the northeast enabled an irregular grid bordering the eastern side of the Queen's Park Savannah.[15]

In 1917, after several surrounding districts were officially incorporated into Port of Spain, the city comprised 1,793 acres (2.8 square miles). While the total population of the city was 33,787 in 1891, it grew to 54,100 in 1901 and to 61,580 in 1921. In addition to the expansion of the city's boundaries, this growth was due to continued migration from the countryside and outside the island, and to natural increase. The 1911 census showed that the city's population density ranged from 407 people per acre in an impoverished downtown area adjacent to the Dry River to 9 people per acre in upscale areas adjacent to the Queen's Park Savannah.[16]

The Port

Since its founding, the city of Port of Spain had developed in relation to its harbour. During the early nineteenth century, the port comprised a wet strip of land on the south side of Marine Square and a jetty. In the course of the century, land was gradually reclaimed below Marine Square down to South Quay and then beyond to constitute an expanded area for Queen's Wharf. By the end of the century, land was also being reclaimed west of St Vincent Street to expand the St Vincent Wharf. These two wharves served as the central transportation hub for the city and the island. The main north-south streets of the city terminated at or below South Quay, while the St Joseph Road, the primary route into the city from the east, ended at Marine Square.

Complementing these roadways and a coastal steamer service between Port of Spain and other points around the island was the Trinidad Railway, which serviced both passengers and freight. The railway opened in 1876 with a line from the capital to Arima. By the end of the century, this route had been extended to Sangre Grande and additional lines had opened to San Fernando and Princes Town and to Cunupia and Tabaquite.[17] Railway tracks approached the port from the east, crossed the Dry River over an iron bridge, and continued near Queen's Wharf, passing repair and paint shops for railway cars, a machine shop, a "Round House" with a turntable for cars, a freight shed and a fish market (the "Southern Market"), before reaching the railway station, with its offices and waiting rooms. From here the tracks continued past the port's lighthouse towards the large Custom House. From these main tracks various sidings diverged to a crane directly at the edge of the Queen's Wharf, to the Custom House, and to the St Vincent Wharf (see figure 1).

West of the railway station was the Commercial News-Room, a building that in 1888 also housed the Harbour Master's Office and the West India and Panama Telegraph Company. J.H. Collens noted that the News-Room was "liberally supplied with the principal English and many of the foreign newspapers, magazines, journals and periodicals. It serves as a sort of exchange or bourse for the merchants, and business men generally assemble at an early hour and discuss the burning question of the day". Collens added that, outside the Telegraph Company, "You will usually find a small crowd of men and boys congregated around the board, where are posted, as soon as they arrive, the latest telegrams from Europe." The imposing Custom House, constructed in

1880 along Queen's Wharf, comprised a series of long bays with gabled roofs. It was later modified to include a two-storey addition on St Vincent Wharf and a four-storey tower with bands of arched windows and an observation deck. In 1897 the *Port-of-Spain Gazette* described the Custom House as containing an attractive courtyard with a fountain, ornamental palms, and orchids suspended from galleries. The building lent a stately order to the docks and became a landmark for arriving passengers.[18]

Between South Quay and Marine Square to the north was a dense commercial area that included numerous warehouses for storing cocoa and other products. Among the many firms with facilities here were Gordon Grant and Company; A. Cumming and Company; Leon Agostini and Company; G. Ralston and Company; Leon Centeno; Permuy and Romero; and E.P. Masson. In some cases, the second levels of warehouses were used as residences or hotels. At the eastern end of this area, on the west side of the Dry River, were the Laguerande slaughtery and cattle pens. On the east side of the river was an area known as "the La Basse", which included a shipyard, sawmill, lumberyard, foundry and machine shop, ice-manufacturing company, coconut-oil factory, match factory, another slaughterhouse and cattle pen and the Trinidad Street Car Company.

With its various transportation, storage and service facilities, Port of Spain was well positioned for trade with a variety of ports in South America, the Caribbean, North America and Europe. There was extensive traffic with ports in the southern Caribbean via schooners and steamboats. In addition, Collens listed in 1888 several major steamship lines with regular service, such as the Royal Main Steam Packet Company (with connections to ports in England, France and the Caribbean); Compagnie Générale Transatlantique (with French and Caribbean connections); the London Direct Line; the Atlantic and West India Line (with service to New York); the Dutch Royal Mail Service (with connections in British Guiana, Surinam and French Guiana); and the Orinoco Line (with service up the Orinoco River to Ciudad Bolívar). Trinidad's location near the Venezuelan coast and the mouth of the Orinoco made it particularly well suited for trade with this country. Most of this commerce involved transshipment of goods to and from larger vessels at Port of Spain.[19]

Trinidadian newspapers regularly reported on the arrivals and departures of ships at the city's port. On 21 January 1895, for example, the *Daily News* reported that the *Prins Willem 1* was due from Amsterdam via Paramaribo and Demerara and would sail afterwards to Venezuelan ports, Curaçao, Haitian ports and New York. Meanwhile, the *Bernard Hall* was due from Liverpool via Barbados and would go on to Venezuelan ports, Curaçao and Colombian ports. Traffic at Port of Spain was not only varied but frequent: in 1903 there were eighteen steamers per month from England, six from the United States, two from Holland and seven to Venezuela. Top trading partners during this period included Britain, the United States, Venezuela, other British colonies (combined) and France.[20]

The Gulf of Paria offered an excellent protected harbour for ships at Port of Spain, but water depths near the shore posed a substantial challenge. Small boats could dock at the wharves, and 100-foot and 600-foot jetties assisted moderately sized vessels. Large ships, however, were forced to anchor half a mile to two miles from the wharves and relied on lighters to move people and goods to and from the shore. This inconvenience was a source of much concern to both users of the port and civic leaders. During this period, dredging was carried out as part of the effort to improve the harbour, while the installation of a floating dock in 1907 enabled the accommodation of intercolonial mail steamers and similarly sized boats. An editorial in the *Port-of-Spain Gazette* applauded this installation but emphasized that further improvements remained necessary, "the overwhelming consensus of opinion being that Port-of-Spain is too progressive a city, and its trade and commerce are too important for the almost primitive harbour conditions that prevail". By the 1910s, there was much discussion of the need for a full-scale deep-water port, but opinions differed within Trinidad's chamber of commerce and legislative council on the details of an appropriate scheme and its financing.[21]

While Trinidad's economy was based primarily on agriculture, Port of Spain's harbour district was the central site for exchange and storage, and thus was instrumental to the prosperity of the colony. Agricultural export products arrived in the district by cart, motor vehicle (by the early twentieth century), railway and local steamers, and from here were shipped abroad. Meanwhile, a wide array of imported consumer goods, construction materials and other products arrived for distribution throughout the colony. The port was also the main point of entry for migrants, businesspeople, colonial officials, Venezuelan political refugees and leisure travellers, as well as the point of departure for those seeking their fortune in other lands. Finally, the port was a site for the exchange of information with the wider world, whether in the form of literature, mail, telegrams or the talk of sailors, longshoremen and others who worked at or passed through this locale. By the early twentieth century, the colonial government and business community were seriously investigating plans for improving the port and facilitating economic expansion. In time, the port would also become a key site of protest, as longshoremen, followed by other workers, challenged their position within the colonial economy.

Marine Square

One long block to the north of South Quay was Marine Square, which was anchored at its eastern end by the Roman Catholic Cathedral of the Immaculate Conception and on the west by the St Vincent Wharf. King Street ran along the north side of the square and a street known as "Marine Square South" along the south side. Since the city's main north-south streets intersected the square, there were six blocks of lawns and trees, all bisected by a central east-west walkway from which radiated additional paths. In the roadway at the centre of the square was a fountain with a statue of a child holding a swan (see figure 2).

Along with lower Frederick Street, Marine Square was Port of Spain's commercial centre. Its eastern area had been the main public space of the old Spanish/French creole city, which initially developed in the blocks to the north of this zone. The original Plaza del Marina included a church (one block to the east of its current location) and a military barracks, with troops employing this area for drills and parades. During his term as governor of Trinidad between 1813 and 1828, Sir Ralph Woodford directed German botanist and Town Engineer Baron Schack to plant trees in the square, which by the early 1830s reached St Vincent Street. A new church was designed in a Gothic Revival style by Philip Reinagle, an architect and engineer who served as Woodford's secretary. Construction began in 1816, using limestone from the nearby Laventille quarry, and at the time of the first service in 1832, the 210-foot-long building could accommodate a congregation of twelve hundred. The western façade featured the main entrance, two bell towers and, by 1879, a large clock. During the cocoa boom era, the church grounds were enclosed with a masonry and iron fence and planted with flowers and ornamental shrubs.[22]

At the turn of the twentieth century, towering mahogany and other trees in Marine Square provided an expanse of shaded lawns and walkways. Photographs show a variety of the city's inhabitants using the square: Indians seated on the grass, women shopping, men observing the flow of activity and small groups strolling along the central path. In short, the square offered an open public space at the centre of the city's commercial traffic.

Lining the several blocks along the north and south sides of Marine Square were stores, offices and warehouses, some with residences or hotels on the upper floors. These buildings manifested a Trinidadian creole urban architecture that was typical of many of the main streets of downtown Port of Spain. Constructed of stone or brick, the buildings fronted the pavement and were adjoined or closely sited. They generally consisted of two floors (though some included a third) and often had gable roofs (though hip and mansard roofs were also used). Main façades featured tall (often arched) doors and windows, while dormer windows were common on first or second storeys. Many buildings had balconies projecting over the pavement, often supported with columns and featuring decorative iron railings. In some, these balcony spaces were enclosed with panels of windows and louvres. The overhanging balconies provided shady arcades in which pedestrians could walk and gather, while the abundant doors and windows helped to cool the buildings' interiors.

The many stores along Marine Square offered a wide variety of goods, such as clothing, furniture, household supplies, sporting equipment, books, stationery, photographic albums of Trinidad, groceries, wine and spirits, tobacco and perfumes. Also central to the city's commerce were the Colonial Bank and the Union Club. In 1895 the Colonial Bank was on King Street between St Vincent and Abercromby, but later moved to the southeast corner of Marine Square South and Chacon. The new building was an impressive structure that featured arches and pilasters on its ground and first storeys, with pairs of Demerara windows on the upper level. The roof was edged with a parapet, with a pediment at the centre of the Marine Square façade. Collens noted that the bank was incorporated by royal charter, paid a 10 per cent dividend in 1888 (even with the sugar depression), and was "the very essence and soul of commerce". Meanwhile, the Union Club was initially on Abercromby Street, above King Street, but later moved to the southeast corner of Marine Square South and Abercromby. The new building was designed by George Brown, an architect and builder who migrated from Scotland to Port of Spain in 1882, worked for the construction firm of Turnbull, Stewart and Company, and had a profound impact on Trinidadian architecture before returning to Scotland in 1921. His Union Club consisted of three storeys and an attic, with a hip roof, dormer windows and cresting. Iron columns supported balconies (with decorative iron railings) on the first and second floors, while broad doorways on all three floors facilitated the circulation of both occupants and air and the surveillance of activity in the square. Historian Bridget Brereton says the Union Club was "the premier association for the commercial elite; most of its members at first were English Creoles or Englishmen, but by the early twentieth century many French Creoles were also included". In 1888 Collens noted that visitors considered the club the best in the West Indies and that "gentlemen making a short stay in the colony are admitted by the committee as honorary members for a period of one month, on the introduction of two members of the club".[23]

Marine Square and its immediate area were also the site of the majority of the city's hotels, such as the Family Hotel (popularly known as the Ice House), Hotel de Paris, Wippenbeck's, the Standard Hotel and Hotel Orinoco. Certainly the best known of these was the Family Hotel, on the northeast corner of King and Abercromby. The building consisted of three storeys, with a steep mansard roof with dormer windows constituting the third level. Windowed towers projected from the roof on both the King Street and Abercromby Street sides, and there was an overhanging balcony (shaded by an awning) along the former. C.L. Haley and Company ran a grocery on the ground floor and was the proprietor of the hotel on the first and second floors. An advertisement in Collens's *Guide* provides a sense of this establishment: "a spacious, cool, respectable and comfortable resort for strangers visiting the Island, or residents in it, and where Gentlemen and Ladies, with or without families, can find really comfortable quarters. The Hotel is provided with Baths and all the necessary requisites so greatly needed here; each room has its Electric Bell communicating with the Saloon on the second floor; Food and Liquors of the very best, and terms moderate." The advertisement further noted that the ground-floor store offered natural ice, and meat, fruits and vegetables in ice, as well as "groceries of all kinds, from all parts of the world".[24]

Reviews by visitors to the Family and other hotels varied. In an 1891 article titled "The West Indies as a Sanitarium" for the Philadelphia-based *Times and Register*, a physician named William Hutchinson wrote: "In the capital city, there are several excellent hotels. The Family Hotel, the Hotel Paris, and four or five others, offer all possible comfort. . . . At the 'Paris' good Madame Louise takes personal charge of her guests, and sees that they lack nothing. One gets all native dishes there, and has a chance to try them; while at the 'Family', where tourists mostly go, the cuisine is much more English." On the other hand, writer H.F. Abell contributed an article ("The West Indies as a Winter Resort") to the British *Westminster Review* in 1892 in which he said:

> The Family Hotel, better known as the Ice House, is worthy of no warmer eulogy than "decent", for its sanitary arrangements are very imperfect, and, being the recognized house of call for commercial travellers, it is noisy. Wippenbeck's, in a back street, is the only other place to which an Englishman or woman, with normally sensitive cuticle and nose, could go, although there are grandly named institutions, patronized by Venezuelans and coloured creoles.

Though differing in their assessment of Port of Spain's hotels, these two articles reflect late nineteenth-century efforts in the United States and Britain to promote the Caribbean as a destination for health and recreation, as well as for business.[25]

The hotels in and near Marine Square were well positioned to accommodate the various business and leisure travellers arriving at the port, along with Trinidadians travelling to the city by railway or the main roads. Advertisements and articles in the local newspapers suggest that city residents also frequented these centres of social interaction and refreshment. In January 1914, for example, the Royal Standard Hotel on Charlotte Street advertised its "breakfast" (midday meal) menu as including saltfish pie, curried salmon and white rice, black pudding and eggs, lamb kidneys on toast, pork cutlets and mashed pumpkin, sirloin steak and salad, table wines, liqueurs, fruits and coffee. Later that year, the Standard Hotel on South Quay publicized its special Christmas-season luncheon and dinner menus. Musical events were a further attraction: in November 1919 the *Argos* newspaper reported that the Hotel McKinney (formerly the Family Hotel) had introduced jazz to the Trinidadian public. Lovey's Band, a top local orchestra, performed, while a "fine assembly of youth and beauty was in attendance, dazzling the pure white walls of the spacious hall".[26]

Marine Square's cardinal points led to four other important public spaces in the city. At its western end was the St Vincent Wharf, which at the turn of the century was being expanded more than two blocks west along King Street. From the southern point of the square's centre, a broad street ("Almond Walk") extended down to South Quay. The street's long centre strip featured two parallel rows of almond trees, while its sides were lined with multistoreyed buildings used as warehouses, stores and residences. The writer Alfred Mendes recalled that his Portuguese grandfather ran a wholesale store here, filled with Madeiran furniture, fireworks, wine, onions, salted fish and assorted other items. In the afternoon, Portuguese merchants gathered under the shade of the almond trees to drink wine and play cards. This attractive boulevard was also a popular site for evening promenading as well as for more unusual activities. In 1895 the *Port-of-Spain Gazette* published a note that "the attention of the police is directed to the fact that on Almond Walk open gambling is taking place daily. Full grown men sail little chips down the gutters and gamble on the results." That same year an electric tramline began running on tracks in the middle of the boulevard, which led to the removal of the trees as well as the fountain in the centre of Marine Square. In 1906 Almond Walk was renamed Broadway.[27]

At the eastern end of Marine Square, beyond the cathedral, was Columbus Square, which consisted of three plots of land. A triangular plot at the east end was created by the St Joseph Road splitting to form King Street and Marine Square South. Within the square were tamarind trees, royal palms, ornamental shrubs and a circular fountain with a statue of Columbus, facing west. The statue was a gift from Hippolyte Borde (a wealthy cocoa proprietor) in 1881, the year the square was officially opened by the governor. Since the St Joseph Road served as the main point of entry into the city from the east, travellers regularly encountered the square with the cathedral in the background – a composition that clearly asserted the position of Europe and Christianity in the formation of Trinidadian society. The square was also enlivened every third Thursday of the month at 5:00 p.m. with a concert by the Trinidad Police Band.[28]

Frederick Street

Frederick Street originated at the north point of Marine Square's centre and continued approximately a mile north to the Queen's Park Savannah. It was the city's leading commercial street and a main route for public processions of all types. Among the most popular photographic views of Port of Spain during the late nineteenth and early twentieth centuries were images of lower Frederick Street shot from Marine Square, showing prominent stores on both corners (see figure 3). For a brief period, however, this area lay devastated. On 4 March 1895, a fire destroyed the blocks on both sides of Frederick Street, from Marine Square up to Queen Street. British and American naval forces that happened to be anchored in the harbour assisted with fighting the blaze, including blowing up and tearing down buildings, owing to an insufficient water supply. Total damage was estimated at five million dollars. The *Port-of-Spain Gazette* editorialized on the "criminal neglect of the Government for not having long ago . . . taken the obvious and ordinary precautions, to guarantee the finest town in the West Indies against such a fearful catastrophe".[29]

Fortunately, the major businesses were insured, as well as documented on Goad's 1895 insurance map, which had been completed a few weeks before the fire. In fact, the disaster allowed the stores along Frederick Street to be rebuilt in a grander style. This reconstruction was directed by architect George Brown of Turnbull, Stewart and Company. Architect/architectural historian John Newel Lewis notes that Brown inserted steel frames within masonry walls, raised the height of the floors, used slender cast-iron columns and railings to support and ornament overhanging first-floor balconies, and capped roofs with lantern lights (box-shaped roof extensions with multiple windows).[30] The result was terraces of stores with fireproof solidity, graceful façades and well-lit and ventilated interiors.

In his 1897 guidebook to Trinidad and neighbouring territories, James Stark offered a detailed description of the innovative commercial architecture of Frederick Street:

> As a consequence of the fire, a new and much more handsome Frederick street has arisen, and the wealth that was there before the fire has very materially increased. Port-of-Spain can boast of handsome public buildings, and it can also boast of emporiums of commerce that would do credit to a European or American metropolis. On both sides of Frederick street, and facing Marine square, are the ornate glass fronts of spacious department stores, with shelves lined with staple goods in all lines of merchandise, and with the latest novelties that make their appearance in the old or new world. . . . New blood is always coming into the business life of Trinidad, and the colony is in close touch with all the parts of the globe, and readily assimilates to itself new ideas. The colonists are always on the move, frequently

going "home", as they term a trip to Europe, to get the latest tips in their various lines of business.

The architecture of these large bazaars is worthy of special description, for it is pretty, substantial, light and airy, and fairly fire-proof. They are iron-framed buildings, with stone and concrete outside walls, and are two-storied, with what are called lantern roofs of iron and glass. The first story is one immense compartment, and the second is really a gallery with a broad well, through which light, shining through the blue glazing of the lantern roof, sheds a soft radiance over the whole store. The second story and the roof are supported by ornamental iron columns capped with Corinthian or composite capitals. The fronts are decorated with large plate-glass windows, overshadowed by light iron galleries, and as these extend in one line down the whole length of Frederick street on both sides, it gives the thoroughfare a handsome appearance. Plate-glass fronts, iron galleries, and lantern roofs succeeding one another make the *tout ensemble* most harmonious.[31]

Stark's guidebook also included advertisements and photographs of the stores that he described. Exterior and interior photographs of Smith Bros. and Company ("The Bonanza"), for example, reveal abundant goods and customers, while ad copy proclaims the "Largest and Most Varied Stock of Fancy and Staple Dry Goods in the West Indies" and enumerates such products as millinery, silks, cashmeres, straw hats, tropical helmets, portmanteaus, tweeds, iron bedsteads, steamer chairs and ladies' and gents' walking boots and shoes. The photographs appearing in Stark's guide, as well as in various other books and postcards of the period, were shot by Felix Morin and other local photographers. They represent a vibrant, modern retail landscape, with people posed in front of the profusion of goods in the massive display windows along the Frederick Street arcades. Unlike the pre-1895 landscape, the names of the stores now appear on large signs, on fabric panels suspended from the balconies and even on the city's new tramcars. Clearly, merchants employed all promotional techniques available to attract local residents and visitors to their emporia. Here customers could experience and purchase the latest merchandise delivered by Port of Spain's international commerce. In 1917 A. Hyatt Verrill, one of the city's most fervent visitors, described Frederick Street as "kaleidoscopic in color, crowded with life" and observed: "Wonderful linguists must be the clerks in Trinidad's stores, for within a space of ten minutes the man behind the counter may be called upon to wait on customers in as many tongues."[32]

Brunswick Square

Two blocks north of Marine Square was Brunswick Square, which constituted an entire block bordered by Frederick, Knox, Abercromby and Hart Streets.

While Marine Square (the centre of the old Spanish/French creole city and commerce) was open and intersected by busy streets, Brunswick Square was enclosed and the focal point of the newer British colonial city and government. Its formal design featured a large circular path with a fountain in the centre, from which radiated ten straight paths to the perimeter. The multi-tiered fountain, donated in 1866 by merchant Gregor Turnbull, displayed bronze sculptures of a bathing woman, child, two mermaids and a merman (see figure 4). Throughout the square were lawns, shrubs and a variety of roble, poui and other trees. A low railing that initially enclosed the square was later replaced by a tall iron fence with spikes.

In the early nineteenth century, this space was known as "Place des Armes" and served as a parade ground for military troops. In 1810 the colonial government selected the field as the site for a new Anglican church, though the townsfolk protested this decision, since they used this space for leisure and recreation. When Sir Ralph Woodford arrived as governor in 1813, he ordered the largely finished church to be torn down and turned the square over to the cabildo (town administration) for public use. He then directed his secretary, Philip Reinagle, to design a new church on the block to the south of the square. Work on this Gothic Revival structure began in 1816 with limestone from the Laventille quarry; additional stone, iron and glass were imported from England. The church was consecrated in 1823 and dedicated as Holy Trinity Cathedral in 1872. Its lavishly designed interior included a state pew where the governor's staff sat in official dress, a marble statue of Woodford and memorial tablets for leading British families.[33] The attractive grounds of the cathedral were surrounded by an iron fence and contained a parsonage and garden. Two rows of tall palm trees graced the entranceway to the southern portal of the church from Queen Street.

By the early twentieth century, there was considerable public interest in enhancing the appearance of Brunswick Square and ensuring decorum in its use. In an editorial in 1910, the *Port-of-Spain Gazette* described efforts to level grass plots in the square as "a commendable move in the right direction towards the improvement of this popular public recreation ground of the city". However, it also called for the completion of paving the paths, the installation of more seating and the addition of plants "more in accordance with the ideas of public gardens prevailing in other towns both in the West Indies and in older countries". Two years later, the newspaper affirmed continued work on the square, "this lung of the city", but called now for the fresh painting of the perimeter fence: "Surely for the sake of the reputation of the town in the eyes of visitors, many of whom necessarily pass through or near it, this square should be kept in spick and span order, and a coat of paint could easily be given the railing a little more often than is customary at present." During this period, there was also public concern about the variety of people who frequented the square and their activities there. For example, the *Gazette* editorialized against "beggars and loiterers" and condemned those individuals who slept in the square at night. It described as particularly objectionable three regular inhabitants, "the sight of whom on this public thoroughfare is alike a nuisance to those using the square, and a blot on the civilization of the colony". As part of continued efforts to elevate the amenities and use of the square, there were calls for the erection of a bandstand to better accommodate concerts by the police band. In 1917, in the midst of World War I, the mayor of Port of Spain opened a bandstand in the northern portion of the square. This elegant octagonal structure consisted of a masonry base with iron rail and a roof resting on ornamented iron columns. Concurrent with the bandstand inauguration, the square's German name of "Brunswick" was replaced by "Woodford", in honour of the governor who had reserved this space for public enjoyment.[34]

On the west side of Brunswick Square were the Government Buildings, which extended along the entire block. The original structure, designed by Superintendent of Public Works Richard Bridgens in 1844, consisted of two buildings linked by a passageway. This austere Georgian complex was modified and embellished over the years and, after receiving a coat of red paint in 1897 in honour of Queen Victoria's diamond jubilee, became popularly known as the "Red House". The northern building contained the offices of the governor and colonial secretary, the legislative council chamber and other departments, while the southern one housed the courts and additional offices. In 1903 a large crowd burned and gutted the buildings in what became known as the "Water Riots", a protest against the colonial government's water policy for the city. After the riot, a new complex for the government and courts was designed in a French Renaissance style by Daniel Meinerts Hahn, chief draughtsman of the Public Works Department.[35]

The magnificent new Red House, approximately 400 feet long, included northern and southern two-storey wings and pavilions (with mansard roofs) and a taller central block with a dome, cupola and spire (see figure 5). There were arcades on both floors of the wings, while the pavilions featured arched windows and pilasters and second-storey galleries with columns, entablatures and pediments. On the ground floor of the central block, there was a passageway with a fountain, while the upper level comprised an open space surrounded by arches. Initially, the complex's grounds consisted of plain lawns, but, over time, trees and shrubs were planted, thus creating a typical colonial Caribbean composition of a grandiose public building presiding over an ordered tropical environment. In short, the Red House was the premier public space in Trinidad for the display of European imperial stateliness, authority and control.

On 4 February 1907, the new building was officially opened by the governor,

Sir Henry Jackson, with a special session of the legislative council. The governor arrived from his residence with an escort of the mounted constabulary (police) and was received by the police guard of honour and band. He and other officers wore Windsor uniforms, the members of the council were attired in levée dress, and the Crown's law officers wore wig and gown. Special seating was provided for the public, which included many of the colony's prominent citizens. Within the ornate legislative council chamber, the governor welcomed the attendees and delivered a speech for the occasion: "These fine buildings are infinitely more suitable to the steadily growing importance of the Colony, as well as to the needs of this Council and of the Public, than those which they replace, and had their construction been undertaken merely as an improvement which the growth of the Colony demanded, and our resources justified, then my task to-day would be easier than it is." Following comments on the recent riot and an attribution of faults to both sides in the confrontation, he continued:

> To-day we leave that episode of the past behind us for ever, and we turn a fresh page in the history of Trinidad. It lies before you open and unsoiled, and on you, Honourable Gentlemen, and your successors, chiefly depends what is to be written thereon. Your work is to be done in this spacious, lofty and well-proportioned Chamber, and shall we not try and mould our policy on the same lines? Let it be broad minded, with nothing narrow and self seeking in it, let our aims be lofty, and our measures carefully planned and justly proportioned to the needs of the people. If we succeed in this, then indeed will all the bitterness pass from our memories, and the whole people of the Colony will be able to point with pride to this beautiful group of buildings as the seat of a Government holding their confidence and labouring for their good.

The governor went on to discuss the prospects of the colony and then formally declared the council chamber open, with a performance of the national anthem by the band and the audience on their feet.[36] So, with an appeal to the architectural balance and expansiveness of the recreated Red House, the governor attempted rhetorically to define an order for a contentious Trinidad. At the Red House that day, a new colonial space literally became a model for a colonial society.

Various other public buildings were located around the perimeter of Brunswick Square or nearby. Directly to the west of the Red House, one block off the square, were the Police Barracks, another key space of colonial authority. This massive polychrome stone complex formed a hollow square, stretching across Lower Prince (Sackville) Street from St Vincent to Edward Street. Designed in an Italian Gothic style and completed in 1876, the northern and eastern sections of the building featured long arcades on the ground and first floors, with a 70-foot parapeted clock tower accentuating the eastern side. The interior parade ground was used for drills by the resident forces. Collens noted that the "spacious, well-ventilated dormitories present a smart and orderly appearance, as do the store-rooms and kitchen, etc., clearly indicating a military supervision". He added that the "armoury contains Snider rifles, revolvers, swords, all brightly burnished, and ready for immediate use, if need be". In 1888 the fire brigade was housed at the Police Barracks, but around 1895 moved its headquarters to the south side of Brunswick Square, where it occupied an attractive two-storey stone building with a central four-storey tower. In 1902 a new public library opened on the north side of the square, replacing a smaller building on Chacon Street. Constructed with local blue limestone and imported yellow brick, this two-storey building featured spacious arcaded galleries on its southern and western elevations, with a balustrade lining the upper level. Corresponding arched doors with sidelights and transom panels provided much ventilation and light to the interior reading rooms. A cast-iron fence on a concrete base surrounded the building and its narrow yards. In 1897 the *Port-of-Spain Gazette* observed that the old library's public reading room "affords an opportunity for young men, no matter what their social position, of improving their minds, enabling them to understand the issues of the day whether social, scientific, or political". Indeed, the library, with its prominent new position on Brunswick Square, became an important space for public debate in the following decades.[37]

Finally, Brunswick Square was also the centre of the Port of Spain municipal government. In 1899 this body relocated from the south side of the square to a building on the north side, to the east of the library's new site. This structure dated back to the early nineteenth century and apparently originally consisted of three separate units. The municipal administration initially occupied only the western unit, but by 1907 occupied the entire premises. Constructed in a Spanish style, the building featured thick masonry walls, a series of tall doorways on the ground floor, a first floor that projected over the pavement and was supported by a colonnade, and courtyards in the rear. Sash windows and louvres on the overhanging first floor and a small second-floor extension in the centre of the building were probably later additions.[38] While the Red House was isolated by lawns and eventually a fence, the town hall and its shady arcade were integrated with the street and its traffic.

As noted above, tensions between the colonial and municipal governments escalated at the close of the nineteenth century, and the governor abolished the latter in late 1898. Thus it was the governor's appointed commissioners and the town board who occupied the new town hall for several years. However, local community leaders continued to advocate the restoration of an elected municipal body during this period. After an elected city council was established in 1914, the town hall became the site of a more independent management of local affairs and for the definition of a political destiny distinct from that propounded by the colonial government across Brunswick Square.

East, West and Uptown

Frederick Street divided the city into east and west sectors, while Park Street served as a general border for the division of downtown and uptown. The eastern and western portions of downtown included both commercial and residential buildings, with a higher concentration of stores, offices and bars in the two blocks on either side of Frederick. In general, the buildings on the eastern side of the city were older and more dilapidated and their occupants more impoverished. Residents of other parts of the city generally perceived this eastern area as chaotic, unsanitary, dangerous and morally inferior. In contrast, the western sector of downtown included higher-income as well as poor inhabitants. While eastern Port of Spain was hemmed in by the Dry River and the hilly East Dry River district, the city was expanding across the relatively flat terrain to the west. During the late nineteenth and early twentieth centuries, there was much construction of new buildings in this western area, and new neighbourhoods took shape. These neighbourhoods generally had a lower population density than eastern Port of Spain, where migrants continued to crowd into limited housing units. The eastern side of downtown also included more speakers of French Creole. Sometimes referred to as the "French Shores", this district embodied the city's francophone past, while the western areas pointed towards its anglophone future (see figure 6).[39]

An important public facility on the east side of the city was the Eastern Market, which was owned by the municipal government and included spaces on both sides of George Street, north of Queen Street. On the western side was an enclosed yard with a central market building and stalls for additional vendors; to the east was an open space known as Market Square, which also contained the Eastern Government School. Additional market facilities were eventually constructed here. While Frederick Street was a site for appreciating and buying diverse imported products, the Eastern Market was a place for the exchange of local produce, meats, fish and other goods. A wide range of vendors and customers from the city and beyond arrived here daily. Collens observed: "Between the hours of 7 and 8 a.m., especially on Sundays, business here is of the liveliest, and the mixture of nationalities, amongst both buyers and sellers, makes the site always interesting to strangers." Managing commerce in this busy locale was an ongoing concern. In 1913, for example, the *Port-of-Spain Gazette* called for the introduction of "more modern sanitary improvements", with particular attention to unhealthy meat stalls and vegetable vendors' use of the floor rather than tables. The newspaper also noted that, on the pavements, streets and entrances surrounding the market, there were unlicensed vendors who blocked traffic and sapped revenues.[40]

A short distance south of the Eastern Market was another well-known institution: the Angostura Bitters Factory, housed in a long two-storey building on George Street. Used as a flavouring for drinks and as a tonic, Angostura Bitters were invented by the German-Venezuelan J.G.B. Siegert, who had been appointed by Simón Bolívar as surgeon general of a military hospital in Angostura (later renamed Ciudad Bolívar). In 1875, a few years after Siegert's death, his sons moved their bitters factory to Port of Spain in order to more effectively serve the global market for this unique product, which was protected by a secret formula. The factory was originally on Marine Square, but in 1881 moved to George Street. Here it became a sightseeing destination for early tourists in Trinidad, given that the bitters were one of the island's best-known exports. An advertisement in 1897 proclaimed that the product was "Registered in All Countries of the World"; "Awarded the Highest Distinction and Most Honorable Mention at the Exhibitions of London, Paris, Vienna, Philadelphia, Santiago de Chile" and other cities; and "Analyzed and Highly Praised and Recommended by Leading Chemists and Members of the Medical Profession of Berlin, London, Philadelphia, &c, &c". The attractive wrapper for bitters bottles included instructions for use in four languages.[41]

The majority of other factories in Port of Spain were either in "the La Basse", to the east of Queen's Wharf, or in the small neighbourhood of Corbeaux Town, west of Brunswick Square and the police barracks. Named after the vultures that were common in Port of Spain, Corbeaux Town was an old district that encompassed London, Sackville and Charles Streets, and bordered the sea until the initiation of a large land-reclamation project in the 1930s. In addition to housing for mainly low-income residents, it included an iron foundry, slaughterhouse, tannery, sawmills, boatyards and facilities for fishermen.[42]

During the late nineteenth and early twentieth centuries, the Port of Spain municipal government developed a new upscale district to the north of Corbeaux Town in an area known as the Ariapita Estate or Shine's Pasture. J.N. Brierley, a police officer of this era, noted that this space had previously served as "a grazing land for decrepit mules and half-starved cows" and was "occasionally rented to circus proprietors". In 1889 the borough council began laying out lots along Richmond Street and eventually plotted areas farther west. At the centre of this new development was Victoria Square, which constituted an entire block between Park and Duke Streets and was filled in with rubble from the gutted Red House after the 1903 Water Riot. In an editorial in 1907, the *Port-of-Spain Gazette* noted that the town board was planning to erect a railing around the square and advocated additional improvements, such as laying out footpaths (either concrete or finely crushed blue stone), planting more trees, levelling irregularities in the lawns and erecting a fountain. In an editorial three years later, the *Gazette* acknowledged that an iron railing had been installed on a low concrete wall and footpaths laid out, but again called for paved paths and more trees, as well as improved lighting and the erection of either a bandstand or a statue of the late King Edward. In a 1914 article, titled "The Transformation of Shine's Pasture: A Fashionable Residential District", the *Gazette* reported:

> A short visit paid to this still growing district would surprise the visitor who has not passed there, say, for some ten years. The fine cottages that have sprung up, so ornate and commodious, are a credit to the city authorities who decided to transform the locality into what it presently is, as also to those who invested and to the builders. With a fine square and well kept streets, there are the houses which are – most of them, what a man's house should be – "his monument, the first thing in which he expresses to the world his sense of what is beautiful and fit for himself and for those that he loves".[43]

Directly northwest of Victoria Square was the Lapeyrouse Cemetery, comprising some 20 acres with a central road lined by samaan and palm trees, a surrounding stone wall and an arched entranceway. Collens provided a sense of the cemetery's appearance and use in the late 1880s. Protestants were buried to the north of the main road and Catholics to the south, though in earlier years this division had not been observed. Sculptures on the grounds by Señor Palacios (a local Venezuelan artist) included *Une Pleureuse, Grief,* a statue of the Virgin and a bust of Dr J.G.B. Siegert of Angostura Bitters fame. There were also attractive mausoleums for the Montbrun, Tinoco, Huerne, and D'Abadie families, as well as granite obelisks in memory of Gregor Turnbull and D.L. Todd. All Souls' Eve was a particularly impressive occasion at the cemetery: "All classes of the Roman Catholic community, and even many of the Protestants, illuminate the graves of their deceased relatives and friends with candles, presenting a most remarkable spectacle to the unaccustomed English eye." During this period, the keeper of Lapeyrouse was Pierre-Gustave-Louis Borde, author of the two-volume *Histoire de l'île de la Trinidad sous le gouvernement espagnol* (Paris, 1876 and 1882).[44]

The Lapeyrouse Cemetery was at the western edge of the central city and within the area generally considered "uptown". Extending several blocks from Park Street to the Queen's Park Savannah, uptown was predominantly residential, though it also included some commercial and public buildings. Overall it had a significantly lower density of buildings and population than downtown and housed a substantially larger number of middle- and upper-class residents. Particularly fashionable was an area in the northwest known as "Tranquillity". During the early 1880s, the colonial government (which owned this land) began laying out streets and lots and, by the turn of the century, had developed a shady neighbourhood with upscale homes. For example, the writer Alfred Mendes's father was a prosperous businessman who owned a large house during the 1910s on Stanmore Avenue, across from the tennis courts in the private Tranquillity Square. Uptown's central public space was Lord Harris Square, named after a governor (1846–1854) who was remembered especially for expanding public education. Like Victoria Square, Lord Harris Square was filled in with debris from the ruins of the old Red House and constituted an entire block with trees, lawns and radiating footpaths. By the early twentieth century, it was enclosed with an iron railing on a low masonry wall. At the centre were a fountain and a sculpture of Lord Harris on a pedestal (erected in 1905). In 1914 the constabulary band was scheduled to perform concerts here on the third Monday of each month.[45]

Directly south of Lord Harris Square was St Joseph's Convent, founded in 1836 and the principal Catholic school for girls. Collens described it as "devoted to the education of girls of the better classes, who wear neat uniform dresses, with different coloured sashes and ribbons to distinguish their grade or standing in the school". Directly east of the convent and facing Frederick Street was St Mary's College, the principal Catholic school for boys. Founded in 1863, the school offered courses in languages, history, geography, science, mathematics and music, while its facilities included a chapel built of prefabricated iron, a theatre/lecture hall and a gymnasium. Initially, the language of instruction at both St Mary's and St Joseph's was French; the former shifted to English during the 1870s and the latter followed suit during the 1890s.[46]

Two major government institutions stood northeast of Lord Harris Square: the Royal Gaol and the Colonial Hospital. The Royal Gaol occupied an entire block, surrounded by a 22-foot stone wall. Above the iron gate at its entrance on Frederick Street was the motto "Pro rege et lege" ("For king and the law"). The prison contained 182 cells, with a daily average in 1886 of 586 prisoners, including 57 women. Wardens dressed in blue uniforms with red piping and were armed with short staffs, and male inmates wore canvas suits and different-coloured caps (with black designating felons). Men were assigned to hard labour and various trades, while women carried out needlework, washing and breaking fine metal. Indian indentured labourers serving sentences were employed in the grounds of the governor's house and the Botanic Gardens. Both floggings with a cat (long whip) and executions were administered at the prison. Two blocks to the east of the Royal Gaol was the Colonial Hospital, on the extensive grounds of a former military barracks. Designed by a local architect (Mr Samuel), this building measured 400 by 64 feet and featured an arcade on the ground floor and tall windows with Demerara shutters on the first. Surrounding the structure were tidy lawns, planted with a variety of trees and shrubs. Though the hospital was built to accommodate 400 patients, it averaged 525 a day in 1886. Patients were classified into four grades in accordance with their payments (with paupers admitted free).[47] In later decades, additional buildings were constructed to form a larger medical complex.

THE QUEEN'S PARK SAVANNAH

To the north of the central city was the Queen's Park Savannah, a large expanse of open land consisting of more than 200 acres (see figure 7). This irregularly shaped park was bordered by the uptown district to the south, New Town to the southwest, St Clair to the west, the Botanic Gardens and grounds of Government House to the north and Belmont to the east. While the various roads surrounding the Savannah carried different names over the years, they were known by 1912 as Queen's Park West on the south, the Maraval Road on the west, the Circular Road on the north, and Queen's Park East on the east. In the early nineteenth century, the lands of the Savannah, Botanic Gardens and Government House constituted the Paradise and Hollandais estates. In 1817 and 1819, during the administration of Governor Ralph Woodford, the cabildo purchased these lands and transferred them to public use. From this point through the early twentieth century, the Savannah was used for pasturing cattle. By 1828 it was also being employed for horse racing and in 1854 a grandstand was erected for spectators of the annual races.[48]

During the cocoa boom era, the Savannah was a locale in which a cross-section of the city's population engaged in a variety of formal and informal recreational activities. Major horse races continued to be held here during the Christmas season, and in December 1900, the *Port-of-Spain Gazette* captured the scene at one of these events:

> As usual at this ever popular race meeting, the stands were all packed. The number of ladies present was particularly noticeable. The crowd flocked to the savannah on foot and formed along the whole length of the barriers enclosing the course. . . . The East Indian population, whose love of horse racing is almost proverbial, supplied a large proportion of those who were to be seen wandering about the savannah enjoying the proceedings. . . . Here and there over the savannah, were the usual booths, stalls and tents for the sale of drinks and light refreshments as well as the tables and other contrivances for gambling. The Police band was in attendance and during the afternoon played some very pleasing selections.

The Savannah was also a site for other equestrian competitions and for polo, which was popular with the Trinidadian elite.

Meanwhile, the Savannah was the centre of Trinidad's vibrant cricket tradition until the Queen's Park Cricket Club relocated to St Clair in 1896. At the Savannah, the club had a portion of land surrounded by a wooden fence and in 1887 added a pavilion with a Moorish Revival dome. The first official intercolonial cricket match here took place against Barbados in 1893 (before a crowd of four thousand) and the first contest against an English team in 1895, with unfortunate losses by Trinidad at both events. Even with the departure of the Queen's Park Cricket Club, the sport continued to be played at the Savannah, as did football (soccer), rugby, hockey and golf. Among the more unusual activities occurring in the Savannah at the close of the nineteenth century were a performance by a tightrope-walker and a parachute jump by a balloonist who had launched from Victoria Square. In addition to sports and performances, the Savannah was a popular location for informal gatherings and promenades. Pedestrians strolled the Pitch Walk that ran beneath shady trees around the park's perimeter, while carriages, and later automobiles, drove the surrounding streets. In 1902 an electric tramcar began running around the border of the park. In 1917 the ever-exuberant A. Hyatt Verrill described dusk at the Savannah:

> And marvelously beautiful and enchanting is the savanna as the great red sun sinks behind the Venezuelan mountains across the gulf and darkness descends with tropical swiftness upon the land. From speeding motor cars and open windows bright beams of light glint through shrubbery and gleam on ghostly palm trunks, casting mysterious shadows across the broad white road. Upon the soft scented breeze are borne the merry sounds of laughter and of music. Over the dusky, dim savanna the fireflies dance like troops of elves, and against the star-studded, velvet sky the mountains loom.[49]

While the residents of Port of Spain visited the Savannah regularly for leisure activities, the park was also a site on special occasions for official reviews of the Trinidad Constabulary and other local forces. These ceremonial events attracted much interest from the residents of the city. In 1911, for example, the *Port-of-Spain Gazette* reported on a parade for the visiting Sir Ian Standish Monteith Hamilton, inspector general of oversea colonies of the British empire. By 9:00 a.m. the various forces had assembled in the Savannah, while a large crowd of spectators waited in the grandstand and surrounding grounds. After an initial review of the units, the inspector general took up his position at the saluting base, where assorted local dignitaries also gathered. The forces then performed a march-past "to the strains of a lively air" by the constabulary band, followed by a procession of the mounted units, also to musical accompaniment.

Proceedings concluded with the units marching back to their parade grounds in the city, while the visitor retired to Government House.[50] On occasions such as these, the Savannah served as a space for the display of Trinidad's colonial order, as manifested in military uniforms, music and choreography.

In addition to functioning as an expansive recreational and ceremonial venue, the Queen's Park Savannah defined the character of its surrounding spaces, which contained a variety of prominent public buildings and grandiose mansions. At the top of Frederick Street, just south of the Savannah, was the Victoria Institute, an elegant two-storey building consisting of a central area with a portico and two flanking sections with bay windows and Dutch gables. This centre of scientific study, education and the arts opened in 1892 in commemoration of Queen Victoria's golden jubilee, which had occurred five years earlier. In his sketch of Trinidad for the 1893 World's Columbian Exposition in Chicago, Henry James Clark described the institution's collections:

> Among some of its more interesting contents are a fine collection of stuffed birds, representative of the ornithology of the island, presented to the colony by the late Dr. Leotaud; a very fine and valuable collection of shells, the gift of the widow of the late Robert William Keate, who was Governor of the colony from 1857 to 1864; an interesting collection of reptiles and insects presented by the late Dr. Court; and many minor collections and specimens.

Like many local museums, the Victoria Institute appears to have served as a repository for the peculiar belongings of the deceased. However, Clark noted that it was also a meeting place for the Central Agricultural Board, the Medical Council, the Scientific Association, the Field Naturalists' Club and the Literary Association. In 1902 Collens reported that the institute had been enlarged the previous year to include reading rooms and a recreation room for billiards, chess, draughts, ping pong and other activities. In addition, classes were offered in Spanish, drawing, painting, bookkeeping, shorthand, business correspondence, cooking, dressmaking, agriculture and building construction. By 1912 there were a lecture and performance hall, orchestral and choral groups, a debating society and tennis courts. The institute also periodically presented art exhibitions. In 1895, for example, it organized a show comprising works in oil, watercolours and crayon, as well as photographs (including prints by L.F. Sellier). The newspaper *Public Opinion* applauded the exhibition for bringing more recognition to local artists. In short, the institute was a place in which Trinidadians of various socioeconomic backgrounds could pursue diverse interests in learning, artistic expression and recreation. In 1920 the institute was destroyed by fire, but managed to reopen three years later in a similarly designed building.[51]

On the grounds adjacent to the Victoria Institute was the Prince's Building, a one-storey structure raised on piers, surrounded by a verandah and approached by a semicircular drive from Queen's Park West. The building was erected quickly in 1861 to receive Prince Alfred (the second son of Queen Victoria) and, though he never arrived, other princes were later entertained here. More important, the building became "a place of public amusement for the general use of the inhabitants of the Colony" and in 1909 was leased by the colonial government to the town board for community purposes. Over the years, it served as a venue for "innumerable concerts, dances, theatrical performances, agricultural and other shows and exhibitions, amateur boxing contests, bazaars, entertainments of various sorts, lectures and public meetings". While many of the performances were locally produced, there was also a wide array of visiting shows, such as "Dr. Richards, the great Illusionist", who in 1911 performed for the governor's entourage and a large gathering, "among whom the beauty and fashion of the city were well represented". In 1914 the Favourite W.S. Harkins Players were in town for twelve days, presenting each night a different play, including *The Liar*, *The Confusion* and *Alias Jimmy Valentine*.[52]

The Prince's Building also served as a site for political rallies. In 1912, for example, Alfred Richards, a local pharmacist and president of the TWA, chaired a "monster meeting" in connection with a visit by Joseph Pointer, a Labour Party member of parliament. An audience of several thousand crowded in and around the building. Richards spoke first and offered a motion: "That in the opinion of this meeting the time has come when the Government of this Colony should be reconstituted on an elected basis." After a seconding of the motion and loud applause from the crowd, W.E. Beckles, the mayor of Arima and another TWA member, moved: "That in the opinion of this meeting the Municipality of Port-of-Spain should be restored by Royal Charter." There was again a seconding and more applause. Then Pointer addressed the gathering, saying he had come to Trinidad not only to consider matters of representative government but also to learn of "the condition of life and labour under which the people of the island were living". He questioned the conservatism of the Trinidadian elite and said he was prepared to return to the Colonial Office in London, where he would say he had been "commissioned by a mass meeting of the people of Trinidad" to request that they be granted "legislative powers of some kind".[53]

The Prince's Building also provided accommodation for Queen's Royal College during the late nineteenth century. Founded by the colonial government as the Queen's Collegiate School in 1859, this institution was reconstituted under its new name at the Prince's Building in 1870. In 1904 the school opened in its own building on the west side of the Savannah. This ornate two-storey structure, designed by Daniel Meinerts Hahn, was built with red-tinted concrete and blue limestone and included six classrooms, a large lecture hall and offices. The front façade of the central block featured arcaded galleries on both floors and a 93-foot tower to which a clock was later added. Extended wings contained sets of tall windows divided by pilasters that were capped with small towers at the roofline. At the front of the school's lawn was an iron fence with massive masonry gateposts, while sports fields were at the rear. Though it was non-sectarian in constitution, Queen's Royal College attracted primarily Protestant boys, including many who would go on to become leaders in various spheres of Trinidadian society. In 1911 a ten-year-old C.L.R. James entered the school as a scholarship winner. Here he "mastered thoroughly the principles of cricket and English literature"; studied Latin, French and Greek; and "learnt and obeyed and taught a code, the English public-school code".[54]

Three blocks to the west of the Prince's Building on Queen's Park West was the Queen's Park Hotel. This was designed in the 1890s by George Brown, who used as its centrepiece a house previously belonging to Frederick Warner, a prominent attorney. Brown built extensions to the east and west of the original residence, and during the following decades, the owners added other components. The two-storey hotel was a masterpiece in the architectural style promoted by Brown at the turn of the century. Built of masonry and wood, the sprawling complex consisted of multiple sections with gabled roofs of different pitches (embellished with turrets and finials) and a spacious verandah on the ground floor. Its walls were lined with sash windows and louvred panels, while intricate fretwork adorned the eaves and panels between verandah posts. A variety of palms and other tropical foliage surrounded the complex, and the perimeter was defined by concrete walls, iron fencing and elegant concrete fenceposts.

Established by a group of local investors and managed by a Swiss hotelier, the Queen's Park Hotel opened in January 1895 to much fanfare. The *Daily News* reported that "business operations will begin on an extensive and up to date style reminiscent of the Metropolitan Hotel, London and other larger establishments of the kind in large centres of civilization. The building is spacious – one of the largest in the island, cool, airy and situated in one of the most healthy and desirable parts of the town". The newspaper added that the hotel was "well-appointed and of the highest order" and that it would "undoubtedly prove a boon and blessing to tourists". After expansions during the early twentieth century, the hotel featured some eighty guest rooms (with plunge and shower baths), as well as a private drawing room, writing room, ladies' room, billiards room, smoking room, barber shop, ballroom, breakfast gallery, dining room, extensive wine cellar and a garden in the centre of the complex.

The hotel's location on the Savannah was integral to its appeal. In his 1904 *Book of Trinidad*, writer T.B. Jackson said:

> This celebrated hotel is situated in the finest and coolest part of Port-of-Spain, overlooking that beautiful and glorious Savannah. . . . Here can be seen from the verandahs every afternoon games of football, cricket, baseball, golf races, or polo matches.
>
> The hotel is commodious and up-to-date in every detail. . . . Its rooms are large and airy, and entirely free of those troublesome insects often met with in tropical hotels.
>
> It has the choicest surroundings, and is known as the starting point from which all the places of beauty and interest in the colony can be visited. . . . Across the road from the hotel the visitor can take a comfortable electric car, which will convey him to any part of Port-of-Spain. . . .
>
> The hotel is famous for its excellent Cuisine and large stock of fine old Vintage, and well deserves the name given to it by the *Montreal Gazette*, "The Hotel *par excellence* of the West Indies". . . .
>
> Well out of the heat and dust and glare of the business part of Port-of-Spain, yet by cab, tram, bicycle, "Shanks' pony" or telephone, absolutely within touch with it, the Queen's Park Hotel enjoys a unique position in the centre of the fashionable part of Port-of-Spain and of its coolest, loveliest quarter.

Certainly, visitors to Trinidad experienced the Queen's Park Hotel as a tranquil refuge. For example, the American poet Ella Wheeler Wilcox wrote in a 1909 travel book: "Not until the broad cool verandas of the Queens Park Hotel are reached, does nervous irritation with boatmen, and cabmen give way to nobler sentiments of appreciation of scenery and climate." From her rooms on the north side of the hotel, Wilcox observed the varied activities on the Savannah, including the drives by well-to-do citizens around the park in the late afternoon. Though the Queen's Park Hotel attracted many tourists, it also became a social centre for the Port-of-Spain elite. Local historian Olga Mavrogordato recalls that it served as the site for various dinners and dances, including the presentation of debutantes and the annual Old Year's Dance.[55]

At the turn of the twentieth century, the Queen's Park Hotel contrasted sharply with other hotels in Port of Spain, all of which were downtown. Instead of the commerce and congestion of Marine Square and surrounding streets, this new facility, with lavish furnishings and modern amenities, offered repose within a spacious, beautiful and healthy natural environment. Large verandahs and abundant windows enabled guests to view the hotel's gardens, the expansive Savannah and the mountains in the distance. This picturesque scenery was complemented by the Savannah district's significance as a place of leisure and prestige, with various spaces for recreational activities and the homes of many of the city's wealthiest residents. In addition, the Queen's Park Hotel provided visitors with a new way of orienting themselves within Port of Spain. Instead of staying in hotels near the port, they could now, on arrival, be quickly carried to the Savannah, where they could take advantage of various forms of transport to explore the city and surrounding countryside. In essence, the hotel's goal was to construct for its guests a memorable experience of comfort, convenience and serenity within a prosperous tropical colony.

Natural beauty and elite residence in Port of Spain reached their epitome on the north side of the Savannah in the Botanic Gardens and Government House, the home of the governor. David Lockhart, Trinidad's botanist, laid out the Botanic Gardens in 1820 (during the administration of Ralph Woodford) and obtained some of his plants from an older garden in the nearby British island of St Vincent. Subsequent botanists expanded the gardens to include an immense array of species for scientific study and aesthetic appreciation. The gardens stretched along the north side of the Circular Road and featured a variety of paths along which visitors could contemplate a wealth of tropical plant life. Visitors could also climb a 300-foot hill for a view of the gardens, the Savannah and the city beyond. Among the numerous species under cultivation, J.H. Collens mentions the palmyra, talipot, sabal and rotang palms; bamboos; eucalyptus, nutmeg, samaan, mango, tonga-bean, Liberian coffee and camphor trees; and various flowering shrubs such as frangipani and oleander. Meanwhile, Henry James Clark was particularly impressed by the poui, traveller's, Brazil-nut, leopard-wood and cannonball trees. He observed that the gardens "present an endless succession of new and beautiful forms, ranging from the most delicate mosses and tiny film-ferns to the stately palms and giant forest trees – a field for contemplation and study as wide as it is wonderful". He advised early-morning visits to the gardens, "their shady walks and groves being, especially at that time, deliciously cool, while the air is made fragrant by the perfume of flower and blossom, and the morning breeze is laden with the aroma from the nutmeg and other spice trees".[56]

In 1899 Lady Broome, a writer and the wife of Governor F. Napier Broome (1891–1896), commented on the nursemaids and babies who frequented the gardens (especially during police-band concerts twice a week) and noted that she enjoyed sending her Government House guests on tours of the gardens with their superintendent. However, Lady Broome also emphasized another dimension of this horticultural wonder:

> Pages might be written on the scientific value of the beautiful gardens which surround this tropical palace [Government House], as well as of the opportunity they afford of studying insect life. . . . But the serious business of the gardens is really to make experiments in the growth and cultivation of the various economic products of the island – raising seedling canes, coffee, and cocoa, and determining which variety would most successfully repay culture. It is a mistake to regard them only from the ornamental point of view, though their beauty is very striking, for they are chiefly valuable for their practical results.[57]

In short, Trinidad's Botanic Gardens were one component of the vast British imperial enterprise of botanical research that was centred at Kew Gardens in London and encompassed gardens in colonies throughout the world. This enterprise constituted a well-organized network for the circulation of plants, personnel, and information. While Trinidad's Botanic Gardens provided residents and visitors with a peaceful space for leisure and contemplation, they also served as an important site for experimentation aimed at increasing the colony's value as a source of agricultural products.

On the eastern side of the Botanic Gardens was Government House, which was erected around 1875 to replace an earlier residence for the governor nearby (see figure 8). The front elevation of this massive two-storey limestone structure faced the Savannah to the south and included three distinct parts. The western section featured a triple-arched entryway, a gallery on the first floor, and a hipped roof, while the eastern section consisted of a single arched entryway, a porch with a balustrade on the first floor and a square parapet with a flagpole. The longer central section included two floors of colonnaded galleries and a transverse gabled roof; dormer windows were later added here and to the western section. With various other components extending to the rear, Government House clearly asserted authority and grandeur within the Botanic Gardens. The view of the building from the south was particularly impressive. Gravel walkways in the gardens met at a fountain surrounded by urns, while a path to the fountain's north was flanked by flowerbeds, shrubs and palms and continued to a balustrade that marked the perimeter of the house's front lawn.

The abundance of nature outside Government House continued into the interior. In 1895 the American journalist Elizabeth Bisland described the main entrance through the parapet-topped east section:

> One's first impression upon entering the great square marble-paved hall, with a staircase wound around three sides of it, is of cool greenery; in the turn of the stair, on the broad landing half-way up, in the corners, in the archway leading to the dining-room, and down the shadowy-mirrored vista of the drawing-room, one sees plants and plants, and again plants. Palms twenty feet in height, ferns, dracaena – purple, red, yellow, white – blooming orchids, calladiums freaked and splotched with a thousand tints; endless feathery and satin-leaved things with long Latin names banked in every available corner.

The building's openness to the surrounding environment also impressed Lady Broome:

> It was certainly an ideal house for entertaining. I always declared that the balls gave themselves, and there was never the slightest trouble in arranging any sort of party in the large rooms, which were always as cool as possible after sunset. The

ballroom was lofty, open "to all the airts that blow", and possessed a perfect floor. Then when you have Kew Gardens for decorative purposes growing outside your windows, there is not much difficulty in producing a pretty effect. Indeed, the entire house was arranged for coolness, from the great hall which went up the whole height of the building, to the wide verandahs which surrounded it on three sides.

Indeed, balls at Government House typically involved both the interior rooms and exterior grounds. In April 1914, for example, Sir George and Lady Le Hunte held a party for the visiting Princess Marie Louise of Schleswig-Holstein, a granddaughter of Queen Victoria. Seven hundred guests attended. A reporter from the *Argos* described the scene:

> The entire grounds and Botanic Gardens were most elaborately illuminated, particularly the enclosure on the southern side, which was attractively set off in the form of a square, with several flags, those of the Union Jack being the most prominent, upon which were hung myriads of variegated electric bulbs, the effect being most pleasing and picturesque.
>
> The spacious ball room was tastefully decorated in an appropriate scheme of red, white and blue, with very effective lighting and an abundance of flowers, in which were entwined tiny electric lights, dangling about in every direction. North of the ball room a huge tent was erected for the bar, which was replete with the choicest and most delicious wines and best cigars and cigarettes.

At 9:30 p.m. the governor escorted the princess into the grand hall to a rendition of "God Save the King", after which she was seated on a dais specially prepared for her. Subsequently there was dancing, with music provided by an orchestra of over thirty string instruments under the direction of Lionel Belasco, one of Trinidad's top musicians at the time. Selections included lancers, waltzes, two-steps and paseos (a calypso-like genre). At midnight a lavish dinner was served both in the hall and the outdoor tent.[58]

To a large extent, Government House and its surrounding grounds encapsulated the composition and significance of the Queen's Park Savannah district as a whole. The Savannah was a low-density residential and recreational area in which there was a premium on order, control, peacefulness and cultivated nature. In this, it differed greatly from the high-density, heterogeneous commercial, industrial and residential spaces of downtown Port of Spain. For both residents and visitors, the Savannah offered a realm of leisure and contemplation – an alternative to the commotion of downtown. Moreover, its visual coherence carried much appeal. At the turn of the century, local firms sold numerous postcards of palm trees, gardens, elegant buildings and other attractive scenes in the Savannah district. With the homes surrounding the park belonging to the city's most prominent inhabitants, the area carried a high social status. Nonetheless, middle- and working-class people also made extensive use of the Savannah grounds and frequented some of the buildings on its perimeter, such as the Victoria Institute, the Prince's Building and Queen's Royal College. Occasionally, the Savannah even became a site for public meetings that protested the prevailing social and political order.

SURROUNDING DISTRICTS

Surrounding central Port of Spain and the Queen's Park Savannah were several other primarily residential districts, which varied greatly in layout, architecture and socioeconomic characteristics. With the migration of people of all classes out of the crowded central city, the population of these districts grew during the cocoa boom era. The official incorporation of much of this land into the city during the first few decades of the twentieth century in turn posed new challenges for municipal administration. In a 1910 editorial, the *Port-of-Spain Gazette* called for the integration of this wider urban area:

> Port-of-Spain must stretch out its civic arm and extend its boundaries from the old toll gate on the St. Joseph Road, to the ridges of the hills that lie in a half moon shape around the town . . . quite to Four Roads, and keep of course to the sea as the other boundary. Within these borders all must be gathered in as citizens of Port-of-Spain, and with some slight initial exception all must be treated alike.[59]

Equality in the improvement of the infrastructure of Port of Spain's diverse districts remained an ideal rather than a reality as the twentieth century developed.

To the east of the central city, beyond the Dry River, was the low-income district of East Dry River, including Laventille. In contrast to the flat terrain and street grid of the central city, this area consisted of steep hills that residents circumambulated through a maze of winding lanes and paths. It was initially settled during the late eighteenth and early nineteenth centuries by planters and their enslaved workers, who grew cocoa, coffee, cotton and eventually sugar. By the time of emancipation, many of these estates had been abandoned. During the following decades, various African-descended residents of the area were joined by many migrants from Trinidad's plantation districts and other British Caribbean islands. This population typically worked in service occupations in the city, in agriculture or in the district's quarries, which supplied limestone for the construction boom of the late nineteenth and early twentieth centuries. While some people were squatters, many bought or leased parcels of land for their homes. Since there was minimal government regulation of the area, inhabitants constructed a dense and free-form landscape of routes, yards and small wooden houses in accordance with their own intentions and means. Given the steep terrain, they frequently added stairs to paths and employed piers of varying lengths for supporting their houses. Though a strong sense of community developed among the people of East Dry River, residents of other parts of the city generally perceived the district as unsanitary, dangerous and disreputable.[60]

While outsiders considered East Dry River's landscape a forbidding realm, it also contained several well-known landmarks. Near the top of Laventille Hill was Fort Chacón, built in the early 1790s as an observatory and named after Trinidad's last Spanish governor. Frederick Treves included a description of the remains of this structure in his 1908 travel book: "Its walls are of astounding thickness; its paved court, that once echoed with the clang of arms, is now a wild garden, a mere tangle of green, a court whose silence is broken only by the patter of rain and the song of birds." Further south was Fort Picton, erected by Governor Thomas Picton in 1797, after the British conquest of the island. This 40-foot-high Martello tower was built with walls 4 to 6 feet thick and accommodated cannon, quarters for troops and storerooms. Perched on a hill on the western side of the district, across the Dry River from Queen Street, was the United Brothers Masonic Lodge. Built by French settlers in 1804, this small masonry and wood building featured a gabled portico with Doric columns. While the lodge was chartered by France during the 1790s, it shifted its allegiance to Pennsylvania after the British conquest and to Scotland with the War of 1812. However, its prominent members continued to keep minutes in French for many years. Also near the Dry River were the first of a series of fourteen brick and limestone Stations of the Cross (see figure 9), which led up the hill to Our Lady of Laventille Church at the summit. Between 1885 and 1891, a Portuguese confraternity built a new stone church here, attached to a tall white belfry and statue of the Virgin that could be seen from throughout the central city. Each May, pilgrims gathered in the city in the early morning and spent a day in devotion as they ascended the hill.[61]

North of East Dry River and east of the Savannah was the district of Belmont. After emancipation and the abandonment of sugar and coffee estates, the population of this area grew through settlement by various peoples of African descent, including Africans liberated by the Royal Navy from the transatlantic slave trade. During its early period, Belmont was known as "Freetown" and, like East Dry River, was a centre for the perpetuation and re-creation of African-derived religious and other cultural practices. Folklorist Andrew Carr notes that, during the latter nineteenth century, the district included communities of Dahomean, Igbo, Kongo and Mandingo peoples. A Rada (Dahomean) compound on the Belmont Valley Road served as a social centre and included the house of a religious leader, a chapel, a shed for dance ceremonies and shrines for Elegba and Ogou (spirits associated with crossroads and iron). In 1888 the compound held a special *Gozen* ceremony and invited members from a Yoruba settlement in East Dry River to participate. A procession to a nearby spring, departing around 5:00 a.m., was led by a devotee possessed by Agwé (spirit of the sea), followed by Rada drummers, girls with goblets resting on their heads, Yorubas playing *shekeres* and other members of the two communities. After the goblets were filled at the spring, the procession returned to the compound for additional rituals.[62]

During the latter nineteenth and early twentieth centuries, Belmont developed into a vibrant working- and middle-class community, as people sought better housing than what was available in the crowded and decaying central city. After the turn of the century, there were efforts to lay out regular streets, build bridges and improve drainage and sewers. In 1905 a Belmont Improvement Ordinance was implemented with revenues from the colonial government, the Port of Spain commissioners and the householders themselves. In 1910 the *Mirror* editorialized on advances in the "flourishing district" of Belmont: "Almost every crooked and winding alley has been converted into a comfortable street with concreted sidewalks, new and artistic cottages have sprung up, the old stagnant drain with its miasmatic germs that ran through the whole place, threatening the lives and health of the inhabitants, has been made into a splendid concrete channel." That same year, the *Port-of-Spain Gazette* acknowledged that "the district has been converted into a very desirable residential suburb of the city" and mentioned "hundreds of new dwellings of a superior class that are already springing up in all directions". However, the newspaper also called for a better system of street lighting ("after all efficient street lighting is one of the first requirements of any decently managed municipality") and claimed that the Belmont Improvement Ordinance had actually exacerbated flooding in parts of the suburb. In 1912 Belmont was incorporated within the city of Port of Spain.[63]

To the northeast of the Savannah was St Ann's. In the late nineteenth century, this district still included various small agricultural estates, but was increasingly becoming a locale for middle- and upper-class homes. Government House, in the Botanic Gardens, was considered part of St Ann's and northeast of it was a prominent residence known as Coblentz. In the late nineteenth century, it belonged to Joseph Leon Agostini, a cocoa proprietor and merchant, first president of the chamber of commerce, and member of both the legislative council and municipal government (including a term as mayor). Reputed to have ninety-nine windows, Coblentz House was the site of many lavish parties during this era. Farther up the St Ann's Road was the lunatic asylum, relocated from Belmont at the beginning of the twentieth century. Historian David Trotman notes that in 1900 the asylum housed over four hundred patients, who were admitted in accordance with various medical categories of the age: "maniacal and dangerous, quiet chronic, melancholy and suicidal", and "idiotic, paralytic, and epileptic".[64] Later known as the St Ann's Hospital, this institution developed into an extensive complex of buildings.

To the west of the Savannah was St Clair, the most elite neighbourhood in Port of Spain. Originally a sugar estate, this area was bought by the colonial government in 1879 and used as a stock farm for cattle and horses and as a dairy. The government began laying out the east-west St Clair Avenue in 1889 and, after the farm was removed in 1899, developed a grid of streets to the north with a small park in the centre. St Clair was a planned community with covenants controlling the value, setback and spacing of houses, as well as restrictions on the types of secondary structures that could be built on lots. During the first decade of the twentieth century, six grandiose homes were constructed on the Maraval Road, to the north of Queen's Royal College and facing the Savannah. From the south, these included Hayes Court, a relatively sedate structure completed by the firm of Taylor and Gillies for the Anglican bishop; the residence of physician and civic leader Enrique Prada, built by George Brown and featuring a circular drive, porte-cochère, large verandah, and contrasting rooftops; the home of the merchant Lucien Ambard, a baroque extravaganza of towers, domes, balconies and ornamental ironwork, designed by a French architect; the Romanesque residence of the Catholic archbishop, built by George Brown, with a central square tower and arcades surrounding both floors; a house occupied initially by Joseph Leon Agostini, built with white coral limestone and featuring a flat roof, central gallery with Moorish arches and a symmetrical array of windows and pilasters; and the home of the Stollmeyer family, designed by Taylor and Gillies in the style of a Scottish castle with fine brick and stonework, a parapeted tower and a turret. The originality and lavishness of this cocoa boom ensemble of homes defined St Clair and the western side of the Savannah. Architect/architectural historian John Newel Lewis refers to the houses as "Queens of the Bands" (after the most elaborate costumes in Carnival masquerades) and asserts: "The highly cultivated individuality of the Trinidadian is frozen in these splendid palaces."[65]

North of this district's homes was the St Clair Experimental Station, which the *Port-of-Spain Gazette* surveyed in an article published in 1911:

> Where the stately buildings of St. Clair lift their heads in greeting to the stranger in search of things beyond the ordinary is to be found the main entrance to the Government Experimental Station. The surroundings are exceedingly picturesque; to the East the sun is not yet at its zenith; the tile-covered roofs, and the varying colours of the adjoining cottages and mansions, blend in the making of an Arcadian picture of which the tropics alone can boast parentage.

Inside the grounds, government officers grew orange, mango, pawpaw, cocoa, nutmeg, cinnamon, clove, rubber, palm, camphor, samaan and mahogany trees, as well as various other plants, all in the interest of the scientific advancement of agriculture in Trinidad. Later in 1911 the *Gazette* applauded the station on the "progressive move" of expanding its visiting hours so that the public could more fully appreciate its work.[66]

Adjacent to the southern end of St Clair and southwest of the Savannah was the district of New Town. This suburb was laid out as a grid of nine long blocks during the 1840s and initially attracted prosperous residents from the central city. Two elegant stone churches were built: All Saints for Anglicans, completed in 1846, and St Patrick's for Catholics, initiated in 1858. By the latter 1850s and 1860s, landowners were subdividing the district's lots and its population grew to include residents of various income levels. During the early twentieth century, centres of social interaction in the area ranged from the elite Savannah Club on Queen's Park West to the Cavalry calypso tent on Woodford Street, constructed each Carnival season as a shed covered with coconut branches.[67]

To the south of New Town and St Clair (and west of Lapeyrouse Cemetery) was Woodbrook. Formerly a sugar estate, this area was purchased in 1899 by the Siegert brothers, owners of Angostura Bitters. With some tenants already living on the property, the Siegerts extended a grid of streets, naming many after members of their family. In 1900 the Port of Spain town commissioners took over the maintenance and development of the streets. In his 1901 *New Illustrated Guide to Trinidad*, Paget reported that the area had been "converted into building lots and laid out with streets on the principle of the model estates in England. The whole property . . . promises to be a thriving and attractive suburb for the artisan class." During the early twentieth century, many working people did leave the crowded central city for better housing opportunities in Woodbrook. By 1910 the *Port-of-Spain Gazette* observed that Woodbrook "affords a residential quarter where clerks and better class artisans and the like find some of the home comforts and decencies that are denied them in the older quarters of the town owing to congestion that there exists, and this class of people are gradually improving the place and displacing a less desirable type of residents". The *Gazette* argued, however, that the town board was not giving sufficient attention to the improvement of the district's streets.

In 1911 the town board purchased Woodbrook from the Siegert family and implemented more regulations on its development, including requirements for lot sizes, setbacks and the minimum value of dwellings, as well as a limit of one dwelling per lot. In addition, the board began tearing down substandard housing. As it became more difficult for the poorest sector of the city's population to live here, Woodbrook was increasingly occupied by better-off working- and middle-class residents. Meanwhile, the municipal government maintained ownership of the district's lots (and in some cases its houses) as a source of revenue, a position that generated controversy with tenants who could afford to buy. Though the government strictly controlled the residential composition of Woodbrook during this period, it did permit the establishment of businesses on some street corners and set aside land for parks, schools, churches and a new cemetery. The Woodbrook Savannah became a popular site for various types of recreation and for travelling circuses and other shows. A highlight of 1914, for example, was the appearance of Arlington and Beckmann's Oklahoma Ranch Wild West, with 550 people and horses, "Calgary Stampede Champions", automobile polo featuring "Death Defying Drivers", "Barbarous Mexico Steer Wrestling", "5 Tribes of Indian Warriors" and a "Big Frontier Street Parade".[68]

To the northwest of Woodbrook were the St James Barracks. Constructed during the 1820s and among the oldest structures still standing in Port of Spain today, these Georgian-style buildings featured long rows of rooms fronted by colonnaded galleries. Initially, they housed British troops, with a capacity of approximately four hundred men. After the troops were relocated to Jamaica and St Lucia in the late 1880s, the buildings were handed over to the Trinidad Police for residence and training.[69]

West of the barracks were the lands of the old Peru sugar estate, a plantation that had been worked by Indian labourers. After the plantation closed, Indians continued to live here in a settlement called "Peru Village"; eventually the district as a whole became known as "St James". At the turn of the twentieth century, Peru Village constituted the primary concentration of Indo-Trinidadians in the Port of Spain area, since a relatively small number lived in the city proper. Visitors to Port of Spain during this era considered the village an exotic destination. In 1895 a writer for the *New York Observer and Chronicle* offered a few impressions of the settlement:

> The village . . . is a single long street of miserable wooden huts, thatched with straw or covered with corrugated iron. . . . All life is open to the view. There are men in turbans and dingy white robes gathered at the thigh, who move about in various avocations, or driving teams of hump-backed Indian cattle. . . . Some of the jewelers, who make the bangles with which the women are universally adorned, and who are in fact by this means the savings banks of their husbands, were at work under sheds over charcoal fires, and with no apparent implements except a pair of pincers and a small hammer.

This observer also described a Hindu temple as a hexagonal shed, 20 feet in diameter: "It was open to the gaze of every passer, and within could be seen some images and religious paraphernalia, and an elderly priest was engaged in sprinkling some sort of incense around the room." In addition, St James included many Muslims and became a site for Muharram observances, known in Trinidad as "Hosay". This event featured street processions with drummers and *tadjahs* – elaborate representations of the tomb of the martyred Hussein, the grandson of the prophet Mohammed. Hosay's participants and spectators included both Muslims and Hindus, as well as Afro-Trinidadians. In 1919 the Port-of-Spain City Council debated the possibility of annexing St James, but there were concerns about costs, given the area's substandard housing, water supply and drainage. When the district was finally incorporated in 1938, it added over 250 acres and approximately ten thousand residents to the city.[70]

By the end of the cocoa boom era, Port of Spain had evolved into a complex landscape comprising several major districts and myriad component places, each with distinct socio-spatial characteristics and significance. Within this dense landscape, people observed a range of conventional ways of enclosing or demarcating space, ornamenting structures and cultivating the natural environment. At the same time, they perceived locations as settings for particular kinds of activities, from industry, commerce and transport to governance, domestic life and recreation. Individual places and wider districts, in turn, carried varying degrees of social prestige, depending on the levels of wealth and power associated with them. People's perspectives on the city were shaped by where they lived, but also by their typical movements through the landscape. Common patterns of circulation generated more broadly shared experiences – large numbers of the city's residents, for example, regularly visited the harbour district, Marine Square, lower Frederick Street, Brunswick Square and the Queen's Park Savannah. Through ongoing observations and communication with each other, people developed extensive colloquial knowledge of the city, and, as the cocoa boom era developed, this knowledge was increasingly influenced by newspapers, pamphlets, books, postcards and other publications. Literary and visual materials, however, offered only partial depictions of the city. While low-income areas and surrounding districts were occasionally examined, publications focused on the main public and commercial spaces of the central city and on sites in and around the Savannah. Overall, writers and photographers of the cocoa boom era constructed an image of Port of Spain as an orderly, progressive city – an attractive and rewarding locale for investors, workers and travellers.

2. THE CITY AS A WHOLE

IN THE COURSE OF THE COCOA BOOM ERA, the people of Port of Spain constructed their landscape in ways that expressed both commonalities and differences within Trinidad's evolving social order. The population of the growing city shared the basic needs of an expanded infrastructure, a far greater supply of housing and the availability of outdoor spaces for leisure and public gatherings. However, construction practices and uses of space during this period manifested not only collective goals but also high levels of social inequality and conflict. In both the older central city and newer districts, government officials implemented a variety of projects to develop streets, the water supply, drainage, electricity and public transport. While some initiatives benefited the population as a whole, poorer areas of the city continued to receive less investment than more prosperous ones. Meanwhile, construction firms and individual builders erected houses at an exceptional rate throughout the city. These buildings, the largest portion of the urban environment, assumed a variety of forms, ranging from the extravagant mansions for the wealthy around the Queen's Park Savannah to the extremely crowded "barrack yards" for the poor in the city's centre and the small self-built structures on its edges. During this period, builders also perfected a Trinidadian-creole detached house type that could be produced at different scales and degrees of ornamentation. Patterns in housing design, size and location closely reflected the city's social hierarchy as well as people's aspirations for improved living conditions and social mobility during these years of general economic growth. Finally, the city's streets, squares and parks offered public spaces not only for conviviality and recreation but also for the organization of large-scale events, such as imperial celebrations, political rallies and protests. Customary forms of assembly and movement in these highly visible places were a means by which the city's populace periodically affirmed and critiqued its collective existence.

In short, infrastructure, housing and public spaces during the cocoa boom era constituted basic urban systems through which Port of Spain's inhabitants articulated social distinctions and their interdependence. In their ongoing modification and use of the landscape, they both perpetuated the inequalities of the colonial order and envisioned a more inclusive civic community.

THE URBAN INFRASTRUCTURE

Rapid population growth within Port of Spain and surrounding districts during the cocoa boom posed immense infrastructural challenges for government officials and civic leaders, while also raising issues concerning the definition of the limits of the city. By the turn of the twentieth century, municipal boundaries were far more circumscribed than the expanse of contiguous densely settled areas that constituted the city's actual sphere. Thus, officials were in a position either to exclude large portions of the urban area from basic services or to expand municipal boundaries and attempt to improve the material conditions of a broader population. While requiring a large financial investment, a wider definition of the city would benefit more people, address public health concerns, and lend greater credibility to civic rhetoric that Port of Spain was a modern, progressive place.

In an editorial published in 1910, titled "The Unification of Port-of-Spain", the *Port-of-Spain Gazette* advocated a more inclusive concept of the city:

> One of the most pressing problems ... is how to preserve a unity of treatment that is fair and just to the inhabitants of Port-of-Spain taken collectively and to the city as a whole. Port-of-Spain is admittedly a difficult city to administer. It is a town that has grown and is still growing at a very rapid rate, and, more complicating than anything else, it is a town that is so shut in by a range of hills and couple of malarious and malodorous swamps that it can no longer extend ... by a gradual, perceptible and organized growth. Belmont, Laventille and the suburbs of that district present to-day the most typical examples of what the growth of Port-of-Spain has been like. On the other side of town, thanks to the Messrs Siegert and other landowners there has been some attempt at systemized suburban extension, while the Government at St. Clair has possibly gone to the other extreme and placed too many restrictions on the development of its estate. Otherwise the manner of Port-of-Spain's growth has been almost as neglected as Topsy's, its tentacles have run here, there and everywhere in a most unregulated manner, and consequently the problem of the unification of Port-of-Spain and the uniform and equal treatment of its citizens is one that presents unusual difficulties. But it is one that must be settled.

The *Gazette* continued:

> A wide and well defined boundary and something like equal treatment for all who live within it is the only way out of many of the present town problems. Of course we do not mean that as much should be spent on a back street of Laventille or Woodbrook as on some of the show places of the town, but every street in town should be put in order in rotation – and kept so.[1]

For the *Gazette*, Port of Spain was a sprawling and generally chaotic phenomenon in immediate need of greater control and systematic servicing. The coherent functioning of the city, it argued, depended on infrastructural improvements across the urban area, though it qualified this assertion by suggesting that more central and upscale locales (with higher visibility) deserved preferential treatment.

At the heart of infrastructure debates during this period was the fact that the actual provision of services to the residents of Port of Spain and surrounding districts was a complex process in which financing and management were shared by the colonial and municipal governments. Moreover, the details of these arrangements changed over time, particularly with the colonial government's abolition of the borough council and appointment of commissioners in 1899, the establishment of a town board in 1907 and the restoration of a more independent city council in 1914. Given these complexities, the improvement and eventual annexation of outlying areas proceeded slowly and with much administrative and fiscal wrangling. During 1896 and 1897 the borough council indicated that it was willing to incorporate Belmont and other districts, but only on condition that the colonial government first address the poor state of their streets, water supply and drainage. After the demise of this body, the new town authorities did in fact implement a Belmont Improvement Scheme (1905) and a Woodbrook Improvement Scheme (1907), which facilitated the city's annexation of Woodbrook in 1911 and Belmont in 1912. The 1912 municipal expansion also included a substantial portion of the low-income East Dry River district – the area along the western side of the Laventille Hills, from Belmont to the sea. In 1917 the wealthy district of St Clair was incorporated, while Mucurapo (west of Woodbrook) and St James were not added until 1932 and 1938 respectively. Most of impoverished Laventille was never incorporated, but neither were the more prosperous contiguous areas of Maraval, St Ann's and Cascade. This gradual and uneven extension of Port of Spain's official boundaries across urbanized settlements suggests a general broadening of concepts of civic responsibility, but also that the definition of the city was affected by factors specific to disparate outlying districts.[2]

Additional perspectives on the evolving morphology of the Port of Spain area and the limits of the city are offered by maps produced during and after the cocoa boom. Goad's 1895 *Insurance Plan of Port of Spain* includes the grids of downtown, uptown and New Town, as well as the initial grid of Woodbrook between Colville and French Streets and a few other early streets here. Peru Village (St James), further to the west, is off the map. Meanwhile, the only portions of East Dry River shown are those near the river, such as the area of Piccadilly and St Paul Streets; the beginning of the Laventille Road; and, further north, Sorzanoville, with Observatory Street and the initial portions of Quarry, Basilon and La Carriere Streets. A few of the main streets of lower Belmont are indicated: Belmont Circular Road, Erthig Road and Norfolk

Street, along with the initial sections of the Belle Eau, St François Valley and Belmont Valley Roads. Girod's 1912 *Plan of Port of Spain and Suburbs* depicts a very different city. To the west of the central core is the full grid of Woodbrook (as far as the new municipal boundary along the Maraval River) and, to the north, the grid of St Clair. West of Woodbrook, straddling the Western Main Road, are "Peru Lands", with such early streets as the Long Circular, Lee Lum and Bournes Roads. East Dry River is now included as far east as the new municipal line, with documentation of numerous streets, several quarries and such locales as Essex Place, Scott Place, Clifton Hill and High Woods. Much of the irregular grid of lower Belmont is filled in and the roads of upper Belmont are indicated as far as the municipal line. To the northeast of the Queen's Park Savannah, several streets are shown in St Ann's and the adjacent Cascade valley. In 1931, a decade after the cocoa boom, the colonial government's Lands and Surveys Department issued a map of Port of Spain that recorded even further suburban growth, including an extensive grid for St James (the former Peru Lands). Moreover, this map delineates individual lots within blocks in outlying districts as well as in the central core, thus demonstrating a higher level of attention to the city as a whole.[3]

With Port of Spain's rapidly growing population and expanded settlement during the cocoa boom, a central issue for colonial and municipal governments was the improvement of the water supply. During the early 1850s, the colonial government established a waterworks on the Maraval River in the Maraval valley to the northwest of the city. In the 1880s, historian Louis A.A. de Verteuil offered a description of this system:

> Three reservoirs have been constructed in the latter [Maraval] valley at about three miles from town, and a main pipe of 12 inches bore, reduced to 10 inches, brings the water to the lowest end of the town and the wharves. It is distributed through every street by sub-main and branch pipes, varying from six to two inches in diameter; hydrants are also disposed at every 500 feet, more or less, for protection against fire. . . . The local supply is calculated at 2,500,000 imperial gallons per day, or 77 gallons per individual, the population being 31,858 inhabitants. There are, at present, 3,802 service pipes, supplying about 3,700 houses.

De Verteuil also noted an additional dam and reservoir in the St Ann's valley, to the northeast of the city. Goad's 1895 insurance plan of Port of Spain indicated a daily average supply of more than 2.5 million gallons from the Maraval reservoir and more than 400,000 gallons from St Ann's.

Though these two reservoirs provided a substantial supply, water was not reaching the city's inhabitants equally and much was being wasted. In 1881 a government committee reported:

> In nearly every yard, and at almost every house, passers in the street will hear the sound of water running, and, as the gutters show, to waste, in addition to which baths of unnecessary and previously unknown dimensions have been constructed, fountains erected, and gardens irrigated to an extent that could not have been contemplated, and certainly not provided for when the water supply was brought to Port-of-Spain.

The baths referenced here (known as "plunge baths") contained hundreds of gallons and were popular in elite residences, especially around the Queen's Park Savannah. For example, St Clair resident Eugene Cipriani had in his garden a 1,000-gallon, marble-floored Roman bath, replenished by a continuous flow of water. By 1900 there were 1,380 baths in the city with a capacity of more than 100 gallons and their users were estimated to consume an average of 187 gallons each per day. At the other extreme were the thousands of people who competed for water at communal standpipes in the barrack yards of the central city or in poorer outlying areas that received very limited supplies. With the continued increase of the population across greater Port of Spain, the colonial government developed additional water sources in Diego Martin (to the west), St Clair and Cascade. Moreover, it passed an ordinance in 1896 that authorized the implementation of water meters and higher rates in an effort to curtail waste. However, this ordinance was retracted owing to heavy opposition from the public and the municipal government. In 1902 conflict between the citizenry and the colonial government over the supply and regulation of water surfaced again and escalated to the level of large-scale protests and a riot the following year (discussed below). During subsequent years, water remained a major challenge. In 1914, for example, the *Mirror* editorialized against the government's efforts to regulate the use of water and called for the development of expanded resources to meet the demands of the growing city: "If the people of the town are to enjoy the health that they should, and the town be as clean as it is essential that it should be, there must be a full and uninterrupted supply of water even at the driest time of the year."[4]

The removal of water from Port of Spain was similarly an ongoing concern. The colonial government introduced an underground sewerage system in the late 1850s to early 1860s and approved an expanded scheme in 1889. However, installation of sewers across the urban area was slow and uneven. For example, sewers constructed in Belmont during the first decade of the twentieth century effectively serviced only the lower part of this district, and a system was not implemented in Woodbrook until the late 1930s. Meanwhile, the Dry River, on the densely populated east side of the city, posed a particular drainage challenge. During storms, the river sometimes flooded surrounding areas, while during the dry season pools of standing water posed a significant public health threat. In the early twentieth century, the *Port-of-Spain Gazette* frequently called on the government to address the conditions of this watercourse, referring to it as an "open sewer" and an "excellent breeding place for mosquitoes and for miasma and for infection of well nigh every class". The newspaper emphasized that the river threatened the health of the entire city, not just impoverished residents in its immediate vicinity. By 1912 the government was beginning sewerage work in the hilly East Dry River area to lessen run-off into the river, though a full-fledged scheme involving paving the river bed did not occur until the 1930s. An additional project of the cocoa boom era was concreting drains at the sides of city streets. This reduced the pools of water that, according to police officer J.N. Brierley, had afforded "a comfortable resting place and singing ground for the nice little frogs which so frequently enliven the place of their habitation by their melodious (?) piping".[5]

Regular cleaning of streets was another critical element of public health in Port of Spain. By the mid-nineteenth century, the city employed crews of scavengers (garbage collectors), though, as a visitor explained in 1890, these were assisted by an auxiliary workforce:

> I made the intimate acquaintance of the Port-of-Spain street-cleaning department. It is a wonderfully efficient organization and could teach New York, London, and Paris lessons in street-cleaning economy. It is composed entirely of vultures . . . these accommodating municipal servants not only clean the public thoroughfares but own them as well. They hold animated caucuses in the parks and market places, and require pedestrians to step aside when met on a narrow sidewalk. Under ordinary circumstances they are a jolly and complacent brotherhood, but good-fellowship vanishes in the presence of offal.

Eventually, municipal authorities assigned street-cleaning entirely to human employees and in 1905 hired Henry Reading, a local marksman, to eliminate many of the corbeaux, which had previously benefited from legal protection. In his first four months of work, Reading delivered 3,405 carcasses to the town dump, for which he was paid nine cents each. Increased attention to Port of Spain's sanitation was formalized in the colonial government's Public Health Ordinance of 1915, and in 1917 the democratically elected city council took over the government's local sanitation department in its efforts to improve conditions throughout the municipality.[6]

Along with addressing water and sanitation, governmental officials worked to electrify Port of Spain at the end of the nineteenth century. Some streets had been lit with kerosene or gas since the 1870s, but electricity promised a more fully illuminated and modernized city. The borough council awarded a contract to the Trinidad Electric Light and Power Company, which succeeded in lighting some of the city's streets on 5 March 1895. Though electricity certainly excited Port of Spain's populace, there were also concerns about its safety. A legislative council paper in 1898 featured a report by an outside engineer who warned of dangers caused by the unregulated installation of electrical and telephone lines. Nonetheless, the electrification of the city proceeded. In a 1904 advertisement, the Electric Company summarized its services: "Buildings of all Descriptions Wired for Lights, Bells, Annunciators, &c., &c. Temporary Lighting of Buildings and Gardens – A Speciality." The company also noted that it supplied power and installed motors for all purposes. Along with transforming the look, sound and capacities of the urban landscape, electricity appears to have attracted more people to the streets at night. In 1907 the *Port-of-Spain Gazette* editorialized:

> First of all it should be said that few, if any, Colonial cities have improved as much as Port of Spain has done within the last decade. . . . Less than a decade ago Port of Spain at night was a city of the dead . . . but the habits of the people are changing. They walk around, or ride in the car nightly, in the streets and suburbs of the town, or around the Savannah. Shops are springing up whose principal trade is done after night fall, and Port of Spain is as lively as most cities of its size any where from seven o'clock on to after nine. . . . But while Port of Spain is getting to be a city that is used at night very freely by respectable people, they have not that protection in the streets which they should have. . . . Ladies complain bitterly that if they go out alone or with companions of their own sex only, they are often followed and accosted by apparently respectable men. . . . Then again men walking out alone are not free from being accosted by loose women in any street in the town. Especially is this likely to happen at street corners waiting for the car, and it is a more than usual evil in the two principal streets of the town – Frederick street and Marine Square.

So, electrification extended traffic and commerce into the night, which in turn facilitated forms of encounter undesired by much of the public. The *Gazette*'s suggested solution was more police and yet more lights: "Crime and immorality flourish in the dark a hundred fold more than they do in the light."[7]

An additional element of the changing urban infrastructure was public transport. Around 1883 the Trinidad Tramways Company initiated mule-tram service from its stables near the railway station on the Queen's Wharf. It operated two routes: one up St Vincent Street and on to the southwest corner of the Savannah at Tranquillity Boulevard (later renamed Cipriani Boulevard), and another up Frederick Street and around the eastern side of the Savannah to near the Botanic Gardens. While mule-trams continued to run into the early twentieth century, the Belmont Tramway Company introduced an electric tram service in 1895, with cars imported from Philadelphia. On 26 June Lady Broome, wife of the governor, inaugurated this first electric line, which ran from the railway station up Frederick Street to Belmont, where it looped through several streets. The cars were decorated with flags, bunting and flowers for the occasion and cruised at fifteen miles per hour. From a newspaper account, local historian Carlton Ottley relates that "the crowd along the route was most enthusiastic and danced and screeched and waved their hands, hats and heads, and ran alongside and tried in every way to express their pleasure and admiration". In 1901 the Canadian-based Trinidad Electric Company purchased the Belmont Tramway Company, as well as the Trinidad Electric Light and Power Company, and developed additional tram routes. J.H. Collens reported in 1912 that tram service was running from 6:00 a.m. to 11:00 p.m., with four routes from the railway station to Belmont, St Ann's, St Clair and Four Roads, to the west of St James. A fifth route circled the Savannah and began service at 4:30 p.m., the traditional time for promenading. Passengers on any of the four main routes could switch cars at the Transfer Station on the southwest corner of Frederick and Park Streets. In 1918 the Trinidad Electric Company initiated an additional eastern route from the railway station along South Quay and the Eastern Main Road, thus providing service to the people at the southern end of East Dry River and Laventille.[8]

As the electric trams became an established part of life in Port of Spain, they helped to integrate downtown with surrounding districts. By the end of the cocoa boom years, many of the lower-lying neighbourhoods of the urban area were connected through this efficient form of transport. Moreover, trams afforded passengers the thrills of faster mobility and new experiences of the varied landscape of their expanding city.

HOUSING

With the rapid increase of Port of Spain's population during the cocoa boom era, there was an ongoing demand for additional housing among all social classes. New construction occurred primarily uptown and in districts surrounding the central city, as people moved out of downtown or migrated from other parts of Trinidad and abroad. Nonetheless, a substantial portion of the population continued to live in the downtown area. Here typical middle-class housing consisted of buildings that were adjoined or closely built, sited at the pavement or the street, and comprised two storeys, though some had one or three. Many people lived above ground-floor shops. Meanwhile, a large portion of the low-income population lived in "barracks" – generally single-storey buildings with a series of adjoining rooms, in yards in the interior of blocks. In contrast to the high-density, mixed commercial/residential environment of downtown, uptown and surrounding districts were predominantly residential, with detached houses and yards of varying sizes. Trees and gardens were far more common, particularly in middle- and upper-class areas, where they sometimes obscured the houses themselves.

Goad's 1895 insurance map indicates the density and quality of houses in uptown and surrounding areas, with individual blocks coded as "closely built", "detached (eight to forty feet apart)", and "scattered (over forty feet apart)", as well as "poor & probably uninsurable", "ordinary & poor buildings mixed", and "better class, well built as a rule". In general terms, density decreased and quality increased from the southern to the northern portions of uptown. East Dry River included a variety of densely built and detached dwellings of poor and mixed quality, while Sorzanoville (the northern portion of this area) contained detached houses of mixed quality and even a block of scattered, better-class homes between the Dry River and Observatory Street. Belmont and New Town both included houses of a range of qualities, though the former had a generally lower density. The blocks of early Woodbrook contained detached dwellings of poor and mixed quality.[9]

The growing demand for new housing in Port of Spain during the latter nineteenth and early twentieth centuries coincided with innovations in construction technologies that helped to meet this need. In his historical study of architecture in Trinidad, John Newel Lewis offers a summary of these developments. Most important, pre-cut standardized wood members for framing houses were extensively imported from North America. In addition, advances in the fretsaw during the 1860s facilitated the production of fretwork, the ornamental wood pieces used to decorate houses. By the turn of the century, concrete, concrete blocks and clay blocks were also being used in constructing homes, though wood-framing continued. In fact, many houses during the first half of the twentieth century featured a combination of wood and concrete, with the latter becoming more popular as the century progressed.[10]

Two of the largest firms in house construction during this era were Turnbull, Stewart and Company and Taylor and Gillies. Newel Lewis notes that Turnbull and Stewart had a workshop on Richmond Street, where architect George Brown directed the mass production of standardized fretwork and other wood components for houses. In addition, Brown coordinated a force of some four hundred workers constructing houses around Port of Spain. Meanwhile, Taylor and Gillies, also based on Richmond Street, maintained a wide range of wood supplies and was manufacturing concrete blocks by the early twentieth century. In a 1904 advertisement, the company said it provided architectural and construction services, with "Estimates and Plans for all classes of Buildings, Additions, Repairs and Sewerage Work supplied with despatch at reasonable rates".[11]

By the early twentieth century, there was a common Trinidadian-creole detached house type for the middle and upper classes, varying in size and elaboration in accordance with the means and preferences of its residents (see figure 10). Comprising one or two storeys, the house was framed with wood and raised on masonry piers. External walls were filled with nogging (stone or brick debris mixed with cement) and finished with plaster. The house had a steep-pitched gable roof, often with dormer windows, though hip and mansard roofs were also employed. Roofs were generally covered with slate tiles or corrugated galvanized-iron sheets and often featured finials. Ventilation was facilitated by numerous louvred windows and doors, flanked by additional louvres, while interior walls contained vented areas near the ceiling. Fretwork in a range of geometric patterns adorned gables, eaves, transoms, verandah posts and other building elements. A gallery (sometimes including a balustrade or low wall) graced the front of the house and occasionally extended on other sides as well. Kitchen and bath facilities were separate from the house. Surrounding the house was a yard with plentiful trees, shrubs and flowers, while the yard perimeter was marked with a masonry wall or wall combined with iron fencing. The wall typically featured corner- and gateposts, often with post caps in pyramidal or spherical shapes.[12]

The elaborate fretwork was certainly one of the most prominent features of this house type, and observers have often admired Trinidad's "gingerbread houses". Fretwork, however, had practical as well as aesthetic qualities. John Newel Lewis notes that, in such houses, "light and air were filtered through the eaves, the fretwork, the hanging plants, the galleries, the jalousies, windows and flowing curtains". He adds that fretwork also helped to protect vulnerable parts of houses from wind and rain and may have interfered with the directional signals of bats seeking to hang under eaves.[13]

The Trinidadian-creole house type reached its greatest elaboration in the idiosyncratic homes of the elite at the turn of the twentieth century. By this point, the cocoa boom was generating extensive wealth that could be ostentatiously displayed in large houses with unique variations on the basic type or in entirely different architectural styles. In addition, large yards, walls and dense foliage enabled the upper class to achieve a degree of privacy within the busy urban environment. The six grandiose mansions on the northwest perimeter of the Savannah – in a profusion of styles ranging from George Brown's creole elaboration for the Prada family to the Stollmeyers' Scottish castle – exemplify the exuberance of elite house design in Port of Spain during the first decade of the twentieth century. However, there were many other extraordinary homes in the area of the Savannah. Three diverse examples are the Boos, Boissière and Gordon family houses, all of which were surrounded by lush yards and boundary fences or walls.

The Boos house, on the wide Cipriani Boulevard south of the Savannah, was built by George Brown in 1883 and was one of his first projects in Trinidad. It was a large two-storey masonry and wood structure with a gabled roof, crestings, dormer windows and finials. The front elevation had a prominent lantern light in the centre of the roof and spacious galleries on both floors. Rather than fretwork, the house featured decorative wood panels, principally between columns in the lower gallery. (Newel Lewis notes that this house predated the common use of fretwork.) The Boissière house, on the Savannah near Cipriani Boulevard, was designed by local architect Edward Bowen in 1904 and remains a masterpiece of the gingerbread style (see figure 11). This one-storey structure was constructed of wood and masonry and featured several gabled roofs with crestings and finials. Its front façade contained a central gable with two windows, a tiled and balustraded verandah with sets of double doors, a porte-cochère supported by iron columns, and two turret-roofed units at the corners. Windows (some frosted or painted) were flanked by louvres, while elaborate fretwork and other decorative elements graced the house overall. The Gordon home, opposite the Savannah between the Prince's Building and the Queen's Park Hotel, was built by Taylor and Gillies in 1904. Known as "Knowsley", this massive two-storey orange-brick and limestone structure featured four intersecting gable roofs with crestings and a front elevation that included a central porte-cochère (with a balcony on top) and, at the corners, two towers – one turreted and the other parapeted. Elegant columns supported the porte-cochère and lined marble-floored galleries around the house.[14]

These elite houses were truly exceptional – only a minute percentage of Port of Spain's population enjoyed such accommodation. Much of the city's working class lived under very difficult circumstances. Many working people uptown and in districts around the central city occupied small wood-frame houses with one or two rooms, perhaps with some of the features of the basic creole house type if income permitted. Others lived in structures pieced together from assorted discarded materials. In St James, many houses were *tapia* structures, with thatched roofs and walls of plaited pieces of wood or bamboo, filled with clay and grass or leaves. Barracks, however, were the primary form of housing for Port of Spain's poor, and existed throughout much of downtown, as well as in blocks on the north side of Park Street and in districts to the east and west of the central city. An architectural form apparently derived from the island's plantations, a typical barrack was a building with a row of rooms approximately 10–12 feet square, with each room accommodating a whole family. A barrack could be constructed of masonry or wood and was frequently raised on piers. Each of its rooms had a single door and window with a wooden shutter. Thin wooden partitions between the rooms ended a couple of feet below the ceiling. Often, several barracks surrounded an unpaved yard, which might also contain detached single-room structures. The residents of a yard shared one or more water pipes and latrines. Barrack yards were often in the interior of city blocks and were entered through passageways from adjacent streets (see figures 19 and 20).[15]

As a result of urban migration during the latter nineteenth century, Port of Spain's barrack yards were extremely crowded spaces. Buildings continued to deteriorate owing to heavy use and insufficient maintenance, there was minimal privacy and the threat of disease was ever present. During the early twentieth century, some downtown barrack-dwellers moved to areas to the east and west in search of better housing. However, many remained and tried to improve their rooms and yards as best they could. Though barrack conditions generated many tensions, the yards were also spaces for camaraderie, mutual assistance and collective activity.

Meanwhile, barrack yards were a subject of ongoing criticism by much of the city's middle and upper classes. Since the yards were often in close proximity to businesses and better-quality housing, there were various concerns about their material conditions and occupants. During the early twentieth century, the *Port-of-Spain Gazette* frequently editorialized against the yards as a threat to the city and its prospects. In 1909 the paper stated categorically: "The unsatisfactory and thoroughly unwholesome conditions prevalent in most, if not all, the barrack yards of the city have often in times past been referred to by us as matters requiring and urgently demanding the attention of the Government with a view to the speedy amelioration of evils the magnitude of which it is almost impossible to exaggerate." In addition, the editors asserted that the yards clearly contributed to "a very large portion of those disease [*sic*], immorality, and other attendant evils prevalent in the town" and applauded the legislative council's consideration of a public health ordinance that would require registering existing yards and licensing new ones. It further recommended an authority for cancelling the licence of any yard known to be "a place of evil repute": "That would do much to rid the town of several well known nests of vice at present producing handsome profits we doubt not to the owners, and rendering the surrounding district unbearable for all other classes of people."[16]

The threat of barrack yards to public health was certainly a major issue during this period, and it was known that they generated higher levels of tuberculosis than other types of housing. In 1910 Dr G.H. Masson, a physician and civic leader, took dramatic action by organizing an exhibition of a barrack room at the Prince's Building in conjunction with an agricultural show. The *Mirror* reported on the characteristics of the display. Since the barrack room was not raised off the ground, air could not circulate underneath and the floor was perpetually damp. In addition, the room contained a partition to create a back space for sleeping, where fresh air and light could not reach. Ventilation was also hampered by rags stuffed into spaces in the walls, a practice of barrack dwellers who believed that night draughts caused sickness. Also on display was an exhibit of an alternative for healthier living: a structure raised off the ground and fitted with multiple jalousie windows. Other components of the exhibition were a microscope with a display of tuberculosis bacilli and a specimen of an affected lung in the process of decay. The *Mirror* commended this "splendid practical demonstration by Dr. G.H. Masson of the danger that arises from inhabiting stuffy ill-ventilated rooms and the comparative ease with which wholesome conditions can be secured by means of cleanliness and ventilation".[17]

In spite of such efforts to increase public awareness, tuberculosis remained a serious problem in Port of Spain. A 1912–1913 *Report of the Trinidad Association for Prevention and Treatment of Tuberculosis* listed 845 patients treated for the disease, 531 of whom lived in barrack yards or in "front barracks" (structures opening onto the streets). In addition, all the deaths reported appeared to have occurred near streets with barrack yards. Typhoid fever was also a threat. In 1918 the *Argos* reported on the city council's Public Health Committee and said a medical officer had identified twenty-three buildings on the St Joseph Road (in the southeast of the city) as "unfit for human habitation". The area in question was 188 by 98 feet and included approximately one hundred rooms with four hundred tenants. The *Argos* noted that the space was the same size as a single residential lot in St Clair. The council, however, did not pass a motion to serve a notice to the area's landlords.[18]

Public perceptions of barrack yards concerned not only disease but the activities of their dwellers. During this period, a sense of moral outrage pervaded the reporting of the *Port-of-Spain Gazette*. In June 1910 the newspaper condemned "the daily and nightly brawling, accompanied with the foulest of language and gesture and action, which go on in many of these barrack yards, to the annoyance of the more peaceable inhabitants of the yards, and still more so of the neighbours who are perhaps of a better class". It also observed that there were several barrack yards "in the heart of the city which, from a peaceful and decent past, are fast degenerating into the centres of all that is obscene, indecent, and rowdy". In December of that year, the *Gazette* said it had received several complaints of a "great nuisance caused in that section of St Vincent Street lying between Duke and Park Streets by the large number of common prostitutes and other lewd and disorderly characters who seem to have flocked there, and occupy rooms in the several barrack yards situated in the vicinity of the Grass Market". In February 1913 the paper editorialized about complaints concerning barrack yards in this same area: "The other evening, having occasion ourselves to pass down this street, we were astonished beyond measure, that it should be possible for such a commotion, such volleys of vile and obscene language, and such general disorderliness, both on the pavement and in the yards, to be in progress, without the intervention of the constable on duty." In a general observation on the city's barrack yards, the newspaper described:

hordes of the lowest men and women the town can produce, women whose rooms are to all intents and purposes brothels and so known to such members of the police who frequent these yards, – men who make Sundays hideous with boxing matches and fights and ribald songs after a drunken spread; while all the time the little children who usually throng these yards, are the witnesses of a course of conduct that may ensure their growing up to be the criminal classes of the next generation.

In May 1913, the *Gazette* summarized its position: "Barrack-yards are evil institutions, vile through and through, and ought not be allowed to remain in the city of Port of Spain. How can you get a moral people living under the barrack-yard system, or a people that are healthful, sanitary, free from vice and fit to take their part in the duties of our common citizenship?"[19]

Clearly, there were different codes of acceptable behaviour manifested in the activities of some barrack-yard dwellers and the commentary of the *Gazette*. Working people in the city's barracks had their own expressive styles, pastimes and methods of coping with the exceedingly difficult conditions under which they lived. Meanwhile, the *Gazette* and other middle- and upper-class observers demonized them, identified them with their material environment and held them responsible both for crime in the city and for depreciating the value of property near their yards. However, the newspaper was also critical of government authorities, the police and the owners of the barracks. It called for better housing for the poor, argued for the need to implement and enforce more regulations on barrack yards and commented that many barracks were owned by prominent members of the community. Meanwhile, the *Argos* specified that some members of the city council itself were landlords.[20] Certainly, the vested interests of landlords, who received high rents from marginal housing, curtailed the passing of legislation pertaining to the yards and the enforcement of those regulations that were adopted.

Though Port of Spain's middle and upper classes perceived the barrack yards as a threat to health and morality, they also benefited from having a large labour force close at hand, in the heart of the city. The residents of the yards worked as domestics, laundresses, seamstresses, craftsmen, longshoremen, general labourers and in various other occupations essential to the homes and businesses of the city. Though these individuals were attracted to Port of Spain by the prospect of work, limited housing options forced them into barracks or other substandard buildings. Here high rents and low wages furthered their impoverishment. Meanwhile, the city's upper and middle classes continued to benefit from the financial rewards of the cocoa boom economy and from the availability of new housing in the expanding suburbs. In its May 1913 editorial, the *Port-of-Spain Gazette* asked how the barrack-yard system could produce people "fit to take their part in the duties of our common citizenship".

Indeed, civic equality in Port of Spain would require not only political rights but greater access to decent housing and economic opportunity.

CELEBRATIONS AND PROTESTS

The social hierarchy that structured Port of Spain's landscape during the cocoa boom years was dramatized in various public performances staged by the population at prominent sites in the city. Throughout this period, colonial officials and community leaders mounted imperial celebrations in observance of such events as the arrival of new governors, coronations, royal birthdays and ceremonial send-offs and returns of military troops. At the same time, various groups held political rallies and protests that challenged the organization of the colonial regime. In addition, the pre-Lenten Carnival (discussed in chapter 5) offered an extraordinary opportunity each year for creative exploration of the complexities of local society and the broader human condition. In staging this range of performances, Port of Spain's inhabitants employed the city's most central and visible spaces, especially Marine Square, Brunswick Square, the Queen's Park Savannah and Frederick Street – the primary route connecting downtown with the Savannah. Given the multifunctional character of these spaces and their constant traffic, they were ideal arenas for dramatic display and persuasion. Here participants articulated their diverse values and concerns through a variety of expressive resources, including building decorations and illuminations, visual props, uniforms and other costumes, speeches, music and choreographies. Such large-scale appropriations of the urban environment constituted a civic theatrics that enabled the population repeatedly to examine its commonalities and differences.

Imperial celebrations were designed to mark a transition or anniversary in imperial rule, display imperial power and achievement and elicit expressions of loyalty to the crown from its subjects. Two examples of such events in 1897 were the arrival of Sir Hubert Jerningham as governor (following colonial service in Mauritius) and Queen Victoria's diamond jubilee. On 2 June a government launch brought Sir Hubert and Lady Jerningham to shore, where they were welcomed by a large crowd at the Custom House. For the occasion, the building's courtyard, which had a fountain, palms and orchids, was decorated with flags of various nationalities. From here, the couple was driven in a landau to Government House, on the north side of the Queen's Park Savannah. The *Port-of-Spain Gazette* reported: "On the South Quay and on the route homewards were gathered crowds who were loud in their cheerings accompanied with the waving of hats, handkerchiefs &c., which Sir Hubert gracefully acknowledged. The bells of the Cathedral of the Immaculate Conception and

Church of the Sacred Heart were also pealed for the occasion." Though Sir Hubert had desired a subdued arrival, this request "did not prevent the masses, irrespective of colour, class, creed or nationality, offering His Majesty's new Representative a hearty and, what is more appreciable, spontaneous ovation on his arrival to assume the reins of Government in the 'Land of the Hummingbird,' universally admitted to be the 'Pearl of the Antilles'". At Government House, the Light Infantry Volunteers served as the guard of honour, with a contingent of the police also present. At noon the chief justice swore in Sir Hubert in Government House's council chamber.

After an address from the legislative council and reply from the governor, the town clerk read an address on behalf of the borough council and the inhabitants of Port of Spain. He said:

> we esteem it our special good fortune that at the present moment when many important questions affecting the position, rights and functions of the Municipality are awaiting settlement, there will be at the head of the Government of this Colony one whose well known liberal views and sympathetic attitude towards the free development of Municipal Government, inspire us with the fullest confidence that any representatives from the Mayor and Burgesses of Port-of-Spain, the oldest representative Institution in the Island, will receive full and impartial consideration.

The governor replied, "In regard to the old institutions of this colony . . . I am not likely to let them lose their rights and privileges (Applause). I have at all times stood up for all the elective assemblies." However, he added that he had not yet studied the details of the Port of Spain Borough Council's wishes. In fact, he abolished the body a year and a half later.[21]

In June 1897 Trinidad and Tobago also joined colonies throughout the empire in celebrating Queen Victoria's diamond jubilee, marking her sixty years on the throne. In preparation for the event, stores on Frederick Street advertised such items as ladies' untrimmed hats, feathers, quills, ribbons, flags, bunting and decorative cloth. On Sunday, 20 June, special services were held at local churches. Governor Jerningham arrived at the Cathedral of the Immaculate Conception to a guard of honour from the Light Infantry Volunteers, with the Artillery Band and Trinidad Police Band also in attendance. For the Mass, there was "an orchestra comprising the leading musicians of the city". At noon on 22 June, the actual day of the jubilee, the governor reviewed local forces in the Queen's Park Savannah, while a flag was lowered at Government House to a salute of seventeen guns. There were various expressions of loyalty at the Savannah, including a presentation from Mayor Henry Alcazar on behalf of the people of Port of Spain. Three nights later, a lavish jubilee ball was held at Government House, where "the avenue was brilliantly lighted with flambeaux made of coco-nuts" and "the gardens in front of the residence were tastefully lighted up by fairy lamps arranged in figures on the turf, among others . . . a Device of a V.R. and Crown".[22]

Another elaborate imperial celebration during this period was the coronation of George V at Westminster Abbey on 22 June 1911, after the death of Edward VII. During the previous decades, George had served in the Royal Navy and travelled widely in the empire, including three visits to Trinidad. The *Port-of-Spain Gazette* exclaimed:

> Throughout the scattered dominions of an empire over which the sun never sets, the magnificent pageant which was being enacted in the great metropolis found a re-echo in various forms of celebration, but undoubtedly the sacring of the "Sailor King" must strike a note of peculiar interest to the inhabitants of Trinidad, re-awakening as it does, treasured memories of his personal visits to this outpost of empire. Such was the feeling that pervaded every nook and corner of the island whence poured forth the tributes of unswerving loyalty and devotion to the throne and person of a monarch. . . . The day of crowning broke fair, and was ushered in betimes with the chiming of joy bells which rang out from all the churches in the city.

At 7:30 a.m. there was a parade at the Queen's Park Savannah of the local forces, including the Light Horse Volunteers, Light Infantry Volunteers, Constabulary, Mounted Constables and Cadet Corps from Queen's Royal and St Mary's Colleges. Also present was a company of bluejackets from HMS *Aeolus*, apparently in port for the occasion. The governor arrived on horseback to the firing of minute guns and a rendition of "God Save the King" from the constabulary band. After inspecting the troops, he took up his position at the saluting base, where he greeted local military veterans and other servants of the empire. After more cannon fire, the troops delivered a royal salute (with "God Save the King" again as accompaniment), cheered the king and marched in a column. The governor then addressed the commanders of the various units at the saluting base and returned with a cavalry escort to Government House, while the troops went to their respective headquarters in the city. Later that morning, there were special services at local churches:

> The Cathedral of the Immaculate Conception was arrayed in festive garb for the Coronation Celebration. From the tower floated on one side the Union Jack and on the other the Papal standard. In the Interior streamers of white and royal red were tastily [sic] festooned, while the columns were decorated with lovely banners in various colours. The Sanctuary and High Altar were most effectively arranged, flowers and ornamental foliage having been used to great advantage. Over the baldachino [sic] of the Tabernacle was suspended a device of an imperial crown canopied in red.

While the governor sent representatives to the various churches, he attended Holy Trinity Cathedral, where the interior was decorated with flags and streamers and the constabulary band contributed to the musical portions of the service.[23]

In the late afternoon, the governor returned to the Queen's Park Savannah for presentations by representatives of Trinidad's Indian community and friendly societies. Among the former were officers and members of the East Indian National Association. In an address read and presented to the governor in book form, barrister George Fitzpatrick said: "We, who form the community of Indians in Your Majesty's Colony of Trinidad and Tobago . . . desire humbly to express our loyalty to the Throne and person of Our August Sovereign." The governor responded that he "knew that His Majesty would feel very great satisfaction in knowing that so many thousands of his Indian subjects had found a happy and prosperous home in the island of Trinidad". After this exchange, the proceedings shifted to the friendly societies, mutual-aid organizations that had predominantly working-class memberships but also included some middle-class participants. The governor greeted officers of those organizations in attendance: the Ideal Union Friendly Society, Mountain Rose Lodge, Mount Paran Songs of Consolation Lodge, "Good Hope" Landship Friendly Society, Western Star Lodge and Woodbrook United Friendly. Male and female members of the societies wore regalia and carried banners. At the Savannah the next day, there were athletic events and an assembly of schoolchildren who formed a square and lifted red, white and blue flags in an arrangement representing the Union Jack. This display was followed by the singing of "Rule, Britannia!" and an address from the governor.[24]

In an editorial after the celebrations, the *Port-of-Spain Gazette* observed:

> The behaviour of the people, too, was excellent, and their loyalty not only unimpeachable, but most enthusiastic. Go where one would among the great crowds that thronged Port-of-Spain during the celebrations it was impossible to find disorder, bad temper or disloyalty. Never, we suppose, has there been in the principal aspects of Port-of-Spain such crowds as there were on the evening of the illuminations. Frederick Street, especially, was packed with humanity like sardines in a tin.

The newspaper added that many expected "that a section of the people would have attempted to behave as they do at Carnival time" and make the streets "hideous with ribald dance". However, such activity did not occur.[25]

An additional imperial celebration that took shape during the early twentieth century was Empire Day. This event was annually observed across the empire on Queen Victoria's birthday (24 May), after her death in 1901. In Trinidad, Empire Day focused on the patriotism of children, with a large assembly at the Queen's Park Savannah, though there were also athletic events at the St

Clair Oval. In 1909 the celebration at the Savannah was led by J.H. Collens, chief inspector of schools (and author of the 1888 *Guide to Trinidad*). This observance included many of the elements typical of other imperial celebrations at this locale: an inspection and speech from the governor, the parading of the local forces and performances by the constabulary band. The more than twenty-eight hundred participating students carried banners with the names of their schools, as well as Union Jacks and other flags, and sang "Rule, Britannia!" and similar songs of imperial loyalty. Students from the Tranquillity Girls' Practising School presented a tableau that represented Britannia and her colonies. The *Port-of-Spain Gazette* reported that there was a large attendance for the event both in the grandstand and surrounding grounds. In addition to children's and sporting activities, Empire Day featured expressions of patriotism in church sermons and in newspapers. In 1914 the *Argos*, a periodical frequently critical of the colonial regime, proclaimed in an editorial: "To-day the differences of opinion among the sons of the Empire, though many, are largely matters of detail: the underlying principles which tend to unity are one, and, we venture to state, indivisible." It concluded: "No ocean, no desert, shall be a barrier to our patriotism. Prosperity shall only enhance our unity and emphasise our patriotic ideal. And we shall stave with iron rods all foreign elements that may tend to impair the harmony of the greatest of Empires since the beginning of time, thus making it possible that the brotherhood of man shall continue living a fact for ever."[26]

It is difficult to assess the views of the general population of Port of Spain towards Empire Day, coronations, and other imperial celebrations during the late nineteenth and early twentieth centuries. The *Port-of-Spain Gazette* may have exaggerated the degree of public enthusiasm for these events, or the gathering of crowds may have been motivated as much by curiosity and desire for a diversion as by patriotism. It seems likely that opinion during this era ranged from strong support for the empire through affirmation of the ideals of the empire, but dissatisfaction with the local colonial administration, to opposition to the imperial system as a whole. In any case, participation in imperial celebrations was complemented by the staging of diverse political rallies and protests. Certainly the most dramatic uprising of this period was the 1903 Water Riot, an event that began as a carefully organized demonstration.

The water protests and ensuing riot were motivated by the colonial government's proposal in March 1903 of a new Waterworks Ordinance, which would create a water authority (to be controlled by government officials) and would subject homeowners with large baths to higher rates or to the use of meters. As noted above, water had become a highly contentious issue in Port of Spain by the end of the nineteenth century. In essence, the city's residents felt entitled to an unlimited supply of water and resisted virtually any regulation of consumption. Many wealthy citizens maintained massive baths, while the practice of leaving taps running was common throughout the city. Port of Spain did, in fact, have a substantial water supply, encompassing the Maraval waterworks, the St Ann's reservoir and additional sources implemented by 1903. The growth of the city, however, placed increasing demands on this supply, especially during the dryer months of the year. In an effort to control consumption, the government proposed metering and an increase of rates in 1896 and again in 1902, but withdrew these measures owing to public opposition. This opposition was aimed not only at the specific policies but at Walsh Wrightson, the director of public works, who was widely perceived as overbearing and antagonistic towards the people of the city. Particularly unpopular was Wrightson's programme of cutting off property owners' water pipes that had defective taps or were found running. The Public Works Department had been executing this policy since 1901 and accelerated its efforts in early 1903 on the ground that such action was necessary to ensure sufficient water for the city during the dry season.[27]

Opposition to the proposed Waterworks Ordinance of 1903 and to the government's general management of water was led by a group called the Ratepayers' Association. Formed in 1901, this organization comprised some 185 members and represented the 6,793 Port of Spain property owners who paid water rates. Its generally middle-class membership included a number of attorneys, such as Emmanuel Mzumbo Lazare and Edgar Maresse-Smith, and other well-established citizens. John Newbold, a former mayor, served as president. While the organization's primary objective was to protect the interests of rate-paying citizens, it was also a vocal proponent of democratic government. It condemned the 1898 abolition of the Port of Spain Borough Council, on which many of its members had served, and advocated the introduction of elected members to the legislative council. In short, the association's critique of the government's water management was interrelated with broader opposition to the authoritarian character of the crown colony system.[28]

After the government's publication of the Waterworks Ordinance on 5 March 1903, the proposal was vehemently criticized in the local press. Opposition was also expressed on placards posted around the city:

> The terms of the proposed Waterworks Ordinance are inacceptable to the people of Port-of-Spain. If this measure were to become law the inhabitants of this Town would be placed under the despotic control of the Water Authority. . . .
> *Fellow Citizens it is our duty to resist.*
> We have been deprived of our Municipality, Taxation is uncontrolled, and Representation is denied us! Such a state of affairs is unworthy of ourselves, of our country, and of the great Empire to which we belong. We can obtain nothing except by our own efforts, and we appeal to every inhabitant of this town to

rally round us and support us in the great struggle we are about to enter upon to secure our rights and defend our liberties as becomes free and loyal subjects of His Majesty the King.

On 14 March the Ratepayers' Association held a mass meeting at the Queen's Park Savannah to further mobilize opposition to the bill. Among the speakers was John Newbold, who, without having read the ordinance, suggested that it would empower Wrightson and his men to invade the sanctity of homes to inspect pipes (while women were bathing) and that low-income residents could be deprived of water altogether. On 16 March the ordinance was slated for discussion by the legislative council at the Red House, but the council's claim of disorderly conduct by spectators led to the meeting's being rescheduled to the following week. A couple of days later, the Ratepayers' Association placarded Port of Spain with signs that read, "Higher rates will mean higher rents", adding that the poorest people would receive no water. A rumour then spread that poor people would be charged five cents a bucket for water. Finally, on 21 March, the association held another meeting, this time at Brunswick Square, with some two thousand people in attendance. Among the issues addressed was the government's announcement that, for the council's meeting on 23 March, the public would be admitted to the council chamber only by tickets issued in advance. Association speakers advised the crowd that they had a right to be admitted to the chamber without tickets.[29]

The government mobilized the police force in preparation for possible disorder during the 23 March noontime meeting of the legislative council. Early that morning, thirty-five policemen, armed with Martini-Enfield rifles and bayonets, were hidden in the colonial secretary's office on the ground floor of the Red House, below the first-floor council chamber. At 10:45 a.m. sixty-four policemen, equipped with staves, were stationed in and around the building. Meanwhile, the Ratepayers' Association rallied supporters. A number of Indo-Trinidadians, presumably hired by the association, paraded the streets, ringing bells and carrying placards that read: "Come to the Red House at 12 o'clock to-day or you will have to pay more rent." At around 11:20 a.m. several leaders of the association, surrounded by a large crowd, arrived at the public entrance to the council chamber on the western (St Vincent Street) side of the building. After refusing admittance tickets, they tried to force their way in, but were resisted by police. They then led much of the crowd to Brunswick Square, on the eastern side of the building, and began delivering speeches. Soon after the start of the council meeting, a large crowd of men, women and boys began circling around the Red House (see figure 12). They shouted, sang "God Save the King" and "Rule, Britannia!", and beat tin pans and empty oil containers in an effort to disrupt the council's business. Emmanuel Lazare and another attorney waved flags as they led the marchers. Another attempt to enter the building was again resisted.

Eventually, some members of the crowd began throwing stones through the Red House's windows; others seized the governor's carriage and dumped it in the sea, several blocks away. By 1:30 p.m. the crowd, now numbering five to six thousand, had begun an attack on the council chamber itself by hurling bottles, bricks and stones. As police reserves arrived, protesters forced their way into the Red House's central courtyard, from which they continued throwing stones up at the chamber and occupied ground-floor offices. By 2:30 p.m. the building was on fire, with flames spreading rapidly. An official read the Riot Act from the building's western and eastern galleries. The police then began firing both from the building and out on the surrounding streets. After various police manoeuvres, sixteen members of the public were dead and forty-three were treated at the Colonial Hospital. Two women died of wounds from bayonets, the use of which had not been authorized. The fire destroyed the Red House, except for its walls and a vault. Though stationed on Brunswick Square, the fire brigade had been slow to respond, possibly out of sympathy with the protesters. Later in the day, the police and naval troops from two British ships in port began patrolling the town, while the local Light Horse Volunteers provided additional security. Two days later, a contingent of the Lancashire Fusiliers arrived from Barbados.[30]

The British commission of enquiry after the riot attributed the event to public opposition to the proposed ordinance, the requirement of admission tickets for the council meeting and the agitation of the masses by leaders of the Ratepayers' Association. However, the commissioners also suggested that the government mishandled the public presentation of the ordinance and that it seemed "to have taken refuge in a policy of stolid, if not unsympathetic, isolation, which has ended in a kind of cleavage existing between rulers and ruled".[31] Certainly, the lack of opportunity in the crown colony system for political participation forced local debate to take place in other settings in Port of Spain, such as streets, squares and parks. Here there was oratory, signage, music and marching – of a vigorous but generally peaceful nature. Occasionally, however, incidents sparked violent confrontations. In the case of the Water Riot, exclusion from the public space of the council chamber appears to have been a critical factor in precipitating the uprising. This exclusion led to the crowd's rallying at nearby Brunswick Square and circling the Red House, and the eventual attack on the building itself as the premier setting and symbol of colonial rule in Trinidad.

Clearly, water was an effective issue for inspiring popular protest at the turn of the century. Though the proposed Waterworks Ordinance primarily affected the city's upper- and middle-class residents as property owners, the Ratepayers'

Association was able to mobilize the working class to its cause, in part by suggesting that their rents would increase if water rates were raised. Moreover, piped water was essential to the entire population and the expanding urban landscape, from the large compounds of St Clair with their lush gardens and extravagant baths to the barrack yards of downtown where standpipes were central to cooking, bathing, laundering and social interaction. Though there was extreme inequality in access to the supply of water, the city's population as a whole perceived the threat of the 1903 ordinance as emblematic of the more general constraint of the colonial regime on their lives.

Another dramatic sequence of protests (and celebrations) took place in Port of Spain in 1919, after the end of World War I. The celebrations honoured local men who had served abroad in the British West Indies Regiment, while the protests were motivated both by the troops' overseas experiences and by the living conditions in Trinidad to which they returned. During the war, there was substantial price inflation in the island without corresponding increases in wages. At the end of the war, a reorganized TWA responded to the growing discontent as a strong advocate of working-class rights and demands. Meanwhile, men who had joined the British West Indies Regiment out of eagerness to serve the cause of empire were subjected to pervasive racism and humiliating treatment by British officers, as well as unequal wages, in North Africa and Europe. They returned proud of their service but further determined to combat injustice in their home societies.[32]

The first contingents of returning troops arrived on 26 May 1919 and were greeted with elaborate celebrations. In preparation for their arrival, the townspeople had constructed a temporary triumphal arch on the St Vincent Wharf, a second arch on Broadway that represented "Commerce" and a third at the Queen's Park Savannah and Frederick Street, representing "Agriculture". The *Port-of-Spain Gazette* reported: "Flags, and bunting and festooning were everywhere in evidence. . . . The Frederick Street stores were all gaily bedecked, and along the route to the Savannah, private residences vied with one another in the decorative scheme." The soldiers arrived at the wharf around 11:00 a.m. to the cheers of large crowds, the sounds of ship sirens and a rendition of "Home! Sweet Home!" by the constabulary band. Various other units of the police and local forces were also in attendance. Near the customs warehouse was a reception platform where the mayor of Port of Spain welcomed the troops and praised them for their service. The men then marched in rows of four up Broadway and Frederick Street to the Savannah. The *Argos* noted that, along the way, spectators were "clinging on to them and hurrahing enthusiastically despite the attempts of the police to restrain them". In the grounds near the Victoria Institute, at the top of Frederick Street, schoolchildren assembled and waved small flags. In the Savannah were cadets from Queen's Royal and St

Mary's Colleges and a stand for government officials, from which the acting governor welcomed and commended the heroes.³³

In Trinidad, as throughout the empire, official postwar peace celebrations were held on 19 July. The *Argos* reported:

> There was hardly any private residence or business house from which some patriotic device was not displayed. All the public buildings were decorated and some of them illuminated. . . .
>
> The illumination of the Red House by electricity was beyond reproach and at intervals the remaining lights were put out so that the Crown and the words Victory and Peace appeared with special prominence. The Town Hall, too was nicely illuminated and the display of the King's message of Peace on the Frederick Street side was a very thoughtful act.

The day of celebration began with the sounding of church bells, whistles, and sirens from both land and sea. At the Savannah, there was a parade of the local forces, returned soldiers (though many refused to take part) and some British sailors from HMS *Dartmouth*. Friendly societies and thousands of schoolchildren also participated. Later in the day, the *Argos* related that "several hundreds of the lower classes enjoyed themselves a la carnival, by forming themselves into swell bands and indulging in calypsoes to the strain of bottle and tin music". There were also dinners, dances and bonfires.³⁴

During the following days, there were more celebrations, but also a night on which returned soldiers and other local men attacked British sailors around the city. In response to these occurrences, the *Port-of-Spain Gazette* accused the *Argos* of fomenting "race hatred" by republishing "exaggerated" reports from newspapers in Britain, where recently there had been attacks by whites on blacks in such cities as Liverpool and Cardiff. According to the *Gazette*: "And in the returned man from the British West Indies Regiment who has, or fancies he has, a grievance against the Empire in general, these disloyal people find ready and willing assistants in their campaign. Especially so is this the case with regard to those returned soldiers who previous to their enlistment were wharf idlers or, in some cases, even convicted criminals." The *Gazette* added that it was the duty of the authorities to do whatever was necessary to prevent "the establishment of anything resembling Bolshevism in Trinidad". The *Argos*, in turn, dismissed any connection between its reports and the attacks on British sailors and asserted, "the primary objective of our existence is to reflect accurately the views of every section of the community especially as our rulers and nominated members of the Legislature, the latter particularly, are absolutely ignorant or affect to be, of conditions that surround the humbler classes of this colony".³⁵ As this exchange indicates, the return of the British West Indies Regiment troops in 1919 intensified social divisions within

Trinidadian society. While the streets of Port of Spain were transformed into a ceremonial landscape of patriotism to commend the troops, they also served as a venue for the expression of anti-imperial sentiment.

Later that year, Port of Spain's docks became the site of a labour conflict that had a pervasive impact on the society. Dockworkers occupied a key position within Trinidad's colonial economy as the individuals who loaded ships with the island's agricultural commodities and unloaded incoming goods. Moreover, their interaction with sailors facilitated knowledge of black consciousness and workers' movements throughout the Atlantic world. On 15 November stevedores went on strike, demanding better wages from shipping companies. They were represented by the TWA and held public meetings in Woodford Square and various other locations in the city. Shortly after the initiation of the strike, shipping companies began hiring strike-breakers to unload boats. This generated tensions that exploded on the morning of 1 December, when strikers engaged in a series of attacks on strike-breakers on the docks and the police arrived in an effort to control the crowds. A sense of the scene by late morning is offered by the *Trinidad Guardian* (a newspaper established in 1917 and generally supportive of business interests and the colonial government):

> On resumption of work at the American Steamers' Warehouse the behaviour of the crowd assumed a serious aspect. The striking stevedores who had warned the strike breakers not to resume work after breakfast stormed the warehouse and attacked those of the men who had ignored the threat and had returned to work. An attempt on the part of the clerks, checkers and foremen to resist the first wave of the attackers broke down, and the stevedores in full strength and reinforced by their women folk flooded the warehouse, pursued, and held the strike-breakers, hustling them one by one out into the street where they were received by a noisy mob who continued to clout and chase their victims off the water front.

By the afternoon, the demonstrations had spread to the city's main commercial streets and beyond:

> During the remainder of the day the mob paraded the city attacking the provision stores on Broadway and ordering their closing down. In its wild career a crowd of strikers and excited women came upon Mr. Gioannetti of the R.M.S.P. Co. who had just come ashore from the Chaleur and was on his way to the Company's office in St. Vincent Street. He was held up and completely surrounded, receiving several blows with sticks from desperate men in the mob which was shouting, "Heave! heave!" . . .
>
> The crowd gathering in excitement during the latter part of the day overflowed to the suburbs of the city penetrating as far as St. James where the suburban shopkeepers, following the example set by urban shops, closed down. . . . The rumshop saloons throughout the city were shut down in obedience to orders issued by the

military and Broadway went out of business earlier than usual. . . . The greater part of the mob was composed of parentless small boys who are a law unto themselves and took a holiday interest in these demonstrations of rowdyism, driving on the tramcars . . . insulting and threatening the conductors and motormen to their hearts' content. The usual nightly guard of the Treasury was doubled and precaution was taken in mounting a police picket for the night around the plant of the Electric Company.[36]

In response to the demonstrations, the government mobilized its mounted volunteer units (consisting mainly of businessmen) to augment the security provided by the regular police force. Though the police patrolled the city the following day, the demonstrations continued. Crowds harassed the domestic servants of the well-to-do at the Eastern Market, marched along Marine Square and Frederick Street (ordering shops to close), and searched for strikebreakers on the wharf. In Woodbrook, strikers moved along Ariapita Avenue with sticks and pieces of iron, accompanied by boys shouting "Close down! Close down!" On 3 December the dockworkers reached an agreement with the shipping companies in which they received a 25 per cent wage increase. The TWA held a rally at Woodford Square to announce the settlement:

> From early morning Woodford Square was thronged with the stevedores waiting on the fulfilment of the promise of a compromise with the shipping agents which was extended to them on Tuesday as a result of the deliberation of the Conciliation Board. . . . Mr. A.F. Brathwaite, Acting Secretary of the Workingmen's Association, subsequently addressed a large concourse in Woodford Square about 1 p.m. As soon as it was noised around that a decision had been arrived at through every gate in the square poured swarms of men, along with not a few of the womenfolk.

After Brathwaite's speech and the stevedores' assenting to return to work, the meeting concluded with the singing of "God Save the King" and loud cheering.[37]

In the aftermath of the settlement with dockworkers, the *Trinidad Guardian* published several editorials in which it warned of the potential for "anarchy" in Port of Spain, with "agitators" provoking class conflict. It called on the colonial government to protect all citizens against "the triumph of mob law" in the city and asserted that the "responsible men of Port of Spain" were "determined to protect themselves, their property and their town against the attacks of the spurious Bolshevists who are endeavouring to undermine the foundations and destroy the fabric of decent existence in this colony". Meanwhile, the settlement with the dockworkers stimulated further strikes by members of other occupations in the city (including Indo-Trinidadian porters and scavengers), as well as among workers elsewhere in Trinidad and Tobago. In response to the growing labour militancy, the chamber of commerce held a special meeting at its News-Room headquarters near the wharves, and members of the business community organized their own security unit, known as the "Colonial Vigilantes". In the following weeks, the government brought in a contingent of British troops from Jamaica and arrested close to a hundred individuals involved in the strikes. In January and February 1920, it also passed a Strikes and Lockout Ordinance that curtailed the right and ability to strike, and a Sedition Ordinance that enabled broad suppression of literature and other activity that criticized the colonial regime.[38]

Though the strikes came to an end, working people (including men, women and children) in Port of Spain and beyond had demonstrated their ability to disrupt the colony's commerce and to assert demands for a greater share in its profitability. Mobilization for protest in central public spaces in the city was established as an effective means of exercising power in a society where economic advancement was difficult and political participation remained severely limited.

In the course of the late nineteenth and early twentieth centuries, Port of Spain continually expanded in size, became more densely settled and encompassed an ever greater variety of constructions. Thousands of people moved to the city or its outskirts in search of new lives, while authorities and builders struggled to create a material environment that could accommodate them. While the colonial and municipal governments implemented wide-ranging initiatives to improve living conditions, a high level of socioeconomic inequality remained. In addition, governmental and elite promotion of public order was frequently contested by the broader populace. As the cocoa boom developed, Port of Spain became an increasingly contentious place in which a heterogeneous population pursued a range of interests and agendas, while also attempting to negotiate a shared existence.

Patterns of social interdependence and difference were clearly manifested in developments in infrastructure, housing and public space. New streets and transportation systems increased mobility within the city and connections with places across Trinidad and beyond; management of the water supply and drainage addressed concerns over public health; and the miraculous medium of electricity enhanced the mechanization, illumination and sophistication of the city. Though these advances supported civic leaders' rhetoric of progress, boosterism ignored the fact that many of the city's inhabitants struggled with poor roads and drainage and limited access to utilities. During this period, builders also erected numerous new wood and concrete houses occupied by a wide cross-section of the population, from skilled workers to the elite. While building size and accoutrements varied with income, owning or leasing a house signified socioeconomic achievement, domestic well-being and participation in a socially graded community. However, more than a third of the population continued to live in extremely crowded barrack yards that were stigmatized as sites of moral failure, family breakdown and disease. Finally, the city's residents made extensive use of a growing number of outdoor public spaces, which they occasionally transformed by organizing large-scale communal performances. While imperial events displayed an ideology of political unity and consensus, protests demonstrated deep divisions and discontent.

The people of Port of Spain remained highly diverse in material possessions and social status, but collectively they managed to construct a unique creole landscape in the course of the cocoa boom years. Though this landscape had antecedents in the Old World and parallels elsewhere in the Caribbean, there was a distinctively Trinidadian quality to the densely built multistorey buildings of downtown, detached houses in uptown and surrounding districts, networks of narrow streets, shady squares and enclosed yards, and luxuriant but orderly gardens. It was an environment with a certain aesthetic coherence and one that its inhabitants recognized as their own. Thousands of craftsmen and labourers worked on infrastructure projects, laid out squares and parks, and erected buildings. Thousands more homemakers, domestic servants, gardeners, scavengers and other workers maintained the environment on an ongoing basis. In producing and occupying this landscape, people developed a community with capacities for cooperative organizing and action. Though the community was hierarchical, its relatively compact size and high density intensified social interaction, awareness and interdependence. This was a place where encounters with varied others were inevitable and constant. Access to wealth and power varied widely among Port of Spain's residents, but most imagined the possibility of improving their lives, the wider community and its governance. The city that they built was a materialization of both these inequalities and these aspirations.

PART 2

THE INTERWAR ERA, 1920–1940

Figure 13. Trinidad War Memorial, west side. Designed by Louis Frederick Roslyn, completed 1924. Photograph by Tucker. Postcard published by Davidson and Todd.

Figure 14. New Railway Headquarters, completed 1924. Photograph by Tucker. Postcard published by Davidson and Todd. The Michael Goldberg Postcard Collection, Alma Jordan Library, University of the West Indies, St Augustine, Trinidad and Tobago.

Figure 15. Treasury Building. Designed by Herbert Brinsley, completed 1938. Marine Square in foreground. Photograph by H.O. Thomas. Postcard.

Figure 16. Queen's Park Hotel. Central addition designed by William F. Brown; completed 1939. Postcard published by Y. De Lima & Co.

Figure 17. Metro Cinema. Designed by Herbert Brinsley, completed 1933. Renamed the Globe Cinema in 1934. Photograph by Kerr. Courtesy Adrian Camps-Campins.

Figure 18. De Luxe Theatre. Designed by C. Hume, completed 1937. Courtesy Adrian Camps-Campins.

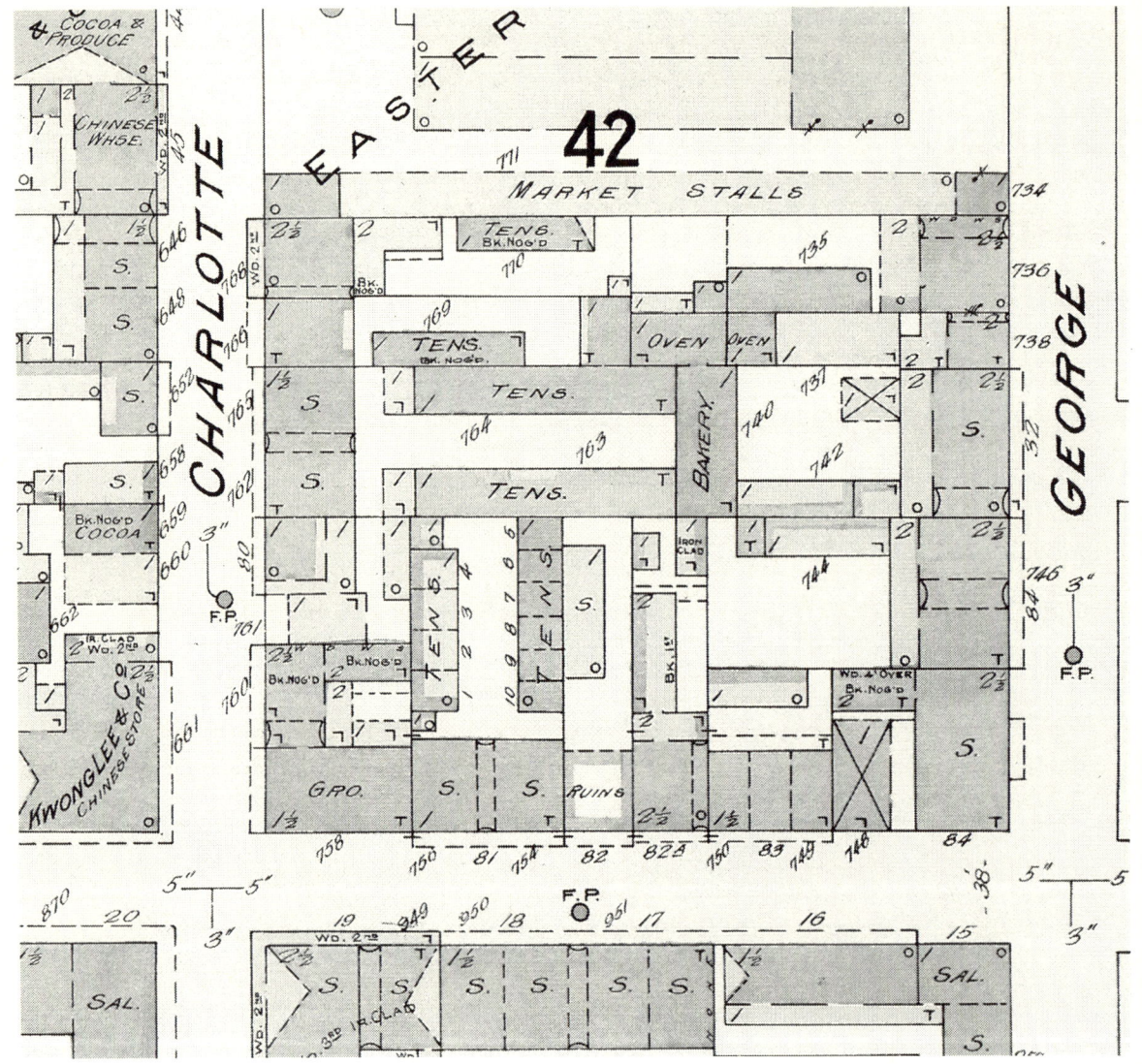

Figure 19. Plan of barrack yards inside the block of Queen, Charlotte, and George Streets, below the Eastern Market. "Tens." are tenements. Detail from sheet 8 of *Insurance Plan of Port of Spain, Trinidad*, by Chas. E. Goad (London: Chas. E. Goad, 1895). Digital Library of the Caribbean, George A. Smathers Libraries, University of Florida, Gainesville, FL.

Figure 20. Barrack yard, 1950s. Low-income housing typical of the cocoa boom and interwar eras. The National Archives of the United Kingdom, ref. CO1069/399.

Figure 21. Carnival, Marine Square at Frederick Street, 1920s. Note members of a devil band and a sailor band. Courtesy Adrian Camps-Campins.

3. THE ENHANCEMENT OF THE CITY

DURING THE TWO DECADES AFTER WORLD WAR I, the inhabitants of Port of Spain pursued a range of construction projects intended to improve the city's material conditions and efficiency, increase its aesthetic beauty and enable new types of collective experience. These initiatives were spearheaded by a variety of government officials, planners, architects, entrepreneurs and community leaders, all of whom propagated compelling visions of an enhanced city. In the aftermath of the war, a citizens' group created a scenic memorial park with an elegant monument to honour Trinidad's deceased servicemen and mark the territory's participation in this epoch-defining global event. By the 1930s, architects were beginning to experiment with modernist designs in various prominent commercial and public buildings. These streamlined structures suggested a desire to surpass the legacy of European aesthetics embodied in the historical revival architecture that characterized the cocoa boom era and continued to dominate the urban landscape. During this period, entrepreneurs also built numerous lavish movie theatres that offered a new form of popular entertainment and enchanting encounters with distant lands. Finally, the colonial and municipal governments implemented various infrastructure schemes, ranging from a massive reconstruction of the Port of Spain harbour and land-reclamation project to improvements of streets, bridges and drainage. All in all, the construction projects of the interwar era employed technological innovations and new aesthetic forms that promised a more productive and sophisticated future for a city determined to better define its significance within the Caribbean and the world at large.

The people of Port of Spain carried out these diverse modifications of their landscape in the context of a substantial restructuring of Trinidad's economy and increasing popular protest against crown colony governance. Economic developments during the interwar era were driven by local factors, evolving world markets and the global depression after 1929. The first major change was the decline of the cocoa industry, which had fuelled the colony's growth and the expansion of its capital city during the preceding decades. As a result of worldwide overproduction, prices of cocoa dropped dramatically in the early

1920s. While they increased again for a few years in that decade, by 1930 Trinidad planters were facing not only a challenging market but also an infestation of their trees by witches' broom disease. The colonial government pursued various plans to assist the industry, which remained an important component of the colony's economy but never regained its former dominance. Meanwhile, the sugar industry also contended with global overproduction and low prices, though local production continued to increase during the interwar era and by 1927 sugar had again become the island's leading export crop. In July 1933 the *Trinidad Guardian* ran a front-page article that announced the largest sugar crop in the island's history and noted that Usine Ste Madeleine had achieved the greatest output ever delivered by a sugar factory in the British empire.

Though sugar, cocoa and other agricultural industries continued to employ large portions of Trinidad's workforce, the most significant economic development of this era was the oil industry. After sustained drilling in southern Trinidad at the beginning of the twentieth century, private companies were increasing production by the 1910s and supplying the Royal Navy, among other customers. By 1914 United British Oilfields of Trinidad and Trinidad Leaseholds were running refineries at Point Fortin and Pointe-à-Pierre respectively (the latter loaded ships through a viaduct that ran over a mile out to sea). With continued exploration, drilling, infrastructure expansion and technological advancements, the growth of the industry was phenomenal: 125,112 barrels of crude in 1910, over two million in 1920, over five million in 1927, and more than thirteen million in 1936. By this point, Trinidad was the largest producer of oil in the British empire, though its output constituted only 1 per cent of world production. While companies such as Trinidad Leaseholds and Apex Oilfields reaped huge profits, the industry paid relatively small royalties to the Trinidad government and employed only a tiny fraction of the colony's workers.[1]

Trade statistics for the interwar years reflect Trinidad's evolving economy. In 1920, 44 per cent of exports went to the United Kingdom and 26 per cent to the United States, with cocoa constituting 48 per cent of the total, sugar 36 per cent and oil 6 per cent. In 1931, 26 per cent of exports went to the United Kingdom and 32 per cent to the United States, with oil accounting for 47 per cent of the total, sugar 22 per cent, and cocoa 20 per cent. By 1936, oil and related products comprised 59 per cent of exports; sugar, molasses and rum 24 per cent; and cocoa 9 per cent.[2]

Economic developments in Trinidad during the interwar years were accompanied by major political changes. First was a modification of the colony's constitution to allow for the election of six representatives in the twenty-six-member legislative council. There were high property/income requirements for voters and even higher requirements for candidates, but the election in 1925, with 6 per cent of the population as registered voters, offered a small opportunity for democratic participation after 128 years of centralized imperial governance. Advocacy of an electoral franchise had been mounted by a middle-class reform group and especially by the TWA, which had grown in size and influence since the strikes and protests of 1919. Based in Port of Spain, with branches around the colony, the TWA was the principal organization for the expression of Afro-Trinidadian working-class concerns, though it also attracted some Indo-Trinidadian support. In 1923 the TWA elected as its president A.A. Cipriani, a French creole who had a background in racehorse training and cocoa and had served as a captain in the British West Indies Regiment during World War I (through which he gained much popularity with the troops). A consummate orator, Cipriani easily won the Port of Spain seat in the 1925 election. Most of the members of the TWA would not have met the voter-eligibility requirements, but they voiced their support through public rallies and other means.[3]

The election campaign and workers' issues in general were enthusiastically covered by the *Labour Leader*, the TWA's newspaper. By August and September 1924, several months before the February 1925 election, the newspaper was reporting on "monster meetings" at the Prince's Building and in Woodford Square. In a description of the latter, the paper exclaimed:

> The surging mass of humanity which had foregathered in dribblets [*sic*] even as early as 3 o'clock reached its maximum about twenty minutes past four, when all sorts and conditions of wage-earners stood in mass formation, packed like sardines in a tin for fully two hundred yards around and about the bandstand, which was utilised as a point of vantage from which the addresses were delivered. . . .
>
> The entire atmosphere seemed to be impregnated with the thought of the man who was to address, in the great cause for which he stands. . . .
>
> It was to Cipriani as an individual . . . that so many thousands of dusky-skinned devotees seemed to have been drawn, and these all listened with rapt attention to every syllable that fell from the lips of a man who seemed to be under the spell of a high and noble inspiration.

Similarly, a *Labour Leader* report on a January 1925 meeting at the London Electric Theatre in Woodbrook observed that "every crevice of the spacious hall was filled and, hanging on to the windows, walls and other points of vantage could be seen a sea of faces peering eagerly into the room". The paper proclaimed that, with this meeting in Woodbrook, Cipriani was carrying "War into Enemy's Camp" and that his speech left the "Opposition Staggering before the Wind".[4]

The excitement in Port of Spain continued on election day itself. In a description of the town hall (the polling station for the city's southern ward), the *Trinidad Guardian* reported:

> From the opening of the station it was a scene of unparalleled excitement. Coincident with the first rush of voters came an enormous crowd representing voteless thousands while on their heels followed bands gaily attired acclaiming their particular candidates, decorated motor lorries with bands of music, men and women with banners. They swarmed Knox Street from Frederick to Pembroke Streets and occupied the portion of Frederick Street near the Town Hall.

After the announcement of the election results that evening at the town hall, Cipriani addressed the crowd in front of the building. While there was particularly strong interest in the election in Port of Spain, colony-wide voter turnout for districts with contested seats was 44 per cent.[5]

Over the course of the next decade, Cipriani and the TWA (renamed the Trinidad Labour Party [TLP] in 1934) consistently advocated workers' issues, such as an eight-hour workday, minimum wages and workers' compensation; civil service reform to create more opportunities for the local population; and democratic self-rule within the framework of the British empire. The TWA/TLP built ties with the labour movement and party in Britain, continued to hold rallies in Port of Spain and other districts and, through its newspaper, offered a substantially different perspective on local and world affairs than that of the *Trinidad Guardian* and the *Port-of-Spain Gazette*, both establishment papers. Cipriani and the TWA/TLP, however, had limited success in achieving real improvements in the lives of working people, given that the legislative council remained heavily weighted towards the interests of capital and authoritarian rule and that there was elite opposition throughout the society to most reform efforts. Nonetheless, Cipriani and his party created a new level of political awareness and involvement among the Trinidadian masses during this period. Political scientist Selwyn Ryan suggests that Cipriani was "the first genuinely 'national' political leader to emerge in Trinidad and Tobago" and was "the instrument by which large numbers of individuals who had previously experienced no basic attraction towards one another came to develop feelings of national kinship and identification".

By the mid-1930s, however, support for Cipriani and the TLP was waning. Economic conditions for the working class deteriorated during the global depression, with growing unemployment, higher consumer prices and continued low wages. Workers sought more militant solutions to their plight and a leadership that would bring concrete change. Oil and sugar workers were especially dissatisfied, given strong earnings for companies in these sectors, but no corresponding improvement in wages or in working and living conditions. Protest marches between 1933 and 1935 were followed in 1937 by island-wide strikes and violent demonstrations, the most severe assault on the colonial order in Trinidad's history. During the mid-1930s, new leaders also emerged, particularly Uriah Butler and Adrian Cola Rienzi (formerly Krishna Deonarine), both of whom had been associates of Cipriani. Butler, who had migrated to Trinidad from Grenada to work in the oil industry, organized the British Empire Workers and Citizens Home Rule Party in 1936 and was a powerful speaker whose rhetoric combined critiques of inequality with Christian visionary imagery. He was a catalyst of the 1937 strikes, which began in the southern oilfields. After the strikes, Rienzi, an attorney and political activist, led the organization of both the Oilfield Workers Trade Union and the All Trinidad Sugar Estates and Factory Workers Trade Union, and contributed to the formation of the Federated Workers Trade Union (which was based in Port of Spain). The crisis of 1937 dramatically exposed the exploitation and impoverishment of working people in Trinidad and resulted in the dispatch of commissions of inquiry from the Colonial Office in Britain. In the late 1930s and early 1940s, Britain gradually adjusted its economic and political policies in the colony and implemented various programmes for improving social welfare. During this same period, the union movement expanded and constitutional reform continued, culminating in universal adult suffrage for the 1946 election, with nine members of the legislative council now popularly elected.[6]

PERSPECTIVES ON THE GROWING CITY

As economic and political forces were reshaping Trinidad during the interwar era, Port of Spain continued to grow in size. Several districts on the edges of the city were officially incorporated within its boundaries: Mucurapo, a residential area to the west of Woodbrook, in 1932; Gonzales Place, in the eastern hills, in 1936; the St Clair Experimental Station – land formerly used for agriculture – in 1937; and the communities of St James and Cocorite, to the northwest of Woodbrook, in 1938. While the city proper consisted of 1,793 acres in 1917, it had expanded to 2,382 acres by 1938. Population grew from 61,580 in 1921 to 70,334 in 1931 and to an estimated 88,698 in 1938, owing to the incorporation of these new districts as well as continued migration and natural increase.[7]

The incorporation of St James was especially significant, given its large Indo-Trinidadian population. Owing to ad hoc development during the nineteenth century on former sugar-plantation lands, this district lacked a standard urban infrastructure and was perceived by the citizens of Port of Spain as a health threat, especially to nearby Woodbrook. While the improvement and annexation of St James had been discussed as early as 1919, it was not until 1937 that the colonial government passed legislation to this effect, with the approval of the Port of Spain City Council. The ordinance arranged for the costs of improvements to be shared by the colonial and municipal governments, along with two principal landowners. On 1 June 1938, St James became part of Port of Spain, adding over 250 acres and a population of approximately ten thousand. Improvements carried out by the municipal government and supervised by the city engineer, T.H. Scott, included widening streets to 33 feet (including drains and footpaths), laying out new streets, paving and repairing streets and upgrading the entire drainage system. By this point, St James included a street grid that memorialized the Indian heritage of many of its residents, with names such as Calcutta, Madras, Bombay, Agra, Bengal, Benares, Lucknow and Ganges. Moreover, the Western Main Road, the district's commercial strip, served as a major artery for traffic between the city and Trinidad's northwest peninsula. After it was incorporated, this area's unique landscape and institutions became integral components of the city, rather than an exotic zone on its margins.[8]

One of St James's most prominent institutions was the Haji Gokool Meah Masjid on the Western Main Road. While there had been an earlier mosque in the district, this impressive structure was built by Gokool Meah in 1927 as a gift to the community. Brought from India as a child by his mother in the mid-nineteenth century, Gokool worked as an indentured labourer, eventually bought land in Diego Martin for cultivating cocoa, acquired additional property in the city and, by the 1930s, owned a major cinema business. In addition to his entrepreneurship, he was renowned for his piety and charity. His masjid, with a capacity of five hundred people, was built on a rectangular plan with a central dome, minarets at the corners, and pointed arched windows. In order to allow the mihrab (prayer niche) on the main façade to face Mecca, the building was sited at an angle to the street. A masonry wall with an iron fence at the front of the property was constructed in the standard style of the city. While the masjid was the centre for Muslim devotions in St James, the district also continued to serve as a major site for Hosay, the observance of the martyrdom of Hussein during Muharram. Each year community members constructed tadjahs – elaborate representations of Hussein's tomb. In 1933 the *Trinidad Guardian* reported on this mobile and transient form of religious architecture:

> Indians of St. James and Diego Martin, who for the last ten days have been preparing for the Hosein festival, paraded their miniature temples through the streets of St. James on Friday night to the accompaniment of drum-beating, singing and rejoicing of throngs of followers.
>
> Beautifully decorated with coloured beads and bits of glass the temples – the largest of which was nearly fourteen feet high – were examples of the architectural skill of the makers.
>
> There were four perfect miniature representations of Indian Mosques, glitteringly decorated and perfumed. . . .
>
> It took nearly six days to cover their frames with coloured paper.

The next day the tadjahs were brought out again and, as was the custom, thrown into the sea near Mucurapo Road.⁹ Hosay attracted large and diverse crowds each year and was considered by the broader populace to be one of the definitive traditions of St James.

With the growth of population in St James and other outlying districts, as well as in central Port of Spain, government officials faced further challenges in managing urban infrastructure and became increasingly aware of the need for more systematic planning. An early call for town planning appeared in 1924 in a short article in the *Port-of-Spain Gazette*, signed "L'Inconnu":

> Most citizens of Port-of-Spain are proud of the capital city of the colony, which is undoubtedly the "Queen City" of the British West Indies. Even those who do not say much about Port-of-Spain echo in their hearts the words of Kipling: "Of no mean city am I." . . .
>
> With this feeling of civic pride existent, even if quiescent, in the hearts of all classes of ratepayers, it is passing strange that the Corporation has not set to work a really effective and permanent Town Planning and Improvement Committee. . . .
>
> Its duties would be, of course, to plan for the improvement of the city in every conceivable shape and form, and to see to it that Port-of-Spain grows more beautiful and more attractive year after year . . . Port-of-Spain should grow and acquire merit in the eyes of the world and esteem in the regard of her citizens on a definite plan, in which the beautiful, as well as the convenient, should find place.

Discussion of town planning intensified during the 1930s. In 1934, for example, the *Trinidad Guardian* editorialized on the first scenes of Port of Spain encountered by visitors when, arriving by steamship, they left the docks and headed north to South Quay:

> What does the new arrival see when he passes the Customs House and sets his face expectantly citywards?
>
> The best answer to this question will be found in a visit to those waste areas of ground abutting the tram lines in South Quay.
>
> Rubbish of every kind litters the ground. Goats and chickens wander where they will.
>
> People chaffer over plantains from Venezuela or fowls from Tobago, erect shelters out of old tarpaulin, or light smoky fires to cook al fresco meals. It is all very care-free and Bohemian, but hardly the sort of introduction to the Colony's capital City calculated to make a favourable impression on strangers.

A few months later, the *Guardian* applauded the erection of new office buildings on Marine Square and contrasted these with the seaside western end of the square, where fishing nets were spread about and conditions resembled those of South Quay. The newspaper suggested developing a park in this area and trimming trees to allow an unimpeded view of the Catholic cathedral at the eastern end of the square.[10]

During the 1920s and 1930s, Port of Spain's city engineer and the director of the government's Public Works Department were the main figures responsible for planning and improving the municipality's infrastructure and appearance. By 1932 the government had also formed a town-planning committee, chaired by the surveyor-general and sub-intendant of crown lands, and in March 1937 established a town-planning board comprising the colonial secretary (chairman), surveyor-general, director of medical services, director of works and transport, crown solicitor, city engineer, San Fernando town engineer and Herbert G.W. Brinsley (an English architect living in Trinidad). The board's charge was to "advise Government concerning the lay-out and development of any area, other than a single building lot, within the Colony". In addition, the government secured the expertise of a town planner from England, R.B. Walker, who arrived in July and was asked to develop a plan for the balanced commercial, residential and recreational use of the large area of land that was being reclaimed from the sea as part of Port of Spain's Deep Water Harbour Scheme. Walker also addressed the problem of ribbon residential development along main roads in the colony, exacerbated by the expansion of bus services.

Eventually Walker and local officials began work on a comprehensive planning programme for Trinidad, which was formulated in conjunction with a new Town and Regional Planning Bill (passed by the legislative council on 16 December 1938). In introducing the bill, the attorney general noted that it was based on the English Town and Country Planning Act of 1933 and similar Irish legislation of 1934, but adapted to the specific circumstances of Trinidad. The objective of the bill was "to secure orderly and progressive development, proper sanitary conditions, the co-ordination of roads and public services and the preservation of amenities", under the direction of a planning and housing commission. Planning proposals would begin with surveys that examined such issues as topography, population trends, commercial centres, labour needs and traffic conditions, followed by the preparation and implementation of actual town or regional planning schemes. In response to previous concerns expressed by the chamber of commerce, the attorney general affirmed that the new bill would also protect the rights of private landowners.[11]

Town planning and improvements during the interwar era were motivated primarily by local needs but also by concerns about increasing the appeal of Port of Spain to tourists and investors. In 1924 the president of the chamber of commerce announced plans for a committee to develop the island's tourist trade further, and that same year the *Trinidad Guardian*'s publishing company released a 150-page booklet titled *Trinidad: The Riviera of the Caribbean*. The publication offered a poetic account of the island's many attractions and amenities and was distributed to ocean liners and other outlets. By the 1930s, there was in fact an increase in the number of cruise ships docking at Trinidad and of tourists generally, as well as a wider spectrum of visitors than the elite clientele at the turn of the century. In a promotional article for the *Guardian* in December 1937, Wilson Minshall, secretary of the Tourist and Exhibitions Board, reported forty-seven thousand tourists during the previous year, including fifteen thousand cruise-ship passengers. Minshall suggested that Trinidad could reap far greater economic rewards from tourism and noted the importance of advertising to compete more effectively in this global industry. In 1937 the government also formed a street nuisances committee to address both the harassment of tourists by touts and knick-knack sellers and the broader problem of increasing noise in the city, generated principally by the blowing of motor-vehicle horns. Meanwhile, Mayor Alfred Richards suggested that tourist guides should be educated, appointed by a bureau and uniformed.[12]

Though civic leaders remained concerned about Port of Spain's image, travellers' accounts of the city during the interwar era offered generally favourable impressions. In 1930 the guidebook author Algernon Aspinall asserted that Port of Spain "stands out as the cleanest, brightest, and best-cared-for town in the British West Indies". He noted the "excellent service of open electric trams that hum up and down the main streets with clanging bells", the many shops "where every conceivable necessity of life can be purchased" and the house gardens which, instead of trim English lawns, featured a profusion of poinsettias, bougainvillaeas, hibiscus, allamandas, plumbago and crotons. In 1931 A. Hyatt Verrill reprised his enthusiastic 1917 report on the city, saying: "When the visitor steps ashore at Port of Spain he enters a surprising town, a bustling, modern, busy city in which English, Spanish, French and Hindustani are heard on every side, for Port of Spain is a truly cosmopolitan place." He also noted the city's chromatic variety: "Everything is colorful. The buildings are painted every hue of the rainbow. Gaudily painted canvas sun-awnings hang above the sidewalks. Flaming flowers bloom everywhere, and, thronging the streets and shops, are people of a score or more races, each apparently striving to outdo all others in the brilliancy of garments." Some visitors, however, had more negative views. For example, British writer Owen Rutter complained in 1933: "Everyone tells you that 'Port of Spain is so cosmopolitan.' That was not my impression of it at all." Rutter suggested that the city's diverse social groups kept to themselves, which did not allow for "widened vision or a multiplicity of interests". In addition, he described the city as "unlovely", architecturally "without character" and lacking "any intellectual life".[13]

While Port of Spain attracted a growing number of tourists during the 1920s and 1930s, it also remained a destination for migrants from the Trinidadian countryside, Tobago and other Caribbean territories. Here newcomers found an array of economic, educational and leisure opportunities. For example, Edric Connor, who would later gain fame in England as a baritone and actor, arrived in the city in 1929 from the close-knit village of Mayaro, on Trinidad's remote southeastern coast, where his father was a shoemaker. At sixteen, he had won a scholarship to study a craft at the Royal Victoria Institute, which assigned him to an apprenticeship in the boiler-making department of the Trinidad Government Railway. For Connor, Port of Spain was a new "horizon", a place to experience the wider world and improve himself. In addition to working for the railway, he took night classes in physics at Queen's Royal College and, over time, participated in the Royal Victoria Institute's choir and dramatic society, worked as a reporter for the *Trinidad Guardian*, served as a vocalist and drum major for the police force and fire brigade, and employed his engineering skills at a construction firm. However, the city was also a place of hazards, ambiguities and scheming individuals. After being poorly treated at the home of a church acquaintance of his mother, he moved into a shelter intended primarily for young ex-offenders, on Duncan Street, in the eastern section of downtown:

> There was something fascinating there. Life was raw. The market place was just around the corner on Nelson Street. . . . There was nothing offensive here but poverty. The men played whe whe and loved the women; there was nothing else to do. It was the height of the depression. . . .
>
> It was a tough district. On Besson Street, near the police station, a man smoked a stick of dynamite and blew his head off to prove his love for a woman. Family life here was never a private affair. The streets rang with the cries of the vendors. The whistle of scavengers and the clip-clopping of mules. The exultant cries of sex. Dogs barked and cockerels crowed proudly. These noises were the Symphony of Life.

Connor also encountered a variety of street characters in the city such as a wayside preacher known as "Nosegay", who one Good Friday staged a crucifixion of himself on Piccadilly Street by the Dry River. After preaching and singing with his followers in the market that morning, Nosegay carried a heavy cross through the streets to the spot he had prepared for his performance. Spectators converged from throughout the neighbourhood to witness this remarkable event. Nosegay quietly instructed his accomplices to tie (rather than nail) him to the cross and to throw pebbles (rather than stones) at him. By midday he decided it was time to come down and, when his followers were reluctant to end the drama, he exclaimed: "Take me down! You sons of bitches! What the hell, you all think I'se Jesus Christ?" Nosegay's aborted escapade remained part of the oral lore of Port of Spain for years.[14]

THE TRINIDAD WAR MEMORIAL

One of the most visually imposing and symbolically resonant additions to the Port of Spain landscape during the interwar years was the Trinidad War Memorial, which was unveiled in June 1924 in the newly created Memorial Park (see figure 13). This open space, formerly known as the "Little Savannah", was at the northern end of Frederick Street, across from the Royal Victoria Institute and directly below the Queen's Park Savannah. The towering new monument served to recognize all Trinidadians who had served in World War I and to memorialize those who had died. As the first public monument to honour local people, it contrasted with the statues of Columbus and Lord Harris, in their respective squares, and the mermaids who graced the fountain in Woodford Square. A few days before the ceremonial unveiling, the *Labour Leader* (the newspaper of the TWA) editorialized that Memorial Park would forever "represent a people's gratitude and loving tribute to their loyal sons" and the sacrifices they made "in the great struggle of right against might".[15]

The planning of the memorial extended over several years. In 1916 the mayor of Port of Spain, Enrique Prada, proposed the erection of a memorial and moved that a committee of the city council be formed to consider the matter. A committee did meet but decided to postpone further discussion until the conclusion of the war. In 1919 a public meeting of various citizens was held at the Royal Victoria Institute, with Governor John Chancellor presiding. Though there was debate at this meeting about an appropriate site for the monument, it was decided to place it in Marine Square at the head of Broadway. This gathering also established the planning entity that would become known as the Trinidad War Memorial Executive Committee. While debate over the monument's location continued, the executive committee reconfirmed Marine Square, though eventually it moved the site slightly to the east (off centre) to avoid having to reroute the Broadway tram tracks. Fundraising for the monument progressed over the next couple of years, with the colonial government providing the bulk of the money, but dissatisfaction with the site remained. In a retrospective article on the memorial at the time of the unveiling, the *Port-of-Spain Gazette* noted: "Opposition from many influential sections of the public continued to the choice of the new site, and especially it may be mentioned that representatives on behalf of returned soldiers, relatives of the fallen and the Trinidad Working Men's Association urged the selection of a worthier position for our war memorial." In a similar article, the *Trinidad Guardian* observed that in November 1922 the executive committee "decided to refer the question of the site for the memorial to a representative meeting for reconsideration in view of the fact that there was a great deal of dissatisfaction with the 'cart stand' site which had been selected, and that the Government had expressed its willingness to hand over the Little Savannah to the city council for the purpose of the memorial if the meeting adopted that site". The government's condition for this transfer of land was that the city council maintain it as a park in perpetuity. At this point, the committee and the governor (now Samuel Wilson) agreed that the Little Savannah would serve as the site and designated the city engineer, T.H. Scott, to oversee the construction of the memorial.

Back in 1919, while the site was being debated and funds were being raised, Governor Chancellor took a leave of absence in England and there contacted Louis Frederick Roslyn (1878–1934), an accomplished sculptor. Chancellor forwarded plans and photographs of the Marine Square site to Roslyn, who prepared designs for the memorial. These designs were subsequently displayed for public comment at Maillard's department store on Frederick Street. Communication with Roslyn continued and Wilson, while visiting England in 1923, finalized arrangements with the artist for the design at the new site and for the transport of the monument's components to Trinidad. When shipments began arriving in February 1924, the city engineer initiated construction.[16]

Roslyn's Trinidad War Memorial was solidly in the European tradition of allegorical public monuments. It rested on a granite platform with four shallow surrounding steps that cascaded to the ground, while its four-sided base and central shaft were both made of white Portland stone (a type of limestone). The shaft rose almost 42 feet; near its top were carvings of lions' heads at the four corners, as well as scrolls and other decorative elements. Surmounting the shaft was a bronze statue of a winged Victory figure, standing on a globe and holding a wreath with her raised left arm and a palm branch with her right arm. Below the figure, at the top of the base, were the bows of ships, sculpted in Portland stone and extending to the north and south. The north bow contained a bronze figure of a woman holding a wreath, while a figure of a woman reading a scroll rested in the south bow. On the west (front) side of the monument were bronze sculptures of a soldier with a rifle standing over a fallen comrade. In lieu of a statue, the east side featured carvings on the shaft of an assembly of trophies, flags, a crown and a trident. An inscription on the front of the base (bordered by a gold cord) read: "1914–1918, In Honour of All Who Served, In Memory of Those Who Fell." Bronze plaques on the other three sides of the base listed the names of the soldiers who died in the war.[17]

The *Port-of-Spain Gazette* reported that Roslyn's basic design concept was "to represent victory through sacrifice". Hence the winged Victory figure stood on a globe symbolizing the worldwide war, with a wreath of sacrifice in one hand and a palm of victory in the other. The ships' bows on the monument's base were emblematic of the roles of the Royal Navy and Merchant Marine in the conflict. The female figure in the south bow was reading "the scroll of Fame", while the figure on the north was a Red Cross nurse, whose laurel wreath symbolized "the tender care of the sick and fallen". The front sculpture represented courage, with the armed soldier "standing guard over and defending a dying comrade".[18]

By the time of the unveiling of the Trinidad War Memorial in June 1924, Rosyln was already well known for his creation of sculptures and designs for various war memorials around Britain. His monument for Trinidad most closely resembles his Oswaldtwistle War Memorial, unveiled in Oswaldtwistle, Lancashire, in January 1922. Though proportioned differently from the Trinidad monument, the Oswaldtwistle memorial has a stepped platform, base and shaft, with a winged Victory figure at the top. Statues of standing and fallen soldiers are positioned in front, and ships' bows with female figures on the sides. Given that the Oswaldtwistle memorial was unveiled two and a half years before the Trinidad memorial, it seems likely that the former served as a model for the latter. However, this is not certain, since Rosyln was initially contacted by the Trinidad governor in 1919 and prepared a design that year or in 1920, albeit for Marine Square rather than the Little Savannah site. It is unclear how Roslyn may have modified his design for Trinidad during the following years.[19]

The Trinidad War Memorial was situated at the centre of the roughly rectangular block that was renamed Memorial Park. Its western orientation perhaps signified the departed soldiers but also took advantage of the scenic background of trees at the Holy Name Convent, directly east of the park. A paved circular area, approximately 18 feet in diameter, surrounded the monument, while paved walkways led here from gates at the cardinal points of the block. The *Port-of-Spain Gazette* reported that young palms were planted on the sides of the walks and around the central area, but early photographs do not show these plantings (though benches do appear). Most of the park consisted of lawn, with shade trees at the perimeter. The *Gazette* also mentioned iron fencing surrounding the park, but it is unclear if this was completed in time for the unveiling or how it was modified during the following years. Nonetheless, early photographs show iron fencing on a low masonry wall, with tall four-sided gateposts and swing gates at the four entrances. Each gatepost held an elegant iron lamp with three spheres.[20]

The scenic appearance of Memorial Park was enhanced by the surrounding area, which included the Queen's Park Savannah, prominent public buildings and upscale residences. The *Gazette* noted that the memorial's "striking gracefulness and impressiveness is greatly enhanced by the beauty of its situation, and the remarkably appropriate symbolism suggested by its background of tall palm trees in the grounds of the Holy Name Church, and the Colonial Hospital". The paper added that the proximity to the convent seemed "to speak the blessing of Mother Church on all those who fell and whose names are inscribed, and at the same time holding forth as a consolation to the bereaved relatives". Meanwhile, the *Labour Leader* editorialized that those who had opposed the relocation of the monument must feel that "the selection of the 'up town' as against the 'down town' site was justifiable and sound as not only does it compare favourably with most Memorials in the world, but, on account of its sequestered environment, Memorial Park will form one of the prominent beauty spots of Port-of-Spain".[21] In the end, the city's populace was convinced that the memorial belonged in a dignified park, a setting of tranquillity and contemplation, rather than in the crowded centre of the commercial Marine Square.

The unveiling of the memorial on the afternoon of 28 June 1924 was much anticipated but not without controversy. Contention centred on Trinidad's two groups of veterans, from the Merchants and Planters' Contingent and the British West Indies Regiment. At the beginning of the war, the former group had excluded darker-skinned men, thus leading to the formation of the latter. At issue for the unveiling was the placement of sentries at the four corners of the monument. The unveiling ceremony was centred on the west side, which meant that the sentries at the northwest and southwest corners would have the most prominent positions. It was agreed that the northwest sentry would represent the Royal Navy, a contingent of which was in port on HMS *Ormonde*. The British West Indies Regiment insisted that, as the larger force, it should provide the sentry for the southwest corner, while the Merchants and Planters' Contingent contested this, and, two days before the unveiling, threatened not to attend if it were not given prominence. On the day before the unveiling, however, the contingent reluctantly agreed to the positioning of its sentry at the southeast corner. A sentry at the northeast represented others who had served in the war.[22]

Along with the positioning of the four sentries, the spatial configuration of personnel for the unveiling included the governor (Samuel Wilson), the mayor of Port of Spain (Gaston Johnston) and other colonial and municipal officials on the west side of the monument; the British West Indies Regiment to the north; the Merchants and Planters' Contingent to the south; and the constabulary and other local forces to the east. Families of those who had served and the general public filled the park and beyond, while Boy Scouts directed and assisted the crowd. The *Port-of-Spain Gazette* observed that the assembly consisted of "men, women and children of all ranks", while the *Trinidad Guardian* said: "The whole scene presented an appealing picture: satisfying to the eye and stirring to the imagination – this calm, inspiring gathering of the military, of men who survived the war, official and civic dignitaries, officials of representative institutions, clubs, associations and commercial houses, and a huge mass of the general public, to applaud the consummation of a worthy effort." The arrival of the governor was marked by the constabulary band's rendition of the royal salute (the first six bars of "God Save the King"). The ceremony itself consisted of prayers for the dead, a speech from the governor, the governor's removal of the Union Jack that veiled the monument (to the strains of "God Save the King"), additional prayers, a minute of silence and the band's performance of "Reveille", along with a rocket signal from the Royal Victoria Institute and the ringing of church bells. At this point, the governor officially handed over the memorial to the City of Port of Spain, which became its owner and caretaker. Mayor Johnston accepted the memorial with a speech. After noting that the city had initiated the memorial movement that reached its fruition today, he said:

> I can safely promise on behalf of the citizens of Port-of-Spain that everything in their power will be done to discharge the duty that has been undertaken in their name, – the duty of making this little savannah a garden worthy of imperishable memories of which this beautiful monument is intended to be the hallowed emblem. The Port-of-Spain City Council feels deeply honoured to be deemed the worthy guardians of the Colony's most valued historic possession.

After the mayor's acceptance speech, the laying of wreaths and the departure of the governor, the crowd moved inward to take a closer look at the memorial.[23]

Immediately after the day of the unveiling, commentary began to appear on proper public behaviour towards the memorial. A statement in the *Gazette*, signed "L'Inconnu", asserted:

> Yesterday, with befitting solemnity and appropriate ceremonial, the War Memorial of this colony was unveiled, testifying for all time to the part which this colony took in the Great War....
>
> It is as a war shrine that it should be looked upon in the days to come. Our memorial should be guarded with tender and reverent care and surveillance not only by those who have the direct charge of it, but by every person who approaches it. Around it is no place for idle levity; for lewdness, for the sort of conduct that we have far too much of in our parks and open spaces at nights. And every member of the public can help to see that the memory of our dead is respected in the shadow of the shrine we have erected to them.

A couple weeks later, the commandant of the local forces issued an order that the public, when passing the memorial, "should salute in the same manner prescribed for the Local Forces". Soon thereafter the *Guardian* reported that some people were saluting or lifting their hats, while adding: "It has been observed that among the lower orders few pay attention to the appeal but it is hoped that as time goes on they will follow the lead given them by others." While physical gestures may have varied, the memorial remained a site generally cherished by the Port of Spain public and, on Armistice Day that year, citizens again laid wreaths, made principally of Flanders poppies, and observed minutes of silence at the memorial.[24]

The chief significance of the Trinidad War Memorial was that it was a monument planned and executed by the local community in honour of its own heroes. Though it was designed by an English artist in a European allegorical style, it represented Trinidadians and inscribed their names in bronze for all to see. Moreover, local people, under the direction of the city engineer, built the monument and laid out the surrounding park, a new space of beauty and serenity within the urban landscape. The memorial represented Trinidadians of widely varying backgrounds and affirmed an ideal of unity, in spite of the social differences that characterized their service during the war and their existence afterwards. Local commentators interpreted the memorial as a civic shrine that exemplified public duty and service, as well as a monument that marked Trinidad's participation in a global event that defined the era. During the following decades, the memorial was extensively photographed from various perspectives and, through the publication of postcards, became an iconic image of Port of Spain. The municipal government maintained its commitment to the care of the park, while the local population continued to visit for reverent or casual moments of peace.

NEW BUILDINGS: REVIVALIST TO MODERNIST

While the war memorial was a particularly powerful symbolic addition to the Port of Spain landscape during the interwar years, the local populace also constructed a wide range of new public and commercial buildings during this era. At the same time the war memorial was being erected near the Savannah, labourers were working on another monumental structure downtown: the colonial government's new railway headquarters, which was on the south side of South Quay and stretched two blocks from Broadway to Charlotte Street (see figure 14). Completed in 1924, this expansion of the old station consisted of a neoclassical two-storey concrete-block building that faced Broadway and featured, along with a subdued central section, two imposing pavilions, each with a pediment, pilasters and a large rectangular entranceway crowned with an arch of windows. Rows of windows and pilasters lined the sides of the pavilions, and their roofs included balustraded parapets. A long colonnaded concourse, providing access to the tracks, continued to the east and culminated in an additional two-storey building. With abundant waiting rooms, offices and other facilities, the station remained centred within the transportation hub of Queen's Wharf. The government's 1931 map of Port of Spain shows multiple railway tracks arriving from the east, some terminating at the station and others continuing further west to the Custom House and the St Vincent Wharf. Along with the Custom House (which contained the Harbour Master's Office), other structures on the wharf included the Harbour Constabulary Station; the lighthouse; sugar, cocoa, petroleum and other warehouses; and a locomotive workshop and engine shed. In addition, tramlines ran along South Quay, Broadway and Charlotte Street, with side tracks to a carriage shed three blocks east of the railway station. To the north were the many warehouses, stores and other commercial buildings of the Marine Square district.

Several months before the opening of the new railway headquarters, the *Labour Leader* announced: "Within the next few months Port-of-Spain will be able to boast of the finest Railway Station in the West Indies, and one which will compare favourably with any similar structure in the largest cities of the world. This statement, however, does not take away one feather weight from our oft expressed opinion that so expensive a building is quite unnecessary for the needs of a service like ours." Indeed, there appears to have been minimal public enthusiasm for the new headquarters, as there was limited support for the Trinidad Government Railway itself. At the time, the railway, as well as the government's coastal steamer service, was consistently losing money, in part because of a general economic downturn but more because of the increasing competition from omnibuses, lorries (trucks), taxi cars and private cars. Given the attraction of independent and flexible automotive transportation, many people perceived the railway as inefficient for moving goods and passengers, and a drain on public funds. Road congestion, however, was also a growing concern, as was the need for better transport for the residents of Port of Spain's eastern suburbs. While there were train stops in this area, the Trinidad Electric Company applied for a licence to extend tram service further to the east and, by the time the new railway headquarters opened, the *Trinidad Guardian* was advocating tram service as a more effective option for these districts. Nonetheless, the government remained committed to the railway as an important component of the island's economic development. The erection of a grand new headquarters building in neoclassical style seemed to symbolize its continued determination to control a centralized island-wide transportation system.[25]

Another example of architectural historicism during this period was the 1924 addition to St Mary's College on Frederick Street in uptown Port of Spain. Designed by George Rosenthal in a Mediterranean Revival style, this two-storey building included two asymmetrical sections. The south section featured ground-level arched entryways into galleries perpendicular to the front façade and a similar plan of arched openings and galleries on the first floor. Between the arches were bays of windows. The north section contained galleries along the front façade, with columns and balustrades and series of double doors into interior rooms. Both sections had hipped roofs, with a dormer window on the south and two lantern lights on the north. Also erected at this time were an arched gateway into the grounds, an iron fence on a low wall, and the college's war memorial, a 16-foot-high monument bearing bronze plates with the names of the school's deceased.

While the new building was designed in a historicist style, its purpose was to address the inadequacies of the existing facility, the school's growing number of students and the need for modern scientific education. The southern section housed a library and lecture room, which were "cool, spacious, and airy" and "well lighted by large windows". The northern section included three classrooms on the ground floor and, on the first floor, a 30-by-54-foot science room (with gas and water appliances), a chemistry storage area, a photographic darkroom and rooms for physics, botany and biology, "all airy and comfortable". The *Trinidad Guardian* assessed the new facility at the time of its opening: "Remodelled and enlarged at the cost of $45,000 and calculated to meet the improved requirements of modern education the building, situated as it is in a residential portion of the town, forms a substantial adornment to the locality and will afford greater scope for the continuance and furtherance of its work of usefulness in the community in moulding and fashioning the lives and characters of the young."[26]

While architects working in Trinidad continued to employ revivalist styles during the 1930s and into the 1940s, they also began to experiment with modernist designs. With its clean lines, streamlined surfaces and reduction or elimination of historical references, modernism offered a vision of a technologically driven international future, rather than the encrusted legacy of a European colonial past. Architects and builders incorporated modernist designs gradually and often combined them with revival styles. Their most prominent experiments during this period involved commercial and public buildings, but they also began introducing new concepts to domestic architecture.

The pursuit of modernist design occurred in conjunction with a building boom in Port of Spain and throughout Trinidad that was developing by 1933, despite the global depression and continued challenges within Trinidad's economy. Including both new construction and renovation, the boom was propelled in part by low prices for building materials. Timber imports for the first five months of 1934 increased to 4.1 million board feet from 3.2 million during the same period in 1933, while there were also growing imports of cement, steel, galvanized iron and roofing materials. In addition to new commercial buildings downtown, new homes were built across the city and in the northern suburbs of Maraval and St Ann's, including the area of Coblentz Avenue and Cascade Avenue/Road (now part of Cascade). Though prices for building materials were increasing by 1937, construction continued. In 1939, for example, there was much new work along the Eastern Main Road, including the orderly layout of residential plots in lower Laventille, the purchase of a building site by Fernandes and Company (a rum distillery) and the erection of a storage facility by Messrs J. Fogarty Limited (furniture makers).[27]

The building boom of the 1930s provided an opportunity for innovations in engineering and architecture. Certainly the key figure in the exploration of modernist design in Port of Spain during this period was the English architect Herbert G.W. Brinsley. A fellow of the Royal Institute of British Architects, Brinsley had settled in Trinidad in 1919. In addition to the new San Fernando Town Hall (1930), he designed many buildings in Port of Spain, including the Metro/Globe Cinema (1933), the new hall for Bishop Anstey High School (1933); the Neal and Massy Garage (circa 1934), the Alston Building (circa 1935), the new Treasury Building (1938), the Electricity Board's transfer station at Frederick and Park Streets (renovation, 1938), and numerous large houses.[28] Brinsley's new garage for the Neal and Massy Engineering Company, a car dealership, stood on Edward Street, between Park and Duke Streets, and was built by George F. Huggins and Company. Exceeding 20,000 square feet, the building featured three long bays, each with a pair of large garage entrances. Above each set of entrances and a simple marquee that extended the length of the front façade was a band of windows, each intersected by a streamlined pilaster that culminated in a free-standing stepped pediment. The building's walls were reinforced concrete, steel columns supported the bays, corrugated asbestos sheets provided insulation for the roof, and windows and skylights were made with a glass that diffused sunlight into a mild green glow. Brinsley employed similar engineering and Art Deco elements in his design for a new building for Alston and Company, a major import-export firm. This building, constructed by W.A. King, faced Marine Square South, between St Vincent and Abercromby Streets, and extended all the way to South Quay. Built with a steel frame, the three-storey structure comprised a central projecting section and two side sections. Each featured a bay of doors on the ground floor with bays of windows above, while the façade as a whole was integrated by a stepped roofline. A marquee of steel and heat-reducing Calorex glass protected the entrances. The ground floor of the building housed Alston's shipping offices, along with its cocoa department at the Marine Square end and merchandise department at South Quay. The upper floors included additional offices and the roof contained a lookout station for viewing the harbour.[29]

In a 1934 article on the new design trends in Port of Spain, the *Trinidad Guardian* proclaimed:

> Amid one of the greatest building booms Trinidad has ever known, a new style of architecture is creeping in to adorn the face of the City and bring Port-of-Spain into line with modern cities throughout the world.

> This is ultramodern architecture – the style that knows no nooks and crannies for dirt to gather, yet violates none of the canons of good design and will forever remain a thing of grace and beauty.

The *Guardian* contrasted the new commercial structures downtown with surrounding buildings, which it described as a hodge-podge of different ideas and styles employed by various architects over the previous half-century. The newspaper also commented on the use of modernist design in residential districts "where houses, instead of running to the size of small hotels with much ornate trimming and tracery, are more compact and attractive and so situated in their grounds as to form a pleasing scene".[30]

Herbert Brinsley's masterpiece was the new Treasury Building, which, after the Deep Water Harbour Scheme, was the second largest construction project in Port of Spain during the interwar era. This massive complex at the western end of Marine Square filled an entire block between Marine Square North (formerly King Street), Edward, St Vincent and Treasury Streets, with building sections surrounding a courtyard. The former treasury and bonded warehouse on this site were destroyed by fire in 1932. Initially the government considered both this site and one on the south side of Marine Square for the new treasury and retained Herbert Savage as the architect. However, Savage's elaborate neoclassical proposal was determined to be too costly to build. By 1934 the government had decided on the northern site and recruited Brinsley as the new architect. In collaboration with the Public Works Department, which was responsible for construction, Brinsley prepared a plan that would house not only the treasury on Marine Square but also the post office (with its main entrance on St Vincent Street) and the Agricultural Bank, while later the internal audit department was added. Construction began in March 1936 and continued for over two years, with more than four hundred workers employed by June 1937.

Brinsley designed the Treasury Building in a style now often referred to as "Stripped Classical" or "Modern Classic" (see figure 15). The front two-storey section on Marine Square consisted of a central block and two long wings, each of which comprised two parts with distinct setbacks. The central block's portico featured a base with three steps, six towering pillars, and an upper area with a low-stepped roofline and a Portland-stone relief carving of the colony's coat of arms. In the expansive flat-roofed wings, engaged pillars alternated with inset vertical window bands. The basic structure was built of steel and concrete, with a plinth of polished dark granite rising 5 feet from the ground and smooth cast-stone blocks (made in a nearby public works factory) employed as a veneer on the remainder of the exterior. Overall, the front elevation combined classical monumentality with modernist austerity, a fitting image for the new financial centre of an aspiring colony.

The treasury's interior was similarly elegant. Limestone from the Laventille Hills was used to make terrazzo for walls and floors in lunchrooms, washrooms, corridors and similar spaces, while marble, Portland stone and faience were employed for the entrance (which contained an electric elevator) and public spaces of the post office. Also included in the building were black glass counters with bronze grilles, steel furniture and globe-shaped lamps. To preserve the general appearance of tidiness, electric and telephone wires were routed through ducts in the floors, and plumbing ducts were also hidden. Finally, there was much attention to the maintenance of a cool and comfortable workplace. The roofing comprised layers of cork and bitumen felt, while the ample inset windows included roller blinds that shielded the sun and louvres for ventilation. Occupants moved into the building over several months, with part of the audit department arriving around 1 June 1938 and the remainder of the agencies settling in by October. The post office, including its 649 private letterboxes, opened to the public on 24 October. Clearly, the new Treasury Building was an impressive addition to the city and greatly enhanced the appearance of the western end of Marine Square, where visitors continued to arrive by ship. In time, the adjacent space on the square was filled with orderly parking places in response to the growing popularity of automotive transport.[31]

During 1938 another prominent modernist structure was under construction at the other end of the city: a new addition to the Queen's Park Hotel on the Savannah. During the 1920s and 1930s, this hotel remained the premier venue for accommodating visitors and a popular gathering place for the Trinidadian elite. *Trinidad: The Riviera of the Caribbean*, the tourism promotional booklet published in 1924, described it as comprising approximately two acres of land and a hundred guest rooms. The hotel's setting remained central to its appeal: "Away to the north lie the high hills which surround the town, and over which float everchanging shadows, thus rendering them wonderfully beautiful to the eyes of travellers sitting in the wide open verandahs which surround the ground floor of the Hotel." The booklet added that the hotel had a "delightfully cool, open restaurant" and well-stocked bar, a magnificent ballroom next to a palm garden, its own electric generator and ready access to electric tramcars that passed every fifteen minutes. In fact, the hotel expanded its ballroom at the end of 1924 to hold seven hundred guests. A cool atmosphere was created within this space by a colour scheme of cream and green, a flood of lighting from the walls and ceiling, and electric fans. The hotel featured a series of cabaret dances during its 1925 season to show off the new facility.[32]

Though the Queen's Park Hotel had a grand reputation, the English writer Alec Waugh offered a sardonic portrait of the venue in his travel book *Hot Countries*, published in 1930. Referring to the hotel as the "Baracuda", he complained of baths being located down a winding maze of corridors, delayed responses to his requests for an inkpot, the incessant noise of car horns around the Savannah, the dining room crowded with passengers from a cruise ship, a loud tourist dance at night and, as a final irritation, bedbugs. When Owen Rutter, another English writer, visited Port of Spain in 1933, he argued with local businessman George Huggins about whether Waugh's report of bedbugs was accurate. Rutter reported that there were no bedbugs during his stay and that the food and service were good, as was the Queen's Park Hotel Super Cocktail, made with local rum, Angostura Bitters, grenadine, lime juice and Italian vermouth. In 1938 the writer John Vandercook said:

> The Queen's Park . . . is one of the famous inns of the American tropics. The Queen's Park is old and it verges on shabbiness. But its broad verandah and its great open dining room have for a generation been one of the classic meeting places of the West Indies. Passing tourists, in for the day, throng it in their hundreds, fit easily into its pleasant scheme, and, to their visible satisfaction, fail to dominate it. The Q.P. is a place for "regulars". Planters and business men, fliers and experienced voyagers come to it. Nowhere else does one realize so clearly that despite the changing times and the multiplicity and variety of the islands, there is still a compact, special Caribbean world, with interests, purposes and friendships of its own.[33]

While the Queen's Park Hotel continued to function as a fashionable meeting place for both locals and visitors, it was obvious during the late 1930s that improvements were needed. By 1937 the management was contemplating a multistorey addition, which in May 1938 generated heated debate within the city council on whether the planned structure would comply with building regulations and enhance or diminish the ambience of the Savannah. Nonetheless, the central portion of the existing hotel complex was torn down and construction went ahead. By the end of January 1939, the new addition (with ninety-two guest rooms) was accommodating cruise-ship passengers, even though work was not entirely completed.[34]

The addition was designed in an Art Deco style, with strong vertical and horizontal lines, by William F. Brown, an English-born architect who had settled in South Florida (see figure 16).[35] The front elevation, facing the Savannah, consisted of a ground floor with an open porch and four floors of guest rooms, divided into three vertical bays by engaged pillars. Each room contained a series of louvred windows and doors that opened onto a balcony, which was semicircular for the central bay and rectangular on the sides. The two pillars featured ornaments (web shapes, parallel lines and floral designs) and neon lights, while vent gaps in the porch walls created accents perpendicular to these. When completed, the overall composition consisted of a streamlined white tower emerging from the centre of the rambling gingerbread buildings of the turn of the century, thus creating a striking juxtaposition of two eras of architecture and accommodation in Port of Spain.

In an account of a tour of the new addition, a *Trinidad Guardian* reporter narrated that guests entered through a neon-lit spacious hall containing a reception office and information bureau. Also on the ground floor were an inquiry office for Pan American Airways and a sunken bar, featuring a horseshoe-shaped counter (in black and red with chrome strips) and a representation of a setting sun as a backdrop. Guest rooms on the floors above were graced with varnished maple floorboards, modern steel furniture ("glittering in the rays of the sun and contributing to the general atmosphere of splendour"), and baths tiled in green, yellow, cream or blue. On top of the building was a roof garden, accessible by elevator and providing both a view of the surrounding city and a solar-heating plant for hot-water baths. The roof's bandstand and dance floor inspired the reporter to comment: "One can just imagine the influence that will be wrought on lovers dancing beneath the spell of a tropical moon and the starlit canopy of heaven to the strains of some lilting waltz." In a travel book published in 1941, Amy Oakley affirmed the sophistication of the new addition: "The ancient caravansary at Trinidad has largely been rebuilt on modern lines – for is it not a stopping-place for those ultra-modern Cosmopolitans, the passengers of Pan-American Airways?" Oakley stayed in the new building, where her room provided "the last word in taste and comfort", and observed that tourists and business associates continued to mingle in the lobby and cocktail bar.[36]

The accommodation of Pan American passengers and crew was indeed another important element of operations at the Queen's Park Hotel. This airline's business in Trinidad began on 22 September 1929, when Charles Lindbergh (with his wife and a crew of three) flew a seaplane from San Juan, Puerto Rico, to Port of Spain, as part of the inauguration of US airmail service from Miami through the Caribbean to South America. Lindbergh's plane and a second one carrying Pan American president J.T. Trippe and additional mail landed in the city's harbour, while throngs of well-wishers watched from the shore. A reception was scheduled at the Union Club on Marine Square, but, owing to large crowds, the party was instead taken directly to Government House on the Savannah. By December of that year, Pan American had established a seaplane facility at Cocorite, to the west of St James, and landed its first passengers there in February 1930. In 1936 the company initiated flights of its express thirty-two-passenger Clipper to Cocorite, but by 1939 had shifted to land-based aviation at Piarco, an airfield in north-central Trinidad that was also used by other airlines. With its growing service to Trinidad, Pan American developed a close relationship with the Queen's Park Hotel. An unsigned copy of a 1934 contract shows that the hotel agreed to set aside eighteen single rooms and six doubles for Pan American passengers and staff, to refurbish the rooms and to have them ready for occupancy by March 1935. In return, Pan American agreed to provide a payment and to publicize the hotel in its literature. While the airline may have started to use these rooms by the mid-1930s, it built its own wing on the southeast corner of the hotel complex in 1939. A 1944 letter from Pan American to the hotel refers to the renewal of a 1939 agreement (and annual payment) for priority rights to eighteen singles and six doubles in an old building and ten singles and twenty-one doubles in a new building (presumably the section built by the airline). In any case, the accommodation of Pan American passengers reinforced the status of the Queen's Park Hotel as a centre for the latest developments in international travel.[37]

MOVIE THEATRES

Among the most popular buildings in Port of Spain during the interwar era were several movie theatres, which screened films (mainly American and British) throughout the week and attracted regular audiences of differing socio-economic classes. With their impressive exteriors, lavish interiors, advanced electronic technologies and moving images of exotic locales, romance and adventure, the theatres were places of fantasy where the city's populace congregated for a new type of leisure experience. They also served as venues for various forms of live entertainment.

A few of the city's movie theatres predated the interwar era. In 1911 the English brothers Marcus and Reginald Davis opened the London Electric Theatre (later renamed the Astor Cinema) on the southwest corner of Baden-Powell and French Streets in Woodbrook. An advertisement in the *Mirror* promised "'The World Before Your Eyes', showing the Finest Living Pictures – Travel, Adventure, Drama, Sport, Comedy and Current Events". In an article on the opening night, the newspaper reported: "The lighting is brilliant inside and out, everything has been done to secure the comfort and safety of the audience and there are several emergency exits. The attendants were in spotless uniform and the manager gave personal supervision, while a lady pianist played throughout the entertainment. The pictures were very good indeed, especially the viewing of Niagara, in which the rushing, foaming water was represented perfectly." Lamenting that Port of Spain had previously not had a venue for such amusement, the *Mirror* concluded that "the promoters of the Electric Theatre have placed an attractive and rational entertainment in comfortable surroundings within the reaches of all classes". With the well-known musician Lionel Belasco taking over as pianist and eventually manager, the London continued to offer varied programming. An advertisement in the *Port-of-Spain*

Gazette in 1914, for example, listed the French film *Zigomar* and performances by Miss Annie McRillop, "the Popular Vocalist", and Syd Martin, "the Prince of Comedians". The London's main competitor during these early years of Trinidad's cinema industry was the Olympic Theatre, opened by Belasco and Doris Legg in 1916 at the northeast corner of Erthig Road and Pelham Street in Belmont. An advertisement in the *Trinidad Guardian* in 1920 listed Lillian Gish in *Innocent Magdalene*, with *Twin Triangles* and *Twenty Thousand Leagues Under the Sea* as coming attractions. Around this same time, local writer Alfred Mendes recalls seeing a theatrical troupe at the Olympic and enjoying "the dancing, the acrobatics, the tableaux representing classical themes, and the singing in Italian, Spanish, and Portuguese".[38]

In 1924 the London and the Olympic contained approximately seven hundred and six hundred seats respectively, but the new theatres built during the 1920s and 1930s assumed much larger proportions. First was the Empire Theatre, opened by the American George Rosenthal in 1920 with a main entrance on St Vincent Street and a back entrance for pit seating on Edward Street at the intersection of Tragarete Road. (A theatre's "pit" contained its cheapest seats, close to the stage/screen.) The Empire had a capacity of fifteen hundred seats, a fifty-by-forty-foot stage, stage scenery for plays and concerts (painted by Lee Lash Studios of New York), a range of lights for stage illumination and two alternating projectors to enable the continuous screening of films. On the day of the opening, the *Trinidad Guardian* reported: "On entering one is confronted with a brass chandelier consisting of 18 lamps which, when lighted, will present a most charming effect. On turning to the right or left is a stair on either side leading to a lounge gallery which will be adorned with oil paintings of two famous film stars. Here friends may gather before pictures are shown." The programme for the opening night included a performance of von Suppe's *Poet and Peasant Overture* by the constabulary band, a series of newsreels, songs by two local vocalists, Charlie Chaplin's *A Dog's Life*, a performance by Spanish dancer La Crisaldia and *The Romance of Tarzan* in seven parts. By 1930 the Empire was screening "talkies" and local audiences were able to experience sounds as well as sights from abroad.[39]

While the Empire remained Trinidad's leading cinema for over a decade, lavishness in theatre design reached a new level with the opening in March 1933 of the Metro on the southwest corner of Park and St Vincent Streets, one of the busiest intersections in Port of Spain. Directly below Tragarete Road and near the Empire, the Metro was developed by Nur Mohammed Gokool, managing director of Metro Theatres Limited, a firm established in association with Metro-Goldwyn-Mayer (MGM), which was expanding its Latin American and Caribbean operations at the time. The son of Gokool Meah (wealthy landowner and benefactor of the St James mosque), Nur Gokool initially intended to become a physician. He lived and studied in Britain and Ireland for many years before returning to Trinidad and entering the cinema business with his father and brother. Though the Metro was a major success, the Gokools renamed it the Globe in 1934, after a dispute with MGM over the company's requirement for exclusive screening of its films. Over time, Nur Gokool established additional theatres in Trinidad and other Caribbean territories and became a major supporter of civic causes in Port of Spain and across the island.

The architect of the Metro was Herbert Brinsley, who designed the building in a Mediterranean Revival style, perhaps in an effort to augment the romance of the movie world (see figure 17). W.A. King held the main construction contract and employed some hundred men for the job. Built with a steel frame and reinforced concrete, the theatre nearly filled its 177-by-124-foot corner site. Its prominent tower at the corner of Park and St Vincent Streets featured a projecting hip roof with corbels, red Spanish tiles, and a neon-lit red globe at its apex. Elongated arches framed entrances and windows on the north and east sides of the tower, with the entrances sheltered by marquees. Arched windows and pilasters defined the north and east sides of the main building, and there was a balustraded roof garden to the west of the tower. While patrons for house, balcony and box seats entered through the tower, the entrance for pit seating was farther down St Vincent Street. Stairways in the main lobby led to the balcony and box seats, a refreshment bar and tea room and the roof garden. The lobby also displayed large colour photographs of MGM stars, such as Greta Garbo, Norma Shearer, Joan Crawford and Clark Gable.

The 104-by-80-foot auditorium contained a total of 1,761 seats on opening night, though this number was later slightly reduced because of safety concerns. Seating included rattan armchairs in the boxes, upholstered chairs elsewhere in the balcony and enamelled wooden chairs in the house and pit. Brinsley supervised the interior design, which featured a saxe-blue and sunshine-yellow colour scheme and geometric patterns that the *Trinidad Guardian* described as "charmingly refreshing and modernistic, though not violently so". At the top of the stage's proscenium arch was the figure of a nymph that symbolized "the Spirit of Film", while sculpted masks representing tragedy and comedy adorned adjacent oriel windows that had wrought-iron grilles and tiled roofs. An elaborate scheme of white and coloured lights on the ceiling and walls illuminated the auditorium, and large mechanical ventilators, concealed behind the oriel windows, were designed to completely recirculate the air every six minutes. The Western Electric Company sent down a specialist to instal a projection and audio system that would provide the most advanced exhibition of sound films, and there was special attention to acoustics, including the use of acoustic boards on the auditorium walls, which simulated Bath stone. The *Guardian* suggested: "The Metro Cinema is Mr. Brinsley's most ambitious creation in Trinidad, and he has to be congratulated in conceiving a building of a dignity befitting the premier house of entertainment in the Island, yet of a quiet originality and a romantic jollity in harmony with the purpose – that of giving pleasure."[40]

The opening of the Metro on 18 March was a grand affair. The governor and his wife officially patronized the event, many local dignitaries attended and a congratulatory telegram from MGM, bearing the names of several of its stars, was pinned up in the theatre lobby. A "Film Correspondent" for the *Guardian* described the scene:

> Beneath the snowy lighting of the Metro's modernistic pale blue ceiling there assembled last night the greatest audience ever gathered at any theatrical entertainment in Trinidad. . . .
>
> Outside in the streets huge crowds blinked before the illumination that proclaimed the importance of the occasion. Thousands watched a ceaseless stream of cars unload their occupants before the steps of the theatre. . . .
>
> I feel as though this building was Mr. Gokool's Taj Mahal, – a memorial to a beautiful dream, the fruition of a life of work in beautiful, cosmopolitan Trinidad. Last night the Capital was indeed a beautiful Metropolis, the brightest gaiety and perfection of the [site] made strangers think of the thrilling, crowded life of the great capitals of Europe or America which they have loved.

Along with a performance of Rossini's *William Tell* Overture by the constabulary band, the programme included *The Rogue Song*, a musical directed by Lionel Barrymore and starring the baritone Lawrence Tibbet, and several shorts: a Hearst newsreel, *The Pyjama Party, Volley and Smash* (depicting tennis), and *Riding the Rails*. *Riding the Rails* was a picture on the Trinidad Railway by Louis Tucker, a local filmmaker who also created news shorts with material imported from Britain. The Humming Bird, the *Guardian*'s social columnist, gave a glowing account of the evening. She affirmed that the theatre would "enhance the civic dignity of Port-of-Spain", but believed there was one flaw: "The noble lines of the building are not given sufficient background, as they would have been if the theatre had been built near where the Princes' Building now stands." While Gokool chose to locate his theatre within the dense commercial and residential fabric of the central city, the Humming Bird would have preferred to see it in the environment of the Queen's Park Savannah.[41]

The next major figure to enter Port of Spain's growing cinema industry was Timothy Roodal, who was born and educated in southern Trinidad. There he acquired oil-bearing lands and founded Oropouche Oilfields Limited. In the 1930s and 1940s, Roodal served on the San Fernando Borough Council (including terms as mayor), was a member of the legislative council, served as vice president and president of A.A. Cipriani's TLP and was active in numerous civic undertakings. After entering the movie business in San Fernando in 1931, he eventually acquired cinemas in other parts of Trinidad, as well as in Barbados and British Guiana. In 1940 he purchased the Ambard house, the most ornate of the series of mansions on the Maraval Road side of the Savannah. The first of several cinemas that he established in Port of Spain was the Roxy, which opened on 13 October 1934, at the intersection of Tragarete Road, St Clair Avenue and Damian Street in Woodbrook, adjacent to King George V Park and St James. The Roxy was a large white structure with two floors of verandahs featuring columns and balustrades. A projecting semicircular central section housed what the *Trinidad Guardian* described as an "illuminated sign displaying the name 'Roxy' in letters painted on white translucent cubes". The theatre's interior was designed in white, blue and gold, with seating for a total of twelve hundred patrons in the balcony, house and pit. Devoted exclusively to MGM films, the theatre opened with *Dancing Lady*, starring Joan Crawford and Clark Gable. The *Guardian* noted that this spectacular musical comedy featured hundreds of chorus beauties who, in one scene, could be seen thirty times at once, via a maze of mirrors. As mayor of Port of Spain at the time, Cipriani opened the Roxy and, in a brief speech, said it "stands with one foot in Woodbrook, one in St. Clair and one foot in St. James, and therefore caters to every section of the community, the classes and the masses".[42]

In 1937 three more cinemas opened in Port of Spain: the St James Theatre on the Western Main Road at Madras Street on 6 March, the Royal Theatre at Charlotte and Observatory Streets on 22 May and the De Luxe Theatre at Keate and Pembroke Streets on 29 May. While the first two generally catered to patrons of more modest means, the De Luxe's uptown location was very prestigious – across the street from the Royal Victoria Institute and near Memorial Park and the Prince's Building. The theatre was owned by the British Colonial Film Exchange, which had been established several years earlier by a group that included William P. Humphrey, another leading figure in Port of Spain's cinema industry. The architect, C. Hume, employed an Art Deco design, which contrasted with the historical revival styles of the city's earlier theatres (see figure 18). The De Luxe's streamlined front elevation was divided by four engaged pillars, with a simple marquee bisecting the central two. A series of stepped rooflines crowned the façade, while vertical grilles (with abstract floral motifs) and window bands were featured between the pillars. The interior of the cinema was similarly modern and innovative. A *Guardian* reporter described a "colour scheme of green and grey, set off by glistening chromium metal bands", which provided "a restful and harmonious atmosphere for the enjoyment of films in comfort". In addition, there was an "ingenious use of lighting effects and curtain draw-backs", as well as "deep spring cushioned seats throughout, soft rubber inlaid flooring, modernistic furniture, running ice-water in lobbies and foyer and decorative fountains in which gold-fish swim in multi-coloured baths". Most significant, the De Luxe contained no pit, which meant that its affluent clientele would not be troubled by the lively exclamations of the patrons who typically filled these low-cost seats. The opening-night movie was Warner Brothers' *The Charge of the Light Brigade*, though the theatre also scheduled a grand charity night several days later that featured a travelogue; *Trinidad Cocoa Industry*, a Technicolor film produced by Cadbury (the British confectioners); and *The Battle*, an "All-British Super-Production". An advertisement for this latter event promoted the De Luxe as "Port-of-Spain's Latest and Best Cinema" and "The Very Last Word in Luxury, Comfort and Beauty!"[43]

In general, Port of Spain's cinemas of the 1920s and 1930s offered a new type of architectural space and collective experience in the city. Their exotic façades, bright lights and bold signs commanded the attention of passersby and drew them into lavish interiors that served as gateways to the other worlds of the movies themselves. While large churches and government buildings had dominated the urban landscape for decades, the cinemas were grand public buildings devoted to popular entertainment. They attracted a wide cross-section of the population to film screenings throughout the week, as well as to occasional dramatic or musical performances that featured both local and visiting artists. Though the theatres' auditoriums functioned as civic gathering places, their spatial divisions maintained the society's class distinctions, with differential pricing and comfort for the pit, house, balcony and boxes. Moreover, theatres in different neighbourhoods of the city catered to different audiences. By the 1930s, the London in Woodbrook and the Olympic in Belmont were second-run cinemas with lower prices, while the Gaiety on the St Joseph Road in eastern Port of Spain also offered cheaper pricing.

Nonetheless, Port of Spain's diverse population generally watched the same movies, whose settings, stars, stories, dialogue and music became part of the shared knowledge of the community. Such knowledge was amplified by ongoing coverage of the movies in articles and advertisements in the local newspapers. A concern of some officials during the 1930s was that cinemas were being dominated by American movies. In 1932 the government passed a Cinematograph Ordinance that authorized the governor to set a quota for the screening of British films, though the precise percentage apparently remained a matter of debate. Meanwhile, cinema owners Timothy Roodal and Sarran Teelucksingh (both members of the legislative council at the time) argued that there were not sufficient British films to meet the quota and that they were less popular. So Port of Spain (and Trinidad as a whole) continued to absorb a constant stream of images and ideas from Hollywood. During a legislative council session in 1932, Teelucksingh said: "Showing the American films in this Colony has practically made this Colony like the United States – in their words, in their thoughts, in their actions and in many other ways you can see the American principle manifesting itself upon the individual who witnesses American films." However, the local population's response to Hollywood was creative. Some cinema patrons, especially those in the pit, maintained a vibrant dialogue with each other and the films' characters during screenings. Outside the theatres, young people in particular experimented with the ways in which the stars talked, walked and otherwise behaved. In 1934 Ivy Achoy, film correspondent for the *Trinidad Guardian*, reported: "Greta Garbo, Marlene Dietrich, and Norma Shearer, are household words in homes of Trinidad. Trinidad girls try to dress like these [stars], walk like them, talk like them, and expect their boy friends to make up to them like Clark Gable, Cary Grant, and Fredric March." Whether through such youthful emulation or more general discussion and evaluation, patrons actively engaged the worlds of the movies. The city's theatres served not only as major sites of external cultural transmission but also as venues of local imagination.[44]

INFRASTRUCTURAL IMPROVEMENTS

While entrepreneurs built Port of Spain's cinemas as new venues of fantasy during the interwar era, colonial and municipal government officials remained engaged in efforts to improve the city's basic foundation – its port, roads, bridges, drainage and electricity. By the mid-1930s, the colonial government was implementing its Deep Water Harbour Scheme, the largest construction project in the city's history. Its primary objective was to facilitate and expand the colony's commerce. Since the shallowness of the harbour forced large ships to anchor two or more miles from the docks, an inefficient system of lighters continued to be used for transporting cargo and passengers to shore. Dredging the harbour and building a new quay would enable large freighters and passenger ships to reach land directly. A second objective was to reclaim land from the sea to the west of downtown and south of Woodbrook, which would provide new space to develop the city. The government had proposed a new harbour scheme in 1929, but for several years the business community expressed concerns about costs and whether the project would be big enough to service the number of large ships visiting Trinidad. However, it moved forward in 1934, when the Colonial Office approved a financing plan and provided a grant for interest payments. The new harbour was designed by engineers associated with the Crown Agents for the Colonies; the primary construction contract was awarded to Edmund Nuttall, Sons and Company of Manchester; and S.R.H. Beard served as the resident engineer. Work began in 1935 and continued to 1939, with an average of eight hundred men (mainly local) employed daily.

The engineering of the Deep Water Harbour Scheme was a multifaceted feat. Workers constructed a quay wall that began near the western end of Marine Square and extended 3,300 feet west. This was achieved by driving two parallel rows of steel sheet piles into the sea bed, removing water and seabed material from the area between the pilings and pouring in concrete. Outside the quay, workers dredged a new harbour channel and basin to a depth that measured 30 feet at low tide. This required removing over six million cubic yards of material and pumping some of it to the zone inside the quay wall, thus enabling the buildup of new land. When the project was completed, workers had reclaimed 160 acres of land from the sea, extending from Marine Square to Mucurapo Point, near the southwest corner of Woodbrook. The sea edge, defined by the new quay wall and extended further west by a rubble bank, had been shifted an average of 1,100 feet to the south. Since Woodbrook was now no longer adjacent to the sea, engineers had to devise a new system for water drainage from this district. The final elements of the project were constructing in the dock area railway tracks, roads and five massive steel transit sheds for storing cargo.

By early 1939 much of this work was completed and Port of Spain now possessed a quay that could dock six to seven large ships at a time. The first merchant vessel to arrive was the Harrison Direct Line's *Governor*. With a draft of 26.5 feet, the *Governor* steamed easily through the dredged channel on the morning of 16 February and berthed at the quay to load 7,000 tons of sugar bound for Europe. A crowd observed with delight this major advance in the island's maritime commerce. On 12 October *The Times* of London reported that the colonial government had assumed management of the new harbour from its contractors and anticipated lower shipping costs and increased prosperity for Trinidad.[45]

The government's development of the new harbour was paralleled by planning for the reclaimed lands beyond those utilized by the dock facilities. This was a primary assignment for R.B. Walker, the government's town-planning consultant, who arrived in Trinidad in July 1937. Walker prepared an elaborate plan for the area that featured a central plaza, boulevards, businesses, stores and residences. A perspective drawing of his vision appeared on the front page of the *Trinidad Guardian* on 8 October 1938. Though this plan never materialized, improvements were carried out on Wrightson Road, an important route immediately north of the reclaimed land. To direct this work, the government Public Works Department hired in 1937 Ranjit Kumar, an Indian-born, British-educated engineer who had arrived in Trinidad two years earlier planning to develop an Indian film industry. Kumar expanded the old Wrightson Road into an 80-foot-wide divided highway, while also addressing drainage problems. When work ceased in 1940, the new route reached to the southwest corner of Woodbrook (near the Mucurapo sewage-pumping station) and extended in the east from its previous point of origin in Corbeaux Town through reclaimed land to connect with Marine Square and South Quay, thus forming a major corridor from downtown to the city's western districts. In addition, R.E. Deane, curator of the Botanic Gardens, coordinated the planting of the highway's central strip with grass and flowering shrubs, which, along with their ornamental value, helped to demarcate the opposing lanes of traffic and reduce the glare of headlights.[46]

While the colonial government's Deep Water Harbour Scheme further developed Port of Spain's position within a global network of maritime commerce, the municipal government continued to work on a variety of basic infrastructural improvements to the city itself. The city council and the city engineer, T.H. Scott, built and enhanced roads and bridges, expanded the system of sewers, and in 1938 opened a new steel-frame extension of the Eastern Market on George Street. However, it was the city council's paving of the bed of the Dry River that generated the most public attention. Running through Belmont and then along the low-income area on the eastern side of downtown, this small river flooded during the rainy season, stagnated during the dry season and was perceived as a serious threat to public health. Plans for the river were developed as early as 1898, but no funding was secured for their implementation. During the 1920s, the city council rallied new support for the project and worked out a financing arrangement with the colonial government. Scott devised a new plan that involved regrading the riverbed, making some adjustments to its course, building concrete retaining walls and constructing a concrete bed with a recessed channel in the centre. Local workers laboured from 1930 to 1934 to improve over two miles of the river's course, while the city council affirmed the completion of the project as one of its major achievements of the interwar era.[47]

Another large project of the city council during this period was attempting to acquire ownership of the municipality's electric power supply, which included the electric tramway system. In 1901 the colonial government had awarded a thirty-year concession for electrical power to the Trinidad Electric Company, a Canadian-owned firm. At the end of the concession, the government had the option of approving an extension, taking over the power supply itself or allowing the municipality to do so. By the late 1920s, the Canadian firm was discussing with the government its desire to extend its concession, while the city council was expressing (with much public interest) a strong desire to take over the company for the benefit of the local population. The council observed that the Canadian firm made no payments to either the colonial or municipal government, but charged consumers high rates. By the early 1930s, Mayor Cipriani was leading a complex legal initiative to acquire the company. Though litigation reached the British Privy Council, which decided in favour of the acquisition, the city council was unable to finalize a purchase, owing in part to a lack of support from the colonial government in Trinidad. In 1937 the Canadian firm finally yielded ownership and the governor turned the supply over to an island-wide Trinidad Electricity Board, which comprised members of both the colonial and municipal governments. Though the council was successful in removing electricity from foreign ownership, it did not obtain control over the municipality's electrical works until 1946. In 1961 these works were again merged with an island-wide government agency.[48]

The city council's concern during the 1930s with the electrical supply was interrelated with plans to upgrade the municipality's public transport system. In 1937 an electrical specialist advised that the electric tram rails were in poor condition and recommended replacing trams with electric trolleybuses. Though the council also considered petroleum-powered buses, it adopted a Trinidad Electricity Board report in 1938 and decided on the gradual replacement of trams with trolleybuses. The board ordered trolleybuses manufactured by an English firm and in 1941 initiated service from the railway station downtown to Ariapita Avenue and Mucurapo Road. By 1950 trolleybuses had replaced all trams in Port of Spain, thus ending a mode of transport that had been introduced to the city (along with electricity) in 1895.[49]

A final major event for the city council during the interwar era was the celebration in 1939 of the silver jubilee of its restoration as an elected, self-governing body in 1914. Though 25 June marked the actual anniversary, the council scheduled festivities to coincide with Discovery Day – an annual observance on the first Monday in August of Christopher Columbus's arrival at Trinidad in 1498. In an effort to highlight its achievements and generate greater public appreciation of its work, the council organized an entire week of activities. Celebrations began on Thursday, 3 August, with a ceremonial planting of twenty-one trees at Memorial Park. Under the supervision of R.E. Deane of the Botanic Gardens, the councillors took turns planting queen of flowers and flamboyant trees in an alternating pattern on the western and southern sides of the park, while a twenty-first tree was planted by Enrique Prada – town clerk and first mayor of the restored municipal government. Each tree was given a tag indicating the name of the councillor, his municipal ward, the date and the words "Silver Jubilee". That night there was a concert of vocal and instrumental music at the Prince's Building, including a jubilee song composed by Gladstone Arrindell, a tramcar motorman with the Trinidad Electricity Board. Saturday morning opened with the blowing of sirens and chiming of church bells, while later there was a gymkhana (equestrian event) at the Queen's Park Savannah. Various municipal and other buildings around the city were adorned with bunting and flags, and that night crowds were attracted to colourful illuminations displayed on the town hall, Prince's Building and Eastern Market.

On Saturday night there was also a municipal dinner at the Hotel Sand in St Ann's. After a generally congratulatory speech by the governor (the main guest of honour), Mayor Cipriani delivered an address in which he asserted that "beautiful Port-of-Spain, with her wonderful drainage, well paved streets, beautiful buildings, health, cleanliness, development and prosperity are in themselves living examples of our work and progress and a complete answer to our critics". Cipriani also took the opportunity to condemn crown colony rule, noting that it crippled a country's development. But then he shifted his thoughts towards the future:

> if I look a little further on at our chief city of this beautiful Colony, I see, before long, Port-of-Spain reaching and stretching out towards the highest tops of those pretty hills overlooking the city and I see on those hills ranges of bungalows and modern buildings. I see properly paved roadways and waterways and I see Port-of-Spain embracing the true setting that nature has destined for her and again I look forward to work done by my friend the Town Planner.
>
> I am sorry he is not here tonight but one cannot help visualising the Garden City that will be ours and the beautiful new gateway that will be Port-of-Spain's between Wrightson Road and the sea.

Celebration of Port of Spain's past, present and possible future continued during the following days. There were special church services on Sunday, activities for children on Monday (typical of Discovery Day), a calypso competition on Tuesday night at the Prince's Building (during which contestants sang on various topics, including the history of the city) and a municipal workers' dance at this same venue on Wednesday night, which attracted some six hundred employees from all departments.[50]

Throughout the proceedings, the city council had on sale a commemorative silver-jubilee booklet as part of its efforts to better acquaint the public with its history of service to the community. A schematic illustration of the Port of Spain landscape on the booklet's front cover captured the council's vision of its success: a bright sun shining over surrounding hills, a paved Dry River, a modern electric power plant with radiating electrical lines, a set of orderly new workers' homes (in juxtaposition to a group of dilapidated houses), a children's playground, a water supply station and, at the bottom of the image, the city seal and the dates "1914–1939". Inside the front cover were a dedication – "To those who, throughout all the years, have laboured faithfully to improve the city and to uplift its people" – and a dignified photograph of the councillors posed in what appears to be the town hall. The various articles that followed outlined the city's history from the nineteenth century to the present, with particular attention to developments since 1914, including the restoration of elected government, paving the Dry River, acquiring the electric company, incorporating St James and advances in public health. Also included were photographs of the council's various construction projects: new bridges, streets, workers' homes and the addition to the Eastern Market. The booklet's authors observed that Port of Spain "has grown from a quiet sea-port town into a fast, industrial city of lofty spires, a modern deep-water harbour, up-to-date buses, wide streets, ideal drainage; so changed is its countenance that it is almost unrecognizable".⁵¹ Indeed, the city council, the colonial government, private entrepreneurs and the people of Port of Spain themselves had fashioned a new city that embodied the latest trends in technology, architectural design and recreation.

In carrying out major new constructions and civic enhancements during the interwar era, government officials and business leaders in Port of Spain drew on a variety of architectural styles and technologies imported from abroad and collaborated with diverse foreign designers and engineers. To a large extent, they pursued projects through a web of relationships with the imperial government in London and commercial firms in both the United Kingdom and the United States. However, the evolving urban landscape was not simply an expression of British colonialism or American expansionism. It was also shaped by the myriad local individuals who actually built and used it. Most of the labour for the city's new constructions, ranging from the gigantic harbour scheme to small municipal bridges, was supplied by local workers with their own traditions of aesthetics and craft skills. Moreover, there were architects and building specialists who were born in Trinidad, as well as individuals who had lived there for long periods of time. For example, T.H. Scott, though from Scotland, was appointed city engineer in 1915 and, except for a brief period of employment with Gordon Grant and Company, served in this position until his retirement in 1941. In an address in his honour, the mayor said Scott (along with the town clerk, Enrique Prada) "have so identified themselves with the land of their adoption that we have long come to regard them as if they belonged to us".⁵² Similarly, Herbert Brinsley, though born and educated in Britain, had lived in Trinidad for over a decade before beginning his prominent architectural projects in Port of Spain and had a firm knowledge of local climatic conditions, construction materials and aesthetics.

In short, the people of Port of Spain created a landscape during the 1920s and 1930s that was practical and sensible to them. Combining local and foreign resources and expertise, they produced buildings, streets and other outdoor spaces that sustained a distinctively Trinidadian way of life and sense of beauty. Their government was principally controlled by Britain, the economy favoured few local people and class distinctions were deeply embedded in the urban environment and its use. Nonetheless, it was an environment that was ultimately their own – a place that they inhabited and gradually recreated as they envisioned a more democratic and prosperous future. So, as the city council carried out its silver-jubilee celebrations and lauded its accomplishments to date, the populace as a whole continued to seek progressive change within their expanding city.

4. THE HOUSING AND LIVES OF WORKING PEOPLE

THE VARIOUS NEW CONSTRUCTION PROJECTS of the interwar era continued to define Port of Spain as a progressive city engaged with current world trends in architecture, commerce and entertainment. However, the majority of the city's working people remained in housing of exceedingly low quality, often consisting of a single room for an entire family. During the interwar years, there was vigorous debate concerning working-class housing conditions, based on the assumption that such domestic spaces were fundamental to civic order, morality and health. Both colonial and municipal government authorities proposed plans for demolishing or renovating the most seriously deteriorated buildings in the central city and constructing new "model" homes for workers in less congested districts. Though there was some progress, these plans were substantially impeded by the interests of landlords and the vast scale of the problem. By the 1930s, working people were increasingly protesting poor housing and high rents, along with low wages, unemployment, inflation and the basic inequities of Trinidad's economy. While there had been workers' protests in Port of Spain after World War I, the demonstrations of the 1930s intensified in frequency and militancy and encompassed the whole island. Workers appropriated and disrupted key public, industrial and commercial spaces to voice their demands and obtain recognition. This mass mobilization was interrelated with a growing working-class consciousness and contributed to more fundamental changes in the society during and after the 1940s.

During the late 1920s and 1930s, there also emerged a new group of writers who examined the housing, lives and discontent of working people. Associated with *The Beacon* literary magazine, Alfred Mendes, C.L.R. James and other authors explored the domestic and recreational spaces of Port of Spain's working class and vividly represented these environments in fiction. This literature more sharply defined concepts of a Trinidadian people and the injustices of colonial society. In addition, Port of Spain continued to be described by visiting writers. At the end of the 1930s, for example, the city was visited by three particularly keen observers: the British novelist and journalist Arthur

Calder-Marshall and the American anthropologists Melville and Frances Herskovits. Calder-Marshall constructed a detailed "portrait" of the city, with attention to its varied places, ethnic groups and social classes in the context of the inequalities of the Depression era. While the Herskovitses did most of their research in a remote Trinidadian village, they also briefly documented a religious community in the eastern Port of Spain district of Laventille and highlighted the presence of West African–derived cultural traditions and creativity in the city.

HOUSING CONDITIONS AND GOVERNMENT PLANS

During the interwar era, Port of Spain's working class continued to reside in several house types of varying size and characteristics. The 1931 census indicated that the city's population of 70,334 lived in 5,494 houses with one room, 3,432 with two rooms, 5,213 with three or more rooms and 1,791 "barracks, compounds, tenement houses, etc.". Working people with higher levels of skills and more secure incomes often lived in houses with two or more rooms – typically a version of the basic Trinidadian-creole house type constructed with wood and nogging (or concrete); a gabled roof of corrugated-iron sheeting; ample windows, doors and vents; a verandah; perhaps some ornamentation and a yard with a boundary wall. In areas such as Woodbrook and Belmont, some people gradually improved and expanded their houses as their resources permitted. However, the city's much larger population of lower skilled workers (many of whom were marginally employed or unemployed) typically lived in one-room accommodation of poor quality. Detached single-room structures pieced together with wood and other available materials were common throughout the city, especially in the hillier areas on the east side. While building in Woodbrook and lower Belmont followed regular street grids and lots, construction in the eastern hills was more improvised and flexible. In June 1933, for example, the Port of Spain Local Sanitary Authority discussed what it perceived as the "new village" of John John at the southeastern edge of the city, with particular concern about the residents' daily dumping of garbage in a drain that ran through the area. The lands in question were owned by both the colonial government and private parties. One city councillor asked how John John came into existence: "Was it grown up like a mushroom?" Others suggested that it emerged "accidentally", without lots being laid out. A few years later, a medical specialist described John John as "an entangled conglomeration of unsightly ruinous huts and privy cesspits placed helter-skelter on a sloping, steep and slippery hillside – a danger to health, life and limb for the local residents and a menace to the surrounding city population".[1]

While some of Port of Spain's working people lived in small detached houses (or in subdivided larger homes and boarding houses), many continued to occupy the central city's barrack yards – spaces typically located in the interior of city blocks and consisting of buildings with rows of single-room accommodation for whole families (see figures 19 and 20). In 1930 there were at least 25,000 barrack dwellers (a third of the city's population), and, by 1937, 42,820 (half the population). Though some residents continued to move out to surrounding districts, there was ongoing migration from rural parts of Trinidad and from other islands into the city. In 1931 the population density on the eastern side of the central city exceeded 100 people per acre and, in some blocks, reached 290 people per acre.[2]

Perhaps the most vivid description of a barrack yard during this period was published in *The Beacon* in 1931 by a seventeen-year-old named James Cummings, who lived with his mother (a laundress) in a barrack owned by the archbishop of Port of Spain. Cummings provided a thorough account of this type of housing:

> How miserable and disgraceful it is to see the agglomerated mass of human souls known as the working class overcrowded in those ten by twelve boxes, known as "barrack rooms"....
>
> What are the barrack-rooms in which these unfortunate victims of Dame Fortune live? They are like the boxes horses are shipped in. A long line of ten by twelve boxes, nailed together with a window and a door allotted to each....
>
> The walls are dirty, and the roof, which is about twelve feet high from the elevated part to the rotten flooring, is black and sooty from want of paint....
>
> They [the occupants] have the undying ambition to keep a decent home, but where is the room for such? Their small bed, for no more than two, is barred off by a cloth screen, or a wooden blind about six feet high covered with a wall paper. The balance of this room can only contain a little table for dining.

Cummings goes on to describe the minimal ventilation in the barracks, the partitions between rooms which do not reach the ceiling, the infestation of insects and the muddy yards where residents cooked and shared decrepit lavatories. In reference to social interaction in the yards, he wrote: "These barrack-rooms also have a great moral influence on children.... All sorts of conversations are vociferously exchanged between the tenants.... In some of the yards many sleepless nights are passed through the gaming, liquor-drinking, and prostitution of some of the neighbours. The little children are shown the regrettable step to degradation." Cummings also observed that the barrack dwellers paid rents between $3.50 and $4.50 a month for a room and were afraid to complain about the conditions of the yards to the "merciless, callous-minded agents" who collected payments on behalf of owners. (Such rents were very high, relative to typical earnings for working people at the time.)[3]

High rents, in fact, were a major problem throughout the interwar period. In the years immediately after World War I, the prices of many necessities increased rapidly, and by January 1920, both the *Argos* and the *Trinidad Guardian* were calling on the colonial government to amend a Profiteering Ordinance to control the inflated house and land rents charged by landlords. The two newspapers also noted the related issue of insufficient availability of housing. A few months later, the *Guardian* urged the city council to move forward with a plan to address the acute need for both more and better housing for the poor, observing that many residential buildings in the downtown area were being taken over by businesses. The presence of homeless people living on the streets was also a serious problem. In 1924 the *Guardian* wrote: "The spectacle of destitute men and women of many races sleeping in the squares and on pavements, covered and uncovered, has long been a nightly eyesore of Port-of-Spain." Observing that the homeless generally returned to the pavements after arrests and jail sentences, the paper advocated the establishment of a municipal night shelter as a remedy. In 1929 the *Labour Leader* similarly editorialized on homelessness, saying, "It would be only necessary for one to make a nocturnal excursion around certain prominent public avenues of the city when and where the abominable sight will be revealed." On police roundups of the homeless (many of whom were physically disabled), the *Labour Leader* commented, "It is more of a disgrace to find on many a pleasant morn, a vast army of men, women and children, very dirtily clad and in some cases almost nude, trooping to the District Court, under Police escort, for the purpose of paying a sanitarily attired Magistrate an early and unwelcome visit." The paper deplored this "Street Parade of unfortunates", the inhumanity and costs of jailing the homeless and "the recent scandalous and wanton waste of taxpayers money in providing spacious housing accommodation for six Senior Government Officials, all of whom are already too well paid, instead of utilising it in the direction of adequately housing the deserving poor of the land".[4]

While government plans for addressing housing conditions in Port of Spain date back at least to the World War I era, the first substantial action did not occur until 1930, when the city council appealed to the colonial government for a loan to build workers' homes and begin to ameliorate slum conditions. With government support, the council constructed twelve homes at South Quay. In May 1931 the *Labour Leader* opined: "A couple of months hence, it is anticipated that in these highly sanitary dwellings, one dozen families of the working man will be safely and comfortably housed, free from the detestable contamination that obtains so largely in the barrack yard, where, usually, vice is at a premium and virtue at a discount." At the end of June, the governor formally opened the South Quay Workers' Homes, while the *Labour Leader* commented: "The erection of these Homes, although merely an experiment, sounds the death knell of that most pernicious system of barrackyard landlordism, which Captain Cipriani [the mayor] has been denouncing in and out of season, and which the Governor did not hesitate to describe as a blot on the fair name of the Colony." Though twelve houses were a small start, the governor had recently appointed a joint colonial/municipal committee, chaired by Cipriani, to investigate the housing situation further, including a plan to build at least two hundred workers' homes at Gonzales Place – a portion of land owned by the city to the southeast of Belmont.[5]

Over the next several years, there was much discussion of the housing problem in Port of Spain but minimal progress in implementing actual remedies. By 1933 Dr G.H. Masson, the city medical officer of health, was preparing new reports on housing conditions in an effort to propel the city council into action. In February of that year, he observed that overcrowding in the city was escalating and posing a serious danger to public health: "The ordinary barrack yards being full to overflowing, an increasing number of dwelling-houses originally built for occupation by single families is being divided up with matchwood or cloth screens into cubicles without regard to air space or ventilation and let at astonishing high rentals." He added that some of these houses could be discovered only by chance, since their exteriors did not reveal the subdivision of interiors. By June Masson was developing a census of barrack yards, with sanitary inspectors carrying out inquiries and compiling statistics. They discovered one yard on the St Joseph Road (on the eastern side of the city) with close to three hundred people living in approximately sixty rooms, and other yards with as many as ten people sleeping in a single room.[6]

Meanwhile, the colonial government proposed the creation of a housing commission that it would jointly administer with the city council as a public trust. Though financing was provided mainly by the government, the city would acquire and reconstruct housing in slum areas, while the commission would then rent or sell properties to workers. However, there was strong opposition within the city council to the proposal, since government representatives would chair and constitute the majority of members on the commission. Several councillors argued that the city should have the right to control its own housing plans. As debate over the proposed commission continued within the city council, working people themselves voiced their demand for concrete action on the housing crisis. On 6 July 1933, for example, some three hundred attended a meeting in Woodford Square to call for new workers' homes, with writer/activist Algernon Burkett as the principal speaker. Later in the month, *The People* (a new labour-oriented newspaper) said workers were being "badly let down" by city councillors and suggested that these individuals would not be elected if the municipal franchise included working people. The newspaper also reiterated a point often made by the press and other observers: implementation of a housing plan was hindered by the fact that many councillors themselves owned slum properties. Though *The People* called for prompt action, it also felt that a housing programme should be managed by the city.[7]

In May 1934 the city council finally agreed to the establishment of a joint housing commission, which would be chaired by the colonial treasurer and include three additional government representatives and three municipal representatives – Mayor Cipriani and councillors Garnet McCarthy and Tito Achong. The commission was to spend £40,000, half on reconditioning existing housing and half on new homes to be constructed and managed by the city council in Woodbrook and Gonzales Place. In addition, some slum housing would be destroyed. In 1935 the government passed a Slum Clearance Ordinance, while the city council went ahead with a plan to build a hundred workers' homes at Gonzales Place. When it was completed in April 1936, the Gonzales Place development consisted of a grid of fifty single homes and fifty duplexes, closely built, with small yards and balustraded concrete walls lining the streets (see figure 25). The houses were raised on piers and comprised plaster-finished wood-frame and nogging walls, gable roofs, and louvred doors and windows. The single homes contained a front and back room, with a door and window on the front façade, while the duplexes included adjoining front and back rooms and a façade with two windows in the centre and the doors at the ends. Overhanging roofs at the rear provided some space for cooking and other domestic chores. Essentially, the structures were small-scale versions of the Trinidadian-creole house type, stripped of porches and ornamentation.[8]

Though the Gonzales Place development was orderly and its houses reasonably attractive, it remained unoccupied for over a year. By 1937 Mayor Alfred Richards and Tito Achong, the city's acting medical officer of health, were determined to move forward with housing initiatives and, with the advice of the city engineer, T.H. Scott, began serving notices to owners of dilapidated residences in accordance with a 1934 amended Public Health Ordinance, which provided for a simpler and cheaper course of action than the 1935 Slum Clearance Ordinance supported by former mayor Cipriani. Initial plans focused on "Slum Clearance Block No. 1", which extended from Marine Square up to Prince Street, between Duncan Street and the Dry River (in the oldest sector of the city). While the residents were targeted for the occupation of Gonzales Place, they were reluctant to move. One factor was the proposed rent of $4.00 per month for a detached home and $3.50 for a duplex, though some people were probably paying this much for barrack rooms. In addition, barrack dwellers may have preferred the convenience of living in the centre of the city to the relatively remote location of Gonzales Place. For example, laundresses and seamstresses would have been close to many clients, while dockworkers, porters and general labourers were in proximity to various sources of employment.

Moreover, barrack yards provided individuals with social networks essential to survival, in spite of their abysmal material characteristics.⁹

On 26 May Dr Achong organized a tour of Slum Clearance Block No. 1 for Governor Murchison Fletcher and Acting Colonial Secretary Howard Nankivell, officials who (by the standards of the Colonial Service) had considerable sympathy for working people. The team visited a variety of sites, including No. 4 Marine Square, which happened to be owned by city councillor and former mayor Gaston Johnston. The governor engaged in cordial conversation with the area's occupants (at times without immediately identifying himself) and attempted to better understand their living situations and reluctance to relocate. After the tour, he recommended that the city council reduce the rents for the Gonzales Place homes and provide lorries (trucks) to help people transport their belongings. The city subsequently lowered rents to $3.50 and $3.00 for detached houses and duplexes respectively and arranged for transport. On 1 June residents of Block No. 1 began paying deposits at the town hall for the Gonzales Place homes and on 3 June the *Trinidad Guardian* reported: "Today municipal motor lorries will roll over the streets of Port-of-Spain as slum dwellers proceed to Gonzales Place with smiling, happy countenances to live under healthier conditions."¹⁰

While the occupants of Block No. 1 were relocating to Gonzales Place, Mayor Richards and Dr Achong advocated that the city should immediately begin constructing more workers' houses, given the enormous need and the availability of government funding. In preparation, Achong began surveying other city areas for slum clearance. At a 10 June meeting of the city council, however, Gaston Johnston and several other councillors sharply criticized the mayor's actions and asked for the issue of slum clearance and housing to be referred to a committee (with discussion closed to the public). The mayor refused, saying "vested interests" would overthrow the whole initiative. A special meeting of the council on 14 June was even more heated. Protesters arrived at the council chamber with banners proclaiming their demands: "Down with the enemies of the Slum Clearance Scheme", "The Slum Clearance Scheme must begin immediately", "The Barrack Yard and its filth must go", "Demand homes for all workers, employed and unemployed". While the mayor insisted on proceeding with house construction, opposing councillors again requested the formation of a committee to discuss details. In addition, council member George Cabral argued that some of the available government funding was intended for reconditioning existing properties – an approach undoubtedly appealing to landlords. As the public gallery became noisy, another councillor, Albion Gooding, shouted back: "You want us to build houses for you people to live in for nothing?" Soon afterwards, the mayor adjourned the meeting to avoid further trouble. Continued insults from the crowd outside the town hall required Gooding to seek sanctuary in an office, while one councillor, C.M. Lastique, told the town clerk he would not be intimidated and, for the next meeting, would bring his poui (a hardwood stick used in traditional Trinidadian stickfighting). Debate on housing remained contentious in the council during the following weeks.[11]

While opposition within the city council hampered public housing plans during the late 1930s, a bigger challenge was the scale of the need. As noted, more than forty thousand people lived in barrack yards in 1937 and many more occupied other substandard housing. Clearly, an enormous investment of government resources was necessary to address the housing problem seriously. An impetus for more systematic planning and social welfare was offered by the island-wide strikes and protests of June 1937, which occurred during the same period as the heated housing debates in the city council. A report from the Colonial Office's commission of inquiry into the disturbances, released in 1938, strongly recommended government action in improving housing. Meanwhile, R.B. Walker, the government's town-planning consultant, who had arrived from England in July 1937, was at work on an island-wide housing scheme. In December 1938, the legislative council passed both a new Slum Clearance and Housing Ordinance and its Town and Regional Planning Ordinance. The first of these established a planning and housing commission that was controlled by the government and had broad powers to address slum conditions throughout the colony and build workers' homes. Included in the legislation were plans for extensive surveys of housing needs and long-term investment in new construction. By 1940 the government was building a few hundred workers' homes in Morvant (also to the east of the city) and additional homes in St James and other areas, but these schemes too were on an insufficient scale.[12]

A basic assumption underlying the ongoing housing debate was that proper homes were fundamental to the order and stability of society. Through developing planned neighbourhoods with "model homes", the authorities hoped to produce a working class whose domestic life would more closely resemble middle-class concepts of respectability. Such homes would contrast sharply with the various types of "slum" housing, which were considered congested, haphazard and depraved settings. Barrack yards in particular were perceived by many commentators as spaces of degradation and vice that corrupted their occupants, especially children. In addition, commentators frequently described barrack yards as a public health hazard – sources of disease that affected not only their residents but the whole city. The city's medical officer of health consistently emphasized the threat of contagion and the dire need for a healthier urban environment and populace.

While suitable housing was considered essential to a progressive city, the responsibility for ensuring its existence remained an open question. Should landlords be expected to maintain their properties in decent condition and charge reasonable rents? Should government establish codes for such conditions and control the inflation of rents? Should government provide funding for constructing workers' homes and for rent subsidies? What were the specific roles of the colonial and municipal governments in addressing all these issues and implementing effective plans? Working people themselves engaged in this debate by demanding access to decent housing at fair rents. However, their protests during this period went beyond the question of housing alone to challenge the whole economic structure of the society. In short, they asserted that wages in the colony were too low to afford adequate housing (as well as other necessities) and were indefensible in relation to the profits realized by many employers. The fundamental objective of their demonstrations was gainful employment and equitable wages, which in turn would enable them to secure and maintain houses in accordance with their own wishes. This multifaceted struggle over working-class housing remained unresolved during the interwar era and was interrelated with broader political and moral debates about the future of Trinidadian society.

Though working people, landlords, employers and government officials were the main figures in Port of Spain's housing struggle, independent social welfare workers also emerged as an important force during the interwar era. Both the colonial and municipal governments, as well as churches, had long maintained some basic charitable institutions and services for those residents of the city in greatest need. For example, the colonial government provided a house of refuge for the aged and chronically ill, the city maintained the Ariapita Asylum for the infirm and impoverished until the early 1930s, the Catholic Church ran the Belmont Orphanage and the Salvation Army had a centre downtown. In 1921, however, a new form of social welfare began to take shape: the Coterie of Social Workers, founded by Audrey Jeffers (1896–1968). Raised in a large house in the elite St Clair, Jeffers studied social science in London, where she was a founder of the Union of Students of African Descent and a member of the Trinidadian activist F.E.M. Hercules's Society of People of African Origin. Her coterie in Trinidad consisted mainly of black and mixed-descent middle-class women and focused primarily on helping working women and their children. The group opened the first of several "breakfast sheds" in 1926 to provide noontime meals to working-class children, established the St Mary's Home for blind girls and women in 1927, and founded the Maud Reeves Hostel for Working Girls and the Anstey House for middle-class young ladies in 1935. In addition, the group organized various Christmas, Mother's Day and other activities, and advocated rights and opportunities for women and girls. Through her leadership of this social welfare movement, Jeffers became one of the most prominent women in Port of Spain during the interwar era.

Moreover, she was the first woman elected to the city council (1936) and was nominated to the legislative council in 1946 and 1951. At the coterie's opening of a day nursery in the depressed neighbourhood of John John in 1940, Jeffers said: "A lot of people have asked why we have come to John John, and some have even expressed fears for our safety. . . I am glad that we are doing social work here, where the people feel that they have been forgotten."[13]

THE BEACON GROUP

While various government officials, journalists and social workers explored the domestic environments of working people during the interwar era, this sphere was also extensively studied and portrayed by an emerging group of local creative writers. By the late 1920s and early 1930s, there was a loose network in Port of Spain of individuals (later known as the Beacon group) that included such figures as Alfred Mendes, C.L.R. James, Albert Gomes, R.A.C. de Boissière and Ernest A. Carr. Mendes and James published and edited two issues of the magazine *Trinidad* in late 1929 and 1930, and Gomes published and edited its successor, *The Beacon*, from 1931 to 1933. In addition to short stories and poems, *The Beacon* featured commentary on such topics as West Indian literature and other arts, the Port of Spain municipal government, electoral politics, barrack housing, divorce legislation, scholarships for girls, poor pay and working conditions for female employees in stores on Frederick Street, black consciousness and affairs in India. In his autobiography, Mendes says *The Beacon* "shook and shocked the island into an awareness of values which had been taboo to its people" and that "its antennae caught the winds of change blowing from every corner of the world and translated them in terms of Trinidad's social, economic, moral, and cultural life". Later, some of these writers also published novels and various books of non-fiction.[14]

Mendes, James and Gomes were the leading figures of the Beacon group, and their particular biographical trajectories through Port of Spain provided them with unique knowledge of the city's varied landscape and inhabitants. Born to a Portuguese merchant and planter family, Mendes (1897–1991) initially lived in a cottage in Belmont, but in 1904 his father built a house in the new Victoria Square, on the west side of downtown. After secondary school in England, he joined Trinidad's Merchants and Planters' Contingent and fought in France during World War I. He returned to Trinidad determined to be a novelist and short-story writer: "Such acumen as I possessed convinced me that the material available to me in the West Indies would be new to fiction and as rewarding and rich as any other to be found in any other part of the world." While working in his father's provisions warehouse on Charlotte Street, he devoted himself to writing *Pitch Lake*, his first novel. He met C.L.R. James in the early 1920s and the two assembled a variety of local writers who called themselves the "Trinidad Group". Eventually, Mendes moved to a house on Richmond Street (one block from Victoria Square), where by 1933 his library included two thousand books as well as a classical-music record collection. This house was one of the places where the writers' group met to discuss colonialism, socialism and art.[15]

In preparation for writing about barrack-yard life, Mendes spent an extended period in one of these settings:

> What I did in order to get the atmosphere, to get the sort of jargon that they spoke – the vernacular, the idiom – what I did was: I went into the barrack-yard that was then at the bottom of Park Street just before you came into Richmond Street, and I lived in it for about six months. I did not completely live there, but I ingratiated myself. . . . I slept there frequently, and a lot of the incidents that appear in my second published novel, *Black Fauns*, were taken almost directly from my experience with the barrack-yarders.

During this period, Mendes wrote short stories (some of which were published in England and the United States) and worked on novels. In early 1933 he met Aldous Huxley, who was visiting Trinidad. Huxley read his manuscript for *Pitch Lake*, recommended it to Duckworth in London and wrote an introduction for the 1934 publication in which he commented that it had "none of the romanticism which generally characterises the tropical tale". In 1933 Mendes moved to New York, where he continued writing fiction (including *Black Fauns*), worked for the Works Progress Administration Writers' Project and interacted with other writers, such as Richard Wright, Countee Cullen, William Saroyan and Ford Madox Ford. By 1940, however, he had lost confidence in his writing – he burned the manuscripts of several unpublished novels – and returned to Trinidad. During the 1940s, he contributed arts criticism to the *Trinidad Guardian* and worked as a bookkeeper at the Port of Spain harbour. In the course of the 1950s, he rose to the position of general manager of the port, where he was forced to balance his socialist sympathies with the need to negotiate with a strong longshoremen's union.[16]

While Mendes's family accumulated considerable wealth, the parents of C.L.R. James (1901–1989) belonged to the growing Afro-Trinidadian middle class. James spent his early years outside Port of Spain, particularly in Tunapuna on the Eastern Main Road. His family's house was adjacent to the town's cricket grounds, which, as a small child, he observed intently through a bedroom window. Meanwhile, he developed a passion for literature and learning from his mother, a voracious reader of novels, and received instruction from his father, a schoolteacher. A precocious child, he won a secondary-school scholarship at ten and enrolled in Queen's Royal College in Port of Spain. Here he was, by his own account, a rebellious student but nonetheless read widely in Latin, Greek, French and especially English literature and history. He also excelled on the cricket field at Queen's Royal College, which, for the school's heterogeneous students, was a special realm of collective order and achievement. After graduating in 1918, he began teaching at the school, continued his pursuits of cricket and literature, published in the TWA's *Labour Leader*, and developed relationships with Mendes and other writers in Port of Spain. In 1932 he migrated to England, where he published *The Life of Captain Cipriani: An Account of British Government in the West Indies* (1932); *Minty Alley* (1936), his only novel; cricket commentary for the *Manchester Guardian*; and *The Black Jacobins* (1938), a highly insightful study of the Haitian Revolution. From the late 1930s onward, James lived at various times in the United States, England and Trinidad, engaging in wide-ranging political and labour activism and publishing extensively on such topics as Marxist theory and movements, the works of Herman Melville and politics in the Caribbean and Africa. In 1963 he published *Beyond a Boundary*, his extraordinary synthesis of personal memoir and reflections on cricket, social history, politics and art.[17]

Like Mendes, Albert Gomes (1911–1978) was born to a Portuguese family, but one with considerably less property. He grew up in a wooden house in Belmont, next to one of his father's several provisions shops. Immediately behind the house, three large families lived in barrack rooms, which Gomes recalls as a place of "loud laughter" and "anguished cries". He attended college in New York from 1928 to 1930 and, upon returning to Trinidad, joined the literary circle led by Mendes and James, which had "a common bond of detestation of hypocrisy, obscurantism and general claustrophobia of Trinidadian society". From 1931 to 1933, Gomes published and edited *The Beacon* on a monthly basis, with moral support from his mother, money from his father and the enthusiastic participation of writers both in Port of Spain and around the island. The magazine offered provocative challenges to the Trinidadian status quo, resulting in "frequent visits from the police, denunciation from the pulpit, pressure from both church and state, increasing opposition from the commercial community, and a chronic lack of funds". After *The Beacon* ceased publication, Gomes worked in a pharmacy owned by his father, but continued writing for newspapers and compiled a collection of local fiction and poetry titled *From Trinidad* (1937). However, his career was shifting towards union organizing and politics. In the late 1930s, he helped build the Federated Workers Trade Union and recruited municipal workers into it, including the predominantly Indo-Trinidadian scavenger gangs – "the street-sweepers and those who burrow, often on their bellies, into the dark and malodorous labyrinth of underground drains beneath the surface of Port of Spain's streets".

Gomes was elected to the city council in 1938 and the legislative council in 1945. By 1946 he was also serving on the government's executive council and in 1950 was appointed to the influential position of minister of labour, commerce and industry.[18]

The editorship of the literary magazines *Trinidad* and *The Beacon* by Mendes, James and Gomes introduced the Trinidadian public to a remarkable range of local fiction. Stories by James and Mendes were particularly strong and offered vivid accounts of the circumstances of Port of Spain's working people. For example, James's "Triumph" (1929) opens with a quasi-sociological description of barrack yards: the narrow passages from streets into the yards, the low buildings with their series of small rooms, the inadequate water and sanitation facilities and the heaps of stones and wire lines where the resident women bleached and dried laundry as an occupation. The narrator of "Triumph" says the yards have lost their picturesque life of twenty-five years earlier, when calypso singers and other Carnival figures performed late into the night. Now performances must end at 10:00 p.m., electric lights illuminate the streets and there is more police interference. However, "life, dull and drab as it is in comparison, can still offer its great moments". Thus begins a story in a barrack yard on Abercromby Street, involving the friendship of Mamitz and Celestine, their antagonism with Irene, and the various men who circulate through their lives. Mamitz has lost the tram conductor who was "keeping" her (giving her money), but attracts a scheming and gambling man of pleasure and, later, a butcher; Celestine is kept by a policeman; and Irene by a cabman. With Celestine's support and the magical effects of a "bush" (herbal) bath, Mamitz eventually triumphs over the jealous Irene. For James, the barrack yard is a site of impoverished living conditions and social tensions but also of close bonds and mutual support. Moreover, it is a space in which day-to-day life is organized by exceptionally strong women.[19]

Mendes's "Sweetman" (1931) portrays a different type of relationship between women and men. A "sweetman" is a fancy-dressing man who attracts women and receives money from them, rather than the reverse. Maxie, the sweetman in this story, is a dougla (someone of mixed African and Indian ancestry) and a calypsonian, a typically flamboyant and impressive figure in Port of Spain. The story takes place during a dance held by the "Workingman's Friendly Society" in the upstairs room of the "Creole Cafe", on Prince Street in the heart of downtown. The narrator describes the scene: "The Creole Cafe was gaily decorated in the rumshop-fashion with strings of paper-flags, candle lanterns and multicoloured streamers. Black girls, brown girls, light-skinned mulatto girls, dressed in bright and satiny colours, laughing raucously and chattering like black-birds in the early morning, shuffled with their partners in slow sensuous movements round and round the room." With a band providing the music, Maxie and his companions (other sweetmen) enjoy the occasion. However, the jealous and hot-tempered Mamitz, who is supporting Maxie, is outraged when he dances with a previous paramour. She charges onto the dance floor and, with a knife, strips him of the suit that she had bought for him.[20]

While "Triumph" and "Sweetman" depict contrasting financial relationships between women and men, Mendes's "Her Chinaman's Way" (1929) illustrates additional types of housing arrangements. Maria, the main character, at first lived in a barrack yard, where she was supported over time by stevedores, porters, messengers, cabmen, a barber and a "foreman-porter at the Customs' Warehouses". After receiving a bush bath from a friend in the yard, she attracted and had a child with Hong Wing, who owned a provisions shop in addition to engaging in opium-smuggling. Initially, the couple lived on the premises of the shop (as was typical in Trinidad), but Maria eventually persuaded Hong Wing to obtain a two-room residence (with "drawing room" and bedroom) on Charlotte Street, an arrangement she considered "more respectable". The story itself centres on Maria's attraction to a carter-man and an ill-fated scheme to leave Hong Wing.[21]

Mendes's short stories were initial experiments for the extended portrayal of the barrack-yard setting and character types that appear in *Black Fauns* (1935). Virtually this entire novel is set in a single yard, with only occasional references to events occurring elsewhere in Port of Spain. The narrator offers a brief description of the scene: "The rooms were about twelve feet by twelve, and in this particular barrack, built on land standing away from the street, all the doors and windows gave onto the yard which was seventy-five feet wide by thirty feet deep; so that the two rows of rooms, extending along the width of the yard, faced each other." Also in the yard are a breadfruit tree, a pile of bleaching stones and clotheslines for laundry, coalpots in front of the rooms for cooking, a latrine and an open gutter. All the residents of the yard are women, most of whom wash laundry for other residents of the city. Men make only occasional appearances, with the exception of the yard matriarch's grown son, who visits from New York for a few weeks and seriously disrupts the dynamics of the place. In essence, the yard serves as a stage for the dramas of the women's lives, with characters entering and exiting as in a play. In fact, the bulk of the novel consists of the women's dialogue, in Trinidadian speech. In the yard itself and their individual rooms, the women (of various ages and backgrounds) assist and scheme against each other; banter and argue; discuss men, religion and Trinidadian society; and occasionally engage in physical confrontations.

Black Fauns also includes performances of various folk traditions typical of working-class life. For example, Ma Christine (the matriarch) is a herbalist, with a supply of "roots, barks, leaves and grasses in her room; gully root, herbe-à-femmes, guérir root, fever grass and so on". At one point, she prepares a bush bath in her room to help the young and timid Martha secure a new man. After boiling a bath-pan outside her door at midnight, she brings the pan inside, closes the door and window, lights three tall candles and bathes Martha while delivering an incantation. Later the women hold a wake for the troublesome Christophine's man, Seppy, who was killed by a car – the new form of transportation that contributed to the loss of his job as a horse-cab driver. Seppy is laid out in an ice-refrigerated "dead-box" in Christophine's room, with candles around his head. Since he had been the vice-president of the "St. Nicholas Society", the members of this organization arrive for the wake with rum and pelau (a dish of rice, meat and vegetables). As the night progresses, there are eulogies, hymn-singing, praying and a speech from the president of the society. The next afternoon, members of the society arrive for the funeral procession, which includes a large purple banner, men adorned with the organization's insignia and six young women in white dresses and mauve shoulder-straps. As the novel continues, tensions among several of the women escalate to a tragic climax, though the narrator suggests that the community of the yard will survive. Overall, the novel provides a vivid portrayal of an intimate world controlled principally by working women, even though their lives are constricted by the wider forces of the city's economy and legal system. In addition, it is a sustained attempt to represent women's voices and the nuances of their speech styles.[22]

While Mendes's *Black Fauns* explores barrack-yard life, James's *Minty Alley* (1936) focuses on a different sort of domestic setting: the yard of Mrs Rouse, who runs a small cake-making business. The novel opens with Haynes, the twenty-year-old protagonist, in the house of his mother, a school headmistress who has recently died. Haynes has promised his mother that he would keep the house, and contemplates how he can manage the mortgage with his low salary as an assistant in a bookstore, and rental income from rooms on George Street (a downtown area of barrack and other substandard housing). In response to his plan to rent out his mother's house and live elsewhere, his servant Ella mentions a room for rent at nearby Minty Alley, but adds that the residents of the house are "ordinary people, sir. Not your class of people". However, the room is cheap and Haynes takes it, thus beginning his discovery of working-class life and a growing understanding of himself. References to "Victoria Street" in the narrative suggest that James conceptualized Minty Alley as intersecting Victoria Avenue in uptown Port of Spain, an area of mixed housing types and income levels during the 1920s. The narrator offers a description of No. 2 Minty Alley: "The house was built in a simple style, square and containing five rooms, drawing-room and dining-room on one side and three bedrooms on the other. But at some time after it had been built, two rooms had been added to the original structure on the side opposite the kitchen, which was a separate building about ten feet away." Haynes rents one of these rooms, and, through a peephole in the wooden wall, begins to observe the activities of the yard, which centre on the kitchen – a building with open windows and doors where the assorted members of the household bake cakes and carry out other chores.

With the exception of a few brief scenes, the subsequent action takes place within the yard and buildings of No. 2 Minty Alley. As the novel progresses, Haynes evolves from a passive spectator (and reader of books) to an active participant in this micro-landscape, developing friendships with its occupants and a romantic relationship with Mrs Rouse's teenage niece, while also advising Mrs Rouse on a range of personal and financial challenges. In fact, much of the novel revolves around concerns with No. 2 as property, domestic space and economic enterprise, with ongoing discussion of the mortgage, rents, boarding payments, cake-baking business and finances of the yard's residents. Though there are deep bonds among the members of the household, there are also various tensions, which explode when Benoit, Mrs Rouse's man of eighteen years, runs off with and marries Nurse Jackson, an alluring but capricious boarder. Benoit and the nurse move through several housing arrangements, ending up in a small room on George Street, where Benoit has a stroke. After he is abandoned by his wife, Mrs Rouse decides to bring Benoit from the hospital back to No. 2 (of which he is a co-owner): "he and me build the house. We sweat and we strain to build it, and while it standing there I can't see him want a shelter." But Benoit dies at the hospital and she sells the house. In the closing scene, Haynes (who has moved out) walks by No. 2 and sees a new family in the home, with a child at a piano in the drawing room. The property has become a space of aspiration for another of the city's households.[23]

In contrast to the tight focus on a working-class yard in *Minty Alley* and a barrack yard in *Black Fauns*, Mendes's first novel, *Pitch Lake* (1934), has a more expansive range: Port of Spain's Portuguese community and the wider urban landscape during the 1920s. The Portuguese minority in Trinidad had an intermediary status between the French-creole elite and the Afro- and Indo-Trinidadian masses, and was itself divided between small shopkeepers and more prosperous business owners. The novel follows Joe, a twenty-two-year-old Portuguese man, as he attempts to navigate his way in Trinidad's complex class and colour structure, represented especially in his three different romantic interests. The story opens with Joe moving on from his father's depressing rum shop in San Fernando, where he has worked for six years. While on the train north, he "remembered he was leaving San Fernando and the rum-shop for good and was going to Port-of-Spain where everything would be different with him". In Port of Spain, he lives with his brother and sister-in-law in "a neat little cottage, with a front gallery and a bay-window, built about ten feet from the pavement". References to the chimes of the Sacred Heart Church on Richmond Street suggest that the house is in the pleasant Victoria Square area, where Mendes himself lived for a time. The cottage's gallery included a Madeira wickerwork suite, while the drawing room featured an oak-stained floor, several small carpets, a mahogany table, rockers and a piano. The full bed, chest of drawers and washstand in Joe's bedroom were similarly impressive: "What a difference to what he had been accustomed to in his little back-room on the rum-shop premises!" Joe's primary concern during his first couple of days in the city is to buy a dress suit that "would be a symbol of his resolutions: there always to remind him of his social aspirations". As the plot develops, he moves through a variety of spaces in Port of Spain, ranging from an upscale Portuguese club to a cheap hotel on Charlotte Street, as well as the provisions department of a large firm where he finds employment as a salesman. In the end, his new life collapses in what the narrator suggests is the morass (or pitch lake) of Trinidad's class and colour values and expectations. While Joe initially experiences Port of Spain as a realm of excitement and opportunity, its prejudices and snobbery ultimately make it a place of confinement. Meanwhile, the United States figures in the background of the novel as a possible destination for further escape.[24]

Through such stories, Mendes, James and other *Beacon* writers revealed spaces and inhabitants of the city that previous literature had generally represented in superficial ways. They led readers inside working-class yards and explored the complexity of their social organization and economic activities. In narrating the interaction and dialogue of various characters, they captured local patterns of thought and demonstrated the richness of Trinidadian speech. They also documented customary forms of architecture, domestic furnishings, cuisine, dress, courtship, leisure, artistic expression and spirituality. Of course, they wrote from their particular middle-class perspectives, which led at times to a certain voyeuristic fascination with degradation, intrigue and sensation. In fact, James self-consciously addressed this dynamic in his depiction of the middle-class Haynes observing the affairs of No. 2 Minty Alley through the peephole of his room. Even with such social distance, however, *Beacon* writers were able to imagine and portray individual working-class lives. Moreover, yards were not the only concern of their fiction. They comprehended these spaces as part of the larger realm of Port of Spain, while also writing stories that dealt with other settings in the city (as well as other parts of Trinidad). In general, they examined how colonialism and social inequality structured the urban landscape and limited the opportunities of its inhabitants. But they also disclosed how people took possession of their environment, managed to persevere and built communities. This affirmation of local places, communities and forms of expression was the foundation for a new type of literature in Trinidad.

WORKERS' DEMONSTRATIONS

While *Beacon* writers were exploring the housing and lives of working people in literature, the voices of the workers themselves were increasingly heard in the streets of Port of Spain and elsewhere in Trinidad. During the 1930s, workers organized in public spaces a variety of demonstrations ranging from celebrations of May Day and the abolition of slavery to strikes and protests. At these carefully staged and highly visible events, they articulated their concerns over unemployment, low wages, rising rents and the general oppressiveness of colonial society and governance, while seeking recognition on their own terms. In essence, public demonstrations were a critical means by which workers communicated among themselves and with employers and government authorities. As the decade progressed, demonstrations became an increasingly effective instrument through which workers developed a fuller understanding of their position within the colonial socioeconomic order and of their capacity to challenge this order through collective action.

During the 1930s, May Day served as a regular occasion during which Trinidad's working men and women displayed their numbers in the streets. May Day celebrations were organized by the TWA, which, during the first several years of the decade, continued to attract a strong following. The *Labour Leader*, the TWA's newspaper, offered an effusive account of the occasion in 1931:

> On Sunday last, with King Sol in happy mood, all Trinidad witnessed the celebration of May Day, when, in a spirit of heightened joyousness, the officers and members of over seventy sections of the Trinidad and Tobago Workingmen's Association gathered together under the emblematic Red Flag of Labour and Socialism.
>
> Long before 2 pm., hundreds of interested onlookers thronged the Woodford Square enclosure, and these, together with the large army of workingmen and workingwomen in this colony, erected a well set stage for the purpose of carrying into effect the 1931 celebration of May Day.
>
> Capt. Cipriani, under whose Presidency the Trinidad Workingmen's Association is conducted, arrived a few minutes before the time appointed for the parade, and, in customary eloquent manner, addressed the gathering in a few short words, exhorting them to maintain order throughout the day's proceedings so that nothing might have contributed to mar the event.
>
> Leaving Woodford Square the procession, headed by the Executive Committee of the Trinidad Workingmen's Association and accompanied by a brass band,

proceeded up Pembroke Street, down Oxford Street into Dundonald Street, on to the Grand Stand at the Queen's Park Savannah. Along the route of march, there was in evidence a goodly number of banners which bore the objects and aims of the respective sections of the Association. The lusty singing of Labour's favourite hymn "Stand Firm Workingmen", (composed by the late Mr. William Howard Bishop) was heard to advantage. . . .

On housetops, through windows and on either side of the route of the march, men, women and children viewed what to them was undoubtedly one of the largest and most imposing ceremonies ever witnessed in this colony.

The procession included core elements of labour demonstrations of the era: the leadership of Cipriani, sections of workers from various trades, identifying banners, disciplined marching, a brass band and singing. The street route followed was the most direct path from Woodford Square to the grandstand in the Queen's Park Savannah, and passed through the heart of the uptown area, including the block along the south side of Lord Harris Square. After the crowd gathered at the grandstand, the band performed another labour hymn, followed by speeches from a minister and Cipriani.[25]

In 1933 there was a meeting at the TWA's Liberty Hall on Prince Street to discuss both the route of the May Day parade and the day on which it should be held. While Cipriani favoured the most direct route from Woodford Square to the Savannah, Comrade Alexander, the assistant secretary of the TWA, suggested a longer route, since the purpose of the procession was "a demonstration before their employers of the number and organization of the working people". There was also debate concerning the practice of holding the celebration on a Sunday, rather than 1 May, in order to avoid losing a day of wages. Comrade Henry, general secretary of the TWA, argued that 1 May would have a greater impact than Sunday, "when most employers of labour are either out of town or in their beds". In the end, the potential for increased visibility was overridden by more practical concerns in a vote to hold the parade along the usual short route on Sunday. In addition, Cipriani said he hoped representatives of country branches of the TWA would participate and bring their banners with them. The procession took place as planned, with sections, banners and band music, followed by speeches from Cipriani and others at the Savannah. The mass gathering also approved a resolution in which they called on both the colonial and municipal governments to move forward with providing relief for unemployment.[26]

During the early 1930s, working people (especially those of African descent) also rallied to celebrate the centenary of the abolition of slavery in the British empire. The fiftieth anniversary of emancipation had been observed in 1888, a half century after the end of the "apprenticeship" period in 1838. Five decades later, there were initial observations in 1933, the centenary of the passing of the

Slavery Abolition Act, and a more extensive schedule of programmes in 1934 to mark the commencement of abolition on 1 August 1834. On the Sunday before 1 August, members of the TWA marched with banners from Woodford Square to the grandstand in the Savannah, where they were joined by members of friendly societies. At the Savannah there was a variety of speakers, including Cipriani, who proclaimed that the West Indies were ready for nationhood and observed: "The air tingles with freedom but there is something that rankles. That is that we should still be called 'subjects.' We are British, yes, but subjects, no." The rally closed with a resolution of loyalty to the King and the singing of the national anthem. Emancipation Day, 1 August itself, was declared a public holiday and celebrated with Carnival festivity, including masquerading and dancing in the streets. At the Queen's Park Oval in lower St Clair, there were masquerade and calypso competitions and the mayor unveiled a painting of William Wilberforce ("the great Liberator"). Other activities during the week included special church services, an address by the acting governor to schoolchildren, a concert of "Negro music" at the Royal Victoria Institute, debates by literary and debating clubs and "Slavery Through the Ages" – a multi-evening historical pageant staged at the Prince's Building by the Paragon Dramatic Association and the National Association of African Progeny. Though the TWA used the emancipation centenary as a public occasion to articulate the freedom of workers and West Indian self-government, the *Trinidad Guardian* said its message to the people of Trinidad was "to forget origin, forget colour, forget prejudice and turn our thoughts entirely to the great British Empire of which we are a part".[27]

While May Day and Emancipation events were essentially celebrative in form, major protests by working people also took place during 1933 and 1934. On 19 June 1933, the TWA organized a demonstration of unemployed men and women in the city. After gathering at Besson Street, an impoverished area to the east of Marine Square, they took a circuitous route through the southeastern quadrant of downtown: up Piccadilly Street, along Prince Street, down George Street, along Marine Square, up Henry Street, again onto Prince Street and into Woodford Square. Perhaps this roundabout route through a low-income district enabled them to attract more followers. In any case, some eight hundred people marched in an orderly fashion, with no band or chanting, but carrying banners that said: "No work – no rent", "Too much depression – we want work", and "Stop the landlord exploitation". As they crossed Woodford Square towards the Red House, they were met by a police detachment. Comrade Alexander, assistant secretary of the TWA and spokesman for the marchers, told the police that they wished to meet with the governor to request work for the unemployed and reinstatement of a rent-restriction ordinance. A police inspector relayed the message to the governor, who, after observing the marchers from the portico of his office in the Red House, said he would be willing to meet with representatives in two days.[28]

The next major march of unemployed labourers originated not in Port of Spain but near Caroni Sugar Estates Limited in west-central Trinidad. On 20 July 1934, approximately 650 sugar workers and sympathizers marched along highways to Port of Spain and were met on the Eastern Main Road, at the edge of the city, by government officials and police. The labourers' objective was to meet with the acting governor to explain that they wanted work and, if none were available, relief, since they were starving. A delegation of six men was led to the Red House, where they were able to meet with Howard Nankivell, a deputy of the governor. Nankivell was sympathetic to their plight and said he would address the issue of unemployment with estate owners, while advising those in greatest need to seek relief from the district warden. This message was accepted by the marchers, who returned home. However, there were also violent demonstrations by workers in the Caroni area and other sugar districts during this period.[29]

Meanwhile, working people began to form more militant organizations as alternatives to Cipriani's TWA (renamed the TLP in 1934). In early 1934 Jim Headley, Elma François and Jim Barrette created the National Unemployed Movement in Port of Spain. Headley, a seaman, had been active in the Young Communist League and National Maritime Union in the United States, where he also interacted with the Trinidadian radical activist George Padmore. Barrette was an oilfield worker and companion of François. Originally from St Vincent, François migrated to Trinidad around 1919 and was initially active as a speaker for the TWA. Sociologist Rhoda Reddock notes that François would "go to Woodford Square and 'take on any group of fellas'. Her approach was to sit on a bench next to perfect strangers and use the newspaper to start political discussions. In various areas of the town, on street corners, she would inquire about its history and the living conditions". The National Unemployed Movement took shape after François became disillusioned with the TWA's gradualist approach to workers' issues and through her interaction with Headley and Barrette. By the end of 1934, François, Barrette and other activists reorganized the National Unemployed Movement as the Negro Welfare Cultural and Social Association (NWCSA), owing in part to the influence of Rupert Gittens, who had recently been deported from France for his involvement with the French Communist Party. The NWCSA addressed not only issues of unemployment and poverty but also broader concerns of education, labour organizing and political transformation. In addition, it actively recruited women and emphasized cooperative work between men and women. Reddock says François held the position of "organiser" or "organising secretary" within the organization and was perceived as its main ideologue.[30]

The National Unemployed Movement/NWCSA organized a variety of "hunger marches" and was instrumental in popularizing this form of demonstration across Trinidad. A particularly prominent use of the method occurred in March 1935 in connection with a strike by workers at the Apex Oilfields in southern Trinidad. When Cipriani refused to sanction the strike, labour advocate Uriah Butler led workers on a hunger march to Port of Spain. Though Cipriani was able to stop the march before it reached the city, the demonstration helped to establish Butler as a new leader of oilfield workers.[31]

While the NWCSA developed links with Butler and the growing labour movement in southern Trinidad, by October 1935 it was also coordinating demonstrations in response to Italy's invasion of Ethiopia, an event that sparked widespread outrage in Trinidad and across the Caribbean, given this African nation's long resistance to European imperialism. The NWCSA organized a mass meeting in Marine Square on 10 October (four days after the invasion) and distributed in advance ten thousand leaflets about the slaughter of Ethiopians. Over two thousand people attended the meeting, some with placards stating "Down with Mussolini", "Away with Fascism", and "Down with the Enemies of the Negro". Members of the crowd also protested at the Catholic cathedral on the square, the Italian consul's office and Woodford Square. Meanwhile, dockworkers affiliated with the TLP and NWCSA refused to unload or load Italian ships, in keeping with a ban by international dockworker unions. Support for Ethiopians was also offered by the fundraising drives of various associations, such as an Ethiopian Flag Day organized by social workers Audrey Jeffers and Beatrice Greig for the Friends of Ethiopia and a flag day coordinated by the Daughters of Ethiopia (followers of Marcus Garvey). In early November, there were mass meetings to observe the fifth anniversary of the coronation of Haile Selassie as Emperor of Ethiopia, and in May 1936, protests intensified when it became clear that Britain would not provide effective support for the Ethiopian people. Elma François was the featured speaker on the crisis at a large meeting organized by the NWCSA in Woodford Square on 29 May. During this period, Cipriani, who was mayor of Port of Spain as well as president of the TLP, frequently prohibited the NWCSA from holding meetings in Woodford Square. Though he remained a supporter of workers and the Ethiopian cause, the NWCSA represented a significant threat to his authority.[32]

While the various demonstrations of 1933–1936 mobilized large numbers of workers and increasingly displayed the level of their discontent, the strikes and protests of June 1937 were more dramatic in execution, island-wide in magnitude and far-reaching in their impact on the colonial order. Dissatisfaction among oil workers in southern Trinidad had been steadily growing, owing to their low wages in relation to the increasing cost of living and a variety of unfair labour practices within the industry. Uriah Butler intensified his speeches around the oilfields and suggested that there would be a strike sometime in June. At midnight on 18 June, workers at a Trinidad Leaseholds field near Fyzabad began a sit-down strike that continued through the early morning hours of 19 June. Later that day the government sent a police contingent to Fyzabad with the objective of arresting Butler on the ground of inciting violence. By evening the police found him addressing a crowd in Fyzabad and tried to apprehend him. Butler escaped, but in the ensuing confrontation between the police and the crowd, two officers were killed. Over the course of the next several days, there were violent disturbances at the refinery in Port Fortin, in downtown San Fernando, at Usine Ste Madeleine (the largest sugar factory), at the Waterloo and Woodford Lodge sugar estates, in the southeastern town of Rio Claro and in Port of Spain. There were also strikes at numerous other places around the island. In its efforts to contain the growing disorder, the colonial government mobilized not only its regular police force but also the Trinidad Light Horse (now a mechanized unit) and the Trinidad Light Infantry Volunteers. In addition, two ships of British troops arrived on 22 and 23 June.[33]

By 22 June strikes and protests were disrupting Port of Spain. Early that morning, labourers, carpenters and masons working on the new Treasury Building in Marine Square demanded higher wages from the government's director of public works and transport. When the director told them he would discuss the matter later, they began a sit-down strike, but eventually left peacefully when instructed by the police. While most of the men returned home, some joined a group of NWCSA members who had gathered on the street nearby. This group then went to the site of the Deep Water Harbour Scheme and ordered workers there off the job. As the workers went to the scheme office to request increased wages, the police and a detachment of armed volunteers arrived. The *Trinidad Guardian* described the scene:

> The crowd, though restive, maintained order until they were called by leaders of the Association to demonstrate in a tangible way their sympathy with the oilfield workers.
>
> A man motioned the gathering to the open space before Gordon Grant and Company, Limited, where, amidst singing and shouting and the display of banners, a man named Bharat harangued them to action.
>
> He advised the gathering to march through the town and stop every man from working.
>
> On the banners displayed were the words: "Not bayonets and blood, but more pay", "Sympathy with the Strike", etc.
>
> The crowd then brought their meeting to a close and marched towards the Customs where carters were temporarily stopped from performing their daily duties.

Several hundreds gathered and, as it was apparent that trouble might ensue, the doors of the Custom House were closed.

The gathering then proceeded towards the Port-of-Spain Railway Station along South Quay and up Charlotte Street. Here they halted on Marine Square and, after leaders had conferred, the crowd made a sudden dash – howling and yelling – towards the Syrian Stores and J.T. Johnson corner store demanding that they close at once.

When the workers moved up Frederick Street, shouting closing orders, storeowners quickly pulled shutters down over their doors and windows. The workers then turned east on Prince Street and south on Duncan Street, along which they returned to Marine Square. From the square, they went east along the St Joseph Road and then back again on South Quay, where they entered the grounds of the railway station, shut down the railway workshop and tried to stop a train from leaving the city. Apparently this train was carrying a supply of rifles and ammunition to San Fernando, to be used in suppressing the uprising in southern Trinidad. As the train left, the crowd became more confrontational and a truckload of members of the Trinidad Light Infantry Volunteers arrived. After gunfire and the wounding of one man, the workers reassembled at Woodford Square, where they listened to speeches and sang hymns.[34]

The next day most shops reopened but employees remained on strike at the Harbour Scheme, Treasury Building and other public works projects. At this point, scavengers employed by the city council also went on strike. HMS *Exeter* arrived in the harbour and platoons of British troops began patrolling the streets with machine guns, while aeroplanes from the ship circled the city. Over the following days, a variety of other workers also went on strike, including lightermen (who worked the small boats for carrying cargo and passengers from ships in the harbour), stevedores, customs cartermen and some railway employees. The strikes of the scavengers and dockworkers were particularly critical. With garbage piling up in the streets and posing a public health hazard, Mayor Alfred Richards awarded the scavengers a 50 per cent pay increase and arranged for police protection so that they could carry out their essential duties without interference by other strikers. Meanwhile, the dockworkers' strike was forcing ships to move on to ports outside Trinidad to unload their goods. In addition to raising the possibility of a food shortage, this meant that goods would have to be transshipped back to Trinidad later at substantial expense. While a government mediation committee (chaired by Acting Colonial Secretary Nankivell) pursued negotiations with various categories of workers, Governor Fletcher personally entered into discussions with lightermen and stevedores. Gradually, the city's diverse workforce accepted pay increases and other changes in working arrangements, with the dockworkers being the last to reach an agreement.[35]

Across Trinidad, the majority of workers were back on their jobs by 5 July. In total, fourteen people were killed and fifty-nine wounded during the disturbances. In response to the crisis, the Colonial Office sent a commission of inquiry to the island, which took evidence from a wide range of individuals from early September to mid-October. In its report, published in 1938, the commission concluded that the underlying cause of the disturbances was the workers' "general sense of dissatisfaction for which there was no adequate means of articulation through recognized machinery of collective bargaining". A major consequence of the strike was the formation of unions. While some labourers obtained improvements in their wages and working conditions at the time of the strikes, it was through the ongoing pressure and negotiations of unions over time that more substantial gains were achieved. Finally, the uprising had consequences for Governor Fletcher and Acting Colonial Secretary Nankivell: the Colonial Office removed them from their posts in December 1937 and May 1938 respectively, in part because of their expressions of empathy with the workers.[36]

During the strikes and protests of 1937 and those of the preceding years, working people engaged in a level of collective action and expression unprecedented in Trinidad's history. The frequency and coordination of demonstrations in streets, roads, squares and other public places far exceeded that of the cocoa boom era. Workers increasingly appropriated key public, industrial and commercial spaces for staging events and demanding recognition. While protesters during the cocoa boom era also employed such spaces, the geography of the rebellion of the 1930s was different. The prominent strikes and protests of 1919 were concentrated in Port of Spain; those of the 1930s occurred across the island. In 1919 striking longshoremen led the disruption of the island's commerce, while the major disturbances of the 1930s were initiated by workers in the oil and sugar industries, the main productive sectors of the colonial economy. Though these industries were based in southern and central Trinidad, Port of Spain remained a destination for protest. Workers carried out hunger marches to the city with the goal of communicating their grievances directly to the central government authorities. In addition, workers in Port of Spain mounted a variety of demonstrations during the 1930s and, three days after the strike of oilfield workers at Fyzabad in 1937, began strikes and protests in the centre of the capital. The initial strikes at the Treasury Building and Deep Water Harbour Scheme disrupted the two major public works projects of the time, while the strikes at the docks again undermined the city's position as the hub of the island's commerce. In short, workers in Port of Spain and across Trinidad during this era were successful in temporarily transforming locations of economic production and trade into spaces of uncertainty and danger. In response, the government moved swiftly to regain control of these spaces through aggressive police action and, in the case of the June 1937 uprising, mobilizing volunteer regiments and British troops. Order was soon restored. However, workers emerged from the events of 1937 with a greater sense of their ability to create public demonstrations and threaten normal activities in the city and elsewhere. In the following months, they formed new organizations and, over time, union halls became additional spaces for assembly and expression.

ARTHUR CALDER-MARSHALL AND THE HERSKOVITSES

At the end of the 1930s, the consciousness and activities of working people were documented in two unique studies by visitors to Trinidad: English fiction writer and journalist Arthur Calder-Marshall (1908–1992) lived on the island for three months in 1938 and published *Glory Dead* the following year, and the American anthropologists Melville Herskovits (1895–1963) and Frances Herskovits (died 1972) spent a similar length of time there in 1939 and published *Trinidad Village* in 1947. While Calder-Marshall devoted most of his research to Port of Spain, the Herskovitses carried out the majority of their fieldwork in the village of Toco in the remote northeastern corner of the island. However, they included an appendix in their book with descriptions of a Yoruba-derived Shango (Orisha) yard and ceremony in the eastern Port of Spain community of Laventille. As a journalist, Calder-Marshall explored life in the city in the context of British colonialism, the depression and the labour movements of the 1930s. He claimed that Afro-Trinidadians had "lost their original culture" and were "evolving a new culture along working-class lines".[37] As ethnographers, the Herskovitses examined Trinidadian Orisha practices as a New World adaptation of an ancient West African religion. Their book overall is concerned with long-term processes of cultural continuity and change and gives relatively little attention to the economic and political developments of 1930s Trinidad. Though their subjects and perspectives differ, both Calder-Marshall and the Herskovitses offer evocative accounts of the environments, experiences and creativity of working people in the city at the close of the interwar era.

In his foreword to *Glory Dead*, Calder-Marshall says he could have followed the lead of Charles Kingsley, author of *At Last: A Christmas in the West Indies* (1871), and described the beauties of Trinidad's varied natural environments. However, he was fascinated by the Trinidadian people and the complexities of their contemporary predicament. He notes: "The plan of life, the medley of different races, the conflict of economic forces baffled me at first. But gradually I came to see clearly the system underlying what at first seemed pure confusion." This system is slowly revealed in the first part of *Glory Dead*, a sixty-four-page narrative titled "A Portrait of the City". In explaining his method, Calder-Marshall writes: "Out of imaginary, but typical incidents, I have tried to build up a portrait of the capital, which will give the reader that strange and yet familiar atmosphere that is so difficult to define in abstract words." The result is a composition of numerous vignettes, depicting a wide range of places, people and activities in the city over a period of twenty-four hours, from midnight to midnight.[38]

The "Portrait" opens at a soft-drink stand on the Port of Spain docks, where there is a gathering of local men and American sailors – including a drunken sailor retrieved from the city by the US Shore Patrol. As a church clock chimes 12:00 a.m., Calder-Marshall's camera-like view pans the downtown area and focuses on homeless men and women sleeping on the pavement near the Anglican cathedral in Woodford Square, a squad of policemen marching down St Vincent Street, a group of mainly female vendors resting with their baskets of produce at the new Eastern Market building on the east side of George Street and patrons of late-night cafés, along with participants in a card game out in Belmont. As the night progresses, a rainstorm moves in and the homeless seek shelter in the arcades of the town hall and stores on Frederick Street, while men on the night shift at the harbour scheme continue working under carbide lights, operating the pipeline that suction-dredges mud from a half mile out in the gulf. By 4:30 a.m. passengers are gathering at the bus-company garage, where they decide whether to ride the company buses or take advantage of the cheaper pirate buses lingering nearby. At dawn, cocks crow, the harbour dredge continues groaning, Indo-Trinidadian boys hawk the morning papers at the waterfront and a calypso blares from a gramophone in a George Street parlour.

As the morning progresses, downtown fills with people, pedlars lay out their goods along Frederick Street and Marine Square, trams and buses move along their routes (ringing bells and sounding horns), tourists arrive on a cruise ship at the docks (where they are accosted by taxi drivers and hotel touts) and carts haul imported goods from the customs sheds to the stores of Huggins, Alston and Gordon Grant. A sick child suffers in a shack facing the Dry River, while a lady in Maraval gossips with friends at a bridge party and Mrs Ranji (a Woodbrook resident) contemplates how to profit from the sale of her house. On Frederick Street, men hawk the goods of the leading stores as women arrive from Woodbrook, Laventille, St Clair and St Ann's. "Here black and white mix, yellow and chestnut, as nowhere else at no other time. Indian women wearing *saris*, Chinese schoolgirls, high-brown mistresses." Though there is much interaction, "most feel not the similarity of human beings but their difference". Mrs Wilson, the wife of a British official, converses in a cordial but patronizing manner with Mrs Tournevant, a woman of mixed ancestry who knows that *her* husband, a commission agent and slum lord, has a higher income. Meanwhile, a middle-aged American woman staying at the Queen's Park Hotel tries to seduce César de Montfort, a taxi driver who owns a three-quarter share in a Ford V8. An Indo-Trinidadian man argues with a cashier at a weigh-house over the price for his sacks of copra, stevedores fight for limited jobs at a warehouse on Chacon Street and an Afro-Trinidadian man in Woodford Square expounds to a gathered group on exploitation in the colony and the greatness of Uriah Butler, with encouragement from a police informer.

By 11:30 a.m. it is time for "breakfast" (lunch). Businessmen assemble at the Union Club on Marine Square and enjoy cocktails on the club's gallery, journalists from the *Trinidad Guardian* and lightermen from the harbour eat in a parlour on St Vincent Street, clerks and shop girls ride home on buses and trams, and the destitute obtain soup, bread and saltfish at the Salvation Army Hostel. During the afternoon, a young Syrian man tries to sell dresses and knick-knacks door-to-door in Woodbrook, an Afro-Trinidadian attorney defends his client in the police court, members of the NWCSA and the TLP discuss local politics in a rum shop (adorned with pictures of a Venezuelan dictator, Adam and Eve, Lord Baden-Powell and a pin-up girl) and an Indo-Trinidadian woman buys some meat at a Chinese delicatessen. At 4:00 p.m. the shops on Frederick Street close, professional men gather at respectable drinking establishments, a Cockney argues with an Irishman at a bar (while an American oil driller watches) and gramophone dance parties take place at homes across the town. Another storm sweeps in, forcing everyone inside to the sound of slamming windows and rain pounding on galvanized-iron roofs.

At night people dine, if they have food, and play games: bridge, poker, rummy, whappy, all-fours, fantan or dice. Those with money buy tickets for the best seats in the leading cinemas, while those of lesser means attend the second-run theatres. Some sit on the porches of their homes and watch fireflies, while others walk arm in arm across the Queen's Park Savannah or kiss on benches in the squares. Prostitutes follow a route down Frederick Street, across Marine Square, up Charlotte Street and back to Frederick via Queen Street. Some of these visit the Oxford and the Cambridge, two clubs adjacent to each other. At the Cambridge, a crowd of American sailors dance with local women to the music of piano, guitar, saxophone and drums. "At the head of the stairs the bouncer stands like a ringmaster watching the bar, the dance-floor and the bedrooms round the courtyard." By 10:00 p.m. most people in the city have turned off their lights and shut their windows. A man, woman and four children try to sleep in a 12-by-10-foot barrack room – the man has not had regular work since supporting unionization during the recent strikes. At the Country Club, the tourists who arrived earlier in the day dance with the local elite to the sounds of the band and the frogs and cicadas in the surrounding trees. Again vendors gather for the night at the market, while the homeless find shelter in doorways. A group of American sailors arrives at the wharves – a drunken one insults the local men gathered at the soft-drink stand. A fight breaks out, with bottles from the stand as ammunition, but is soon ended by the local police and US Shore Patrol. As the city's clocks begin to strike midnight, the Shore Patrol assures the soft-drink vendor that Uncle Sam will pay for his losses.[39]

As the above scenes suggest, Calder-Marshall offers a vivid account of the geography of Port of Spain and the characteristics of many of its varied locales. In essence, he tries to capture recurrent patterns in the disparate sights and sounds of the city. His composition of "typical incidents" reveals diurnal and nocturnal rhythms in the life of the city that collectively constitute the distinctive quality of its milieu. Through his montage, he juxtaposes a wide range of scenes, often highlighting differences in individuals' social positions and conditions. Though there is much tension and conflict among the populace, he also demonstrates that Port of Spain is a socio-spatial system, a realm in which diverse inhabitants and visitors are interrelated and interdependent. This is the "plan of life" that he found in what initially appeared to be confusion. His "Portrait" covers myriad forms of economic relations and activity, as well as common diversions and pastimes. For Calder-Marshall, Port of Spain is clearly a city of colonial racism and exploitation but also a place with an undeniable verve and joie de vivre.

In the following chapters of *Glory Dead*, Calder-Marshall describes other places around Port of Spain and more fully examines the inequities of colonial society. At this point, he also introduces Jean "Tony" de Boissière, his primary guide to the city and the individual to whom his book is dedicated. De Boissière was a member of an old French-creole family, had studied in New York, travelled across Europe and North Africa, and was working for the *Port-of-Spain Gazette* when Calder-Marshall met him a couple of weeks after arriving in Trinidad. According to Calder-Marshall, de Boissière had "invaluable contacts and information", "mixed without embarrassment with people of any class or colour", and utterly ignored the conventions of the local bourgeoisie, who warned the visiting author against associating with him. He adds that de Boissière "got from life a greater enjoyment than any man I have known". Like many rebellious artistic figures of the 1930s, de Boissière was loosely associated with the Beacon group of writers. Alfred Mendes recalls that, though he always wore "outlandish garments" and claimed that "his life was a work of art", he was in fact bitter and full of malice. During the late 1930s and 1940s, de Boissière published and edited *Callaloo* and *Picong*, two periodicals which, in the words of Mendes, "served the purpose of lampooning the affectations and hypocrisies of the people who placed the emphasis on respectability". In a book published in 1958, Edgar Mittelholzer (a Guyanese novelist who lived in Trinidad for several years) suggests that, thanks to the guidance of the outcast de Boissière, Calder-Marshall depicted Port of Spain as "one vast shanty-town of hovels, a disgrace to the British government". While *Glory Dead* obviously portrays the city as much more than a conglomeration of slums, de Boissière's position at the margins of polite society certainly facilitated Calder-Marshall's access to a wide range of working-class locales, and his biting critique of the bourgeoisie resonated with the visitor's strong socialist sympathies.[40]

Calder-Marshall had a low opinion of domestic architecture in Port of Spain and was particularly appalled by the housing of the poor. However, his guide for a tour of housing was not de Boissière but Dr Marcano, the city's public health officer at the time. First the two visited a boardinghouse and adjacent restaurant in the centre of the city. The boardinghouse included a room that combined a dining space with partitioned sleeping cubicles, a garret with approximately a dozen bed-size closets and a run-down shower closet, while the restaurant featured eating rooms filled with flies and a bathroom with a crate of live chickens and an ice-box. As Dr Marcano charged about these and other premises, issuing a constant stream of orders in response to infractions, it was clear that the occupants regarded him as something of a "paid nuisance" who only increased their misery. The tour then moved on to barrack yards. Here Calder-Marshall observed buildings with single rows of small rooms as well as "back-to-backs" with double rows. Some rooms had five or more occupants, cooking took place outside, lavatories and showers were minimal and profits for landlords could reach 20 or 30 per cent. Some occupants could not afford the rents for the new workers' houses at Gonzales Place; and when barracks were condemned, they were sometimes replaced with equally substandard detached houses. In other cases, the former barrack occupants moved into larger houses that were subdivided into multiple units and deteriorated through overcrowding. It was apparent to Calder-Marshall that a concerted solution to the city's housing would not occur soon. The colonial government claimed that it had ceded authority to the municipal government, and the city council, elected through a mainly middle-class franchise, continued to include a significant number of members with vested interests in barrack properties. Calder-Marshall concluded that improvement in housing would come from the persistent demands of the workers themselves, but at present, they had even greater concern with securing food, clothing and employment.[41]

Meanwhile, Tony de Boissière assisted Calder-Marshall in contacting various labour and cultural organizations in Port of Spain. Among these was Rupert Gittens's L'Ouverture Club, a middle-class organization in Belmont devoted to the appreciation of the cultural traditions of peoples of African descent. Calder-Marshall delivered a lecture on modern literature at the club and discussed writers' growing attention to the political conditions of their societies. This precipitated a sharp response from a rotund white man in the audience who turned out to be Albert Gomes. Though a champion of working people, Gomes argued "art for art's sake" and art as "universal". Calder-Marshall was also a guest of honour at the club's first-anniversary banquet, attended by men in tuxedoes and women in evening gowns. The programme featured such items as a piano solo, Gittens's recitation of a Langston Hughes poem, a young woman's recitation of a poem by Gittens on Toussaint L'Ouverture and, eventually, dinner and dancing. In addition, Calder-Marshall spoke at six different union meetings, activity that attracted the attention of the police. Among his topics were the importance of cooperation over individualism, the global context of workers' movements and the mechanics of union-building. He also interacted with the NWCSA and once, when passing through Woodford Square, encountered this organization holding a meeting with Clement Payne as chairman and Elma François speaking from a packing crate. Soon the police broke up the gathering, on the ground that the mayor had not granted a permit. The NWCSA leaders sang "The Internationale" and Payne shouted across the square: "Comrades . . . I call you to witness that this square is OUR SQUARE."[42]

Calder-Marshall gained further understanding of Port of Spain's socio-spatial order when he tried to organize a production of the play *Waiting for Lefty* by Clifford Odets. He and de Boissière used the seamen's union hall on George Street for auditions, with the hope of filling the parts with union members. However, Rupert Gittens felt that L'Ouverture could more effectively handle the play. Unfortunately, the seamen perceived the L'Ouverture people as spies, while L'Ouverture viewed George Street as a low-class district. After Calder-Marshall recruited a few additional actors from Woodbrook (where he was living), the production moved to a hall north of Woodford Square, considered a neutral location. But when the lighter-skinned recruits from Woodbrook indicated their discomfort at sharing the stage with the darker-skinned members of L'Ouverture, Calder-Marshall flew into a rage and abandoned the production.[43]

An American lady, who had spent just one evening in Port of Spain, once told Calder-Marshall: "There was something I didn't like about the place at all, something evil, something corrupt." He felt there was an element of truth in this observation and indicates that his "Portrait" shows the forms this corruption takes. Though the "Portrait" documents various schemes of deception and trickery, he seems to conceptualize the city's corruption more deeply in terms of prejudice, oppression, indifference and poverty. In summing up his thoughts, he writes that the Trinidadian worker's "position in the structure of the British Empire is that of a wage-slave whose labour is exploited, a consumer on whom the trash of the home market is unloaded, and a dependent who finally has no say in his own Government". However, he also has great confidence in the collective organizing of working people and concludes that labour "represents the creative force that alone can bring the island from that darkness and unhappiness".[44]

In 1939, a year after Calder-Marshall's visit to Trinidad, Melville and Frances Herskovits arrived with the intent of examining Trinidadians' retention of West African cultural practices. Ten years earlier, the couple had stopped at Port of Spain while in transit to New York from Surinam, where they had been doing fieldwork with African-descended Maroon communities in the interior of this Dutch colony. During their brief time in port, they read a letter in the *Trinidad Guardian* "from an aroused citizen expressing indignation at certain practices then being carried out near the capital by Negroes who were worshippers of Shango". They vowed to return soon to research this phenomenon, but for the following decade, devoted their attention to other research, including fieldwork in Dahomey (Benin) and Haiti and the publication of *An Outline of Dahomean Religious Belief* (1933), *Rebel Destiny: Among the Bush Negroes of Dutch Guiana* (1934), and *Suriname Folk-Lore* (1936); as well as *Life in a Haitian Valley* (1937) and *Dahomey: An Ancient African Kingdom* (1938), which were written by Melville Herskovits alone. By the time of their 1939 trip to Trinidad, the Herskovitses thus possessed a broad framework for examining the retention and reinterpretation of African-derived cultural traditions in the Americas.[45]

After arriving in Port of Spain in June 1939 and dining with Governor and Lady Young and other local residents, the Herskovitses selected Toco as the site for their fieldwork, on the assumption that Shango worship and related African-derived ways of life would be stronger in this mainly Afro-Trinidadian village far from the capital city. After completing their research, however, they concluded that a history of slavery, colonial domination and the Afro-Trinidadian's "drive to achieve the benefits in living that he observes have accrued to the Europeans" together produced in Toco cultural patterns in which the economy and institutional structures were largely European. Nonetheless, the people of Toco had reinterpreted a variety of African-based customs in such cultural domains as spirituality, music and verbal art. For example, the Herskovitses provide much documentation of reinterpretation in reverence towards ancestors through burials, wakes and other ceremonies; a variety of magical, divination and other spiritual beliefs; the Spiritual Baptist faith (which synthesized West African and Protestant religious systems); an emphasis on eloquence, wit and competitive exchange in speeches during court cases and in other types of verbal performance; and the stylistic characteristics of such dance/music genres as the bongo, belé and reel. In addition, they recorded some more direct African retentions, such as Yoruba-language songs performed by Margaret Buckley, an elderly woman whose Yoruba-speaking parents had been born in West Africa and probably liberated from a slave ship by the British Navy between the 1840s and 1860s. However, the Herskovitses did not discover in the village any practice of the Yoruba religion, which had been the initial objective of their research.[46]

The Herskovitses *were* able to document Yoruba religious traditions back in Port of Spain, shortly before their return to the United States. In "Notes on Shango Worship", they describe a visit to a Shango yard in Laventille, on the eastern edge of the city:

> The complex of houses which constitute the cult-center of one Shango group is perched high on a hill above the capital, on a street that is but a short distance from a main road. To the west can be seen the city, the harbor, and the distant Venezuelan Andes. The compound is surrounded by a fence, the lower part of which is crudely made of flattened gasoline tins, topped with the round ends of the metal casks in which pitch is stored.

The several buildings in the yard included the house of the group's priestess and her husband and an adjacent second house, with unspecified residents. Facing the second house and sloping downhill was the "tent", an open structure with a perimeter railing and a galvanized-iron roof. A 25-foot-long thatched passageway connected the tent to the *chapelle*, a 6-by-10-foot structure that was raised on posts and featured a doorway screened by red and white curtains – colours representing the deity Shango. Flanking the chapelle was a cook-house. In addition, the Herskovitses noted that pigeons continually circled the yard, while "sensa-fowls" (chickens with erect feathers) ran about the grounds, in accordance with an African-derived belief that such creatures have the ability to dig up any evil charms.[47]

Within this asymmetrical, multifunctional compound, the chapelle served as an inner sanctuary – a space that contained the presence of various deities of the Yoruba pantheon. Practitioners represented the deities with specific colours and objects and identified them with particular Catholic saints – a syncretism that had developed over time in Trinidad through the recognition of corresponding qualities between the two sets of beings. A table near the door of the chapelle was dedicated to the river deity Yemanja, to whom the priestess of the compound was devoted. This display featured a blue-and white colour scheme, a dish with a stone resembling a fish, a second dish with nut-like objects called *après Dieu* ("after God") that offered protection and a large chromolithograph of St Anne (with whom Yemanja was associated). A table for Shango, the deity of thunder and lightning to whom the priestess's husband was devoted, was in a secondary position, since the husband held a lesser rank in this religious community. Above this table were various chromolithographs – the largest depicting St John the Baptist (associated with Shango) and others for such figures as St Philomène (Oshun, of the river and sea), St Michael (Ogun, associated with iron and war) and St Catherine (Oya, of the wind). Also in the chapelle was a third table for miscellaneous deities and a rack for storing dance-ceremony paraphernalia, such as an axe and shepherd's crooks for Shango and an anchor for Oshun. When the community held nighttime dance ceremonies in the nearby tent, they left the door to the chapelle open so that the deities, when invoked, could freely leave and possess their devotees.[48]

The tent contained benches on its four sides for participants in ceremonies, while spectators watched from outside the railing. Suspended from the roof of the tent were eight double-headed drums of various sizes and names, three of which were employed to form a battery for a particular ceremony. The drummers sat facing the chapelle, with a lighted candle in front of them. A sense of their music is provided by the several audio recordings that the Herskovitses made at this compound, including a song for Eshu – the messenger deity who is the first invoked at a ceremony. In this recording, a male lead engages in call-and-response singing with a female chorus, accompanied by three drums, a *shac-shac* (gourd rattle) and a piece of iron struck as a timekeeper. During the evening, the ensemble's music guided the dancing of the congregants, some of whom eventually became possessed by particular deities and enacted their characteristic behaviours. During possessions, these individuals (or assistants) sometimes retreated to the chapelle and reappeared with ritual objects. Much dramatic activity ensued in the tent as the night progressed. Then, gradually, the possessed individuals regained their normal human consciousness and successively engaged in a final ritual:

> They danced in subdued fashion until, turning from the drums, they remained standing in one place, their eyes glued to the doorway of the *chapelle*. Suddenly on a dead run, they would make their way toward it, leaping in the air as they approached the steps, and hurling themselves in a kind of dive onto the floor, to lie prostrate in the small shrine, with their feet projecting from the doorway.[49]

In addition to describing this public ceremony, the Herskovitses discuss Shango groups' recruitment of new members. Renowned for their specialized knowledge and healing gifts, group leaders attracted individuals who sought assistance for various maladies. After a successful healing, a leader might inform the client that a deity desired his or her devotion and encourage the person to become involved in the public ceremonies of the group. Meanwhile, other people were attracted by the vibrant dancing of Shango ceremonies and might be informed by a leader that this attraction was motivated by a deity. Finally, some individuals gained membership in a Shango group through their family (often from a grandmother or great-grandmother), with the inheritance revealed by divination or a sudden possession by a deity. In all these cases, the call of a deity was followed by a ritual in which the group leader washed the head of the initiate with leaves and other substances in order to prepare him or her for service to the deity and future possession. After this consecration, the initiated person created a small shrine in his or her home, followed various ritual protocols and participated in ceremonies at the leader's compound.[50]

Though the Herskovitses spent only a short time in Laventille, their transatlantic perspective on African-derived cultural traditions enabled them to describe the Shango yard coherently, affirm its West African antecedents and provide a sense of how it functioned as a domestic/religious sphere for the construction of an extended spiritual family. The focal point of the Laventille yard (like Shango yards in general) was the chapelle, which, as a container of spiritual power, oriented the ceremonial drummers and dancers and sustained the religious community as a whole. In contrast to this enclosed space, the tent was an open area for public ceremonies at which both participants and visitors were welcome. Here the religious family was periodically renewed and expanded through performances. Finally, the yard's houses and kitchen provided living space for the group's priestess and others. As a locale that was conceptualized, designed and managed by Afro-Trinidadian working people, the Shango yard contrasted sharply with much of the landscape of Port of Spain, especially the central city with its grid layout, elite-controlled public and commercial spaces and exploitative barrack housing. Within the yard, people honoured African deities and ancestors; recreated African forms of verbal, musical, choreographic and visual expression; healed the afflicted; and built a supportive community. As an alternative realm of knowledge, aesthetics and action, the Laventille yard and similar compounds around the city existed at the edge of the British colonial system and were sources of local empowerment complementary to the worker demonstrations and organizing that characterized Trinidad during the upheavals of the 1930s.[51]

5. THE SPATIALITY OF CARNIVAL

EVERY YEAR DURING THE INTERWAR ERA, masqueraders, musicians and spectators filled the streets of Port of Spain in celebration of the festival of Carnival on the two days before Ash Wednesday. There were bands of devils, with scampering imps taunting chained beasts; bats in tight faux-fur outfits and enormous wings; clowns dressed in ludicrous assemblages of disparate materials; Wild Indians who danced in serpentine lines and sang in esoteric "languages"; Midnight Robbers who delivered speeches on their destructive careers and demanded payments in lieu of further harm; Yankee Minstrels sporting stylish suits and performing versions of American "plantation songs"; bad-behaviour sailors who rolled on the ground to soil their white uniforms and accost observers; and groups whose elaborate costumes portrayed everything from ancient civilizations to visions of the future. Masqueraders moved in all directions through the city to the sounds of rhythms beaten with pieces of bamboo and metal; the strumming of guitars and banjos; the melodies of flutes and clarinets; and crowds singing the refrains of popular calypsoes. Along with these street festivities, the city's populace held numerous Carnival-season balls in social clubs, hotels and private homes, where costumed attendees danced to music provided by bands ranging from small ensembles to the top orchestras of the land. With thousands of people travelling to Port of Spain from other districts in Trinidad or abroad, the city became an annual centre of mass revelry – a site for exceptional freedom of movement, consumption and expression.

This variety of Carnival activity was staged and understood by the local population in terms of spatial distinctions within the city. While outdoor spaces offered greater possibilities for physical mobility, diverse social encounters and a multiplicity of sights and sounds, indoor venues provided more contained and predictable experiences. In addition, there were contrasts during the interwar era between revelry in the crowded downtown commercial district and at the more spacious and genteel Queen's Park Savannah. As they engaged in their annual celebrations, different sectors of the society negotiated the use and significance of this range of urban spaces. Some activities displayed social boundaries and differentiation, while others involved unusual interactions and convergences. Though there was much innovation in the Carnival of the interwar years, patterns of differentiation and interaction were derived from festive traditions that emerged during Trinidad's pre-emancipation era and developed during the latter nineteenth and early twentieth centuries.

THE DEVELOPMENT OF CARNIVAL

Before the abolition of slavery in the 1830s, the European elite in Trinidad held masquerade balls and engaged in house-to-house visiting and street promenades during the several-week-long Carnival season that preceded Ash Wednesday. Free people of colour followed similar customs within their own circles, while enslaved Africans were generally excluded from participation in the festival except by special invitation as performers. By the 1830s, however, Africans were holding their own Carnival dances and street processions, and, in the years after 1838, they gradually took over the street celebration of the festival. At this point, Europeans and the mixed-descent middle class largely withdrew from street activities but continued to engage in house visits and indoor dances. By 1847 the street Carnival was, in the description of a traveller, a "squalid splendour": bands of ten to twenty individuals, nearly naked and coated with black varnish; a man fettered with a padlock and long chain; revellers wearing white masks and carrying hardwood sticks; groups of women with bodices of distinguishing colours; individual masqueraders such as Pulcinellas, pirates and Turks; a personification of Death with horse bones; South American Indian figures played by immigrant workers from the Spanish Main; and even an occasional white man in a black mask.[1]

By the 1860s and 1870s, the Carnival was performed in Port of Spain's streets primarily by *jamettes* (*diamètres*) – a term used at the time to refer to people who lived beneath the "diameter" of respectability. During this period of extensive movement to the city, both from rural areas of Trinidad and from neighbouring Caribbean territories, migrants crowded into the barrack yards of the central city or found marginal housing in the surrounding districts. While some of this population was able to secure regular employment, jamettes typically lived off occasional jobs, petty crime, prostitution and gambling. As they settled into their new urban environment, they organized themselves into bands associated with particular neighbourhoods. In the late 1870s, for example, there were s'Amandes from the wharves, Bois d'Inde from eastern Prince Street, Cerf-Volants from Duncan Street, Bakers from near the Eastern Market, Danois from near the Dry River, Peau de Canelle from the uptown Royal Gaol area, Maribones from Belmont, Free-grammar from Corbeaux

Town, and Corail from New Town. The bands included kings, queens and other hierarchical positions, and were roughly divided into two sectors: the predominantly French Creole-speaking population on the eastern side of Port of Spain (known as the "French Shores") and an increasingly English-speaking population on the western side, with Henry Street serving as a dividing line. Essentially, the jamettes created an urban underworld, with its own spatial organization, economy, social groupings and expressive styles that contrasted with the values and aesthetics of the colonial culture of respectability.[2]

Long-standing rivalries between the jamette bands often erupted in violence during Carnival Monday and Tuesday. One vehicle for the expression of these feuds was *kalinda* – a traditional configuration of stickfighting, dance and music that was widely practised in Trinidad during the nineteenth century. At various times throughout the year, people gathered in yards to watch successive pairs of combatants engage each other with hardwood sticks in movements of attack and defence that involved choreography but frequently had bloody results. Musical accompaniment for the fights included a *chantwell* (lead singer) and chorus performing call-and-response songs in French Creole with a battery of African-derived drums. The most elaborate manifestation of kalinda occurred during Carnival. From midnight of Carnival Sunday until dawn of Carnival Monday, the city's jamette bands engaged in a custom known as *Canboulay*, which consisted of stickfighters and their supporters moving through the streets with torches, sticks, drums and other percussion instruments. When two bands met, their lead stickfighters entered into an initial round of combat, which was then followed by fights between other contestants. Stickfighting was also connected with the performances of Pierrots, a Carnival masque that probably had a historical relation to the European clown of the same name, but which Trinidadians developed into a figure who was both elegant and belligerent, rather than comical. The Pierrot costume consisted of a satin gown constructed of triangular pieces of various colours, tipped with small bells; a heart-shaped breastpiece with such ornaments as sequins, spangles or small mirrors; a headpiece comprising a protective iron pot covered by a velvet beret; and a long multicoloured satin train, carried by an attendant. Like stickfighting bands, Pierrots were territorially based. When encountering each other, they first exchanged elaborate, boastful speeches composed from Shakespearean orations or excerpts of other English literature. They then typically engaged in combat with whips, followed by sticks; for protection, each contestant wound his satin train around one arm to form a shield.[3]

While most stickfighters and Pierrots were men, women played an active role in jamette bands as singers, supporters and sometimes combatants. During the nighttime Canboulay in 1868, for example, there were several bands of predominantly women parading the streets in "fantastic costumes": Mousseline, Dahlia, Black Ball, Don't-Care-a-Damn, Magenta, Maribone and True Blue. The Mousselines, led by Mamselle Janette, were dancing on Duke Street when they were attacked by the Dahlias, led by Elizabeth Simmons. Both bands were armed with sticks in what appears to have been an east-side (French Creole) versus west-side (English) confrontation. During the latter nineteenth century, there were also many other famous female jamettes, such as Bodicea, Piti Belle Lily, Alice Sugar, Annie Coals and Myrtle the Turtle. According to one legend, Annie Coals and Myrtle the Turtle fought over the grave of the well-known chantwell Hannibal the Mulatto after his death in 1873. When a crowd assembled at the cemetery, Bodicea composed an impromptu song, tore off her dress and led the group in a provocative dance.[4]

The jamette Carnival generated extensive condemnation from the upper and middle classes, and by the late 1870s, a new police chief, Captain Baker, was determined to suppress it. After a few years of government efforts to curtail stickfights, the French Creole-speaking and English-speaking jamette bands joined together for the Canboulay of 1881 to attack the police force, when it tried to seize their sticks and torches. A three-hour battle ensued in the eastern downtown streets between several hundred jamettes and 150 policemen, with 38 of the latter being injured. Around 3:30 a.m., many of the police returned to their barracks, but tensions remained high. After the borough council asked for conciliation, the governor visited the Eastern Market in the late afternoon and addressed a crowd of Carnival revellers, assuring them that if they remained peaceful, the police would not trouble them for the remainder of the festival. The next year's Carnival was peaceful, but a resurgence of violence in 1883 led to the passing in 1884 of a Peace Preservation Ordinance, which empowered the governor to prohibit by proclamation torch processions, drumming, dances and assemblies of ten or more people with sticks.[5]

While stickfighting and drumming continued during the Carnival season, the Peace Preservation Ordinance essentially eliminated Canboulay processions from the early Monday morning of the Carnival and paved the way for further regulations during the 1890s, such as a requirement that the combative Pierrots apply for permits and a ban on a "pissenlit" masque that was considered obscene. Meanwhile, Ignacio Bodu, a businessman, began holding organized masquerade competitions in Marine Square with the objective of improving the moral and aesthetic quality of Carnival. With the curtailment of the jamette dimensions of the festival after 1884, the middle and upper classes began to reappear on the streets, especially in horse-drawn carriages and, by the early twentieth century, cars and lorries (trucks). A popular custom for these masqueraders was to drive about in their decorated vehicles and engage in mock battles by throwing confetti. During this same period, there appears to have been an increase in upper- and middle-class participation in masquerade balls and dances in halls and private residences during the Carnival season. One elite setting for fancy-dress balls was the Queen's Park Hotel; in 1907 the *Port-of-Spain Gazette* reported on its decorated ballroom, prizes for best costumes and such masqueraders as a prehistoric man, cowboy, toreador, Cleopatra, Egyptian woman, Early Victoria and Welsh girl. In 1910 the newspaper noted what would have been a humbler affair: a fancy-dress dance at the Trinidad Mutual Friendly Society Hall, with masqueraders including Japanese, Chinese, gypsies, sailors, ranchmen, Rajah Tourists and Rose of Sharon.[6]

By the turn of the century, the Carnival was also attracting the interest of a small number of American tourists and journalists. In 1901 a correspondent and a photographer for *Collier's Weekly* documented the festival in Port of Spain and spent much of their time at the Ice House Hotel, on the advice that this Marine Square location was a good vantage point for observing the event. On Monday morning, the pair watched a group of clowns pass the hotel and later saw an ensemble of minstrels that included a man in a cutaway suit playing a violin, a second man with a guitar and a third dancing on stilts (a masque known as *moko jumbie*), as well as a few women who, with matching dresses and powdered skin, beat tambourines and tin pans. After this performance, the stilt dancer bent down to collect donations in his hat before the group moved on to its next audience. The *Collier's* correspondent also described activities inside the hotel:

> The Ice House was a hotel, with the barroom and the ballroom combined in one large hall on the first story. As we ascended the stairs there were many people both going up and coming down, and from above could be heard the sound of loud talking, and music, and strained laughter. The hall was filled with Carnival folk. The air was hot, and smelled strong of cheap perfume and cigarette smoke.

An orchestra in the centre of the room played continuously, while "the women in their short skirts whirled about in a crazy kind of dance" and "the men danced with the women, or wandered about aimlessly, or drank at the bar". The room's doors and windows were open to the balcony, where revellers who had had too much were sleeping in chairs. In general comments on activity across the downtown area, the correspondent noted that the streets were "densely thronged with people" and that there "seemed to be no one in authority to govern the proceedings of the Carnival".[7]

While Carnival continued to be performed both in the streets and in indoor venues, by the early twentieth century a new type of intermediate festive space had emerged: the Carnival-band tent. Each season masquerade bands built these structures in barrack yards or other available spaces for the purpose of gathering members and rehearsing songs that they would sing on the streets during Carnival Monday and Tuesday. Frames were constructed from bamboo poles, while roofs were typically made of coconut-palm branches. Charles Jones, an early twentieth-century chantwell/calypsonian known as the "Duke of Albany", provides a sense of these venues:

> [They were built] of bamboo, with coconut palms for a roof, lovely lace curtains, with ribbons to hold them in place and in the centre of the Tent, on a table set there for that purpose, a lovely bowl of Roses or other Flowers. For seats there were benches made of bamboo set around the Tent or a few chairs. There were no electric lights. In place of that lamps made of tin or large bottles called Flambeaux were placed all around the tent, giving a lovely soft glow to the surroundings.

Money for constructing tents was commonly provided by prominent citizens who enjoyed Carnival music, and well-to-do men often attended the Carnival band rehearsals. During these events, a chantwell stood on a chair, box or other platform in the tent and taught the band choruses for the season's new songs. These songs often dealt with recent local events, as did other songs that the chantwell might perform after the rehearsal period. In addition, chantwells sometimes visited each other's tents and engaged in contests of song. At the end of the evening, a tent's band passed around a "bouquet" – a tray with fresh flowers on which people could make donations.[8]

The songs performed in these tents typically had multiline stanzas and were accompanied by ensembles that included flute, clarinet, violin, guitar, cuatro (a small four-stringed guitar) and bass – instrumentation that was also common in nearby Venezuela. Though French Creole was the primary language of traditional song at the turn of the century, masquerade-band chantwells increasingly composed their songs in English. They also often employed grandiloquent rhetoric, which resembled the bombastic orations of Pierrots. This emerging song form contrasted with the call-and-response singing led by chantwells during stickfights in yards or when stickfighting bands paraded the streets during Carnival. Kalinda songs had shorter stanzas, often used French Creole, and, after skin drums became less common, were accompanied by tamboo bamboo, ensembles consisting of different-sized pieces of bamboo that were struck or stamped as percussion instruments. String-band songs in English had a higher social status than kalinda songs in French Creole. However, the two forms were interrelated, both drew on other Trinidadian and Caribbean musical genres, and both were increasingly referred to as "calypso" (with various pronunciations and spellings) during the early years of the twentieth century.[9]

Prominent masquerade bands of the early twentieth century were typically called "social unions" and favoured fancy costumes. Carnival advertisements from leading stores of this period provide a sense of the composition of these outfits. In 1907, for example, Wilsons Limited advertised such materials as coloured prints, muslins, velvets, plushes, silks, satins, gold and silver tinsel, trimmings, flowers, feathers and ribbons; the Smith Brothers' Bonanza store featured many of these same items, as well as wire, cloth and paper masks, Yankee hats, gladiator helmets, gold and silver crowns and coronets, striped stockings, beads and spangles, Japanese kimonos and clown suits. Among the best-known fancy masquerade bands of this period were Artillery, Standard, Calvary and White Rose. According to Charles Jones, Artillery's chantwell (Henry Forbes) wore a "lovely costume of velvet, with his sword, gloves on, cape thrown over his right shoulder, and like other chantrels a lovely plume in his hat". The band's king and queen wore majestic outfits and glittering crowns, while other members were dressed in identically coloured costumes of "the best silk obtainable". When two fancy masquerade bands met on the streets during the Carnival, their chantwells challenged each other with song verses. The bands also competed for prizes at masquerade competitions sponsored by merchants on Marine Square, as well as by other establishments such as the Petit Glaciere Bar on Chacon Street. In 1908, for example, the Bonanza held a competition in Marine Square that attracted fourteen bands, and awarded first prize to the Tiger Cat Social Union of Belmont. This band carried a painted banner proclaiming that it was the king of Belmont and depicting a tiger tearing the flesh of a lion. The image was a reference to a rival Belmont band – the Crown Lion Social Union, which won third prize and carried a banner with an illustration of a dead tiger at the feet of a lion and the legend: "Here lies all that remains of tigercats."[10]

Second prize at the Bonanza's 1908 competition went to Khaki and Slate, a band of devils wearing costumes in colours that reflected its name. According to barrister and Carnival researcher Bruce Procope, Khaki and Slate was formed as the first devil band by Patrick Jones and Gilbert Scamaroni in 1906 and consisted of sixty to seventy men and women in "jab jab" costumes: the men in close-fitting merino overalls with horns, tails and wings, and the women in scalloped satin dresses. The band also included "presidents" in costumes with additional ornamentation and a Lucifer who wore a crown. In 1909 Jones co-organized a red dragon band and in 1910 formed Demonites, which included a Beelzebub (enclosed in a cage and bound with chains) and a dragon that was carried in the air on poles. In 1911 Jones introduced Satan, who carried a book and pen "to record sins". Various other devil bands were also established during this period. With their retinue of characters, these bands devised elaborate choreographies that they rehearsed in their tents and performed on the streets during the Carnival. Devil bands were particularly popular with masqueraders into the 1920s and have continued to have a presence in the Carnival since then.[11]

Fancy-dress bands, devils, clowns, sailors, Indians and various other masqueraders actively participated in the merchant-sponsored competitions that were intended to "improve" the Carnival during the early twentieth century. Meanwhile, stickfighters, along with their tamboo-bamboo accompanists and other supporters, also continued to appear in spite of efforts to suppress them. Much stickfighting took place in city yards during the weeks leading up to the Carnival. In 1933 a writer calling himself "Mask" contributed an article to the *Trinidad Guardian* in which he recollected Carnival activities of the early twentieth century. He noted that stick contests were held within a ring enclosed by a bamboo fence and added:

> Holes about 9 inches in diameter were dug all around the fighting arena; and liberal supplies of ordinary table salt placed around each. These were the blood holes. As soon as a combatant received a cut on the head or face, he went to one of these holes, and let the blood flow into it. He would then apply a handful of the salt to the wound, tie it up, and return to the ring for revenge.

Mask also described a "dangerous game" played only by experts: a coin was placed on the ground and several stickfighters surrounded it with the objective of picking it up. The combatants might engage in strikes and parries for hours without anyone successfully retrieving the coin.

Stickfighting bands also ventured onto the streets during the Carnival itself. In an article published in *The Beacon* in 1932, Joseph Belgrave recalls that "the men of the different bands from Belmont, Corbeau Town, Tie-pins (those from George Street and that vicinity), and also from other districts paraded the streets carrying sticks. They wore beautifully decorated costumes made of velvet, whilst some of them wore tweed or flannel trousers, silk shirts and silk handkerchiefs with pieces of ribbon attached to their trousers or shirts." In 1907 the *Port-of-Spain Gazette* had reported on a court case involving one such stickfighter – a man named Arthur Betty. On early Carnival Monday morning that year, the St James, Woodbrook, Man-o'-war and Rosehillan stick bands joined forces and paraded the streets, led by Betty and five other men dressed as *negres jardin* (another name for the elegant costume worn by stickfighters). Around 10:00 a.m., at the corner of Henry and Queen Streets, they engaged in a fight with the powerful Typin band of George Street, defeated them and "caused them to retire in disorder". Though the combined band was repeatedly warned by the police to end their disturbance, they meandered through the streets until they reached the vicinity of the Queen's Park Savannah, where they attacked the Belmont band. Here they were again confronted by the police, who managed to capture only Betty. Though he pleaded not guilty, Betty was convicted and sentenced to three months' imprisonment with hard labour.[12]

During the early twentieth century, the press routinely criticized the Carnival not only for its disorder and violence but also for what were described as lewd gestures and dances and sordid, meaningless or monotonous song lyrics. Moreover, many masquerades were perceived as lacking "picturesqueness". Condemnation of the Carnival was particularly strong in the articles and editorials of the *Port-of-Spain Gazette*, a publication associated with the French-creole elite and the leading newspaper of the era. At times the *Gazette* even argued that, if the objectionable elements of the Carnival could not be eliminated, the event should be abolished altogether, though it also appeared to recognize that such action would be virtually impossible, given how deeply the festival was rooted in popular tradition. After the chaotic 1907 festivities, the *Gazette* editorialized:

> The Carnival has been celebrated this year with a good deal of vulgar animation. . . . Fighting with sticks, stones and bottles was in evidence in more than one place and there was, worse than all, the indecent behaviour of the women in the streets who seemed to imagine that because their faces were hidden they had unbridled licence to misconduct themselves. The effect of the Carnival is, we are sorry to say, debasing. The minds of the younger ones are demoralised and polluted by the disgraceful scenes witnessed in the streets and other public places. . . . The tourists who were here on Monday saw the populace at its worst. They witnessed the debaucheries at the restaurants and the unseemly contortions in the streets and in fact the impressions they took away could not have been flattering to the community as a whole. Some of these scenes were in our knowledge snapshotted and will be used against Trinidad's people in future.

Indeed, more than two hundred tourists had arrived in Trinidad and were seen observing and photographing the Carnival around the city. During this period, civic leaders were trying to attract more American tourists to the island, and the *Gazette* continued to voice its concern that these efforts would be undermined by unrestrained Carnival revelry, even while noting that the visitors appeared to be "enjoying themselves immensely".[13] In addition, the increasing affordability of portable cameras meant that visitors could create and disseminate their own images of Port of Spain – images that might challenge the photographs of elegant public buildings and other orderly scenes sold through postcards and guidebooks.

On the Sunday before Carnival in 1910, the *Gazette* said in an editorial that it again expected the Carnival to be "tawdry, common place and barbarously vulgar". It then posed the question of why Carnival still existed and answered: "There is such a thing as going too far in interfering with the liberties of the common people, especially when the classes above them would have to be allowed their masquerade dances and other amusements outside the streets." The newspaper also voiced doubts about the effectiveness of masquerade competitions in improving the Carnival, arguing that these events "have had absolutely no effect on the moral tone of the Carnival, but have simply improved some of the costumes slightly". In preparation for the 1912 Carnival, the *Gazette* published an editorial that referenced recommendations by a "correspondent" for a more substantial remedy:

> Our correspondent suggests that a Committee of ladies and gentlemen should take the Carnival in hand and "organise competitions to take place on the Savannah on masquerade days between costume bands, donkey riders, chorus and glee-singers, string-bands, decorated carts and carriages. Also chariot races, a Spanish floral tournament and anything else that would render the meeting attractive: only approved bands to be admitted within the racing enclosure." In our correspondent's opinion this would draw the rabble from the dusty streets and the vicinity of rum shops and barrack yards and afford to all concerned a much more healthy and wholesome form of amusement. The trouble is that the great majority of those who support the Carnival by active participation therein do not want to be drawn away from the vicinity referred to above. They want to make the Carnival an orgy, which for years they have succeeded in doing.

So, with these editorials,[14] the *Gazette* acknowledged that there were two realms of Carnival: the festival performed by the masses in the crowded streets of downtown and the celebrations of the middle and upper classes that were held principally in indoor venues (but which also involved riding through the streets in vehicles). The popular street Carnival could not be abolished if the indoor Carnival were permitted to continue. Thus the intriguing suggestion of the correspondent: why not recreate Carnival as a wholesome family affair in the spacious and beautiful Queen's Park Savannah? Here the festival would be surrounded by elegant homes, the Prince's Building, the Queen's Park Hotel, Government House and the Botanic Gardens, rather than the rum shops, barrack yards and other unsightly spaces of downtown. Surely such a setting would advance civic leaders' efforts at improving the moral and aesthetic tone of the event. The *Gazette* had doubts, however, as to whether the people would participate in a Savannah Carnival.

MASQUERADES DURING THE INTERWAR ERA

In fact, downtown-versus-Savannah concepts of Carnival became a central tension in the festival in the years after World War I. Essentially, much of the Trinidadian elite advocated a reconstruction of Carnival at the Savannah, while a majority of middle- and working-class supporters of the festival continued to affirm its traditional downtown location. The controversy emerged in January 1919, when, after wartime restrictions on the street celebration of the 1917 and 1918 Carnivals, it became apparent that Governor John Chancellor might again issue prohibitions against the festival. Fearing an ongoing curtailment of the rights of the people to engage in their customary street revelry, a group of concerned citizens organized a delegation to meet with the governor to assure him that the Carnival could be held without disorder. Among the several delegates were James Wharton, manager of the *Argos* newspaper; Arthur Raymond, the newspaper's editor; and Dr A.H. McShine. Meanwhile, Emmanuel Mzumbo Lazare, a prominent attorney and another member of this circle, suggested the idea of organizing the festival in the Savannah, where it could be more effectively contained and controlled. Though Lazare's suggestion raised concerns among his colleagues, it appealed to the governor and was picked up by the *Trinidad Guardian*, which began planning a "Victory Carnival" at the Savannah. Popular opposition to a Savannah Carnival quickly swelled, with the *Argos* taking the lead in organizing the Downtown Carnival.[15] Both groups were committed to creating an orderly, disturbance-free festival and to "improving" the event by rewarding costumes that were inoffensive and of high aesthetic quality. To this end, both committees organized formal masquerade competitions, with downtown dry-goods merchants in particular supporting prizes for the Carnival of their district and Major Randolph Rust (an oilman and civic leader) and other prominent businessmen supporting the Savannah Carnival. During the following weeks, an intense rivalry played out between the two newspapers and interest groups over the location, character and future of the Carnival.

In order to mobilize its supporters, the *Argos* Carnival committee organized a series of meetings on Prince Street at the Hall of the Faithful Brothers of the Souls in Purgatory Friendly Society (the hall's overhanging first-floor gallery was adorned with flags and the word "Victory" illuminated by coloured electric lightbulbs). In a report on the final meeting, the newspaper said: "The hall was packed to its utmost capacity with an enthusiastic gathering of all classes, including ladies, which is an undoubted sign of the whole hearted manner in which the people are supporting the ARGOS Carnival scheme." Among the speakers was Alfred Richards, who argued that if the people played Carnival in the Savannah, they would be surrendering their rights and would be forced to carry out their masquerades at this location every year. His speech received a lively response from the audience:

> They were not going to walk from Marine Square up to the savannah to exhibit themselves to those who were not their friends. (Hear, hear.) . . . They must not be led by those who do not appreciate their mode of Carnival. Those who advised

them to go up to the savannah did nothing for them during the 4½ years of war. (Hear, hear.) (A voice: Correct illustration sir.) Did they think that those strangers could teach them to play Carnival? (No-o-o-o)

In addition to its public meetings, the *Argos* ran advertisements, such as: "The 'Argos' Competition. Play Your Carnival as in the Good Old Days. Join the Argos Competition in and around Marine Square. Enjoy Your Carnival Down Town."[16]

Meanwhile, the *Trinidad Guardian* vigorously promoted its campaign for a Carnival at the Savannah. Masquerade competitions were to be held at the grandstand, which was lent to the Savannah Carnival committee by the Trinidad Turf Club, the colony's elite horse-racing organization. On the Sunday before Carnival Monday, the newspaper proclaimed: "The Victory Carnival of 1919 begins tomorrow and will be an epoch-making day in the annals of this Colony's history . . . it shall mark the period where the Trinidad Carnival ceased from being a disorganised and inane revelry and became a picturesque and edifying spectacle worthy of support and of the fair reputation of the Island." It added that "no place seems so suited for displaying the bands to the best advantage as Port-of-Spain's spacious beauty spot, the Queen's Park Savannah" and that spectators would be able "to view the competition without the discomfort and sense of suffocation which arise as a necessary result when the competitions are held in the commercial portions of the town". The *Guardian* claimed that a large number of masquerade bands had registered for its competition and noted that it was not expecting bands to abandon the Downtown Carnival but to participate in the festivities at both locations.[17]

Perhaps the least biased accounts of the results of the 1919 Carnival were provided by the *Port-of-Spain Gazette*. In a report on Carnival Monday activities, the *Gazette* said: "The 'Argos' Scores. 'Guardian's' Up-Town Idea Falls Flat." While the competition at Marine Square attracted many masquerade bands and a large and orderly crowd of observers, the Savannah Carnival was poorly attended. On Carnival Tuesday, masses of people again gathered downtown, while only a few bands appeared at the Savannah later in the afternoon. The *Guardian*, however, did have success with its planned parade on Tuesday night of decorated cars and other vehicles filled with affluent revellers. The manager of the Trinidad Electric Company had coordinated the construction of arches (illuminated with hundreds of multicoloured lights) along the southern perimeter of the Savannah from Cipriani Boulevard to Charlotte Street. After nightfall, the procession of vehicles through the arches and around the Savannah attracted a large crowd of spectators.[18]

During the 1920s, advocates of a Savannah Carnival further pursued efforts to employ the park as a spacious and comfortable alternative to the congestion, dust and heat of the Downtown Carnival, which continued to thrive. By 1924 and 1925, when the Savannah Carnival competition was organized by the *Sporting Chronicle* newspaper, participation by masqueraders was growing, especially on Carnival Tuesday. Both the *Trinidad Guardian* and the *Port-of-Spain Gazette* voiced strong support for Carnival activities in the Savannah, while also acknowledging that downtown would remain a popular site. In an editorial in 1924, for example, the *Gazette* said it did not accept the common opinion that masqueraders preferred the downtown streets close to their homes and would never venture to the Savannah. In calling for further improvement of the festival for both residents and visitors, the paper affirmed the use of the park, at least on Tuesday. In an editorial in 1925, the *Guardian* reminded its readers that six years earlier, it had said, "The Queen's Park Savannah with its ample space and central situation has no superior for suitability of purpose and beauty of scene in any city in the world." It noted that its recommendations for an improved Carnival were now being fulfilled, especially in the "picturesqueness" of masqueraders' processions around the Savannah in decorated cars and lorries.[19]

By the 1930s the geography of a Downtown and a Savannah Carnival was well established, with each sphere comprising a variety of outdoor and indoor spaces for festivity. Marine Square, Frederick Street and the surrounding downtown streets remained the traditional centre of the festival and the site of the densest crowds and most intense artistic displays (see figure 21). While Carnival officially began at 6:00 a.m. on Monday, some revellers in "ole mas" (old masquerade) outfits frequently appeared on the streets before this hour. "Ole mas" was a broad concept that encompassed a variety of types of old or outlandish costumes. Some people simply wore rags or bizarre assemblages of garments, while others cross-dressed as men or women or made satirical statements with props and signs. Also popular were impersonations of various characters, ranging from policemen to Bajan (Barbadian) cooks, deserted mothers seeking child support (with babe in arms), and shoe-shiners (who requested payment for mimed shines). As the sun rose, the performers of various traditional masquerades appeared, following well-established patterns of costuming, choreography and vocalization. There were clowns (in bizarre costumes constructed with multifarious elements), bats (with wingspans exceeding 10 feet) and the ever-popular devil or dragon bands. In reference to the latter, the *Trinidad Guardian* noted Bad Demons indulging in "amusing cries and stunts" in 1933, and in 1934 described the Hell Population band, which included His Satanic Majesty (carrying a giant key) and a "fearsome-looking creature, in black and gold scales" restrained by chains. Also on the streets in 1934 were Sons of Demons – "a sinister-looking band, resplendent in purple and gold", accompanied by "a monster in gold scales who disported himself on the ground in a most realistic fashion." Bruce Procope discusses how dragon bands often engaged in a choreographed performance known as "Crossing the Water". When encountering a gutter containing water, a band's imps provoked their chained beast into crossing it. After much hesitation, the creature accomplished the crossing with an acrobatic leap and thus, as a fiery creature of hell, avoided contact with water. A favourite spot for this performance was the corner of Frederick and Duke Streets.[20]

Several traditional masquerades involved significant American influences, acquired through print publications and movies, encounters with visitors to Trinidad or travels to the United States. Among these were Midnight Robbers, which emerged from Trinidadian portrayals of American cowboys during the early twentieth century and were common by the interwar era. Dressed in black outfits with broad-brimmed hats and capes, these fearsome figures sported fake guns and daggers and delivered elaborate speeches in which they boasted of their exploits and threatened their rivals. Also common were Yankee Minstrel masquerades, which were based on turn-of-the-century American minstrel shows and performed by Afro-Trinidadians in elegant suits and blackface or whiteface. For example, the *Argos* mentioned the Mobilean Yankee Band, USA Yankee Band and Columbian Yankee Band in 1920, while the *Trinidad Guardian* noted in 1924 that several bands of minstrels delivered "the latest hits and coon songs". (That year the paper also reported a Ku Klux Klan band with white gowns, headdresses and masks, as well as mock weapons.) A photograph in the *Guardian* in 1939 shows a group of minstrels in whiteface, with black-and-white suits and canes; a caption adds that they performed hit songs. Another popular portrayal of this era was millionaires, inspired by the growing number of tourists visiting Trinidad. Male masqueraders often sported flannel pants and Panama hats, females wore flannel skirts and carried handbags, and both pinned dollar bills of various denominations on their outfits. Finally, sailor bands became increasingly common as the century progressed. Though these masquerades were modelled on the navies of various countries, American sailors made a particularly strong impression. Large bands of masqueraders in sailor uniforms represented the various personnel and activities of US Navy ships, while "bad-behaviour" bands parodied the drunken antics of sailors on shore leave, such as falling on the ground or harassing ladies. In a 1930 letter to the editor of the *Port-of-Spain Gazette*, a lorry-rider thanked the police for banning sailors from attacking "respectable people" with animal bladders, while in 1933 the *Guardian* noted a bad-behaviour sailors' band that "rolled on the ground, then rose and sang a refrain".[21]

Also popular during the 1930s were "historical" and "original" masquerade bands. Historical bands portrayed scenes from around the world, from ancient to recent times. A few well-received presentations in 1934 were

Tut-Ank-Amen's Mummies, which carried a pyramid from which emerged a golden-faced mummy; Greek Soldiers, featuring Helen of Troy and a Trojan Horse; and Punjabi Defenders of the Empire, who wore turbans, waistcoats and pantaloons, and sang "Rule, Britannia!" Original masquerade bands typically addressed contemporary topics or were constructions of fantasy. In 1939 a band that attracted much attention was Slum Clearance, in which a group of children portrayed relocating slum dwellers and sang, "It is Morvant we going." They were accompanied by a "medical officer of health", "sanitary inspector" and "policeman" who maintained order.[22]

During Carnival Monday and Tuesday, downtown filled with thousands of exuberant masqueraders and onlookers. While bands and other revellers moved in various directions through the crowded streets, Marine Square served as a focal point and a venue for masquerade competitions on both days. The primary competition, under the patronage of the mayor, was held at the northern end of Broadway, where a temporary stand was erected for spectators. During the 1930s, competitions were also held at the eastern end of the square or at Besson Street, two blocks further east. In 1933 the *Trinidad Guardian* reported:

> All traffic on the roads surrounding the Square was jammed. It was the greatest concourse of people ever seen in the district in its history.
> At times the great mob grew to such proportions that it was entirely beyond control.
> Police were helpless, but the people were nevertheless orderly.
> There was an incessant stream of people flowing from all parts of the town.
> All colours imaginable were in evidence – green and gold, and scarlet and yellow, and blue and red and white, crimson and scarlet, fresh and brilliant.

Among the prize-winning bands at the eastern Marine Square competition that year were Algerian Warriors, Punjabi Social Union, Dixie Boys, Three Star Comedians, Saracen Band, Eastern Sheiks, Bedouin Chiefs, Railroad Tourists, Texas Petty Officers Band, Flying Demons, Gipsy Girls, Mohammed the Great and His Moslems, Fruit Destroyers, Bad Behaviour Sailors, Good Samaritans, New World Hunters, Metro Clown Band, Afghanistan Chiefs, Rameses Egyptian Kings and Satan and his Red Dragons.[23]

While the Marine Square competitions attracted a cross-section of the city's population, the Hotel de Paris, on lower Abercromby Street, was a gathering spot for a more elite crowd as well as some grassroots masqueraders and singers. In 1933 the *Guardian*'s social columnist, "The Humming Bird", reported that old friends gathered here to be entertained by masked bands and calypso singers and noted that "the ballroom was thronged with young folk dancing the much-loved Trinidad 'breakdowns', to cheery music". The following year the newspaper described revellers playing ole mas at the Paris on Monday morning, filling the hotel's ballroom and palm court. Masquerades ranged from blue-faced minstrels performing plantation songs to individuals in costumes that combined a Cupid and Roman soldier. On Tuesday an upscale crowd returned to the hotel and the *Guardian*'s reporter commented: "What was a most bewildering feature of the morning was the rapidity with which people changed their personalities." A charming young woman ("decorously and smartly dressed") would disappear, and reappear fifteen minutes later as a disreputable and annoying ole-mas figure.[24]

While wealthier Trinidadians gathered at the Hotel de Paris or played masquerades in cars and lorries that offered a degree of isolation and protection when venturing into the centre of the city, many preferred to celebrate Carnival at the Queen's Park Savannah, which by the 1930s was attracting a wider cross-section of masqueraders. At the Savannah, the Trinidad Turf Club's grandstand was the site of the "Carnival Pageant", a competition that was staged under the patronage of the governor and featured a similar range of masquerade bands and individuals to those who appeared at the downtown competitions: devils, bats, clowns, Indians, Midnight Robbers, Yankee Minstrels, millionaires, sailors and a variety of historical and original portrayals. In the late afternoon, activities at the grandstand were complemented by the popular parade around the Savannah's perimeter of decorated cars and lorries, filled with well-to-do masqueraders who engaged in "warfare" with each other and spectators by throwing confetti and streamers. In 1939 the *Trinidad Guardian* observed: "Some of the decorated lorries are astonishingly elaborate works of art. Some are constructed to resemble ships, some castles, some airplanes. Dozens of boys and girls in pretty allegorical costumes man these artistically decorated 'floats' and vigorously do battle with people who stand on balconies and stands, and hurl harmless missiles at the masqueraders."[25] While some lorries represented historical or original themes, others advertised the goods of local merchants. Advertising bands and individual masqueraders were also common downtown, as stores took advantage of the publicity afforded by large crowds of Carnival revellers.

Processions in lorries and cars were a popular and relatively safe mode of Carnival festivity for the upper and middle classes, but equally important were indoor dances that were held in the weeks preceding Carnival, as well as on Carnival Monday and Tuesday. Such dances enabled celebrations with peers in contained spaces, removed from the congestion, social diversity and unpredictability of the outdoor Carnival. Among the most prestigious balls were those held at the Prince's Building and Queen's Park Hotel on the south side of the Savannah and at the Country Club, less than a mile to the northwest of the park. The Country Club organized its premier dance for the season on the Carnival Saturday. In 1934 this coincided with the opening of a new ballroom by the governor and dancing to two twelve-piece orchestras: Roy Rollock's band and MacLean's Jazz Hounds. The Humming Bird's account of the Country Club's 1939 ball was especially effusive:

> The decorations that night surpassed anything Mr. Nothnagel and Miss Rostant have yet done for Carnival and struck a note as flamboyant and gay as the revelry in progress.
>
> Big triangular frames covered with multi-coloured paper decked the posts which were swathed with more coloured paper.
>
> The lights were most originally done with pink skirts and red sashes, and confetti, serpentines and balloons expressed the Carnival spirit reflected in the gay demeanour of the dancers.

The Country Club, like other indoor venues for Carnival balls, awarded prizes for the best masquerades. Contestants in 1939 included individuals portraying Crinoline Lady, Spanish Lady, Mussolini and Mechanical Man; couples representing Marie Antoinette and Louis XVI and Cuban Dancers; and bands playing Hungarian Gypsies, Snow White and the Seven Dwarfs and Cocoa Producers' Profits.[26]

On Carnival Monday night, the Prince's Building held an annual charity ball. In 1937 Governor and Lady Fletcher sat on a dais that was "transformed by the decorator into a miniature garden with a lawn and beds of anthurium lilies and roses, while the rest of the hall was made brilliant by twinkling lights and bunting". Prize-winning bands included Sultan and his Attendants, Buccaneers and Seaforth Highlanders. On Tuesday night (the "last lap" of Carnival), the Queen's Park Hotel held its main ball. In 1934 this event was attended by approximately eight hundred people, the majority in costume. During the Carnival season, dances were also organized at a variety of other indoor venues, such as the Portuguese Club, the Kosmos Club, the Maple Club, the Sailors and Soldiers' Club and Hotel Sand, as well as in many private homes. Attending a series of such dances was an exciting annual pastime for many upper- and middle-class Trinidadians.[27]

Though Carnival continued to be celebrated throughout Trinidad during the interwar era, Port of Spain remained its centre. For the main days of the festival, thousands of people from other districts crowded into trains, buses and cars to travel to the city, often in costume. In addition, a growing number of American tourists were attracted to the festival during the 1930s, as were visitors from other Caribbean territories, such as British Guiana, Barbados, Grenada, St Vincent, St Lucia and Dominica. In 1939 the *Trinidad Guardian* estimated that Port of Spain's population would increase threefold for the Carnival.[28] As the city developed as a popular destination for festivity and entertainment, the huge crowds brought growing benefits to hotels, restaurants, stores and the economy in general. In turn, civic leaders became increasingly concerned over visitors' perceptions of the Carnival and the city. Though there were various organizations for the development of Carnival during the 1930s, the government appointed in 1939 a permanent Carnival Improvement Committee, with a mandate to improve the "general tone" and management of the festival, advance competitions and control the content of calypsoes.[29] Much of the criticism of Carnival during this era involved denunciations of lewdness in some masquerades, dancing and calypso lyrics. A challenge was how to curtail objectionable elements without diminishing the licence for revelry and expression that many residents and visitors desired. The award of masquerade and calypso prizes was one way in which authorities attempted to steer the festival in preferred directions. Both downtown and Savannah competitions were managed by business and civic leaders and emphasized order and improvement, though the activities and experiences of Carnival at these two locales continued to differ during the 1930s. Downtown there was a larger working-class presence, dense crowds moving in multiple directions and more aggressive revelry, while at the Savannah wealthier sectors of the population could display themselves in the grandstand and in their cars and lorries with a greater level of comfort and security. However, the organizers of Carnival in both districts were committed to developing the festival as a clean and attractive spectacle for a city with expanding commercial prospects.

CALYPSO DURING THE INTERWAR ERA

The kaleidoscopic variety of costumes on the streets during Carnival was accompanied by an equally wide array of sounds: the singing, chanting and speeches of diverse masqueraders, along with the playing of myriad percussion, string and wind instruments. Within this cacophonous soundscape were the chantwells who led the members of the larger fancy masquerade bands in songs as they paraded around the city. As noted above, chantwells rehearsed these songs with their followers in Carnival-band tents in the weeks before Carnival Monday and Tuesday. In the years after World War I, however, some shifted from rehearsing band songs to performing programmes of their compositions for paying audiences. Such chantwells gradually became known as "calypsonians" and their venues were increasingly called "calypso tents". The more successful singers eventually broke away from masquerade bands and achieved reputations as independent artists, with grandiose sobriquets such as Lord Executor, Atilla the Hun, Roaring Lion and Growling Tiger. Each Carnival season, they earned income from performing their new calypsoes in tents and other venues, while for the rest of the year they typically sustained themselves through occasional concerts, assorted other jobs and the support of admirers. Calypsonians were popular figures in the street world of Port of Spain – stylish dressers, witty observers of the human condition and consummate showmen. Though many people valued their entertainment, guardians of propriety considered them disreputable and subversive.[30]

Throughout the interwar era, chantwells/calypsonians appeared in bamboo-frame tents that were temporarily erected each Carnival season in barrack yards and other open spaces around the city. Atilla recalls that construction was carried out by a *gayap* – an informal group of workers assembled for the occasion. Men often cut bamboo in the St Ann's hills to the north of the city, built their tent and then held a celebration when the work was completed. Lion suggests that bamboo and coconut branches were cut at groves nearest to the tent sites and similarly notes completion celebrations with rum, pelau and other dishes. The group that erected a tent was responsible for its disassembly at the end of the Carnival season.[31]

In 1919 a reporter for the *Trinidad Guardian* visited several tents and provided brief descriptions of venues on Woodford Street in the western neighbourhood of New Town and on George Street in the French Shores district on the east side of downtown:

> At Cavalry, Woodford Street, there was a marked display of enthusiasm. A large benab [shed] covered over with coconut branches and liberally decorated with flags and paper balloons had been erected on a spot opposite the A.M.E. Church. Inside the benab had been placed in neat rows along the sides several benches on which those who were privileged to gain admission were seated. A small charge of a couple of cents was exacted for entry, but this did not deter people from turning up in large numbers to listen to the airs which should prove exceedingly popular. Long before nine o'clock, the hour fixed for the proceedings to begin, spectators made their way to Woodford Street, so that when Mr. E. Briggs and his musicians opened their programme with a lively composition, fully four hundred persons surrounded the benab. The musical instruments of the band here consisted of four pieces – a violin, flute, quatro and guitar[,] their blending, soft and low, being very good indeed. Several prominent numbers of the community who were present, expressed themselves as being quite pleased with what they heard, the airs being principally patriotic. At George Street, [where] the "Bamboo Band" had also entrenched themselves under a coconut leaf covered hut, the crowd of spectators was not so large as in New Town, but what they lacked in members they made up for with their spirited approval of the tunes which were being rehearsed. Here the musical paraphernalia were confined to the popular "instruments" of the proletariat, which consisted of lengths of hollow reeds of bamboo, a small grater operated on by a musician with a stick, a "schack-schack" [gourd rattle], and the inevitable empty gin flask with a spoon as a beater.

Though the design of these two band tents appears to be roughly similar, the Woodford Street venue was clearly of higher status, given its west-side location and its employment of a string band (typically used to accompany the more elaborate form of English-language calypso). On the other hand, a *Guardian* reporter noted the following year the pleasure of strolling the French Shores after dark and listening to the sounds of calypso refrains accompanied by bamboo percussion. He added that the movements of the female dancers in the tents were particularly appealing and made a strong impression on the sailors, soldiers and other overseas visitors who regularly attended these venues.[32]

Carnival researcher Errol Hill argues that chantwell Chieftain Douglas's opening of a tent for his Railroad Millionaires band in 1921 marked an important moment in the conceptualization of these venues as devoted to calypso performances for audiences. Douglas's tent, at 26 Duncan Street in the French Shores, had a more elaborate design and more comfortable accommodation than previous structures. Though he still used bamboo for the tent frame, he constructed the roof with tarpaulins borrowed from the Government Railway (his daytime employer), rather than with palm fronds, which were susceptible to leaks when it rained and required sprinkling sawdust on the floor to mitigate mud. He also replaced the customary kerosene flambeau torches with gas lamps and rented three hundred chairs for his audience, instead of using bamboo benches. Douglas held performances between 8:00 and 10:00 p.m. three nights a week and advertised his shows through printed tickets, with a charge of six cents for a chair and four cents for standing room. At one end of the tent, there was a stage for the calypso singers and an ensemble consisting of a flute, clarinet, cuatro, guitar, bass and occasionally a violin. A chorus of approximately forty band members sat near the stage. Initially, Douglas himself would sing for the entire two hours, but in later years, he invited guest calypsonians to perform. Finally, Douglas positioned and lit his tent so that potential patrons could peer in from the street and assure themselves before entering that they would feel safe inside.[33]

During the 1920s, calypso tents and calypsonians received considerable support from middle- and upper-class individuals, both as audience members and general patrons. Lion recalls that business- and professional men assisted with the expenses of building tents, renting chairs, hiring musicians and advertising, which now included not only tickets, but leaflets, posters and town criers. Some of these men also served as managers of tents. Meanwhile, growing tent attendance and increasing ticket prices constituted a new stream of revenue that enabled the best calypsonians to earn some income during the Carnival season. From their interactions with prosperous patrons, calypsonians also obtained stories that they could use in composing songs. Calypso audiences thoroughly enjoyed songs about scandals involving affluent and powerful members of the society, though such compositions also inspired condemnation from elite commentators.³⁴

By the early 1930s, the builders of calypso tents were beginning to use galvanized-iron sheets for roofs, which provided even more protection from rain than Douglas's tarpaulins. However, it appears coconut branches were still used to provide partial covering on the sides of tents. Meanwhile, Lion notes an innovation in lighting to attract patrons:

> It was a lighted lantern on which the name of the tent was written and hung on the front gate, facing the street. The lantern was a three-cornered wooden structure, covered all around with transparent coloured paper; and inside of it was a piece of wood, about three inches in width, nailed across at the bottom. On this floor a candle was placed and the reflection of this light was seen some distance away.

During this period, Douglas continued to enhance his tent: in 1931 he moved from Nelson Street to 74 Henry Street, where he opened a venue (the "Crystal Palace") with a galvanized-iron roof and electric lights. In the midst of the 1933 Carnival season, however, he returned to Nelson Street, where he opened a tent a few doors away from the Salada Millionaires Syndicate tent, which featured Atilla and Lion. By this point, calypso tents each had a slate of calypsonians who took turns performing in the course of the evening. At the end of a show, performers often engaged in a "calypso war", during which they improvised verses of self-aggrandizement and denunciation of each other.³⁵

In January 1933 the English writer Owen Rutter visited Trinidad and stayed at the Queen's Park Hotel, where he met a young American woman who was attending calypso tents every evening. One night Rutter and the woman went to a tent on Henry Street where "a canvas enclosure had been rigged up, with bamboo supports and an iron roof covered with fronds of palm". The singers and accompanying ensemble performed from a platform stage, which was draped in red cloth that displayed "Tenant's Union" in white letters. A chorus of women in hats and silk dresses sat on benches at right angles to the stage. In front of the stage were chairs (where Rutter and his escort sat), while an area farther back, railed with bamboo, contained raised benches as cheaper seats. The next night Rutter went with *Beacon* writer Alfred Mendes to the Railroad Millionaires tent at 44 Nelson Street. The programme for the evening featured Douglas, Atilla, Lion, Inveigler, Albany and Controller, suggesting the Railroad Millionaires and Salada Millionaires calypsonians had been combined for this occasion. After the show, Rutter and Mendes continued their carousing on the town with stops at a dance hall and a fancy masquerade ball at the Hotel Gonzales. At the latter venue, they picked up two partners and then went to a Chinese coffeehouse and eventually to the country house of one of Mendes's friends, where they danced, drank and listened to gramophone records.³⁶

Calypso tents in the French Shores section of downtown continued to attract middle- and upper-class patrons (both local and foreign) during the interwar years. Though the disreputable character of this district was part of its appeal, visitors also had concerns about safety during their nighttime excursions. According to Lord Beginner, another prominent calypsonian of the era, such patrons were becoming afraid of the east-side tents by the late 1920s and early 1930s, which led to the establishment of some tents on the west side of downtown, particularly on St Vincent, Edward and Park Streets. Nonetheless, major calypso tents continued to operate in the east during the 1930s. In 1937, for example, the White Star tent (then on Henry Street) could seat approximately eight hundred people, while the Advertisers' Union Tent on Queen Street could accommodate five hundred. In 1939 both the east and west sides of the city featured prominent tents: the Trinidad Calypso and Musicians Advertising Association at 47 Nelson Street and the Trinidad Calypsonians Union at 100 St Vincent Street. The *Port-of-Spain Gazette* reported that the Nelson Street tent was "well ventilated and lighted and a pleasant atmosphere prevailed".37

While tents served as the primary venue for calypso performance during the interwar era, calypsonians also appeared in movie theatres, where they typically sang between or after film screenings. One of the earliest singers to perform in cinemas was Phil Madison, a vaudevillian from British Guiana. During the Carnival season of 1920, Madison and Berkeley (another vaudevillian) appeared at the London Theatre in Woodbrook in a "Grand Cinema Carnival" that also included jazz and string bands, dancing, throwing of confetti, and Charlie Chaplin in *The Pawnshop*. During the 1925 Carnival season, the London held a calypso competition that featured Executor, Marlborough, Douglas, Albany and Modern Inventor singing about a cricket match between Trinidad and Barbados. Meanwhile, the Olympic Theatre in Belmont held a similar competition, but with singers from Barbados as well as Trinidad. The larger cinemas that opened during the 1930s also featured calypso shows; in 1937, for example, the Roxy in Woodbrook held an "Intercolonial Calypso Competition" with Bill Rogers of British Guiana against Tiger and Radio, accompanied by the Ambassadors Orchestra. The following season, the writer John Vandercook visited Trinidad and attended a theatre calypso show in which Atilla, Lion, Radio, Pretender and Houdini sat on chairs on the stage and took turns singing at a microphone on such topics as the 1937 strikes and the state of the cocoa market. During this era, calypsonians also performed in various other public venues, as well as in the private homes of the wealthy. In 1939 the Carnival Improvement Committee organized a high-profile calypso competition at the Prince's Building that featured Tiger, Atilla, Pretender, Caresser, Ziegfield, Ras Kassa and Lion. The judges crowned Tiger "Calypso

King" of the season for a song about the labour movement, and Mayor Cipriani delivered a speech in which he assured the large audience that the Carnival Improvement Committee had no intention of banning ole-mas portrayals as part of its efforts to clean up the festival.[38]

By the 1930s, calypsonians were composing songs on a vast array of topics. Many calypsoes commented on events in Trinidad, from the general, such as Tiger's critique of social inequality in "Money Is King" (1935), to the specific, such as Atilla's analysis of bias in the British government's report on the 1937 strikes in "Commission Report" (1938). Also common were songs that praised the qualities of Trinidad, such as Tiger's "The Beautiful Land of Iere" (1938), and songs that described local cultural traditions, such as Growler's "Trinidad Loves to Play Carnival" (1939). In addition, calypsonians regularly offered commentary on world affairs, such as Atilla's "Emancipation Centenary" (1933) on remembering Britain's abolition of slavery in 1833, Tiger's "The Gold in Africa" (1936) on the Italian invasion of Ethiopia, Beginner's "King George's Silver Jubilee" (1935) on the monarch's twenty-five years on the throne, and Lion's "The Invasion of Poland" (1940) on the outbreak of World War II in September 1939. Perhaps the most popular calypso theme, however, was the intricacies of male-female relationships. Calypsonians offered various male viewpoints in songs like Radio's "Man Smart, Woman Smarter" (1936), Executor's "My Troubles with Dorothy" (1938), Atilla's "Not Me with Matrimony" (1938) and Lion's "I Am Happy to Be in Love" (1938).

Many calypsoes on Trinidadian topics focused on life in Port of Spain. Such songs were derived from the calypsonians' close observation of a variety of settings, social groups and personalities around the city, and their ongoing fascination with both typical and novel events in this complex environment. Frequently, they sang about basic material concerns, such as housing and domestic conditions. In "Slum Clearance" (1939), for example, Beginner assesses the impact of government demolition of barrack and other housing for the poor in the centre of the city, after the Public Health Ordinance of 1934 and the Slum Clearance Ordinance of 1935. He observes that the government was tearing down buildings in the name of improvement without providing sufficient new housing to which displaced people could move. Meanwhile, crowded living conditions inspired various calypsoes about troublesome neighbours. In "Next Door Neighbour" (1938), Tiger complains of daily aggravation from a single woman and her several children. Rather than washing clothes to earn money and cooking for her children, the woman peeps into his kitchen each morning and begs for food. Tiger takes up this topic again in "Ah Neighbours, Neighbours" (1940), describing how a woman next door complains at night about his light, his coughing and sneezing and his using smoke to keep mosquitoes away. However, he eventually gains some peace when the neighbour and her husband are arrested and jailed for stealing chickens. In "Malicious Neighbours" (1939), Lion comments on nosy neighbours who spread gossip through barrack yards by peeping through curtains and jalousies, using mirrors to peer into windows and even employing earphones better to hear conversations. In the refrain for this calypso, Lion claims such individuals can be found all over Port of Spain.

As an alternative to crowded barrack-yard living, calypsonians fantasized about living in bungalows, the attractive one-storey houses with verandahs that were being built during the first half of the twentieth century in various neighbourhoods outside downtown. In "I Am Going to Buy a Bungalow" (1938), Lion looks forward to living with a pretty woman in his own house, outfitted with a Zenith radio, a Simmons bed from the store of J.T. Johnson, a coverlet from Salvatori and a pillow. He adds that the services of Dr Marcano, Mr Claude and Mr Wooding (a well-known Port of Spain doctor and two attorneys) will further ensure his comfort. In "I Don't Want No Bungalow" (1938), Atilla claims that he does not aspire to this type of house, owing to a fear that a boom in rents would force a return to living in a barrack room. However, he does desire a feather bed from Waterman's, a coverlet from Kirpalani's, a Zenith radio, an Armstrong bicycle and top medical and legal services. Clearly, these enumerations of consumer goods and services by Atilla and Lion not only evoked a dream world of comfort but also saluted businessmen and professionals who patronized calypso tents.

Growler offered even more incredible fantasies as well as promotions. Not satisfied with a bungalow and local women, he says in "Only Foreigners" (1938) that he will have, happily ensconced together in a three-storey house, a woman from India or Egypt, one from Syria and a third from America. Here he will live like a king with a golden bed, a V8 car from McEnearney, a plane to fly him to Venezuela, a Zenith radio from Sa Gomes, a Brinsmead piano from Strong's and a microphone to broadcast his voice. In "Leave Me Alone Dorothy", performed the following year, Growler suggests that he is now happy with three Trinidadian women: one of Chinese ancestry who is an accountant and grocery cashier, one of Venezuelan descent who left her husband and sold her property and one of Portuguese background who provides him with fine suits and cigars from Germany. The accoutrements of his home now include ostrich-feather pillows, electric fans, a telephone and a swimming pool. Finally, Growler's "History of Woodbrook" (1938) lauds the development and qualities of this residential community, with its pleasant bungalows, shady squares, children's playground, Queen's Park Oval for cricket, pharmacies, market, dance hall and billiard saloon.

Other calypsonians also commented on Port of Spain's public sphere of streets, stores and other gathering places. In "The New Shop Law" (1939), Executor protests class-biased legislation that forced small and large stores to close at the same time, thus preventing smaller business owners from serving (and benefiting from) working people who needed to shop in the evening.³⁹ Executor comments on the law's impact on the poor, notes protests against it in Woodford Square and laments that the city's streets will now be subdued at night. However, nightlife of other types also figured in calypso. In "The Rats" (1936), Tiger describes prostitutes at such locations as Queen Street and Marine Square and accuses them (rather than their clients) of being an insidious and violent threat to the city. Executor repeated this theme in "In the Dew and the Rain" (1939), noting prostitutes at the corner of George and Prince Streets and elsewhere in the city. He holds them accountable for their way of life and blames them for corrupting young men. Calypsonians also commented on other denizens of the city's streets. In "Gambo [sic] Lai Lai Before the Court" (1939), for example, Executor narrates an incident involving this city character known for his elaborate, nonsensical orations. When one day Gumbo Lai Lai, dressed in a Sunday suit and puffing on a cigar, interfered with a woman on the street, the police arrested him and threw him in jail, despite his loquacious speech on his innocence.

Scandals and other unusual occurrences in the city were a perennially popular subject for calypsonians. In "Country Club Scandal" (1933), Radio tells the story of how a government officer (known by audiences to be the inspector general of the constabulary) was caught in a liaison with a high-society woman. In "Treasury Scandal" (1937), Atilla relates the disappearance of $200,000 in cash from government coffers, the denial of responsibility by employees, the likelihood of clever corruption and his own plight as a man without access to such wealth. Though the intrigue of impropriety was especially appealing, calypsonians also reported on other kinds of newsworthy events. In "Graf Zeppelin" (1934), for example, Atilla sings of a German airship that flew over Trinidad in 1933. With much precision, he describes the sounds and movements of the zeppelin, as well as the enthusiastic response of people on the ground as they marvelled at this feat of engineering. There were also calypsoes on local disasters, such as Lion's "Customs Fire" (1939) on the destruction, right before the previous Christmas, of an American customs warehouse at the harbour. Lion suggests that hams and other specialty groceries that people were expecting for the season were now being enjoyed by fish at their own Christmas party.

Finally, there were the many possibilities for romance, or at least fantasies of romance, in the city. In "Anacaona" (1935), Beginner describes a show at the Empire Theatre in which the enticing movements of a rumba dancer mesmerize not only him but also patrons from the pit to the balcony. Beginner says that he would give up his own woman if he could make the visiting Anacaona his wife. Exotic love is also the subject of Tiger's "Señorita Panchita" (1938), in which he meets a wealthy Venezuelan tourist on Frederick Street. After bilingual introductions and mutual infatuation, he takes the young lady by taxi to meet his family but soon realizes that the relationship would not last. On the other hand, Tiger sings in "Darling Kimberlin" (1938) of a woman who would provide him with breakfast at the Queen's Park Hotel, lunch at the Country Club, dinner at Hotel Sand, a thousand dollars from the Royal Bank and various other luxuries, including a Lincoln Zephyr and De Soto. Moreover, she would arrange for him to have top attorneys and a physician, eye doctor and dentist. In "Romance in the Moonlight" (1940), Lord Invader relates a somewhat simpler wish – to meet an aristocratic girl from a church choir at the Queen's Park Savannah at night. He advises the girl not to tell her mother of the meeting, since he is a lowly calypsonian.[40]

As this sampling of songs suggests, calypsonians were familiar with a wide range of settings in Port of Spain and offered commentary from a variety of perspectives. In crafting their compositions, they assumed such diverse personas as outraged citizens, aggrieved neighbours, bemused spectators, boastful ladies' men and inveterate dreamers, while offering stories or observations in a language rich with humour, hyperbole, irony and wordplay. The audiences who gathered in the calypso tents were thrilled by their verbal dexterity and ability to chronicle and analyse the life of the city. At these venues, the calypsonians developed unique voices and collectively constructed a genre of expression that was rooted in the local environment and paralleled the local literary movement that was also taking shape at this time. Moreover, the tents constituted a new sphere of public opinion and social critique, beyond what was offered in newspapers. Here artists of primarily working-class backgrounds found an opportunity to articulate their thoughts and engage the attention of a cross-section of the society. While tent performances were applauded by many, they were also seen as a threat by some sectors of the elite. In response, the colonial government implemented a Theatre and Dance Hall Ordinance in 1934–1935 that applied to various types of venues but was clearly aimed at curbing the speech of the calypsonians, particularly songs deemed to be profane or obscene or that were "insulting to any individual or section of the community". Policemen were stationed in tents to monitor infractions of the ordinance, but, with clever lyrics, calypsonians were sometimes able to circumvent their control.

Though the calypsonians' tent performances had a substantial impact on Trinidadian society, they were ephemeral events. The recording of some of their compositions during this era, however, preserved and disseminated their voices. While American companies had sporadically recorded calypso since the 1910s, the first records by major calypsonians were cut when Atilla and Lion travelled to New York for sessions with ARC in 1934. In the following years, Atilla, Lion, Beginner, Tiger, Executor, King Radio and Caresser travelled to New York to record with Decca, while RCA Victor and Decca sent teams to

Trinidad for recording sessions with various artists during the Carnival season. A key figure in arranging calypso recordings during this period was Eduardo Sa Gomes, the owner of Sa Gomes Radio Emporiums in Port of Spain and San Fernando (advertised as "The Five Palaces of Good Music"). The sale of the calypsonians' records in Sa Gomes's shops, along with their occasional performances in New York nightclubs, significantly added to their local celebrity. With the distribution of records, their audience expanded beyond Trinidad to include fans in other parts of the anglophone Caribbean and in the United States, where even President Roosevelt indicated his appreciation of the art form. In fact, calypso became a part of Trinidad's unique appeal for tourists. The small but increasing number of Americans and other visitors who arrived for the Carnival season hoped to hear calypso performances as well as to watch masquerades in the streets.[41]

At Carnival time, Port of Spain's residents and visitors constructed an alternative version of the city by appropriating a variety of spaces and recreating them as sites of festivity and artistic expression. The normal flow of traffic and commerce in the city was suspended as masqueraders organized themselves in bands, paraded through the streets and attracted crowds of onlookers. Even lorries and cars were transformed into moving stages for celebration. The city's landscape assumed a wholly different appearance. Instead of the day-to-day activities of a Depression-era Caribbean city, there were scenes ranging from the Christian hell to classical Greece, medieval England and Indian cultures of the American Plains. In their masquerades, revellers assumed personas other than their customary selves. They became clowns, bats, sailors, soldiers, policemen, millionaires or denizens of all sorts of faraway places. Men dressed as women and women as men. Such costumed fantasies were complemented by the equally imaginative language of Carnival. Bands of Wild Indians recited esoteric chants, Pierrots Grenade (comical versions of the older Pierrots) delivered nonsensical orations, Midnight Robbers boasted of absurd exploits and calypsonians composed songs that ranged from elegant treatises of social realism to ludicrous flights of fancy. In essence, Carnival was a time of experimentation – of disruption of the quotidian city and exploration of other possibilities. There were increased expressions of aggression and sensuality, parodies of the powerful, and general outrageousness and comedy. Revellers carried out all these performances in a spirit of competition, as they attempted to surpass their peers and impress their audiences. While there were numerous formal masquerade contests at outdoor and indoor locales, Carnival overall was an occasion for endless informal encounters and displays of invention.[42]

Revellers exploited the particular material and social characteristics of spaces in the city. Downtown remained the heart of the festival. This dense zone of stores, offices, warehouses, barrack yards and other housing was the home of many of the participants in the Carnival and a landscape that they fully understood. Moreover, the grid of streets offered many possible routes for processions, while the rows of multistorey buildings limited sightlines and allowed for surprise encounters at corners. In contrast, the Queen's Park Savannah was an open expanse of lawns and trees. The elite's processions in lorries and cars on the long streets surrounding the park offered a controlled and predictable experience, as did parties in the elegant houses and upscale venues nearby. Thus the production of Carnival in both downtown and Savannah locales dramatized the city's socio-spatial order. Class distinctions were clearly displayed, but there were also interactions across such boundaries. More grassroots residents of the city gradually participated in the masquerade competition at the Savannah, while some middle- and upper-class individuals patronized calypso tents and ventured into the streets downtown.

The significance of Carnival for Port of Spain's inhabitants was also interrelated with their understanding of the city's other large-scale public events – imperial celebrations and political demonstrations. Like Carnival, both these types of events involved large numbers of people appropriating major streets, squares and the Queen's Park Savannah for public display and communication. Imperial celebrations reinforced colonial authority and hierarchy with their orderly marching of troops, patriotic music, speeches by the governor, expressions of loyalty by citizens, and church services. Political demonstrations, on the other hand, challenged authority and hierarchy through the assembly and marching of working people; speeches, songs and signs of protest; and occasional acts of violence. The festive traditions of Carnival incorporated elements of both imperial celebrations and demonstrations but created far more complex portrayals of the society. Masquerades included fancy bands with their kings, queens and other royalty; historical bands that represented the royalty of Britain and other lands; assorted bands of sailors and soldiers; and individuals costumed as policemen and other figures of authority. In these portrayals, however, authority and hierarchy were both displayed and parodied. Meanwhile, there was much social and political criticism in masquerades and calypso, but this was conveyed in a generally humorous mode and in the context of revelry. Carnival participants essentially played with the structure of Trinidadian society, revealing and questioning its inequalities. Indeed, Carnival was an event that expressed a wide range of human concerns, desires and fears. While imperial celebrations and political demonstrations had specific purposes and predetermined routes through the city, Carnival was multiplex both in intent and spatial movement.

At its most fundamental level, Port of Spain's Carnival was a profound expression of local imagination and empowerment. By the 1930s, working people had been celebrating the festival on the streets for a century and had created myriad genres of masquerades, music, choreography and verbal art. Every year, they gathered in their yards and tents to take over the city's public sphere and lead the society in fantasy and merriment. Their carnivalized city, however, was also shaped by the forces of British colonialism. In addition to displays of authority and social hierarchy in some masquerades, the colonial government closely monitored the festival, issuing an ongoing series of regulations, deploying substantial police contingents, actively censoring calypsoes and joining other elites in attempting to channel the revelry into improved forms. At the same time, the Carnival was a response to the multifaceted impact of the United States on Trinidad. Indian, minstrel, Midnight Robber, millionaire and sailor masquerades all revealed a fascination with America. Among their various topics, calypsoes addressed events in the United States and, by the 1930s, were typically performed by ensembles in swing-band styles that featured brass, reeds, guitar, piano, bass and drums. The appearances of calypsonians and ensembles in cinemas further linked them to the world of American entertainment, as did their recordings with American record companies. During the 1930s, there was also the increasing arrival of American tourists for the Carnival. While their numbers were small compared to the immense crowds of local people, their interest in the festival was regularly noted in the press. In short, American social types, artistic forms and actual visitors all added to the re-creation of the city during Carnival as a place of revelry and excitement. Though significant to the local populace at the time, this American presence in the Carnival would be dwarfed by the invasion of the island that occurred a few years later with the escalation of World War II.

PART 3

WORLD WAR II AND THE POSTWAR YEARS, 1940–1962

Figure 22. Docksite, US Army, April 1942. US Army Signal Corps, World War II, Trinidad, Book #2. National Archives of the United States, photo #150118. 111-SCA-3049, SC 326259.

Figure 23. Barracks, St Clair Cantonment, US Army, November 1941. US Army Signal Corps, World War II, Trinidad, Book #1. National Archives of the United States, photo #125967, 111-SCA-3048, SC 150114.

Figure 24. USO No. 2, Mucurapo, March 1944. Eleanor Roosevelt delivers a message from President Roosevelt, accompanied by Major General J.D. Patch (*at left*), William Childs, director of the facility (*at right*), and a band of musicians. Official US Navy Photo. General Records of the Department of the Navy, Box 80-G-624. National Archives of the United States, photo #22364.

Figure 25. Gonzales Rhythm Makers, Leotaud Street, Gonzales, circa 1943. Note houses completed by the city council in 1936. Photograph by Edric Connor. Edric and Pearl Connor Papers, Alma Jordan Library, University of the West Indies, St Augustine, Trinidad and Tobago.

Figure 26. PNM March for Chaguaramas, 22 April 1960. Eric Williams, at left. Photograph by Sampson Studios. Courtesy Ivar Oxaal.

Figure 27. Government flats ("the Plannings") on Duncan Street, facing north, 1950s. The National Archives of the United Kingdom, ref. CO1069/399.

Figure 28. Perspective drawing of "Type A" house in Diamond Vale. Designed by Lionel Fernandez, Homes International, completed 1962. Detail of exhibit 13 in Trinidad and Tobago. *Diamond Road Housing Project, Diego Martin Valley* (Trinidad: Ministry of Housing and Local Government, 1961). Courtesy the Trinidad and Tobago Ministry of Housing and Urban Development.

Figure 29. New Town Hall. Designed by Prior, Lourenco and Nothnagel, completed 1961. Note portion of Carlisle Chang mural *Conquerabia* visible at back of courtyard. Woodford Square is in the foreground. Photograph by H.O. Thomas. Postcard published by H.O. Thomas. The Michael Goldberg Postcard Collection, Alma Jordan Library, University of the West Indies, St Augustine, Trinidad and Tobago.

Figure 30. Queen's Hall. Designed by Colin Laird, completed 1959. Photograph by H.O. Thomas. Postcard published by H.O. Thomas.

Figure 31. Trinidad Hilton Hotel. Designed by Warner, Burns, Toan and Lunde; completed 1962. Postcard.

Figure 32. Paschim Kaashi Hindu Mandir. Designed by Jang Bahadoorsingh and John Newel Lewis, completed 1962. Postcard published by Y. De Lima & Co.

Figure 33. Aerial view of Port of Spain and harbour, 1960s. Note Queen's Wharf and St Vincent Wharf in centre, the 1937 Deep Water Harbour Scheme improvements on the left, and the 1940s reclamation (Sea Lots) on the right. Also visible are the seven-storey Salvatori Building on the eastern side of Independence Square, Woodford Square farther back to the left, and the Queen's Park Savannah in the background. Postcard published by Y. De Lima & Co.

6. THE CITY AT WAR

THE ARRIVAL OF AMERICAN ARMY, navy and civilian personnel in Trinidad during World War II dramatically transformed the landscape of Port of Spain, generating within a year a new topsy-turvy world in which public spaces became military bases filled with tents and barracks, massive quantities of strange equipment and supplies arrived on the docks, fleets of trucks and jeeps constantly sped through the streets, distant parts of the island became accessible through new roads and nightlife flourished with endless dancing and carousing. Suddenly there were thousands of white men living in or passing through the city. In contrast to colonial officials, wealthy business owners, tourists or movie stars, these men cleared land, erected buildings, moved cargo, marched in formation, played baseball, chewed gum and cavorted boisterously in the streets. The tempo of life in the city, already brisk, further accelerated as the Americans and the local population hurried to revamp the city and the island as a major defensive position against enemy German forces that threatened the Atlantic world.

In constructing and operating military bases in Port of Spain and elsewhere in Trinidad, the Americans possessed and controlled substantial portions of the island that were previously private property or government lands. While there were numerous army bases throughout the territory, the largest (Fort Read) was in an extensive area between Arima and Sangre Grande, while the primary navy base (Chaguaramas) occupied much of the northwest peninsula of the island. Port of Spain contained several smaller bases and functioned as the command, transportation and recreation centre for the entire military undertaking. The city was a node that connected bases throughout the island as well as a port that enabled the arrival of large quantities of supplies and personnel on an ongoing basis. The variety of bases that the United States quickly established had a unique status within the wider landscape. To some extent, they were alien spaces – tightly contained and regulated zones that featured construction technologies and forms that contrasted with the local built environment and that functioned with substantial independence in terms of legal jurisdiction, material provisions, medical care, leisure activities and religious worship. However, they were also deeply interrelated with the surrounding environment and society in terms of the employment of thousands of local labourers, the use of local transport systems and utilities, and the servicemen's pursuit of off-base recreation. For American authorities, the bases posed a constant challenge of balancing socio-spatial containment and interaction in the execution of a military mission. Meanwhile, British colonial officials tried to demonstrate Anglo-American cooperation in the war effort while also seeking to maintain their own authority in the face of encroaching American power and influence. Finally, the local population eagerly pursued the numerous economic opportunities that the bases offered, was intrigued by the exciting wartime atmosphere, but strongly resented the sense of superiority and entitlement displayed by many Americans and was often critical of the military's disruption of its landscape and mores.

THE CONSTRUCTION OF AMERICAN BASES

The construction of American bases in Trinidad, as well as in other Caribbean territories, was driven by the needs of both the United States and Britain as World War II escalated. Britain urgently required more warships to strengthen its navy and counter German attacks, while the United States sought additional Atlantic bases to more effectively defend its territory and its interests across the Americas. The needs of the two countries were met through a destroyers-for-bases agreement, negotiated in August and September 1940 and formally signed on 27 March 1941. Through this exchange, the United States provided Britain with fifty aged destroyers, while Britain gave the United States ninety-nine-year leases on land for base-building in Newfoundland (then a British colony), Bermuda, the Bahamas, Jamaica, Antigua, St Lucia, Trinidad and British Guiana. The largest bases were established in Newfoundland, Bermuda and Trinidad, with the latter being the most important location. Trinidad's strategic significance lay in its proximity to South America (less than ten miles from Venezuela) and the establishment of bases here was intended to protect several key American and Allied interests. The Panama Canal to the west was critical to US military strategy and commercial enterprise, with sea lanes to South America passing near Trinidad. In addition, there were vital oil deposits in Trinidad and Venezuela; major refineries in Trinidad, Aruba and Curaçao; and substantial bauxite resources in British Guiana and Surinam. Bauxite, an aluminium ore essential for aeroplane manufacturing, was transshipped from British Guiana through Trinidad. Meanwhile, there were various military threats in the region. Some American strategists believed that a Nazi attack on the Caribbean and the United States could be launched from the Vichy

French–controlled Dakar area of West Africa, across the Atlantic, and north from Brazil, perhaps facilitated by sympathetic German residents and business interests in South America. Moreover, Martinique and Guadeloupe were also under Vichy administration, and by early 1942 German U-boats were torpedoing merchant ships in the Caribbean.[1]

So, with the outbreak of the war, the small island of Trinidad assumed, in the words of US Army historian Lieutenant Robert A. Johnson, "a new and world-wide importance as a key spot in military strategy and a stronghold for the defense of the Western Hemisphere". On 10 October 1940, an American committee, known as the "Greenslade Board", arrived in Trinidad to select sites for military bases. The colony's governor, Sir Hubert Young, offered them the Caroni Swamp southeast of Port of Spain, with the dual objectives of reclaiming this land for productive use and consolidating army and navy bases in one location in order to minimize the disruption of local life and transport. After US engineers advised that it would take years to convert the swamp into usable land, the board selected the Cumuto Reserve (southeast of Arima) for the main army base and the island's northwest peninsula for the navy base. The governor's resistance to these sites resulted in further negotiations over the following months, including direct discussion between US officials and Prime Minister Winston Churchill.[2]

On 17 January 1941, Trinidad's legislative council met to discuss a bill that would amend the colony's Land Acquisitions Ordinances (1925–1933) and enable the government to acquire the proposed sites for transfer to the Americans. Several members of the council expressed concerns about leasing the northwest peninsula, since this area included various beaches that were heavily used for recreation by a cross-section of the population of Port of Spain and northwestern Trinidad. The director of medical services, for example, noted that beaches along the island's western coast were unsuitable owing to discharges from the Orinoco River, so the northwest peninsula beaches were essential to the health and well-being of the community. Meanwhile, trade unionist Adrian Cola Rienzi hoped the Americans would not bring Jim Crow segregation practices with them, that they would pay fair wages and respect collective bargaining and that they would be subject to local courts. After much discussion, the council passed the bill, in part thanks to assurances from US authorities that they would try to provide some public beach access. The council observed that, if restrictions on beaches proved necessary, this would be a worthy sacrifice for the war effort and affirmed that the bases, for the next ninety-nine years, would represent "the fusion of the two great English-speaking Democracies".[3]

The destroyers-for-bases agreement signed in London on 27 March 1941 included detailed terms for the location and administration of the US bases in the eight Atlantic colonies, and a lease signed on 22 April in Port of Spain by the Trinidad governor and the American consul to the colony actually transferred thirty-two square miles of land here. Along with the Cumuto Reserve and the northwest peninsula, the United States obtained lands for an auxiliary airfield near Longdenville in west-central Trinidad and for a recreation area at Saline Bay on the northeast coast (the latter facility was never developed). The agreement also enabled the United States to acquire additional lands in Trinidad, obtain access to water supplies, control waters in the northern part of the Gulf of Paria (in the vicinity of the naval base), use 1,200 feet of the new quay and two of the large transit sheds at the Port of Spain harbour and extend this quay up to an additional 3,000 feet.[4]

The army and navy development of the bases in Trinidad began before the agreement and lease were signed, with the two services working independently, each with its own design and construction personnel, American civilian contractors and large pools of locally recruited labour. In the case of the army, work was directed by the Corps of Engineers' US Engineer Department (USED), for which Major David A.D. Ogden, district engineer, served as the local commanding officer. Promoted to lieutenant colonel and then to colonel during his time in Trinidad, Ogden was a graduate of West Point and the Army Engineering School and had worked for the corps in various capacities, including teaching at MIT for four years, serving in the Panama Canal Zone, supervising the construction of the Illinois Waterway and being chief of operations for the Works Progress Administration in Los Angeles. By December 1940 Ogden was establishing a USED headquarters in Port of Spain and coordinating surveys of lands selected for bases. The USED's design and engineering contractor was Caribbean Architects-Engineers, a firm created in 1941 by Voorhees, Walker, Foley and Smith (a well-known architectural practice) and Parsons Brinkerhoff (a major engineering company) specifically to bid for the army's Caribbean-base projects.[5]

The army's primary construction contractor for the Trinidad bases was the Walsh-Driscoll Construction Company, a joint venture formed by the Walsh Construction Company and the George F. Driscoll Company. Walsh, the leading partner, had a portfolio that included such projects as the Grand Coulee Dam, the Los Angeles Water District Aqueduct and the Queens-Midtown Tunnel. The Corps of Engineers' contract with Walsh-Driscoll, signed on 7 February 1941, was on a cost-plus-fixed-fee basis – a contract structure, justified by the wartime emergency, that enabled the company to be reimbursed for an initially unknown scope of work and ever-escalating level of expenses. While the USED originally estimated that the contract would cost $50,000,000, it had reached $100,000,000 by the time work was completed in Trinidad and several other southern Caribbean territories. Like the USED and Caribbean Architects-Engineers, Walsh-Driscoll maintained offices in both New York and Port of Spain for the development of bases. After the contract was signed, the firm's New York personnel office began recruiting construction workers from across the United States, but faced considerable competition for skilled men, given the growing wartime economy. Though the personnel office attempted to eliminate "undesirable applicants and vacationists", it still had to settle for "a more than normal percentage of semi-skilled and unskilled employees", whom it hoped to train in Trinidad. Meanwhile, most of the vast supply of construction materials and equipment (such as cranes, bulldozers, concrete mixers, barges, railroad cars and trucks) would be shipped from the United States, a further challenge with the increasing demand for warehouse and vessel cargo space during the war.[6]

In spite of such obstacles, Walsh-Driscoll persevered and in early March 1941 sent its first large contingent of employees to Trinidad. This group immediately took over work initiated by USED personnel on the large expanse of land reclaimed from the sea through Port of Spain's Deep Water Harbour Scheme during the 1930s. This area, leased by the colonial government to the United States, soon became known as the "Docksite" base and served as the army's port in Trinidad. At the same time, Walsh-Driscoll began work with USED and Caribbean Architects-Engineers at the Cumuto Reserve, the major army base out in the countryside. In its 7 April issue, *Life* magazine ran an article on base-building in Trinidad and, in adventure-inflected prose, commented: "Here in the steamy, shadowy heart of Trinidad's ancient jungle, U.S. engineers and surveyors tediously uncover and plot the contours of the land on which no manmade walls ever before were reared." The article's lead photograph depicted two men looking out over a densely vegetated landscape, with a giant triangle containing "U.S.A." inscribed on the image. The caption noted that it was within this triangle that the base would be constructed. Other photographs showed surveyors struggling through the thick forest; architects, engineers and draftsmen working intently on plans at the operation's headquarters in Port of Spain; and a smiling Major Ogden. Soon the army and its contractors were also developing bases on the small islands of Chacachacare and Monos, which guarded the northern entrance to the Gulf of Paria off Trinidad's northwest peninsula. By early May, Walsh-Driscoll was employing twenty-seven hundred local workers, in keeping with Ogden's stated policy of using as much local labour as possible. In an article published two years later in the army's local periodical, *Trinidad News Tips* (*TNT*), a writer for the USED reminisced on this initial period of base construction: "Buildings sprang up everywhere, seemingly overnight. Roads were built where formerly there were only narrow, winding trails, and in many cases where dense forests existed. Each day more of the terrain in the leased areas was developed for military purposes and countless new projects were quickly completed. Boat after boat docked at the new wharf in Port-of-Spain and soon Americans were commonly seen everywhere." Indeed, a sense of urgency and determination, as well as flexibility, pervaded the base-building enterprise. In a summation of its work in Trinidad, the Walsh Construction Company noted that its assignment was constantly changing and that "engineering and design, instead of preceding construction, paralleled it, or, in many instances, lagged behind". This pressure to complete jobs accelerated with the increasing arrival of regular army troops on the island.[7]

The first non-construction troops to enter Trinidad were ten members of the Army Signal Corps, who arrived on 19 March to begin work on communication facilities. On 24 April approximately five hundred Army Air Corps officers and enlisted men, previously stationed in the Panama Canal Zone, docked at Port of Spain and were subsequently housed in tents at Trinidad's Piarco airfield, where their planes landed a few days later. Sergeant Paul J. Schmitt contributed a piece to *TNT* on this contingent's initial experience:

> Our arrival here caused quite a bit of excitement among the native population, who at first thought we had come to take over the place. Many of them had never seen an American soldier before, and we were looked upon much in the manner of freaks in a side-show. Our trip from Port-of-Spain to Piarco Airport, which was to be our home for the next seven months, again made us feel that we were exhibits in a museum; something to be stared at in wonder. All along the route, the well worn greeting of the tropics: "Hello Joe", was hurled at us by everyone . . . from that day on, we were to be known as "Joe".

On the night of 5 May, the first ground troops, under the command of Brigadier General Ralph Talbot Jr, arrived at Port of Spain, and began unloading 8,000 tons of equipment and supplies the following day. Again there were crowds of Trinidadians present, who greeted them with "The Yanks are here" and "Hello Joe", and there was further excitement that afternoon when a contingent marched through the streets of the city. After a few days of sleeping on their ship, the troops moved into tents pitched on the Docksite base, where the USED and Walsh-Driscoll had already prepared mess halls, warehouses, showers and latrines.[8]

Whitehall and the Institute for the Blind

The US Army established the headquarters for its command in Trinidad at Whitehall, an elegant house in the series of large private homes along the Maraval Road facing the Queen's Park Savannah. In early 1941 Major Ogden negotiated a lease for the house with representatives of the estate of N.M. Henderson (the owners) and set up offices here for the USED and Caribbean Architects-Engineers. It was in the spacious rooms of this house that design work was carried out for the various army bases around Trinidad. When General Talbot arrived with his ground troops in May, however, he quickly determined that he would not be locating his headquarters at Docksite. Army historian Lieutenant Johnson explains:

> General Talbot was, however, impressed with the fact that a good Headquarters for the initial Trinidad Base Command was, in the eyes of the Colonials, imperative to the prestige of the American flag. He felt that if headquarters were set up in a flimsy shack on the mud flats near the docks, such action would be misunderstood both by the Government and the populace at large, so he made arrangements with the District Engineer, Trinidad District, to take a limited space in the Colonial Mansion, "Whitehall", near the Governor's residence and offices.[9]

Certainly, the location of the command headquarters at Whitehall affirmed the prestige of the US military, while the prominent display of an American flag and guards outside the building displayed its power. Moreover, the proximity to Government House on the north side of the Savannah facilitated ongoing discussions with the Trinidad governor, while the presence in the area of elite homes, clubs and the Queen's Park Hotel encouraged officer interaction with local society.

However, the allocation of only a few rooms at Whitehall to General Talbot and his staff was clearly inadequate and a degree of friction existed between Talbot and Ogden, who held separate commands within the US Army. With Talbot taking precedence, the USED and Caribbean Architects-Engineers eventually moved to buildings belonging to the Institute for the Blind on Ariapita Avenue in western Woodbrook, near Mucurapo Point. After this move, Talbot and his staff occupied all of Whitehall and coordinated an increasingly complex military presence on the island. The general's command included not only Trinidad itself but the entire "Trinidad Sector", which stretched from French Guiana in the east to Venezuela in the west and St Lucia in the north; over time bases were established throughout this region. As greater numbers of troops arrived in Trinidad and other territories, the army arranged for a higher level of military leadership within the sector. On 12 January 1942, Major General Henry C. Pratt became the new commanding officer and was succeeded on 30 March 1943 by Major General Joseph D. Patch. While Talbot's relationship with Governor Young was somewhat tense, both Pratt and Patch worked hard to maintain harmonious relationships with the colonial government, and appear to have been well admired by local society as well as the troops. Within Trinidad, the American presence continued to escalate, with army troop strength peaking at approximately fourteen thousand in mid-1943. In addition, navy personnel on the island probably peaked in May 1944 at almost seventy-seven hundred, under an entirely separate command at Chaguaramas.[10]

With Whitehall functioning as the army command headquarters, the army engineers developed their new offices at the Institute for the Blind. These were on a 3-acre plot of land that the institute leased from the Port of Spain City Council. In May 1941, the institute obtained the consent of the city council to sublet the premises to the army and also granted the army permission to erect additional buildings there. By July, construction of the housing of the USED and Caribbean Architects-Engineers was nearing completion. Meanwhile, the USED had already created athletic grounds on a field nearby (with provisions for baseball, volleyball and other sports) and by April 1942 finished work on a recreation building that it called "The Castle Club", presumably in reference to the castle of the Corps of Engineers' logo. The Castle Club included offices, a kitchen and cafeteria and a ballroom with a stage, piano, phonograph and loudspeaker system. Administered by a council of USED and Caribbean Architects-Engineers personnel, the club served breakfast and lunch, was open every evening and held dances on Tuesday and Saturday nights. Its formal opening took place on 11 April, with the ballroom decorated with American and US Engineer flags and beer and soft drinks served to five hundred guests. Music was provided by the eight-piece Castle Club Orchestra, consisting of Trinidadians who also served as USED chauffeurs.[11]

Docksite

While Whitehall on the Queen's Park Savannah served as the US Army's command headquarters, the Docksite base on the reclaimed land along the harbour functioned as its logistical nerve centre. This was the point of entry for most troops, equipment and supplies, as well as the departure point for personnel and materials travelling to other bases in the Trinidad Sector. For much of the war, ships were constantly arriving at Docksite, while trucks and jeeps streamed in and out. Thus, land that the Trinidad government had intended to develop as a new commercial, residential and recreational area within the city was taken over by the United States to support its growing military operations. Moreover, Docksite's location on the busy Wrightson Road, adjacent to both downtown and Woodbrook, meant that its myriad activities were on continuous display to the local populace.

The Docksite base was a complex, multipurpose zone in which the USED and its contractors erected and modified a wide range of structures over more than two years (see figure 22). Of principal importance were the wharves. Along with using 1,200 feet of the quay constructed by the Trinidad government during the Deep Water Harbour Scheme, the army carried out additional dredging in the harbour, installed a 500-foot offshore emergency wharf with connecting trestle, and built a 900-foot permanent wharf and retaining wall and numerous rows of warehouses for handling the vast quantities of supplies arriving at the port. Meanwhile, Docksite served as a major camp for troops stationed in Port of Spain or passing through to other bases. Much of the housing consisted of rows of tents, each fronted with a wood-framed screen as a guard against mosquitoes and bats. While the site was initially referred to as "Tent City", some troops eventually lived in barracks which, along with mess halls and other service buildings, were generally long one-floor, wood-framed structures, with wood-plank siding and screened windows. Gable roofs with overhanging eaves provided some protection against sun and rain. Another critical component of the base was a hospital complex that consisted of both wood-frame buildings and tents and included wards, clinics, an x-ray room, operating room and laboratory. There was also a post exchange (store), post office, chapel, recreation hall (with a library and facilities for games and music), open-air movie theatre (which also featured boxing) and a two-storey administration building for Walsh-Driscoll. The base was organized in a grid of roads and duckboard walkways (later replaced with gravel paths), wired with electrical poles and surrounded by a chain-link fence. A few ornamental plants were added to open spaces, which were dusty during the dry months and exceptionally muddy during the rainy season that began shortly after the arrival of the first ground troops.[12]

Certainly the most popular development at Docksite was the United Services Organization (USO) Club, which opened on 20 April 1942 on Wrightson Road near French Street. Funded by several religious organizations, USOs offered a variety of leisure activities, as well as food and lodging, for American army, navy and other military personnel stationed throughout the world. Trinidad's USO filled an acre of land and consisted of a complex of interconnected one- and two-storey hip-roofed buildings surrounding a central patio. Shortly before it opened, a *TNT* correspondent described it:

> this building is a magnificent revelation of everything that is essential for the diversion and recreation of the service man far away from home. On the southern wing there is a study, library, large lounge, showers, and a billiards room. Between the two wings will be the offices for administrative staff. In the lower northern wing there is [a] modern soda fountain with a patio; a club room that may well be used for small group meetings; a theatre that may be used for the production of plays as well as dances. There is an upper floor to this wing that will be used as living quarters for the director and hostesses, and a projection room for the theatre.

Another wing is being added to house a restaurant, and there dormitories are to be added where men from the outlying cantonments may receive rooming accommodations when on leave.

Comfortable furnishings were featured throughout the complex, and a special lounge and powder rooms were provided for "lady guests and hostesses". The main lobby was lined with writing desks; the library included "thousands of good, wholesome books"; the game room offered checkers, cribbage and cards; and a covered promenade bordered the central patio and contained a snack bar that featured a soda fountain of particular interest: "By electric compression, the many-mouthed fountain will produce a variety of iced drinks – orange, lime, coca-cola, strawberry and sodas." The eight-hundred-seat auditorium (theatre) was a flexible space that could be used for theatrical shows, movies, dances and even roller-skating. By December 1942 a cafeteria was added and a 150-bed dormitory opened the following month. *TNT* referred to the club as the "Grand Central Terminal of the Caribbean" and noted that it was one of the largest USOs in the world. By May 1943 there were seventy-five people on its payroll and monthly attendance exceeded one hundred thousand. In addition to its military clientele, the club used guest cards to admit civilian contractor personnel and local women.[13]

The St Clair Cantonment

Soon after the arrival of ground troops in Trinidad in May 1941, the army began developing plans for a second base in Port of Spain. Critical of Major Ogden's selection of the dock area as a site for a tent camp, General Talbot noted that trucks were breaking through the crust of the reclaimed land there and that the area would likely become a sea of mud with the beginning of the rainy season. Talbot thus negotiated with Governor Young for an additional site and succeeded in obtaining the entire King George V Park, an appealing 16-acre green space at the intersection of St Clair and Woodbrook, across the street from the Roxy cinema. Since the colonial government leased the park to the city council at a token rent, it was necessary first to obtain this body's consent to the transfer. The council quickly voiced its support, in part due to assurance from the general that "no trees will be felled and that he will personally interest himself in the maintenance of the aesthetic amenities of the area and seeing that the camp presents a creditable and attractive appearance".[14] Thus the citizens of Port of Spain again surrendered a public space for the war effort and accommodated a military base at a prominent location adjacent to residential districts.

In developing what became known as the St Clair Cantonment, the army and its contractors did devote much effort to creating an aesthetically pleasing base that would complement the pleasant homes and yards of St Clair and northwestern Woodbrook. They retained the park's shady samaan trees and augmented its landscape with additional trees and shrubs. A plan for the camp published by the *Trinidad Guardian* on 10 July shows approximately twenty-four buildings neatly distributed throughout the park's elongated grounds, which stretched from Serpentine Road on the west to Elizabeth Street on the east. Surrounding a central assembly area and a green to the west were troop barracks, a mess hall, a post exchange, a dispensary and two headquarters buildings (the base included some administrative personnel associated with the central command at Whitehall). To the east, adjacent to Elizabeth Street and the elite homes of St Clair, were the houses of the commanding officer and chief of staff (each with a circular drive in front), officers' barracks, a guesthouse and the officers' mess and club. Enclosed with a perimeter fence, the camp's various buildings were connected by a network of roads and paths and serviced with electrical poles, a water supply and sewer pipes. Barracks followed a design similar to that used by Walsh-Driscoll for housing some of its employees at Docksite: long one-storey wood-framed buildings rested on concrete piers and were surrounded by shallow drainage moats; wood-plank walls were lined with screened windows and narrow vents; railed wooden steps provided access to doors; and gable roofs included overhanging eaves (see figure 23). Other camp buildings also featured this general design.

Photographs and written descriptions of the St Clair Cantonment suggest that the plan published in early July was modified somewhat in implementation. There was an enclosed theatre set apart from the rest of the camp so that "the noise of the pictures being shown late at night will not disturb the men who wish to retire early". The theatre's attractive interior featured a panelled ceiling, a stage and movie screen, rows of wooden armchairs and benches, and potted plants. In addition to the officers' club, there was a non-commissioned officers' facility, surrounded by flower beds and featuring "new shrubbery, grass, and the famous star-shaped garden". Inside this building were a stage, bar, tables, armchairs and reading lamps. An important addition to the base in 1943 was WVDI, the armed-forces radio station whose studio, control room and offices were housed in an Army Signal Corps building. This popular station transmitted both US radio programmes ("flown to Trinidad within a few days of their broadcast") and locally produced programming.[15]

Overall, the St Clair Cantonment contrasted with Docksite in a manner similar to the Queen's Park Savannah area and downtown Port of Spain. Both Docksite and downtown were hectic, congested areas with mixed commercial and residential functions, centred on the seaport and ground-transport systems, while the St Clair Cantonment and the Savannah area featured more substantial housing arranged in quieter park and garden settings. If Docksite confirmed Trinidadians' fears of American disruption of their society, the St Clair Cantonment suggested a more temperate and refined US presence.

Mucurapo, Laventille and Rapsey

An additional requirement for troop barracks arose in May 1942 with the arrival of the 99th Coast Artillery regiment, consisting of almost twenty-five hundred African American soldiers. Since segregation in the US Army continued during World War II, these men were housed in camps separate from white troops for the eighteen months that they remained in Trinidad. The 99th served at various locations around Trinidad; in Port of Spain their principal camps were at Mucurapo, Laventille Hill and Rapsey (probably on the northern edge of the city). While neither the *Trinidad Guardian* nor *TNT* provides information on the layout or material characteristics of these camps, a glimpse of their activities can be gleaned from *TNT* columns contributed by 99th members, such as "Laventille News Meal" by Corporal James O. Mann and "The Rapsey Rapsey-dees" by Corporal Walter Eskridge. For example, on 15 December 1942, Corporal Mann wrote: "We had a Jam session the other week. It was strictly on the beam. The Clam [bake] was groovy as a ten-cent Flick. Janes from all over town came to dig some of the fine Jive that Sgt. Peters and the Ack Ack band puts out. The meeting was called to order with Do you wanna jump Children." For *TNT*'s 1 January 1943 issue, Corporal Mann commented on Christmas activities: "To start the day off right was a parade at Rapsey. It was a pleasure to see our Battalion commander pin good-conduct medals on soldiers of this regiment. . . . Our chaplain held a special service on the parade ground, and during the holidays the La Petite Musicale rendered Christmas Carols that really did put the boys in the spirit." On 1 February 1943, Corporal Eskridge of Rapsey wrote:

> Why is it that the Fort Read boys come into town on that one pass per week, swear that there is no place like Arima and Sangre Grande, yet these same boys can always be found in good old Port-of-Spain? . . .
>
> We were down to the dance at Mucurapo and really had a fine time. The music was fine and the boys must be getting better with their jive judging from the collection of fine chicks that were there.[16]

By October 1942 US military officials were looking for a site in Port of Spain to construct a segregated USO club for the African American troops and suggested to the colonial government land between South Quay and the St Joseph

Road, which the city council intended to use for a housing scheme. Eventually, the military's plans shifted to Mucurapo Point (an area where it was already leasing land) and, in May 1943, "USO No. 2" opened there. According to a contributor to *TNT*:

> USO 2 is completely equipped with every modern convenience and many recreational facilities, including an auditorium, lunch room, game room, billiard room, library and sleeping quarters for troops remaining overnight or for an indefinite period away from their regular station.
>
> The lunch room will serve daily meals prepared with the same exacting care that has made the USO the enlisted man's favorite and most sanitary lunch-room off post.
>
> There will also be entertainment committees such as drama groups and various athletic organizations to make USO No. 2 as comprehensive in its various departments as the main USO at Dock Site.

During a whirlwind goodwill visit to army and navy bases in Trinidad on 12 March 1944, Eleanor Roosevelt visited both the USO clubs. A photograph at USO No. 2 shows her on stage delivering a message from President Roosevelt, accompanied by General Patch, William Childs (director of the facility) and a band of musicians (see figure 24). In the audience are a group of local women and several African American naval troops, probably associated with a construction battalion stationed at Chaguaramas.[17]

Historian Annette Palmer observes that the 99th was the only African American army regiment to serve in the Caribbean during World War II. In Trinidad, tensions developed between this group and white US troops, which sometimes resulted in violent altercations. Conflicts also arose between the black soldiers and local men, generally precipitated by competition over local women. Meanwhile, the local white elite perceived the black troops as agitators, and Governor Clifford pressed for their removal from the island. In November 1943, the army did relocate the 99th, but Palmer notes that this did not reduce the level of violence in wartime Trinidad.[18]

Fort Read

While the US Army established its command, transport and recreational centre in Port of Spain, it also developed numerous other bases around Trinidad: the extensive Fort Read; Edinburgh Field (renamed Carlsen Field in 1943), Xeres Field and Exchange Field in the west-central area of the island; defences of the Gulf of Paria at Chacachacare and Monos in the north and Greenhill in the south; and smaller installations at many additional locations.[19] A consideration of Fort Read, along with the Naval Operating Base at Chaguaramas and the Americans' road-building programme, offers a fuller sense of the significance of Port of Spain within this sprawling military complex.

Fort Read (in its final configuration) was a 27-square-mile base, approximately 23 miles east of Port of Spain. The Eastern Main Road ran through its northern portion and was the site of initial construction work, though eventually six separate cantonments were developed on the base. An early objective was to provide housing for USED personnel, contractors and their families. By October 1941, 150 one-bedroom and two-bedroom houses were under construction for these groups, based on plans that combined design concepts submitted by army engineers, Caribbean Architects-Engineers, and Walsh-Driscoll. Arranged in a grid layout, the houses were one-floor wood-framed structures that rested on 8-foot piers and featured hip roofs with ridge ventilators, windows with screens and louvres, and two external staircases. Each included a combined living and dining room, kitchen, bath and one or more closets. With sections prefabricated in a shop on site, the houses were erected at the rate of one every forty-five minutes. In the words of Mrs Mary Dwyer, who apparently lived in one of the homes: "Although in a foreign country the people of Cottage City are living a typical American life." Occupants played bridge, enjoyed bowling and Saturday-night dances at a recreational hall and decorated their homes with Christmas trees and wreaths for the holiday season.[20]

Meanwhile, work continued on the construction of a wide range of buildings for the increasing number of troops at Fort Read: barracks (both one- and two-storey), mess halls, post exchanges, a massive laundry facility, a hospital complex, chapels, cinemas, a sports stadium and a special theatre: "Built along lines typical of those used for summer stock in the States, the theatre follows a trend towards the rustic. Its walls are paneled and stained and the stage is almost an exact replica of similar stages to which flock vacationing audiences . . . for a summer theatre season in the United States' New England." Fort Read supported both infantry troops and a large contingent of the army air force – by October 1941 the first section of its Waller Field was already in use for aviation. In addition to an initial 5,000-foot runway (later extended to 6,000 feet), Waller Field included two 8,000-foot runways as well as hangars, repair sheds and a drainage system. Though the terrain in the Fort Read area was rough and the vegetation dense, the army and its contractors had by 1943 constructed 1,432 buildings, 130 miles of roads, 345 miles of electric lines and 60 miles of water lines.[21]

Along with its various operational specifications, this extensive complex of facilities in the middle of the forest required protection from enemy planes. A solution to this challenge was coordinated by Lieutenant Colonel Homer Saint-Gaudens, the ranking camouflage officer with the Army Chief of Engineers

Office in Washington. Saint-Gaudens had a background in theatre directing, and during the war, was on leave from Pittsburgh's Carnegie Institute, where he was director of the Department of Fine Arts. He visited Trinidad in June 1941, at the early stage of base-building, and, in an interview with the *Trinidad Guardian* at the Queen's Park Hotel, explained that the objective of the camouflage scheme to be used at Fort Read and other bases was to blur the target as a result "of placement and dispersion of buildings, of the growth of trees, organisation of roads, and of the toning down to a monotone of the variety of surfaces of wood, landing strips and roads". All of this was carried out in a manner that would "conform with the natural landscape so as not to disturb the normal set-up". While a vast quantity of trees was cleared to develop Fort Read, a nursery was also established to grow bamboo, Australian pines and samaan for transplanting where additional camouflaging was needed.[22]

Naval Operating Base, Trinidad

The US Navy's massive operating base at Chaguaramas, on Trinidad's northwest peninsula, supported both seaplanes and ships and was vital in countering German submarine activity in the Caribbean. It was approximately eight miles west of the city, and the initial lease of land for the base included 7,940 acres (12.4 square miles), until a lease executed in December 1942 added 3,800 acres. With its position near major Caribbean sea lanes and its protected harbour within the Gulf of Paria, Chaguaramas eventually became one of the most important naval bases in the world. Similar to the army-base building programme in Trinidad, the development of the naval facility involved a wide range of personnel: the US Navy Civil Engineer Corps, with Lieutenant Commander C.P. Conrad serving as chief engineer; James Stewart Associates, an American firm that held the primary construction contract from January 1941 to June 1943; several contingents of the US Navy Construction Battalion ("Seabees"), who began arriving at the end of 1942 and took over construction work from James Stewart in mid-1943; and a peak of ten thousand local construction workers by the latter part of 1943.[23]

Of the total land acquired on the northwest peninsula, the navy developed 1,200 acres, including separate installations at Carenage Bay (St Peter's Bay), Chaguaramas Bay, Teteron Bay (Pierre Bay), Scotland Bay and in the Chaguaramas and Tucker Valleys. The navy also eventually employed Macqueripe Bay on the north coast of the peninsula and converted the popular Macqueripe Hotel (built during the 1930s) into an officers' club. Construction began in March 1941, the same month that an initial detachment of a hundred marines and other military personnel arrived on the island. Early work focused on

Carenage Bay and involved building a 500-foot pier, seaplane facilities (including ramps, a hangar and a control tower), and the usual range of base buildings. In addition, the navy carried out an extensive dredging operation and removed 13 million cubic yards of material from the bay over the course of two years. Some of this debris was used to infill low-lying swamp areas as part of a malaria-control programme that also included drainage and oil-spraying. As was the case with Walsh-Driscoll's army contract, the scope of work for James Stewart's assignment constantly expanded and encompassed construction at the various sites throughout the base area. Along with a growing number of barracks and general personnel buildings, projects included additional piers, fuel-storage tanks with a total capacity of close to eight million gallons, numerous large warehouses and an entire ship-repair facility at Chaguaramas Bay with an 1,800-foot quay and four finger piers. An extensive system of roads, electrical power, communications and water supply was also developed. In August 1941, the *Trinidad Guardian* commented that, with Chaguaramas and Fort Read, the Americans were creating two cities in the wilderness: "Men, dollars and machinery are putting these cities up at lightning speed for, as the U.S. Navy slogan pointedly states, 'Time is short'." In March 1943 Rear Admiral Jesse B. Oldendorf, commandant of the naval base, presented James Stewart Associates with the Army-Navy "E" Pennant in recognition of exceptional performance in construction work. During the award ceremony at Chaguaramas, James Stewart's operating manager paid high tribute to the local workmen, a large number of whom were present to receive pennant badges.[24]

On 12 March 1944, Eleanor Roosevelt visited Chaguaramas as part of her tour of military facilities in Trinidad and, a few days later, shared her observations of this well-constructed base in her "My Day" syndicated newspaper column:

> I think I am more deeply impressed by the work of the engineering groups and the Seabees on the different bases on Trinidad than anywhere else. . . .
>
> Sunday morning we visited the naval operating base including the naval air station. Everything was planned in expectation of more active opposition in this area than we have encountered, but our very preparation is what has brought about our safety. . . .
>
> The naval base has many acres of citrus fruit, and if properly taken care of, these orchards ought to provide our men with fresh fruit and be a great asset to the fleet and bases in this area.
>
> Sir Bede Clifford and several of the island officials met me on our arrival in Trinidad, and we met again at a dinner at the Officers' Club at Macqueripe. There is a beautiful view of the harbor from this club, and it is in every way a charming spot with a good swimming beach.
>
> We saw the most wonderful recreation area at Scotland Bay which was

> developed by the men on the station and the men from the ships which come in here....
>
> I would like to mention the work of a Colored Naval construction unit which has done such good work that it has earned a wonderful reputation among all the officers.

Indeed, Mrs Roosevelt visited the camp designated for African American Seabees at Chaguaramas and addressed them in their outdoor theatre. Photographs of her visit show both wood-frame barracks and Quonset huts.[25]

While the development of the Chaguaramas base was a grand success from the perspective of the US Navy, it also involved the dislocation of over six thousand people, substantially more than were displaced by the army's Fort Read base in the Cumuto Reserve. Residents from Nicholas Village and the Chaguaramas Bay area were the first to be forced to move; eventually the populations of both Teteron Bay and Scotland Bay were also ordered to relocate. Residents received some compensation for their losses and, in some cases, their disassembled houses were transported to new locations. Meanwhile, the Trinidad government's Lands and Surveys Department laid out a new settlement near the town of Carenage for more than two hundred displaced Teteron families. Adjacent to Carenage Bay, the settlement included streets paved with oil sand, a leased 100-by-50-foot plot for each family, an area where fishermen could keep their boats and mend their nets, and spaces planned for shops and a recreation park. A correspondent for the *Trinidad Guardian* referred to the settlement as a "model fishing hamlet" and opined that "there has been a definite attempt at town planning, something usually lacking in other rural areas allowed to grow in a haphazard fashion, with buildings scattered untidily on any odd spot".[26]

One of those involved in coordinating the relocation of families from the base area was baritone/actor Edric Connor. As noted in chapter 3, Connor studied engineering as part of his range of activities in Port of Spain and eventually gained employment with a construction firm. When James Stewart Associates began work at Chaguaramas, Connor arrived with his own crew of twenty-five men. In his memoirs, he says construction supervisors made him an "expeditor" who facilitated both the removal of local residents and relations with local workers. He claims that he was the person who recommended compensation and transportation for the displaced families, the establishment of a new settlement at Carenage and regular transport and soup kitchens for local workers. When a supervisor asked him about the prevalence of malnutrition among the labourers, Connor suggested, "Feed 'em."[27]

The Churchill-Roosevelt Highway and the North Coast Road

In addition to constructing bases, US authorities carried out two major road-building projects during the war – one to provide a more efficient link between Port of Spain and Fort Read, and the other to connect Port of Spain with an attractive beach at Maracas Bay on Trinidad's north coast. At the time, access to Fort Read was limited to the Eastern Main Road, the only route that connected the city with the bulk of the island to the east and south. This old two-lane road passed through numerous towns and heavily congested areas and thus was incapable of handling the large volume of trucks and other traffic generated by increasing military activity. By early 1942 the Americans were at work on a new thoroughfare to the south of the Eastern Main Road: the Churchill-Roosevelt Highway, which would extend 22 miles from the eastern suburbs of Port of Spain to Fort Read, passing the road to the Piarco airfield en route. At its western end, the highway would connect with a new Lady Young Road, which the Trinidad government was planning to build through the Morvant housing development, over the Laventille Hills, and down to the Queen's Park Savannah. Named to affirm British-American friendship, the Churchill-Roosevelt Highway was a well-graded and well-paved dual-carriageway road with shoulders and drainage. Since work progressed rapidly, it was soon being used by military vehicles and was eventually opened to civilian traffic.[28]

A far more challenging feat of engineering was the construction of the road to Maracas Bay, which the Americans built as a public relations gesture, rather than for military purposes. The navy's development of its base on the northwest peninsula eliminated public access to popular beaches, a situation that was further aggravated by its acquisition of Macqueripe Bay in December 1942. At this point, US authorities agreed to build a road to Maracas Bay, which would offer an alternative for beach recreation. This route, eventually called the "North Coast Road", would extend from the Saddle Road (which ran north from Port of Spain) over steep mountain passes and down the rugged north coast to Maracas Bay. In the late 1930s, the Trinidad government carried out preliminary work on the road, but discontinued its plans because of the war. In March 1943 navy contractor James Stewart Associates began a $500,000 project to continue the road, which was taken over by the Seabees in July 1943 and completed in April 1944. With dynamite, bulldozers and other heavy equipment, crews of Americans and Trinidadians worked their way through the densely forested, mountainous terrain and removed a total of one million cubic yards of earth. When completed, the 7.5-mile asphalt-paved road was 14 feet wide (with 5-foot shoulders), climbed to 1,335 feet and, with extensive switchbacks, never exceeded a 10 per cent grade. During construction, there were two routes under consideration from Pichon Gap in the mountains down to Maracas Bay. In the end, the Americans chose the route closer to the coast, which provided spectacular views of the mountainside plunging into the sea.[29]

As early as 1941, the *Trinidad Guardian* had been advocating a road to Maracas Bay in order to provide a new recreational beach for the local population and a postwar tourist destination, as well as to give fishermen greater access to the north coast and facilitate northern agriculturalists' travel to urban markets. In addition, the newspaper recommended planning the Maracas Bay area itself: "The importance of adequate planning in advance has been exemplified at those of our bathing beaches where the absence of a harmonious plan has resulted in chaotic conditions . . . results will not be satisfactory unless everything is fitted into its right place, and developments prevented from spreading haphazardly over areas where control is essential." As work on the road began in March 1943, the *Guardian* exclaimed: "Maracas, dream baby of our planning experts for many a year, looks at long last as if it is about to come forth as port, playground and production centre with rather charming and intriguing possibilities." In September 1944, after the road's completion, the newspaper continued its call for adequate planning: "Here there is scope for someone with vision to evolve a scheme which will make the area at once a thing of beauty and a joy for ever, for it would be almost sacrilege to allow so charming a spot to be sacrificed to sordid commercialism." Essentially, the *Guardian* appealed to the Trinidad government's growing interest in systematic land-use planning in order to advance a concept of Maracas Bay that would creatively integrate scenic beauty, beach recreation, village houses and other buildings, and commercial fishing.[30]

The US military carried out its extensive base- and road-building programme at a scale and speed unprecedented in Trinidad's history. With large command and operational structures and tens of millions of dollars at their disposal, the army and navy were able simultaneously to pursue multiple construction projects at various places around the island and mobilize a wide range of workers and material resources. Along with the military's own personnel, army contractor Walsh-Driscoll sent over forty-five hundred Americans to Trinidad and vast amounts of construction equipment and materials, including "69,000,000 board feet of lumber, 1,500,000 bags of cement, 6,000 tons of structural steel, 4,000,000 square feet of screening, 12,000,000 square feet of roofing, and 3,000,000 feet of fiber-board". Meanwhile, navy contractor James Stewart Associates also brought in employees and enormous quantities of equipment and supplies. In addition, the military and its contractors hired a substantial Trinidadian workforce: there were 21,692 local labourers employed on army bases in May 1942, the peak period of construction, and approximately

10,000 local labourers on the navy base during 1943, when construction peaked there.[31] The urgency of wartime preparedness necessitated rapid work. Much was accomplished during the first year of the mission and most projects were completed by early 1944.

Throughout the war, Port of Spain remained the operational centre of this activity. Though the largest bases were in rural areas of Trinidad, the city contained the army headquarters, the army seaport and other bases and entertainment offerings that attracted personnel from throughout the island. Moreover, the city linked the Western Main Road to Chaguaramas with the Eastern Main Road and Churchill-Roosevelt Highway to points east (including Fort Read) and points south (such as Carlsen Field) along the Southern Main Road. Military personnel and supplies constantly travelled in and out of the city on this network of roads, as well as on the eastern railway line that passed through Fort Read. In addition, thousands of labourers departed every day from Port of Spain along these roads to work at outlying bases, or on special trains from the city to Fort Read.

The American military bases, whether in Port of Spain or the countryside, were urban landscapes that contrasted sharply with surrounding environments in terms of design, function and population. While barracks and other general service buildings incorporated features that mitigated the heat and rain of a tropical climate, they were designed in simple, standardized forms to facilitate fast construction and immediate use. These structures offered basic necessities for habitation, without the comfortable verandahs, effusive ornamentation and bright colours characteristic of many Trinidadian houses. Spaces around the base buildings were also generally sparse. While military personnel made some effort to plant grass and shrubs, base environments looked nothing like Trinidadian yards, with their profusion of vegetation. The bases, however, did contain many of the facilities of a typical town – along with housing there were dining places, stores, laundries, hospitals, churches, movie theatres and recreation halls, all organized in street grids and supplied with utilities. But the regimentation and austerity of the base landscapes differed greatly from the eclectic character of Trinidadian towns and cities. Moreover, the bases existed not for commerce or manufacturing but to execute a military mission. Their ships, planes, vehicles, depots, fuel tanks, guns and general hardware were foreign to local material environments, while their training exercises, manoeuvres and other martial activities were unlike usual town life. Finally, the population of the bases consisted primarily of young white American men, though there were also some middle-aged men, women and children, as well as African Americans at segregated sites. In the context of Trinidad's population, the Yankees, whether on their bases or out and about, were clearly alien beings. "Hello Joe!"

Through their base-building enterprise, the Americans created alternative urban environments within Port of Spain and across Trinidad – places that displayed different construction processes, material styles and forms of public order. While the landscape of Port of Spain and other urban areas generally evolved in a gradual manner, even during boom times, the bases were built in their entirety over a relatively brief period. Instead of complex colonial environments with diverse historical layers, legacies and pursuits, these were streamlined instant towns organized to win a war.

LIFE IN THE WARTIME CITY

Though the Americans designed their bases as relatively contained environments and communities, they also depended in many ways on services offered by Trinidadians. The local population, in turn, tried to take advantage of the economic opportunities that the bases offered, while still maintaining a sense of control over their lives. Thus ensued a complex set of relationships in which Americans and Trinidadians tried to manage their sudden co-existence within Port of Spain and other base areas around the island. The massive American presence affected virtually every sphere of local life, from the economy and politics to social relations, domestic arrangements and entertainment. At the same time, the Americans gained varying degrees of familiarity with Trinidadian places, customs, speech and forms of artistic expression. Over the period of the war, the two populations indeed learned much about each other through interactions both contentious and cordial. Meanwhile, British colonial authorities in the city tried to accommodate the ever-growing requirements of the US military mission while still retaining sovereignty of the island and control over local affairs. The American presence posed numerous governance challenges, such as addressing land rights and leases, transport and utilities, labour markets, tax issues, housing and food shortages, crime and justice, and the general disruption of the colony's customary social life. In the course of the war, Trinidadians, Americans and Britons negotiated this range of issues and emerged from their experiences of the military enterprise with new perceptions of each other and themselves.

Soon after the United States initiated its base-building projects, Port of Spain became a major centre for housing and transporting construction and other workers. Thousands of people migrated to the city from the countryside and from other British Caribbean territories, in search of jobs that paid better wages than agricultural labour or other types of work within local economies. By 1942 the city's population had reached an estimated 100,585, up 13 per cent from an estimated 88,698 in 1938. While some residents of Port of Spain worked on military bases within the city or engaged in other occupations that supported the Americans, many got work at Chaguaramas and Fort Read. Workers travelling to Chaguaramas assembled at James Stewart Associates' recruitment/transport centre at the corner of the Mucurapo and Western Main Roads in St James. From here they rode in large trucks out to the base. Many of those employed at Fort Read travelled by train, and, for a period, Walsh-Driscoll chartered free morning and evening trains for its workforce. In early August 1941, a reporter for the *Trinidad Guardian* investigated this mode of transport and offered a vivid account of the dangerous conditions. After a day of work in the rough terrain of the Cumuto Reserve, labourers stampeded onto approximately fifty trucks, which carried them to one of the base's railway stations. They then prepared to board the trains:

> When the workmen's train bore down on the crowd, hundreds surged forward, letting the engine pass inches from their chests so restless and eager was every one to be the first to get in. Five carriages, two open wagons and a brake-van made up the train and every one was already packed – a condition accounted for by the fact that the train had come from the Cumuto station some two miles or so away.
>
> But agog as every carriage and truck was, hundreds of the crowd somehow found themselves in and on the train. There was no platform at this end, and this made it yet more risky to get into a carriage. People occupied the seats, sat upon the backrests, stood up in the spaces between the seats, invaded the couplings, thronged the floorboards – 40 persons on the floorboard alone.

The train stopped at the town of Tunapuna, but only slowed at smaller stations, obliging departing passengers to jump to the ground. Though the ride was hazardous, workers made the best of the situation. In the reporter's car, a group of some twenty men "entered into a sort of carnival merriment", singing and beating partitions, pans and bottles. The conversation of another group took a more theological slant, centring on "whether angels wore clothes, but mainly on whether there are black angels as well as white ones". By the time construction at Fort Read peaked (April–June 1942), between twelve thousand and fifteen thousand workers were travelling from Port of Spain to the base each day.[32]

Both in Port of Spain and around the outlying bases, tensions soon developed between Trinidadians and Americans. Many Americans arrived with little or no concept of Trinidad, racist attitudes of superiority towards peoples of African and Asian descent, and a sense of entitlement to carry out their military mission regardless of any local concerns. Army historian Captain James C. Shoultz Jr observes that, when the first construction personnel appeared, the Trinidad Country Club and other leading social establishments in Port of

Spain offered them club membership, but local opinions of these men quickly changed:

> In spite of these first offers of friendship, however, social relations got off to a very bad start. Walsh-Driscoll Contractor and the United States Engineer Department sent for construction work in Trinidad some of the lowest types of individuals from the United States, probably due to the pressure for quick completion of the base, and to the shortage of labor in the United States itself. These people were very quick to make a bad impression on the natives of the island.

American writer Wenzel Brown, who visited Trinidad shortly after the war, offers a more explicit description of this group:

> The Americans overran the hotels, flooded the clubs, threw their money about in the bars. These were not Americans skilled in diplomacy. The first wave was composed mostly of plumbers, carpenters, joiners, technicians, and various other semi-skilled laborers. They had been picked up willy-nilly in recruiting stations in Brooklyn, the Bronx, the water front of Norfolk and Wilmington. There was no time for careful screening. Stumble-bum and conscientious workman labored side by side. But it was the roughest, the noisiest, the most arrogant among the Americans who attracted attention.

Captain Shoultz adds that the arrival of the first army ground troops in May 1941 did not improve relations, noting that "the 33rd Infantry was not a very select group". Both the soldiers and the contractors' personnel were disrespectful towards local women and police, and frequently engaged in fights and other disturbances in the city. Tension was also increased by the Americans' perception that taxi drivers were charging them higher fares.[33]

It soon became clear to US military leaders that abusive and condescending behaviour towards Trinidadians interfered with their mission. Thus they devoted considerable attention to improving relations. In July 1941 General Talbot directed officers to act promptly in response to all incidents involving local people, and an increase in the deployment of military police also helped to reduce misconduct. In addition, the Americans used various media channels to foster better understanding between the two populations. In November 1941, for example, Alfonse Kaufman, a senior engineer with the USED, advised in a letter to *Tropical Topics*:

> Let us, men and women of the U.S.E.D., begin here in Trinidad by conducting ourselves with dignity. Let the people of Trinidad look up to us, not down on us. . . .
> Here in Trinidad, we have leased a home for ninety-nine years and we are really guests of the British authorities. Why not act as if we were guests and try to conform with the wishes of our hosts?

> When we visit Port-of-Spain or other public places outside of the American bases, why not be American the same as we would be in our home town?
>
> In the evening when we go to a public place such as the Queen's Park Hotel, why not wear a coat instead of shirt sleeves and suspenders?

Meanwhile, the army employed public relations officers in an attempt to create favourable coverage in local and external media, and in May 1942, the staff of *TNT* worked with the local Radio Distribution Company to broadcast a programme called *Meet the Americans*. *TNT* also counselled the troops in its own columns. In December 1942, for example, it ran an article, titled "Respect for Trinidadian Law Must Be Shown", in which it observed:

> We, literally, are guests of the people of Trinidad: they have accepted us here as friends and protectors; we walk the same streets, ride the same trolley cars and taxis, work [for] the same cause. Yet, we feel (not all of us) that we are privileged to a certain extent and that feeling manifests itself in an air of independence and disregard for set laws. . . .
>
> A lot of us would like to be back in the United States. In all likelihood, a lot of people in Trinidad also would like to have us back in the United States. . . . While we are here, we should conduct ourselves like soldiers and gentlemen.

Finally, when the army radio station (WVDI) began broadcasting from the St Clair Cantonment in 1943, it attracted a Trinidadian as well as a military audience and thus contributed to increasing familiarity with Americans and their mission in Trinidad.[34]

Perhaps the US military's most prominent display of cooperation with the local population was its participation in the Trinidad government's week-long Civil Defence Rally at the Queen's Park Savannah in May 1943. Intended to heighten public awareness of preparation against enemy threats, the event included a wide variety of exhibitions and demonstrations by the Trinidad Home Guard, British troops, American troops and such organizations as the Air Raid Precautions Services, British Red Cross Society, Women's Voluntary Services, Volunteer Fire Brigade, Boy Scouts Association, Girl Guides Association and the Win the War Association. Certainly the highlight of the rally was a staged attack by the US Army Air Corps on a model village that had been constructed in the Savannah. An estimated crowd of twenty-five thousand watched this closing event:

> The tensest moment in the day's activities came when U.S. Army 'planes cooperating with the defence services to give a touch of realism to this gigantic object lesson, approached the model village constructed in front of the racestand from several directions. . . .
>
> The village with its house, shops, school, church, and rumshop was going about

its normal business when there was an alert followed by a low-level attack by six 'planes. The Home Guard took up their positions and fired their rifles as the 'planes roared overhead. . . .

Shortly afterwards the village is subjected to a high-level attack, and the rumshop is bombed and collapses. Rescue and stretcher parties move in and get to work. . . .

The village has hardly recovered from this attack, when there is a third, in which some of the buildings take fire, and the V.F.B. now turn out with their pumps and hose and the situation is saved.

The lengthy programme lasting until 7:30 p.m. went off smoothly and successfully, and ended in a fitting blaze of light with distant U.S. searchlights directing their friendly beams on the smoking village and milling crowds, as the Police Band played the American and British anthems – a beautiful symbol of the clock-work co-ordination that featured the day's activities.

In such fashion, the Trinidadian public was treated to an "object lesson" in the vulnerability of their local landscape, the vital role that volunteer organizations played in civil defence and above all the military might of the United States. If the rally was organized to demonstrate wartime cooperation between Trinidadians, Britons and Americans, it also made clear the awesome power that the United States now exercised within the island.[35]

While the Civil Defence Rally was a large-scale official display of international cooperation, much social interaction between Americans and Trinidadians during the war took place in more casual and leisurely settings. As has historically been the case wherever military bases exist, the American troops in Trinidad had an insatiable appetite for entertainment and recreation, particularly socializing with local women. Their demand for diversions was intensified by the fact that while in Trinidad, they were carrying out a defensive military mission and not engaged in combat. Thus they constantly struggled with boredom, while their officers worked to maintain morale.[36] The military built a wide range of recreational facilities at the Port of Spain and outlying bases, with baseball and other sports attracting much participation. In addition, officers and enlisted men organized numerous dances on their bases and some regularly attended dances at elite social clubs around the city. Meanwhile, many servicemen pursued entertainment and pleasure in local nightclubs, calypso tents and on the streets. Indeed, an entire socio-spatial organization of leisure developed, in which Americans and Trinidadians participated in various roles.

The first base dance in Trinidad was presented at Docksite at the end of June 1941 by the "Survivors Club", a group of medical personnel. The organizers hired Bert McLean's Orchestra (one of the top bands on the island), invited a hundred local women (with chaperones), and lined up a mid-evening floor show by the Happy Hollow Haylofters, an army ensemble that performed country music. The Humming Bird, the *Trinidad Guardian*'s social columnist, attended and provided a sense of the scene: "The recreation room where the dance was held was beautifully decorated for the occasion by the men themselves, and the scene was a truly tropical one. Bamboo branches and coconut palms intermingled. The bamboos themselves were slit and a beautiful collection of tropical flowers and wild fruit protruded from these slits." The event was a grand success and many more dances were subsequently held after recreational facilities were completed at other bases in and outside the city. By July 1942, Sergeant A. Elwell Reid Jr, contributor to the *Guardian*'s "News from the US Bases" column, noted a schedule of dances that included Tuesday at the Castle Club (the army engineers' facility), Wednesday at the St Clair Cantonment, Thursday at Waller Field, Friday at the USO, Saturday at the Officers' Club and the Castle Club, and Sunday at the Non-commissioned Officers' Club. "What keeps the local gals going[?]," Reid wondered. In addition to the regular dances, there were occasional performances on the bases by various well-known American entertainers, such as Al Jolson, Laurel and Hardy, John Garfield and Chico Marx, who even penned a poem ("The First Time I Saw Trinidad") for *TNT*.[37]

A particularly exciting addition to the military's entertainment offerings was the Trinidad Base Command Follies, founded by Sally Osmon Rowe in early 1942. Before arriving in Trinidad with her husband, Rowe had performed as a nightclub singer in Chicago, Detroit and New York. Sensing a need for more diversions on the bases, she decided to organize a variety show and obtained the support of the army's Special Services Branch, the army band and the Civilian Volunteer Corps. Rowe recruited a range of female and male performers, both civilians and soldiers, and was soon leading rehearsals and designing costumes. Eventually the troupe developed a two-hour show, consisting of music, comedy, magicians, a Donald Duck imitator and "a dancing chorus of eight lovely girls" from Walsh-Driscoll's cottages at Fort Read. This latter group performed "several tricky dance numbers capped by a torrid conga". On 1 April the Trinidad Base Command Follies held their "world premiere" at the coastal-defence base on the island of Chacachacare, where they thrilled the audience; subsequently they appeared before enthusiastic crowds at Docksite, the St Clair Cantonment, Fort Read and other bases with theatres. By June they had also performed twice in British Guiana, seven times in Surinam and were preparing for trips to Aruba, Curaçao and St Lucia, with *TNT* confirming that they would become "the first flying stock company in the history of the U.S. Army theatricals". Meanwhile, Rowe was appointed "Regimental-Hostess" of the US Infantry at Fort Read.[38]

If the Trinidad Base Command Follies were the most successful performing group to emerge from the American military in Trinidad, the USO Club on Wrightson Road became the favourite venue for dances and other leisure activities. A few weeks before its grand opening on 20 April 1942, *TNT* ran an editorial in which it called for the club to operate a "date bureau", which would be of particular value to servicemen who were visiting from outlying bases and did not have friends in Port of Spain. The newspaper suggested that young women could be recruited from the lists of those who had been attending military dances for the past year and that their "particulars" could be obtained from their older female chaperones. In fact, the USO authorities moved forward with a plan of this sort to recruit young white women for club membership. Since there was still substantial distrust of American servicemen in the city, the authorities first recruited from prominent families twenty-one "senior hostesses" who would approve membership cards for the younger women. With this arrangement in place, many women did join the USO and began attending the regular Friday-night dances. They were even provided with transport if they telephoned the club. Meanwhile, the leadership of USO No. 2, the club for African American servicemen at Mucurapo Point, recruited its own set of senior hostesses and women. Further challenges then emerged when the African American 99th Coast Artillery departed Trinidad and was replaced by Puerto Rican troops. These men were admitted to the Docksite USO, which recruited women for them from the city's Spanish-speaking community. However, separate dances were eventually organized for the continental and Puerto Rican troops, as a result of arguments over music preferences. While the US military leadership pursued this officially segregated system in its attempts to control socializing and romance in Trinidad, it is equally clear that the troops often did not follow these directives when they were off the bases. In his detailed study of the sociocultural dynamics of the American occupation, historian Harvey Neptune describes extensive liaisons between white servicemen and non-white local women and argues that the transgressive appearance of these couples in public places threatened Trinidad's racist social hierarchy.[39]

In addition to attending dances and other functions on the bases, American military personnel and contractors also frequented some of Port of Spain's prominent social venues, many of which were in the Queen's Park Savannah area. Sometimes they organized their own events there. In June 1941, for example, an American Club of the West Indies met to plan a dance at the Queen's Park Hotel, as well as other leisure activities that would be open to all Americans resident in Trinidad and their guests. The following month, the army's service detachments held a dance at the Portuguese Club, set up army tents for refreshments in the club's garden, arranged for army trucks to bring young women to the event and taught them the latest jitterbug steps. The group was joined by members of the club and treated to an impromptu fashion show. The Prince's Building was also a popular site for dances. In August 1942, for example, non-commissioned officers from Waller Field (Fort Read) organized a dance there and decorated the ballroom with yellow, green, red and blue crepe paper and a crepe chandelier, illuminated by multicoloured spotlights. The men travelled to Port of Spain in an army convoy, arranged for women (who received mailed invitations) to be transported in Walsh-Driscoll buses and recruited the army engineers' twelve-piece Castleers band to provide the music. The band's theme song was "From One Love to Another", based on Cuban composer Ernesto Lecuona's "Danza Lucumí".[40]

Many servicemen, however, sought recreation not in the upscale settings of the Savannah area but in downtown venues and streets. Both US military and Trinidad government authorities warned against visiting such areas. In a *Seamen's Guide to Trinidad*, for example, Trinidad's information officer wrote: "To combat hooliganism the police are taking strong measures against drunkenness and for your safety you are advised not to frequent places other than those given in this booklet." Among the acceptable establishments listed were the USO Club on Wrightson Road, the British and Allied Merchant Navy Club in St Ann's, the American Seamen's Club (also in St Ann's) and the Sailors and Soldiers Club Harbour Canteen near the docks. However, the booklet also conveniently included the locations of "prophylactic stations" in the city: near Gate 3 of the USO Club, at the Shore Patrol building opposite the Naval Headquarters on Wrightson Road, at the Harbour Police Station on South Quay and at the corner of Park Street and Ariapita Avenue.[41]

The US Army also attempted to restrict the nighttime excursions of the troops. Army historian Captain Shoultz notes that "the bad spots of the town were also located and efforts made to keep soldiers away. One of the worst of these spots was found to be the GREEN CORNER in the heart of Port of Spain, where many of the local prostitutes made contacts. It was also found that the sailors gave much more trouble in this line than the soldiers." At the intersection of Park Street, St Vincent Street and Tragarete Road, Green Corner was a major point of traffic flow between the central city and western districts. In his memoirs, Guyanese writer Edgar Mittelholzer, who lived in Port of Spain during the war, recalls the ambience at Park Street and the corner:

> It is a street of cafés and restaurants and cheap boarding-houses and shops and shop-residences. The trams, at that time, ran through it, and rumbled through Green Corner into Tragarete Road. . . . There is the Green Corner Café, always crowded, and at the corner of St. Vincent Street stands the gaily-postered Globe Cinema, obliquely opposite which is the Plaza dance-hall where a piano or an orchestra seems to play day and night. . . . Traffic rumbles and roars and toots

> . . . and neon signs add to the vulgarity of the scene in the same way they do in Piccadilly Circus and Times Square.

Servicemen and sex workers also gathered at night on Wrightson Road near the USO. In a letter to the *Trinidad Guardian* on 26 October 1944, a resident of the area complained of shouting and singing servicemen, as well as pimps and prostitutes, at the corner of Wrightson Road and French Street, where they waited for buses and taxis. On this same day, *Guardian* editors observed that a new US Army order, designating certain sections of Port of Spain out of bounds for soldiers, had resulted in "the daring migration of questionable characters to the Docksite neighbourhood". It also noted that taxis there were being used for "immoral purposes" and that bawdy houses in the adjacent Woodbrook district were a "blot on the whole community".[42]

One of the areas that undoubtedly most concerned military and colonial authorities was the eastern side of downtown, which for years had been a site of disreputable activity. Among the venues in this district during the war were those run by the notorious gangster Boysie Singh: the adjacent Sunrise and Baltimore (bars and gambling dens) at the corner of Charlotte and Prince Streets, and the twenty-four-hour Dorset Club at the corner of Charlotte and Queen Streets. While another individual ran a restaurant on the ground floor of the latter building, Singh used the top floor for gambling and the middle floor for a bar, dance floor and suite of rooms graced by a contingent of prostitutes whom he recruited from all over Trinidad through contacts made at all-fours card matches. At the Dorset, he also dealt in marijuana from Venezuela and opium from India, as part of his larger black-market operations, which encompassed alcohol, jewellery and guns. By 1944 Singh was immensely wealthy and enjoyed parading the streets with a gold-topped walking stick and dressed in one of his 120 suits – selecting a different colour for each day of the week.[43]

One other popular destination for entertainment was Port of Spain's calypso tents, which the Trinidad government permitted to open for the Carnival season, though it banned the street Carnival from 1942 through 1945. In 1940, before the arrival of the American military, the city's two tents were on Henry and Nelson Streets, on the east side of downtown. From 1942 through 1945, however, they were positioned on the more attractive west side, shifting names and locations between St Vincent, Edward and Duke Streets. During this period, tents continued to be built in yards as temporary structures, comprising bamboo, wood and galvanized-iron sheets. Typically, they included a stage for the calypsonians and instrumentalists, chairs for the audience and decorations such as British and American flags and patriotic posters. Throughout the war, the tents were packed with enthusiastic military personnel. A few days after the 1943 Carnival, the *Trinidad Guardian* observed that "the advent of the United States armed forces to Trinidad resulted in a boom for calypsonians during the season, the novelty of the calypso to them attracting crowded houses every night". The city's dance bands were also fully booked for the season. In addition to their regular appearances in tents, some calypsonians occasionally performed on the military bases and in other venues. For example, Atilla, Lion, Growler and Invader were scheduled for a show at the USO auditorium on 11 March 1943, a few weeks after the close of the Carnival season. In fact, Atilla recalls that, during this period, calypso was becoming an accepted form of entertainment not just during Carnival but at parties and other functions throughout the year. He affirms: "The kaisonian was finding himself in a new awakening and discovering that he was now a celebrity."[44]

During the war, calypsonians continued to use their genre to explore a range of local and international topics. By the 1942 season, however, they were composing many calypsoes that addressed the American presence in Trinidad, and this remained a major theme for the remainder of the war. In a 16 January article for the *Trinidad Guardian*, army correspondent A. Elwell Reid wrote:

> Take a trip down to the R.A.F. Calypso practice sessions at St. Vincent Street some night if you want the straight information as to how the American "invasion" has affected the locals.... Nearly every number has an American twist to it, and they cover all phases of the U.S. in Trinidad from Chaguaramas to Cumuto with a couple of interesting detours on the way, "Wouldst the gift were given us, to see ourselves as others see us!"[45]

Certainly the best-known calypso of this era was Invader's "Rum and Coca-Cola", which he performed at the Victory Tent on Edward Street in 1943. With a lilting melody, the song critiques a breakdown in local domestic relations: mothers and daughters chasing the Yankee dollar at Point Cumana (between Port of Spain and Chaguaramas), aristocratic women out late at night, a newlywed who left her husband for a Yankee, and a police raid on a brothel in St James. Calypsonians wrote many songs of this sort, but also examined changing circumstances as the American troops began to depart. Lion's "Pam Palam" (1944), for example, describes local women who can no longer go dancing at Docksite, afford pretty dresses to wear to the cinema matinee or drive about in jeeps. Similarly, Growler's "Certain Taxi Driver" (1944) offers a metaphorical account of a woman who used to run a Lincoln Zephyr out of Arima and only picked up Yankees at high prices. But now Growler has met her in town at the Savannah, where her car is in disrepair.

Calypsonians also wrote on various other aspects of the war years, from unusual events to general social conditions. In "Scrutinize Their Face" (1944), Tiger relates the story of an American ship's cook who, in port in Trinidad, obtained a naval commander's uniform, dined and partied with the local elite, suggested marriage to one of their daughters and even visited the Chaguaramas base, where he enjoyed the navy's hospitality and recounted war stories. In "Food Distribution" (1944), Atilla addresses how wartime shortages forced most people to stand in long lines at markets, while the people of St Clair enjoyed truck deliveries and well-stocked kitchens. Meanwhile, Tiger advises workers who were earning high wages at the bases to prepare for the hard times that were likely to come after the war ("Save Your Money", 1944). Perhaps the calypso that best summarized wartime experience was Atilla's "No Nationality", which he wrote after the war had ended. He relates how, before the arrival of the Americans, he could travel anywhere in Trinidad, but now is scared to go near Cumuto (Fort Read) and cannot go past Carenage on the northwest peninsula, where a Yankee sentry might shoot him and tell him that he has no right to enter America. Meanwhile, the Americans have disrupted the society with their money, challenged local mores and left women with blue-eyed babies. Atilla concludes that he has no nationality – he knows that he is not an Englishman (the British gave away land for the bases without consulting local people), but he suspects that he is not an American either.[46]

During the war, calypsonians wrote songs on these and other topics for an expanded audience that included many Americans as well as Trinidadians. While calypso continued to serve as a form of social critique within the local community, it also functioned as a generally playful medium of communication between Trinidadians and Americans – a carnivalesque form in which the calypsonians were in charge and defined the situation (in contrast to the authoritarian labour relations on the bases). While the calypsonians dealt with serious ramifications of the American presence, they typically did so in a witty fashion in keeping with the stylistic characteristics of the calypso genre. American audiences, in turn, delighted in the calypsonians' artistry, were thrilled that the songs were often about themselves and seem to have accepted in good humour the way they were portrayed. In short, both calypsonians and Americans perceived these performances as entertaining and enjoyable.

During this period, calypsonians also increasingly viewed their music as a vehicle for defining Trinidad as a place in the wider world and themselves as professional artists. Since the mid-1930s, a number of the top calypsonians had recorded with American record companies and appeared in New York nightclubs. The wartime military bases, in turn, greatly expanded their audience and their opportunities for income and recognition. For most Americans, calypso was a new form of music – one that seemed to capture the ambience and spirit of Trinidad. Calypsonians worked to exploit this interest both in their willingness to perform for Americans in tents and other venues and in their composition of lively songs about these visitors. At the same time, there developed within Trinidad a body of research and commentary on calypso as a unique local art. For example, Edric Connor submitted a letter to the *Trinidad Guardian* in 1943 on the historical development of calypso in Trinidad (as part of a larger exchange on this topic), while in 1944 Charles Espinet and Harry Pitts published a seventy-five-page study of the genre titled *Land of Calypso: The Origin and Development of Trinidad's Folk Song*. With the growth of Trinidad's international significance during the war years, its populace increasingly conceptualized calypso as a creative medium for defining themselves and engaging with others.[47]

Though the American presence increased employment and generated a booming entertainment scene in Port of Spain during the war, it also created various hardships for the local population, particularly shortages of food and housing. By 1942 there were insufficient food supplies in the city, as a result of multiple factors. First was the increased resident population, encompassing American servicemen and contractors as well as migrants from elsewhere in Trinidad and other territories. In addition, there was less food production on the island owing to the substantial number of agricultural workers who left the fields for better-paying jobs in base construction. Finally, food imports were disrupted by the allocation of space on ships for construction materials and other military supplies, and by the threat of U-boat attacks. Decreased food supplies, along with increased demand, in turn raised prices, creating further hardship for the city's population.

In response to this situation, the colonial government initiated a "Grow More Food" campaign. While sugar planters were required to devote a portion of their lands to short-term food production, Harold Neal Fahey (the controller of local food production) called on householders to convert their flower gardens to kitchen gardens or help cultivate food crops in public spaces. Fahey particularly advocated easily cultivated crops, including cassava (which could be used as a vegetable or a source of flour), tannia, dasheen, bananas and Indian corn. In support of Fahey's call, the *Trinidad Guardian* editorialized: "Trinidad must be prepared to sacrifice without queries or quibbles a large part of the beauty of its private gardens and public parks including the Queen's Park Savannah, if food planting is to be placed on a war basis." In support of these initiatives, the government began selling both seeds and plants in depots in Port of Spain and around the island.

One group that was particularly active in the food-growing campaign was the Women's Voluntary Services. Modelled on the organization of the same name in England, the Women's Voluntary Services was established in Trinidad in May 1942 with the objective of mobilizing women to contribute to the war effort in such areas as driving cars and trucks, staffing canteens, operating telephone switchboards, doing clerical work and forming emergency first-aid units. Active members dressed in uniform, while other supporters wore armbands or badges. In a radio broadcast, the organization's president, Lady Clifford, affirmed that "it is a good and necessary thing to see the women of this community, irrespective of race, custom or creed, associating amicably together, and giving their time and energy in this work for the common welfare and safety of our island". As part of its many activities, the Women's Voluntary Services formed garden clubs in various districts of Port of Spain to support both cultivating and trading in produce. By the latter part of June 1942, close to 70 per cent of the city's households had kitchen gardens. However, food production was apparently not pursued in central city squares. When Alderman J. Milton Thorne, at a municipal health authority meeting, called for the immediate cultivation of squares and other available spaces controlled by the city council, the following exchange ensued:

> THE MAYOR [Tito Achong]: Do you suggest we knock down the trees in Woodford Square?
>
> ALDERMAN THORNE: No one suggested that. I would call you a vandal if you did that.
>
> THE MAYOR: I know something of agriculture, and I know if you have not sun you cannot grow crops.

While the city's shade trees were spared, families did modify the spaces around their homes and, to a degree, took food production into their own hands. This was accompanied by food preparation that was less dependent on wheat flour and other imports. By January 1943 the Women's Voluntary Services had even opened a cookery centre, where it demonstrated how to make bread, biscuits and delicacies from cassava and other local products. During the war, the government also implemented price controls and rationing in its efforts to address the food shortage.[48]

The wartime food shortage was accompanied by an equally serious crisis in housing. Port of Spain's insufficient supply during the 1930s was greatly exacerbated by the early 1940s, with the rapid influx of military personnel and migrating workers. While there was a growing demand for all types of accommodation, labourers faced the greatest challenge, since the total quantity of low-income barrack housing had actually decreased during this period. According to the *Trinidad Guardian*, 1,399 barrack-ranges containing 7,773 rooms occupied by seventeen thousand people were razed between 1938 and 1941. Many of these units were replaced by businesses or residential buildings that housed fewer people. With the growing demand for housing, and rising wages, landlords in turn steadily increased rents. Though the colonial government passed rent-control ordinances in October 1941 and February 1943, many tenants were pushed out of their homes. By the end of 1942, hundreds of families in the city were homeless, with some people sleeping in squares, on pavements and in other open spaces.[49]

Meanwhile, the government's Planning and Housing Commission, established in 1938, continued its work during the early 1940s under the chairmanship of Robert Grinnell, an American engineer who had been working in Tobago. The commission surveyed slum conditions downtown and in eastern areas like John John, where small houses were constructed with such materials as scrap wood, cement drums and bags. At the same time, it undertook new housing projects as part of its vision of a more orderly and healthy city in which planned neighbourhoods would replace the communities created by working people themselves. One of its projects was the construction of ninety workers' cottages in a development at the northwestern end of St James. Ready for occupancy by September 1941, these small houses contained two rooms, along with a verandah, kitchen and bath. Though the houses were arranged on open ground, workers were planting lime trees along the streets by the time tenants began moving in from Duncan, Nelson and Queen Streets downtown.[50]

During this same period, the commission implemented a more extensive housing project in Morvant, an area on the eastern slope of the Laventille Hills, which extended from the ridge down to the Eastern Main Road. Construction was carried out on a 360-acre site and by 1941, 440 houses were completed: 168 smaller units in Lower Morvant and 272 larger ones in Middle Morvant. Aimed at workers with higher incomes, the Middle Morvant homes included two bedrooms along with a living room, dining room, kitchen, bath and front gallery. The commission provided the development with water and electrical utilities, and reserved spaces for recreation grounds, schools, churches and shops. It also promoted the area's scenic beauty and named many of the new streets after local trees and birds. The *Trinidad Guardian* reported:

> Under trained and ever-watchful eyes nothing is being omitted that will add to the natural charms of the place. Bearing coconut trees, gracefully studding the landscape, and fruit trees are being saved and cared for to benefit residents and with the help of the Department of Agriculture, the Commission proposes to plant as many more fruit trees as possible at convenient spots and will grow ornamental hedges and flowering shrubs at points where these will lend harmony to the landscape.

In October 1941, as families began moving into Morvant from downtown, the *Guardian* described the new development as a "model township" and noted: "These first residents are reported to be happy at the change from the unhealthy congestion of the southeastern section of Port-of-Spain to the open setting of the Laventille Hills with its health-giving breezes." After 1941 the Planning and Housing Commission built additional houses in Morvant in its attempt to promote this district as an exemplar of a planned community that could reduce slum housing and improve the lives of working people. However, its overall impact on the city's housing problem was minimal, since the number of units was disproportionate to the need and because many low-income workers could not afford to rent them.[51]

By the latter part of 1943 and 1944, the role that Port of Spain and Trinidad played in American military defence was decreasing. With significant Allied victories in Europe and increased activity in the Pacific, there was less need for Atlantic bases to protect the Western Hemisphere. The United States thus began to scale down its troop strength in Trinidad and to return some smaller areas of leased lands in Port of Spain and throughout the island. With this reduction of the American military presence, both the colonial and municipal governments began contemplating plans for new postwar uses of spaces around the city. In 1944, for example, the former engaged in discussions with the US military about the return of King George V Park and a possible purchase of the St Clair Cantonment buildings. However, the buildings were eventually removed and the land again used as a public park. During the final years of the war, the government and its Planning and Housing Commission also undertook projects downtown, particularly the reclamation of an expected 183 acres of land from the eastern end of the old Port of Spain harbour, on both sides of the Dry River. In addition to eliminating mudflats and a malaria breeding-ground, this project was intended to provide land for new docking facilities, government buildings and industrial and commercial uses. For a period, the commission even planned to incorporate within this site an airport designed by Robert Grinnell. However, the feasibility of the airport was questioned, and in July 1944, Grinnell resigned and was replaced as commission chairman by Errol Dos Santos, a local government official.[52]

Another active figure in the Planning and Housing Commission during this period was Anthony Lewis, who had been appointed architect and city planner in September 1943. The son of a Port of Spain family, Lewis held a bachelor's degree in architecture from McGill University and a master's degree in city and regional planning from the Illinois Institute of Technology, and had worked for several months with Caribbean Architects-Engineers on the American bases. In addition to assisting with plans for the reclaimed lands at the harbour, in 1944 he developed a master plan for the deteriorating blocks on the east side of downtown, with the intention "to zone the area for specific functions affording healthy, convenient places in which people may live, work, play and move". Existing slum housing would be replaced with two- and three-storey residential buildings, accompanied by open spaces for recreation and laundry. On 8 October 1944, the *Trinidad Guardian* published a perspective drawing by Lewis that depicted an orthogonal layout of five long three-storey buildings with surrounding lawns and paths, on the block of Marine Square between Duncan Street and the Dry River. During the late 1940s and early 1950s, numerous two- and three-storey concrete apartment blocks of this type were erected along Duncan, Nelson and George Streets. Locally known as "the Plannings", these buildings radically changed the organization and appearance of the east side of downtown (see figure 27).[53]

LITERATURE OF THE WARTIME CITY

The American presence in Trinidad generated extensive commentary in local newspapers and other literature, both during and after the war. As US military activity escalated and then declined, writers worked to chronicle the wide-ranging changes that had occurred in the landscape around them and to describe the different facets and consequences of American-Trinidadian interactions. Among the most revealing accounts of life in wartime Port of Spain are three novels written during the 1950s: Ralph de Boissière's *Rum and Coca-Cola* (1956), Samuel Selvon's *A Brighter Sun* (1952) and V.S. Naipaul's *Miguel Street* (1959).

The three writers differed significantly in terms of their upbringing and early experience in Trinidadian society. Ralph de Boissière (1907–2008) was a mixed-descent member of a prominent Port of Spain family, attended the uptown Tranquillity Boys' Intermediate School and Queen's Royal College, and found employment principally as an office worker. During the 1930s, he was a member of the Beacon group of writers and was active in trade unionism and the NWCSA. In 1947 he travelled to Chicago to study mechanics and the following year migrated to Australia, where he wrote *Crown Jewel* (1952), which dealt with the upheaval of Trinidad during the 1930s, *Rum and Coca-Cola* and other books. Samuel Selvon (1923–1994) was born in southern Trinidad to an Indian father and a mother of Indian and Scottish descent. He attended Naparima College in San Fernando, interacted easily with companions from various backgrounds and considered himself a cosmopolitan Trinidadian, rather than a member of a particular ethnic or religious group. During the war, he served in the local branch of the Royal Naval Reserve and later worked as a subeditor with the *Trinidad Guardian*'s weekly magazine, while also writing poems and short stories. In 1950 he migrated to London, where he wrote *A Brighter Sun*; a sequel, *Turn Again Tiger* (1958); *The Lonely Londoners* (1956), which depicted the life of West Indian emigrants in the metropole; and several other books. In 1978 he migrated to Canada and continued writing.

Younger than both de Boissière and Selvon, V.S. Naipaul was born in 1932 in Chaguanas in central Trinidad, lived in the house of his mother's well-established Indian family (the Capildeos), and moved to Woodbrook in 1938 when his father, a reporter for the *Trinidad Guardian*, was reassigned to the Port of Spain office. During the early 1940s, the family spent two years on the outskirts of Port of Spain, but then lived again in Woodbrook until 1946, at which point they moved to St James. Naipaul attended Queen's Royal College, won a Trinidad government scholarship in 1948, and left for England in 1950 to study English at Oxford. In 1954 he completed his studies, moved to London and began writing, while also working as a freelancer for the BBC Caribbean Service. Though he wrote *Miguel Street* in 1955, two of his other novels were published first. During the following decades, he lived in England, travelled widely, wrote over twenty more books (both fiction and non-fiction) and was awarded the Nobel Prize in Literature in 2001.[54]

De Boissière, Selvon and Naipaul all drew on their personal knowledge of Port of Spain to construct narrative perspectives for their books. Reminiscent of the 1930s novels of Alfred Mendes and C.L.R. James, de Boissière's omniscient narrator in *Rum and Coca-Cola* offers realistic descriptions of various settings in and around the city, chronicles the interrelated lives of characters of various ethnicities and classes, and develops an explicit critique of social injustice. In *A Brighter Sun*, Selvon also employs an omniscient narrator, but one whose views and voice are closer to those of his characters. Narration in standard English is combined with extensive dialogue in (modified) Trinidadian Creole to create an informal, contemplative account of the lives of a small group of working-class characters living in a town adjacent to the city.[55] Finally, V.S. Naipaul's first-person narrator in *Miguel Street* recollects memories from his childhood and youth in one Woodbrook street. With a mix of standard and Creole English, he captures the life of the neighbourhood in a humorous, ironic style typical of male storytelling and banter in Trinidad.

Originally published in Australia in 1956 and republished in a revised edition in London in 1984, de Boissière's *Rum and Coca-Cola* weaves together stories of romantic relationships, labour activities, business deals, political manoeuvring and recreational diversions in a trenchant examination of the American impact on Trinidad from 1941 to 1945. Most of the novel is set in or around Port of Spain, which is represented as the hub of the American occupation. A few early scenes take place at "Coudray lands", a yard on the eastern outskirts of the city in which Marie, her lover Fred and several other characters live in small wooden houses. When Henri de Coudray (a member of an old, well-to-do mixed-descent family) sells the yard, American contractors arrive with a bulldozer, uproot trees and knock down the houses to construct a road. De Coudray also loses two other properties to US authorities: a former family estate on the northwest peninsula where the Americans are developing the Chaguaramas naval base, and a house on Manzanilla beach on Trinidad's eastern coast. With this loss of his family's past, de Coudray becomes ill and dies in his home in town, dreaming of Americans digging a trench for telephone cables through his back garden. The narrator observes:

> Who the real masters of the island were became clearer day by day. Endless streams of military trucks, long trailers carrying bulldozers or tanks, moved between Docksite and Cumuto; planes roared overhead. . . . Out of the mud of the foreshore, out of the inland forests, arose complete American towns. Such was Docksite, with its own streets and wharves, theatre, hospital and administration buildings. George the Fifth Park, at the western end of Port-of-Spain, had disappeared under army huts that sprang up overnight like mushrooms.

While de Coudray loses his land and his life with the arrival of the Americans, other characters in the novel find new opportunities. Principal among these is Marie, who is seventeen at the beginning of the story, orphaned by a Portuguese father and mixed-descent mother, and skilled at surviving through her wit and beauty. After Coudray lands are demolished, she obtains from the bulldozer-driver a nice house in the Santa Cruz valley (to the north of the city) and later moves to a two-bedroom cottage in Woodbrook, where she finds a job in the laundry at nearby Docksite. Soon she develops a relationship with Bob, an American electrician, subsequently befriends Wal, a US Engineer Department employee whom she eventually marries, and has a child. Through Bob and Wal, Marie is able to visit a range of upscale events and settings around the city, such as dinner at the Hotel de Paris (where she earlier worked as a chambermaid), balcony seats at the De Luxe cinema, dances at Docksite and a party with Americans at a house in the exclusive Maraval district. Meanwhile, she opens her own restaurant on Queen Street, where she presides over an enthusiastic clientele of American military personnel and local businessmen. By the latter years of the war, however, Marie's good fortune begins to unravel and her life comes to a tragic end at the Queen Street bridge over the Dry River, on the depressed eastern side of the city.

While the American presence quickly enriches and consumes Marie, the African mechanic Fred (the novel's other principal character) negotiates the changing times with more caution. After the destruction of Coudray lands, he finds a place to live in uptown Port of Spain and begins working as a night-shift driver for the Chaguaramas naval base. Throughout most of the novel, he is torn between relationships with the vivacious and charming Marie and the thoughtful and politically engaged Indra, daughter of an African father (a shopkeeper and city councillor) and a social-climbing Indian mother. He also becomes increasingly involved in organizing local labourers employed at the American bases, where they are paid far less than American civilians and subjected to physical abuse. Eventually, the base drivers mount a strike and succeed in obtaining a pay increase. At the close of the novel, Fred reflects in his rented room on the events of the past few years (during which he has lost both Marie and Indra): "He thought how the white American occupation had broken down walls and snapped ancient chains without freeing him or Mopsy [Marie] or anyone at all. But it had forced ideas upon him, ideas that could be weapons." Here de Boissière ends his multi-stranded story of American possession; British colonial decline; and growing political consciousness, organization and assertion among working people in wartime Port of Spain. While the US military presence disrupted the local landscape and social order, it also opened up new possibilities for the city's inhabitants.[56]

Samuel Selvon's *A Brighter Sun* offers a more tightly focused account of the war years through a narrative of a young Indian couple (Tiger and Urmilla) and their friends and acquaintances, though several chapters begin with listings of various contemporary local events (seemingly gleaned from newspapers) that place the lives of the characters in the broader context of a rapidly changing Trinidad. The novel is set primarily in Barataria, a town straddling the Eastern Main Road on the outskirts of Port of Spain. With the wartime housing shortage in the city, Barataria has filled with new residents – a mix of Africans, Indians and Chinese. Trains, buses and taxis regularly pass through the town, carrying workers to and from Port of Spain, while some residents make a living by cultivating gardens on its southern edge. In essence, Barataria is an intermediary zone between country and city and a microcosm of evolving Trinidadian society.

After their arranged marriage in Chaguanas, in Trinidad's sugar district, Tiger and Urmilla arrive in Barataria one evening to the sounds of a moaning cow and jazz from a radio. They occupy a one-room mud structure with a palm-leaf roof, a few pieces of furniture and an earthen fireplace dug in the ground in the back. Tiger tends a garden, while Urmilla sells milk from their single cow and eventually takes care of their new baby girl. Soon after their arrival, they develop a friendship with their next-door neighbours Joe and Rita, an African couple who live in a concrete-block house with glass windows, electricity, running water and a variety of furnishings. The narrator introduces the world of Port of Spain to the story by providing background on Joe, who was born on George Street to a young woman working as a prostitute. After dropping out of school, Joe got a job at the Chaguaramas naval base and eventually moved with Rita to Barataria. Another figure who has left Port of Spain for Barataria is an Indian named Boysie, who "was mixed up good and proper with the cosmopolitan atmosphere of the city and was at home with anybody".

Though Boysie tends a garden near Tiger's, he regularly visits the city, where he enjoys the nightlife and his African girlfriend. Tiger admires Boysie's freedom from country traditions and eagerly looks forward to his own first visit to Port of Spain. One day the two take a taxi into the city, where Boysie nonchalantly handles Tiger's many questions about the place. Later in the day, Tiger rides on a tram to the Queen's Park Savannah and is impressed by Queen's Royal College and the magnificent houses along the Maraval Road. He dreams that someday he will go to school, study in England to become a lawyer, open an office in Port of Spain, marry a doctor's daughter of his own choosing and live in an elegant house.

Back in Barataria, still working his garden, Tiger teaches himself to read and applies this skill one day to a notice posted in a shop: the Americans will be building a new road on the south side of the town and the gardeners will have to vacate their lands. Thus begins a dramatic change in the affairs of the settlement. Sensing that the road could be a path forward in life, Tiger tells his neighbour Joe that he will gladly give up his garden to take a construction job and save money to build a new house: "You think I want to live in a mud hut all the days of my life? . . . I have ambition." The next day American servicemen arrive in a jeep to survey the land for what would become the Churchill-Roosevelt Highway. When they peer through their theodolite, Tiger imagines the course of the road passing through the fields. He gets a job on a construction crew, buys a book about roads and begins writing down everything that happens in a copybook. As the project progresses and familiar landmarks disappear, the members of the crews start calling each other "Joe", imitate a Yankee drawl and sport sailor and army caps.

Eventually, the workers finish the highway with gravel, asphalt and Barber-Greene paving equipment, and a short ceremony is held near Barataria to mark its opening to civilian traffic. The fame of the road soon spreads across the island – drivers leave their regular routes to experience it, bicyclists race on it, lovers stroll on it in the evenings, farmers sell produce on its sides and visitors enjoy its scenery, all while a constant stream of military truck convoys travel back and forth between Port of Spain and Fort Read. Tiger sometimes walks along the highway at night and reflects on his life, after a family tragedy that has resulted in his wife and daughter's returning to Chaguanas for a period. Meanwhile, he starts to build a concrete house around the perimeter of his hut. At first he works alone but eventually re-establishes relationships with friends, who come on Sundays for a collective "lend-hand" of building (with Joe's house serving as a model) and rum-drinking. By the time Urmilla returns, the house is almost finished, with a galvanized metal roof, flooring and parts of the old hut used to make a larger kitchen. Though Tiger tells Urmilla that he will never go back to working in a canefield, he maintains two beds of lettuce on the side of the house, "to keep my hand in practice". For Tiger, constructing a new house is part of a larger process, pursued throughout the novel, of trying better to understand himself, his marriage, his multiethnic community and their future. At the close of the novel, he joins in the mass celebration of VE Day on the streets of Port of Spain and waits for a reply from the *Trinidad Guardian* concerning a short story that he has submitted about the new highway.[57]

V.S. Naipaul's *Miguel Street* is an even more sharply delimited novel, modelled on his personal experience of living on Luis Street in Woodbrook. Both the fictional and actual streets terminate at Docksite to the south and intersect Ariapita Avenue. The timeframe of the novel (1938–1950) also corresponds to Naipaul's childhood and youth. Though he did not live on Luis Street for this entire period, it was his home during the war's latter years, which are the focus of the novel. In an essay titled "Prologue to an Autobiography" (1984), Naipaul reflects on the process of writing *Miguel Street*. While working in a BBC office in London in 1955, he remembered his Woodbrook neighbour Hat shouting a greeting each morning to Bogart, a family friend who lived in a one-room structure in their backyard. This memory inspired a story about Bogart, which in turn provided a foundation for recollecting and recreating the whole world of the street. Simplification was essential to this literary rendering. While a growing number of Naipaul's maternal relatives moved into the house on Luis Street after 1942, the narrator of *Miguel Street* lives alone with his mother and is easily able to observe and interact with the denizens of the neighbourhood, without excessive domestic encumbrances. Looking back on his childhood and teenage years (like Naipaul's recollections in 1955), the narrator gradually introduces new characters – initially as names, then with passing comments, and eventually in chapters, each of which focuses on one figure. Most characters are not identified by ethnicity – they are simply residents of Miguel Street, urban Trinidadians. As the narrative progresses, the shape of this community becomes increasingly clear in terms of personal relationships, occupations, pastimes, collective sentiment and the daily rhythms of life on the street. Dialogue in Creole, pithy observations, lines from calypsoes of the era and sharp humour all contribute to the setting's ambience. While the narrator's memories jump back and forth in time in the course of his storytelling, he has matured by the end of the novel and leaves Trinidad, as Naipaul himself did in 1950.[58]

The residents of Miguel Street are a varied lot who are generally amused by and tolerant of each other's eccentricities (a common attitude in Trinidad). Bogart lives in his small backyard room, and while the narrator paints a sign for him that advertises a tailoring business, he spends most of his time playing solitaire. He acquired his nickname after *Casablanca* played in Port of

Spain, keeps a picture of Lauren Bacall on his wall and likes to speak with an American accent. Next door to Bogart is Hat, who maintains a cow pen and talks like the British actor Rex Harrison. Hat is something of a leader of the men and boys on the street, constantly reads the *Trinidad Guardian*, seems knowledgeable about most affairs of the neighbourhood and regularly offers wry comments on passing events. A close friend of Hat and Bogart is Eddoes, who drives a blue scavenging (garbage-collecting) cart and thus finishes work early each day. Eddoes is a "saga boy", a fellow who attracts women by dressing in stylish clothes (often following the latest American fashions). This trio of individuals, Hat's brother Edward, the narrator and a few other younger boys frequently gather together to pass the time and observe the many other residents of Miguel Street. There is Popo – a carpenter who works in his backyard galvanized-iron shop on "the thing without a name", making no actual furniture until later in the story. Man-man, who runs for every election and obtains three votes, spends much of his time writing words. When the narrator tells him that he is on his way to school, Man-man devotes the rest of the day to chalking "school" on the pavement, with multiple O's, all the way around the block. The narrator's Uncle Bhakcu, the "Mechanical Genius", constantly tinkers with his car, often rendering it inoperable. Morgan, the "Pyrotechnicist", carries out fireworks experiments in his house, igniting it one night and finally attaining the admiration of his neighbours. At one end of the street is Titus Hoyt, who runs a small school in his house. Mr Hoyt tries to teach the neighbourhood boys Latin on his verandah and then forms the Miguel Street Literary and Social Youth Club, which soon devolves into an occasion for the boys' commentary on the latest movies playing in town.

As the narrator tells stories of these and various other characters, the landscape and community of Miguel Street emerge as an interconnected whole. Within this environment, there is a high level of residential density as well as spatial openness, as manifested in open doors and windows in houses and the use of verandahs and yards as domestic spaces. Yards, in turn, open into the street, where the men and boys gather regularly to talk and the latter play cricket. Occasionally, some of the women join the others on the street to pass judgement on an unusual incident. In essence, the density and openness of the environment facilitate constant social interaction among residents and keen awareness of each other's business. Such landscapes were (and remain) typical of many parts of Port of Spain.

Though the residents of Miguel Street occasionally venture to other parts of the city and beyond, most of the novel takes place in this single locale. However, there is an intrusion on this familiar world: American servicemen from the Docksite base at the end of the street. In his "Prologue to an Autobiography", Naipaul discusses the arrival of the Americans at Docksite, where they raised a flag each morning and lowered it each evening to the sound of bugles. At night one could also hear the outdoor cinema on the base, while a house on the street became a sort of brothel. At the end of the war, when a local contractor began tearing down the buildings at the base, Naipaul's family had the opportunity to gather whatever timber they wanted. Naipaul himself took some to make a gate for his father's recently purchased house in St James.[59] In *Miguel Street*, the Americans similarly invade the neighbourhood. The unpopular George turns his dilapidated pink house into a brothel, while Hat's brother Edward gets a job at Chaguaramas, begins chewing gum and wearing American-style clothes, and holds noisy parties for Americans in his house. He tells the narrator that Miguel Street could pass for a sidewalk in the United States and takes him to watch an open-air movie through the barbed-wire fence at Docksite. Meanwhile, Hat runs a racket in which the narrator and other boys hustle servicemen for gum and chocolate. Finally, Bolo the barber, who cuts hair under a mango tree on Miguel Street, only accepts that the war is over when, in 1947, the Americans begin tearing down the buildings at their base in King George V Park.

The American construction of bases in Port of Spain during World War II had a minimal long-term effect on the built environment of the city, given that they were closed after the war, buildings removed and lands returned for other uses. During the war, however, it constituted a large-scale demonstration of American power: acquisition and control of property, the display of military engineering and architecture, and rearrangement of social relations. Before the war, Trinidadians encountered the United States primarily through movies, magazines and trade goods; passing interactions with visiting tourists, sailors and businesspeople; and a limited degree of travel and migration to the north. The war, however, rapidly introduced thousands of American servicemen and other personnel who became regular inhabitants of the city and the outlying bases. Their impact in their few years of residence was wide-ranging in terms of occupation of land, competition for housing, hiring local labour and reshaping entertainment in the city. Though Trinidadians increasingly questioned the American disruption of their world, many also enjoyed the higher incomes and good times while they lasted.

One core concern among Trinidadians during the war was the possibility that Britain would cede sovereignty over the colony to the United States. During the local debate about the destroyers-for-bases agreement in 1940–1941, an American acquisition of *all* of Trinidad was envisioned as a potential outcome. By November 1941, with the American military presence rapidly developing, journalist Trevor Christie reported in *Life* magazine that "underlying every conversation about the bases is the unspoken fear or hope that Great Britain eventually will hand over the island or the U.S. will take it over". Christie attempted to summarize local opinion on a possible transfer: British officials and local businessmen were in general strongly opposed, a small group of professionals and senior office workers were in favour because they felt the Colonial Office had denied them job opportunities, a large number of the mixed-descent middle class was opposed because of fear of American racism, but the great majority of the masses hoped for a takeover on the theory that "it couldn't be worse than this and it might be better". As the American presence in Trinidad expanded during 1942, however, President Roosevelt reiterated that the United States had no interest in acquiring more territories in the Caribbean. In her examination of wartime experiences across the British Caribbean, historian Annette Palmer notes a general change in opinion on American annexation. At the beginning of the war, many people welcomed the possibility of American sovereignty on the assumption that it would bring greater economic and political opportunity. After several years of American racism, abusive labour practices and troublesome troop behaviour, however, local populations were ready for the United States to depart and opposed suggestions of a takeover.[60]

The American military bases certainly had a lasting impact on Trinidadians' perceptions of the United States and the British empire and on their understanding of themselves. While army activity at Fort Read and Carlsen Field ceased after the war, the Chaguaramas naval base remained in operation (with greatly reduced personnel) into the 1960s and became a symbol of arrogant US imperialism. During these years, Trinidadians were forced to balance apprehension over American military and political interference with support for growing economic relationships. At the same time, the capacity of the United States to transform the island in the course of the war further challenged the significance of British colonial authority for the local population. Britain seemed less commanding as a political and cultural centre and more vulnerable in a rapidly changing world. During the postwar era, Trinidadians' opposition to British imperial rule continued to grow as they envisioned greater control of their land, resources and lives and began to pursue new forms of national sovereignty.

7. THE LANDSCAPE OF INDEPENDENCE

IN THE YEARS AFTER WORLD WAR II, Port of Spain flourished as a site of exceptional creativity in both artistic expression and political organization. Writers, actors, musicians, dancers, painters and sculptors appropriated spaces across the city, formed networks and associations and strove to achieve greater visibility and support for their work. Shows and exhibitions occurred regularly in a variety of indoor venues, while the city's streets continued to serve as a stage for large-scale public performances, such as the pre-Lenten Carnival, with its thousands of masqueraders, and the observance of Hosay, with its towering representations of the tomb of the martyred Hussein. Much of this creative expression utilized or explored elements of the local environment and was promoted by community activists and commentators as a manifestation of an evolving national identity. Certainly the most unusual phenomenon of the era was the development of steelbands, ensembles of young men who made music from metal containers and other objects of the urban landscape. These bands increasingly claimed new spaces within the city and eventually gained recognition as a distinctively Trinidadian art form. Paralleling this postwar artistic ferment and its nationalist promotion was the organization of numerous political parties, including the sudden rise in the mid-1950s of the People's National Movement. Employing Woodford Square as its primary centre, this party advanced mass political education and mobilization, brought a new level of discipline to the political arena, contested the continuation of American military bases in Trinidad and successfully led the territory to independence in 1962. For the celebrations of independence, civic leaders organized a series of events that combined political and artistic expression to dramatize the transition from colonial rule to full self-government and to showcase the nation's achievements. However, the city also functioned during this period as a place for debating the nation's character and prospects, including its ongoing ties to the British Commonwealth and the United States.

Formal decolonization in Trinidad and Tobago was a gradual and peaceful process, worked out through negotiations and constitutional modifications over a period of more than fifteen years. After the institution of universal adult suffrage in 1945, changes to the territory's constitution incrementally increased the number of elected members in the legislative council while decreasing appointed members and the power of the governor. Elections held in 1946 and 1950 featured multiple loosely organized parties and a plethora of candidates, most from middle-class backgrounds. During this period, Albert Gomes emerged as the territory's dominant political figure, particularly after 1950, through his executive council portfolio for labour, commerce and industry. While Gomes had been a strong advocate of workers' interests from the 1930s through the mid-1940s, he now worked to restrain labour and develop favourable conditions for the business community, including the passage of a Pioneer Industries Ordinance that offered tax exemptions in order to attract foreign investors as well as stimulate local entrepreneurship. By the mid-1950s, however, there was considerable public dissatisfaction with the integrity of the administration spearheaded by Gomes. In the 1956 election, Eric Williams's leadership of the tightly organized PNM enabled it to capture thirteen of the twenty-four elected seats in the legislative council. Governor Edward Beetham then arranged the support of four unelected members of the council, which allowed the PNM to form a government. At this point, the main opposition was the People's Democratic Party, under the leadership of Bhadase Maraj, who was also president of the sugar-workers' union and head of the Maha Sabha (a major Hindu organization). Though both the PNM and People's Democratic Party had campaigned as national parties, they appealed primarily to Afro-Trinidadian and Indo-Trinidadian bases respectively and thus established a pattern of ethnic-based politics that would characterize subsequent elections. Once in office, the PNM pursued a variety of infrastructure and economic development programmes, some of which had been initiated by the previous administration. In 1961 the PNM engaged in a fierce election campaign against the People's Democratic Party's successor, the Democratic Labour Party, led by Rudranath Capildeo, an educator (with a PhD in mathematics), attorney and uncle of V.S. Naipaul. The PNM won a decisive victory, instituted further development programmes and continued to prepare the nation for independence.

Complicating Trinidad and Tobago's political trajectory during this period was the initiation in 1958 of the West Indies Federation, a body that comprised most of the anglophone islands of the Caribbean. The formation of the federation was propelled both by nationalists' vision of a larger and more powerful economic and political union and by the British Colonial Office's desire for a consolidated administration that would reduce responsibilities for its Caribbean territories. In 1961–1962, however, the federation collapsed, owing to differences among its constituent members over its goals and structure. Trinidad and Tobago then sought its independence directly with Britain through constitutional conferences in Port of Spain and London, culminating in an agreement between Williams and Capildeo that would safeguard the political interests of the nation as a whole. Independence Day was celebrated on 31 August 1962, three weeks after Jamaica's independence.

The process of decolonization in Trinidad and Tobago took place during a period of strong economic growth. In 1950 imports and exports totalled $169,225,970 and $177,592,231 respectively, while by 1960 these numbers had increased to $504,591,000 and $491,838,000. The expansion of the oil industry was central to this performance. During the early 1950s, discoveries of new oil deposits offshore, as well as on land, greatly increased production, and Trinidad refined high volumes of both domestic and imported oil. Expansion was accompanied by shifts in the ownership of the industry. In 1956 Texaco took over Trinidad Leaseholds Limited (the largest oil company in the territory and the owner of the largest refinery in the Commonwealth), while British Petroleum and Shell also expanded their presence. By 1956 petroleum and petroleum products constituted 81.3 per cent of Trinidad and Tobago's exports, far exceeding sugar at 8 per cent and cocoa at 3.3 per cent. Though sugar exports were proportionately modest, there was substantial growth in this industry during the postwar period, with an increase of acres under cultivation and technological improvements in factories. British trade arrangements supported strong exports, while ownership of the industry was increasingly concentrated in the large British firm of Tate and Lyle. In addition, efforts by both the Gomes and Williams administrations to expand Trinidad's manufacturing sector succeeded in attracting foreign investors (mainly American and British), who established a variety of factories in the metropolitan Port of Spain area and elsewhere in the island. However, manufacturing remained a relatively small portion of the territory's economy. Similarly, hotel facilities and tourism promotional efforts expanded during the postwar years, but this industry never achieved the significance it obtained in many other Caribbean territories. As a whole, economic growth during the postwar era contributed to the expansion of the middle class and generated government revenues that increased public programmes and public-sector employment. However, the level of unemployment remained high, owing to a rapidly growing population and the relatively small number of jobs in the petroleum and manufacturing sectors. Trinidad and Tobago continued to be challenged by pervasive socioeconomic inequality, poverty and grassroots discontent.[1]

STEELBANDS AND THE URBAN ENVIRONMENT

As World War II drew to a close and officials made plans for a postwar Trinidad, a new phenomenon quickly captured the attention of the public: steelbands (see figure 25). When Allied victory in Europe was declared on 8 May 1945 (VE Day), the residents of Port of Spain took to the streets in Carnival-like celebration, with metallic percussion ensembles driving the revelry. Buildings in the city were adorned with multicoloured lights and other decorations, bunting-lined streetcars and the flags of the Allied nations were displayed everywhere. Military posts and ships in the harbour sounded their sirens, while bells chimed at churches across the city. Thousands of people jammed the downtown area, shouting, dancing (some in Carnival costumes saved from before the war), and singing lines such as "Is your moustache we want, Hitler" and "Whole day, whole night, Carnival!" The *Port of-Spain Gazette* reported:

> Somewhat timidly at first, one or two small steel bands felt their way through the thoroughfares seemingly uncertain of the limits to which victory celebrations permitted them to go. . . .
>
> [A]s the day grew older persons from all walks of life threw caution to the winds unable no longer to restrain the tantalising beat of the old pan and steel. Before noon the businessman and his clerk, the carter and the civil servant, the Trinidadian and the visitor joined in the long processions of wild and hectic jubilations.

Such celebrations were repeated a few months later after the defeat of Japan, beginning on the night of 14 August (VJ Day) and continuing for two additional days. As crowds danced and sang in the streets, young men beat rhythms on dustbins (trash cans), utensils, car brake drums and other metal objects. According to the *Trinidad Guardian*, "on both days the steel band boys kept up a deafening din with their improvised instruments which all but crushed recognised orchestras off the streets as revellers showed preference for music thumped out of old iron".[2]

While steelbands made a dramatic appearance on the streets during the VE and VJ Day celebrations, they had actually emerged several years earlier out of tamboo-bamboo bands – ensembles in which different-sized pieces of bamboo served as percussion instruments accompanying Carnival street processions and stickfights in yards during the Carnival season. Though bamboo bands had been incorporating some metal objects since the early twentieth century, a shift to metal percussion accelerated during the late 1930s. Experiments with such instrumentation occurred in several locations around the city. One centre was the yard of Tantie Willie, an Orisha priestess who lived on the Gloster Lodge Road near the city council's housing project at Gonzales Place. According to various accounts, young men who limed (hung out) in this yard did not have bamboo instruments prepared in time for the celebration of the coronation of George VI in May 1937, and instead stripped metal parts from an old car and/or a couple of motorcycles. Meanwhile, developments were also occurring downtown in Hell Yard, an open space surrounded by the Dry River and buildings on Duke and Charlotte Streets. By the late 1930s, youths associated with this yard would sit on the river embankment and beat on car parts, pieces of iron and metal containers. Around this same time, in the southeast neighbourhood of John John, men who worked in a nearby abattoir would relax in the morning and at lunch in old train carriages, where they beat on brake drums and oil tins with their butcher knives and sharpening steels.

However, it was in the Big Yard in the western neighbourhood of New Town that the most elaborate advancement in steel percussion took place. At the corner of Woodford Street and Tragarete Road during the late 1930s, surrounded by barrack dwellings, this yard was a site for liming, stickfighting and tamboo bamboo. For the 1939 Carnival, some younger members of the yard's band proposed the novel idea of going out on the streets with only metal percussion. The group named itself Alexander's Ragtime Band (after a musical film released the previous year) and paraded in black jackets, white shirts and black cardboard ties, directed by Lord Humbugger (Carlton Forde), who sported a scissor-tail coat and top hat. Their instruments included paint cans, biscuit containers and buckets, as well as a gramophone horn and assorted other objects. It was a dazzling performance and sound – one that made a strong impression on that year's bamboo-band percussionists, some of whom had also been experimenting with metal. By the 1940 Carnival, many bands in Port of Spain had discarded their bamboo altogether and adopted all-metal instrumentation. When Decca Records returned to Trinidad that season to record calypsoes, it also captured some of the new "steel music". In reference to this visit, the *Port-of-Spain Gazette* commented, "no longer does the bamboo band hold sway, it having given place to the steel drums with bottle and spoon".[3]

The working-class youths who invented the steelband greatly preferred metallic percussion to bamboo – it was louder, more durable when pounded for long periods of time and more easily obtained. While bamboo had to be cut up in the hills surrounding Port of Spain, metal objects were part of the landscape and sound of the city. Cement drums and paint cans could be found on the land around the Deep Water Harbour Scheme, biscuit drums were available at factories on Duncan and Frederick Streets, two soap factories near John John were a source of caustic-soda drums, and the abattoir in this area offered metal tins and utensils. Dustbins, car parts and pieces of scrap metal were easily found in yards and streets throughout the city, while many homes had cooking-oil tins, pitch-oil tins and buckets. Throughout the 1940s, band "tuners", such as Winston "Spree" Simon, Neville Jules, Ellie Mannette and Anthony Williams, worked with this variety of containers to gradually fashion "pans" with ranges of notes and to improve their acoustic qualities, especially when struck with padded sticks. Their development of a standard ensemble of lead, mid-range and bass pans enabled the orchestration of a wide range of music, including calypsoes, American popular tunes, European classical pieces and Latin American dance-music genres. By the late 1940s, band tuners were increasingly fabricating lead pans from large-volume oil drums, obtained from various transport and industrial facilities. The strong but malleable metal of these containers offered a superior tone quality, while their larger diameter provided a surface on which more notes could be tuned. By the early 1950s, large oil drums had replaced all other types of containers in steelbands, the range of pans contained chromatic scales of notes, and musical arrangements featured more complex harmonies.[4]

For the young steelbandsmen or "panmen", their new music was an expression of their generation – a powerful, contemporary sound that differentiated them from older tamboo-bamboo men and stickfighters. The idea of forming steelbands soon spread throughout Trinidad and Tobago and to other Caribbean territories, but Port of Spain remained the epicentre of creativity and performance. During the 1940s, numerous bands were established across the city; some had associations with the yards of defunct bamboo bands, while others were new organizations. Bands were typically based in specific areas, from which they drew their members and supporters. Among the better-known bands on the east side of the city were Destination Tokyo in John John, Crusaders in St Paul Street, Hill 60 on Clifton Hill, Dead End Kids (later known as Desperadoes) from upper Laventille Hill, Bar 20 in Bath Street, Casablanca in eastern Oxford Street and Rising Sun in Belmont. On the west side of the city were the Oval Boys (later known as Invaders) across from the Queen's Park Oval in Woodbrook, while St James was home to Tripoli, Sun Valley and North Stars. There were also steelbands downtown, but some of these included members from beyond their immediate area. For example, Cross of Lorraine (later known as Trinidad All Stars) was based in Hell Yard but drew members from various parts of the city. Red Army also attracted personnel from throughout the city, and while it kept its pans on Prince Street, a number of its prominent members generally limed at Green Corner, the high-profile intersection of Park Street, St Vincent Street and Tragarete Road. Regardless of their locations, steelbands were tightly knit organizations with a strong sense of collective identity and spatial territory. During and after the war, panmen (who were avid cinema attendees) frequently named their bands after American war movies, other high-action films or related imagery as part of an effort to express a combative stance in relation to their rivals.[5]

Each steelband maintained as its headquarters a "panyard" – where it rehearsed, limed and organized its activities. Like older Carnival-band yards, a panyard was an open space, typically surrounded by residential buildings and sometimes partially shaded by one or more trees. In addition, bandsmen often built simple structures in their yards for storing pans and rehearsing. During the 1950 Carnival season, for example, a *Trinidad Guardian* reporter noted that Casablanca employed bamboo stalks and coconut branches to construct a "hut" for practising. That same year the British writer Patrick Leigh Fermor published an exceptionally vivid account of an earlier visit to the Trinidad All Stars in Hell Yard:

> We all four took a taxi to the street called Piccadilly, on the other side of the dry river, and our new acquaintance led us down an alley-way between heavily populated wooden houses, over a wall and into a large pit built in a bay of the embankment. It was full of young Negroes hammering out, on extraordinary instruments, the noise I had heard. When we appeared with his friend, the leader rose, shook hands, and gave us four little rum kegs to sit on, and went on playing.
>
> The leader, or Captain, was a Negro in his early twenties called Fish Eyes Rudolf Olivier [Rudolph "Fisheye" Ollivierre]. . . . When the din had stopped, he made some introductions. "This is Neville Jules, my second-in-command, and this is my managing director, O. Rudder." The ease of his manner was admirable. "Now I'll show you our yard." He led the way into the centre with the air of a country magnate flinging open the double doors of the ballroom.
>
> It was a piece of waste-land, a-flutter with clothes lines, jammed between the embankment and the back of houses. . . . The band was a little group of young men from the neighbourhood who had installed themselves here and turned it into a stronghold. A large blue banner, embroidered with the name of the group, was stuck in the ground, and, beyond the minstrels, half a dozen familiars were playing gin-rummy on a plank between two kegs. . . . The little enclosure was illuminated by flambeaux.[6]

Leigh Fermor goes on to describe the band's instruments as including kerosene tins, a Vaseline drum, a biscuit container and a car brake drum, while also mentioning such rival bands as Desperadoes, Destination Tokyo and Hill 60. His account captures several common characteristics of steelbands and their yards: an enclosed space, the proximity of housing and domestic activity, the collecting of assorted objects for use by the band, engagement in recreational pastimes as well as music-making (especially at night), military-style leadership and identifying banners and a general sense of a community that contends with adversaries in other districts.

During the war, steelbands generally made music in their yards, given the ban on outdoor Carnival and street processions. However, they sometimes risked excursions with their pans, especially in the winding streets of the eastern hills or in the bed of the Dry River. These outings often took place during the Christmas and Carnival seasons and frequently attracted the police, who sometimes confiscated the pans. The wartime ban on the street Carnival and the bands' limited opportunities for performing in public explains why they were not widely known during the early 1940s. While the VE and VJ Day celebrations introduced steelband music to the city's population at large, the 1946 Carnival established it as a central component of street festivity. In an article subtitled "Steel Bands Lead Happy Revellers on City's Streets", the *Trinidad Guardian* reported: "After nearly six years of war-time restrictions votaries of King Carnival were able to indulge their pent-up feelings in a riot of revelry, transforming the city into a veritable playground, and thronging the streets of the island's towns and villages. At zero hour – 6 a.m. – the anxiously awaiting masqueraders poured into the streets and paraded about to the strains of familiar tunes provided by numerous steel bands and other orchestras." Over the course of the two days of festivity, the paper noted particular acclaim for such steelbands as Red Army, Cross of Lorraine, Tripoli and Casablanca. The steelbands' captivation of the public continued during the following year's Carnival, with the *Guardian* exclaiming: "The infectious quality of steel music caught revellers in its spell to make everyone join hands and dance and sing regardless of colour, class or creed."[7]

While the originality of music on pans was central to the steelbands' appeal, their masquerades were also impressive. Frequently they portrayed military forces, particularly sailors. These masquerades ranged from "fancy" sailors – with highly ornamented uniforms, long noses in the shapes of planes and ships, and intricate dances – to "ship's crew", which offered more realistic representations of naval personnel along with re-enactments of maritime scenes and exercises. Leading the musicians and masqueraders through the streets were flagmen, who performed elaborate twirling choreographies, and individuals who carried banners that identified the bands. With their martial names and masquerades and their aggressive processions through the city, the panmen imaginatively replayed the wartime drama that they had followed in movies and newspapers and observed directly in the manifold military activities within Trinidad itself.[8]

Though the Carnival was the premier setting for steelband music, the bands also performed on the streets for holidays such as Christmas, Old Year's, Easter and Discovery Day, which was held on the first Monday in August and commemorated Christopher Columbus's arrival at Trinidad. Steelbands played a prominent role in the 1946 Discovery Day, the first one after the war. Following a special Mass on Sunday at the Catholic cathedral on Marine Square, Monday began with the ringing of church bells and discharging of rockets. Next there was a ceremony to the east of the cathedral in Columbus Square, where the mayor and other dignitaries delivered speeches to the gathered crowd. Meanwhile, celebrations in the downtown streets assumed the form of a Carnival, with thousands of masqueraders. Most masquerade bands passed Columbus Square, where they laid wreaths at the statue of the mariner. The *Trinidad Guardian* noted that the Invaders Steel Band brought a wreath in the shape of an anchor and added: "Following the laying of wreaths, revellers danced around, singing old ballads to the strains of the steel bands which played a prominent part in the proceedings."9

At Carnival and other celebrations during the postwar years, the music of the steelbands propelled the revelry and appealed to a wide cross-section of the public. However, these were also occasions during which bands expressed rivalries shaped by strong identification with particular territories in the city, competition in musical skill and quality of pans, and efforts to control women associated with their districts. In many cases, the women were simply neighbourhood residents, though some members of some bands (especially Red Army) lived off the earnings of prostitutes. Steelbands generally paraded the city with a combative orientation and sought to dominate space on the streets. When two bands met, a contest ensued both for room to pass and musical superiority, with each band trying to play more loudly than the other and disrupt its rhythm. Occasionally, these musical contests escalated into physical violence, typically sparked by a grievance or minor incident, such as the throwing of a bottle. Then members of the bands grabbed their weapons (knives, razors, bottles, stones and so on) and engaged in battle, while spectators scattered and the police rushed to the scene. The first major incident of steelband violence occurred during the 1947 Carnival, when the *Guardian* reported a clash between two unidentified bands on Duke Street and a total of fifteen cases of wounding during the festival. Over the next few years, there was continued violence during street festivities as well as throughout the year, such as the 1949–1950 feud between Casablanca and Invaders. This conflict was, in part, a manifestation of the traditional east-west rivalry in Port of Spain, enacted by Carnival bands since the nineteenth century. Steelband violence peaked in June 1953 during a special carnival organized as part of a week-long celebration of the coronation of Queen Elizabeth II. While observances were generally peaceful outside Port of Spain, carnival merriment in the city was marred by eight steelband clashes, over a hundred injuries and one fatality. Some observers suggested that much of the violence was precipitated by conflicts between the established steelbands and new bands that had been formed over the past few years by middle-class youths.10

During the weeks following the Coronation Carnival, dozens of letters to the editor appeared in the *Trinidad Guardian* and the *Port-of-Spain Gazette* in which writers, both from Port of Spain and around the country, debated steelbands and Carnival festivity. Condemnation of the bands was vehement and wide-ranging. For example, "Disgusted", while acknowledging earlier support for steelbands, now advocated that they should be banned from parading the streets. Dawson Rondon claimed that "the members of steel bands and their followers are mostly noisy, vulgar, undisciplined, and uncultured" and added that the "only use for a steel pan is to store rubbish". Cecil Quesnel said "the steel band is the hooligans' most dangerous weapon; it is the means of uniting and instilling into them the bravado and the means of fight that they could not get from ordinary music". "Alarmed" described steelbands as "a savage, bestial cult" and called for their suppression, since they appeared to be "the prime cause for the alarming prevalence of crimes of violence and indecency, not only at Carnival, but all through the year". Claudio Carvalho suggested that the steelband "is a deception created by Satan to defeat music that has taken centuries to perfect in God's own voice". "Son of the Soil" argued that, unless steelbands were banned from all celebrations, Trinidad would suffer from a severe loss of tourism revenue. Finally, Cecil Cameron opined that "the steel band and all that goes with it cannot be picked up from the gutter and tossed, still reeking, into the drawing-room" and advised: "The gaol, the lash, public scorn and ostracism – these are the weapons we have; let us use them." However, other observers mounted a defence of steelbands, both in letters and in a public forum held at Whitehall a month later. These individuals argued that the disturbances of the Coronation Carnival were exaggerated in the press, that violence associated with steelbands was often instigated by band followers rather than the musicians themselves and that steelbands were being used as a scapegoat for a general crime wave.[11]

The debate over the disruption of the Coronation Carnival built on a public discourse about steelbands that had been developing since 1945. While steelband music was often enjoyed as a form of revelry during Carnival or similar occasions, much of the population was also unsettled by the phenomenon, given its association with the streets and with young men who were frequently unemployed and often perceived to be rowdy and disreputable. Moreover, Trinidad's colonial institutions continued to promulgate an ideology that denigrated all locally created grassroots cultural practices. On the other hand, a small but influential number of steelband advocates affirmed the music as a unique and valuable form of artistic expression. These opposing views were articulated in a debate in the legislative council in December 1945 concerning a bill that amended the Summary Offences Ordinance to forbid "the playing of noisy instruments on the streets and other public places except during such time as the Governor shall proclaim or with the permission of the Commissioner of the Police". The attorney general said the bill was motivated by an increase in the amount of noise within the city and by complaints received from Cascade, Coblentz and St Ann's (upscale suburbs). Council member Albert Gomes said though the attorney general did not specify steelbands, the bill was obviously inspired by them. Along with questioning the social prejudices of the complainants, Gomes suggested that "those persons who hold the reins of government in this place are more familiar with the environs of certain parts of our city than with those other parts where we find the steel orchestra being preferred to other forms of music". In response, council member L.C. Hannays argued that steelbands could still play in their yards and that the ordinance was "intended to prevent this form of mischief being transferred to a public place". Though the bill passed and the police tried to enforce it, steelbands continued to play in the streets, both with and without permission.[12]

In the following years, Gomes became one of the most devoted advocates of steelbands, particularly in his weekly column ("Behind the Curtain") in the *Trinidad Guardian*. In contrast to dismissals of the steelband as noise and a manifestation of postwar social disorder, Gomes emphasized the sheer inventiveness of the panmen, their determination to create something extraordinary from the debris of the urban landscape and the power of their music as a shared sound for a diverse population during Carnival. In addition, he consistently challenged social snobbery and acceptance of European culture as an absolute model of truth and beauty. In 1949, for example, he sparred in the press with Stanley Best – the representative in Trinidad of the British Council, an organization established to disseminate British culture throughout the world. When Best suggested that West Indians should look to Britain for standards until a strong local culture established its own, Gomes fired back that Trinidadians were no longer willing to simply emulate others and that soon the British Council would have to focus its work on sending abroad the exciting arts of the West Indies.[13]

Among the other leading advocates of the steelband in the postwar era were Beryl McBurnie (dancer and choreographer), C.S. Espinet (journalist and folklorist), C.R. Ottley (educator and local historian) and Lennox Pierre (attorney and Trinidad and Tobago Youth Council official). All these figures were participants in a growing movement of cultural nationalism that affirmed local artistic creativity as an expression of a distinct Trinidadian people and a foundation for local empowerment and self-government. Moreover, they believed that the steelband was a productive and positive activity for unemployed/underemployed youths. In November 1949, with steelband violence escalating, the government appointed a steelband committee to investigate the bands and make recommendations concerning their "cultural and recreational potentialities". In addition to McBurnie, Espinet, Ottley and Pierre, the committee included such figures as the government's principal probation officer and a representative of a football club. It was chaired by Canon M.E. Farquhar, a well-known Anglican priest who, like Gomes, wrote a weekly column for the *Trinidad Guardian* and was a prominent defender of the panmen, particularly in reference to the social conditions in which they lived and the intolerance they faced. Over the next few months, the committee worked with the panmen to resolve current conflicts and form a Steel Band Association. Launched at the Youth Council's centre in Cocorite in April 1950, the association's goals were to maintain peace and promote the common interests of its members.[14]

One of the primary ways in which steelband advocates highlighted the artistic merit and national significance of the bands was to present them in indoor concert settings. These events removed the bands from their usual environment of yard and street and placed them on a stage in formally organized programmes for audiences generally consisting of middle- and upper-class patrons. The first staged presentation of a steelband took place during the war, when Edric Connor (baritone, folklorist and construction contractor) included the Gonzales band in a lecture-demonstration on West Indian folk music on 27 July 1943 at Bishop Anstey High School, the prestigious Anglican girls' school in uptown Port of Spain. Sponsored by the Trinidad Music Association (a classical-music organization), the programme focused on African influences on West Indian folk traditions, a topic that was generally outside the awareness of the genteel audience. Many of the performers were people Connor had helped to evacuate from the rural Chaguaramas area as part of his work for the US Navy. While he lectured, these individuals remained in the stage shadows behind him; when he demonstrated a particular genre of folksong, they joined him as a chorus of singers and drummers. Then there were the performers from Gonzales: "The climax came naturally in the form of drumming and dancing. With the rapt attention of every member of the audience the men from Gonzales Place gave forth upon the 'steel orchestra,' the 'tamboo bamboo' and on substitutes of their own making for the shango drums." The audience was mesmerized throughout the programme, and a demonstration of a bongo (a music/dance genre performed at wakes) even moved them to their feet. The event's reviewer concluded: "Here is a field for interesting research in our own backyard."[15]

While Edric Connor demonstrated the steelband soon after its emergence, programmes organized by Beryl McBurnie (died 2000) during the postwar years showcased its rapid advancement and reached a far larger audience. McBurnie's support of the steelband was part of a range of artistic activities dating back to her youth in Woodbrook. As a young schoolteacher, she had presented concerts and plays while also pursuing dance, her principal discipline. Eventually she became intrigued by local artistic traditions and accompanied folklorist Andrew Carr on research trips into the countryside. During the late 1930s and early 1940s, she spent substantial periods in New York, studying at Columbia University, teaching Caribbean dance and performing at a variety of venues, from the Village Gate to the Museum of Modern Art. Meanwhile, she was directing and choreographing dances for a troupe in Trinidad and was primarily based here after 1945. After several years of rehearsals in her mother's house and shows at places like the Prince's Building and the Empire Theatre, she decided she needed her own space. While on a dance-research trip in South America, she saw an intimate theatre in Cayenne (French Guiana), drew a picture and gave it to architect Aldwyn Beckles for the design of the Little Carib Theatre in the backyard of a house at the corner of Roberts and White Streets in Woodbrook (around the corner from Invaders' panyard). It was a simple masonry and wood structure, temporary in intent, and by the early 1950s subject to demolition threats from the city council owing to safety concerns.[16]

On 25 November 1948, the Little Carib held its formal opening, an event of great significance for Trinidad's nationalist arts movement. The programme booklet featured articles by such individuals as Albert Gomes, Canon Farquhar, C.S. Espinet, Youth Council chairman Jack Kelshall and future prime minister Eric Williams, while a list of the centre's "associates" included many other leading figures in the civic life of Port of Spain. The evening's programme, titled *Talking Drums*, reflected McBurnie's deep commitment to local traditions as well as her modernist experiments. Among the pieces were "Movement" ("The philosophy of good movement"), "Modern Dance", "Folk Play" ("In the Fields"), "Ah Passin'" ("Market Scene"), "Massala" (an Indian spice) and a performance by the Invaders Steel Band. Later in the evening, American bass-baritone Paul Robeson, who was visiting Trinidad at the time, stopped by to deliver a speech, recite Langston Hughes's "Freedom Train" and lay a cornerstone for the building, which was still under construction. In a general review for the new *Caribbean Quarterly*, "E.M." (possibly Guyanese writer Edgar Mittelholzer) wrote: "The Little Carib is an unpretentious building squeezed into a backyard in suburban Port-of-Spain . . . [it] is Beryl McBurnie's concrete expression of her belief in an indigenous West Indian culture." In the following years, the Little Carib thrived as a site for multidisciplinary artistic innovation in the city. McBurnie continued regularly to present Invaders, who often performed the final selection for programmes and provided music for social dancing afterwards.[17]

During the late 1940s and early 1950s, there were various other well-received presentations of steelbands in elite indoor settings. For example, Casablanca, Invaders' archrival, appeared at Whitehall in February 1950 and at the Royal Victoria Institute in May 1951. For the first show, titled "Music of the Caribbean", the band performed calypsoes, "rhumbas", popular dance tunes and marches, with commentary provided by folklorist C.S. Espinet. A reviewer for the *Trinidad Guardian* exclaimed: "At the same place where concerts of classical music are held regularly, the music of the steel band was heard for the first time. It was the local counterpart of Paul Whiteman's taking jazz to Carnegie Hall, some time during the 1920's. The band demonstrated the musical scope of the steel orchestra, and the ingenuity and skill of the men who comprise it." This programme also featured calypsonians Growler and Radio, demonstrating traditional and contemporary forms of calypso, and concluded with the audience dancing ballroom-style to Casablanca's music, which, in the words of the reviewer, proved that "steel band music is not restricted to 'jumping up' in the streets". The following year, at the Royal Victoria Institute, Casablanca performed under the direction of a pianist, Professor Katz, and accompanied tenor Victor Soverall for several selections. The concert was billed as an experiment to determine whether the steelband could be successfully combined with classical musicianship. A reporter for the *Port-of-Spain Gazette* concluded: "So perfect was the blend that the association of the bin and piano was natural. Neither proved out of place."[18]

Further affirmation of the musical achievement of the steelband came in 1952 with its inclusion as an official class in the Trinidad Music Festival. Under the leadership of May Johnstone, the Trinidad Music Association began organizing this biennial festival in 1948 and developed competitions in various vocal and instrumental categories, adjudicated by a visiting British musician. By the time of the 1952 festival, steelband musicianship had reached a high level of proficiency, facilitated by the fully chromatic instrumentation and more sophisticated arrangements advanced by the Trinidad All Steel Percussion Orchestra (an all-star ensemble that the colony sent to the Festival of Britain in London in 1951). For the final night of steelband competition at the 1952 festival, bands were required to play both a test piece (a folksong) and an additional selection in any genre of their choice. The *Trinidad Guardian* reported: "The drums of the steelband throbbed out their heady, exciting rhythms for Dr. Sidney Northcote and a huge, mixed crowd of stiff highbrows and noisy 'pan' enthusiasts at the Globe Cinema last night." In addition to the audience's vociferous appreciation, Dr Northcote said: "We have witnessed man's ingenuity in trying to get beauty out of something that is absolutely waste product." However, he encouraged the panmen to continue working to refine their ensembles. The winning band at the festival was Boys' Town, a little-known outfit from Point Cumana, while Dudley Smith of Belmont's Rising Sun won a class for solo lead pan.[19]

As these developments suggest, various social interests and agendas were shaping the spatial manifestation and significance of the steelband in Port of Spain by the 1950s. For the panmen themselves, their music-making was an experiment that they carried out in their yards, with ongoing efforts to improve the technology of their instruments and the artistry of their performances. New bands were constantly formed and new yards established in most districts of the city. These spaces served not only as sites of musical innovation but also as community centres that attracted nearby residents and reinforced neighbourhood solidarity. Panmen and their followers expressed these affinities and their musical achievements on the streets each Carnival season and at other festive occasions during the year. Competition remained fierce and occasional physical altercations continued, in spite of the efforts of the Steel Band Association to curtail violence. Paralleling this music-making in yards and streets were presentations in elite indoor settings, organized by steelband advocates but actively embraced by the panmen in their effort to obtain new performance opportunities. While these presentations redefined steelband music as a concert art with national significance, they also altered public concepts of the sponsoring institutions. By featuring steelbands, these institutions expanded their image as places that encouraged local grassroots expression in addition to promoting the classical arts of Europe. Meanwhile, steelbands were also playing in a variety of other settings, including stadiums, cinemas, nightclubs and private homes, as a cross-section of the city's population increasingly accepted them as an appealing form of entertainment. This growing acceptance, however, was accompanied by continued perceptions of the bands as interrelated with various forms of social disruption and by frequent calls for firmer control of their public presence. Nonetheless, the panmen had managed to claim a wider array of spaces in the city since their beginnings in secluded yards and forays along back streets during the war. Steelbands now flourished across the city, and, day and night, produced a new urban soundscape.

THE PEOPLE'S NATIONAL MOVEMENT AND THE UNIVERSITY OF WOODFORD SQUARE

During the mid-1950s, the PNM emerged in Port of Spain with an energy and excitement similar to that of the dramatic appearance of steelbands in the public arena in the mid-1940s. While this political party was collectively built by many talented men and women in the city and beyond, it was the extraordinary figure of Eric Williams (1911–1981) who motivated its assembly, envisioned its scope, articulated its principles and led its activities. Williams was born on either Dundonald or Oxford Street in central Port of Spain, the first of twelve children of a lower-level postal official and a homemaker. In his autobiography, he notes that his family was plagued by housing challenges and, during his first twenty-one years, moved eight times to low-rental accommodation around the city. Though the family struggled financially, it maintained a sense of gentility, due in part to his mother's birth in the mixed-descent line of the prominent Boissière family. An avid reader and diligent student, Williams won a scholarship to Queen's Royal College, where his subjects included Latin, French, Spanish and history (with C.L.R. James as one of his teachers). In 1931 he was awarded one of Trinidad's two island scholarships, which enabled him to do a bachelor's degree in history at Oxford. He continued studying history at Oxford at the postgraduate level and received a doctorate in 1938. The next year, Williams began work as a professor of social and political science at Howard University in Washington, DC, which served as a base for a range of activities: lecturing, consulting, research and publication (including *Capitalism and Slavery* in 1944), and extensive travel across the Caribbean, during which he interacted with Fernando Ortiz, Jean Price-Mars and other well-known intellectuals. By 1944 he had a full-time appointment with the Anglo-American Caribbean Commission, which the United States and Britain had established two years earlier to coordinate research and policy in the region. In 1946 this organization became known as the Caribbean Commission (with the inclusion of France and the Netherlands) and moved its headquarters from Washington, DC, to Port of Spain. In 1948 Williams returned to Trinidad as the deputy chairman of the commission's Caribbean Research Council.[20]

In Port of Spain, Williams developed a close relationship with the Teachers' Economic and Cultural Association (TECA), a progressive organization dedicated to advancing the professional interests of teachers and promoting educational and artistic programming to the larger community. TECA was interlinked with many of the city's literary, dramatic and musical groups; ran a bookstore on Park Street; and eventually consolidated its outreach activities in a People's Education Movement. This group, in turn, organized lectures featuring Williams, including presentations on topics in Caribbean history and culture at the public library on Woodford Square. In his autobiography, Williams observes that he made the library his "intellectual headquarters": "If imperialism attacked from Kent House, nationalism would counter-attack from the Public Library" (Kent House was the office of the Caribbean Commission on the northern outskirts of the city). His lectures were aimed at encouraging Trinidadians to formulate their own perspective on their past and current conditions. In an assessment of local education, he asserted: "The West Indian school today despises and disparages its environment. . . . The West Indian school of tomorrow must make a positive fetish of the West Indian environment."[21]

Meanwhile, Williams increasingly resisted the Caribbean Commission's colonial orientation and interference with his lecturing and writing. In May 1955 he received a letter from the organization saying his contract would not be renewed after it expired on 21 June. That night in June he delivered a lecture

("My Relations with the Caribbean Commission, 1943–1955") from the bandstand in Woodford Square, an event organized by TECA's People's Education Movement. Thousands of people jammed the square and remained transfixed as he offered a lengthy account of how his personal experiences reflected the broader reality of colonial oppression in the Caribbean. He concluded: "I was born here, and here I stay, with the people of Trinidad and Tobago. . . . I am going to let down my bucket where I am, right here with you in the British West Indies." In his autobiography, Williams says, "Woodford Square roared its approval, and the roar was heard in London and in Washington. I had crossed the Rubicon."[22]

In selecting Woodford Square for this first mass presentation, TECA and Williams effectively exploited its prominent location and its rich symbolism. An attractive public space in the heart of the city, Woodford Square comprised an entire block with an iron fence around its perimeter that offered both a sense of enclosure and an openness to the surrounding area. This included the Red House (seat of the colonial government), courts, town hall (relocated uptown for much of the postwar era owing to a fire), public library, Anglican cathedral and businesses on Frederick Street – essentially a microcosm of official Trinidadian society and its various discourses. Pathways from the several gates on the perimeter of the square drew people in throughout the day and evening for relaxation and debate on lawns and benches beneath shade trees. The circular bandstand (with elegant ironwork and roof) on the north side of the square provided a stage for both musical performances and speechmaking. For decades, Woodford Square had been the city's most popular meeting space and site of political rallies. It was certainly the most advantageous location in Trinidad for launching a new nationalist mass movement.

On 19 July, Williams and his followers returned to Woodford Square for a lecture titled "Constitutional Reform in Trinidad and Tobago". In a preamble to this speech, he said:

> Somebody once said that all that was needed for a university was a book and the branch of a tree; someone else went further and said that a university should be a university in overalls. With a bandstand, a microphone, a large audience in slacks and hot shirts, a topical subject for discussion, the open air and a beautiful tropical night, we have all the essentials of a university. Now that I have resigned my position at Howard University in the USA, the only university in which I shall lecture in future is the University of Woodford Square and its several branches throughout the length and breadth of Trinidad and Tobago.

Thus Williams gave this central space a new name, which was soon embraced by the population at large (with some individuals even using this nomenclature for addressing letters). In his autobiography, he asserts that the University of

Woodford Square became "a centre of free university education for the masses, of political analysis and of training in self-government for parallels of which we must go back to the city state of Athens". Similarly, sociologist Ivar Oxaal, who did research in Trinidad in the early 1960s, describes the square as "the central institution, the symbol and embodiment" of the process that moved the country to independence.[23]

In defining Woodford Square as a university, Williams expanded its historic role as a central public space of dialogue and learning. A cross-section of people had always gathered here to talk, but Williams brought greater formality to this discourse with lengthy prepared lectures that offered analyses of life in Trinidad in the context of Caribbean and world affairs. His ability to hold the attention of large crowds stemmed from his wide-ranging knowledge, skill in telling compelling stories and appealing professorial image and verbal style, which combined learned speech with the combativeness and wit of calypsonians. All in all, Woodford Square was a site well suited for displaying Williams's authority and charisma and for cultivating mass adulation. Here he fostered popular devotion and deference that he would exploit for political advantage in the upcoming years. While he held rallies throughout Trinidad and Tobago, he attracted the largest following at the University of Woodford Square, which enabled not only the efficient dissemination of ideas but also the populace's physical display of its desire for change.

Shortly after Williams's initial lecture in Woodford Square, a number of core members of the People's Education Movement formed what they called the Political Education Group to explore the possibility of organizing a political party around his leadership. The group frequently met at TECA's bookstore on Park Street, while some of its members also gathered at Kamaluddin Mohammed's Dil Bahar Restaurant on Queen Street. Both Ivar Oxaal and political scientist Selwyn Ryan observe that the group assembled and expanded along friendship lines, which resulted in a primarily urban middle-class membership, including teachers, doctors, lawyers and other professionals. Many were Afro-Trinidadian, though other ethnic groups were also represented. Eventually this collective formed much of the leadership of the new PNM and attracted strong support from the urban middle class generally. However, Williams and the Political Education Group aimed at creating a party that would transcend class differences. The mass lectures at Woodford Square and elsewhere were central to this effort, as was promotion during the postwar era of locally created music (such as calypso and steelband), dance and other art forms as shared national symbols. While these forms of expression were generally associated with grassroots Afro-Trinidadians, their advocates represented them as national achievements and gradually built greater middle-class interest. In discussing this inter-class cultural and political alignment, Oxaal notes that TECA was involved in creole arts activities and that a number of the supporters listed in the Little Carib's 1948 opening-night programme were active in the formation of the PNM. Moreover, Williams wrote an article ("Our West Indian Culture") for this programme in which he said, "It is people like Beryl McBurnie who will improve conditions in the West Indies and upon whom more than anything else the future of the West Indies will depend." In short, the affirmation of local arts during this period contributed to a new form of national consciousness and the rise of the PNM.[24]

The PNM held its inaugural conference on 15 January 1956 at the Good Samaritan Friendly Society Hall on Duke Street and then staged a public launch in Woodford Square on 24 January, with the bandstand decorated with its new party symbol: the balisier (the local name for *Heliconia bihai*). Trinidadians believed that this tall plant with its series of scarlet flowers was a sign of soil fertility. Consequently, folklorist and PNM public relations secretary Andrew Carr wrote in the first issue of the *PNM Weekly* that it symbolized the party's local roots, democratic association and "fertility of ideas for social reform, economic advancement and moral improvement". At rallies throughout Trinidad during the following months, PNM followers regularly employed the balisier to decorate venues, adorn their cars and wave in the air.[25]

The PNM achieved victory on 24 September and held a celebration in Woodford Square two days later. The *Trinidad Chronicle* reported:

> thousands of "students", parents, friends, well-wishers and even babes-in-arms, thronged the "University of Woodford Square" on Wednesday night, to attend the "graduation exercises" of the People's National Movement. . . .
>
> Long before starting time of the meeting (8:00 p.m.), thousands were filing into the square from all directions. They came from the city, they journeyed from the rural districts; men, women, hundreds of them with babies in arms. They occupied all available space, some taking to the trees, others atop the public convenience in the Square to hear the victory songs of the respective winners.

With people also filling the streets surrounding the square, Andrew Carr formally presented Williams and the other victorious candidates, each of whom delivered an address. After supporters garlanded him with balisier flowers and offered him gifts, Williams spoke confidently of a meeting with Governor Beetham about forming a new government and commented on the PNM's plans for the future, including contesting the upcoming municipal and county elections. A month later, after the first meeting of the PNM-led legislative council in the Red House, another immense rally took place in Woodford Square, where Chief Minister Williams and the other members of his executive council spoke to the crowd from a balisier-decorated rostrum.[26] Both rallies displayed for the masses the territory's new middle-class leadership, highlighted their authority and reinforced the position of Williams as the supreme figure. As the new government took shape, Williams strove to maintain tight control over this inner core of individuals and the broader party apparatus.

Though the PNM received votes from throughout Trinidad and Tobago, its strongest support came from urban areas, with their high percentages of Afro-Trinidadian residents. Greater Port of Spain was the party's stronghold, thanks to its large population and institutional structures. As noted, the PNM built its support initially through urban-focused networks of teachers and other professionals, as well as via the city's various arts organizations. It then expanded its support through wider middle-class networks and by engaging the much larger working-class population in the city and beyond. In addition, Williams and many of his close associates lived or worked in Port of Spain, and it was here that they established the party's official headquarters, first in the Hajal Building on Queen Street and then, by the early 1960s, in Balisier House on Tranquillity Street in the uptown area.[27] Though decision-making occurred at the headquarters and in other offices, the University of Woodford Square remained the centre of the party and its staging ground for articulating a vision of an independent nation. This was the place where Williams often gave new speeches and the largest crowds displayed their commitment. It was also easily covered by the city's journalists, whose reports and photographs amplified its significance.

While Woodford Square served as the focal point for the mobilization of the PNM's predominantly African and mixed-descent base, it was also a site for the marginalization of the territory's other ethnic groups, particularly Indians. The majority of Indians lived far from the square and considered the PNM's image of a creole nation one in which they were relegated to a secondary status. Such sentiments were plainly manifested in the 1958 West Indies Federation parliamentary election, in which the Democratic Labour Party contested the PNM and won six of Trinidad and Tobago's ten seats. After this surprising outcome, Williams delivered a speech in Woodford Square in which he condemned Indians as a "recalcitrant and hostile minority" who constituted a danger to nation-building. Ethnic tensions intensified further during campaigns for the 1961 general election. The Democratic Labour Party said PNM hooligans were disrupting its meetings and carrying out other attacks, facilitated by a partisan police force. Though Williams invited his followers to "march where the hell you like", Democratic Labour Party leader Rudranath Capildeo issued even more extreme statements. During a rally at the Queen's Park Savannah, for example, he advised his supporters to break up PNM meetings and proclaimed: "Arm yourself with weapons in order to take over this country . . . get ready to march on Whitehall." While the leaders of both parties employed the power of rhetoric and manoeuvring in public space to impassion their constituencies, they eventually realized the potential for more extensive violence and called for restraint in advance of election day.[28]

Though the PNM held many large-scale rallies in Woodford Square in the early years of its administration, the most dramatic was its march for Chaguaramas, which was launched from the square on 22 April 1960 as a mass demonstration of nationalist objectives. While World War II was long over, the United States continued to hold base lands in Trinidad (and in other West Indian islands) in accordance with the ninety-nine-year lease agreement with Britain in 1941. Holdings in Trinidad included the Chaguaramas naval base in the northwest peninsula, the Waller Field air base southeast of Arima and the Carlsen Field air base near Chaguanas. In 1954 *The Times* (London) reported that the United States had partially released (with recovery rights) Waller Field for the purpose of growing experimental grasses and developing cattle pasturage, while Chaguaramas remained an active base, with approximately thirteen hundred American personnel and sixteen hundred Trinidadian employees. This continuing American military presence at Chaguaramas was a major concern of Eric Williams and the PNM government throughout the late 1950s and early 1960s. Williams constantly portrayed American possession of this site as imperialistic and unjust. While the existence of the base symbolized external domination, reclamation of the land would symbolize Trinidad's sovereignty. In this sense, the claim to Chaguaramas also signified the goal of decolonization from Britain. Williams argued that Trinidad and Tobago, as a territory on the verge of self-government, should not be beholden to an agreement negotiated by Britain during the early years of the war, but should now be a full participant in any discussion concerning its own land.[29]

The Chaguaramas issue was also interrelated with the creation of the new West Indies Federation and the selection of its capital. This was a contentious process that involved various committees over a period of several years, during which Trinidad, Jamaica, Barbados and a few of the smaller islands were all considered as candidates. In January 1956 a Capital Commission released a report based on the principles that the capital should be near one of the three largest cities of the West Indies (Kingston, Jamaica; Port of Spain; and Bridgetown, Barbados) so that it could benefit from these cities' amenities, while a degree of removal (a few miles) would ensure its autonomy. The commissioners (none from the Caribbean) ruled out Jamaica because of its location (far to the west of the other islands) and Trinidad because of perceptions of its politics as unstable and corrupt, and because they believed that its large Indian-descended population would not be loyal to the federation. Their recommendation of Barbados generated outrage from most West Indians, who perceived this island as having a high level of colour prejudice. Williams said this selection "suggests a total ignorance of past West Indian history and a total lack of sympathy with the obvious West Indian aspirations for the future"; he described Trinidad, on the other hand, as entrepreneurial and progressive. Others argued that Trinidad's new PNM government would clean up the territory's politics and that its diverse population was part of its strength. When a Standing Federation Committee met in early 1957, it selected Trinidad for the federal capital and, a few months later, agreed that Chaguaramas would be the most suitable site. In addition to its proximity to Port of Spain (approximately eight miles) and scenic terrain, Chaguaramas possessed some existing facilities and an excellent harbour.[30]

At a meeting in London in July 1957, the United States took the position that it could not cede Chaguaramas, since the base was still needed for defence purposes. Arguing that the 1941 agreement had been made without consulting the Trinidadian people and against the recommendation of the colony's governor, Williams suggested the establishment of a joint commission to investigate a new location for a base in Trinidad. A commission moved forward in 1958 but determined that Chaguaramas was indeed the best location for a military base and that it would not be practical to partition the land for dual use as a capital. In the meantime, the United States was developing a new missile-tracking station at Chaguaramas as part of its Cold War defences.[31]

While debate continued over the status of Chaguaramas, Port of Spain became the temporary capital of the West Indies Federation and remained so throughout the life of this body (1958–1962). Since it was also the capital of the territory of Trinidad and Tobago, this created a complicated political landscape. Materially, the federation's administration took over a multistorey office building (renamed Federal House) directly north of the Treasury Building downtown, its parliament made use of the Red House and its governor general lived in Government House on the north side of the Queen's Park Savannah, thus displacing the Trinidad governor to other quarters. In addition, the local government developed a new residential area (Federation Park) at the northwest end of the city to house federation officials. Meanwhile, the PNM administration had to work within the political context of the federation, which had limited central power and an agenda that was frequently at odds with Williams's goals. By 1960, in fact, Williams was publicly criticizing Grantley Adams (the Barbadian federal prime minister) for insufficient support of Trinidad's demands for Chaguaramas, and accusing the federal government of being a "stooge" of Britain.[32]

Chaguaramas was now a focus of Williams's attention and he spoke out against the base regularly. Among his various condemnations, he claimed that the base's missile-tracking station, installed by the Americans in 1958, was generating "radiation" that was potentially harmful to the Trinidadian people. In August 1959, the PNM government had invited Dr David Evans, an English physicist, to investigate this, but in January 1960 he reported that the emissions were the microwave radiation characteristic of radar and posed no hazard. Williams, however, did not let the issue rest. Instead, he asked Dr Winston Mahabir, his minister of health, to prepare a report on the Evans report. In a chapter of his memoirs titled "Radiation – the Immaculate Deception", Mahabir dismisses the whole outcry as a hoax and says his committee met once, but never reported. Nonetheless, Williams's radiation rhetoric effectively resonated with another claim that the base "exposes us to immediate and direct participation in the nuclear orbit and to the retaliation that [it] will almost certainly evoke".[33] America was not only unjustly possessing Trinidad's land, but was also subjecting it to the dangerous technology of the Cold War.

On 21 March 1960, the PNM held a meeting at Woodford Square at which Williams declared that "Chaguaramas is the principal head of the Hydra of colonialism". In his speech, he lashed out against Britain's domination of and indifference towards its Caribbean territories and again condemned the weakness of the West Indies Federation. He also rejected any agreement between the United Kingdom, the United States and the federation concerning Chaguaramas without the direct participation of Trinidad. He then asserted:

> The war of Independence is on. The opposing divisions are at the crossroads – one leading back to the Colonial dirt track, the other leading on to Independence Highway.
>
> The army of reaction has military power on its side – jet planes, radiation, cruisers, nuclear missile launching submarines. Its base is Chaguaramas.
>
> The army of progress has political power on its side – mass meetings, popular alertness, development programme [*sic*], constitutional ambitions. Its base is the University of Woodford Square.

Other speakers during the evening included Winston Mahabir, Dr Patrick Solomon (minister of home affairs) and Isabel Teshea (vice chairman of the PNM). Teshea disclosed that the PNM was contemplating for 22 April either a march to the gates of Chaguaramas, where it would plant a Trinidad and Tobago flag, or landing a fishing fleet at one of the base's harbours, where it would hoist both West Indies and territorial flags. That date, 22 April, was the second anniversary of the inaugural session of the West Indies Federation parliament in 1958 and a date that Williams had unilaterally set for the federation's independence (with 11:00 a.m. as the designated hour).[34]

The PNM moved forward with plans for a march for Chaguaramas on 22 April, but decided against storming the base itself, which would have been impractical and unnecessary. Indeed, it was possible to make an equally powerful and more visible statement within the landscape of Port of Spain: a rally would be held at Woodford Square, with a march to the US consulate, Government House and the territorial governor's residence in the Queen's Park Savannah area, then returning downtown to Marine Square, where a statue of West Indian patriot A.A. Cipriani had been erected a year earlier. On 22 April, the *Nation* (formerly named *PNM Weekly*) published an issue that outlined the itinerary of the march; guidelines for banners and placards; instructions that bands (including steelbands) were to restrict their music to "West Indian Boys are Marching", "Onward Christian Soldiers" and "Brothers in Co-Operation"; and a notice that the demonstration should be disciplined with "no drinking or carnival jump-up". In discussing the purpose of the march, the paper said it would "establish a new claim to the lands in which we live" and would create a sense among citizens of belonging to a wider community. It added that a national spirit "is the private feeling you experience of possessing and being possessed by the whole landscape of the place where you were born".[35]

The mass rally began early on the designated date. The *Trinidad Guardian* reported that people "poured into Port-of-Spain by rail, road, and sea, the Bird of Paradise making a special night trip with 'Independence Day' passengers from Tobago". By 9:00 a.m. Woodford Square was filled with demonstrators. Learie Constantine, PNM chairman and past cricket star, welcomed the crowds, while subsequent speakers included Simeon Alexander (first vice-president of the Trinidad and Tobago National Trade Union Congress), B.I. Lalsingh (president of the Trinidad and Tobago Businessmen's Association) and Janet Jagan (radical wife of Dr Cheddi Jagan, leader of British Guiana's People's Progressive Party). Williams then delivered a rousing speech in which he observed that "we find ourselves today, on what should have been our historic Independence Day, cheated of our right and frustrated in our aspirations". He applauded the enormous turnout for the occasion and affirmed that "our march in Port-of-Spain is the symbol of our march throughout the West Indies". He noted that West Indian leaders had proven their capacity for self-government and asserted that the march would demonstrate to the world that the West Indies were independent in fact if not yet in law. As he reached the speech's climax, he proclaimed: "A demonstration such as this is not only a political leap forward. It is also a spiritual purification. As we surge forward confidently to meet the future, we bury the past. And so symbolically, as we ready ourselves for the demonstration of a people determined to be free, let us consign to the bonfire the seven deadly sins with which we have been afflicted." Then, in a moment of high drama, Williams tossed seven documents into a fire in front of the bandstand, intoning with each, "Consign it to the flames", and, "To hell with it!" Among these items were the constitutions of Trinidad and Tobago and the West Indies, the British-American Chaguaramas agreement, the report that recommended siting the federal capital in Barbados and, lastly, a copy of the *Trinidad Guardian* (which frequently criticized the PNM at the time). He left little doubt concerning his opinion of this seventh deadly sin: "that purveyor of falsification, that venal pander to colonialism, that betrayer of all the ethics of journalism, that symbol of the lowest form of political life in our community, that most shameless of all monopolies in Trinidad and Tobago".[36]

After this ceremony, Patrick Solomon read a "memorial" (written by Williams) which, in addition to commenting on British colonialism and American expansionism, listed the five demands of the march: independence for the West Indies Federation, full internal self-government for Trinidad and Tobago, revisions of the 1941 British-American bases agreement, the return of Chaguaramas and the right of the West Indian people to decide their own destiny. At 11:00 a.m. Williams hoisted West Indies and Trinidad and Tobago flags on poles in the square, while a steelband performed Handel's "Largo". With rain showers increasing, the crowd then left Woodford Square along its designated route, in what the *Guardian* described as one of the largest political demonstrations ever held in Trinidad (see figure 26). Among the placards and banners carried by the participants were "Yankees Go Home", "Dignity Is Incompatible with Colonialism", "Independence Now", "Road to Independence Passes through Chaguaramas", "Remove Radiation from Chaguaramas to Colonial Office", and "Chaguaramas for Our Capital!" As planned, the protesters presented their memorial to the American consul-general at his office and to the West Indies and Trinidad governors at their residences. During the presentation to the consul-general, Isabel Teshea noted that the memorial had been endorsed at a mass meeting and asked that it be forwarded to the US government (a request which was met that evening). The marchers then returned downtown and assembled around the Cipriani statue in the centre of Marine Square. Representatives of various groups laid wreaths at the statue while Williams, in a closing address, paid tribute to Cipriani, labour leader Uriah Butler and Hubert Young, who, as the governor of Trinidad in 1940–1941, had opposed the location of an American base in Chaguaramas. Williams ended by proposing that Marine Square be renamed Independence Square.[37]

All in all, it was a grand multisensory performance that creatively combined oratory, music, signage, flag-raisings, wreath-laying, a purification ritual and kinaesthetic movement. Spatial equivalencies were established on the scales of city, territory and West Indian region. The marchers' movements from Woodford Square (centre of the people) to the Queen's Park Savannah (with buildings representing British and American power) and back down to Marine Square (redefined as Independence Square) embodied Williams's rhetorical war between the University of Woodford Square and the Chaguaramas base and, at an even broader level, his reference to advancing the West Indies as a whole. In addition, the physical experience of marching enabled a collective "possessing and being possessed" by the local landscape, while the visits to the American consulate and governors' residences constituted specific symbolic acts of reclaiming the land at Chaguaramas and contesting British colonialism. Earlier, when the demonstrators assembled at Woodford Square, it was not necessary to burn down the Red House (as was done during the 1903 Water Riot) but simply to burn seven documents emblematic of colonialism. Similarly, raising West Indies and Trinidad and Tobago flags in the square was an act of claiming sovereignty at regional and territorial levels, including the rightful repossession of Chaguaramas. In short, the demonstration provided the public with a representation of the issues of Chaguaramas and independence alternative to the one generally offered by the *Trinidad Guardian* (though the paper did provide substantial coverage of the entire protest itself).

The march was also successful in attracting increased attention from the British and American governments. In June 1960 secretary of state for the colonies Iain Macleod visited Trinidad to discuss both the federation and Chaguaramas. Concerning the latter and other US bases, he laid out a plan for multiple rounds of talks that would involve Britain, the United States and the federation, including meetings during which the United States would negotiate directly with Trinidad and other territories with American installations. By December 1960, the United States agreed to release most of the land at Chaguaramas, with the exception of portions still in use and some land that would be used jointly with the federation and Trinidad for military purposes. All of Waller Field and Carlsen Field would be released, though in the event of an emergency the Americans had the right to reoccupy some land at Waller Field as well as at Chaguaramas. The United States agreed to review its remaining Chaguaramas base in 1968 and to close it entirely in 1977, unless global security prohibited this. In addition, the Americans agreed to provide financial aid for infrastructural projects in Trinidad and to participate in building a college of arts and sciences at the new University College of the West Indies at St Augustine. Given the continued US presence at Chaguaramas for several years, it appeared uncertain that this area could be used for a federal capital, and in any case, the federation was collapsing by the end of 1961.[38]

On the morning of 10 February 1961, a new West Indies–United States defence agreement was executed at a ceremony in the ballroom at Government House. With the governor general of the West Indies presiding, the agreement was signed by Grantley Adams, as prime minister of the federation, and by Eric Williams and other territorial leaders, as well as a delegation of US authorities. Before the ceremony, there was a parade in the Queen's Park Savannah of troops that included the Royal Navy, Royal Marines, US Navy, US Marines, West India Regiment and Trinidad police. That afternoon an open-house event, with four thousand West Indians in attendance, took place at the Chaguaramas base itself. Here the Union Jack, American flag, West Indies flag and Trinidad and Tobago flag were raised side by side to music supplied by bands from the Royal Navy, US Navy and Trinidad police. Following a joint military parade, a cannon was fired and the Trinidad Police Band offered "Abide with Me" and a bugle retreat, as the flags were lowered with the setting of the sun.[39]

At last Trinidad had planted a flag at Chaguaramas. In addition to gaining recognition of its authority by Britain and the United States, it had worked out an agreement for the repossession of most of its land and for American financial support in compensation for the use of these areas over the past two decades. To this degree, the PNM could declare the march for Chaguaramas a success. But did the march advance the process of independence? In an editorial published a couple of days after the demonstration, the *Trinidad Guardian* asserted that the PNM "seemed to many to be pushing an open door". Indeed, when Macleod visited Trinidad a few weeks later he suggested that the West Indies "hurry up" to independence.[40] Certainly the Colonial Office had mechanisms in place for independence for the federation and self-government for constituent territories like Trinidad and Tobago, even if there were still assorted issues to be negotiated. Then the federation disintegrated, thus permitting Trinidad and Tobago to seek its own sovereignty. Perhaps the multifaceted drama of the demonstration had a greater impact in promoting national consciousness among the Trinidadian population than in convincing Britain to grant independence. In this sense, the march for Chaguaramas could be considered a rehearsal for independence.

THE STAGING OF INDEPENDENCE IN THE CAPITAL CITY

As the capital city of the new nation of Trinidad and Tobago, Port of Spain served as the central site for staging independence celebrations during late August and early September 1962, with Independence Day on 31 August. A wide range of events was held that both marked the transition from colonialism to self-government and showcased the nation's achievements for the local population and for overseas guests and media. Drawing on a long tradition of pageantry for official ceremonies in the city, the primary events took place in and around Woodford Square and the Queen's Park Savannah. Throughout the celebrations, there was affirmation of both the country's natural environment and its local art forms, which were applauded as deeply rooted expressions of a national spirit. At the same time, there was extensive political commentary in speeches and the media through which leaders and observers articulated the meanings of independence, the challenges ahead and the place of the new nation in the wider world.

The planning of the independence celebrations was a large-scale project involving numerous individuals and organizations in Port of Spain and throughout the country. In April 1962, the Trinidad government appointed an Independence Celebrations Committee (ICC) with the charge of organizing events that would "impress upon everyone, especially the country's youth, the evidence of national progress and to project an image of Trinidad and Tobago as a progressive and stable society which would inspire confidence abroad". The ICC comprised a twenty-person executive, twenty-one subcommittees responsible for various facets of the celebrations and forty-seven district committees. At the helm of this sprawling enterprise was Marguerite Wyke, who as chairman managed all affairs, beginning with the executive's first meeting on 23 June at its headquarters in a cottage on the grounds of Government House. Wyke was a prominent figure in artistic and PNM political circles at the time. In addition to practising pottery, painting and poetry, she was in charge of exhibitions for the Festival of the Arts that accompanied the launch of the West Indies Federation in 1958, had served as vice-president of the Trinidad Art Society, and was a member of committees for the country's National Museum and Art Gallery and National Symphony Orchestra. In addition, she had served as a senator for Trinidad and Tobago in the federation and, during her ICC work, was also advising the government's Central Statistical Office on population surveys. Shortly before Independence Day, Wyke reflected on her experience with the ICC for the *Trinidad Guardian*: "It is obvious that we are at last on the threshold of a new national triumph, the triumph of national purpose over ethnic diversities, which is essential for cultural and political maturity."[41]

Paralleling the planning of independence events was the creation of new symbols for the nation. A committee appointed to consider designs for a flag and coat of arms included artists Sybil Atteck, Carlisle Chang, M.P. Alladin and George Bailey (a well-known Carnival masquerade designer), as well as architects Peter Bynoe and John Newel Lewis. In mid-July 1962, the government announced that a design for the flag and the coat of arms had been approved by Britain's College of Arms. The flag consisted of a black diagonal band with white borders against a red background, which the government said carried no "racial significance". The official symbolism was described as follows:

> BLACK represents the dedication of all in one strong bond. It is the colour of strength, of unity and purpose and the wealth of the land.

WHITE is said to represent the sea by which these lands are bound, the cradle of our heritage, the purity of our aspirations and the equality of all men under the sun.

RED was felt to be the colour most expressive of the country and can be said to represent the vitality of the land and its peoples. It is the warmth and energy of the sun, the courage and friendliness of the people.

Thus, the colours chosen, black, white and red, represent the elements of Earth, Fire and Water that encompass all our past, present and future, to inspire us as one united, vital and dedicated people.

Meanwhile, the coat of arms included a shield with the same colours as the flag and images of two hummingbirds and three Spanish ships (in reference to Columbus and commerce). Above the shield was the Queen's Helm (a helmet with visor) and a crest with a palm tree (to which a ship's wheel was added a few weeks later). On either side of the shield as supporters were two new national birds (supplementing the hummingbirds): Trinidad's scarlet ibis and Tobago's cocrico. Below were waves of the sea and the motto: "Together We Aspire, Together We Achieve". In short, the coat of arms merged imagery of the country's colonial history and insular environment with an inspirational statement of its future. Complementing this iconography and the symbolism of the flag was the national anthem, "Forged from the Love of Liberty", which was composed by musician and businessman Pat Castagne. The words of the anthem included a reference to islands in the Caribbean Sea, an assertion of the equality of peoples of different backgrounds and an expression of faith in the future.[42]

As planning for the independence events progressed, Eric Williams said he opposed Carnival revelry as part of the celebrations but did support steelbands at official functions (such as a state ball, state banquet and garden party), since these ensembles were one of Trinidad's foremost products and had an international appeal. In addition, an Independence Calypso Competition, sponsored by the ICC, was held at the new town hall on Woodford Square, with Lord Brynner winning the final round on 15 August for a song that admonished the populace to work together for the good of their country. On 26 August there was also an ICC-sponsored Grand Indian Singing, Musical and Dancing Exhibition at the Queen's Park Savannah, with awards for the best orchestra as well as the best individual singer "who represents in song the spirit of Independence and nationhood". By the week of independence, buildings in the city were illuminated and decorated with the national colours, while a few streets contained suspended representations of local birds, flowers and fruits. That week also brought the arrival of the princess royal, the queen's aunt and her official representative for the celebrations.[43]

The first major independence events took place on 30 August. In the afternoon there was an Independence Youth Festival at the Queen's Park Oval on Tragarete Road. In attendance were close to twenty-five thousand students, teachers and invitees representing Port of Spain-area schools and youth groups. Though rain showers had soaked the Oval, the princess royal "received a screaming welcome accompanied by the waving of thousands of red, white and black flags" as she was driven around the grounds in a convertible. Among the activities that followed were a march-past of uniformed groups; physical-education displays; dances including a belé (African-derived), joropo (Spanish), *kolattam* (Indian) and a piece representing "the growth of the spirit of Independence"; and massed school choirs that sang patriotic songs (accompanied by the police band) and folksongs under the direction of Olive Walke. In addition, Eric Williams delivered an address in which he advised the students that the future of Trinidad and Tobago depended on their scholastic achievement and noted that he had given the nation the watchwords of "Discipline, Production, Tolerance". As well as this invigorating event, there was a gala performance that evening at Queen's Hall, a concert venue and multipurpose centre that opened in 1959 to the northeast of the Queen's Park Savannah. Produced and directed by playwright Errol Hill, with the princess in attendance, this event featured some seven hundred performers from throughout the country, including Beryl McBurnie's Little Carib, the Julia Edwards Dance Group, Olive Walke's La Petite Musicale, Indian and Chinese dance ensembles, country orchestras, steelbands and calypsonians.[44]

Later that night the eagerly awaited rite of passage would occur. In the words of the *Trinidad Guardian*:

> Midnight tonight is Trinidad and Tobago's moment of destiny. At this hour, the country and its 830,000 people, aflutter with the fever of Independence, will inhale their first breath of political freedom as the national flag of red, white and black is hoisted on the floodlit forecourt of the Red House, Port-of-Spain, ancestral home of the Territory's legislature.
>
> The Union Jack, flying over the country for the past 165 years, will come down for the last time signifying "the achievement of a new relationship with Her Majesty and with the Commonwealth."

With dignitaries (including representatives of fifty-one nations) surrounding the flagpole in front of the Red House, the Union Jack was slowly lowered at 11:58 p.m. and received by a rear admiral for the queen, while the Royal Marine Band sounded the "Last Post". At midnight the Trinidad and Tobago flag was quickly raised as nearby crowds in the thousands cheered. This was followed by the performance of the new national anthem, the pealing of church bells across Port of Spain, and the sounding of sirens and guns by ships of several countries in the harbour. After clerics of five religious traditions offered prayers, the princess received the royal salute from the National Guard and Royal Marines, and "God Save the Queen" was played by the combined bands of the Trinidad and Tobago Regiment and police. After this simple but resonant ceremony, church services were held throughout the city and the country.[45]

On the morning of Independence Day, the princess officially opened parliament in the Red House. Detachments of the National Guard, Coast Guard and police marched outside, while large crowds again gathered and cheered legislators as they arrived. Positioned on a dais in the legislative chamber (with constitutional instruments and a parliamentary mace on a table in front of her), the princess first read the throne speech, in which the Government of Trinidad and Tobago pledged "to uphold democracy in the new nation, raise material standards, and inculcate new ideas and values, especially in the young". She then delivered a message from the queen, who welcomed Trinidad and Tobago into the Commonwealth and affirmed that the new nation, with its diverse population living together harmoniously, "will, in spite of its small area, play a full part in promoting co-operation and mutual understanding in the world". In response, Williams (now officially prime minister) asked the princess to convey Trinidad and Tobago's loyalty to the queen and continued the theme of a harmonious country contributing to world peace and progress. Then Rudranath Capildeo, as leader of the opposition, delivered a brief speech in which he said independence was dedicated to the British parliamentary tradition and that Trinidad entered the future with high hopes. After this ceremony, the princess returned to the governor general's residence and, that afternoon, attended a civic reception at the town hall, where she was welcomed by the Trinidad Police Band and a City Police honour guard.[46]

While the major independence celebrations ended on 31 August, other activities took place over the next two weeks. The ICC presented an exhibition on local industry and agriculture on the Prince's Building grounds and continued work on an exhibition on Carnival, calypso and steelband. It also organized displays of local history, architecture, photography, crafts and fine arts for the new National Museum and Art Gallery, which was opened on 4 September by the princess in the former residence of the governor general (Government House). Donald Pierre, minister of education and culture, declared Government House a good choice for a museum and observed that "the stateliness and dignity of what was once the home of the symbol of Imperial power now attach to what is today the home of our national culture".[47]

On the whole, the independence celebrations were an inspirational programme and Port of Spain, as the stage set, served convincingly as a material manifestation of the nation's progress and achievement. The carefully orchestrated events effectively combined the decisive transition to independence with continuity with the past. After all, Trinidad would remain a parliamentary democracy within the Commonwealth and would retain its loyalty to the queen. The central role played by the princess royal in all the main events affirmed this heritage. At the same time, the various military marches and protocols displayed a sense of order and security during the transfer of sovereignty. Nonetheless, the large crowds enthusiastically cheered the arrival of the new dispensation, while their leaders spoke of the future as well as the past. Much of their rhetoric emphasized the unity and harmony required for Trinidad and Tobago's heterogeneous population to successfully construct itself as a nation. The organization of this heterogeneity was, in turn, demonstrated in the youth festival, Queen's Hall show and exhibitions, each of which brought disparate examples of the country's creative expressions together into an orderly whole. In an article appearing in the *Trinidad Guardian* on 19 August, past Port of Spain mayor Dennis Mahabir declared: "Seen in a broader perspective, we are a United Nations in miniature. Indeed cultural synthesis and social unity are the hallmarks of our achievement."[48] It was a compelling trope for the moment – a euphoric vision enhanced by the collective and long-anticipated celebration of independence.

PERSPECTIVES ON THE INDEPENDENCE ERA

While harmony was articulated and displayed in the independence celebrations, deep tensions remained within Trinidadian society, and in the years after the 1960 march for Chaguaramas, there was vigorous debate concerning the prospects of the new nation. At the centre of this debate were Eric Williams and the PNM leadership, and Rudranath Capildeo and his colleagues in the Democratic Labour Party. However, there were also many other voices, including such prominent figures as Albert Gomes, C.L.R. James, V.S. Naipaul, Derek Walcott and the Mighty Sparrow. These individuals all possessed unique perspectives on decolonization, shaped in part by their particular experiences within Port of Spain during the years preceding independence. Their writings suggest a city that was contentious and apprehensive, striving for new possibilities but also uncertain about its character and future.

After his defeat in the 1956 election, Albert Gomes lost his position as the leading political figure in Trinidad. During the campaign season, the PNM vilified him as part of the old guard and its supporters burned his effigy at a Port of Spain street corner a couple of days before the election. But even before this he was being pushed out of the urban milieu that he loved so much. In 1947, while already a member of the colonial government's executive council, he lost his seat on the city council. Then, when one of his daughters was assaulted on the street near their Belmont home, he decided to move:

> Gay, smelly, proletarian Belmont, that felt always so much a part of me, seemed no longer friendly to fair skins like mine. So I moved upwards to Maraval, with its pretence of wealth and pretensions of social superiority, its settler enclave mentality, its elegant homes and inelegant nostalgia.... Exile must have begun then, because I never really felt part of this disoriented, half-paranoid world.... When I left Belmont my heart was left behind.

After losing the 1956 election, Gomes began writing again for the *Trinidad Guardian* and was frequently critical of Williams and the PNM for what he perceived as deficient economic policies, a concentration of power that blurred the distinction between the party and the state, and a misguided effort to reclaim Chaguaramas. In addition, he was an ardent supporter of the West Indies Federation and served in its House of Representatives as a member of the opposition Democratic Labour Party. By early 1962, with the federation collapsing, he recalls: "Day in and day out, I walked the corridors of Federal House, from which there issued only a depressing gloom." He adds that it was "painful to see a noble undertaking slowly dissolving" and to observe the thinning shelves in the Federal House library, which had been a "symbol of the emerging intellectual consciousness of the West Indies". In 1962 Gomes left Trinidad to settle in England, where he wrote his memoirs. For decades he had operated in multiple spheres of Port of Spain and embodied its creative spirit and joie de vivre. Among his varied roles were editor of *The Beacon* magazine and literary enfant terrible, trade union–movement leader and devoted supporter of working people, elected official (in municipal, territorial and federal governments), ally of business enterprise, advocate of calypsonians and steelbands, defender of the suppressed Spiritual Baptists, *Guardian* columnist and all-around man of humour and goodwill. In the end, he could no longer find a place in the city.[49]

While Port of Spain during the independence era was a place of loss for Gomes, it was a site of disappointment for C.L.R. James. After a twenty-six-year absence, James returned to Trinidad in April 1958 as an invited guest for the inauguration of the parliament of the West Indies Federation. Soon afterwards, Eric Williams appointed him editor of the *PNM Weekly* (the *Nation*), where he covered political and cultural topics, strongly supported the march for Chaguaramas and featured a campaign against discrimination in West Indian cricket, focused on the selection of Afro-Barbadian Frank Worrell as captain of the West Indies team. After the Chaguaramas demonstration, however, James had a falling-out with Williams over issues concerning the newspaper and party organization, and resigned or was dismissed from his editorial position. In a small book published in Trinidad in 1962, *Party Politics in the West Indies*, he argued that Williams and the PNM leadership, because of their middle-class position in society, operated on the flawed assumption that they were the rightful political leaders of compliant masses. Since, he asserted, the middle class was in fact isolated from the masses, it lacked effective ideas for building a truly independent nation. In 1962 James returned to his life in England, having given up on the potential of the University of Woodford Square for social transformation. The following year saw the publication of his magisterial *Beyond a Boundary* – a highly original synthesis of cricket history, sociopolitical analysis, aesthetics and memoirs. Within this book's wide-ranging discussions, he examined how top cricket clubs in Port of Spain were divided along lines of class and colour, with their matches serving as occasions for dramatically acting out social tensions. For James, cricket was a mode of "apprehending the world" and a central ritual of West Indian society: during major matches, "every street corner is a seething cauldron of cricket experiences, cricket memories, fears, suspicions, hopes, aspirations".[50]

Like James, V.S. Naipaul returned to Trinidad through an official invitation – the award of a three-month scholarship by the Trinidad government. He arrived in September 1960 for his second visit since leaving for England ten years earlier. Eric Williams then suggested that he write a non-fiction book about the Caribbean (by this point he had already published *Miguel Street* and two other novels). Though hesitant at first, he accepted the idea; spent the next several months in Trinidad, British Guiana, Surinam, Martinique and Jamaica; and published his impressions as *The Middle Passage* in 1962. His chapter on Trinidad opens with his arrival at the Port of Spain docks and the recurrence of an old fear of the island, which he proceeds to examine. He remembers details of the city's architecture, but there are now more neon lights, more cars and steelbands (which he detests). It is a place, he suggests, that lacks community, is driven by competitive individualism, denies itself heroes (with the exception of cricketers) and dwells on stories of failure. It considers itself "modern", but this simply means being enthralled with American products advertised in magazines, while ignoring local goods and regarding British ones as old-fashioned. Audiences are thrilled by the style of Humphrey Bogart and other Hollywood tough guys at movie theatres, while another crowd attends Queen's Hall for a children's dance show with selections like "Ballet of the Enchanted Doll" and "Broadway Melody". There is much talk of Trinidad "culture", but this is something invented by politicians to provide people with a sense of meaning in their lives and to sell to tourists in nightclubs. Only in calypso, a truly local art, do people gain glimpses of the reality of their world, with its class, ethnic and other divisions. Naipaul continues in this vein for more than forty pages, combining detailed descriptions with broad assertions to construct a devastating portrait of a society plagued with anxieties and lost in fantasies. It is a representation that contrasts completely with the promotions of the Independence Celebrations Committee. While his earlier fiction, based on memories, was shaped by a fascination with Trinidadian idiosyncrasies, his return visit revealed an experience of deep alienation.[51]

A more optimistic account of Trinidad is offered by Derek Walcott, who arrived in early 1958 for the production of his play *Drums and Colours* for the federation's West Indies Festival of the Arts. Walcott was born in Castries, St Lucia, in 1930, published his first small book of poetry at nineteen, and had his first play produced at twenty, while also learning to paint. In the early 1950s he attended the University College of the West Indies in Jamaica and then taught and worked as a journalist for three years, while continuing to write poetry and plays. In the course of his 1958 visit to Port of Spain, he became enamoured of the city's dynamism, the openness of its people and its vibrant arts scene. After a period in New York, he returned in 1959 to pursue an artistic career in this promising setting.[52]

By early 1960 Walcott was supporting himself through a job as a staff writer with the *Trinidad Guardian*, a position that enabled him to explore the full range of the city's literary, visual and theatrical arts, which he generally advocated but also subjected to a sharp critical eye. In August 1960, for example, he reviewed the second issue of the literary journal *Opus*, which he suggested needed a more aggressive editorial policy and "something to fight about". He dismissed an essay about the Queen's Park Savannah ("wisely published anonymously") but praised a poem by E.M. Roach, an excerpt of a novel by Oliver Jackman and a literary review essay by Ursula Raymond. Meanwhile, he appears to have attended most art exhibitions in the city. In May 1962, for example, he condemned a show held by the Trinidad Art Society at its Art Centre in the old Woodbrook Market, describing it as "one of staggering triviality" with "an air of genteel desperation". However, he noted two powerful works by Trinidad Art Society president Sybil Atteck ("The Spirit of Carnival" and "Washerwoman") and suggested that Jackie Hinkson, Willi Chen and Pat Chu Foon showed promise. That same year he offered praise for a one-man show by veteran M.P. Alladin at the town hall and encouragement for one by Chen at Nina's Gallery on Frederick Street. Along with covering the work of Trinidad's elite art circle, he visited in July 1960 a multimedia "Backyard Exhibition" on Quarry Street in east Port of Spain, organized by a group of Belmont artists calling themselves the Trinidad and Tobago Co-operative Art Society. Though he believed that much of this show was "awkward and amateurish", he applauded Raphael Samuel's concrete sculptures of steelband figures and Carnival artist Ken Morris's copper plaques. For the Carnival itself, Walcott offered many accolades, lauding such elements as the "surrealist speech" of the Midnight Robbers, the versatility of the steelbands (the festival's "richest invention"), and the "epic theatre" of the large masquerade bands as they crossed the stage at the Queen's Park Savannah.[53]

While working for the *Guardian*, Walcott continued his creative writing. In 1960 he met V.S. Naipaul for the first time and, in a central Port of Spain café, explained his process of composing poems. In 1962 he lectured on the poetic process for a large audience at the Trinidad Public Library, suggesting that poetry has its origin in "the heredity of the folk imagination", involves "both magic and personal industry" and is "a refinement of language and possible invention of new language". For this occasion, he also read from his first major collection of poetry (*In a Green Night*), recently published in London. In a review of this book for the *Trinidad Guardian*, C.L.R. James declared that, after several successful novelists, the West Indies had at last produced a poet with an independent vision and voice. By this point, Walcott was also writing poems about his adopted home, such as "Nights in the Gardens of Port of Spain" – a short phantasmagoric piece on the city's nocturnal qualities. In parallel with his poetic work, he established at the Little Carib a theatrical project that later evolved into the Trinidad Theatre Workshop. Here actors and other artists developed their skills and performed both local and foreign plays. In 1962, for example, he directed and designed the set for a production of Samuel Beckett's *Krapp's Last Tape*. With Slade Hopkinson in the role of Krapp, this was the first presentation of a Beckett play in Trinidad. For the *Guardian*'s August 1962 independence supplement, he contributed an article, titled "The Prospects of a National Theatre", in which he proffered his concept of a West Indian art generated by a shared *genius loci*, based on his assumption that the West Indies would have achieved independence as an archipelago. The separate independence of Jamaica and Trinidad now required concepts of island-specific arts, shaped more by political expediency. Nonetheless, he was hopeful about the development of a national theatre in Trinidad, in part because of its strong tradition of popular performance in the Carnival. After independence, Walcott developed the Trinidad Theatre Workshop into a highly successful arts collective, which presented both his own plays and the works of other writers. During the late 1970s and early 1980s, he gradually relocated to the United States and in 1992 won the Nobel Prize in Literature.[54]

Another major poetic voice of the independence era was the calypsonian Slinger Francisco, known as the Mighty Sparrow. In *Party Politics in the West Indies*, C.L.R. James proclaimed that Sparrow embodied the West Indian nation: "He represents, makes known what the people really think, what they really are and how they speak. Through him the ordinary West Indian speech is given its place." Sparrow was born in Grenada in 1935, and his mother brought him in 1937 to Port of Spain, where they settled with his father, a builder. He became a choirboy at New Town's St Patrick's Roman Catholic Church, taught himself to play guitar and sing calypso, and by 1953 or 1954 was performing at the Lotus Restaurant and other city venues. In 1955 he joined such prominent calypsonians of the period as Melody, Cristo and Spitfire at the Young Brigade ("New Brigade") tent, then based at Dirty Jim's Swizzle Club on South Quay, near the harbour. In 1956 Sparrow captured the nation's enthusiasm when he won the Calypso King competition on the Sunday night before Carnival at the grandstand in the Queen's Park Savannah. Here he delivered "Yankees Gone" ("Jean and Dinah"), a buoyant song in which he asserted that "glamour boys" like himself (rather than American servicemen) now ruled Port of Spain and had the pick of its women. Though this became one of the most popular calypsoes of all time, Sparrow offered a different perspective the following year with "Yankees Back Again", in which he commented on Texaco's purchase of Trinidad Leaseholds Limited and its refinery at Pointe-à-Pierre. He warned that the Americans might buy all of Trinidad and hoped that they would not "capture" Port of Spain. At the same time, he became the foremost calypso champion of the PNM, with his own reputation progressing contemporaneously with this new government. Though he occasionally voiced criticism, his calypsoes generally applauded or defended Williams: "William the Conqueror" (1957), on the defeat of Gomes; "Pay as You Earn" (1958), support for a new income tax; "The Base" (1958), the reclaiming of Chaguaramas; and "Present Government" (1961), condemnation of the political opposition.[55]

Like other great calypsonians before him, however, Sparrow commented not only on politics but also on a range of experience. For example, an altercation with several men outside the Miramar Club on South Quay in 1959 led to a series of calypsoes in which he assumed the role of a city "badjohn" (ruffian), such as "Gun Slingers" (1959), "Ten to One Is Murder" (1959) and "Royal Jail" (1961). Meanwhile, he narrated relationships with women from various perspectives, including cuckolded husband ("Sailor Man", 1957); thwarted seducer of a young woman from the countryside ("Country Girl", 1958); lovesick suitor ("Dorothy", 1959); and irresistible lover ("May May", 1960). In discussing Sparrow's relationship with postwar Port of Spain, calypso scholar Gordon Rohlehr observes that the singer "wears numerous masks, assumes a variety of personas, and speaks in several voices, as he becomes a channel for the dramatic experiences of the world he has entered". In addition, Rohlehr notes that "Sparrow's calypsos sparkled with the self-confidence and machismo of a decade (1956–1966) marked by a new nationalism" that was first region-wide and then territory-centred.[56]

In 1962 the calypso season began inauspiciously, with Sparrow, Melody and several other leading calypsonians performing abroad. However, Sparrow and Melody eventually returned home and appeared at the Original Young Brigade tent, now in the Good Samaritan Hall on Duke Street. Sparrow also performed at the Penthouse nightclub with Melody and at the Bel Air Hotel with Zebra and Brynner. On 4 March he again captured the crown at the Calypso King competition, this time with "Sparrow Come Back Home" and "Federation". In the latter song he lamented the recent disintegration of the federation but also looked forward to the formation of separate independent nations. By this point, he had achieved substantial international fame: soon after the competition, he was off on a tour to British Guiana and then on to London and Paris before ending up in New York for further engagements. However, he returned home in time to participate in Trinidad's Independence Calypso Competition, in which he came second, singing "Model Nation". In this song, he expressed the recurring theme of small Trinidad, with its diverse but harmonious population, serving as an exemplar for the whole world. Indeed Sparrow, through his overseas tours and an RCA recording contract, had become one of the nation's most exciting ambassadors.[57]

For Sparrow and other calypsonians, Port of Spain was a vital locale for engaging audiences and gaining recognition. Here they joined a range of other performers in a variety of shows held in nightclubs, hotels and other venues, both during the Carnival season and at other times of the year. Clearly, the city thrived as an entertainment centre, one that was appealing to many local residents as well as to newcomers from the countryside, other islands and further abroad. It was a landscape of human variety, imagination, pleasure and intrigue, with a unique configuration of aesthetic qualities that included the novel sounds of the steelbands along with other local forms of expression. Throughout the postwar era, government and business leaders tried to capitalize on these resources by developing tourism campaigns and expanding hotel capacity and related services. However, such promotion of arts and entertainment was only one component of a much larger project in the transition to independence. For the PNM administration and its allies, Port of Spain was also a centre for constructing a mass political movement, expanding and diversifying the territory's economy, erecting new housing and public buildings and advancing international relations. Here the nation's populace could demonstrate Eric Williams's watchwords of discipline, production and tolerance within a concentrated and heavily trafficked environment. As dignitaries, journalists and other visitors arrived in Trinidad for the independence celebrations, they could be induced to observe and appreciate Port of Spain as the progressive capital of a model nation.

8. MODERN ARCHITECTURE FOR AN EMERGING NATION

PARALLELING THE DEVELOPMENT of a nationalist movement in postwar Trinidad was the innovative design work of architects, planners and government officials aimed at increasing coherence and functionality in the landscape of Port of Spain, from individual buildings to the city as a whole. The city posed immense challenges: suburbanization accompanied by a rapidly growing population, expanded car usage and unbridled construction propelled by economic prosperity. With escalating competition and debate over land use, both the central and municipal governments renewed their attention to formal town planning and hoped to implement systems and regulations that would save the city from much-feared chaos. This was an age of trained technocrats with theories and methods for improving the socio-spatial order and a penchant for pronouncements and programmes. Similarly, local architects embraced the principles and logic of international modernism in their design of a variety of residential, commercial and public buildings. While such concepts were immensely appealing, architects adapted them to the local natural and cultural environment and thus gradually formulated a Trinidadian creole modernism in both aesthetics and technique. Indeed, the local landscape was highly valued for its unique beauty and other inherent qualities. As a whole, the work of architects and planners during this era involved experimenting with ways of shaping and organizing local space in order to produce new forms of visual experience and modes of living. Modern design promised the citizens of Port of Spain a progressive existence, a means of crafting a forward-looking capital city representative of a soon-to-be-independent nation.

From the launch of its administration in October 1956, the PNM government considered town and regional planning an integral part of its development goals for Trinidad and Tobago. The rapid increase of population not only in greater Port of Spain but also across the territory was generating serious conflict over land for housing, commerce, agriculture and industry.[1] Given its national and populist orientation, the government sought a more systematic and aggressive approach to land-use management that would improve the quality of life for the entire population while also promoting economic growth. In November government officials participated in a ten-day conference on town and country development planning sponsored by the Caribbean Commission (based in Port of Spain). Held at the Trinidad Country Club, this event attracted representatives from throughout the British Caribbean as well as from Dutch territories, Puerto Rico, the United Nations and other organizations. In the course of the meeting, participants prepared forty recommendations on such issues as the role of planning in development programmes; planning research, legislation and implementation; training of personnel; management of rural-urban migration; and support for self-help projects. In addition, the participants mounted an exhibition at the British Council that included plans and models for housing in Trinidad, an illuminated model of a zoned Greater Georgetown (British Guiana), development plans for Castries (St Lucia), photographs of old and new architecture in Curaçao and material related to comprehensive social and economic planning in Puerto Rico.[2] Underlying both the conference and the exhibition was an assumption that the landscape is best designed by experts with specialized technical knowledge, visions of large-scale and efficient environmental systems and the authority to enforce regulations.

Though the PNM government expressed a strong interest in town planning, it did not pursue major new legislation in this area until 1959. By this point, it was clear to various observers that the Town and Regional Planning Ordinance of 1938 was inadequate for the control of growth in Port of Spain, its environs and the island. In a letter to the editors of both the *Trinidad Guardian* and *Trinidad Chronicle*, Peter Bynoe, president of the Trinidad and Tobago Society of Architects, noted that his organization had recently passed a resolution requesting that government urgently enact an ordinance to check "haphazard development". He added that, without such legislation, "no proper neighbourhood units are being considered; there is no zoning; no villages are being planned and the landscape is being butchered by wanton and promiscuous use of land". A few days later, the *Guardian* editorialized:

> A comprehensive plan and legislation for Trinidad would include zoning for residential, industrial, commercial, and recreational purposes; the location of towns and villages; highways; the preservation of trees and wooded areas, and of sites of special historic and architectural interest; and a number of other necessary measures of control. With the present rate of population increase and of expansion in industry and building construction, we face nothing short of chaos unless something is done soon.

Similarly, the *Trinidad Chronicle* warned of "architectural disaster" and said, "haphazard building, uncoordinated development, and low standards of taste could easily turn Port-of-Spain into a nightmare city". However, it also advised that town planning should involve a balanced approach and not unduly suppress private enterprise.³

By this point, the PNM government had already recruited as a consultant Desmond Heap, a prominent town planner from Britain. Heap prepared a report on land management in the territory and drafted new planning legislation modelled on the United Kingdom's 1947 Town and Country Planning Act. On 29 July 1960, the legislative council unanimously passed the Town and Country Planning Bill, which was hailed by both the PNM government and the opposition as "forward-looking and progressive". Included in the bill were provisions for "the orderly and progressive development of land in both urban and rural areas, and the preservation and improvement of amenities; and for the grant of permission to develop land and for other powers of control over the use of land". The bill also conferred "additional powers in respect of the acquisition and development of land for planning and for purposes connected with the matters aforesaid". In short, the new legislation required individuals to obtain the permission of the government to develop land and provided the government with wide-ranging authority to control the use of land for the public good. Premier Eric Williams took particular interest in the legislation, moved the bill himself and located within his own ministry the chief town planner (Joseph Crooks) and a new town-planning section. Williams described the bill as a long-overdue "integration of physical planning with economic planning" and said individual rights to build must be limited in the interest of society as a whole, with consideration for public safety, convenience and the beauty of the environment. As an example of unchecked development, he cited a proliferation of gas stations and cinemas in both Port of Spain and elsewhere. Indeed, a 1962 map of Port of Spain shows that, in the central city alone, there were ten gas stations and nine cinemas.⁴

During the late 1950s and early 1960s, cooperation between the central government and the Port of Spain City Council facilitated several infrastructure-improvement projects. At the beginning of November 1956, the PNM published in its party newspaper an article ("PNM and the Municipalities") in which it explained why it would contest the upcoming municipal elections. While it noted that the central government should support local initiative and self-government, it also suggested that the party system could introduce "uniformity" to municipal government, which would become "the delegate of the central government for carrying out the programme for the country as a whole". A majority of PNM candidates won seats on the city council in that year's election, and the PNM maintained control of the council in subsequent years, under mayors Dennis Mahabir (1957–1960) and Edward Taylor (1960–1962).⁵

Among the initiatives carried out in Port of Spain during this period were improvements of streets, pavements and drainage; installation of more and higher-quality street lights; numerous public housing schemes; and constructing a new town hall on Woodford Square to replace the building destroyed by fire in 1948. In 1962 the central government also launched a major nationwide sewerage programme that included Port of Spain, where cesspits were still common in some districts. There were also city beautification efforts, such as anti-litter campaigns and horticultural projects. In 1958 the *Evening News* reported that the municipal government aimed to keep Port of Spain, as the temporary capital of the West Indies Federation, "clean and worthy of the honour". In addition to police ticketing of merchants for illegal disposal of rubbish and the formation of a Civil Improvement Committee by the Junior Chamber of Commerce, the city enlisted the assistance of the Horticulturist Society, the Botanic Gardens and the Suburbs Beautiful Circle to encourage the cultivation of flowering plants in both public spaces and private yards. By 1962 the municipal government had established its own flower nursery in the Woodbrook (Mucurapo) Cemetery, which the *Trinidad Guardian* observed was "destined to be the botanical reservoir behind the city council's efforts to beautify the Territory's capital". The city engineer, Eric Phipps, conceptualized the nursery, while Fitzroy Asson served as the keeper of this "luxuriant Eden of tropical blossoms which may well cause the neighbourhood host of dearly departed to turn in their graves". Flowers were transplanted to the cemetery from the Imperial College of Tropical Agriculture (recently absorbed by the new University College of the West Indies at St Augustine), sent out to public spaces in containers and, when they began to fade, replaced in a rotational/rejuvenation system.[6]

Some projects were conceptualized but not implemented. In 1960 Joseph Alwin Awon, a private architect-planner, described Port of Spain as "an architectural nightmare" and argued that, if the city were to become worthy of its name as a capital, piecemeal development needed to be replaced by a "scientific approach" and the creation of a master plan. Awon produced a set of seventy plans and other documents as a proposal for the redevelopment of the city and advocated the need for a "civic centre", which he placed near the southeast corner of the Queen's Park Savannah (apparently considering downtown's Woodford Square inadequate). The *Trinidad Guardian* published one of Awon's plans, which shows his civic centre as encompassing the Prince's Building grounds and Memorial Park. In this scheme, Frederick Street has been removed between Keate Street and Queen's Park West to create one contiguous area. The War Memorial is moved south to allow space for a new town hall to the north; the Prince's Building is eliminated; and a theatre, library, concert hall and art museum are positioned to the west of the Royal Victoria Institute.

A large hotel is located on the south side of Keate Street between Frederick and Charlotte Streets. The following year, Eric Phipps, the city engineer, again thinking about what could be accomplished beneath the surface of the earth, outlined for a *Guardian* reporter his vision for contending with Port of Spain's densely built landscape, narrow streets and increasing traffic congestion. His plans included pedestrian passageways beneath busy streets; an underground electric train line with stops at the railway station (south of Marine Square), Woodford Square and the Queen's Park Savannah; and the construction of a tunnel east of Jerningham Avenue into the Laventille Hills which would enable a connection with the St François Valley Road and points east. In response to the apparently sceptical reporter, Phipps suggested that "the plan is not as fantastic as it appears because in this age of atomic fallout, there is going to be need to think of life underground".[7]

While Port of Spain did not develop underground or have its civic centre relocated to the Savannah, the central government carried out two major road-building projects during this era that greatly improved access to the city from the east. In the mid-1950s most drivers from eastern and southern parts of Trinidad entered the capital along the narrow Eastern Main Road, which fed into South Quay and was connected with Marine Square via the St Joseph Road directly east of downtown. In an effort to address the serious congestion of this eastern approach, the government began constructing the Beetham Highway along reclaimed swamp land to the south of the Eastern Main Road. This dual-carriageway road originated at the terminus of the Churchill-Roosevelt Highway (approximately two and a half miles east of downtown), entered the harbour area below the railway yard and station, and ended at a roundabout that connected South Quay, St Vincent Street and Wrightson Road. In addition, a flyover above the Eastern Main Road provided a direct route to Marine Square. When it opened in 1958, the Beetham Highway not only facilitated eastern access to the city but also enabled drivers who were travelling to western districts to bypass the busy Marine Square.[8]

An even more impressive construction project was the completion of the Lady Young Road, which was officially opened in 1959 by Learie Constantine, minister of works and transport. Initiated during World War II, the Lady Young Road extended north from the Eastern Main Road through the new Morvant housing developments and over the steep slopes of the Laventille Hills. Final work on the road brought it down to an intersection with Queen's Park East at the northeastern edge of the Savannah. Though there were other, circuitous routes over the Laventille Hills, the four-and-a-half-mile Lady Young Road was of much higher quality and offered faster access to northern districts of the city. Moreover, it was exceptionally scenic, given its climb of 520 feet from the Eastern Main Road. *Trinidad Guardian* reporter Carl Jacobs referred to it as a "motorist's dream" – "a holiday road, an avenue of escape, a soothing passage and a sightseer's delight".9 Indeed, the road offered stunning vistas of Port of Spain and the Gulf of Paria below. Along the road were quiet areas where drivers could park and contemplate the growing city, with its new housing developments, sleek office buildings, traffic-filled streets and, at night, ever brighter lights.

HOUSING

For both town planners and the population, the availability of housing in greater Port of Spain remained a critical concern during the postwar era. The population of the area continued to grow through both natural increase and migration. Given the shortage of existing residences and limited space for building within municipal boundaries, many people moved into new houses in the valleys and on the hills that surrounded the city. An expanding middle class, boosted by postwar economic growth, was especially attracted to the possibilities of new homes in more spacious and quieter suburban locales, though many middle-income residents remained in districts such as Belmont, Woodbrook and St James. Meanwhile, the large low-income population continued to contend with extremely difficult housing conditions: overcrowding was prevalent, rents were often unaffordable and the availability of accommodation was limited, owing in part to the ongoing demolition of barrack yards and other substandard buildings and the conversion of residential buildings for commercial use. Some of this population moved into new housing projects that were gradually constructed by the central government during the postwar years, both in the central city and outlying districts. Many other people lived in small self-built structures on steep hillsides or in other marginal spaces on the edges of the city.10

During the postwar era, there were also major changes in the design of housing in Port of Spain and its environs. Except for the small houses assembled by low-income residents from wood and any other available materials, builders shifted from the combination of masonry and wood typical of the prewar era to primarily masonry structures, generally constructed of concrete or clay blocks. This change in materials was accompanied by a shift from gable and hip roofs to low-pitched shed roofs or shallow dual-pitched roofs, commonly in the form of corrugated galvanized-iron sheets or asbestos cement sheets. In addition, the wooden fretwork that had been popular for decades on gables, eaves and posts was eliminated. Houses now featured clean, orthogonal lines, though a degree of ornamentation could be achieved through the geometric patterns of openings in ventilation blocks. Floors often consisted of terrazzo or concrete tiles, while aluminium was increasingly employed for window frames, louvres and other building elements. Since air conditioning was rarely used, ventilation and protection from the sun continued to require architectural solutions. Builders positioned houses to maximize the flow of prevailing breezes; used ventilation blocks in both external walls and yard perimeter walls; and continued to employ verandahs, overhanging eaves, gaps between walls and ceilings and louvred windows and doors.[11]

Several local companies manufactured building products to meet the growing demand for this new type of house during the postwar era. With limestone aggregate quarried from the Blanchisseuse area of Trinidad's Northern Range, Bestcrete Limited produced concrete blocks and other concrete materials at its plant on the Churchill-Roosevelt Highway near the junction to Piarco Airport. The company's product line featured over sixty varieties of load-bearing and decorative ventilation blocks (with a range of square, diamond, circular and other patterns). Other well-established companies were Trinidad Clay Products, which produced hollow clay blocks at a factory in Longdenville; Caribbean Mosaic Tile Products, which manufactured terrazzo and concrete tiles in San Juan; and Trinidad Ready-Mix Concrete Company Limited, which maintained a facility in Woodbrook and was a major supplier to building contractors. Meanwhile, Aluminum Industries Limited ran a factory at the Piarco junction of the Churchill-Roosevelt Highway, where it assembled such products as louvre windows, sliding windows and doors, ornamental grilles, porch and lawn furniture and television antennas. In 1962 the company ran an advertisement in the *Trinidad Guardian* that proclaimed: "Be as modern as tomorrow. Live with aluminum – the modern metal."[12]

Low-Income Housing Projects

During the postwar years, much of Port of Spain's working-class population lived in exceptionally crowded and low-grade housing units, in spite of the general growth of the economy and ongoing government programmes to address its plight. The Planning and Housing Commission, established in 1938, continued to focus on clearing slums in the central city and developing new housing projects, but assisted a relatively modest number of families. After assuming office in 1956, the PNM government devoted greater attention and resources to housing problems. First it formed a ministry of housing and local government, which, under the leadership of Gerard Montano, developed various initiatives for both low- and middle-income sectors of the population, while in 1962 the legislature passed a bill to create a National Housing Authority that consolidated the Planning and Housing Commission and two mortgage-lending agencies in an effort to provide more integrated support to families, builders and investors. But the PNM government, like its predecessors, faced a massive challenge: in 1961, Port of Spain's chief health officer released a report indicating that (in 1959) almost half of the city's twenty thousand accommodation units were dilapidated and insanitary, while in 1962 the *Trinidad Guardian* observed that, in certain parts of the city, 70 per cent of the dwellings included bedrooms occupied by more than four people.[13]

During the postwar era, the Planning and Housing Commission carried out extensive work on the eastern side of downtown, which contained some of the worst accommodation in the city. After removing existing structures, it erected numerous two- and three-storey concrete buildings along Duncan, Nelson and George Streets (see figure 27). With their austere façades, uninviting stairwells, cramped apartments and minimal surrounding yards, these buildings radically changed the organization and appearance of eastern downtown. In 1956 *Guardian* reporter John Grimes visited these projects, locally known as "the Plannings", and offered an assessment:

> The original idea behind the construction of these flats was to eradicate the slum centres in that area and all the evils they stand for.
>
> It was supposed to be a social emancipation particularly for the children. . . .
>
> As an economic, social and cultural gamble, the scheme has backfired. The environments from which the slum dwellers were supposed to have escaped have followed them in no little measure, to be made even worse, by the feeling of frustration.

The flats had limited space (especially as families grew) and, since there were no recreational areas, children were forced to play in the streets. In addition, unaffordable rents further impoverished the tenants; some even began subletting rooms for use as brothels. In spite of these problematic outcomes, the Planning and Housing Commission continued building multistorey flats for low-income families during the latter 1950s and early 1960s at various locations around Port of Spain, including Mango Rose (directly east of downtown) and Cocorite (west of St James). The Mango Rose project was planned to include three nine-storey and three four-storey blocks. One nine-storey building (the tallest in Trinidad at the time) was completed by the National Housing Authority in 1963 and included fifty-two flats of various sizes. At least one of the four-storey blocks was also completed by this time and contained flats for sixteen families.[14]

In contrast to these high-rise schemes, the central government also continued to develop housing in the more spacious and scenic area of Morvant on the eastern slope of the Laventille Hills. As noted in chapter 6, families from downtown began moving into government homes in Morvant in 1941. Housing in this district expanded in the following years, with the construction of the Lady Young Road up the slope and the layout of numerous additional streets and utilities. By the late 1950s, the government was developing two new programmes in Morvant with an objective of increasing occupants' investment in their homes: "Aided Self-Help" and "Rental Mortgage". In Aided Self-Help, the government offered materials and supervising technical officers for the construction of houses, while the future residents provided the labour. During 1957–1958 men selected from John John were organized into five teams, each of which collectively built a group of houses for a total of seventy-six (all with the same two-bedroom design). Mobile floodlights were available to facilitate work after dark. On completion, the families owned the houses but were required to pay back the cost of the materials. Meanwhile, Rental Mortgage enabled families to acquire ownership of homes gradually without having to build them themselves. By the end of 1957, thirty-two three-bedroom and twenty-one two-bedroom Rental Mortgage houses were under construction. An article in the *Trinidad Chronicle* in May 1958 included photographs of both the Self-Help and the two-bedroom Rental Mortgage houses, nearing completion. Both types were closely sited one-floor structures with low double-pitched roofs and plain exteriors. The Rental Mortgage houses included a small entry porch at the front left and, from a floor plan published by the National Housing Authority in 1963, appear to have contained a combined living/dining room and a kitchen in front and two bedrooms and a bathroom in the back. During the following years, the Morvant district continued to grow and, by 1960, a Morvant Community Welfare Association was planning to build a public park with volunteer labour.[15]

Perhaps the greatest challenge to housing authorities during the postwar period was Shanty Town – a protean community that developed south of the Eastern Main Road near "the La Basse" (the city dump), less than two miles east of downtown. The Beetham Highway's construction had displaced some Shanty Town residents and its completion in 1958 in turn offered an unimpeded view of their nearby accommodation. So drivers arriving along this grand new entryway to the capital city encountered a corbeaux-infested dump on their left and what appeared to be a chaotic maze of ramshackle houses on their right. In May 1959 the *Trinidad Guardian* editorialized: "On humanitarian, sanitary, and aesthetic grounds the Government cannot burke this issue. No longer can this unpleasant slum be allowed to exist and grow as it is doing, alongside the main access route into the city from the international airport at Piarco."

Though Shanty Town was an embarrassment to officials and many citizens of Port of Spain, it had a life and structure of its own. In June 1959 intrepid *Guardian* reporter John Grimes visited this district of close to two thousand residents in an effort to understand better how it worked. Here he discovered disparate small houses constructed from a variety of materials and noted that one "built on more ambitious lines actually boasts a fence made up of rusted corrugated galvanised iron sheets, old pieces of board, and scraps of tin salvaged from La Basse". With a shortage of remaining land on the north side of the Beetham Highway, the Shanty Town dwellers were now expanding to the south into a mangrove area ("the Mang") near the sea and closer to the La Basse. When Grimes asked one resident how more buildings kept appearing even though the central government and city council were tearing them down, he received the following explanation: "You see the Inspectors come around like today and pull down three or four. Then they don't come back for another month or two. Man, in that time the shacks they bulldozed are not only up again, we have new ones too." The dump not only provided materials for houses but was also the focus of the Shanty Town economy. As garbage trucks arrived daily, residents were ready to salvage bottles, iron, clothing, food, books and other items, and took advantage of a ready market for the sale of cable wire, copper fittings and other pieces of metal. Though the central government was working on a project to rehouse the Shanty Town dwellers, most indicated no interest in Self-Help, Mortgage Rental or any other scheme. They had grown accustomed to their livelihood, were reluctant to take on any long-term financial obligations, and were suspicious of government authorities. Some had been residents of the old housing in eastern downtown. With the initiation of slum-clearance projects there, they were forced out and could not afford the rents in the new multistorey flats. Thus they created Shanty Town.[16]

In spite of their attachment to Shanty Town, some occupants did seek better housing and gained a glimpse of hope in July 1960, when Minister of Housing Gerard Montano announced that they would be relocated to Hirondelle Street in Lower Morvant. However, their accommodation would be four-storey apartment buildings, rather than houses. In September 1961 the government began work on the first two of these buildings (each containing sixteen two-bedroom apartments) and anticipated that they would be completed by 1962. At this point, the *Evening News* asserted that the "blemish" of Shanty Town had become even greater with views afforded by the Lady Young Road and advised that the new housing would provide residents with "the opportunity of starting a new and better life in more wholesome surroundings".[17] Given the amount of commentary that it elicited, Shanty Town appears to have been the most threatening of all low-income settlements in greater Port of Spain during the postwar years. Perhaps this was due in part to the fact that its residents created their own housing and economy in a swampy wasteland at the edge of the city. Surely it was much safer to lodge such individuals in uniform concrete high-rises in a government-controlled residential development.

Elite Homes

During the postwar era, Port of Spain's high-income families generally built new homes in the districts to the north and west of the city, though some continued to select sites within the municipal boundaries. Typically they employed architects and aimed for houses that combined luxury and convenience while also displaying technological and aesthetic innovation. Particular attention was devoted to designs that embraced the beauty of the surrounding tropical environment while minimizing the impact of its intense heat. Architect/architectural historian Mark Raymond suggests that, during this period, Trinidad's architects drew on both the British tropical modernism of figures like Maxwell Fry and Jane Drew and precepts of regional modernism current in the United States. While the former was concerned with the adaptation of modernism to the tropical climate of much of the British Commonwealth, the latter involved incorporating local building materials and architectural forms.[18]

One of the premier new housing developments in Port of Spain during the 1950s was Federation Park – a secluded area to the west of St Clair that was built by the Trinidad government to provide homes on a rental basis for the ministers and officials of the new federal government. This was a carefully planned community with curving streets, cul-de-sacs, and an abundance of green space, including a park and spacious lawns. Yard perimeter walls were set back several feet from the street by grass strips, a layout that contrasted with the traditional siting of walls adjacent to pavements or streets. In late 1957 and early 1958, contractor Austin Fridal built an initial twenty-four three-bedroom masonry houses in pastel shades and, by the end of 1960, there were a total of eighty-five. *Trinidad Guardian* reporter Carl Jacobs visited the development in April 1958 and described it as a "show window for dreamers" and "a federation of designs and features completely new to Trinidad". He added that a "house-to-house ramble through the Park can be an absorbing adventure into the talent and distinctive tendencies of Trinidad's foremost architects". In fact, there was a sign in front of each house indicating the architectural firm responsible for its design: Prior, Lourenco and Nothnagel; Anthony Lewis; or Mence and Moore. Prior, Lourenco and Nothnagel's house was a one-floor structure featuring a spacious verandah at the front left; along the back of the verandah were sliding glass doors for entry to a drawing room, and a large bay of glass louvred windows. The kitchen was at the rear of the house, while bedrooms were on the right. Anthony Lewis's design included, from the left, a bedroom or maid's room, an open carport with round arch, a kitchen, a projecting front room, and a verandah with round arches on the front and right sides. Behind the verandah was the drawing room, while bedrooms were in the rear. Finally, the Mence and Moore house contained two floors, with a floating staircase to the bedrooms on the second level. The upper floor was ornamented with greenheart, a hardwood from British Guiana.[19]

As noted in chapter 6, Anthony Lewis obtained a bachelor's degree in architecture from McGill University and a master's degree in city and regional planning from the Illinois Institute of Technology, where he studied with Ludwig Mies van der Rohe. After working in Port of Spain during World War II and several years developing a private practice in Barbados, he returned in 1948 to Trinidad, where he worked on a range of residential, commercial and public projects – including his highly acclaimed Church of the Assumption (1950) in Maraval, for which he employed Guyanese greenheart, white wooden louvres, local limestone and pink and yellow sandstone that reflected the colours of surrounding poui trees. Lewis's houses in the Port of Spain area during the 1950s often featured locally quarried stone, clean horizontal façades, multiple shed roofs at varying angles, abundant louvres, wide eaves and other techniques for maximizing shade and ventilation.[20]

Lewis was one of several local architects represented in a series of articles, titled "Trinidad's Fine Homes", contributed by feature writer Greig Allan to the *Trinidad Guardian* in 1960. Others included Colin Laird, Oswald Glean Chase, Edwin da Costa Jr, Anthony Selman and John Newel Lewis (who was then a partner at Mence and Moore). In this series, Allan advised on the value of working with an architect, advocated restrained and ornament-free modern design, summarized the design philosophies and methods of his interlocutors and described an example of each man's recent work (with accompanying photographs of exteriors and interiors). Among the general characteristics of the houses examined were careful attention to the unique qualities of building sites, use of local stones and woods, picture windows and sliding glass doors to facilitate external views, screen walls with geometric patterns, free-flowing interior spaces and indoor gardens. For example, Oswald Chase's house for the Nagib Elias family in St Clair was an expansive five-bedroom concrete structure with low-pitched roofs and wide eaves all around. Exterior and interior walls throughout were a few feet short of the roof, with intervening slatted glass panels to enhance light and ventilation. The roof over the large dining room at the centre of the house was raised even further with a wrought-iron grille, enabling a view of trees outside. Open areas above walls, along with ventilation concrete blocks and brickwork, facilitated both the flow of air and the integration of rooms. Bedrooms featured mahogany-framed sliding windows and louvres as well as plastic skylights. Flooring throughout the house consisted of polished concrete tiles.[21]

Chase worked on the Nagib Elias home around the same time that he built a house for himself in the Diego Martin Valley to the northwest of Port of

Spain. In May 1960 he was visited here by *Trinidad Guardian* writer Derek Walcott. Walcott described his arrival:

> The visitor, turning from Diego Martin road down Nagib Elias Drive, looks twice at what appears to be huge lily pads, drifting on to the bank of the nearby river, or stone kraals set in the middle of a new housing area.
>
> Below the five large pads are, on close inspection, circular concrete towers, whose walls are ventilated by upended cement blocks. Within each tower is a room of Mr. Oswald Chase's "psychological house".

From the roof, which resembled a clover leaf, the visitor and his host walked down an incline and entered the somewhat bewildering world of the latter's architectural vision. Walcott asked why the structure was called a psychological house. Chase (who had studied architecture in France, England, Germany and the United States) explained that the human body and its movements are not angular and added: "To me, whenever a man is creating space, he is re-creating womb space. The first experience a child has is in womb-space, and an architect re-creates that experience." Except for one door and window, the entire house was made of concrete, which Chase considered an affordable and easily worked material. The five circular rooms contained open blocks in the walls and around the high ceiling pads for the passage of air and light. There were curved ledges for utensils along the kitchen walls (Walcott avoided commenting on the standard box-shaped appliances) and a lower and deeper ledge in the living room with cushions for seating. Two bedrooms, a fifth room and a dinette space at the centre of the units completed the house. All the interiors were painted blue, which Chase said discouraged flies. In the backyard, by the river, was a curved three-level swimming pool. Chase ended the visit with his plans for the future: "The thing I'm interested in now is a village patterned on the design, a sort of community up in the Northern Range." Walcott promised to return to see this. Clearly, this was an encounter between a pair of artists with imaginations well matched to each other.[22]

Diamond Vale

While Oswald Chase chose the Diego Martin Valley for a unique architectural experiment, thousands of people had been settling here in more conventional homes since the end of World War II. To the west of Cocorite, the Diego Martin Main Road branched off from the Western Main Road and continued north for several miles through this beautiful terrain flanked by the steep hills of the Northern Range. Plantations and small villages developed here during the nineteenth century; by the mid-twentieth century, most agriculture involved smaller-scale cultivation of food crops. Trinidad's growing middle class was particularly attracted to the valley, given the severe shortage of suitable or affordable housing in Port of Spain and its immediate suburbs. During the final years of the war, developers were already building small housing projects in the valley, and new construction accelerated during the postwar era. By 1960 the *Trinidad Guardian* observed, "Diego Martin, the once plush valley of farmlands . . . is fast being converted into a throbbing, pulsing suburban area." Bulldozers were rapidly clearing land, and new housing estates, along with the businesses to serve them, were appearing across the district. This growth was facilitated by an expansion of car ownership. The drive from the valley to work in Port of Spain was relatively short, though by the early 1960s the increase in population and cars was straining the existing roads. In fact, cars were becoming an integral component of the lives of many suburban middle-class families and were cherished for recreational as well as economic purposes. In 1956 the Starlite Cinema, the first drive-in in the British Caribbean, opened at Four Roads, a busy intersection at the southern end of the valley. The Starlite's 100-by-43-foot screen, raised 17 feet above the ground, enabled whole families to be entertained together in the comfort of their own vehicles, and also served as a beacon of the future in this new suburb.[23]

By 1960 the Trinidad government included among its various housing schemes a major new middle-income development in the northern portion of the Diego Martin Valley. As preparations moved forward, Minister of Housing Gerard Montano attended a housing conference in Puerto Rico and was impressed with the town-planning expertise there. Around this same time, the government recruited A.C. Kayanan, the former head of Puerto Rico's planning board, to create plans for a community of approximately two thousand new homes on land that it had acquired, principally from cinema magnate Nur Mohammed Gokool, to the south and north of Diamond Road. A project on this scale, however, required a major investment of capital. Thus the government developed the concept of a partnership with a private firm that would provide not only planning and construction services but also construction financing and mortgage-lending. A further incentive for the firm (and for other companies with an interest in such projects in Trinidad) was legislation that offered a tax holiday. Negotiations for the Diego Martin scheme were successful, and on 5 April 1961, Premier Eric Williams officially opened the Diamond Road Housing Project, a collaboration between the Trinidad government and Homes International (Trinidad) Limited, a subsidiary of the Puerto Rico-based Homes International. A.C. Kayanan was the planning consultant for the project and prepared for the ministry of housing and local government a booklet with extensive analysis and plans for the new community. At the sod-turning ceremony, Williams described the project as the government's greatest triumph in housing to date, while Montano, in a lengthy speech on the details of the project as well as other government housing accomplishments, said, "The ultra-modern development will embrace the concepts of integrated community organization."[24]

Homes International's Diamond Road booklet included maps of the topography, land use and condition of buildings in the Diego Martin Valley overall and at the Diamond Road site. While the accompanying text described the Diamond Road area as including only a few scattered houses, this was belied by the land-use map and the reality on the ground. More than five hundred people were served notice by the government to vacate the area by the beginning of May or see their houses demolished. In addition, their agricultural plots would be destroyed – though these were not shown on the land-use map, they are clearly visible in an aerial photograph also included in the booklet. In a visit to the offices of the *Trinidad Guardian*, representatives of the area's residents indicated that they had not yet received the resettlement accommodation promised by the government and added that they needed land for farming, since this was the only type of work they had ever done. Nonetheless, the farming families were forced out and work continued on the housing project.[25]

Homes International and the Ministry of Housing employed an "organic planning" methodology for the Diamond Road area in which "cells" functioned within a larger "organic structure". Each cell was a "Neighbourhood Unit" that included a primary school as its nucleus, housing and access to recreational, institutional and commercial facilities. The Diamond Road project encompassed parts of three neighbourhood units which, along with adjacent spaces and other units, were intended to comprise a "community", with its own larger institutional centre, in the northern part of the valley. (In addition to the Diamond Road project, three thousand other new homes and accompanying facilities were envisioned for the valley.) Each neighbourhood unit was conceptualized as including a thousand to twelve hundred families on 180 to 200 acres of land, which would enable every child to walk no more than half a mile to a primary school. A new secondary-school building already existed on Diamond Road, a complex of community facilities was constructed across from it and commercial clusters were planned for either end of the road, though only the east one was actually built. Each neighbourhood unit also contained a playground (adjacent to its primary school) and additional "playlots" for preschool children.[26]

The street layout of the development contrasted with that of most districts in Port of Spain. In the words of the planning booklet: "The Plan avoids the strictly gridiron road pattern and the monotony of repeated rectangular blocks which usually tend to bury the family's identity in the impersonality of the resulting urban sprawl. The Plan indicates a circulation pattern consisting of continuous roads which collect traffic from local access roads in the form of loops and culs-de-sac." In addition to its aesthetic qualities, this street plan contributed to the quiet and safety of the neighbourhoods. Streets were given a total reservation of 40 feet (with a 20-foot carriageway) and were separated from sidewalks by green strips to route underground utilities and protect pedestrians from vehicular splashes. Meanwhile, Diamond Road was converted into a wider dual-carriageway boulevard at its central stretch to highlight the secondary school and community buildings there. Flowering perennials were planned for its centre strip.[27]

The Diamond Road project included two basic kinds of one-storey houses, designed by Homes International architect Lionel Fernandez (see figure 28). Type A (by far the more numerous) was sited on a 4,000-square-foot lot (45 feet wide by 90 feet deep), while Type B provided 5,000 square feet. The floor plan for the 836-square-foot rectangular Type A house included a projecting living/dining room and a small front gallery (porch), with a kitchen, three bedrooms, and a bathroom to the rear. Many buyers also chose the optional carport, which was often positioned along the opposite side of the house from the living/dining room. Exterior walls, floors and low-pitched roofs were built with reinforced concrete, windows featured aluminium louvres, interior walls were constructed with concrete or clay blocks and floors were tiled. Both single-pitched and double-pitched roofs were used. In one version of the design, an overhanging shed roof stretched from a wall extending from the edge of the living/dining room across free-standing walls at the porch and carport. Though the elevations were austere, the planning booklet promised "variations in façade, fenestration and colour to assure the entire development its freedom from monotony". In addition, identical houses were not positioned next to each other, and variations in setbacks enhanced ventilation, views and privacy. Houses were surrounded by small lawns to which occupants added a variety of shrubs and trees. Early drawings and photographs of the project show no property perimeter walls, though a Bestcrete concrete blocks advertisement from August 1962 advised: "See the Beautiful Bestcrete Fences Around the Homes." In any case, many residents did eventually build walls (often with railings), which made the development look somewhat less like an American suburb and a little more like a Port of Spain neighbourhood.[28]

In January 1962 Homes International began running Diamond Road "Grand Opening" advertisements with two model homes ready for inspection, though most of the development remained under construction. On 19 January an ad appeared in the *Nation* (the PNM newspaper) which proclaimed: "See and Buy the House of Your Dreams at Diamond Road!" in "the Air Conditioned Diego Martin Valley". The primary image in the ad is a photograph of the head and shoulders of a jacketed young man superimposed on a photograph of Marine Square (recently renamed Independence Square). The man is contemplatively looking upward, in the direction of a drawing of a Diamond Road house placed higher on the page. A couple and small child appear in the house's gallery and carport. The ad's copy advises "a better home built with reinforced concrete and steel can and ought to be yours" and also highlights the reinforced concrete roof, which is "Stronger, Modern, Efficient, Cooler, Dryer, Number One Public Enemy of Bats, Rats, Termites, etc.". Along with noting that the house's high structural quality will minimize maintenance costs, the ad mentions its various rooms, including "a modern fitted kitchen, planned as a functional work centre, and a porch that can be conveniently combined with the lawn for healthy outdoor living". Finally, the ad summarizes house-purchasing costs (the land would remain the property of the Trinidad government) and says the project is sponsored through the government's Five-Year Development Programme. An advertisement appearing in the *Nation* a few weeks later again invited prospective buyers to the project site, so that they could see "the house with all of the comforts of tomorrow . . . today!"[29]

As construction continued during 1962, the Diamond Road Housing Project was renamed Diamond Vale, thus replacing the reference to a rural road with a more pleasant-sounding allusion to life in a settled valley. An advertisement published in the *Trinidad Guardian* on 18 July includes photographs of a man mowing a lawn, a car in front of a carport, happy children and adults in the front yard and a mother and daughter in a kitchen, while an ad appearing on 12 August features a photograph of a spacious street, children playing in a park, a couple with a stroller, and several houses (with no perimeter walls). With the development partially populated, Homes International could now run a new series of advertisements with photographs of residents with their houses and testimonials attributed to them. Mr and Mrs John Joseph of 15 Sapphire Crescent said:

> What we like about Diamond Vale is our strong and beautiful home with its modern design set in a well laid out valley surrounded by the green mountains which give an air of beauty and tranquillity – Our home is a complete home with its tiled floors, built in cupboards and proper water system, as well as its compactness. The rooms are cool, comfortable and so well placed. We think it is the best home value in Trinidad today.

In a similar vein, Mr and Mrs Vivian Rivero of 29 Sapphire Drive related:

> What we like about Diamond Vale is the planning that has gone into it . . . the wide pavements and roads, the under-ground drainage. We like living in this park-like setting with the breeze that keeps our home cool day and night. The house itself is a pleasure to own, the tiled floors make it so easy to clean and there's so much

cupboard space. Being termite proof, we don't expect any maintenance costs for many years to come.³⁰

Such advertisements, appearing during the weeks leading up to Trinidad's independence, both validated the success of a major government project and affirmed the technologies and aesthetics of contemporary housing.

Homes International planned to build 581 houses as the first phase of the Diamond Vale project; some of these were still under construction at the end of 1963. By May 1962, however, the company had signed an agreement with the Trinidad government for a second phase that would include over nine hundred more houses. This second phase proceeded, but a third phase planned for an area to the west of the Diego Martin Main Road was not implemented. Instead, this site was developed as an industrial park, an adjustment to the original plan, which located light industry beyond the eastern end of Diamond Road. Meanwhile, the government was also at work on planning a four-lane highway that would extend from Diamond Boulevard (Road) all the way to the Western Main Road, near the entrance to the valley. The highway would generally follow the course of the Diego Martin River, which was being straightened and widened to facilitate flood control – a serious problem owing to the extensive building on formerly open and agricultural lands. The construction of this highway, along with the conversion of the Western Main Road through Cocorite into a dual-carriage highway, was crucial to providing convenient access from Diamond Vale to Port of Spain and to meeting the general needs of the rapidly growing population in the Diego Martin Valley.³¹

Diamond Vale was certainly a popular residential area for Trinidad's expanding middle class at the time of independence. As a planned community with integrated houses, schools, parks and other facilities, it contrasted with the frenzied, multifaceted growth of Port of Spain, which some observers warned had the potential to become a "nightmare city". At Diamond Vale, young families of the new nation could invest in their future through home ownership and healthy living. Here they were promised a relaxed family-oriented lifestyle, with houses requiring little maintenance, efficient kitchens and a quiet landscape of lawns, curving jewel-named streets and nearby schools and parks. When they needed to travel to Port of Spain or elsewhere, they could set out from their carports in their snazzy new vehicles along the attractive streets of the neighbourhood onto the wide and smooth Diego Martin Highway. Such was modern life and its material environment – streamlined, logical, practical, progressive. Indeed, Diamond Vale was a model community for an independent and forward-looking Trinidad, a landscape that showcased the organization and aspirations of the new nation. Too bad it was situated near the end of the Diego Martin Valley, visible only to its occupants, visitors and the nearby residents of the old agricultural villages who looked on in consternation. So, given the geographic realities of northwestern Trinidad, civic leaders and planners had to contend with Shanty Town at the entrance to Port of Spain and, within the city limits, pursue more focused building projects that could display the progress of the nation.

PUBLIC AND COMMERCIAL BUILDINGS

The expanding economy of the postwar era that generated the construction of many additional homes throughout Port of Spain and its suburbs also supported new office buildings, stores, factories, schools, health facilities, religious centres and other structures around the city, including a town hall, concert hall and major hotel. As was the case with much of the era's elite housing, the design of most of these new buildings was carried out by local architectural firms that adapted the principles of international modernism to the particular climatic conditions and aesthetic preferences of Trinidad. With extensive use of concrete and glass, architects created sleek, unadorned structures that efficiently served their intended functions and suggested the systematic planning of a coherent city of the future. While the landscape still included large public buildings in European historical-revival styles and many two- and three-storey commercial buildings in the Trinidadian-creole tradition, it increasingly featured rectangular surfaces and flat roofs that brought a simplified geometry to its overall composition. Though the new architects created austere buildings, they also aimed for integration with the environment. There was comprehension of the architectural legacy and social patterns of the city, as well as concern with the visibility of the island's botanic wealth and its incorporation into design plans. Some buildings also included the works of local sculptors and painters and thus highlighted the era's broader realm of artistic creativity. This conceptual orientation and its practical application with respect to local realities were central to the evolving creole modernism of public and commercial buildings, as well as housing, during the independence years.

In 1960 the views of several of Trinidad's architects were featured in a special architectural issue of the short-lived literary journal *Opus*. Two of the articles were of a general character: Oswald Glean Chase's dense analysis and evaluation of modernism from Walter Gropius to Alvar Aalto, and Anthony Selman's technical discussion of recent advances in lightweight roof structures based on "strength through form". The other articles addressed architectural practice in the Caribbean. Colin Laird articulated basic concepts of modernism and, while acknowledging the appeal of Trinidad's turn-of-the-century ornamented houses, affirmed the functional simplicity of historic military buildings in islands like Antigua and St Kitts. He argued, "whether it is a building, a group of buildings or a district, the principle cannot be stressed too much – unity, clarity and true expression of purpose, economy of means, simplicity and honesty". Meanwhile, John Newel Lewis said that in Trinidad, population growth, social change, flows of money and new industries were upsetting the traditional way of life. The role of the architect, he suggested, was to try to understand changing needs and to give clients something new – something that would pull them into the future. Finally, Anthony Lewis outlined the relationship between architects and clients and concluded that "the West Indies is now a new nation and in the rapid development of its cities the public must be intimately concerned". Local architecture would either be "the expression of an incoherent, confused people" or would "tell the story of an inspired and aroused people stimulated by the desire to build the best houses, the finest hospitals, the most efficient schools".[32]

Marine Square/Independence Square

Since the nineteenth century, Port of Spain's Marine Square had functioned as both a centre of the city's commerce and a refreshing park with grass plots, walkways and shade trees. In the postwar era, this public gathering-space was substantially transformed by the construction of numerous new commercial buildings in the surrounding area and by the city's changing transport patterns. The growth of downtown and of car ownership resulted in an ever-increasing number of vehicles on the streets, along with greater competition for limited street parking. During the early 1950s, the city council addressed these developments by permitting the conversion of much of Marine Square into parking lots, thus giving car owners priority over pedestrians and city dwellers who enjoyed lingering in this central locale. While some trees were preserved, many of the lawns and walkways were replaced by multiple series of angular parking spaces. Photographs from the 1950s and 1960s show the square filled with cars both in these central lots and along the streets. Even with this additional parking, the local newspapers continued to complain about traffic congestion in the city and a shortage of parking. In 1958, for example, the *Trinidad Chronicle* said the parking lots in Marine Square and downtown streets had "reached saturation point" and asserted that "remedial steps must be taken now to save the shopping centre of the Temporary Federal Capital from becoming one huge mumbo jumbo". When the city council decided in 1960 to protect a couple of remaining open spaces in Marine Square and Tamarind Square to the east, the *Trinidad Guardian* editorialized: "A city which refuses to make the best possible provision for motor traffic but keeps its eyes fixed exclusively on trees, is less than progressive." Meanwhile, traffic continued to increase, with the new Beetham Highway feeding in to the lower city from the east and the addition of various new buildings along Wrightson Road (in the former Docksite area) to the west. By the early 1960s, the central government was investigating multistorey parking garages and was also building a large new bus terminal on lower St Vincent Street (below Marine Square) to encourage an alternative mode of transport.[33]

While Marine Square lost much of its green space during the 1950s, it was enthusiastically selected as the site for a new statue in memory of A.A. Cipriani, popular captain in the British West Indies Regiment during World War I, leader of the TWA and TLP, member of the legislative council, and mayor of Port of Spain eight times. The monument project was organized by the Captain Cipriani Memorial Committee, apparently with the involvement of both the central and municipal governments, and English sculptor James Woolford was commissioned to create a life-size bronze statue based on photographs. When completed in 1959, the statue was placed on a stone pedestal and four-step platform in the centre of Marine Square, surrounded by a small circular traffic island with perimeter and radial pavements and sectors of grass. Facing north towards Frederick Street and the bulk of the city, Cipriani appeared in an oratorical pose, with his right hand raised at his chest and index finger extended and his left arm elevated to waist level. In addition to creating a new aesthetic focal point for Marine Square, the monument was a pivotal moment in public statuary in Port of Spain, since it was the first outdoor representation of a historical figure from Trinidad, differing both from the generic statues of soldiers in the War Memorial at Memorial Park and from a bust of Cipriani in the legislative council chamber at the Red House. The *Trinidad Chronicle* observed that "for a veteran politician like the Captain, it was agreed that his statue should be placed in 'the market places, the squares and all those places where the un-washed people would see it'"; while the *Trinidad Guardian* said, "it has been placed in a conspicuous spot in the city he served with selfless dedication in the municipal and legislative sphere, helping preeminently to awaken public and official thought to the needs of the common man and his right to fuller opportunity".[34]

The unveiling ceremony for the monument took place on 18 April, fourteen years after the day of Cipriani's death in 1945. Mayor Dennis Mahabir presided and among the other speakers were Chief Minister Eric Williams, Dr C. La Corbiniere (federal deputy prime minister) and Iris King (mayor of Kingston, Jamaica). Thousands of spectators crowded the square for the occasion. In a speech titled "Cipriani's Place in West Indian History", Williams described the hero as "the pioneer of the nationalist movement in Trinidad and Tobago" and said that, with the statue's unveiling, "we commemorate our own historical development, our own positive action, our own native history made by native hands recording the lives, achievements and aspirations of our native people". Similar views were expressed by La Corbiniere:

> All over the West Indies there are to be found relics of our political past in the form of statues of former Governors, many of whom in all charity, and in all desire to let bygones be bygones, ought to be forgotten rather than be perpetuated on us. . . .
>
> [I]f we are to erect monuments, let us erect them from now onwards to our sons and daughters who have served nobly and selflessly, and who have inspired and inspirited us by their sterling example.

At the conclusion of the ceremony, representatives of the participating governments and of various organizations laid wreaths at the foot of the statue.[35]

The Cipriani monument was innovative in its affirmation in a central public space of a local man, along with the broader social principles and nationalist goals that he represented. However, the statue was not without controversy. One problem was that many people felt it did not resemble its subject. For example, Alfred Mendes, writer and past general manager of port services, said that Cipriani usually had his arms down and that the sculptor's depiction of his face was disappointing; Albert Gomes, who became a political rival of Cipriani, agreed that the face was inaccurate. Others asked why a local sculptor had not been commissioned for the project. In an opinion piece titled "Art, Beauty Should Unite in Public Places", *Trinidad Guardian* reporter Lloyd Cartar addressed this concern and called for the formation of an advisory body that would supervise artworks in squares and parks.[36]

On 22 April 1960, Cipriani's statue served as the endpoint for the PNM's massive march for Chaguaramas, where Eric Williams called for the renaming of Marine Square as "Independence Square". On 19 April 1961, the Port of Spain City Council voted fourteen to one in favour of the name change in order to commemorate the independence march itself. The contesting vote came from Democratic Labour Party member Louis Rostant, who condemned the concept of naming a square after an event of this sort. In addition, the *Trinidad Guardian* strongly opposed the renaming, as it had the previous year. Essentially, the *Guardian* argued that the public had not been consulted and that the change would eradicate historical reference to Spanish and British development of the square at the water's edge. The newspaper also claimed that many people objected to the name because independence had not yet occurred and that business owners on the square were concerned about the inconvenience and expense of new stationery.[37] Nonetheless, the name change was implemented and the old commercial centre of the city now referenced an expected future of political and economic autonomy, with Cipriani's statue further symbolizing this trajectory.

This redefinition of Marine Square coincided with the erection here of various new streamlined office buildings that contrasted with the remaining old commercial buildings with their stone and brick façades, overhanging balconies and dormer windows. While Herbert Brinsley's Alston Building and Treasury Building had introduced modernist design concepts to Marine Square during the 1930s, the construction boom of the late 1950s and early 1960s brought a more extensive change to the appearance of this urban centre. In 1959, for example, Gordon Grant and Company installed its banking, transportation, insurance and other departments in a new head office building on Marine Square South at the corner of St Vincent Street. Designed by Mence and Moore and built by Arthur Bros and Company, this four-storey, air-conditioned box featured a smooth stone exterior. Tall windows on the middle floors of the north elevation alternated with plain pilasters, while those on the west were inset and protected by vertical metal sun-breakers. An advertisement at the time of the opening proclaimed the structure "A Landmark in the Economic growth of the Federated West Indies, a lasting monument to local Enterprise and Industry".[38]

The most radical addition to Marine Square, however, was the new Salvatori Building, which was designed by Watkins and Partners and erected by the Miami-based McDonough Construction Company during 1959–1960. While the Salvatoris' store, destroyed by fire in 1958, had occupied the prominent northeast corner of Frederick Street and Marine Square North, their new air-conditioned building spanned the entire block between Frederick and Henry Streets and included seven floors, towering 115 feet above the square. Levels one to six were rented out as office space, while the top floor contained two rows of penthouse apartments along the south and north sides of the building. With the exception of two vertical white marble bands, the entire front façade between the ground level and the penthouses consisted of vertical blue aluminium sun-breakers over windows. In response to some comments that the building was "unimaginative and box-like", the Salvatoris said "the box-shape offers functional unity, and that the design is well-up with avant-garde architectural ideas on simplicity, combined with function". Meanwhile, the penthouse apartments were elegantly designed and furnished; those on the Marine Square side of the building each had a 400-square-foot terrazzo patio, separated by ventilation-block screen walls.[39]

By the latter part of 1960, a soundproofed nightclub, simply named the Penthouse, had opened at the Marine Square/Henry Street corner of the Salvatori Building's rooftop. In 1961 Brunell Jones, entertainment reporter for the *Evening News*, observed: "A significant chapter will be written into the pages of post-war show-business tonight: the Penthouse, snazzy pleasure-spot, marks its first anniversary. And the roof-top venue will celebrate in style." Indeed, the resident Choy Aming band was there for the occasion, as were calypsonians Sparrow, Cristo and Zebra. In his breezy reporting on Port of Spain's vibrant nightlife during the early 1960s, Jones regularly chronicled happenings at the Penthouse, along with other clubs through which the city's late-night sophisticates circulated, such as the uptown Tavern-on-the-Green, the GiGi Lounge on Park Street and the downtown Lotus.[40]

The opening of the new Salvatori Building was followed by two other high-rise construction projects on Independence Square: the local architectural firm of Prior, Lourenco and Nothnagel added two floors and a penthouse to its original three-floor design for the Standard Life Building at Independence Square North and Edward Street, while Mence and Moore designed a five-floor building for Furness Withy and Company at Independence Square North and Wrightson Road. Contrasting with these projects was the new Chase Manhattan Bank (1963), designed by Anthony Lewis, at the southeast corner of Independence Square South and Broadway, across the square from the Salvatori Building. Lewis's subdued two-storey structure complemented the old commercial buildings to its immediate east and south. Along with a front façade consisting entirely of plate glass, the bank featured a west elevation of concrete block (California split block) and glass, a flat canopy projecting above the ground floor and a shallow-curved concrete roof. According to architects/architectural historians Geoffrey MacLean and Brian Lewis, Anthony Lewis wanted to create a sense of transparency for this new bank in Trinidad and thus enabled the public to view all operations inside, even the prominently displayed vault. In an additional gesture of respect for the bank's surrounding environment, Lewis included on the interior walls large photomurals of a latter nineteenth-century etching of Broadway and an 1830s lithograph by Richard Bridgens of Port of Spain as seen from the sea.[41]

Town Hall

In Woodford Square, a few blocks north of Marine/Independence Square, the major building project of the independence era was a new town hall, erected on the Knox Street site of the town hall that had burned down in 1948. After the fire, the municipal government was without a permanent home for thirteen years and depended on office space primarily in the Prince's Building at the Queen's Park Savannah. Delays in rebuilding were due both to debates over a site for the new hall and to a shortage of funds. In the end, the city council decided to return to its historic location at Woodford Square, while the PNM government financed the construction as part of its Five-Year Development Programme, again demonstrating its principle of collaboration between central and municipal administrations. On 24 April 1958, a cornerstone ceremony was held, featuring Princess Margaret, who was in town for the opening of the parliament of the new West Indies Federation. After a speech by Mayor Dennis Mahabir (with references to the old Spanish cabildo and subsequent town government) and the lowering of the cornerstone into place by the city engineer, C.R. Farrell, the white-gloved young princess daintily tapped its four corners with a mallet and declared it "well and truly laid".[42]

The new town hall was designed by Prior, Lourenco and Nothnagel, with English-born Alfred Prior and Trinidadian Ferdinand Lourenco as the lead architects and Arthur Brothers and Company serving as the construction contractor (see figure 29). The design included a basic structure of reinforced concrete along with a variety of products from local firms, such as Bestcrete Limited, Trinidad Clay Products, Trinidad Mastic Asphalt, Aluminum Industries Limited and the Modern Terrazzo and Floor Tile Company. Intended to serve the range of functions of a large municipal bureaucracy, the hall was a sprawling one-acre complex comprising several components of various shapes and textures within an overarching orthogonal order. Viewed from Knox Street, its south block consisted of a "ceremonial entrance" into a courtyard flanked by two wings that extended northward. At the front of the courtyard were pillars supporting a covered first-floor walkway that linked the wings; cantilevered stairs led to the walkway, which continued to a structure behind the courtyard that housed the first-floor city council chamber. The block's west wing, with a front façade of reddish blocks and white vertical bands, contained an assembly hall with seating for over six hundred on its ground floor and first-floor balcony (accessed from the upper walkway). The east wing featured a front façade of vertically laid rectangular ventilation blocks and an east elevation (along Frederick Street) consisting of a variety of materials, including square-patterned concrete ventilation blocks, columns faced with small black tiles, and a projecting first floor of windows with vertical sun-breakers. This wing contained the city police station, the mayor's parlour and other offices.

Behind the complex's multifaceted south block was a contrasting central block with a more homogenous appearance: a long, narrow four-storey structure, lined with windows and sun-breakers and extending all the way from Frederick Street west to Pembroke Street. At the two ends of the block were the complex's main public entrances, which led to staircases and elevators providing access to the departments of the town clerk, treasurer, assessor and engineer. Beyond the central block was a three-storey north block that continued along Frederick Street. Like the south block, this structure featured an eclectic mix of materials on its east elevation. Its upper two floors housed the Department of the Medical Officer of Health (with its own entrance for public medical services) and the ground floor contained a public parking garage, much to the excitement of the city's residents. While the mayor's office and the council chamber were air-conditioned, the rest of the complex depended on natural ventilation and sun screening.[43]

A focal point of the new town hall was a mural titled *Conquerabia*, designed by Carlisle Chang (1921–2001) on the back wall of the courtyard at the ceremonial entrance to the complex. Chang was one of Trinidad's most prominent artists at the time. Born in San Juan, a town to the east of Port of Spain, he studied as a youth with Amy Leong Pang, a painter who was a member of the bohemian Society of Trinidad Independents during the 1930s. In 1945 he attended the New York Institute of Photography and, after returning to Trinidad, practised photography for several years, continued to paint and worked in theatre design. During the early 1950s, scholarships from the British Council and the Italian government enabled him to further his education at the Central School of Arts and Crafts in London and the Istituto Statale d'Arte per la Ceramica in Faenza. By 1954 he was back in Trinidad, where he opened a gallery and developed a successful career in a variety of media, including several mural commissions during the early 1960s.[44]

Chang's *Conquerabia* comprised disparate materials, textures and shapes in a manner that complemented the heterogeneous design of the town hall complex itself. Set below a series of windows that lined the first-floor council chamber, the 41-by-7-foot mural spanned almost the entire courtyard and served as a welcoming image for visitors. In explaining the production of the piece, Chang said:

> It was executed in the sand-cast method whereby concrete is poured on to a bed of wet sand which has been moulded in reverse. The surface is thus enriched by a thin patina of sand, and in this work, further embellished with stone gathered from various parts of the territory. Among the most interesting of these are the grey and white stones of Sans Souci [northeast coast], multi-coloured porcelainite from Erin [southwest coast] and a green stone from Tobago.

Bestcrete Limited did the concrete casting, while two collaborators assisted with the stone mosaics.[45]

Chang named his mural after the pre-Columbian battle site that later developed into Port of Spain. His theme was "praise of the City", which he pursued by juxtaposing, on different scales, a variety of schematic images related to local geography and history. At the left and right ends of the composition are large, outward-facing heads that represent the Dragon's Mouth and Serpent's Mouth – names for the narrow north and south passages into the Gulf of Paria. These figures "guard" the city and frame the central sections of the mural. On the serpent's head are images of a Spanish ship and three hills (which were believed to have inspired Columbus to name the island "Trinidad"). To the right of the dragon's head are sketches of several buildings in architectural styles characteristic of Port Spain; below these are two indigenous clubs referencing the battle at Conquerabia. Flanking the architectural sketches are additional symbols related to the city: "the open door of hospitality", "the sun of energy or vitality" (amplified by a multicoloured stone mosaic), a hummingbird and an indigenous-style sculpture of a head. To the right of this grouping is a crown in tribute to British governor Ralph Woodford and a "plan of the Civic Centre" – Woodford Square appears as "the wheel of Life, surrounded by architectural landmarks in topographical order representing in their orderliness the balanced attributes of a progressive community". These images, at the perimeter of Woodford Square's radial paths, include Holy Trinity Cathedral, the Red House, the Hall of Justice, the public library and the old town hall. To the right of this civic centre is a "Tree of Freedom" with symbols of Trinidad's assorted religions, followed by the Serpent's Mouth at the mural's right end.[46]

Through this array of imagery and his use of local construction materials, Chang placed the new town hall project in the context of a landscape with pre-colonial, Spanish and British layers, while also highlighting such civic values as order, tolerance and vitality. As visitors entered the courtyard of the modern town hall, they were inspired to contemplate the generations of human creativity that shaped the place in which they now lived and to conceptualize the city's future in relation to this legacy.

The official opening of the new town hall took place on 27 October 1961. In preparation for the occasion, the building was decorated with flags and bunting and floodlit the night before. The ceremony began with a city police guard of honour and music from the Trinidad Police Band, before some six hundred specially invited guests, along with a cheering crowd across the street in Woodford Square. Mayor Edward Taylor spoke of the site-selection controversy that preceded the city council's decision to return to the location of the old town hall – "forum of many debates in the years gone by" where "the true representatives of the people" maintained a critical stance towards the unrepresentative colonial government. The ever-resourceful Eric Williams then struggled with the ribbon-cutting: "After much difficulty with the pair of scissors provided by the Port-of-Spain City Council," the premier said, "I have to report I am now in a position to declare officially open this imposing monument to the harmonious co-operation between the Central Government and the Port-of-Spain City Council and to dedicate this building to the service of the burgesses of Port-of-Spain." The ceremony concluded with a blessing by an Anglican archdeacon and was followed by building tours and cocktails in the parking garage. That evening a pageant on town history, also titled *Conquerabia*, was scheduled to be performed in Woodford Square so that the general citizenry could participate in the celebrations. However, when a large crowd in the square stampeded the stage and refused to make room for VIPs in a reserved seating area, the event was called off and rescheduled for two nights later.[47]

Mayor Edwards referred to the new town hall as "a monument to civic consciousness", and indeed the building did generate substantial commentary in the press as well as interest on the street. The *Evening News* remarked that the operation of the municipal government at the Prince's Building had been undesirable: "A Town Hall should always be an impressive building situated near the hub of business activity, so that citizens can have an awareness of the business going on and be imbued with a sense of its importance and urgency." On the day after the opening ceremony, the *Trinidad Guardian* said: "The handsome steel and concrete structure will not only be a proud showpiece in the bustling architecture-conscious city, but a lasting monument to the Territory's political coming-of-age. The Territory's revolutionary drama, from colonial status to full internal self-government, has been enacted alongside the 13-year struggle to rebuild the Town Hall destroyed by fire in 1948." The following day, the *Guardian* ran an editorial, titled "Worthy New Civic Centre", in which it said the building "will be ready to play its role as a reception centre for distinguished visitors and to reflect the progressive ambitions of the whole country".[48] For Port of Spain's civic leaders, the new town hall represented a space of self-determination at the political centre of the city and territory. At this spot with a pre-colonial past, as displayed in Carlisle Chang's mural, the nation's populace could imagine a postcolonial future and carry out the capital's business within the various departments of a modern office complex. Here was a building whose elegant design, expansiveness and multifunctional capacity both reinvigorated Woodford Square and symbolized the emergence of Trinidad and Tobago as a self-governing state.

Queen's Hall

In addition to having no town hall during the 1950s, Port of Spain lacked an auditorium dedicated to the performing arts. Thus organizations that produced classical-music concerts, plays and similar programmes were forced to make use of cinemas and other venues. The limitations of such buildings were of particular concern to the Trinidad Music Association, which began organizing the Trinidad Music Festival in 1948. By 1950 association president May Johnstone was advocating the construction of a proper concert hall and gained strong support from Dr Sidney Northcote, a British musician who adjudicated the festival that year and suggested the idea of obtaining an unused aeroplane hangar from Piarco and remodelling it as a performance venue in Port of

Spain. By 1952 the Trinidad government had agreed to donate a hangar, the city council had said it would lease land for the centre in King George V Park (the site of the US Army St Clair Cantonment during the war) and Watkins and Partners had developed design plans. Meanwhile, Johnstone was chairing a theatre concert hall steering committee to raise money for the project, with appeals to a cross-section of Trinidad's population. In order to increase public support, the committee eventually decided to expand the centre's purpose from strictly performing arts to a variety of activities, including exhibitions, conferences, bazaars and indoor athletics. By 1955 the committee had abandoned the idea of remodelling a hangar and decided to hold a design competition for a new hall, with submissions to be evaluated by J.R. Firth, chief architect in the Trinidad Works and Hydraulics Department. In early 1956 Colin Laird was announced as the winner of the competition.[49]

Laird was born in England in 1924 and was initially exposed to architecture and construction through his father, an engineer. He attended the Regent Street Polytechnic School of Architecture in London before volunteering with the Royal Navy Fleet Air Arm during World War II. His aviation training took him to the Piarco airfield in Trinidad, where he married a local woman the day before departing to participate in the Allied invasion of Normandy. After the war, he completed his architectural studies, worked with Thomas Bennett, won the prestigious Soane Medallion of the Royal Institute of British Architects and subsequently assisted Brian O'Rourke with the country pavilion for the 1951 Festival of Britain. In 1952, Laird and his wife returned to Trinidad, where he established a practice that included residential, commercial and public projects. He also developed close relationships with Beryl McBurnie, Carlisle Chang and other figures of Trinidad's postwar nationalist arts movement.[50]

Though Laird prepared design plans for a community/concert hall to be sited in King George V Park, public controversy developed concerning the suitability of this location. Newspaper articles from the period suggest that some residents of nearby St Clair were concerned that the hall would generate too much noise and disruption in their neighbourhood. With this challenge unresolved, the Trinidad government agreed in 1958 to provide land for the hall off the St Ann's Road, near the Queen's Park Savannah. Situated to the east of Government House, this new site had formerly been part of the Botanic Gardens and was being used as an athletic field. At this point, the government also said it would provide $370,000 for the construction of the hall, with an understanding that its citizens' committee would raise additional money for interior furnishings and equipment. On 26 March 1958, a ground-breaking ceremony was held with May Johnstone, and construction began. Furness Withy and Company served as the principal contractor, while the structural engineer was David Kay, a friend of Laird's from the Fleet Air Arm. By April 1959 the building was nearing completion and had been given the name Queen's Hall.[51]

Laird's design for Queen's Hall was radically different from any other structure in Port of Spain (see figure 30). Its defining characteristic was a thin concrete roof that spanned the 80-foot width of the building in the shape of an inverted catenary[52] when viewed from the south or north. The roof contained a fabric of steel to accommodate expansion and contraction, while its distinctive curve continued in the series of concrete supports that lined the east and west sides of the building. Emerging from the roof, towards the back of the hall, was a rectangular fly tower that housed stage equipment. The building's south façade consisted primarily of glass, with stone at the lower left and right sides, a central clay panel that screened a small office for the hall manager on an upper floor and a canopy projecting over the front doors. Substantial portions of the east and west sides of the building were open to the outdoors, with the roof and wide gutters shielding it from sunlight and rain. Surrounding the hall were beautiful grounds, filled with a variety of trees and shrubs. To the south were a parking lot and a circular drive, with a broad expanse of stairs leading up from the drive to the hall's entrance.

Inside the hall was a relatively small lobby with stairs at either side that led to upper promenades. These walkways lined the two sides of the building, providing both access to the central seating area and spaces for patrons of nighttime shows to enjoy the cooler air and sounds of the outdoors. The seating consisted of stackable tubular steel-and-canvas chairs. While there were a few rows of tiered seating, the central area was flat, since the hall was intended to serve multiple purposes, including exhibitions, balls and sports (such as table tennis and boxing). The directors of the hall, however, promised to provide movable sloped platforms for seating when additional funds were raised. Meanwhile, a partition in this area could be moved to accommodate audiences of various sizes, up to approximately one thousand. The components of the stage (including a safety curtain designed by Carlisle Chang) could also be adjusted for different kinds of plays or other performances. At the back of the hall was a standard complement of dressing rooms, workshops and related theatrical support areas.[53]

Though there was widespread public support for the new concert/community centre, there were also concerns that it should serve the territory's population as a whole and not be under the control of the PNM government. Such considerations were voiced on 1 May 1959, when the legislative council voted unanimously to establish a Queen's Hall board to administer the centre. During the discussion preceding the vote, Mitra Sinanan (a member of the opposition Democratic Labour Party from central Trinidad) called on Dr Patrick Solomon (minister of education and culture) and the government "to prove that the cultural development of the territory was not necessarily identifiable with any political movement". Solomon asserted that there would be no discrimination in the use of the hall and assured the legislators that individuals would be appointed to the board on the basis of their interests in the arts or their business acumen, not their political, ethnic or religious backgrounds.[54]

Finally, after a decade of advocacy, planning and fundraising, Queen's Hall opened on 4 June for the first of ten nights of special programming. David Renwick described the scene for the *Trinidad Chronicle*:

> It was a night of glamour, as Queen's Hall, biggest event in local show business history, flung open its glass doors last night. . . .
>
> Big, grumbling American cars wheeled up to the front steps and deposited their well-dressed load.
>
> Policemen swarmed the grounds, peering for gate-crashers. . . .
>
> Crowds perched on the rail opposite the gates and gawked at the glittering first-night audience.
>
> Bathed in amber, from a battery of lights lodged in the ground, Queen's Hall filled up, the tense expectant playgoers claiming their metal seats.

After the crowd settled in, May Johnstone, chairman of the Queen's Hall board, recounted the years of effort required to build the hall and appealed to those present to make it "part of their lives and aspirations". Minister Patrick Solomon and Governor Edward Beetham then delivered formal addresses. Solomon noted that the hall had been called "a triumph of community effort and a symbol of collaboration between Government and the people" and added: "A concert hall of this type – beautiful, modern, technically excellent – is a symbol of all the creative talents of the several peoples now gathered together to form our new nation and it is right that this symbol should be erected in the capital island of the Federation." Finally, Beetham proclaimed that the opening of the hall was "a moment of inspiration when we catch a glimpse into the future and see something of the cultural destiny of our country; a moment of dedication to the task that lies ahead – the task of welding the several racial and cultural groups of our islands into one solid entity".[55]

The initial ten nights were designed to showcase a range of the performing arts in Trinidad, though most of the groups selected were from the elite sector of the society. The opening and closing nights featured a variety show, *The Happy Wanderer*, produced by impresario Pat Castagne. In an effort to provide an overview of the local landscape and its characteristic art forms, the show followed a taxi driver and a British tourist around Port of Spain. The duo started their journey at the waterfront Tourist Board (where general manager Don Bain played himself) and continued to the Eastern Market (where Olive Walke's La Petite Musicale sang "Mangoes"), the Country Club (with assorted dance and song selections), a calypso tent (featuring the Mighty Striker in black tie), the Little Carib (for three dance numbers) and back to the docks, where bass Ken Oxley and his Argonauts serenaded the visitor before his dawn departure. Other nights of programming included dance ensembles, such as the Julia Edwards Dance Group and the East Indian National Dancers; choral groups, such as St Joseph's Convent Choir and St Hilary's Senior Singing Club; a production of George Bernard Shaw's *Caesar and Cleopatra*, featuring several local theatrical companies; and performances by the US-based pianist Daniel Ericourt, both alone and with the Trinidad Philharmonic Orchestra. For the weeks following this opening series, Queen's Hall scheduled diverse local, regional and international groups: the Trinidad Light Operatic Society's production of Gilbert and Sullivan's *The Mikado*, performances by the St Lucian Drama Guild of plays by Derek Walcott and his brother Roderick and concerts by the (US) National Symphony Orchestra, which was on a government-sponsored tour of Latin America.[56]

As its advocates proclaimed, Queen's Hall was a venue unlike any other in Trinidad. Certainly its curved contours and park-like setting differentiated it from the movie theatres and other public buildings within the street grid of central Port of Spain. From the front, the building appeared like a hill emerging from the surrounding grounds and mirroring in miniature the steep hills of St Ann's in the background. Here was a special realm – balanced, tranquil, removed from the commerce of the city and conducive to contemplation and imagination. With its modern design, the building referenced no past architectural style and instead pointed towards a future in which the Trinidadian people would create art as part of the process of exploring and defining themselves as a nation. At the same time, it would serve as a suitable venue for artists visiting from other countries, thus affirming Trinidad and Tobago's engagement with the contemporary arts of the wider world. Finally, its flexible interior space would enable the development of a community centre that could accommodate everything from Shakespeare to table tennis, from an art exhibition to a gala ball.

Though Queen's Hall was used by the public in various ways, the extent of its social inclusiveness seemed to be an evolving endeavour. For decades the Queen's Park Savannah and the buildings around its perimeter had been perceived by working-class Trinidadians as an elite realm, albeit one that they could enter for recreation and education and for events ranging from political rallies to Carnival. Similarly, the drive to build Queen's Hall and its subsequent programming were dominated by elite groups, but the venue also attracted a broader cross-section of the population both as performers and audiences. Given the scope of its use and its social ambiguities, Queen's Hall functioned during the independence era as one of the capital's most visible spaces for reflections on citizenship and the significance of social and cultural difference in the construction of a nation.

The Trinidad Hilton

In 1962, three years after the completion of Queen's Hall, another major facility opened, a couple of hundred yards to its southeast: the Trinidad Hilton. Constructed on the wooded Belmont Hill overlooking the Queen's Park Savannah, this was the largest and most complex single-building project in Port of Spain during the independence era, involving a range of local and overseas organizations and specialists. Initiated by the Albert Gomes administration in 1955, it was intended to expand the capacity and quality of hotel facilities in Trinidad in order to capture a larger share of the growing Caribbean tourism industry of the postwar years. In early 1957 the PNM government adopted the project from its predecessor and made it a key component of its Five-Year Development Programme for the nation. Initially, arrangements with Hilton Hotels International were administered by the government's Hotels Development Corporation, but by 1959 this entity had been absorbed into a new Industrial Development Corporation (IDC). The IDC served as the owner of the hotel and eventually negotiated a contract under which Hilton would run the property for twenty years and receive a third of the profits, with the remaining two-thirds going to the Trinidad government.[57]

The main model for the Trinidad Hilton was the Caribe Hilton, which had opened in San Juan, Puerto Rico, in 1949 as the Hilton's first property outside the US mainland. The Trinidad government was impressed by the substantial revenues that the Caribe generated for Puerto Rico, while the Hilton corporation followed this initial success by developing hotels in many other countries around the world. In her study of Hilton-hotel architecture, Annabel Jane Wharton includes an extended passage from Conrad Hilton's autobiography, *Be My Guest*, in which he reflects on his experience with the Caribe. Hilton writes that, on VJ Day in 1945, his mind "toyed with a vision of hotels . . . being used to draw the peoples of the world into closer understanding". Subsequently, the US Departments of State and Commerce suggested that the Hilton corporation could contribute to foreign aid and goodwill by establishing hotels in cities overseas. Conrad Hilton was soon able to test this idea within American territory through a collaboration on the Caribe, in which his firm consulted on architectural design, hired and trained predominantly Puerto Rican staff and managed the hotel, while the Puerto Rico Industrial Development Company retained ownership and two-thirds of the profits. Along with outlining Hilton's business model, Wharton discusses the design of the ten-storey reinforced-concrete hotel by a young team of Puerto Rican architects: Toro, Ferrer and Torregrosa. As the project moved forward, Oswaldo Luis Toro invited Charles Warner Jr (a student friend from Columbia University's School of Architecture) to assist with interior design. The Caribe's expansive lobby level featured glass curtain walls, which provided a sense of openness to the surrounding landscape and a view of the sea, while its grid of guest-room balconies made it "the first major Modern hotel constructed with this external sign of the repetitive luxury of the hotel's interior space".[58]

A few years after the opening of the Caribe, Charles Warner's New York firm (eventually known as Warner, Burns, Toan and Lunde) served as the principal architects for the Trinidad Hilton; associate architects included both Toro-Ferrer of San Juan and the local Watkins and Partners. Two of Warner's early drawings of the hotel were published by the *Trinidad Guardian* in September 1956. During subsequent years, he made various design changes and was assisted by Frithjof Lunde, who was the firm's resident representative in Port of Spain (an assignment rewarded in part by his eventual marriage to a local air hostess). After favourable soil tests at the site by a US consultant in 1959, the Trinidad IDC received bids from eight general contractors, all of which were higher than estimated and were rejected. The IDC then clarified its specifications, accepted revised bids and in August awarded the primary construction contract to Socoven, a Venezuelan company. Socoven began work, but by the following April encountered what appear to have been financial difficulties. In May the IDC ended its relationship with the firm and awarded a contract to the second-lowest bidder: Holland and Hannen and Cubitts (Trinidad) Limited (the local office of a large British company), in association with Anglin-Norcross Corporation Limited (a large Canadian business). This partnership completed the project in May 1962.[59]

The site for the Trinidad Hilton comprised 25 acres of land that stretched close to 200 feet up the steep Belmont Hill. During the early nineteenth century, the governor's house had stood on this scenic spot. By World War II, only ruins of the house remained, but the site was enhanced when Governor Hubert Young laid out a series of shady paths and planted some three hundred native flowering trees, creating both a wildlife sanctuary and a locale from which the public could enjoy views of the city. In 1958 Hilton architects Warner and Lunde investigated the site's botanic qualities, and by 1960 Frederic Stresau was employed as the landscape architect. A well-known figure from South Florida, Stresau had already designed landscapes for numerous other hotels, including the Arawak in Jamaica, the Riviera Habana in Cuba, El Embajador in the Dominican Republic, the Aruba Caribbean, and the Americana, Eden Roc and Fontainebleau in Miami. He was impressed by the natural beauty of

Belmont Hill, so made few changes to its topography and preserved many of its existing shrubs and trees, including the bamboo groves at the hill's base. Meanwhile, he collaborated with Paul Boland, the head of a nursery that the IDC had established in St Augustine to grow plants for the Hilton, including such species as hibiscus, ixora, crepe myrtle and gardenia. In addition, nearby plantations supplied coconut trees; workers gathered wild plants such as lilies, philodendrons and bromeliads; and Stresau joined local naturalist C.L. Williams on botanic field excursions in the Cumuto forest, Waller Field and the Northern Range. By the time the hotel opened, the *Trinidad Guardian* reported that its surrounding gardens and parks featured fifty thousand trees, shrubs, flowers and ground covers, representing "nearly all the important decorative species to be found in the island". A final aspect of the preparations was the illumination of the plants in the gardens, entranceway and pool area by the New York-based lighting designer Leslie Wheel, who avoided bright colours to create an effect that was "beautiful in a fairyland style rather than flamboyant and bold".[60]

Resting within this lush and highly cultivated landscape was the "upside-down hotel", as it was commonly called in publicity and press coverage (see figure 31). While the Hilton's lobby and other public spaces were in a two-storey central block on the top of the levelled-off hill, its guest rooms descended seven storeys into the wooded terrain. Built primarily of reinforced concrete and concrete blocks, the complex was approached by visitors from the east, along a winding road that connected with the scenic Lady Young Road (completed in 1959). The entrance area consisted of a circular drive, an arcade of shops and an octagonal pavilion, which led across a raised walkway to a vestibule, paved with forest-green ceramic tiles, and on to the spacious upper-level lobby, with a terrazzo floor, potted plants and illumination from a wall of glass and skylight. The glass wall overlooked the casual Pool Terrace restaurant – a two-storey open-air atrium filled with hundreds of plants, including polypodium ferns suspended in metal-and-cane chandeliers. The restaurant's perimeter walls contained wood-and-glass screens over which shades of dried grass and cotton strips were lowered. Outside was the hotel's central terrace, arrayed with palm trees, a dance floor and bar, and pools in the shapes of Trinidad and Tobago, the former augmented with small ponds containing lilies, hyacinths and goldfish.

In addition to the Pool Terrace restaurant, the lower level of the hotel's central block included a variety of other spaces, such as the vibrantly coloured Carnival Bar, overlooking the Savannah, the city and the sea; the lavish Scarlet Ibis and Humming Bird private dining/meeting rooms; and a cool blue-and-white ballroom that opened onto a gallery and afforded another view of the surrounding landscape. The hotel's formal restaurant was La Boucan, in reference to the smoke cooking carried out in an oven within the dining area. Along with international fare, the restaurant offered local foods under the direction of Lucy Aquan, famous for her rice and peas, callaloo, pastelles and shrimp rolls. Below these public spaces were 261 guest rooms, divided between the seven-storey west wing (with a rooftop terrace) and a four-storey south wing. The interiors of the rooms featured multicoloured speckled walls and Danish furniture made of teak and afromosia, while the exterior grid of cantilevered balconies employed lattices and plants to screen adjacent spaces. Accommodation also included suites with floral names and corresponding colour schemes: Jasmine, Anthurium, Hibiscus, Bougainvillaea and Poinsettia.[61]

In a report on the Trinidad Hilton published in 1962, *Architectural Forum* quoted architect Charles Warner as describing the hotel as "a kind of environment rather than a building" and a structure that had "no architectural ego".[62] Indeed, the hotel was creatively integrated with the encompassing landscape – a sort of concrete protrusion on Belmont Hill that was not only surrounded by a profusion of plant life but also invaded by it. Rather than a towering building on a grid plan, it was an enticing resort with a multitude of angles, paths and terraces that offered unanticipated short-range views to guests as they moved around, as well as panoramic observations from the upper levels. While Warner portrayed the Hilton as having no architectural ego, its free-flowing spaces, fecund gardens and centrally displayed pools and bathers certainly expressed forces of the id.

In addition to exhibiting the local tropical environment, the Hilton showcased Trinidadian art. To ensure high quality, the hotel recruited the well-established artist Sybil Atteck (1911–1975) as its "Art and Craft Coordinator". Born in the southern town of Rio Claro, Atteck moved with her family to Port of Spain during the 1920s. In 1928 she began working for the colonial government's agricultural department, where she produced illustrations of botanical specimens; in 1934 she further developed this expertise through a course at the Regent Street Polytechnic and the Kew Gardens herbarium in London. Meanwhile, she painted in her spare time, exhibited her work and in 1943 spearheaded the establishment of the Trinidad Art Society. During the 1940s, she also studied in St Louis at Washington University's School of Fine Arts (with German Expressionist Max Beckmann) and at the Escuela de Bellas Artes in Lima (where she had a special interest in Inca pottery). By the 1950s, she was exhibiting frequently, both in Trinidad and abroad, and was the leading figure in the island's postwar art movement.[63]

Along with directing the Hilton's art programme, Atteck created two works of her own for the hotel: a pair of 27-by-3.5-foot terracotta murals mounted below the ceiling in the lobby. Each mural consisted of a series of low-relief figures, sculpted and fired in pieces and assembled as a mosaic. Towards the eastern side of the lobby was an urban scene with outlines of buildings as a background for a variety of street vendors, a woman and girl with parasols, a policeman directing traffic and a truck driver and bicyclist. Facing this work to the west was a rural scene, featuring mothers and children, fishermen, cane farmers with an oxcart and workers harvesting fruit, all against a background of large leaves. Meanwhile, Carlisle Chang created three murals for the hotel: a 50-by-10-foot painting of scarlet ibises in flight over a mangrove swamp (displayed in the Scarlet Ibis Room), a 23-by-10-foot painting of hummingbirds and wildflowers in a forest scene (in the Humming Bird Room), and a 16-foot series of copper Carnival figures (in the Carnival Bar). This last work, sculpted by Carnival metal artist Ken Morris, included such masqueraders as dragon-band characters, fancy sailors and an American Indian, as well as steelbandsmen. The final major artwork in the hotel was multidisciplinary artist Geoffrey Holder's 32-by-8-foot mural for La Boucan restaurant. This oil painting depicted a leisurely Sunday in the late nineteenth century, with figures in French-creole dress strolling through a softly lit wooded landscape.[64]

Presentations of local arts at the Hilton continued during the events that accompanied its official opening from 14 to 16 June 1962. These events were intended to showcase not only the hotel but also Trinidad as an attractive leisure-travel destination and business opportunity. Hilton had already launched an international publicity campaign for the new hotel, and, on the Sunday before the opening, the *Trinidad Guardian* ran a twenty-four-page supplement that enthusiastically covered its design, services and staff. In the spirit of the nascent space age, the IDC placed an advertisement on the supplement's back cover that featured a drawing of Earth orbited by American and Russian astronauts, with Trinidad prominently highlighted below. Ad copy outlined various financial incentives for investment and advised: "You can also be an Astronaut and land your Industry in Trinidad & Tobago." Promotions continued on Wednesday with the arrival from New York of Conrad Hilton, accompanied by an entourage of some forty VIPs who included journalists from several countries, and celebrities. After a reception at Piarco Airport, the group travelled in a police-escorted motorcade to the hotel.[65]

The grand opening, attended by local elites as well the special guests, kicked off on Thursday with "Trinidad Night", hosted by John O'Halloran, minister of agriculture, industry and commerce (Premier Eric Williams was out of the country). For a cocktail hour on the hotel's rooftop terrace, folklorist and PNM publicist Andrew Carr recruited contingents of three of the top masquerade bands of the 1962 Carnival: George Bailey's Somewhere in New Guinea, Edmond Hart's Flag Wavers of Sienna and Harold Saldenha's Julius Caesar and the Conquest of Gaul, all illustrative of the extravagant portrayals of far-off places and times that were characteristic of the large Carnival bands during the postwar era. After songs from Olive Walke's La Petite Musicale and a dinner of local fare, impresario Aubrey Adams presented the main show for the evening, *The Spirit of Trinidad*, on the grounds to the east of the swimming pools. This production followed a visiting researcher on an eventful excursion around Port of Spain, in a manner similar to the city-tour show (*The Happy Wanderer*) performed at Queen's Hall three years earlier. In Adams's script, "an anthropologist, steeped in conceit and arrogance, is sent out by his (English) University to gather data for a thesis on the culture of the territory". The anthropologist runs into "an incorrigible loafer", who responds to his "haughty request to be taken to see the 'common people'" by introducing him to the Gaza Strip, a group of seedy nightclubs on Wrightson Road known for their "hostesses". After an escapade that almost lands the pair in jail, they venture elsewhere in the city: Hell Yard (the downtown panyard of Trinidad All Stars), the home of an obeahman (an expert in African-derived spiritual practices), the cemetery (presumably Lapeyrouse, where Lord Brynner sang of departed calypsonians), the University of Woodford Square and eventually to the Hilton Hotel for the final entertainment of the night.[66] Thus visitors and local guests alike were treated to a portrayal of Port of Spain that captured both its earthiness and artistic traditions through a dynamic of seeing and being seen. While the Hilton opening offered a new opportunity for Trinidad to present itself to the world, it also involved management and parody of outsiders' images of the place.

Friday, 15 June, was "Inauguration Day" at the Hilton, with much of the ceremony typical of state occasions in Trinidad. Proceedings began in the morning on a temporary dais positioned near a circular plant bed that contained British, Trinidad and Hilton flags and was surrounded by a mounted police guard. Minister O'Halloran officially dedicated the hotel and, along with Conrad Hilton, received gold keys to the facility from Cyril Merry, chairman of the IDC. In a lengthy speech on PNM government projects, O'Halloran said the hotel was "part of the grand design for the economic development of the country" and that it would "surely go on to build a modern tourist industry, that will attract an increasing share of the tourist trade of this part of the world". The police band then offered musical selections as male guests made their way to the ballroom for a banquet (topped off with brandy and cigars), while the women settled into the Pool Terrace restaurant for their meal and a fashion show. At the men's lunch, Conrad Hilton delivered a speech in which he described the hotel as "a cascade of architectural splendour clinging to the cliffs and looking down on your Port-of-Spain like a crown on the brow of the city". He also mentioned the opening of other Hiltons both in the United States and overseas and observed: "Now your fine city of Port-of-Spain is one with

Madrid, Berlin, Cairo, Mexico City, Montreal and Istanbul." That evening there was a cocktail party in the grounds of Government House for invited guests and fireworks in the Queen's Park Savannah for the general populace. On Saturday evening the Hilton celebrations concluded with a charity dinner in the ballroom for the Lady Hochoy Home for Retarded Children, a project of the governor's wife. Titled "A Night in Port-of-Spain", this Spanish-themed event featured the Roberto Iglesias dance company, brought to Trinidad by Hilton, and the Glorification of Spain, the 1962 masquerade band of the Desperadoes Steelband. Members of the steelband also performed.[67]

The Trinidad government, Hilton Hotels International and the local press all described the Trinidad Hilton as a valuable new economic asset for the nation. The hotel would enable Trinidad to capture a greater portion of the growing Caribbean tourist market, ultimately boost business at other local hotels (with more tourist arrivals), demonstrate that the country was a forward-looking locale for business investors, provide jobs (the hotel employed more than four hundred, mostly local staff), and constitute a substantial customer for local agricultural products. As part of its efforts to attract more business to the island, the government also constructed a new terminal building and carried out runway improvements at Piarco Airport. Nearing completion at the time of independence, this initiative further demonstrated economic ambition and renewed claims that the island was a crossroads of the Americas. Moreover, visitors could conveniently travel from Piarco along the Churchill-Roosevelt Highway and then over the new Lady Young Road directly to the Hilton, without having to pass through the congestion and unsightly areas of central Port of Spain. Finally, the Hilton was intended as a fashionable venue not only for visitors but also for the dining, parties and conferences of the local population. The hotel certainly became a new social and business centre in the city, though its pricing made it inaccessible to much of the population.[68]

Viewed from the Queen's Park Savannah, the streamlined white-and-beige outline of the Trinidad Hilton emerged from the trees on Belmont Hill as a new landmark hovering over the surrounding terrain. At the other end of the Savannah was the still successful Queen's Park Hotel, the sprawling set of turn-of-the-century structures with an Art Deco central addition. Both hotels represented luxury and leisure in a garden environment, but they were of different eras. During the heyday of the Queen's Park Hotel, visitors arrived on the island by ship or seaplane, took cabs through the city and enjoyed the electric trams that serviced the Savannah. In the jet age of independence, most visitors arrived at Piarco and could be whisked along highways to the wooded resort of the Hilton. Though both hotels were elite centres, they were created by different social groups: the Queen's Park was a retreat of the old planter and commercial class and its colonial officials, while the Hilton was a construction of the technocrats of the PNM and the emerging nation. With this new facility, Trinidad linked itself to the cosmopolitan network of Hiltons worldwide and was ready for business in an expanding economy of multinational investment and global travel.

Though the Hilton was designed in an international modern style by a New York architectural firm, it fully engaged the Trinidadian environment and was intended to express a local spirit. Its multiple terraces and profusion of windows framed observation of the myriad species of tropical plants that enveloped it, while also offering spectacular views of the Savannah, city and sea on the horizon. At the same time, the hotel's diverse spaces were showcases for local art, much of which also represented the local landscape. Carlisle Chang's murals captured the splendour of tropical flora and fauna, Geoffrey Holder embedded elegant figures in a wooded park and Sybil Atteck's two terracottas displayed complementary visions of the nation: rural agriculture and the excitement of an urban street. Smaller paintings included in the art collection also frequently depicted local scenes. Finally, the Hilton served as a prominent stage for local artistic performance. After its grand opening, dance bands, steelbands, pianists, calypsonians and dancers continued to appear at the venue, either inside or on the central terrace, with its Trinidad and Tobago–delineated pools.

Temple, School, and Television Headquarters

While the Trinidad Hilton was Port of Spain's most grandiose and publicized construction project at the time of independence, three other buildings completed in 1962 offer additional examples of architectural design, civic organization and national aspiration: the Paschim Kaashi Hindu Mandir on Ethel Street in St James, the John S. Donaldson Technical Institute on Wrightson Road and Trinidad and Tobago Television House on Maraval Road. Each of these buildings provided space for social engagement, focused perception, exchange of knowledge and community-building. Like the town hall, Queen's Hall and many other public spaces around Port of Spain, they were centres for dialogue and preparation for life in a postcolonial world.

From the latter nineteenth through the mid-twentieth century, St James's Hindu community worshipped in small temples and in their homes. Planning for the first major mandir began in the 1950s under the leadership of Jang Bahadoorsingh, a prominent businessman who gave a large donation for the project, inspired contributions from others in the community and prepared an initial design based on his observation of temple architectural trends in India. Supporters of the project established a building committee, which worked with the Sanatan Dharma Maha Sabha (Trinidad's main Hindu organization) to lease land from the Port of Spain City Council on Ethel Street in a residential section of southwestern St James. By 1958 work had begun and in 1961 the committee secured additional design services from John Newel Lewis of Mence and Moore.

The perimeter of the site was demarcated by a vented concrete-block wall, with an arched gateway at its western end that opened onto the Ethel Street pavement (see figure 32). Directly inside the gateway was the mandir: a 60-by-70-foot white concrete structure placed on a steel-column foundation with the hope that it might endure for fifteen hundred years. The mandir's walls contained abundant ventilation blocks as well as large glass windows on its north, south and east elevations to facilitate observation by congregants who could not fit inside. Though contrary to Hindu architectural principles, the entrance faced west, presumably because of the Ethel Street gateway. Projecting from the mandir's flat roof were four domed towers; the largest – 60 feet high and featuring six hundred pieces of coloured glass – was a prominent marker of this spiritual centre within the surrounding neighbourhood. Inside the temple, the principal murtis were representations of Krishna and Radha, carved in Jaipur from black and white marble and residing under a silver umbrella made in Benares. Other areas within the compound were similarly impressive. To the east of the mandir was an 8,000-square-foot tiled courtyard with almond trees and a fountain to be illuminated by coloured lights. Beyond this were a 70-by-65-foot cultural hall with a library, musical-instruments shop, pundit residence, dormitories for visitors from country districts and a verandah for wedding receptions and other events. Over time, a variety of religious and ornamental plants were cultivated within the temple grounds.[69]

Paschim Kaashi Mandir opened on 10 March 1962. After prayers and the consecration, there were public proceedings in the courtyard, chaired by Simbhoonath Capildeo, a member of the Trinidad legislature, brother of Rudranath Capildeo, and uncle of V.S. Naipaul. Capildeo said the temple was established for worship by people of all classes, races and creeds, while Bhadase Maraj (president-general of the Sanatan Dharma Maha Sabha) proclaimed that it was one of the best outside India and a tribute to the people of St James. Celebrations continued until midnight, supported by vendors of flowers, fruits and sweets.[70]

While Paschim Kaashi Mandir offered a community space for worship, contemplation and the transmission of ancient spiritual knowledge, the John S. Donaldson Technical Institute was established by the PNM government to advance technical education in the new nation. It acquired its full name in May 1961, after popular Education Minister John Donaldson died in a car accident. While Trinidad's various colleges (elite secondary schools) offered instruction in academic subjects, at the institute youths could study such fields as mechanical and electrical engineering, electrical trades, surveying, architecture, building trades, commercial art, printing, domestic science and banking, as well as physics and chemistry. The school was built to accommodate fifteen hundred students, with instruction by fifty full-time staff and a variety of part-time specialists. When it was officially opened on 4 September 1962 by the princess royal (in town for the independence celebrations), Senator Donald Pierre, the new minister of education and culture, proclaimed it "a symbol of our dedication to discovering and developing the latent technical skills in our community as well as our faith in the future".

Standing on 7 acres of former Docksite land, the institute was designed by Peter Bynoe, a senior architect with the Department of Works, and built by Holland and Hannen and Cubitts (Trinidad) Limited. The reinforced concrete complex had an L-shaped plan, with a main north block consisting of three- and two-storey sections that extended 520 feet along Wrightson Road and a three-storey east block running towards the sea. The main entrance featured a concrete screen wall with a grid of circular vents and two columns supporting a curved projecting bay of windows and vertical sun-breakers, flanked by a 50-foot rectangular box clock tower. The entire complex was open-air, with outdoor terrazzo-tile walkways and cantilevered stairs on the interior elevations. It was conceptualized as a quadrangle, and plans were in place at the time of the opening for one-storey workshops on the south and west sides.[71] The overall design of the institute provided not only isolation from Wrightson Road and nearby port facilities but also, within the compound, spaciousness, modulated sunlight, clean surfaces and an array of classrooms, laboratories and common areas conducive to social interaction and technological learning.

Two months after opening the institute, the Trinidad government began broadcasting from its new Television House on Maraval Road at Marli Street, southwest of the Queen's Park Savannah. This 12,000-square-foot two-storey building was designed by Watkins and Partners and constructed by Arthur Bros and Company, the firm that also built the new town hall and the Gordon Grant Building on Independence Square. Television House's simple front façade featured three solid block sections, separated by areas with windows and vertical aluminium sun-breakers. The central section included a flat-roofed porte-cochère leading to the reception area. Towering above the building was a 150-foot antenna that transmitted to a relay station on a 1,000-foot hill in Trinidad's Central Range. Inside were three studios – the largest was a two-storey space that could accommodate shows before a live audience. The building also contained offices, workshops and rooms for processing, editing and archiving film. Outside was a terrace that could be used for filming shows in daylight.

To operate its television service (Trinidad and Tobago Television [TTT]), the government formed a company in which it held a 10 per cent share, with the remaining interests belonging to Rediffusion (West Indies) Limited (40 per cent), Scottish Television (40 per cent), and the Columbia Broadcasting System (10 per cent). Though it was not yet prepared for full-scale programming at the time of independence, the service rushed to instal and test equipment and managed to broadcast the flag-raising ceremony, opening of parliament and other main events (with some reception sets temporarily installed in Woodford Square and other public places). Regular broadcasting began on 1 November. On the preceding Sunday, the *Trinidad Guardian* published a television supplement in which its industrial reporter asserted: "The light of progress in today's world is largely the dim flicker from a television screen, dazzling many, and kindling more and more reaction and almost religious fervour, as it ceaselessly parades man and his ideas." TTT programming included local and international news, educational shows, movies, local performances and other entertainment. The *Guardian*'s reporter added that "the quasi entertainment-educational focus, will also be trained with the precision of the TV camera's eye, on our growing nation, its people, jobs, factories and developments; building up an awareness of the world at large, of Trinidad and Tobago, and how they relate, one to the other".[72]

So Television House was the centre for a new type of visibility in Trinidad – a mode of exhibition and viewing that arrived literally with independence. TTT staff and its associates began producing imagery of the local environment and population on a scale far beyond what had been achieved by earlier documentary filmmakers. These productions, along with material channelled from abroad, could be viewed at home by those able to afford the fancy television sets advertised in newspapers, or watched on sets in public places. Through its regular programming, TTT enabled a form of mass visualization in which distance was bridged and social access widened. No longer was it necessary to be on location in Port of Spain or anywhere else to see important events, view and listen to political leaders or experience the performances of popular artists. Moreover, television enabled the populace to feel part of the contemporary affairs of the wider world. With technology of this power now available, government authorities ensured that, on the eve of Independence Day, television viewers throughout Trinidad and Tobago could be transported to Woodford Square to watch the lowering of the Union Jack in front of the Red House and the raising of the nation's new flag.

CONCLUSION

FROM THE COCOA BOOM TO INDEPENDENCE, the people of Port of Spain built their city in pursuit of various visions of improvement. Over the decades, they constructed an impressive array of new landscape elements, from streets and parks to houses and public buildings – each of which enabled particular types of activity as well as forms of display and perception. In the dense configuration of the city's spaces, Trinidad's heterogeneous population and visitors converged and, through their encounters, achieved not only practical goals but formulated understandings of each other and themselves. Moreover, they expressed such understandings in the ways in which they talked about the city or represented it in writing or visual media. Through these ongoing processes of environmental design, use and representation, the city evolved as a realm of collective endeavour and imagination, with manifestations of both social difference and commonality. It is in this sense that the landscape served as a central site for the display and negotiation of Trinidad's social order during its transition from British colony to independent nation-state. From the late nineteenth century to 1962, Port of Spain was a focal point for British governance and commerce; for American trade, tourism and (during World War II) military enterprise; and for various forms of local community organizing, artistic expression and empowerment. Ultimately, Trinidadians refashioned the city as their own capital, though its composition continued to be deeply affected by British and American power and cultural forms.

The development of Port of Spain's landscape was shaped both by economic and political events and by changing concepts of urban planning, engineering and architectural design. During the late nineteenth and early twentieth centuries, wealth generated by Trinidad's cocoa boom, along with vigorous assertions of British imperial authority, facilitated extensive new construction throughout Port of Spain and its environs. Colonial officials, architects, engineers and builders employed concepts of public order, principles of aesthetic elaboration and new technologies to produce a landscape that looked very different from that of the pre-boom years. During the interwar era, social discontent and political protest increased and were accompanied by a wider range of expression in the city's architecture, festivity, entertainment and literature. If the cocoa boom was a period for displaying the primacy of British power and for sociocultural containment, the interwar years brought an upsurge of alternative forms of creativity and communication. While architects continued to draw on historical revival styles, they also began experimenting with modernist forms. The startling new look of these buildings suggested a streamlined international future for Trinidad in contrast to the weighty encumbrance of the colonial past. The tumult of the 1930s continued during World War II with the arrival of thousands of American servicemen and civilians, who rapidly built austere bases and new roads and, through their various interactions with local residents, further disrupted the colonial social and political order. Finally, economic advancements and nationalist aspirations of the postwar period were interrelated with visions of a fully modern city and state. In contrast to the aesthetic of elaboration of the cocoa boom years, designers embraced international modernism's aesthetic of simplification, though they adapted this orientation to the local natural and cultural environment. Indeed, the city's populace as a whole, from prominent architects to the myriad individuals who built their own houses, continued to employ local materials, artistic principles and construction techniques. By the time of independence, they had created an urban landscape with a substantially different appearance from that of the cocoa boom era, though one that still felt like home.

The construction of an independent nation and a progressive capital city was a profound achievement. There were, however, substantial limits to decolonization in Trinidad, which remained a member of the British-led Commonwealth and extensively engaged with the United States. A place recreated by the Spanish in the sixteenth century as a colonial outpost and developed by the British from the early nineteenth century as a colonial experiment would not be suddenly transformed with the formal granting of independence. The forces of colonialism continued to shape its fundamental economic and social structures and their spatial manifestations. The economy was still heavily dependent on the export of a few commodities, principally petrochemicals and sugar, and especially reliant on American and British capital and markets. Texaco, British Petroleum and the British sugar conglomerate Tate and Lyle were the dominant corporations within the local arena, while the impact of the increasing number of local factories was relatively small. This legacy of a limited export economy within a small country contributed to the perpetuation of high levels of social inequality. While there was a growing middle class, democratization and a new political elite, much of Trinidad's population continued to contend with minimal opportunities, underemployment, poverty and substandard housing. In short, deep tensions and uncertainties remained within the new nation-state. In the years after independence, Port of Spain would continue to function as a central site for the debate of these challenges and the display of competing social interests and goals.

CAPITAL CITIES OF THE BRITISH CARIBBEAN

While the particularities of Port of Spain's history and cultural composition are unique, the city's general development has much in common with that of other colonial capitals in the British Caribbean from the late nineteenth to mid-twentieth century. During this period, cities throughout the region grew as centres for transportation, externally-oriented commerce, authoritarian governance, popular protest and democratization. In addition, they were locales of pronounced demographic heterogeneity and cultural multiplicity, continually augmented by migration from outlying districts; visits by businesspeople, military personnel and tourists from Europe and North America; and importation of foreign consumer goods. As nodes of transportation and travel, they thus served as key sites of interaction, exchange and image-making among diverse peoples. A broader perspective on these general processes can be obtained through a sampling of research on Kingston, Georgetown, Bridgetown and Nassau, capitals of territories that, along with Trinidad and Tobago, were the first to obtain independence from Britain – Jamaica in 1962, Guyana and Barbados in 1966 and the Bahamas in 1973.

Kingston

Standing on an expansive harbour on the southeast coast of Jamaica, Kingston is the largest city in the anglophone Caribbean. It has long been studied by geographer Colin Clarke, who has traced its socioeconomic and spatial development from its founding in 1692, after the partial destruction of nearby Port Royal by an earthquake, through Jamaica's independence era to recent times.[1] During the eighteenth and early nineteenth centuries, Kingston was the main port for the island's lucrative, slavery-based sugar economy and also carried out substantial trade with Spanish-American colonies. Social stratification in the city during this period reflected the European, African and mixed-descent categories of the plantations, though this hierarchy was not strongly expressed in location of residence (Clarke suggests that "where status is highly ascriptive, space is often unnecessary as a social barrier"). After emancipation in the 1830s and changes in British import policies in 1845, Jamaica's sugar industry declined, Kingston's trade shifted towards the United States, large numbers of rural dwellers migrated to the city and unemployment became a basic feature of urban life. However, this was also an era during which Kingston became the capital of Jamaica (replacing the inland Spanish Town in 1872), a larger commercial district developed in the lower (southern) portion of the city, and the government pursued projects in public transport, electrification, water supply and sewerage. Goad's 1894 insurance map of the city, drawn a year before Port of Spain's, shows a grid of blocks with dwellings of varied density and quality in the expanding city. Clarke notes that, with a massive population influx, residential location became increasingly important as a status symbol. By the late nineteenth and early twentieth centuries, there was growing spatial differentiation along lines of class and colour in the city, with Chinese, Syrian and Indian minorities also concentrated in particular areas.[2]

After labour protests and riots in 1938 (a year after Trinidad's uprising), unions and political parties formed, elections with universal adult suffrage were held (initially in 1944) and the colony gradually moved towards self-government. Postwar administrations tried to stimulate manufacturing among both local entrepreneurs and foreign investors, but the factories established had minimal impact on high levels of unemployment. By 1960 the city's population had reached 379,980, almost a quarter of that of the entire country. Middle and upper classes (often lighter-skinned) were concentrated in northern and some eastern districts of the city, where many lived in concrete homes, owned cars and enjoyed newer shopping facilities. The generally darker-skinned lower class was concentrated in southern districts, including the particularly high-density and impoverished areas of West Kingston. A large portion of this population rented accommodation in single-storey tenements (with one room per household) or in one-room sheds in yards. So, at the time of Jamaica's independence, Kingston was a sharply divided city in terms of social class, residential distribution and environmental conditions.

However, anthropologist Diane Austin-Broos, in an article on representations of Kingston, describes how this beleaguered city was also a destination for British and North American tourists from the turn of the twentieth century to the early 1960s.[3] It was "a tropical locale for the weary retreating from modernity" but one "tempered by more than two hundred years of British civilization" and possessing modern conveniences. During the early twentieth century, wealth generated by Jamaica's growing banana industry propelled the construction of genteel residences and other buildings in Kingston and supported promotion of the city by local writers such as Herbert de Lisser, who lauded its appealing qualities and noted its Myrtle Bank and South Camp Road Hotels, which held frequent balls enjoyed by both the local elite and visitors. During the 1950s, bauxite mining in Jamaica brought another wave of relative prosperity and the city reached its peak as an exotic haven for tourists, a moment captured in Harry Belafonte's global hit song "Kingston Town".

During the post-independence period, however, downtown Kingston eventually deteriorated, owing to persistent economic challenges and rising political violence. Reggae music then disseminated a more complex image of the city – one that articulated social struggle but also community ties and possibilities of transcendence.

Kingston's pre-independence tourism industry is also examined by art historian Krista Thompson, who offers an in-depth analysis of the Myrtle Bank Hotel – the city's premier site for the interaction of locals and foreigners during the first several decades of the twentieth century.[4] In 1891 a group of Jamaican investors opened the Myrtle Bank between downtown Harbour Street and the sea. Postcards showed a stately three-storey brick structure surrounding a tropical garden, while advertisements noted that the building was lit by electricity and "replete with every Modern Improvement". Indeed, the "Pride of Kingston" opened in conjunction with Jamaica's Great Exhibition, which was intended to highlight agricultural products, encourage tourism and signal the colony's position in the modern world. Though the hotel was severely damaged in Kingston's devastating earthquake of 1907, an American proprietor opened a new California Mission Revival-style building in 1910 – this facility faced the sea and became one of the most popular images of Jamaica. In 1918 the hotel was taken over by the United Fruit Company, the leading American firm in the colony's banana and tourism industries. By this point, the hotel had become a social centre for the local white elite, especially a group of families that had arrived in Jamaica during the mid- to late nineteenth century (more recently than the old planter class).

During the interwar years, Americans flocked to the Myrtle Bank, where they pursued both leisure and business deals with its local clientele. Meanwhile, the hotel's saltwater pool became one of its primary attractions, in keeping with the growing popularity of sunbathing and swimming during this period. However, only whites were able to access and enjoy this luxurious setting. In the 1940s, ownership of the Myrtle Bank passed to a local family, and Evon Blake, a well-known Afro-Jamaican journalist, began writing articles that criticized customary discrimination at the hotel and other venues. One day in 1948, convinced that his journalism was not having a sufficient impact, Blake dived into the pool and quickly emptied it of other bathers. Thompson argues that Blake employed the visibility of the pool to call attention to the invisibility of blacks there and also to highlight their broader marginalization in "the fashioning of a modern Jamaica through the harbinger of modernity, tourism".[5]

Georgetown

Far from Kingston, on the northern coast of South America, Georgetown was established by the Dutch at the mouth of the Demerara River in the late 1700s and developed by the British in the nineteenth century. Situated below sea level and protected by an elaborate system of dikes and drainage, the city served as the capital of British Guiana as well as a commercial centre for the territory's coastal sugar industry (worked by labourers of both African and Indian descent) and for the extraction of gold, diamonds, timber and balata from the interior. Historian Juanita De Barros offers an examination of Georgetown during the late nineteenth and early twentieth centuries, with a focus on conflicting uses and perceptions of urban public spaces by different social groups.[6] She argues that the city's elite struggled to maintain order and cleanliness in streets and other outdoor locales, while the poor employed these spaces for recreation and earning a livelihood. Drawing on Victorian fears of urban filth and danger, the elite considered Georgetown a distinctly unhealthy place and devoted much effort to sanitation, which they conceptualized as intertwined with civilization and morality. The city had a force of sanitary officers and workers, but their uneven provision of services resulted in a substantial portion of the poor continuing to live in degraded settings, which contributed to their demonization by the elite. In a similar vein, the elite described the socializing, banter, music-making and gambling of working people on the streets as polluting and threatening. Even dockworkers lingering on Water Street by the harbour were portrayed as vagrants, though their idleness was conditional on the seasonal sugar industry and other fluctuations in British Guiana's economy. Among the most disruptive figures on the streets were the "centipedes" – gangs of stick-carrying petty criminals who created a moral panic during the early 1900s. Centipedes were associated with particular territories in Georgetown, and in 1924 a serious clash broke out between the Berlin Team of La Penitence and the Pepper Sauce Team of Charlestown, during which their captains and members fought each other with sticks.

De Barros also discusses tensions involving hucksters, hawkers, market officials and police in Georgetown's public spaces before wrapping up her study with a detailed analysis of three major riots in 1889, 1905 and 1924. All three disturbances began on Water Street, Georgetown's major commercial thoroughfare, and then spread to other districts in the city and its environs. In both 1905 and 1924, dockworkers struck for higher wages, organized labour parades on Water Street, attempted to elicit support from other workers in the city and invaded shops and homes. In 1905 the major rioting in the city was triggered by police shootings during a strike on a nearby plantation. The next day a crowd of two thousand gathered at Georgetown's Public Buildings (the seat of the colonial government) for a meeting, and, after threats from the inspector general of police, some protesters forced their way into the building and began breaking windows. In 1924 rioters disabled tramcars, stopped a train and disrupted ferry service on the Demerara River. During both disturbances, participants also engaged in drumming, dancing and stick-waving, which, De Barros notes, were traditions associated with popular festivities, including Tadjah (an event that corresponded to Hosay in Trinidad). All three riots were rapidly suppressed by authorities and strongly condemned by elites. In addition, armed forces from other British Caribbean territories were contacted, in part because of concerns about the reliability of the local police and troops. In the aftermath of the 1905 riot, local and foreign forces marched through the city's streets in a show of power, while authorities banned street masquerading during the impending Christmas season. Though the elite re-established order after each of Georgetown's riots, De Barros argues that the poor successfully combined popular traditions and trade unionism to construct "a peculiarly *Guianese* ritual of protest" in their ongoing struggle for a place in the city's public sphere.[7]

Bridgetown

Established in the late 1620s, Bridgetown is on the leeward coast of Barbados, the easternmost island in the Caribbean and one of the earliest English colonies in the region. In a collection of essays commemorating Bridgetown's 375th anniversary, historians Celia Karch, David Browne and Woodville Marshall offer analyses of economic and political developments in the city during the late nineteenth and early twentieth centuries, a period of crisis for Barbados's once lucrative sugar industry. Karch focuses on Bridgetown's complex commercial world and suggests that it was well positioned to adjust to economic challenges.[8] The city was a prominent port of call and coaling station for British and North American steamship lines (with routes to the Caribbean and Latin America), served as a node for the West India and Panama Telegraph Company and was a centre for schooner traffic across the eastern Caribbean. Moreover, it possessed an advanced infrastructure that included piped water, gaslights (replaced by electric lighting in 1910), telephone service and a railway. It was within this advantageous environment that the city's commercial firms expanded their operations during the late 1800s and early 1900s to gain control of the island's struggling sugar plantations, essentially replacing British companies as mortgage-holders, commission agents and suppliers. At the same time, they continued to operate as importers of manufactured goods and as agents for steamship lines and insurance companies. Consisting almost entirely of whites who lived in mansions in Bridgetown's security-patrolled Belleville and Strathclyde neighbourhoods, this prosperous merchant class was at the apex of a stratified commercial world that extended through retailers of various sizes down to street hucksters and hawkers. Karch notes that "everyone was linked together through the credit system dominated by the large commission houses which held the credit strings". She concludes that the large firms succeeded in keeping the economy in Barbadian hands during a time of economic hardship but that "social revolution would take place in another era".

Indeed, there was a growing critique of Barbados's socioeconomic structure during the 1920s and 1930s, an era examined by David Browne in an essay focused on journalist Clennel Wickham (1895–1938) and physician and political activist Charles Duncan O'Neal (1879–1936).[9] O'Neal had absorbed socialist and trade-unionist ideals while studying medicine in Scotland and subsequently befriended Captain A.A. Cipriani in Trinidad, where he worked as a doctor before returning to Barbados in 1924. Based in Bridgetown, both Wickham and O'Neal vociferously addressed the concerns of the island's black masses, such as the severely limited franchise for the elected House of Assembly, labour exploitation and slum housing. Living conditions were wretched for many of Bridgetown's residents. For example, one report of the era noted 226 families living in 179 houses on a 6.25-acre piece of land known as "Cat's Castle", and a government-appointed committee described the city's slum tenantries in general as a "grave social evil, threatening public health, weakening morals and destroying the promise of the future". While Wickham wrote against injustices in articles for the *Barbados Herald Weekly*, O'Neal founded the island's Democratic League and spearheaded the Workingmen's Association, holding open-air political meetings in Bridgetown and expanding the organization into rural districts. He was also a Pan-Africanist, a supporter of Marcus Garvey and, by 1932, a representative of Bridgetown in the House of Assembly.

Political organizing in Bridgetown assumed a more radical dimension in 1937 with the arrival of Clement Payne, a Trinidadian of Barbadian parentage. Woodville Marshall describes how Payne and his lieutenants created, over a period of only twelve weeks, a popular movement that was unprecedented in Barbados.[10] In Trinidad Payne had been a frontline member of the NWCSA and apparently was sent by this group to Barbados in March 1937 to expand its mobilization of working people. By early May he was organizing public meetings in Bridgetown and delivering speeches that examined the Depression-era plight of the masses in terms of class struggle and black nationalism. Local interest was increased by news of the strikes and protests in Trinidad in June 1937. After the police forced his meetings out of public spaces in Bridgetown, Payne relocated to Golden Square, a low-income housing area. On the evening of 26 July, a crowd there discovered that the authorities had deported Payne to Trinidad, and began rioting and clashing with police. The next day, the riot intensified in Bridgetown's commercial district and spread to the countryside. By 30 July, it had been violently suppressed by government armed forces.

Nassau

Founded by the English in 1666, Nassau is on the north coast of New Providence, one small island in the lengthy Bahamian archipelago that stretches from the Gulf Stream off the coast of Florida to the north of Cuba and Haiti. Over the centuries, the city's fortunes have depended mainly on commerce and services, since large-scale plantations did not develop in the Bahamas. Nassau's tourist industry began to take shape in the late nineteenth century, with publications such as *Stark's History and Guide to the Bahama Islands* (1891) and the ventures of American tycoon Henry Flagler, who extended steamship service from Florida, purchased the Royal Victoria Hotel and built the Colonial Hotel. In her study of touristic promotions of Nassau through the 1930s, Krista Thompson focuses on the work of photographers who shot for guidebooks, advertisements, postcards, albums and exhibitions. She argues that these individuals employed two basic visual methods or frames in representing Nassau: the tropical, which highlighted wild and abundant nature, and the picturesque, which emphasized tamed and orderly scenes. The tropical frame included not only images of massive ceiba trees and swaying palms but also depictions of small thatched houses surrounded by lush foliage in the Afro-Bahamian "Over the Hill" district, to the south of Nassau's commercial and governmental centre. Typical of the picturesque frame were images of the manicured gardens at the Royal Victoria Hotel and of clean limestone streets in the central city or upscale residential areas. While the tropical depicted an exotic world outside modernity, the picturesque suggested colonial control of both nature and society. Such imagery not only manifested racist stereotypes but also mirrored the high level of racial segregation in the city (hotels, for example, excluded black visitors).

During the 1920s and 1930s, Nassau's officials and commercial elite renewed their tourist promotion campaign with a variety of infrastructural improvements, including a new steamship line, Pan American Airways service, upgraded utilities, additional hotels and the extensive planting of tropical trees to ensure that the city more fully resembled its touristic image. These investments were focused on the downtown area, rather than the black districts of the city or surrounding areas. For the winter tourist season, authorities also encouraged market women to dress in more colourful attire and tried to remove beggars and loiterers from the streets. However, they faced a more complicated challenge with John Canoe (Junkanoo) – a Christmas-season masquerade tradition in which communities from Over the Hill invaded downtown Bay Street, which was lined with white-owned businesses. Since tourists actually enjoyed these performances, a committee tried to make them more picturesque through offering prizes. In addition, promoters introduced "Native Nights" with local entertainers at hotel nightclubs. Thompson concludes that "Nassau's picturesque qualities went from being a pictorial ideal to a social policy".[11]

Nassau's tourist industry and broader economy were largely controlled by its minority white population, a group that also dominated the Bahamas's House of Assembly, which (like the legislature in Barbados) was elected under a highly restricted franchise. This social order was challenged by the city's Afro-Bahamian workers in a riot in 1942 and a general strike in 1958 – two events examined by historian Gail Saunders.[12] The first protest was a manifestation of the involvement of the Bahamas in World War II. Like Trinidad, the territory was included in the American-British destroyers-for-bases agreement of 1940–1941, and while the primary US base was on the outlying island of Exuma, the American and British governments developed two joint military facilities on New Providence: Main Field, south of Nassau's Over the Hill district, and Satellite Field, near the western end of the island. During 1942 more than two thousand workers built the bases, under the direction of the US Army engineering department and an American contractor. Soon after the project began, the workers demanded higher wages. After gathering at Main Field, they marched through the city with machetes and other weapons (while singing patriotic songs) and eventually rioted on Bay Street, where they smashed windows and looted stores. Saunders suggests that while the wage dispute and wartime tensions were the immediate causes of the uprising, underlying factors included racial discrimination, poverty, urban overcrowding, limited employment opportunities and lack of political representation.

While the 1942 riot brought little improvement in the conditions of working people, advancement did occur during the 1950s, with the formation of the Afro-Bahamian-based Progressive Liberal Party (which won a few seats in the House of Assembly) and increased labour organizing. When, in late 1957 and early 1958, Nassau's taxi drivers contested competition from buses run by hotels and tour companies, the Bahamas Federation of Labour called a general strike, which included workers from the hotels and other sectors of the city's economy. In addition to essentially shutting down the tourist industry, working people picketed and boycotted businesses on Bay Street. Saunders argues that the strike, as a broad protest against conditions in the Bahamas, motivated the Colonial Office to initiate new trade-union legislation, election reforms and constitutional changes that in 1964 provided internal self-government for the territory.

As the above literature suggests, the late nineteenth to mid-twentieth century was an era of both dynamic growth and escalating social tensions in the capital cities of the British Caribbean. Cities expanded rapidly in physical size as well as population as they attracted ever-increasing numbers of migrants from rural districts. Construction was intensive and varied, ranging from new public buildings, commercial facilities, hotels and elite homes to the small structures erected by the poor in inner-city yards and outlying areas. In addition, governments pursued large-scale improvements in harbours, roads, water supplies and electrification in efforts to manage growth and promote their cities as modern centres. These wide-ranging forms of construction materialized existing social orders, particularly systems of inequality. Stratification was displayed not only in housing quality but also in unequal infrastructural investment and services in diverse urban areas. Differences in material conditions, in turn, supported elite discourses of cleanliness, morality and cultural superiority. Degraded and overcrowded districts were condemned as unsanitary and the poor themselves were depicted as retrogressive. Such discourses were accompanied by policing of the movements and activities of the poor in public spaces and by social conventions that restricted darker-skinned people in general from certain locations. Structures of social inequality were also reinforced by the development of tourism industries. Though tourism was lauded by civic leaders as a progressive force, it channelled state resources towards the production of exclusive spaces, further enriched elites, offered mainly low-wage jobs to the masses and exacerbated racial discrimination.

While the capital cities of the British Caribbean were oppressive places, they were also important sites for diverse expressions of opposition to prevailing social orders. Local journalists and other writers critiqued urban environmental conditions and social inequities. Meanwhile, working people created masquerades and other performances through which they occupied central public spaces. In addition, they organized strikes that disrupted economic activity (from shipping to tourism), participated in labour marches through main commercial streets and joined in political rallies that offered a chance to hear and watch leaders who articulated new visions of their societies. Occasionally, protests erupted into riots during which participants brandished weapons, destroyed property belonging to elites and, in the case of the 1904 uprising in Georgetown, even attacked the primary buildings of the colonial government. All these modes of demonstration took advantage of the visibility of central urban spaces to mobilize large crowds and create threatening spectacles. Such spectacles disrupted the complacency of elites, encouraged recognition of injustice and contributed to processes of social and political reform. By the 1940s and 1950s, labour unions and political parties were developing as major agents of change within capital cities and societies as a whole. By the 1960s, these cities were redefining themselves, both to their citizenries and the wider world, as centres of independent nation-states.

THE SIGNIFICANCE OF THE LANDSCAPE OF PORT OF SPAIN

For Port of Spain, like other capitals of the British Caribbean, the late nineteenth to mid-twentieth century was a period of multifaceted environmental and symbolic constructions. It was an era during which the dynamics of power and creativity in city-building were deeply interrelated with the building of a society and a nation. As a material composition, the urban landscape was a large-scale utilitarian and artistic work, collectively produced by myriad planners, architects, engineers and builders over the course of decades. In crafting disparate public, commercial and residential spaces and successfully integrating them, these legions of individuals developed a local tradition of technology and aesthetics and attempted to provide the broader population with a suitable place to live. However, the landscape was also a realm of political engagement and civic formulation. Like any city, Port of Spain was a proposition for public life – a site for expressing and negotiating differences in the pursuit of collective existence. Thus its streets, squares, association halls, government buildings and other shared areas provided critical spaces for political debate and the propagation of ideals. Given these ongoing civic, technological and aesthetic activities, the city served as a showcase for the colony and, during the post–World War II era, for the emerging nation. Here the diverse Trinidadian populace displayed its concerns and accomplishments to itself and to the equally varied people who arrived on the island's shores.

While Port of Spain remained the centre of the nation-state after independence, its profile began to shift and, in time, became somewhat less differentiated from the rest of the territory. During the 1960s and subsequent decades, there was massive change in settlement across the island. The population of Port of Spain within its municipal boundaries gradually decreased through continued suburbanization and the development of a dense "East-West Corridor", which today stretches across much of the northern part of the island. There was also population growth and expansion of urban settlement in west-central and southwest Trinidad. Meanwhile, Pointe-à-Pierre and Point Lisas, along the central west coast, emerged as rival seaports, while Piarco Airport continued to develop as a major transit hub for both passengers and freight. Other centres of intellectual and political activity also increased in influence.

In 1960 the Imperial College of Tropical Agriculture in St Augustine became the Trinidad campus of the University College of the West Indies, which went on to establish instruction and research in numerous academic disciplines. During this same period, the Indian-based Democratic Labour Party, the primary opposition to the PNM, retained its headquarters in central Trinidad and continued to evolve through various name changes. As the United Labour Front, it joined with other opposition parties in the 1980s and was briefly part of a government. In 1989 it became the United National Congress and, under the leadership of Basdeo Panday, won the general election in 1995. Over the following twenty years, elections resulted in victories for both the PNM and United National Congress.[13]

In addition to Port of Spain's declining municipal population and the rise of other centres, the city faced an array of social challenges during the post-independence years, including a growing disillusionment with postcolonial governance. The National Joint Action Committee, a loose coalition of university students, radical trade unionists and activists, condemned the PNM for policies that it argued were dependent on foreign capital, benefited the local white elite and failed to improve significantly the living conditions of the masses. Leaders of the National Joint Action Committee articulated concepts of "Black Power" and in early 1970 mobilized support from primarily young grassroots Afro-Trinidadians in Port of Spain and other northern urban areas. Major demonstrations were mounted in the streets of the city, an ongoing "People's Parliament" was held in Woodford Square and numerous downtown businesses were firebombed. Twenty years later, there was another alarming display of discontent in the city. In July 1990 the Jamaat al Muslimeen (a primarily Afro-Trinidadian group with a mosque in Mucurapo) tried to overthrow the government. The group stormed the Red House, where it held the prime minister and several other ministers hostage, after first firebombing the police headquarters across the street, and took over the state-owned television station. Six days of arson, looting and violence followed before the government was able to apprehend the rebels and restore order.[14]

While the events of 1970 and 1990 were the most dramatic uprisings of the postcolonial era, Port Spain became increasingly crime-ridden and violent, especially with the growth of international drug traffic from the 1980s onward. By the end of the twentieth century, crime was a major theme in discussion of the city, from statements by government officials and journalists to everyday conversation. Along with this discourse of outrage and fear, people installed ever more burglar bars on their doors and windows, thus creating a landscape of self-imprisonment that eroded spatial openness and civic culture. In addition, Port of Spain continued to struggle with problems common to many cities: insufficient and expensive housing, unemployment and underemployment, poverty, inadequate utilities and escalating traffic congestion. Accompanying all of this were major changes in the built environment. The strength of the nation's petrochemical sector from the mid-1970s to early 1980s and from the late 1990s into the first decade of the twenty-first century propelled building booms in the city that involved the demolition of many older residential and commercial structures. High-rise buildings appeared downtown and later in Woodbrook. The disappearance of large portions of the pre-independence city was astounding. While new construction clearly brought many benefits, some people expressed dismay over the loss of cherished buildings and the declining familiarity of the city as a whole. In 1985 a group formed Citizens for Conservation, initially to oppose the demolition of a house associated with George Brown on the Queen's Park Savannah. The organization went on to work for the preservation of many other heritage sites and was instrumental in the development of legislation during the 1990s for a National Trust of Trinidad and Tobago.[15]

In conjunction with the pervasive change of the post-independence decades, there were growing expressions of a concept of time that differed from that of the pre-independence era. As this study has suggested, ideas of progress were widely articulated by the people of Port of Spain from the late nineteenth century through independence. Visions of progress remained in the post-independence decades, but were increasingly countered by narratives of decline. Many people perceived a city plagued by crime, poverty and social conflict at levels that seemed to be beyond government solution. The discourse of decline, however, rarely took the form of colonial nostalgia. From the late nineteenth to mid-twentieth century, concepts of progress were motivated to a substantial degree by opposition to colonial rule and by the expansion of power and benefits for the local population. Disillusionment with this rhetoric of progress among many of the city's residents during the post-independence era was based on their assessment of what seemed like insurmountable problems of the contemporary moment. People had little or no desire to return to the past, but wondered what could be done in the present.

In spite of massive change and turmoil and the growth of other settlements in Trinidad, Port of Spain has remained the definitive centre of the nation-state and a key site for the expression and negotiation of postcolonial challenges. Given its current predicament, what is the value of research on the colonial city such as the study offered here? Certainly a deeper understanding of Port of Spain's current circumstances can be obtained through examining its history, especially the period of the late nineteenth to mid-twentieth century when much of the city was built. The spatial structures of the colonial landscape have continued to shape the city up to the present. Systems of elite control and socioeconomic hierarchy that were fundamental to the built environment are perpetuated in the inequalities of power and wealth in the contemporary city. At the same time, patterns of grassroots dissent, community collaboration and local innovation that were embedded in the colonial landscape remain as capacities in the city today. Thus historical analysis of the characteristics of diverse spaces and their overall organization as an urban environment can offer a broader perspective on spatial constraints and potentialities at present. Similarly, there is much to be learned from historical study of large-scale public performances and of representations of the city in verbal and pictorial forms. Carnival, political demonstrations and national celebrations of the present continue to draw on performance traditions developed during the colonial era, while contemporary literary and visual depictions of the city also employ and critique tropes from this period. In short, historical study of manifestations of colonialism and decolonization in the built environment can enable a fuller comprehension of power and creativity in the city today, including both locally generated and transnational forces.

In addition, the study of the colonial and postcolonial landscape of Port of Spain can reveal patterns in how Trinidadians have comprehended the history of the broader nation-state. In an article published in 2007, historian Bridget Brereton outlined several competing perspectives on Trinidad's past, including: (1) a British imperial narrative (now defunct) of conquest of the island from Spain, firm colonial governance and successful economic management; (2) a French-creole narrative that has emphasized plantation development prior to British conquest, advancement of the cocoa industry during the late nineteenth and early twentieth centuries and an experience of marginalization, first in relation to British colonists and later as a tiny demographic minority with decreased power; (3) an Afro-creole narrative that stresses the centrality of people of African and mixed descent to the pre-emancipation plantation economy, their anti-colonial activism by the late nineteenth century and the forging of a Trinidadian-creole culture (including iconic Carnival arts); (4) a post-independence Afrocentric narrative that highlights the struggles of people of African descent, criticizes Afro-creole perspectives as neocolonial and affirms African cultural roots and continuities; and (5) an Indocentric narrative that articulates the hardships of Indian indentureship, provision of labour for profitable agricultural industries, discrimination by other sectors of the population and the strength of Indian-derived cultural traditions. (In addition, Brereton notes interpretations of Trinidad's history based on social class, which at present are employed most fully in academic historiography.)[16]

As Trinidad's capital, Port of Spain has been a central space in the formulation and display of all these narratives through practices of building, place-naming and public performance. In the course of their 165 years of administration of Trinidad, British colonists constructed numerous public spaces and buildings in the city that, in their appearance and names, affirmed imperial power and achievement. Throughout this same period, French creoles claimed the city as a centre of their community and, with other segments of the local population, developed a unique commercial and residential architecture that exhibited their success, particularly during the cocoa boom. Meanwhile, the city contained the island's largest Afro-creole population, which built various neighbourhoods, established a range of organizations, led anti-colonial protests in public spaces and promoted Carnival arts and other forms of creole culture as national symbols. While there had been early expressions of Afro-centric views in Garveyism and the opposition to the invasion of Ethiopia, this perspective was asserted most forcefully in the street protests of 1970 and in the ensuing endorsement of the African dimensions of local cultural traditions, including the practices of the city's Orisha compounds. Finally, the Indocentric narrative, though articulated most extensively in the landscape of central Trinidad, was also displayed in the transformation of the Peru sugar estate into Peru Village and eventually the district of St James (with its Indian street names), as well as in the creation of temples, mosques and associations in the city more broadly. Moreover, interactions in Port of Spain between Indians and other groups encapsulated the wider dynamic of ethnic relations in Trinidad, as did the arrival in the city of national administrations led by Basdeo Panday and Kamla Persad-Bissessar. In short, various locales, buildings and public performances in Port of Spain have all served as resources with which Trinidadians have constructed narratives of their history, while the city's newspapers and other media have enabled further dissemination and debate of these perspectives.

In articles published in 2006 and 2012, historian David Trotman explored how such visions of Trinidad's past are inscribed in the landscape of Port of Spain through monuments and toponyms. For the most part, the city's squares, parks and streets have retained their colonial names, while almost all monuments from the colonial era also still stand. However, the appearance and significance of some public spaces have changed. Downtown Columbus Square, for example, is "now the haunt of increasing numbers of destitute vagrants, homeless drug addicts and other victims of the unequal wealth creation and distribution of the post-independence years" (while Discovery Day has been replaced by Emancipation Day on August 1). Uptown, Lord Harris Square has also deteriorated. In 1994 the statue of this nineteenth-century governor at the square's centre was vandalized during a night of revels and the broken pieces were apparently sold by a drug addict for $20. However, they were eventually recovered "when a man of 'no fixed place of abode' was found in possession of three bags containing the body parts of the statue at a slum near the city dump". Though there was public debate on rebuilding the statue

(Harris was a reform-oriented administrator), an empty pedestal exists at present within the park's dry fountain. While other colonial monuments remain intact, post-independence leaders have erected only a few new ones: statues of a group of steelbandsmen, the calypsonians Kitchener and Sparrow, and Mahatma Gandhi (a statue of cricket star Brian Lara is a more recent addition). Trotman argues that the minimal modification of Port of Spain's place names and statuary after 1962 was due initially to Eric Williams's concept of colonialism as a reality shared by all segments of Trinidad's population and thus an inclusive past from which to build a new nation. In addition, he suggests that Trinidadians "have invested so much energy in creating community identities linked to those names that they have subverted the original intention of the colonial inscribers and divested colonial names of their previous associations. Any official aggressive attempt at renaming may well meet with resistance".[17]

Indeed, the landscape of Port of Spain is best comprehended as containing multiple layers of history and symbolic significance. Over the course of centuries, it was a place that attracted people who arrived under varying circumstances from many locales. In their efforts to survive and ideally improve their lot, they interacted within a spatially constituted and continually evolving web of relationships. The landscape served as a medium of their association and potential as they claimed space and erected structures in accordance with diverse social and aesthetic goals. Every inhabitant left a mark through new constructions or the often subtle material modifications of day-to-day life. Given these ongoing processes, Port of Spain's landscape can be appreciated today as a central compendium of the imagination and achievements of the Trinidadian people. Through careful scrutiny of this densely organized environment, it is possible to obtain glimpses of the lives of successive generations of residents. Their presence lingers on in a well-crafted gingerbread house, a clean concrete-block meeting hall, a wall-lined street, a tidy garden. In such constructions, one can discover an enduring urban community with its own configuration of values and expectations.

At present, Port of Spain continues to function as an intimate, rather than grand, urban landscape. It is a city conducive to walking and social contact. Acquaintances are frequently encountered in the streets or on the verandahs of their homes. Parks and squares are lush and generally tranquil, though Woodford Square fortunately still attracts a range of orators and audiences. The architecture is immensely varied and excursions through the city almost always bring surprises – a building recently renovated, or demolished and replaced by something else. Both shade from the sun and shelter from sudden rain can be found beneath expansive trees or commercial arcades and awnings. Lively conversation permeates markets, stores and other gathering places, while continuously circulating shared taxis serve as a mobile civic forum as well as offices of personal advice and moral support. Assertions of authority, orthodoxy and superiority are frequently met with questioning or derision. The display of wit is applauded, idiosyncrasy accepted. Collective organizing, whether in formal associations or more impromptu activities, thrives across the city, as do entrepreneurship and artistic innovation. In spite of its transformations and challenges, Port of Spain remains in the end a unique urban landscape, one of much value to Trinidad and the world at large.

NOTES

Introduction

1. D.W. Meinig, introduction, in *The Interpretation of Ordinary Landscapes: Geographical Essays*, ed. D.W. Meinig (New York: Oxford University Press, 1979), 6; Peirce F. Lewis, "Axioms for Reading the Landscape: Some Guides to the American Scene", in Meinig, *Interpretation*, 12; Yi-Fu Tuan, "Thought and Landscape: The Eye and the Mind's Eye", in Meinig, *Interpretation*, 90; Denis Cosgrove, *Social Formation and Symbolic Landscape* (Madison: University of Wisconsin Press, 1998 [1984]); James S. Duncan, *The City as Text: The Politics of Landscape Interpretation in the Kandyan Kingdom* (Cambridge: Cambridge University Press, 1990). See also D.W. Meinig, "The Beholding Eye: Ten Versions of the Same Scene" and "Symbolic Landscapes: Some Idealizations of American Communities", in Meinig, *Interpretation*, 33–48 and 164–92; Peirce Lewis, *New Orleans: The Making of an Urban Landscape*, 2nd ed. (Santa Fe: Center for American Places, 2003); Yi-Fu Tuan, *Space and Place: The Perspective of Experience* (Minneapolis: University of Minnesota Press, 1977); Denis Cosgrove, "Geography Is Everywhere: Culture and Symbolism in Human Landscapes", in *Horizons in Human Geography*, ed. Derek Gregory and Rex Walford (Totowa, NJ: Barnes and Noble Books, 1989), 118–35; and James Duncan and Nancy Duncan, "(Re)reading the Landscape", *Environment and Planning D: Space and Society* 6 (1988): 117–26. Another seminal figure in landscape studies was John Brinckerhoff Jackson. In *Discovering the Vernacular Landscape* (New Haven: Yale University Press, 1984), Jackson defines a landscape as "a composition of man-made or man-modified spaces to serve as infrastructure or background for our collective existence" (8).

2. For overviews of the concept of landscape and of landscape research since the early 2000s, see George L. Henderson, "What (Else) We Talk About When We Talk About Landscape", in *Everyday America: Cultural Landscape Studies after J.B. Jackson*, ed. Chris Wilson and Paul Groth (Berkeley: University of California Press, 2003), 178–98; Don Mitchell, "Cultural Landscapes: Just Landscapes or Landscapes of Justice?" *Progress in Human Geography* 27 (2003): 787–96; Don Mitchell, "New Axioms for Reading the Landscape: Paying Attention to Political Economy and Social Justice", in *Political Economies of Landscape Change: Places of Integrative*

Power, ed. James L. Wescoat Jr and Douglas M. Johnston (Dordrecht, Netherlands: Springer, 2008), 29–50; Don Mitchell and Carrie Breitbach, "Landscape: Part I", in *The Wiley-Blackwell Companion to Human Geography*, ed. John A. Agnew and James S. Duncan (Chichester, West Sussex: Wiley-Blackwell, 2011), 209–20; Hayden Lorimer, "Cultural Geography: The Business of Being 'More-Than-Representational'", *Progress in Human Geography* 29 (2005): 83–94; Mitch Rose and John Wylie, "Animating Landscape", *Environment and Planning D: Space and Society* 24 (2006): 475–79; John Wylie, *Landscape* (London: Routledge, 2007); and Mitch Rose and John Wylie, "Landscape: Part II", in Agnew and Duncan, *Companion to Human Geography*, 221–34. Henderson and Mitchell call for greater attention to how landscapes reproduce social inequality in both their material constraints and ideological representations, while also functioning as a means through which people can construct more equitable and just social arrangements. Meanwhile, Lorimer, Rose and Wylie articulate modes of landscape research that investigate practice, performance, experience, affect and bodily movement. Such work, they suggest, enables a more holistic comprehension of human interaction with the landscape than methods focused on visual and verbal representations, which tend to present static accounts of landscape scenes and interpretations that reduce open-ended interactions to fixed meanings. Additional perspectives are offered by Tim Cresswell, "Landscape and the Obliteration of Practice", in *Handbook of Cultural Geography*, ed. Kay Anderson, Mona Domosh, Steve Pile and Nigel Thrift (London: Sage, 2003), 269–81; Veronica della Dora, "Travelling Landscape-Objects", *Progress in Human Geography* 33 (2009): 334–54; Nuala C. Johnson, "Political Landscapes", in *The Wiley-Blackwell Companion to Cultural Geography*, ed. Nuala C. Johnson, Richard H. Schein and Jamie Winders (Chichester, West Sussex: Wiley-Blackwell, 2013), 173–85; Tim Bunnell, "Urban Landscapes", in Johnson, *Companion to Cultural Geography*, 278–89; and Daniel A. Friess and Tariq Jazeel, "Unlearning 'Landscape'", *Annals of the American Association of Geographers* 107 (2017): 14–21.

3. Among the considerations of all architects, engineers, city planners and builders working in Port of Spain was Trinidad's tropical climate. Approximately 10 degrees north of the equator, the island featured an average daytime temperature of 84 degrees Fahrenheit in the early 1920s, close to the midpoint of the period under examination here. Temperatures were usually moderated by breezes, principally from the northeast. Rainfall varied widely in different parts of the island, with a general annual range of 60 to 80 inches in Port of Spain. Much of the rain fell during the wet season of June to December. See *Handbook of Trinidad and Tobago* (Port of Spain: Government Printing Office, 1924), 11; and Preston E. James, "A Geographic Reconnaissance of Trinidad", *Economic Geography* 3, no. 1 (1927): 87–88.

4. My examination of performances draws on analytical approaches developed in the field of folkloristics by such figures as Richard Bauman and Roger Abrahams. For a recent statement by Bauman on the social organization and dynamics of these special modes of communicative display, see "Performance", in *A Companion to Folklore*, ed. Regina F. Bendix and Galit Hasan-Rokem (Malden, MA: Wiley-Blackwell, 2012), 94–118. For Abrahams's examination of performance traditions

in the anglophone Caribbean, see *The Man-of-Words in the West Indies: Performance and the Emergence of Creole Culture* (Baltimore: Johns Hopkins University Press, 1983).

5. This interpretation of the significance of landscape elements in terms of their design/position, use and representation roughly corresponds to Victor Turner's analysis of symbols in terms of their positional, operational and exegetical meanings. See *The Forest of Symbols: Aspects of Ndembu Ritual* (Ithaca: Cornell University Press, 1967), 50–51. However, while Turner restricts exegetical meaning to the oral interpretations of local people, I am considering representation to encompass the interpretations of both locals and visitors in a variety of media.

6. For overviews of research on the history of colonialism, see Ann Laura Stoler and Frederick Cooper, "Between Metropole and Colony: Rethinking a Research Agenda", in *Tensions of Empire: Colonial Cultures in a Bourgeois World*, ed. Frederick Cooper and Ann Laura Stoler (Berkeley: University of California Press, 1997), 1–56; and Frederick Cooper, *Colonialism in Question* (Berkeley: University of California Press, 2005). Stoler and Cooper emphasize the comprehension of colonial regimes as complex and unstable systems negotiated by varieties of actors with differing motivations and goals within particular times and places. A review of recent historiography of the British empire is offered by Durba Ghosh in "Another Set of Imperial Turns?" *American Historical Review* 117 (2012): 772–93. For an examination of British imperial imagery and pageantry, see David Cannadine, *Ornamentalism: How the British Saw Their Empire* (Oxford: Oxford University Press, 2001). For general discussions of colonial cities, see Anthony D. King, "Colonial Cities: Global Pivots of Change", in *Colonial Cities: Essays on Urbanism in a Colonial Context*, ed. Robert J. Ross and Gerard J. Telkamp (Dordrecht, Netherlands: Martinus Nijhoff, 1985), 7–32; Anthony D. King, "Writing Colonial Space: A Review Article", *Comparative Studies in Society and History* 37 (1995): 541–54; Nezar AlSayyad, "Urbanism and the Dominance Equation: Reflections on Colonialism and National Identity", in *Forms of Dominance: On the Architecture and Urbanism of the Colonial Encounter*, ed. Nezar AlSayyad (Aldershot, UK: Avebury, 1992), 1–26; Brenda S.A. Yeoh, "Power Relations and the Built Environment in Colonial Cities", in *Contesting Space in Colonial Singapore: Power Relations and the Urban Built Environment* (Singapore: NUS Press, 2013 [1996]), 1–27; and Robert Home, *Of Planting and Planning: The Making of British Colonial Cities*, 2nd ed. (London: Routledge, 2013). Yeoh advocates examination of the built environments of colonial cities as expressions of social conflicts and negotiations, involving both the programmes of colonizers and the day-to-day life of colonized groups.

7. Derek Walcott, "The Antilles: Fragments of Epic Memory", in *What the Twilight Says: Essays* (New York: Farrar, Straus and Giroux, 1998), 71–77 (quotation, 74). Walcott describes Port of Spain as a model of an ideal Caribbean city in this 1992 Nobel Prize acceptance speech. For overviews of urbanization in the Caribbean, see Malcolm Cross, *Urbanization and Urban Growth in the Caribbean* (Cambridge: Cambridge University Press, 1979); Robert B. Potter, ed., *Urbanization, Planning and Development in the Caribbean* (London: Mansell, 1989); Robert B. Potter et

al., "Urban Dynamics and Townscapes", in *The Contemporary Caribbean* (New York: Prentice Hall, 2004), 269–312; and Rivke Jaffe, ed., *The Caribbean City* (Kingston: Ian Randle, 2008). For region-wide examinations of Caribbean architecture, see Jack Berthelot and Martine Gaumé, *Kaz antiyé jan moun ka rété / Caribbean Popular Dwelling* (Guadeloupe: Editions Perspectives Créoles, [1982?]); Edward Crain, *Historic Architecture in the Caribbean Islands* (Gainesville: University Press of Florida, 1994); Paul Oliver, ed., "Caribbean", in *Encyclopedia of Vernacular Architecture of the World* (Cambridge: Cambridge University Press, 1997), 3:1699–1725; and Andrew Gravette, *Architectural Heritage of the Caribbean: An A–Z of Historic Buildings* (Kingston: Ian Randle, 2000). The book by Berthelot and Gaumé and other early works are critiqued by Jay D. Edwards in a review essay: "The First Comparative Studies of Caribbean Architecture", *New West Indian Guide* 57, nos. 3–4 (1983): 173–200. For general discussions of Caribbean history, including settlement patterns, see Eric Williams, *From Columbus to Castro: The History of the Caribbean* (New York: Vintage Books, 1984 [1970]); Sidney W. Mintz, *Caribbean Transformations* (New York: Columbia University Press, 1989 [1974]); B.W. Higman, *A Concise History of the Caribbean* (Cambridge: Cambridge University Press, 2011); and Franklin W. Knight, *The Caribbean: The Genesis of a Fragmented Nationalism*, 3rd ed. (New York: Oxford University Press, 2012). Research on anglophone Caribbean cities during the late nineteenth and twentieth centuries is discussed in the concluding chapter of the present study. Examples include Juanita De Barros, *Order and Place in a Colonial City: Patterns of Struggle and Resistance in Georgetown, British Guiana, 1889–1924* (Montreal: McGill-Queen's University Press, 2002); Woodville Marshall and Pedro Welch, eds., *Beyond the Bridge: Lectures Commemorating Bridgetown's 375th Anniversary* (St Michael, Barbados: Barbados Museum and Historical Society and University of the West Indies, 2005); Colin Clarke, "Kingston: A Creole Colonial City (1692–1962)", in *Decolonizing the Colonial City: Urbanization and Stratification in Kingston, Jamaica* (Oxford: Oxford University Press, 2006), 1–44; and Krista A. Thompson, *An Eye for the Tropics: Tourism, Photography, and Framing the Caribbean Picturesque* (Durham: Duke University Press, 2006). For a discussion of research on decolonization in British territories, see O. Nigel Bolland, "Historiography of Decolonization in the Anglophone Caribbean", in *Beyond Fragmentation: Perspectives on Caribbean History*, ed. Juanita De Barros, Audra Diptee and David V. Trotman (Princeton, NJ: Markus Wiener, 2006), 265–96.

8. In the mid-1940s, for example, Trinidad's population of 557,970 was 46.88 per cent African, 35.09 per cent Indian, 14.12 per cent "mixed", 2.74 per cent European, 1.01 per cent Chinese, and 0.16 per cent Syrian/Lebanese. Port of Spain's population of 92,793 was 57.25 per cent African, 7.77 per cent Indian, 24.82 per cent "mixed", 6.97 per cent European, 2.63 per cent Chinese, 0.51 per cent Syrian/Lebanese and 0.05 per cent "not stated". See Lloyd Braithwaite, *Social Stratification in Trinidad* (Kingston: Institute of Social and Economic Research, University of the West Indies, 1975 [1953]), 6; and Suzanne Stephanie Goodenough, "Race, Status and Residence, Port of Spain, Trinidad: A Study of Social and Residential Differentiation and

Change" (PhD diss., University of Liverpool, 1976), 252. In this study, I use the terms "African" and "Afro-Trinidadian", as well as "Indian" and "Indo-Trinidadian", interchangeably. In addition, I generally use "Trinidad", rather than "Trinidad and Tobago", since my argument concerns this single island, which has a substantially different history and social organization than Tobago. Britain united Tobago with Trinidad in 1889.

9. Linda A. Newson, *Aboriginal and Spanish Colonial Trinidad: A Study in Culture Contact* (London: Academic Press, 1976), 116–21; Francisco Morales Padrón, *Spanish Trinidad*, ed. and trans. Armando García de la Torre (Kingston: Ian Randle, 2012), 43–51; K.S. Wise, "Conquerabia or Cumacarapo", in *A Photographic Album of Trinidad at the Turn of the Nineteenth Century*, by Gérard Besson (Port of Spain: Paria, 1985), 1–2; Gérard Besson and Bridget Brereton, *The Book of Trinidad*, 3rd ed. (Port of Spain: Paria, 1992), 1–5; Joyce Lorimer, ed., *Sir Walter Ralegh's* Discoverie of Guiana (London: Ashgate, 2006), 19–33 (Raleigh's place designations appear first on 20). K.S. Wise, an early president of the Trinidad Historical Society, argues that in 1595 "Cumacarapo", "Conquerabia" and "Puerto de España" were all names for present-day Mucurapo and that the more easterly site was not yet settled. Newson also suggests that Puerto de España may initially have been located at Mucurapo but was rebuilt at the easterly site by 1678 (117).

10. Newson, *Aboriginal and Spanish Colonial Trinidad*, 117–19; Morales Padrón, *Spanish Trinidad*, 154–64; Carlton Robert Ottley, *The Story of Port of Spain* (St James, Trinidad: Charran Educational, n.d. [1962]), 2–4.

11. Bridget Brereton, *A History of Modern Trinidad, 1783–1962* (Kingston: Heinemann, 1981), 13–31; Newson, *Aboriginal and Spanish Colonial Trinidad*, 184–93 (see 192 for a map of the city at the end of the eighteenth century); Ottley, *Story of Port of Spain*, 3–7; John Newel Lewis, *Ajoupa* (Trinidad: John Newel Lewis, 1983), 51–63. Brereton notes a sharp decline in Trinidad's already diminished indigenous population during the period of 1777–1797, due to such factors as illness, migration to the mainland and the birth of mixed-descent offspring from interactions with Europeans and Africans (*History of Modern Trinidad*, 20–21).

12. Brereton, *History of Modern Trinidad*, 32–75; Ottley, *Story of Port of Spain*, 10–41; Olga J. Mavrogordato, *Voices in the Street* (Port of Spain: Paria, 1996 [1977]), 37–43; Michael Anthony, *The Making of Port-of-Spain* (Port of Spain: Key Caribbean, 1978), 21–31; Asad Mohammed, "Colonial Influences on Urban Form in the Caribbean, Illustrated by Port of Spain, Trinidad and Tobago", in Jaffe, *Caribbean City*, 24–42. For a map of the city drawn sometime after the 1808 fire, see Besson and Brereton, *Book of Trinidad*, 109.

13. Goodenough, "Race, Status and Residence", 35–191; Suzanne Stephanie Goodenough, "Race, Status and Ecology in Port of Spain, Trinidad", in *Caribbean Social Relations*, ed. Colin G. Clarke (Liverpool: Centre for Latin American Studies, University of Liverpool, 1978), 17–24; Ottley, *Story of Port of Spain*, 44–76; Anthony, *Making of Port-of-Spain*, 33–61. For a map of Port of Spain prepared by Manuel Sorzano in 1845, see Besson and Brereton, *Book of Trinidad*, 252. Much information on Port of Spain is included in general histories of Trinidad during the latter half of

the nineteenth century: see Donald Wood, *Trinidad in Transition* (Oxford: Oxford University Press, 1968); Bridget Brereton, *Race Relations in Colonial Trinidad, 1870–1900* (Cambridge: Cambridge University Press, 1979); Brereton, *History of Modern Trinidad*; and David V. Trotman, *Crime in Trinidad: Conflict and Control in a Plantation Society, 1838–1900* (Knoxville: University of Tennessee Press, 1986).

14. Anthony Trollope, *The West Indies and the Spanish Main* (New York: Harper and Brothers, 1860), 214–30 (quotations, 216); Charles Kingsley, *At Last: A Christmas in the West Indies* (London: Macmillan, 1880 [1871]), 86–94 (quotations: Marine Square and stores, 87; people, 90; houses, 91).

15. For discussions of Port of Spain's population and social structure in the nineteenth century, see Wood, *Trinidad in Transition*; Brereton, *Race Relations*; Brereton, *History of Modern Trinidad*; Bridget Brereton, "The White Elite of Trinidad, 1838–1950", in *The White Minority in the Caribbean*, ed. Howard Johnson and Karl Watson (Kingston: Ian Randle, 1998), 32–70; and Trotman, *Crime in Trinidad*. Brinsley Samaroo has cited the number of Indians brought to Trinidad at about 147,000 ("Seeking a Space in the Politics: Muslim Efforts to Join the Political Process in British Guiana and Trinidad in the 20th Century", *Man in India* 93, no. 1 [2013]: 201).

16. Bridget Brereton, "The Birthday of Our Race: A Social History of Emancipation Day in Trinidad, 1838–88", in *Trade, Government and Society in Caribbean History*, ed. B.W. Higman (Kingston: Heinemann, 1983), 69–83; Bridget Brereton, "Jubilees: How Trinidad and Tobago Remembered Victoria's Jubilees, the Jubilee of Emancipation, and the Centenary of British Rule", *Journal of Caribbean History* 46, no. 1 (2012): 1–32 (quotation, 19).

17. Other valuable architectural studies of Port of Spain include Mohammed, "Colonial Influences" (2008); an article by Colin Laird on cocoa boom-era houses (1954); Colin Laird (2007) interviewed by Mark Raymond and Marcos Barinas; and two booklets by faculty and students at the Azrieli School of Architecture and Urbanism (Carleton University) on the Trinidad Public Library and two cocoa boom-era houses (2011, 2012). An additional perspective on the residential composition of the city is offered by Ronald Briggs and Dennis Conway (1975). See bibliography for full citations.

Chapter 1

1. For overviews of Trinidad's economy during the late nineteenth and early twentieth centuries, see Brereton, *Race Relations*; Brereton, *History of Modern Trinidad*, especially 82–95, 205; and Eric Williams, *History of the People of Trinidad and Tobago* (Port of Spain: PNM Publishing, 1962), 152–67. See also James Henry Collens, *A Guide to Trinidad*, 2nd ed. (London: E. Stock, 1888), 250–59, 273–79; and Chester Lloyd Jones, *Caribbean Interests of the United States* (New York: D. Appleton and Company, 1916), 41–45.

2. For examinations of politics in Trinidad during the late nineteenth and early twen-

tieth centuries, see Brereton, *Race Relations*; Brereton, *History of Modern Trinidad*, especially 136–53; Williams, *History of the People*, 168–96; and Alvin Magid, *Urban Nationalism: A Study of Political Development in Trinidad* (Gainesville: University of Florida Press, 1988).

3. James Anthony Froude, *The English in the West Indies Or, The Bow of Ulysses* (New York: Charles Scribner's Sons, 1888), 81, 88; J.J. Thomas, *Froudacity: West Indian Fables by James Anthony Froude Explained* (London: New Beacon Books, 1969 [1889]), 92; Algernon Albert Burkett, *Trinidad: "A Jewel of the West"* (London: Francis and Company Printers, [1914?]), 9, 17.

4. Brereton, *History of Modern Trinidad*; Williams, *History of the People*; Magid, *Urban Nationalism*. Elected members of the city council gradually replaced appointed members between 1914 and 1917. In this study, I use "colonial government" and "municipal government" to distinguish between the British administration of the colony of Trinidad and Tobago and the local administration of Port of Spain. Note that the governor and other top colonial officials comprised the government's executive council, in addition to serving on the larger legislative council.

5. For information on Goad and his business, see the *Dictionary of Canadian Biography Online*, accessed 28 April 2016, http://www.biographi.ca/009004-119.01-e.php?BioId=40860. Goad's *Insurance Plan of Port of Spain* is online in the Digital Library of the Caribbean, George A. Smathers Libraries, University of Florida. http://ufdc.ufl.edu/CA02000002.

6. Sellier advertisement, *Public Opinion*, 5 January 1895, 4; Morin advertisement, in *Stark's Guide-Book and History of Trinidad*, ed. James H. Stark (Boston: James H. Stark, 1897), unpaginated. For a historical study of postcards in the Caribbean, see John Gilmore, *Glimpses of Our Past: A Social History of the Caribbean in Postcards* (Kingston: Ian Randle, 1995).

7. Collens, *Guide to Trinidad*, (quotations, iv, 52). Collens arrived in Trinidad around 1876 and published the first edition of his *Guide* in 1886. While working on this book, he served as the superintendent of the Boys' Model and Normal School; later he was appointed the inspector of schools in Trinidad. He was also active in various community organizations and, from 1892 to 1915, compiled the *Trinidad Year Book*. See Brereton, *Race Relations*, 56.

8. Henry James Clark, *"Iere," The Land of the Humming Bird* (Port of Spain: Government Printing Office, 1893), 53.

9. J. Paget, *New Illustrated Guide to Trinidad* (Trinidad: Government Printing Office, 1901), 16, 20–21.

10. Robert T. Hill, *Cuba and Porto Rico, with the Other Islands of the West Indies* (New York: The Century Company, 1903), 367; Frederick A. Ober, *Our West Indian Neighbors* (New York: James Pott and Company, 1904), 411; Frederick A. Ober, *A Guide to the West Indies and Bermudas* (New York: Dodd, Mead and Company, 1908), 458.

11. Ida M.H. Starr, *Gardens of the Caribbees: Sketches of a Cruise to the West Indies and the Spanish Main* (Boston: L.C. Page and Company, 1904), 1:282, 285, 291. For a discussion of Starr and her book, see Aisha Khan, "Portraits in the Mirror: Nature,

12. Frederick Treves, *The Cradle of the Deep: An Account of a Voyage to the West Indies* (London: Smith, Elder, 1908), 57–58 ("main thoroughfares"), 59 ("most delightful"), 78 ("so prodigal").
13. A. Hyatt Verrill, *The Book of the West Indies* (New York: E.P. Dutton and Company, 1917), 146, 148–49.
14. Stephen N. Cobham, *Rupert Gray: A Tale in Black and White*, ed. Lise Winer (Kingston: University of the West Indies Press, 2006 [1907]). For background on Cobham, see the introduction by Bridget Brereton et al. (ix–lv). Quotations from the text: railway station, 7; at work, 14; Botanic Gardens, 51; with the countess, 55. While Rupert Gray embodies the progressiveness of Port of Spain, the novel's villain, Jacob Clarke, writes a letter to the British press that is a parody of local promotional literature: "The city stands on a plain sloping from northern and eastern heights down to the haven called the Gulf of Paria, an enormous mud-hole swarming with monsters.... Among the highlands overlooking the town roam fierce wild bulls... The town is close and hot, with low-roofed houses innocent of ventilation. ... The squares and thoroughfares are disagreeable through the abuse of ill-kept urinals" (89–90).
15. Approximations of the size of blocks and width of streets (along with many other details presented below) are from Goad, *Insurance Plan of Port of Spain*. On the paving and renaming of streets, see J.N. Brierley, *Trinidad: Then and Now* (Trinidad: Franklin's Electric Printery, 1912), 164–65; Ottley, *Story of Port of Spain*, 79; and Anthony, *The Making of Port-of-Spain*, 64, 73–74. Ordinance No. 32 of 1901 ("Relating to the re-naming of streets and re-numbering of houses in Port-of-Spain") is cited in *Trinidad and Tobago Blue Book, 1901–2* (Port of Spain: Government Printing Office, 1902), K1. For the sake of simplicity, I use post-1901 names throughout this study. After he arrived in Trinidad in 1874 to serve in the police force, one of J.N. Brierley's first assignments was to organize a police beat-patrol system for Port of Spain. He notes that this was greatly facilitated by the city's regular street grid (*Trinidad: Then and Now*, 126–27, 163).
16. Goodenough, "Race, Status and Residence", 38, 248, 258, 274. Goodenough notes that some of the residents of surrounding districts were included in the 1901 population for Port of Spain, even though these districts were not officially incorporated into the city until later (249). Brereton states that in 1891 the population of Port of Spain and surrounding areas was approximately fifty thousand, one quarter of the total population of Trinidad (*Race Relations*, 12).
17. Brereton, *Race Relations*, 14–15.
18. Collens, *Guide to Trinidad*, 78; "Arrival of Sir Hubert and Lady Jerningham", *POSG*, 3 June 1897, 5.
19. Collens, *Guide to Trinidad*, 27–29. On commerce with Venezuela, see Augustus, "Trinidad", *New York Observer and Chronicle*, 1 August 1895, 129–30; T.B. Jackson, ed., *The Book of Trinidad* (Port of Spain: Muir, Marshall and Company, 1904), 77–78; and Ober, *Our West Indian Neighbors*, 411. Jackson notes that "very many

companies engaged in Venezuela in trading, mining, or other industries have their headquarters in Trinidad" (78).

20. "Latest Shipping News", *Daily News*, 21 January 1895, 2; Hill, *Cuba and Porto Rico*, 367; *Trinidad and Tobago Blue Book, 1901–2*, W1–W2; James Henry Collens, ed., *Trinidad and Tobago Year Book, 1903* (Port of Spain: Government Printing Office, 1902), 168–69.

21. Editorial, *POSG*, 7 August 1907, 7. On the limitations of the harbour, see Louis A.A. de Verteuil, *Trinidad: Its Geography, Natural Resources, Administration, Present Conditions and Prospects*, 2nd ed. (London: Cassell and Company, 1884), 272. For debate on port improvements, see *POSG*, 28 April 1912, 6; 28 April 1912, 9; 7 May 1912, 9; 7 September 1912, 2; and *Argos*, 5 April 1918, 11; 21 July 1918, 7.

22. Collens, *Guide to Trinidad*, 64–65, 92–95; Brierley, *Trinidad: Then and Now*, 133–36; Mavrogordato, *Voices in the Street*, 38–39, 60–62; Anthony, *Making of Port-of-Spain*, 28; Anthony de Verteuil, *Temples of Trinidad* (Port of Spain: Litho Press, 2004), 28–35, 47. De Verteuil notes that the church was dedicated as a cathedral in 1851. For photographs, see "Roman Catholic Cathedral" on UWISpace, an online repository at the University of the West Indies at http://uwispace.sta.uwi.edu/dspace/.

23. See Stark, *Stark's Guide-Book*, for advertisements for stores on Marine Square; and Collens, *Guide to Trinidad*, 90–92, on the Royal Bank and Union Club. On the Union Club, see also Brereton, "White Elite of Trinidad", 58. For background on George Brown, see Mavrogordato, *Voices in the Street*, 122–24; Newel Lewis, *Ajoupa*, 189–203; and John Newel Lewis, "Trinidad and Tobago, Architecture", in *Dictionary of Art*, ed. Jane Turner (New York: Grove, 1996), 31:334–35. Named after the Demerara region of Guyana (formerly British Guiana), a Demerara window is a top-hinged louvred panel that can be propped open with a support. Note that, in this study, "first floor" and "first storey" refer to the second level of a building.

24. Collens, *Guide to Trinidad*, unpaginated advertisement following 259.

25. William F. Hutchinson, "The West Indies as a Sanitarium", *Times and Register*, 3 January 1891, 3; H.F. Abell, "The West Indies as a Winter Resort", *Westminster Review* 137, no. 1 (January 1892): 281.

26. *POSG*, 8 January 1914, 10; *POSG*, 22 December 1914, 12; "'Jazz' at Hotel McKinney", *Argos*, 22 November 1919, 5. In addition to serving travellers and the local populace, some of the hotels in downtown Port of Spain were a place of refuge and reconnoitring for individuals involved in political conflicts in nearby Venezuela. For example, a raid at the Hotel Orinoco on Broadway in 1914 uncovered thousands of rounds of ammunition, while ex-dictator Cipriano Castro was found hiding at a house in the city ("Smart Detective Work", *Argos*, 20 March 1914, 5). Towards the end of the cocoa boom era, *Argos* reported that hotels and other "places of amusement" were becoming increasingly popular with residents of the city: "So-called hotels, recreation clubs, dancing classes and a dozen and one other forms of attraction, are springing up like mushrooms in the heart of our city. Of course, it is alleged that at these places which are not confined to any particular element of the community dancing is a secondary consideration" ("Those Places of Amusement", *Argos*, 22 April 1918, 2).

27. Alfred Mendes, *The Autobiography of Alfred Mendes, 1897–1991*, ed. Michèle Levy (Kingston: University of the West Indies Press, 2002), 8; Mavrogordato, *Voices in the Street*, 49, 74; "Gambling on the Street", *POSG*, 7 January 1895, 3. Collens identifies the trees as *Terminalia catappa*, with a fruit that resembles an almond (*Guide to Trinidad*, 65). For a photograph after 1895, see "Almond Walk" (National Archives of the United Kingdom, CO 1069-392-68) on Flickr at https://www.flickr.com/.

28. For historical details on Columbus Square, see de Verteuil, *Trinidad: Its Geography*, 270; Collens, *Guide to Trinidad*, 66; and C.S. Assee, "The Old Memorial Squares of Port-of-Spain", *POSG*, 8 June 1924, 17.

29. Editorial, *POSG*, 6 March 1895, 2; "The Big Fire in Port of Spain", *New York Times*, 19 March 1895, 9; Stark, *Stark's Guide-Book*, 34–37.

30. Newel Lewis, *Ajoupa*, 195–97; Newel Lewis, "Trinidad and Tobago, Architecture", 334.

31. Stark, *Stark's Guide-Book*, 37–38. The Boston-based James Stark was an author and publisher of several guidebooks on the Caribbean.

32. Ibid., unpaginated advertisements and photographs; Verrill, *Book of the West Indies*, 149–50.

33. On the history of Brunswick Square and Holy Trinity Cathedral, see Collens, *Guide to Trinidad*, 64, 100–104; Brierley, *Trinidad: Then and Now*, 127–33; Anthony, *Making of Port-of-Spain*, 27–28; Newel Lewis, *Ajoupa*, 91–95; Mavrogordato, *Voices in the Street*, 55–57; Michael Anthony, *Historic Landmarks of Port of Spain* (Oxford: Macmillan, 2008), 23–25, 28–29; and de Verteuil, *Temples of Trinidad*, 47–54.

34. Editorial, *POSG*, 31 May 1910, 7 ("commendable move"); editorial, *POSG*, 4 August 1912, 3 ("lung of the city"); editorial, *POSG*, 5 October 1910, 7 ("beggars and loiterers"); editorial, *POSG*, 14 September 1910, 7 (on bandstand); Ottley, *Story of Port of Spain*, 87. In 1912 Brierley acknowledged the improvement of Brunswick Square from the "wretched condition" that he first encountered in 1874, but, like the *Gazette*, called for more work on its footpaths and the planting of flowerbeds and ornamental shrubs (*Trinidad: Then and Now*, 127–28).

35. On the history of the government buildings designed by Bridgens and Hahn, see Collens, *Guide to Trinidad*, 69–73; Newel Lewis, *Ajoupa*, 211–13; Mavrogordato, *Voices in the Street*, 72–73; and Judy Raymond, *The Colour of Shadows: Images of Caribbean Slavery* (Pompano Beach, FL: Caribbean Studies Press, 2016), 156–61. Born in coastal Venezuela to a family that had settled in Trinidad and was engaged in trading between the two, Hahn was educated in Hamburg and at the polytechnic university in Berlin. After two years of employment in England, he returned to Trinidad to join the Public Works Department. See Anthony de Verteuil, *The Germans in Trinidad* (Port of Spain: Litho Press, 1994), 41–42.

36. "Opening of the New Council Chamber", *POSG*, 5 February 1907, 4–5.

37. Collens, *Guide to Trinidad*, 81; "The Public Library", *POSG*, 15 June 1897, 5; Crain, *Historic Architecture*, 164–66; Anthony, *Historic Landmarks*, 32–36; Azrieli School of Architecture and Urbanism, *A Tale from the Old Library* (Ottawa: Azrieli School of Architecture and Urbanism, Carleton University, 2012), 16–25, 48–60. The Azrieli booklet contains extensive descriptions and photographs of the library's exterior and interior, as well as recommendations for its restoration.

38. See Municipality of Port-of-Spain, *Golden Jubilee of the Restoration, 1914–1964* (Port of Spain: Granderson Bros, 2003 [1964]), 23–24; and Mavrogordato, *Voices in the Street*, 102–3.
39. On the eastern side of downtown, particularly in the vicinity of Charlotte Street, there was also a concentration of Chinese residences, businesses and eventually associations. See Goodenough, "Race, Status and Residence", 160, 339; and Kim Johnson, *Descendants of the Dragon: The Chinese in Trinidad 1806–2006* (Kingston: Ian Randle, 2006), 62–73.
40. Collens, *Guide to Trinidad*, 91; editorial, *POSG*, 6 August 1913, 9. For a photograph of the old Eastern Market, see "Market House" (National Archives of the United Kingdom, CO 1069-392-38) on Flickr.
41. Mavrogordato, *Voices in the Street*, 85–87; Anthony, *Making of Port-of-Spain*, 59; Stark, *Stark's Guide-Book*, unpaginated advertisement.
42. Goodenough, "Race, Status and Residence", 109.
43. Brierley, *Trinidad: Then and Now*, 173; Ottley, *Story of Port of Spain*, 72, 78; editorial, *POSG*, 30 August 1907, 7; editorial, *POSG*, 24 November 1910, 7; "The Transformation of Shine's Pasture", *POSG*, 24 January 1914, 7.
44. Collens, *Guide to Trinidad*, 268–69.
45. Brierley, *Trinidad: Then and Now*, 136–37, 167–69; Mendes, *Autobiography*, 41–42; Ottley, *Story of Port of Spain*, 79; Port of Spain City Council, Minutes, 20 July 1914.
46. Collens, *Guide to Trinidad*, 247–48; Anthony de Verteuil and Miguel Browne, eds., *St. Mary's College, 1863–1988: 125th Anniversary* (Port of Spain: St Mary's College, 1988), 7–9; Brereton, "White Elite of Trinidad", 49.
47. Collens, *Guide to Trinidad*, 116–23. For photographs of the hospital, see "Colonial Hospital" on UWISpace.
48. "Queen's Park Not a Gift to Government", *Trinidad Guardian* (*TG*), 3 February 1943, 2; Mavrogordato, *Voices in the Street*, 53.
49. *POSG* quoted in Carlton Robert Ottley, *Trinidad Callaloo: Life in Trinidad from 1851–1900* (Diego Martin, Trinidad: Crusoe, 1978), 87 (see also 79–83); Verrill, *Book of the West Indies*, 154–55; Paget, *New Illustrated Guide*, 25–27; Mavrogordato, *Voices in the Street*, 54.
50. "Review of Local Forces", *POSG*, 12 April 1911, 5.
51. Clark, "*Iere*", 64; Collens, *Trinidad and Tobago Year Book, 1903*, 49–50; James Henry Collens, ed., *Handbook of Trinidad and Tobago* (Port of Spain: Government Printing Office, 1912), 22; "Fine Art in Trinidad", *Public Opinion*, 11 January 1895, 3; "The Fine Art Exhibition", *Daily News*, 17 January 1895, 2; "The Fine Art Exhibition", *Daily News*, 19 January 1895, 3; Mavrogordato, *Voices in the Street*, 96. Anthony de Verteuil (*Germans in Trinidad*, 43) says Daniel Meinerts Hahn, architect of the 1907 Red House, was responsible for an expansion of the Victoria Institute in 1897 – this may have been the addition that Collens dates as 1901. Antoine Léotaud, a collection donor noted by Clark, was a well-known physician and author of *Oiseaux de l'île de la Trinidad* (1866), a book in which he examined the bird species of Trinidad in comparison to those of Venezuela. For more on his career, see Selwyn R. Cudjoe, *Beyond Boundaries: The Intellectual Tradition of Trinidad and Tobago in*

the Nineteenth Century (Wellesley, MA: Calaloux, 2003), 168–72. In conjunction with Trinidad's commemoration of a century of British rule in 1897, L.M. Fraser, editor of the *Port-of-Spain Gazette* and a former chief of police, organized an exhibition at the Victoria Institute. Bridget Brereton describes this historical presentation as focused on governors and elite white families, with only three of approximately two hundred artefacts related to Afro-Trinidadians and none pertaining to Indo-Trinidadians ("Jubilees", 20–21).

52. Municipality of Port-of-Spain, *Golden Jubilee*, 41 (quotations on use); "Tattlings: The Illustrious Dr. Richards", *Argos*, 31 August 1911, 4; Prince's Building advertisement, *POSG*, 27 March 1914, 5. See also Mavrogordato, *Voices in the Street*, 78–79.

53. *Mirror*, 12 October 1912, quoted in Citizens' Committee of Port-of-Spain, *Souvenir: Silver Jubilee, Port-of-Spain City Council* (Port of Spain, 1939), 14–21 (quotations: resolutions, 15–16; Pointer, 18, 21). For more on the TWA and Joseph Pointer's visit to Trinidad, see Brinsley Samaroo and Cherita Girvan, "The Trinidad Workingmen's Association and the Origins of Popular Protest in a Crown Colony", *Social and Economic Studies* 21, no. 2 (1972): 205–22.

54. C.L.R. James, *Beyond a Boundary* (Durham: Duke University Press, 1993 [1963]), 23–24. For historical details on Queen's Royal College, see Williams, *History of the People*, 204–6; Mavrogordato, *Voices in the Street*, 114–15; Anthony, *Historic Landmarks*, 61–63; and Anthony de Verteuil with Adrian Camps-Campins, *The Great Eight* (Port of Spain: Anthony de Verteuil, 2015), 90–113.

55. "The Queen's Park Hotel", *Daily News*, 16 January 1895, 3; advertisement reprinted in Besson, *Photographic Album of Trinidad*, 111; Jackson, *Book of Trinidad*, 137; Ella Wheeler Wilcox, *Sailing Sunny Seas* (Chicago: W.B. Conkey Company, 1909), 228–29; Mavrogordato, *Voices in the Street*, 98–99. For photographs of Frederick Warner's house and its incorporation into the hotel, see de Verteuil, *Great Eight*, 36–37; and "Queen's Park Hotel" on UWISpace.

56. Collens, *Guide to Trinidad*, 58–62; Clark, "Iere", 57–60 (quotations, 57–58).

57. Lady Broome, "Colonial Memories", *Cornhill Magazine* 7, no. 38 (August 1899): 160–65 (quotation, 165).

58. Collens, *Guide to Trinidad*, 57–58; Elizabeth Bisland, "Life in an English Government House", *Harper's Bazaar* 28, no. 52 (28 December 1895): 1070; Broome, "Colonial Memories", 159–60; "The Government House Ball", *Argos*, 16 April 1914, 6. Collens says Government House was designed by a Mr Fergusson "on the Indian model" (57). In 1896 the building included a drawing room, ballroom, dining room, billiard room, smoking room, governor's office, seven bedrooms and five dressing rooms that could be used as additional bedrooms. See *Trinidad Blue Book, 1896* (Port of Spain: Government Printing Office, 1897), KK1.

59. Editorial, *Port-of-Spain Gazette*, 27 November 1910, 7.

60. On the settlement of East Dry River, see Goodenough, "Race, Status and Residence", 77, 119–22, 187–89; Goodenough, "Race, Status and Ecology", 21; Roy Mc Cree, "History and Development", in *Behind the Bridge: Poverty, Politics and Patronage in Laventille, Trinidad*, ed. Selwyn Ryan, Roy Mc Cree and Godfrey St Bernard (St Augustine, Trinidad: Institute of Social and Economic Research,

University of the West Indies, 1997), 33–44; and Bridget Brereton, "EPOS and Cultural Heritage: Historical Framework", unpublished manuscript for the University of the West Indies, St Augustine, RDIF Project "Leveraging Built and Cultural Heritage for Economic Development in East Port of Spain", 2013, 1–7.

61. Brereton, "EPOS and Cultural Heritage", 8; Treves, *Cradle of the Deep*, 66; National Trust of Trinidad and Tobago, *The Built Heritage of Trinidad and Tobago* (Port of Spain: National Trust of Trinidad and Tobago, 2012), 52–53; de Verteuil, *Temples of Trinidad*, 38–44, 143–49.

62. Wood, *Trinidad in Transition*, 240; Mavrogordato, *Voices in the Street*, 70–71; Goodenough, "Race, Status and Residence", 120; Andrew Carr, "A Rada Community in Trinidad", *Caribbean Quarterly* 3 (1953): 35–48.

63. Ottley, *Story of Port of Spain*, 78, 84; Goodenough, "Race, Status and Residence", 185–89, 276–77; editorial, *Mirror*, 6 April 1910, 4; editorial, *POSG*, 20 May 1910, 4 (quotations); editorial, *POSG*, 30 November 1910, 7.

64. Trotman, *Crime in Trinidad*, 158. On Leon Agostini and Coblentz, see Mavrogordato, *Voices in the Street*, 89–90, 121–22; Brereton, *Race Relations*, 51, 61; and Anthony de Verteuil, *The Corsicans in Trinidad* (Port of Spain: Litho Press, 2005), 145–66.

65. On the development of St Clair, see Mavrogordato, *Voices in the Street*, 92–93; and Colin Laird, "Trinidad Town House", *Caribbean Quarterly* 3, no. 4 (1954): 188–98. For discussions of the Maraval Road mansions and their owners, see Mavrogordato, *Voices in the Street*, 103–13; Newel Lewis, *Ajoupa*, 237–61 (quotation, 259); and de Verteuil, *Great Eight*. De Verteuil compiles numerous photographs, including images of the houses' boundary railings (116–17), and notes that many of their furnishings were made by local craftsmen (56–57). While Mavrogordato and Laird date the government purchase of the St Clair Estate to 1884, Goodenough ("Race, Status and Residence", 115) and Anthony (*Making of Port-of-Spain*, 86) cite 1879.

66. "St. Clair Experimental Station: A Pleasant Survey of Its Area", *POSG*, 12 February 1911, 2; and editorial, *POSG*, 15 October 1911, 3.

67. Goodenough, "Race, Status and Residence", 113–14; Anthony, *Making of Port-of-Spain*, 35, 51; Mavrogordato, *Voices in the Street*, 67, 75; de Verteuil, *Great Eight*, 44, 51; "Carnival Bands at Practice", *TG*, 23 February 1919, 4–5.

68. Paget, *New Illustrated Guide*, 27; editorial, *POSG*, 27 November 1910, 7; Wild West show advertisement, *Argos*, 23 March 1914, 6–7. On the development of Woodbrook, see editorial, *POSG*, 3 November 1911, 9; Ottley, *Story of Port of Spain*, 78; Municipality of Port-of-Spain, *Golden Jubilee*, 38–40; Goodenough, "Race, Status and Residence", 277–78; Mavrogordato, *Voices in the Street*, 64–65; and Anthony, *Making of Port-of-Spain*, 103–5, 110.

69. Mavrogordato, *Voices in the Street*, 58–59.

70. Augustus, "Port of Spain", *New York Observer and Chronicle*, 15 August 1895, 193–94. Another travel account of Peru Village appears in Starr, *Gardens of the Caribbees*, 292–95. Goodenough reports that Hosay was first held in the village in 1863 ("Race, Class and Residence", 163); and Ottley includes a description of the event in 1896 from the *Port-of-Spain Gazette* (*Trinidad Callaloo*, 85–86). During the 1870s and

1880s, Hosay processions were also held in downtown Port of Spain (see Cudjoe, *Beyond Boundaries*, 230–31). For a historical and ethnographic overview of this tradition, see Frank J. Korom, *Hosay Trinidad: Muharram Performances in an Indo-Caribbean Diaspora* (Philadelphia: University of Pennsylvania Press, 2003). On the Port of Spain City Council's discussion of annexation of St James, see "City Council: Expansion of the City", *TG*, 28 November 1919, 9. Annexation statistics are included in Port of Spain City Council, *City of Port of Spain Silver Jubilee, 1914–1939* (Port of Spain, 1939), 36. For a general sketch of the history of St James, see Anthony, *Making of Port-of-Spain*, 231–35. For a photograph of St James in the early twentieth century, see "Coolie Town, St. James" (GoldF3_118B) on UWISpace.

Chapter 2

1. Editorial, *POSG*, 27 November 1910, 7.
2. On the infrastructure and annexation of the districts surrounding central Port of Spain, see Williams, *History of the People*, 173–74; and Goodenough, "Race, Status and Residence", 272–82, 569. For a discussion, at the end of the cocoa boom era, on the possibility of annexing St James, see "City Council: Expansion of the City", *TG*, 28 November 1919, 9.
3. Goad, *Insurance Plan of Port of Spain*; Girod, *Plan of Port of Spain and Suburbs*; Trinidad and Tobago, Lands and Surveys Department, *Port of Spain* (Trinidad: Lands and Surveys Department, 1931).
4. De Verteuil, *Trinidad: Its Geography*, 273–74; Goad, *Insurance Plan of Port of Spain*; *Commission of Enquiry into the Recent Disturbances at Port of Spain, Trinidad* (London: His Majesty's Stationery Office, 1903), 15–19; Williams, *History of the People*, 174, 180–81 (quotation of 1881 report, 180); de Verteuil, *Great Eight*, 9–11; Rita Pemberton, "Water and Related Issues in Nineteenth-Century Trinidad", *Journal of Caribbean History* 40, no. 2 (2006): 235–52; editorial, *Mirror*, 1 June 1914, 4.
5. On sewers, see Municipality of Port-of-Spain, *Golden Jubilee*, 8; Ottley, *Story of Port of Spain*, 58, 80; and Goodenough, "Race, Status and Residence", 276–84. On the Dry River, see editorial, *POSG*, 1 July 1908, 7; "The Dry River", *POSG*, 6 February 1910, 3; editorial, *POSG*, 30 November 1910, 7; "Legislative Council: Dry River Improvement Scheme", *POSG*, 16 January 1912, 7; and editorial, *POSG*, 2 November 1912, 9 (quotation). On street drains, see Brierley, *Trinidad: Then and Now*, 163–65 (quotation, 164).
6. Victor Smith, "Trinidad", *Chautauquan* 10, no. 4 (January 1890): 452; Ottley, *Story of Port of Spain*, 80; Goodenough, "Race, Status and Residence", 100, 279; Municipality of Port-of-Spain, *Golden Jubilee*, 12.
7. Ottley, *Story of Port of Spain*, 62–63; Anthony, *Making of Port-of-Spain*, 60; "The Electric Light", *POSG*, 7 March 1895, 2; "Electrical Systems, Port-of-Spain", Council Paper No. 168, *Trinidad Royal Gazette, July to December 1898* (Port of Spain: Government Printing Office, 1899), 2533–42; Electric Company advertisement in Jackson, *Book of Trinidad*, unpaginated; editorial, *POSG*, 26 May 1907, 7.

8. Collens, *Guide to Trinidad*, 271; Collens, *Handbook of Trinidad and Tobago*, 30; Ottley, *Trinidad Callaloo*, 54–55 (quotation, 55); Anthony, *Making of Port-of-Spain*, 66, 71; Mavrogordato, *Voices in the Street*, 48–49; Allen Morrison, "The Trams and Trolleybuses of Trinidad and Tobago", accessed 1 May 2016, http://www.tramz.com/tt/tt.html. The various routes of Port of Spain's electric trams are indicated on the Lands and Surveys Department's 1931 map of the city. Morrison's website includes many valuable photographs and historical details. He notes that Port of Spain had one of the earliest electric tram systems in Latin America and the Caribbean, preceded only by Nuevo Laredo, Rio de Janeiro and Panama City.
9. Goad, *Insurance Plan of Port of Spain*.
10. Newel Lewis, *Ajoupa*, 11, 14, 200–201, 289–91.
11. Ibid., 200–201, 257, 293; Taylor and Gillies advertisement in Jackson, *Book of Trinidad*, unpaginated.
12. Houses of this type appear in archival photographs and can still be observed in various neighbourhoods of Port of Spain, though they are increasingly being demolished.
13. Newel Lewis, *Ajoupa*, 221, 225. Newel Lewis includes drawings of various gingerbread houses on 220–28.
14. For additional information on these three well-known houses and their original occupants, see Newel Lewis, *Ajoupa*, 191–93, 251–52; Mavrogordato, *Voices in the Street*, 116–17, 119–20; Anthony, *Historic Landmarks*, 51, 56, 60; and de Verteuil, *Great Eight*, 63–89. An in-depth study of the Boissière house (with numerous photographs and drawings) is presented in Azrieli School of Architecture and Urbanism, *A Tale of Two Houses* (Ottawa: Azrieli School of Architecture and Urbanism, Carleton University, 2011). Floor plans show a drawing room, dining room, bedrooms and a study in the house, along with an outbuilding (13 feet to the south) with a kitchen, storage room and bathing facilities, including a Roman bath (18–19). This booklet also contains a detailed study of a smaller gingerbread house that was built in 1920 on Piccadilly Street, at the eastern edge of downtown. For a post-independence photograph of Knowsley, see "Knowsley" (GoldF6_13A) on UWISpace. For further discussion of elite houses in Port of Spain, see Laird, "Trinidad Town House", 188–98. Laird argues that these detached townhouses were derived from the designs of plantation houses.
15. On tapia construction, see Goodenough, "Race, Status and Residence", 123; Newel Lewis, *Ajoupa*, 83, 171–72; and Ruskin Punch, "Trinidadian: Indian", in *Encyclopedia of Vernacular Architecture of the World*, ed. Paul Oliver (Cambridge: Cambridge University Press, 1997), 3:1723. For an excellent examination of the characteristics of barrack yards, see James Cummings, *Barrack-Yard Dwellers* (St Augustine, Trinidad: School of Continuing Studies, the University of the West Indies, 2004), especially xv–28. See also Goodenough, "Race, Status and Residence", 101, 104, 259–63. Goodenough says Port of Spain's barracks were generally built during the 1870s and 1880s (259). In *Inward Hunger: The Education of a Prime Minster* (London: André Deutsch, 1969), Eric Williams notes that in 1911 barracks constituted 40 per cent of the rooms in Port of Spain, typically furnished with "the bed of boards without mattress, the box substitute for chairs, the tin cup, the absence of knives and forks, the oil lamp or candle, the coal pot" (17).

16. Editorial, *POSG*, 20 April 1909, 7.
17. Editorial, *Mirror*, 31 January 1910, 4.
18. 1912–13 tuberculosis report quoted in Cummings, *Barrack-Yard Dwellers*, 7–8; "City Council Meeting", *Argos*, 29 August 1918, 4.
19. "Barrack Yard Nuisances", *POSG*, 1 June 1910, 7; "A Disorderly Quarter", *POSG*, 4 December 1910, 3; editorial, *POSG*, 7 February 1913, 9; editorial, *POSG*, 29 May 1913, 11.
20. Editorial, *Argos*, 31 August 1918, 2.
21. "Arrival of Sir Hubert and Lady Jerningham", *POSG*, 3 June 1897, 5 (quotations on cheering crowds); "Address of the Municipality", *POSG*, 3 June 1897, 3 (quotations of town clerk and governor). See also "Our New Governor", *POSG*, 2 June 1897, 5.
22. Advertisements, *POSG*, 1 June 1897, 1–2; "Jubilee Sunday", *POSG*, 22 June 1897, 6–7 (quotation on orchestra, 6); "Diamond Jubilee Celebration", *POSG*, 24 June 1897, 2; "The Diamond Jubilee Ball", *POSG*, 27 June 1897, 5 (quotation on Government House). For a discussion of Queen Victoria's 1887 golden jubilee, as well as the 1897 event, see Brereton, "Jubilees", 5–12.
23. "Coronation of King George V", *POSG*, 25 June 1911, 2 (quotation on sailor king); "The Coronation Celebration", *POSG*, 25 June 1911, 6 (quotation on cathedral); "Trinidad Since the Royal Visit", *POSG*, 22 June 1911, 5. According to Collens, the Light Horse Volunteers consisted mainly of planters, while the Light Infantry Volunteers comprised mainly clerks and artisans (*Handbook of Trinidad and Tobago*, 37).
24. "Addresses on the Savannah", *POSG*, 25 June 1911, 7 (quotations); "Coronation Sports" and "The Brigades and the Schools", *POSG*, 25 June 1911, 9. The East Indian National Association was founded in 1897 in Princes Town in southern Trinidad (see Brereton, *History of Modern Trinidad*, 109–10, 115). For more on friendly societies, see a lecture delivered by Chas. H.A. Attale in 1910 at the Victoria Institute ("Victoria Institute", *Mirror*, 26 May 1910, 4). Attale noted that friendly societies, which focused on medical and funeral benefits, were derived from England, emerged in Trinidad in the early 1870s and began to prosper after the passing of the Friendly Societies Ordinance in 1888. He cited approximately 124 societies registered in Trinidad (with a total membership of about eleven thousand) and asserted: "As a member of a Friendly Society I take pride in stating that these Societies have stood the test of time, and have succeeded to such an extent as to demonstrate the fact that our people can unite for good and are capable of managing their own affairs." David Trotman cites 160 friendly societies with bank deposits in 1910 (see *Crime in Trinidad*, 111).
25. Editorial, *POSG*, 29 June 1911, 9.
26. "Monday, The Official Celebration", *POSG*, 26 May 1909, 5; editorial, *Argos*, 23 May 1914, 1. See also *POSG*, 26 May 1909, 4–5; and *POSG*, 26 May 1912, 5, 10.
27. *Commission of Enquiry*, 15–23; Williams, *History of the People*, 180–81; K.O. Laurence, ed., "The Trinidad Water Riot of 1903: Reflections of an Eyewitness", *Caribbean Quarterly* 15, no. 4 (1969): 7, 21. The commission of enquiry into the Water Riot was carried out on behalf of the secretary of state for the colonies. Three commissioners

arrived in Port of Spain in late April 1903 and remained for almost a month, during which they examined 146 witnesses concerning the riot and its surrounding circumstances. Their thirty-two-page report included extensive details about the incident and its context. However, the local public perceived the commissioners to be biased towards the colonial officials (see Laurence, "Trinidad Water Riot", 20). For an in-depth discussion of water management in Port of Spain, the riot and its aftermath, see Magid, *Urban Nationalism*, 105–60.

28. *Commission of Enquiry*, 25; Laurence "Trinidad Water Riot", 20; Brereton, *History of Modern Trinidad*, 149.
29. "The Water Question", *POSG*, 10 March 1903, 4 ("terms of the proposed"); *Commission of Enquiry*, 22–23, 27–29 ("Higher rates", 28); Laurence, "Trinidad Water Riot", 7. In addition to the public opposition to ticketing, the commission determined that approximately half of the tickets were given to government clerks (24). For additional coverage of the mass meetings and general opposition to the ordinance, see *POSG*, 14 March 1903, 7; 15 March 1903, 4–5; 17 March 1903, 4–6; and 22 March 1903, 4–5, 7.
30. *Commission of Enquiry*, 4–12 ("Come to the Red House", 6); "Water Question in Legislative Council", *POSG*, 25 March 1903, 4–6.
31. *Commission of Enquiry*, 24–25, 31–32 ("taken refuge", 25). For additional perspectives on the events, see editorials in the *POSG*, 26 March 1903, 4; and 27 March 1903, 7.
32. See Samaroo and Girvan, "Trinidad Workingmen's Association", 205–22; Brereton, *History of Modern Trinidad*, 157–61; and Kelvin Singh, *Race and Class Struggles in a Colonial State: Trinidad 1917–1945* (Kingston: The Press, University of the West Indies, 1994), 14–23.
33. "Our Returned Heroes", *POSG*, 27 May 1919, 13; "When Our Boys Came Home", *Argos*, 26 May 1919, 5–6B ("clinging on", 5); Anthony, *Making of Port-of-Spain*, 116.
34. "Peace Celebrations", *Argos*, 20 July 1919, 6; "The Peace", *POSG*, 20 July 1919, 10. On the opposition of many returned soldiers to the peace-day celebration at the Savannah, see Tony Martin, "Revolutionary Upheaval in Trinidad, 1919: Views from British and American Sources", *Journal of Negro History* 58, no. 3 (1973): 315.
35. "The Attacks on Sailors", *POSG*, 25 July 1919, 11; editorial, *Argos*, 26 July 1919, 2. See also "Clash Yesterday", *Argos*, 22 July 1919, 2.
36. "Industrial Situation", *TG*, 15 November 1919, 8; "The Shipping Strike", *TG*, 16 November 1919, 16; "The Strike Situation", *TG*, 18 November 1919, 9; "The Stevedores' Strike", *TG*, 26 November 1919, 6; "The Shipping Strike", *TG*, 2 December 1919, 8 (quotations).
37. "The Strike Situation", *TG*, 3 December 1919, 6; "The Strike", *TG*, 4 December 1919, 8 (quotation). See also "Intimidating the Government", *Argos*, 6 December 1919, 7.
38. Editorial, *TG*, 4 December 1919, 8; editorial, *TG*, 6 December 1919, 8; editorial, *TG*, 7 December 1919, 8 ("responsible men"). The *Trinidad Guardian* also reported on other strikes in the city that month (5 December 1919, 8–9), while the *Argos* noted that some city council workers and shop clerks had gone on strike in November (21 November 1919, 5; 26 November 1919, 5). A report on the chamber of commerce meeting appears in *TG*, 7 December 1919, 9. For discussions of the 1919 strikes in

Port of Spain and beyond, see also Samaroo and Girvan, "Trinidad Workingmen's Association", 213–15; Tony Martin, "Revolutionary Upheavals"; Brereton, *History of Modern Trinidad*, 160–65; and Singh, *Race and Class Struggles*, 22–36. Martin notes that, by 11 December, the Colonial Vigilantes included 270 members, recruited mainly from the businessmen's Union Club on Marine Square (323–24). One of the publications targeted by the Sedition Ordinance was Marcus Garvey's *Negro World*. Brereton observes that sailors brought Garveyite literature into Trinidad (161), while Martin writes that the TWA "maintained close ties with Garveyism until the 1930's" (317).

Chapter 3

1. See *Trinidad and Tobago Disturbances 1937, Report of Commission* (London: His Majesty's Stationery Office, 1938), 12–25; Williams, *History of the People*, 216, 226–30; Brereton, *History of Modern Trinidad*, 199–209; and Singh, *Race and Class Struggles*, 158–59. On sugar production in 1933, see "Trinidad Produces Record Sugar Crop", *TG*, 9 July 1933, 1. On the Pointe-à-Pierre viaduct, see *Trinidad: The Riviera of the Caribbean* (Port of Spain: Trinidad Publishing, 1924), 77.

2. Algernon Aspinall, *The Pocket Guide to the West Indies* (London: Sifton, Praed, 1923), 112; "Crude Oil Output Gains in Trinidad", *New York Times*, 6 March 1932, E8; *Trinidad and Tobago Disturbances 1937*, 12. While trade statistics offer a sense of economic change in Trinidad during the interwar era, an overview of the economy's spatial organization was published in 1927 by Preston James, a geographer at the University of Michigan. Working in the regional landscape tradition of Berkeley geographer Carl Sauer, James examined the interrelationship of Trinidad's diverse natural environmental/climatic conditions and its cultural patterns. He defined cocoa, sugar, coconut, oil/asphalt and other regions across the island, and described how Port of Spain functioned as the port for agricultural products and the anchor of a highway and settlement strip that ran east along the piedmont of the northern mountain range. In addition, James considered the effects of the fall in cocoa prices in 1920–1921 and noted that some farmers were shifting to other crops, such as coconuts, coffee, fruits, rubber and sugar. He further observed that the prosperity of the cocoa industry affected economic conditions throughout Trinidad and, on the basis of communication with a former professor at Trinidad's Imperial College of Tropical Agriculture, argued: "Interesting correlations may be worked out between the yield of cacao, and the earnings of merchants, the earnings of the street railway in Port of Spain, the purchase of jewelry, and many other things." See James, "Geographic Reconnaissance of Trinidad", 87–109 (quotation, 101).

3. See Williams, *History of the People*, 216–21; Selwyn Ryan, *Race and Nationalism in Trinidad and Tobago: A Study of Decolonization in a Multiracial Society* (Toronto: University of Toronto Press, 1972), 28–35; Brereton, *History of Modern Trinidad*, 164–68; and Singh, *Race and Class Struggles*, 124–27.

4. "Representative Government", *Labour Leader*, 9 August 1924, 7; "Representative

Government", *Labour Leader*, 13 September 1924, 5 ("surging mass"); "The Cipriani Election Campaign", *Labour Leader*, 10 January 1925, 7.

5. "Trinidad's First General Election", *TG*, 8 February 1925, 11; Williams, *History of the People*, 221.

6. See *Trinidad and Tobago Disturbances 1937*; Williams, *History of the People*, 221–38; Ryan, *Race and Nationalism*, 35–69 (quotations, 38); Brereton, *History of Modern Trinidad*, 168–90; and Singh, *Race and Class Struggles*, 131–85. The workers' protests of the 1930s are discussed in more detail in chapter 4 of the present book. See also C.L.R. James's first book, *The Life of Captain Cipriani: An Account of British Government in the West Indies* (Nelson, UK: Coulton, 1932). In the context of a general analysis of colonial society and politics, James offers an account of Cipriani's leadership in the West Indies Regiment, his efforts in the legislative council and his work in the Port of Spain City Council, where he also spent many years. James asks: "What sort of people are these who live in the West Indies and claim their place as citizens and not as subjects of the British Empire?" (10). For a brief interview with Cipriani during the latter part of his period of major influence, see Owen Rutter, *If Crab No Walk: A Traveller in the West Indies* (London: Hutchinson and Company, 1933), 113–15. The strikes and protests in Trinidad during the 1930s were part of a larger movement of demonstrations that swept across the British Caribbean during this decade. A royal commission of inquiry led by Lord Moyne visited various territories during 1938 and 1939 and its report became a framework for colonial policy in the region during the 1940s. See Singh, *Race and Class Struggles*, 186–91.

7. Port of Spain City Council, *City of Port of Spain Silver Jubilee*, 36 and unpaginated map. It appears that the 2,382 acres cited for 1938 do not include land added by reclamation during harbour improvements. On population trends, see also Goodenough, "Race, Status and Residence", 248–49.

8. "Special St. James Bill Soon", *TG*, 21 February 1937, 1; "St. James Inclusion Draft Bill Ready", *TG*, 19 March 1937, 1–2; editorial, *TG*, 29 May 1937, 6; editorial, *TG*, 10 November 1937, 6; "St. James Inclusion Tomorrow", *TG*, 31 May 1938, 1; "Port of Spain Becomes Largest City in British West Indies", *TG*, 2 June 1938, 2; Port of Spain City Council, *City of Port of Spain Silver Jubilee*, 34–36. The *Port-of-Spain Gazette* reported that on the day of incorporation "many market women who could not restrain their feelings of happiness were heard asking the question – 'Are we actually living in Port-of-Spain?'" ("Port-of-Spain's New Suburb", 2 June 1938, 4).

9. De Verteuil, *Temples of Trinidad*, 177–78. An early postcard photograph of the Haji Gokool Meah Masjid appears as "Mohammedan Mosque, St. James Village" (GoldF7_3C) on UWISpace. On Hosay in St James during the 1930s, see "Temple Thrown in the Sea", *TG*, 7 May 1933, 2; Ivy Achoy, "Celebration of 'Hosein' Festival Ends", *TG*, 26 April 1934, 1–2; and "Hosay Festival Ends", *TG*, 3 March 1939, 3 (includes photograph of tadjahs). In addition to the mosque in St James, Muslims erected the Jama Masjid at Queen Street and the Dry River in 1941–1942. Designed, built and funded in part by Mohammed Ibrahim (a baker), this structure featured a balustraded roof, towers with domes in a variety of shapes and extensive windows. Its prominent downtown location and unusual design inspired numerous postcard

photographs. See de Verteuil, *Temples of Trinidad*, 185–87, for historical details and UWISpace for images. Meanwhile, Hindus in St James did not build a major mandir until the late 1950s/early 1960s. Before this, they worshipped in small temples and in their homes (see de Verteuil, *Temples of Trinidad*, 211–12).

10. L'Inconnu, "Town Planning", *POSG*, 16 March 1924, 10; editorial, *TG*, 25 July 1934, 8; editorial, *TG*, 6 October 1934, 6.

11. "Town Planning Expert Coming", *TG*, 24 January 1937, 1; "Town Plan Expert", *TG*, 7 March 1937, 1; "Town Planning Board Formed", *TG*, 17 March 1937, 1 ("advise Government"); editorial, *TG*, 7 July 1937, 8; editorial, *TG*, 8 October 1938, 8; editorial, *TG*, 9 December 1938, 6; "Orderly Town-Planning Designed in New Bill", *TG*, 17 December 1938, 6 ("secure orderly"), 11. See also Robert Home, "Transferring British Planning Law to the Colonies: The Case of the 1938 Trinidad Town and Regional Planning Ordinance", *Third World Planning Review* 15, no. 4 (1993): 397–410. Home argues that Trinidad's 1938 Town and Regional Planning Ordinance served as a model for similar legislation in other British colonies in the Caribbean and West Africa. He notes that R.B. Walker obtained a diploma in town planning and civic architecture from the University of Liverpool, and at the time was one of the few town planners who had both practical knowledge of the 1932 English Planning Act and previous experience working in a colony (Nigeria) (400, 409). While officials pursued town planning in Trinidad during the 1930s, other observers also continued to offer their recommendations. In June 1938, for example, a writer calling himself "Pericles" recounted a "reverie" in the *Trinidad Guardian* in which he rebuilt and beautified various districts of Port of Spain in his mind ("Port-of-Spain Can Be Made into the Gem City of the Caribbean", 5 June 1938, 2).

12. Editorial, *TG*, 6 December 1924, 8; *Trinidad: The Riviera of the Caribbean*; "Trinidad's Biggest Tourist Season Nearly Ended", *TG*, 26 March 1933, 1, 3; Wilson Minshall, "Scenery Brings Dollars to Everyone", Christmas Magazine, *TG*, 5 December 1937, 12; editorial, *TG*, 10 January 1937, 4; "Respectable Educated Tourists Guides Urged by City Mayor", *TG*, 17 January 1937, 2. A much smaller version of *Trinidad: The Riviera of the Caribbean* was published in 1919.

13. Algernon Aspinall, *A Wayfarer in the West Indies*, 2nd ed. (London: Methuen, 1930), 66, 68, 70–71; A. Hyatt Verrill, *West Indies of Today* (New York: Dodd, Mead and Company, 1931), 185, 187; Rutter, *If Crab No Walk*, 43, 47–48, 50.

14. Edric Connor, *Horizons: The Life and Times of Edric Connor, 1913–1968* (Kingston: Ian Randle, 2007), 1–41 (quotations, 27–28, 29). Whe whe is an illegal form of lottery that was brought to Trinidad by Chinese immigrants.

15. Editorial, *Labour Leader*, 25 June 1924, 6.

16. Editorial, *POSG*, 28 June 1924, 11; "History of the Trinidad War Memorial", *TG*, 27 June 1924, 5.

17. See "Trinidad's War Memorial", *POSG*, 29 June 1924, 7; and numerous photographs of the monument and park on UWISpace. At the unveiling ceremony, the bronze statue of the standing soldier was holding a rifle. This statue also appears in most photographs of the monument over the course of its history. However, some photographs from the interwar era show a different soldier – one with a rifle strapped

to his back. It is possible that the original statue was damaged at some point and that a substitute was temporarily employed. After World War II, "1939–1945" was added to the front inscription to redefine the memorial and honour the soldiers who served in that conflict as well. Except for this addition, the memorial appears today essentially as it did in 1924.

18. "Trinidad's War Memorial", 7.
19. Roslyn also used winged Victory figures for several other British memorials, including the Blackley War Memorial (unveiled May 1921), the Buxton Memorial (unveiled September 1920), the Bexhill War Memorial (unveiled December 1920), the Greengates War Memorial (unveiled November 1921), and the Wetherby War Memorial (unveiled April 1922). For details on the first of these, a photograph of the figure and a brief biographical note on Roslyn, see Terry Wyke with Harry Cocks, *Public Sculpture of Greater Manchester, Public Sculpture of Britain* (Liverpool: Liverpool University Press, 2004), 8:139–40, 460. See the Louis Frederick Roslyn article on Wikipedia for photographs and dates of the other monuments, as well as additional biographical details. Vintage photographs of the full Oswaldtwistle War Memorial appear in "Red Rose Collections", an online archive of the Lancashire County Council (see https://redrosecollections.lancashire.gov.uk/).
20. See "Trinidad's War Memorial", 7; and photographs in UWISpace. An article in the *Labour Leader* on 26 July 1924 suggests that the paving of the walkways and the park fence were incomplete at that time ("Memorial Park", 8).
21. Editorial, *POSG*, 28 June 1924, 11 ("striking gracefulness"); "Trinidad's War Memorial", 7 ("Mother Church"); editorial, *Labour Leader*, 25 June 1924, 6.
22. Editorial, *TG*, 26 June 1924, 8; A.S. Bowen, letter to the editor, *TG*, 27 June 1924; "Trinidad's War Memorial", 7. On recruitment for the Merchants and Planters' Contingent and the British West Indies Regiment at the beginning of the war, see James, *Life of Captain Cipriani*, 24–26.
23. "Trinidad's War Memorial", 7 (quotations on assembly and mayor's promise); "Trinidad War Memorial", *TG*, 29 June 1924, 11.
24. L'Inconnu, "A Day of Remembrance", *POSG*, 29 June 1924, 11; editorial, *TG*, 16 July 1924, 6 ("should salute"); editorial, *TG*, 22 July 1924, 8 ("been observed"); "Armistice Anniversary", *TG*, 12 November 1924, 11. The memorializing of Trinidadians lost in the war extended beyond the monument at Memorial Park. Queen's Royal College and St Mary's College both erected small memorials in their school grounds for collegians who died while serving. See "Queen's Royal College War Memorial", *TG*, 8 July 1924, 9; and "St. Mary's College", *TG*, 5 October 1924, 11.
25. Trinidad and Tobago, Lands and Surveys Department, *Port of Spain* (Trinidad: Lands and Surveys Department, 1931); "The New Railway Station", *Labour Leader*, 9 July 1924, 5. On train, tram and automotive transport, see editorial, *TG*, 19 February 1924, 8; editorial, *TG*, 4 January 1925, 10; and editorial, *TG*, 22 February 1925, 10. Debate concerning the railway continued in the 1930s. See, for example, editorial, *TG*, 14 May 1933, 6; and "Road vs. Rail in Trinidad", *TG*, 13 June 1933, 8.
26. "St. Mary's College", *TG*, 5 October 1924, 11 (quotations); "St. Mary's College", *TG*, 7 October 1924, 3. Revival architecture and scientific advancement were similarly

combined in a 1925 building for the Imperial College of Tropical Agriculture. The college was an institution of higher learning and research that had opened in 1922 at St Augustine, approximately eight miles east of Port of Spain. It offered courses in agricultural education for students from throughout the West Indies and the British empire. Designed in a neoclassical style by H.C. Corlette, a British architect, the new two-storey flat-roofed building was constructed with reinforced concrete and steel beams. Columns lined a central block with galleries, while pilasters continued the scheme on wings on either side. The building contained laboratories for agronomy, botany, entomology, mycology and chemistry, as well as a lecture hall, classroom, library and offices. For a description, plan and photograph, see "Imperial College of Tropical Agriculture", *TG*, 17 February 1925, 7; and "Imperial College of Tropical Agriculture", *TG*, 18 February 1925, 5. In 1960 the college became the Trinidad campus of the University College of the West Indies.

27. "City's Reconstruction Drive Progresses", *TG*, 4 July 1933, 3; "Port-of-Spain Extends in All Directions", *TG*, 29 April 1934, 1–2; "Building Boom in Trinidad", *TG*, 4 July 1934, 1; "Building Costs Soar", *TG*, 14 March 1937, 1; "Port-of-Spain Is Expanding Eastward", *TG*, 20 August 1939, 4.

28. On the career of Herbert G.W. Brinsley, see Sidney Rodin, "'Rogue Song' Metro's Opening Film", Metro Theatre Special Issue, *TG*, 12 March 1933, 1; "Bishop's High School Hall Opened", *TG*, 28 April 1933, 3; "Ultra-Modern Architecture Comes to Port-of-Spain", *TG*, 1 July 1934, 1–2; "Local Material to Be Used in Erection of Electricity Board's New Office", *TG*, 2 June 1938, 2 (photograph, 1); and various articles cited below. Among Brinsley's projects in England, before migrating to Trinidad, was the London Guarantee and Accident Company building in Lincoln's Inn Fields. The date cited for the construction of the new San Fernando Town Hall is 1930 in Michael Anthony, *Towns and Villages of Trinidad and Tobago* (Marabella, Trinidad: Printmaster, 2001), 259.

29. "New $40,000 'Garage' Expected to Be Erected on Edward Street This Year", *TG*, 12 May 1934, 1; "Ultra-Modern Architecture", 1–2 (drawing by Brinsley of the Neal and Massy Garage, 2); "Imposing New Commercial Building to Be Erected on Marine Square", *TG*, 5 October 1934, 1. A design drawing of the Alston building in this last article shows a front elevation with flat rather than stepped roofs. Another downtown Art Deco structure of this period was the McEnearney and Company building at Richmond and Charles Streets. See Gérard A. Besson, *The History of the ANSA McAL Group of Companies* (Port of Spain: ANSA McAL, 2006), 86–87 (photograph, 91).

30. "Ultra-Modern Architecture", 1–2 (quotations, 1).

31. "Plans for New Treasury", *TG*, 17 May 1933, 1; "Plans for a New Treasury" (drawing), *TG*, 1 September 1933, 2; "New Treasury Building Plans", *TG*, 24 May 1934, 1; "New Treasury Building to Cost £74,000", *TG*, 5 October 1934, 1; "New Treasury Ahead of Schedule", *TG*, 18 February 1937, 1; "New Treasury to Be Completed This Year", *TG*, 16 June 1937, 9; "Treasury Building Makes Rapid Progress", *TG*, 24 November 1937, 3; E.G. Lytton Anderson, "Our New Treasury", Christmas Magazine, *TG*, 5 December 1937, 27, 30; "Audit Department Moving into New Treasury Building",

TG, 1 June 1938, 2; "'Grey House' Move in Occupants", *TG*, 18 October 1938, 11. Carlton Ottley says the cornerstone for the Treasury was laid on 8 March 1936 (see *Story of Port of Spain*, 89). On stripped classical/modern classic architecture, see Robert M. Craig, "Modern Classic in American Architecture", *Grove Art Online, Oxford Art Online*, Oxford University Press, accessed 8 May 2016, http://www.oxfordartonline.com/subscriber/article/grove/art/T2085956.

32. *Trinidad: The Riviera of the Caribbean*, 24–25; "Queen's Park Hotel", *TG*, 21 December 1924, 10.

33. Alex Waugh, *Hot Countries* (New York: Farrar and Rinehart, 1930), 187–96; Rutter, *If Crab No Walk*, 45–46; John W. Vandercook, *Caribbee Cruise: A Book of the West Indies* (New York: Reynal and Hitchcock, 1938), 260.

34. "City Hotel Makes Big Plans", *TG*, 21 March 1937, 1; "Council Debate Hotel Extension Plans", *TG*, 27 May 1938, 7; The Humming Bird, "Talk of Trinidad", *TG*, 27 January 1939, 4.

35. Brown's portfolio in South Florida included both Mediterranean Revival and Art Deco projects. See an unpaginated directory in Ivan A. Rodriguez and Margot Ammidown, *From Wilderness to Metropolis: The History and Architecture of Dade County, Florida, 1825–1940* (Miami: Franklin Press, 1982); and the architectural database "Miami Beach Art Deco Historic District", https://www.ruskinarc.com/mdpl/ArtDecoDistrict.

36. "Q.P.H. to Become Most Magnificent Hotel in WI", Christmas Magazine, *TG*, 11 December 1938, 9, 59 (quotations, 9); Amy Oakley, *Behold the West Indies* (New York: D. Appleton-Century Company, 1941), 395–96. The back cover of the 1938 *Trinidad Guardian* Christmas Magazine includes a colour drawing by William Brown of the new hotel addition embedded in the older structures. For a collection of photographs, advertisements and historical notes on the Queen's Park Hotel from its opening in 1895 to its demolition in 1996, see Michael Rego, *Queen's Park Hotel, Port of Spain, Trinidad*, West Indies History Booklet No. 2 (Wakefield, UK: Michael Rego, 2009). While working on the Queen's Park Hotel addition, William Brown also served as the architect for the Macqueripe Hotel, which began construction in August 1938. This beachside luxury complex was on Trinidad's northwest coast, some ten miles from Port of Spain. In contrast to his Art Deco Queen's Park Hotel, Brown designed the large three-storey Macqueripe Hotel in a Spanish Mission Revival style, similar to the Mediterranean Revival architecture that was also popular in Miami. Brown's colour drawing for the front cover of the 1938 *Trinidad Guardian* Christmas Magazine shows this hotel perched on a densely wooded hillside, with additional facilities below on the beach. See also "Seaside Hotel at Macqueripe", Christmas Magazine, *TG*, 11 December 1938, 8.

37. "Lindbergh Party Reaches Trinidad", *New York Times*, 23 September 1929, 1; "Clipper Reaches Trinidad", *New York Times*, 21 July 1936, 15; Anthony, *Making of Port-of-Spain*, 135, 149, 244; Mavrogordato, *Voices in the Street*, 99. The Pan American 1934 contract and 1944 letter are housed in the Pan American World Airways, Inc., Records, 1927–1991 (Box 562, Folder 16) at the Special Collections of the University of Miami Libraries.

38. On the London, see advertisement, *Mirror*, 1 February 1911, 3; "The London Electric Theatre", *Mirror*, 3 February 1911, 6 (quotations); advertisement, *POSG*, 27 March 1914, 5; Ivy Achoy, "Onward March of Cinemas in Trinidad", Pictorial Christmas Supplement, *TG*, 9 December 1934, 11; and "Can Nine Cinemas Pay in Port-of-Spain?" Christmas Magazine, *TG*, 5 December 1937, 16. On the Olympic, see advertisement, *TG*, 17 February 1920, 14; and Mendes, *Autobiography*, 67. Ivy Achoy, a cinema correspondent for the *Trinidad Guardian*, offers detailed notes on Trinidad cinemas from 1911 to 1934. Along with comments on the London and the Olympic, she observes that the American George Rosenthal arrived in Trinidad in 1916, leased the St Ann's Hall in Port of Spain, and called it the "City Cinema". There he screened serial thrillers, which attracted patrons from the London. Lynne Macedo notes that moving pictures were first exhibited in Trinidad at the Prince's Building, between 1900 and 1910. See "The Impact of Indian Film in Trinidad", in *Beyond the Blood, the Beach and the Banana: New Perspectives in Caribbean Studies*, ed. Sandra Courtman (Kingston: Ian Randle, 2004), 298. For a brief overview of Port of Spain's cinema scene from the 1910s to the 1930s, see also Anthony, *Making of Port-of-Spain*, 177–80, 207.

39. *Trinidad: The Riviera of the Caribbean*, 28–29; "Scenery for New Theatre", *TG*, 9 June 1920, 7; "Empire Theatre", *TG*, 25 September 1920, 14 (quotation); "Empire Theatre", *TG*, 26 September 1920, 9; Achoy, "Onward March of Cinemas", 11. Achoy reports that, before Rosenthal established the Empire, films were screened in a tarpaulin tent at the corner of Edward Street and Tragarete Road, the location that later became the theatre's pit entrance.

40. "City Super-Cinema to Open in March", *TG*, 1 February 1933, 2; "Palatial New 'Metro' Cinema to Open on March 11", *TG*, 23 February 1933, 1–2; Rodin, "'Rogue Song' Metro's Opening Film", 1 (quotations); "Fewer Seats for the Metro", *TG*, 17 March 1933, 1; Ivy Achoy, "'House Full' Tonight at Opening of Metro", *TG*, 18 March 1933, 1–2; Anthony, *Making of Port-of-Spain*, 179–80. For biographical details on Nur Mohammed Gokool, see Lloyd Sydney Smith, ed., *Trinidad: Who, What, Why* (Port of Spain: n.p., 1950), 259. On the renaming of the Metro, see "New Name for Metro", *TG*, 11 February 1934, 2.

41. Achoy, "'House Full' Tonight", 1–2; advertisement, *TG*, 18 March 1933, 12; Film Correspondent, "Brilliant Scenes at First Night of Metro", *TG*, 19 March 1933, 1; The Humming Bird, "Talk of Trinidad", *TG*, 21 March 1933, 5. An advertisement for Tucker Picture Productions in the *Guardian* on 19 March 1933 (22) describes the company as "The All-Trinidad Journal of the Screen". An advertisement in *The People* on 29 April 1933 (2) proclaims that Tucker films are "Trinidad's Own Motion Pictures" and "as good as those made abroad", while adding that patrons should demand them when visiting their cinemas. Ivy Achoy says Tucker began exhibiting newsreels of local events in 1925 and that his films give "Trinidad a chance to see herself as others see her" ("Onward March of Cinemas", 11).

42. Smith, *Trinidad: Who, What, Why*, 86; Mavrogordato, *Voices in the Street*, 110; "City's Sixth Cinema to Open on Saturday", *TG*, 11 October 1934, 1 (quotation on Roxy sign); "New St. James Cinema Christened", *TG*, 13 October 1934, 1, 3; "The

Mayor Presides at Roxy Premiere Last Night", *TG*, 14 October 1934, 1, 6 (quotation of Cipriani, 1). A photograph of the Roxy appears in an advertisement in the *Trinidad Guardian*, 23 May 1937, 24–25.

43. "New Theatre Open Last Night", *TG*, 7 March 1937, 1; "The Governor to Attend Opening Show of Royal Cinema Tonight", *TG*, 22 May 1937, 6; "Cinema Premiere", *TG*, 27 May 1937, 1 (includes photograph of the De Luxe); "New Cinema Opens", *TG*, 1 June 1937, 8 (quotations on interior); De Luxe advertisement, *TG*, 1 June 1937, 9. Another photograph is featured in "The New De Luxe Theatre", *POSG*, 30 May 1937, 6. See Achoy on the founding of the British Colonial Film Exchange ("Onward March of Cinemas", 11).

44. On the pricing of different theatres in Port of Spain, see "Can Nine Cinemas Pay", 16. On the Cinematograph Ordinance and the debate it generated, see editorial, *TG*, 14 September 1933, 6; and Gordon Rohlehr, *Calypso and Society in Pre-Independence Trinidad* (Port of Spain: Gordon Rohlehr, 1990), 285–86 (Teelucksingh quotation, 286). See Achoy ("Onward March of Cinemas", 11) for her comment on the imitation of Hollywood stars. By the 1930s, a few theatres in Port of Spain were also screening films from India (see Macedo, "Impact of Indian Film", 302). By 1938 10 per cent or less of all films (features and shorts) exhibited in Trinidad were British. See Kim Johnson, *From Tin Pan to TASPO: Steelband in Trinidad, 1939–1951* (Kingston: University of the West Indies Press, 2011), 143.

45. "New Harbour at Port of Spain", Business and Finance, *The Times* (London), 12 October 1939, 14. The most extensive account of the Deep Water Harbour Scheme is "Trinidad's Gateway to the World", Christmas Magazine, *TG*, 5 December 1937, 8, 10. Other sources include "£1,000,000 'Deep Water Harbour' Loan Approved by Secretary for Colonies", *TG*, 23 September 1933, 1; "Trinidad Merchants Denounce Proposed Deep Water Harbour", *TG*, 29 September 1933, 3; "Trinidad Harbor Plan Approved", *New York Times*, 23 March 1934, 13; "Port of Spain to Deepen Harbor", *New York Times*, 24 November 1934, 7; "New Quay Wall to Be Finished This Month", *TG*, 20 October 1938, 1; "New 3,300ft Quay Wall Completed", *TG*, 2 November 1938, 2; "Harbour Works Completion Set for August 31", *TG*, 27 January 1939, 4; "New Quay Busy as 'Governor' Loads Sugar", *TG*, 17 February 1939, 1. For photographs, see "Port of Spain Harbour Works" (National Archives of the United Kingdom, CO 1069-396-8) on Flickr.

46. Editorial, *TG*, 7 July 1937, 8; "Town Planner's Scheme Approved", *TG*, 17 September 1937, 1; drawing by office of R.B. Walker, *TG*, 8 October 1938, 1; "Modern Avenue Along Wrightson Road Planned", *TG*, 19 February 1937, 2; "Wrightson Road Beautifying Scheme Begins", *TG*, 2 November 1938, 7; "Wrightson Road Extension", *TG*, 3 November 1938, 1; Bridget Brereton and Primnath Gooptar, *Ranjit Kumar (1912–1982): Bridging the East and West* (Trinidad: n.p., 2013), x–xi, 57–65. In addition to discussing Kumar's various engineering projects, Brereton and Gooptar examine other dimensions of his multifaceted career, including service on both the Port of Spain City Council and the legislative council. For visual documentation of the 1930s land reclamation and expansion of Wrightson Road, compare Trinidad and Tobago, Lands and Surveys Department, *Port of Spain* (1931) with Trinidad and

Tobago, Lands and Surveys Department, *Sketch Map of Port of Spain* (Trinidad: Director of Surveys, c. 1945).

47. On general municipal projects, see "Improvements for City in 1938", *TG*, 7 December 1937, 2; Port of Spain City Council, *City of Port of Spain Silver Jubilee*; and Citizens' Committee of Port-of-Spain, *Souvenir: Silver Jubilee*. On the Dry River project, see editorial, *TG*, 20 July 1934, 6; and Port of Spain City Council, *City of Port of Spain Silver Jubilee*, 30–32. This booklet includes a discussion and diagrams concerning the superiority of the city engineer's scheme to that of an earlier one proposed by the colonial government's consulting engineer from England.

48. Port of Spain City Council, *City of Port of Spain Silver Jubilee*, 32–33; Municipality of Port-of-Spain, *Golden Jubilee*, 33. See also James, *Life of Captain Cipriani*, 71–78.

49. "Port-of-Spain Tramway System Doomed", *TG*, 5 March 1937, 1, 2; "City Council Vote for Trolley Buses", *TG*, 19 October 1938, 1, 8; editorial, *TG*, 14 September 1941, 6; Morrison, "Trams and Trolleybuses".

50. "City Council Plans Jubilee Celebration", *TG*, 2 June 1939, 5; "Trees to Mark City Council Jubilee", *TG*, 2 August 1939, 3; "21 Trees Planted to Mark Jubilee", *TG*, 3 August 1939, 3; "Trinidad Spends Full Discovery Week-end", *TG*, 9 August 1939, 1; "Governor Lauds City's Work", *TG*, 9 August 1939, 3, 12 (quotation of Cipriani); "'Atilla the Hun' Wins Jubilee Calypso Contest", *TG*, 10 August 1939, 3; "Silver Jubilee Celebrations Closed", *TG*, 11 August 1939, 5.

51. Port of Spain City Council, *City of Port of Spain Silver Jubilee* (quotation, 29). A group calling itself the "Citizens' Committee of Port-of-Spain" also published a commemorative booklet in 1939: *Souvenir: Silver Jubilee, Port-of-Spain City Council*. This group comprised supporters of Alfred Richards, a current city councillor, former mayor and rival of Mayor Cipriani.

52. "City Council Pays Tribute to Retiring Engineer", *TG*, 1 May 1941, 12. Before migrating to Trinidad, Scott served as city engineer of Inverness, Scotland. In addition to directing the construction of the war memorial, the paving of the Dry River, and numerous other municipal projects, he assisted a variety of community organizations in Port of Spain.

Chapter 4

1. *Trinidad and Tobago Blue Book, 1935* (Trinidad: A.L. Rhodes, MBE, Government Printer, 1936), 331 (1931 statistics); "New Village in Port-of-Spain?" *TG*, 23 June 1933, 2; *Trinidad and Tobago Disturbances 1937*, 41 (quotation of medical specialist). For a general discussion of housing in Port of Spain during the first half of the twentieth century, see also Goodenough, "Race, Status and Residence", 248–316.

2. Populations of barrack dwellers are cited in Singh, *Race and Class Struggles*, 112. Population densities in 1931 are shown in a map in Goodenough, "Race, Status and Residence", 270.

3. James Cummings, "Barrack-Rooms", in *From Trinidad: An Anthology of Early West Indian Writing*, ed. Reinhard W. Sander (London: Hodder and Stoughton, 1978),

240–44. For biographical notes on Cummings, see Sander, *From Trinidad*, 303–4; and Albert Gomes, *Through a Maze of Colour* (Port of Spain: Key Caribbean, 1974), 23–24. After being involved in Trinidad's emerging trade-union movement, Cummings migrated in 1957 to England, where he pursued his education and worked for many years as a government officer in community relations. In 2004, seventy-three years after the appearance of "Barrack-Rooms" in *The Beacon*, he published in Trinidad a comprehensive book on barrack yards and their occupants: *Barrack-Yard Dwellers*. In addition to discussing various types of barrack structures and the social characteristics of their inhabitants, he examines typical adult and children's pastimes, religious practices, bush medicine and the general ambience of downtown Port of Spain.

4. Editorial, *Argos*, 14 January 1920, 3; editorial, *TG*, 29 January 1920, 8; editorial, *TG*, 17 April 1920, 8; "Poor of the City", *TG*, 26 November 1924, 9; editorial, *Labour Leader*, 14 September 1929, 8.

5. In an impassioned speech to the city council in 1937, Mayor Alfred Richards offered many details on the history of government housing plans from 1916 to the present (see "Mob Scenes in City Council", *TG*, 15 June 1937, 1–2). See also Singh, *Race and Class Struggles*, 112–13. Coverage of the South Quay Workers' Homes and additional plans at the time is included in editorial, *Labour Leader*, 16 May 1931, 8; and editorial, *Labour Leader*, 4 July 1931, 8.

6. "Emergency Call to Wipe Out Slums", *TG*, 17 February 1933, 2; "City Barracks 'Atrocities' Revealed", *TG*, 8 June 1933, 3.

7. Editorial, *TG*, 6 May 1933, 6; "Government's Plan for Slum Clearance", *TG*, 21 June 1933, 1; "City Council Attack Government Housing Scheme", *TG*, 22 June 1933, 1; editorial, *TG*, 18 February 1934, 6; "300 Citizens Demand Acceptance of Housing Scheme", *TG*, 7 July 1933, 2; "The Workers Badly Let Down", *The People*, 22 July 1933, 6; "Municipal Morality", *The People*, 29 July 1933, 10–11.

8. "Government and City Council Agree on Slum Clearance Scheme", *TG*, 10 May 1934, 1; "City Council Appoints Representatives on Slum Clearance Commission", *TG*, 11 May 1934, 1–2; "Mob Scenes in City Council", 1–2; *Trinidad and Tobago Blue Book, 1935*, 98. For photographs of the Gonzales Place houses, see *TG*, 3 June 1937, 1; *POSG*, 2 June 1937, 6; *POSG*, 3 June 1937, 6; and Port of Spain City Council, *City of Port of Spain Silver Jubilee*, following 32. As of 2014, many of these houses remain in Gonzales Place.

9. "Workers' Town Empty for Year", *TG*, 4 February 1937, 1; "Slum Clearance Policy Change", *TG*, 21 April 1937, 1–2, 14; editorial, *TG*, 30 May 1937, 6; "Trinidad Last Week", *TG*, 6 June 1937, 3; "The Mayor and Deputy-Mayor Clash", *TG*, 22 January 1937, 2, 8. For a photograph of a yard in Slum Clearance Block No. 1, see Port of Spain City Council, *City of Port of Spain Silver Jubilee*, following 32. On barrack-yard dwellers' perceptions of Gonzales Place as a remote and unfamiliar area, see Cummings, *Barrack-Yard Dwellers*, 150–51.

10. "Surprise Visit to Clearance Areas", *TG*, 27 May 1937, 1; "Motor Lorries to Move Slum Families", *TG*, 30 May 1937, 1; "Rent of Workers' Homes at Gonzales Place Reduced", *TG*, 30 May 1937, 5; "Slum Dwellers to Move Tomorrow", *TG*, 1 June

1937, 1; "Slum Move Out Starts Today", *TG*, 3 June 1937, 1–2. In a report dated 16 June 1937, Dr Achong included Gaston Johnston's name among those landlords who had received closing orders, adding that he thought some of these individuals might "become afflicted either with inertia or forgetfulness" (see "Closing Orders Issued to 'Slum' Owners", *TG*, 18 June 1937, 2). For a photograph of Fletcher, Nankivell and Achong visiting a slum yard, see Citizens' Committee, *Souvenir: Silver Jubilee, Port-of-Spain*, 48.

11. "Slum Dwellers to Move Tomorrow", 1; "More City Slum Areas to Be Cleared", *TG*, 16 June 1937, 1; "Mayor Unwilling to Delve to Root of Slum Problem", *TG*, 11 June 1937, 3; "Mob Scenes in City Council", 1–2 (quotations: banners, 1; Gooding, 2).

12. *Trinidad and Tobago Disturbances 1937*, 35–36, 83; "Island-Wide Housing Plan", *TG*, 23 December 1937, 1, 15; editorial, *TG*, 26 December 1937, 6; "Slum Clearance and Housing Bill Passed by Legislative Council", *TG*, 10 December 1938, 2, 4; Michael Anthony, *Port-of-Spain in a World at War, 1939–1945* (Port of Spain: Ministry of Sport, Culture and Youth Affairs, n.d.), 29–31. For a general discussion of housing programmes in the British Caribbean, see Richard Harris, "The Evolution of Urban Housing Policy in the British West Indies, 1929–1960s", in Jaffe, *Caribbean City*, 43–68. Harris (58–59) argues that housing initiatives were motivated by local unrest, increased British funding and US pressure (with housing in Puerto Rico serving as an example).

13. Collens, *Handbook of Trinidad and Tobago*, 17; "City Poor Deprived of Shelter", *Labour Leader*, 2 May 1931, 11. On Audrey Jeffers, see Rhoda E. Reddock, *Women, Labour and Politics in Trinidad and Tobago: A History* (London: Zed Books, 1994), 164–81, 238–40; and Innette Cambridge, "Audrey Jeffers: Key to Trinidadian Philanthropic and Social Service Heritage", in *Caribbean Heritage*, ed. Basil A. Reid (Kingston: University of the West Indies Press, 2012), 175–94. The dates for the founding of the coterie's institutions are from Reddock; Cambridge offers some slightly different years. The quotation from Jeffers appears in Anthony, *Port-of-Spain in a World at War*, 32.

14. Mendes, *Autobiography*, 76, 85 (quotation). For a selection of short stories, poetry and commentary from *Trinidad* and *The Beacon*, see Sander, *From Trinidad*. Sander also offers an introduction to and biographical notes on the Beacon group writers in this volume and provides an in-depth study in *The Trinidad Awakening: West Indian Literature of the Nineteen-Thirties* (Westport, CT: Greenwood, 1988).

15. Mendes, *Autobiography*, 11–19, 26–29, 41–43, 64–75 (quotation, 64–65).

16. Sander, *From Trinidad*, 7 (Mendes quotation); Mendes, *Autobiography*, 76–103, 130–39; Aldous Huxley, "Introduction to the 1934 Edition", in *Pitch Lake: A Story from Trinidad*, by Alfred Mendes (London: New Beacon Books, 1980 [1934]), 7. See also Levy's introduction and chronology in *Autobiography of Alfred Mendes*, xv–xxxi, 168–73.

17. James, *Beyond a Boundary*, 3–34; Paul Buhle, *C.L.R. James: The Artist as Revolutionary* (London: Verso, 1988), 7–28; Paget Henry and Paul Buhle, eds., *C.L.R. James's Caribbean* (Durham: Duke University Press, 1992), 17–27, 56–62, 271–73.

18. Gomes, *Through a Maze of Colour*, 3–53 (quotations, 5, 16, 19, 40). See also Brinsley Samaroo, foreword to *Through a Maze of Colour*, by Gomes, ix–xvi.
19. C.L.R. James, "Triumph", in Sander, *From Trinidad*, 86–103 (quotation, 88).
20. Alfred Mendes, "Sweetman", in Sander, *From Trinidad*, 118–30 (quotation, 122).
21. Alfred Mendes, "Her Chinaman's Way", in Sander, *From Trinidad*, 103–18.
22. Alfred Mendes, *Black Fauns* (London: New Beacon Books, 1984 [1935]). Descriptions: yard, 88–90 (quotation, 90); bush bath, 52–55 (quotation, 52); wake and funeral procession, 100–113, 127–28. Another male visitor to the yard is Mr de Pompignon, the well-dressed and smooth-talking agent for the yard's owner. Pompignon extracts rent from the women, scolds them for their contentiousness, and courts the young Martha.
23. C.L.R. James, *Minty Alley* (London: New Beacon Books, 1971 [1936]). Ella quotation, 21; references to "Victoria Street", 55, 244; description of No. 2 Minty Alley, 26; Mrs Rouse quotation, 237.
24. Mendes, *Pitch Lake*. Joe quotation on leaving San Fernando, 46; description of cottage, 50–55 (quotations, 50, 55); reference to Sacred Heart Church, 63; Joe quotation on dress suit, 63.
25. "1931 May Day Celebration", *Labour Leader*, 9 May 1931, 4. William Howard Bishop was a past general secretary of the TWA and publisher of the *Labour Leader*.
26. "T.W.A. Meeting", *The People*, 22 April 1933, 11 (quotations); "Trinidad May Day Celebration", *The People*, 13 May 1933, 2, 9–12. *The People*, a new newspaper published and edited by Leonard Fitzgerald Walcott, launched in April 1933. In "Workers All", the editorial in its inaugural issue, the paper said "workers" was "a term that embraces all classes of men and women in this Island" and added that "we intend to agitate continuously for better living conditions for that section of workers that is least able to give expression to its views" (*The People*, 15 April 1933, 4). The periodical indeed became a strong advocate of working-class issues, as well as the concerns of people of African descent.
27. "Emancipation Week Starts in Trinidad", *TG*, 29 July 1934, 1, 12; "Trinidad Celebrates Emancipation in Pulpit and Park", *TG*, 31 July 1934, 1; "Trinidad Workers Celebrate Centenary of Emancipation of Slavery", *TG*, 31 July 1934, 3 ("the air tingles"); editorial, *TG*, 1 August 1934, 6 ("forget origin"); "Crowds Witness Masked Pageantry at the Oval", *TG*, 2 August 1934, 9. For coverage of 1933 centenary events, see *The People*, 5 August 1933, 2, 6, 12; and *The People*, 12 August 1933, 6–7.
28. "Big Demonstration of Workers", *The People*, 24 June 1933, 9; "Constabulary Break Up Unemployed March on the Red House", *TG*, 20 June 1933, 3 (banner messages). Comrade Alexander was the individual who, at a TWA meeting two months earlier, had advocated a longer route for the May Day march.
29. "Unemployed Labourers Stage Demonstrations in Sugar Districts", *TG*, 21 July 1934, 1, 3; editorial, *TG*, 26 July 1934, 6; Brereton, *History of Modern Trinidad*, 171.
30. Rhoda E. Reddock, *Elma François: The NWCSA and the Worker's Struggle for Change in the Caribbean* (London: New Beacon Books, 1988) 1–18 (quotation, 11); Reddock, *Women, Labour and Politics*, 135–38.

31. Brereton, *History of Modern Trinidad*, 171–73; Reddock, *Elma François*, 14–15; Reddock, *Women, Labour and Politics*, 135–38.

32. Reddock, *Elma François*, 18–22; Kevin A. Yelvington, "The War in Ethiopia and Trinidad, 1935–1936", in *The Colonial Caribbean in Transition: Essays on Postemancipation Social and Cultural History*, ed. Bridget Brereton and Kevin A. Yelvington (Kingston: The Press, University of the West Indies, 1999), 208–14 (placard messages, 209).

33. "Oilfield Strikers Clash with Police", *TG*, 20 June 1937, 1, 13; "Oilfield Strikes under Control", *TG*, 22 June 1937, 1, 2; "Ajax Arrives: Exeter Due Today", *TG*, 23 June 1937, 1, 4; *Trinidad and Tobago Disturbances 1937*, 57–74. For discussions of the 1937 strikes and protests, see Ryan, *Race and Nationalism*, 44–67; W. Richard Jacobs, "The Politics of Protest in Trinidad: The Strikes and Disturbances of 1937", *Caribbean Studies* 17, nos. 1–2 (1977): 5–54; Brereton, *History of Modern Trinidad*, 177–88; Roy E. Thomas, ed., *The Trinidad Labour Riots of 1937: Perspectives 50 Years Later* (St Augustine, Trinidad: Extra-Mural Studies Unit, University of the West Indies, 1987); and Singh, *Race and Class Struggles*, 158–85.

34. "City Strike", *TG*, 23 June 1937, 1 (quotation), 4; *Trinidad and Tobago Disturbances 1937*, 65.

35. "All Quiet in City", *TG*, 24 June 1937, 1; "Strike 'Peace' Negotiations Open", *TG*, 25 June 1937, 1–2; "Lightermen Strike Delays Shipping", *TG*, 25 June 1937, 1–2; "City Scavengers Get a 50 Per Cent Wage Increase", *TG*, 26 June 1937, 2; "'Bus Strike Continues", *TG*, 27 June 1937, 1, 13; "8-Hour Day for Skilled Government Labour", *TG*, 1 July 1937, 1–2; "City Strikers Drifting Back to Work", *TG*, 2 July 1937, 1; "Longshoremen Report for Work", *TG*, 3 July 1937, 1–2.

36. *Trinidad and Tobago Disturbances 1937*, 6–7, 66, 72, 81 (quotation), 107. On Fletcher and Nankivell, see Brereton, *History of Modern Trinidad*, 182–83; and Singh, *Race and Class Struggles*, 173–74.

37. Arthur Calder-Marshall, *Glory Dead* (London: Michael Joseph, 1939), 13–14.

38. Ibid., 12, 18. For a biographical sketch of Calder-Marshall and a brief assessment of his writing, see Phil Baker, "Arthur Calder-Marshall", in *Oxford Dictionary of National Biography*, ed. H.C.G. Matthew and Brian Harrison (Oxford: Oxford University Press, 2004), 36:831–33. Calder-Marshall was twenty-nine when he arrived in Trinidad. He was joined by his wife for the last three weeks of his visit (Calder-Marshall, *Glory Dead*, 160).

39. Calder-Marshall, *Glory Dead*, 23–86 (quotations: interactions on Frederick Street, 42; at the Cambridge, 76).

40. Ibid., 144–45; Mendes, *Autobiography*, 84–85; Edgar Mittelholzer, *With a Carib Eye* (London: Secker and Warburg, 1958), 11. In his comments on travel literature about the Caribbean, Mittelholzer does not identify Calder-Marshall or de Boissière by name. Sander notes the dates for the publication of *Callaloo* and *Picong* (*From Trinidad*, 304).

41. Calder-Marshall, *Glory Dead*, 98–121. Following 112 are photographs of a barrack yard, substandard detached houses, new workers' dwellings at Gonzales Place and a decrepit larger house that has been subdivided.

42. Ibid., 146–75, 206–9, 213–21 (quotation, 207).
43. Ibid., 176–84.
44. Ibid., 93 ("something corrupt"), 238 ("position in the structure"), 284 ("creative force").
45. Melville J. Herskovits and Frances S. Herskovits, *Trinidad Village* (New York: Octagon Books, 1964 [1947]), v–viii (quotation, v). For biographical details on Melville Herskovits and a bibliography, see Alan P. Merriam, "Melville Jean Herskovits, 1895–1963", *American Anthropologist* 66 (1964): 83–109. A note on the death of Frances Herskovits appears in "Notes and News", *Africa: Journal of the International African Institute* 42 (1972): 334. For a historical discussion of the Yoruba-derived Shango/Orisha religion in Trinidad, see David V. Trotman, "Reflections on the Children of Shango: An Essay on a History of Orisa Worship in Trinidad", *Slavery and Abolition* 28, no. 2 (2007): 211–34. Trotman observes that there was a relatively small percentage of Yorubas in Trinidad during the pre-1834 slavery era and argues that Orisha worship took shape between 1839 and 1869, when the British released Africans (including Yorubas) from the slave ships of other countries and brought them to the Caribbean to work on plantations. In Trinidad, the Yoruba reconstituted their communities, especially near urban centres (218). While at present the religion is generally referred to as "Orisha" or "Orisa" (after the term used for Yoruba deities or spiritual powers), it was typically called "Shango" during the 1930s. Trotman suggests that an emphasis on the powerful orisha of Shango may have been an attempt to unify this religion of many deities in a manner similar to earlier efforts by the rulers of the city of Oyo to consolidate their control of Yorubaland through the use of Shango (218–19). For another historical examination of Yoruba cultural traditions in Trinidad, see Maureen Warner-Lewis, *Guinea's Other Suns: The African Dynamic in Trinidad Culture* (Dover, MA: Majority Press, 1991; repr., Kingston: University of the West Indies Press, 2015).
46. Herskovits and Herskovits, *Trinidad Village*, v–vii, 23 (quotation), 256–317. For an examination of the Herskovitses' fieldwork in Trinidad, their audio recordings, and their documentation of Margaret Buckley, see *Peter Was a Fisherman: The Trinidad Field Recordings of Melville and Frances Herskovits*, vol. 1, notes by Donald R. Hill et al. (Rounder CD 1114, 1998, compact disc).
47. Herskovits and Herskovits, *Trinidad Village*, 326–27, 335 (quotation, 326).
48. Ibid., 327–33.
49. Ibid., 333–39 (quotation, 339). On the song for Eshu, see *Peter Was a Fisherman*, track 12.
50. Herskovits and Herskovits, *Trinidad Village*, 321–26.
51. The Shango compound described by the Herskovitses bears some resemblance to traditional extended family compounds in Yorubaland, which also combine multiple enclosed and open spaces for a variety of activities. See John Michael Vlach, "Affecting Architecture of the Yoruba", *African Arts* 10, no. 1 (1976): 48–53, 99. For three diagrams that show the continuation of asymmetrical, multifunctional Orisha yards in late twentieth-century Trinidad, see James T. Houk, *Spirit, Blood, and Drums: The Orisha Religion in Trinidad* (Philadelphia: Temple University Press, 1995), 151–53. In Trinidad, an Orisha tent is also called a *palais* (palace).

Chapter 5

1. Andrew Pearse, "Carnival in Nineteenth-Century Trinidad", *Caribbean Quarterly* 4 (1956): 180–187.
2. For discussions of the jamettes and their bands, see ibid., 188–89; Brereton, *Race Relations*, 166–70; Trotman, *Crime in Trinidad*, 167–69, 181–82; and John Cowley, *Carnival, Canboulay and Calypso: Traditions in the Making* (Cambridge: Cambridge University Press, 1996), 72–80. While the term "jamette" referred to both males and females in the nineteenth century, it was later restricted to disreputable women.
3. For discussions of kalinda and Pierrots, see Errol Hill, *The Trinidad Carnival: Mandate for a National Theatre* (Austin: University of Texas Press, 1972), 25–30; Jacob D. Elder, "Color, Music and Conflict: A Study of Aggression in Trinidad with Reference to the Role of Traditional Music", *Ethnomusicology* 8 (1964): 128–36; Jacob D. Elder, "Kalinda: Song of the Battling Troubadours of Trinidad", *Journal of the Folklore Institute* 3 (1966): 192–203; Andrew Carr, "Pierrot Grenade", *Caribbean Quarterly* 4 (1956): 281–82; Rohlehr, *Calypso and Society*, 52–54; Donald R. Hill, *Calypso Calaloo: Early Carnival Music in Trinidad* (Gainesville: University Press of Florida, 1993), 25–31; Cowley, *Carnival, Canboulay and Calypso*, 80–82; and *West Indian Rhythm: Trinidad Calypsos on World and Local Events, Featuring the Censored Recordings – 1938–1940*, notes by the Classic Calypso Collective (Bear Family Records BCD 16623 JM, 2006, 10 compact discs with book), 266–67, 275.
4. On the 1868 bands and clash, see Cowley, *Carnival, Canboulay and Calypso*, 59–60. On other female jamettes, see Andrew Pearse, ed., "Mitto Sampson on Calypso Legends of the Nineteenth Century", *Caribbean Quarterly* 4 (1956): 259–62.
5. Brierley, *Trinidad: Then and Now*, 318–30; Brereton, *Race Relations*, 171–73; Cowley, *Carnival, Canboulay and Calypso*, 84–101.
6. Brereton, *Race Relations*, 173–74; Ottley, *Trinidad Callaloo*, 75–77; "Fancy Dress Ball", *POSG*, 14 February 1907, 4; "The Mutual Friendly Society Dance", *POSG*, 9 February 1910, 5. For a visitor's narrative account of participating in the Carnival by driving through the streets in a carriage and throwing confetti and other material, see "The Carnival", *Mirror*, 7 February 1910, 1–2.
7. Guy H. Scull, "The Merry Carnival of Mi-Carême in Trinidad", *Collier's Weekly* 26 (30 March 1901): 18–19. This article also includes photographs of minstrels, clowns, a band with a banner identifying itself as the "Golden Arrow Social Union" and other masqueraders. I acknowledge Ray Funk for providing a copy of this informative document of the turn-of-the-century Carnival. For another description of a moko jumbie band in the early twentieth century, see F.A. Crichlow, "Carnival, 1891–1941", in *Trinidad Carnival*, ed. James H. Smith (Port of Spain: n.p., 1946), 39. Crichlow notes that the stiltwalkers performed contortions to "the screech of fifes and jangling triangles", while another member of the band collected donations from observers.
8. Charles Jones, *Calypso and Carnival of Long Ago and Today* (Port of Spain: n.p., 1947), 13 (quotation), 17; Rafael de Leon, *Calypso from France to Trinidad: 800 Years of*

History (Trinidad: n.p., c. 1980s), 179–81; Mask, "Carnival of Yore", *TG*, 19 February 1933, 18. Rafael de Leon was the calypsonian Roaring Lion; he was born Hubert Rafael Charles and revised his name over the years.

9. On the emergence of calypso and its forms, language, instrumentation and social contexts, see Chas. S. Espinet and Harry Pitts, *Land of Calypso: The Origin and Development of Trinidad's Folk Song* (Port of Spain: Trinidad's Commercial Printery, 1944); Raymond Quevedo, *Atilla's Kaiso: A Short History of Trinidad Calypso* (St Augustine, Trinidad: Department of Extra-Mural Studies, University of the West Indies, 1983); Daniel J. Crowley, "Toward a Definition of 'Calypso'", *Ethnomusicology* 3 (1959): 55–66, 117–24; Errol Hill, *Trinidad Carnival*; Rohlehr, *Calypso and Society*; Donald Hill, *Calypso Calaloo*; Cowley, *Carnival, Canboulay and Calypso*; and *West Indian Rhythm*. Quevedo, the calypsonian Atilla the Hun, wrote most of his study in the latter 1950s (and used the idiosyncratic spelling of "Atilla" for his sobriquet, rather than the "Attila" of his namesake). One of the earliest calypsoes in English was "Jerningham the Governor", which was composed for the 1899 season by Norman le Blanc, chantwell for the White Rose Social Union. The song condemned Jerningham for abolishing the Port of Spain Borough Council (see Rohlehr, *Calypso and Society*, 44, 59; and Cowley, *Carnival, Canboulay and Calypso*, 144–45).

10. Wilsons Limited advertisement, *POSG*, 3 February 1907, 2; Bonanza advertisement, *POSG*, 6 February 1907, 3; Jones, *Calypso and Carnival*, 31; "The Carnival", *POSG*, 4 March 1908, 5. For examples of other competitions, see "The Carnival", *POSG*, 24 February 1909, 4; and "The Carnival", *POSG*, 1 March 1911, 5.

11. Bruce Procope, "The Dragon Band or Devil Band", *Caribbean Quarterly* 4 (1956): 275–77, 280.

12. Mask, "Carnival of Yore", 18; Joseph Belgrave, "Reflections on Carnival", in Sander, *From Trinidad*, 41; "Carnival Disorders", *POSG*, 13 February 1907, 5. For detailed descriptions of a clash between the rival Belmont (east) and Corbeaux Town (west) stick bands in the early twentieth century, see F.A. Crichlow, "Carnival Magic Grips City", *TG*, 3 March 1946, 1; and Crichlow, "Carnival, 1891–1941", 36–38. Crichlow also states that rival bands of Pierrots typically met in one corner of Brunswick Square to combat each other with words and whips.

13. Editorial, *POSG*, 14 February 1907, 7 ("vulgar animation"); "Tourist Visitors", *POSG*, 12 February 1907, 7 ("enjoying themselves").

14. Editorial, *POSG*, 6 February 1910, 7; editorial, *POSG*, 29 December 1911, 9.

15. See Arthur Raymond's recollections of these events in "Origins of the Savannah Carnival and the Development of the Down Town Celebrations", in *The Humming Bird Carnival*, ed. Aubrey E. James, (Trinidad: n.p., 1960), 8–10. As well as serving as editor of the *Argos*, Raymond was secretary of the Downtown Carnival committee.

16. "'Argos' Committee Carnival Meeting", *Argos*, 27 February 1919, 5; advertisement, *Argos*, 23 February 1919, 4.

17. "The Queen's Park Savannah Festival", *TG*, 2 March 1919, 7.

18. "The Carnival", *POSG*, 4 March 1919, 9 (quotation); "The Carnival", *POSG*, 5

March 1919, 8; "The Queen's Park Savannah Festival", 7; editorial, *TG*, 26 February 1925, 8. For other discussions of the 1919 Carnival controversy, see Rohlehr, *Calypso and Society*, 87–97; and Cowley, *Carnival, Canboulay and Calypso*, 208–14.

19. Editorial, *POSG*, 6 March 1924, 7; editorial, *TG*, 26 February 1925, 8.

20. For references to ole mas, see "The Carnival", *Argos*, 18 February 1920, 5; "Carnival", *TG*, 17 February 1920, 8; and Cummings, *Barrack-Yard Dwellers*, 95. Photographs of a clown and a bat appear in "What You Saw on Carnival Day", *TG*, 26 February 1939, 30. References to devil bands appear in "All Trinidad Falls under the Spell of Carnival", *TG*, 28 February 1933, 1; and Ivy Achoy, "Carnival Down Town", *TG*, 14 February 1934, 2. On "Crossing the Water", see Procope, "The Dragon Band", 279. An excellent overview of traditional masquerades is provided by Daniel J. Crowley, "The Traditional Masques of Carnival", *Caribbean Quarterly* 4 (1956): 194–223.

21. For descriptions of Midnight Robbers, see "The Carnival", *POSG*, 4 March 1919, 9; Daniel J. Crowley, "The Midnight Robbers", *Caribbean Quarterly* 4 (1956): 263–74; and Errol Hill, *Trinidad Carnival*, 90–91. On Yankee Minstrels, see "The Carnival", *Argos*, 18 February 1920, 5; "Carnival", *TG*, 4 March 1924, 7; "What You Saw on Carnival Day", 30; Crowley, "Traditional Masques", 216–17; and Donald Hill, *Calypso Calaloo*, 156–59. On millionaires, see "Carnival", *TG*, 5 March 1924, 7; and Jones, *Calypso and Carnival*, 53. On sailors, see "X", letter to the editor, *POSG*, 9 February 1930, 13; "All Trinidad Falls under the Spell", 1; Crowley, "Traditional Masques", 200–204; Errol Hill, *Trinidad Carnival*, 93–94; and Stephen Stuempfle, *The Steelband Movement: The Forging of a National Art in Trinidad and Tobago* (Philadelphia: University of Pennsylvania Press, 1995), 28–30.

22. "King Carnival's Reign Ends in Riot of Sunshine and Revelry", *TG*, 14 February 1934, 1; "King Carnival Starts 2-Day Reign", *TG*, 21 February 1939, 1.

23. "Carnival Closes with a Riot of Gaiety", *TG*, 1 March 1933, 1 (quotation); "All Trinidad Falls under the Spell", 1.

24. The Humming Bird, "Talk of Trinidad", *TG*, 28 February 1933, 5; Mrs Gault MacGowan, "Bands of 'Old Masks' Invade City Hotel", *TG*, 13 February 1934, 2; Mrs Gault MacGowan, "Scenes in City Hotel", *TG*, 14 February 1934, 2–3 (quotation, 2). In addition to serving as a downtown centre for gatherings of the elite on Carnival Monday and Tuesday, the Hotel de Paris held a fancy-dress dance on the Saturday night before Carnival.

25. "King Carnival Starts 2-Day Merry Reign", *TG*, 19 February 1939, 2.

26. Charles Espinet, "Revellers and Calypsos Herald 1934 Reign of King Carnival in Trinidad", *TG*, 11 February 1934, 1; The Humming Bird, "Talk of Trinidad", *TG*, 21 February 1939, 4.

27. The Humming Bird, "Talk of Trinidad", *TG*, 10 February 1937, 15; "King Carnival's Reign Ends in Riot", 1; "Revellers Herald Monster Trinidad Carnival", *TG*, 26 February 1933, 1; Espinet, "Revellers and Calypsos", 1, 16.

28. "All Trinidad Falls under the Spell", 1; Ivy Achoy, "Trinidad Falls under Spell of King Carnival", *TG*, 13 February 1934, 1; "Carnival Invasion of Trinidad Continues", *TG*, 24 February 1933, 1; "King Carnival Starts 2-Day Merry Reign", *TG*, 19 February 1939, 2.

29. Editorial, *TG*, 11 January 1939, 8; "Permanent Carnival Committee Appointed", *TG*, 14 January 1939, 1.
30. On the emergence of independent calypsonians and their lifestyle, see Quevedo, *Atilla's Kaiso*, 35–54; Rohlehr, *Calypso and Society*, 110–24; and Donald Hill, *Calypso Calaloo*, 89–91. The class and ethnic backgrounds of calypsonians varied but the majority were working-class Afro-Trinidadians. For profiles of several prominent figures of the interwar era, see Quevedo, *Atilla's Kaiso*, 89–112; Donald Hill, *Calypso Calaloo*, 92–113; and *West Indian Rhythm*, 122–33. Executor and Atilla were atypical in that they attended the prestigious St Mary's College. While the elder Executor's life deteriorated during the 1940s, Atilla was elected to the Port of Spain City Council in 1946, later served as deputy mayor and was elected to the legislative council in 1950.
31. Quevedo, *Atilla's Kaiso*, 35; de Leon, *Calypso from France to Trinidad*, 189.
32. "Carnival Bands at Practice", *TG*, 23 February 1919, 4–5; "Carnival Rehearsals", *TG*, 28 January 1920, 8.
33. Errol Hill, *Trinidad Carnival*, 65.
34. De Leon, *Calypso from France to Trinidad*, 186–88, 195–96; Hollis "Chalkdust" Liverpool, *From the Horse's Mouth* (Diego Martin, Trinidad: Juba, 2003), 62–63; Rohlehr, *Calypso and Society*, 114–15. De Leon (Lion) lists various prosperous managers of tents, such as Reynold Wilkinson, civil servant; Johnny Khan, advertising agent; Jimmy Smith, accountant; and A.A. Cipriani, planter and political leader (195–96). In an interview with calypsonian/Carnival researcher Hollis "Chalkdust" Liverpool, Lion notes that attorneys Gaston Johnston and L.C. Hannays assisted calypsonians legally and financially (62–63).
35. De Leon, *Calypso from France to Trinidad*, 189, 191 (quotation, 191); Rohlehr, *Calypso and Society*, 120, 136. On calypso wars, see Errol Hill, *Trinidad Carnival*, 76–77.
36. Rutter, *If Crab No Walk*, 102–8 (quotation, 102). See also "Major Rutter 'Discovers' the West Indies", *TG*, 27 August 1933, 18. Rohlehr suggests that calypsonians from the Railway Millionaires and the Salada Millionaires tents joined together in 1933 to perform a "calypso drama", a musical skit in which the singers portrayed individual characters (*Calypso and Society*, 136–37).
37. On Beginner's comments on east and west tents, see Liverpool, *From the Horse's Mouth*, 33–34; and Rohlehr, *Calypso and Society*, 115–16. On tents in 1937 and 1939, see "Calypso Tent Practices Start", *TG*, 15 January 1937, 11; "Calypso Sung on H.E.", *TG*, 17 January 1937, 3; "Calypso Practice Begins", *POSG*, 18 January 1939, 11; and Rohlehr, *Calypso and Society*, 327 29.
38. London advertisement, *TG*, 17 February 1920, 14; London and Olympic advertisements, *TG*, 19 February 1925, 14; Roxy advertisement, *TG*, 6 February 1937, 16; Vandercook, *Caribbee Cruise*, 272–73; "No Intention to Ban 'Old Mask' from Carnival", *TG*, 17 February 1939, 11. On vaudeville and calypso, see de Leon, *Calypso from France to Trinidad*, 77–79; and Donald Hill, *Calypso Calaloo*, 156–59.
39. For discussions of the complexities of store-closing legislation from the 1910s through the 1930s, see Singh, *Race and Class Struggles*, 101–11; and *West Indian Rhythm*, 207–8.

40. Lyrics for most of the above calypsoes concerning Port of Spain can be found in *West Indian Rhythm*. This set of ten compact discs and a book constitutes an extraordinary calypso source: a reissuing of 267 recordings made by Decca in Trinidad from 1938 to 1940, along with transcriptions of lyrics, notes and articles. "The Rats" and "Treasury Scandal" are included in the compact disc *Calypsos from Trinidad: Politics, Intrigue and Violence in the 1930s*, notes by Dick Spottswood (Arhoolie/Folklyric CD 7004, 1991); "Graf Zeppelin" is included in the compact disc *Calypso Pioneers, 1912–1937*, notes by Dick Spottswood and Donald Hill (Rounder CD 1039, 1989); and "Anacaona" is included in the compact disc *Calypso Breakaway, 1927–1941*, notes by Dick Spottswood and Keith Warner (Rounder CD 1054, 1990). Partial lyrics for "Slum Clearance" are cited in Rohlehr, *Calypso and Society*, 189–90; and a few lines of "Country Club Scandal" appear in Quevedo, *Atilla's Kaiso*, 57.

41. On the Theatre and Dance Hall Ordinance of 1934–1935, see Rohlehr, *Calypso and Society*, 288–96 (quotation, 290). Rohlehr also discusses colonial government censorship of calypso records, beginning in 1937 (296–315). On the recording of calypso and Eduardo Sa Gomes, see Donald Hill, *Calypso Calaloo*, 114–44; and *West Indian Rhythm*, 30–32, 111–15, 213–16. For a New York radio broadcast of calypso in 1937 and Roosevelt's interest in the genre, see "Calypso Broadcast Tomorrow", *TG*, 25 February 1937, 1. Michael Eldridge discusses the calypsonians' trips to New York during the 1930s and the American reception of their recordings in "There Goes the Transnational Neighborhood: Calypso Buys a Bungalow", *Callaloo* 25 (2002): 620–38. He argues that their bungalow songs of this era were an expression of their desire for American-style success and comfort, as well as a means of appealing to American images of domesticity.

42. People's appreciation of this alternative city was increased by the fact that Carnival Monday and Tuesday were not official holidays; many businesses, government offices and schools remained open until midday. This continued presence of the quotidian city highlighted the extraordinary characteristics of the festive city. The *Trinidad Guardian*, however, questioned the advisability of attempting to work in the midst of Carnival (see editorial, 28 February 1933, 6).

Chapter 6

1. On the strategic significance of Trinidad and the Caribbean, see Robert A. Johnson, "History of the Trinidad Sector and Base Command", vol. 1 (United States Army, Caribbean Defense Command, 1945), 16–34, 312 (hereafter HTS1); Robert A. Johnson, "History of the Trinidad Sector and Base Command", vol. 3 (United States Army, Caribbean Defense Command, 1946), 8–11 (hereafter HTS3); "Caribbean Bases Protect US from Danger of Invasion", *TG*, 2 September 1941, 5; "US to Spend More on Trinidad Base", *TG*, 15 February 1941, 1; Samuel Eliot Morison, *The Battle of the Atlantic, September 1939–May 1943* (Boston: Little, Brown and Company, 1988 [1947]), 144–48; Howard Johnson, "The United States and the Establishment of the Anglo-American Caribbean Commission", *Journal of Caribbean History* 19,

no. 1 (1984): 30–33; and Gaylord T.M. Kelshall, *The U-Boat War in the Caribbean* (Annapolis, MD: Naval Institute Press, 1994), 1–24. For a discussion of Trinidad's oil refineries during World War II (including the production of high-octane aviation fuel at Pointe-à-Pierre), see George E. Higgins, *A History of Trinidad Oil* (Port of Spain: Trinidad Express Newspapers, 1996), 119–22. On the development of the destroyers-for-bases agreement, see Johnson, HTS1, 20–21, 30–31; and Fitzroy André Baptiste, *War, Cooperation, and Conflict: The European Possessions in the Caribbean, 1939–1945* (Westport, CT: Greenwood, 1988), 51–61. For a general analysis of the American presence, see Harvey R. Neptune, *Caliban and the Yankees: Trinidad and the United States Occupation* (Chapel Hill: University of North Carolina Press, 2007). "History of the Trinidad Sector and Base Command" is a five-volume typescript prepared for the US Army Office of the Chief of Military History shortly after the war. Lieutenant Robert A. Johnson wrote volumes 1, 3 and 4 in Port of Spain, while Captain James C. Shoultz Jr wrote volumes 2 and 5 at Fort Read.

2. Johnson, HTS1, 25–31, 45 (quotation). An article in the *Trinidad Guardian* suggests that the Greenslade Board proposed the Cumuto Reserve and the northwest peninsula before the governor recommended the Caroni Swamp ("US Gets 2 Sites for Bases Here", 12 January 1941, 1–2). Steven High outlines a similar sequence of events in *Base Colonies in the Western Hemisphere, 1940–1967* (New York: Palgrave Macmillan, 2009), 33–34.

3. "Legislature Debate on US Base Leases", *TG*, 18 January 1941, 1, 3, 9 (quotation).

4. "Sites for US Bases in Trinidad", *TG*, 23 January 1941, 1; "US Base Courts Given Jurisdiction Over Brit. Subjects", *TG*, 28 March 1941, 1, 11–12; editorial, *TG*, 28 March 1941, 6; Johnson, HTS1, 318–28.

5. "Construction Chief of US Bases: Major David A.D. Ogden", *TG*, 16 July 1941, 7; "Congratulations, Colonel Ogden", *Tropical Topics* 1, no. 8 (May 1942); Johnson, HTS1, 47; Walsh Construction Company, *Caribbean Area, 1941–1943* (n.p.: n.d.), 8; and Philip Nobel, "Who Built Mr Blandings' Dream House?" in *Architecture and Film*, ed. Mark Lamster (New York: Princeton Architectural Press, 2000), 63–64. Nobel notes that, during World War II, architectural and engineering firms began forming cooperatives in order to compete more effectively for large military contracts. The USED office in Trinidad published the unpaginated magazine *Tropical Topics* during 1941–1942 and included information on construction activities, recreational opportunities for its personnel and the novelty of life in Trinidad.

6. Johnson, HTS1, 329–35; Walsh Construction, *Caribbean Area*, 3–13 (quotations, 9–10).

7. Walsh Construction, *Caribbean Area*, 10, 37–38 (quotation, 37); "Trinidad Bastion: US Starts Building Base on British Isle", *Life* 10, no. 14 (7 April 1941): 77–81 (quotation, 78); "Labour Terms for US Army Base", *TG*, 25 January 1941, 5; "4,000 Trinidadians Engaged on US Projects", *TG*, 11 May 1941, 5; "US Engineers Proud of Work '2 Thousand Miles from Home'", *TNT*, 15 May 1943, 12. In November 1941, *Life* ran a second article on the bases in Trinidad, covering both construction work and the Americans' interactions with the local society. See Trevor L. Christie, "Life's Reports: Yankees in Trinidad", *Life* 11, no. 20 (17 November 1941): 16–27.

Trinidad News Tips (*TNT*) was published by the US Army command in Trinidad during 1941–1943, first as a magazine and then in a newspaper format. The periodical featured lively commentary by servicemen on their activities and experiences on the island, along with original cartoons, poetry and short stories.

8. Johnson, HTS1, 48–58; "Signal Corps 'Real' Pioneer of Trinidad", *TNT*, 15 May 1943, 5; Paul J. Schmitt, "A First Anniversary", *TNT*, 15 April 1942, 4; "More US Army Units Reach Here", *TG*, 7 May 1941, 1.

9. Johnson, HTS1, 58–59. On Ogden's establishment of the USED headquarters at Whitehall, see idem, 47.

10. On the relocation of the USED and Caribbean Architects-Engineers, see ibid., 59, 71. On the boundaries of the Trinidad Sector, see ibid., ii, and maps following 11. After 16 July 1941, there were technically two commands at Whitehall: the Trinidad Sector and the Trinidad Base Command; on 1 June 1942, these were renamed the Trinidad Sector and Base Command (see "Base Headquarters Expands Rapidly", *TNT*, 15 May 1943, 4). On Generals Pratt and Patch, see Johnson, HTS1, 270, 308; and *TNT*, 1 April 1943, 1–3. On peak troop strength, see James C. Shoultz Jr, "History of the Trinidad Sector and Base Command", vol. 2 (United States Army, Caribbean Defense Command, 1947), 19 (hereafter HTS2); and High, *Base Colonies*, 34, 179.

11. "US to Lease 'Blind' Home", *TG*, 14 May 1941, 3; "Recreation Plans for US Soldiers", *TG*, 22 May 1941, 7; "News from US Bases", *TG*, 26 July 1941, 5; "The Opening of the Castle Club", *Tropical Topics*, May 1942. While the *Trinidad Guardian* suggests that the USED's relocation to the Institute for the Blind took place in early August, army historian Robert L. Johnson records the move as occurring in January 1942 (HTS1, 59).

12. Johnson, HTS1, 52–53, 342–44; Walsh Construction, *Caribbean Area*, 47–48 and photographs on 68–78; "Postal Station for US Boys", *TG*, 15 May 1941, 1; "Recreation Plans for US Soldiers", *TG*, 22 May 1941, 7; "News from the US Bases", *TG*, 19 July 1941, 7; Samuel Grasberg, "Base Medical Services Are 'Tops'", *TNT*, 15 May 1943, 7; "Business-Like Quartermaster Also Proud of Soldierly Traits", *TNT*, 15 May 1943, 10. The National Archives of the United States holds collections of photographs of various bases in Trinidad, including Docksite. See US Army Signal Corps, World War II, Trinidad, Book #1 (125967, 111-SCA-3048) and Book #2 (150118, 111-SCA-3049).

13. "USO Plans to Open New Building in POS", *TNT*, 1 April 1942, 4 ("magnificent revelation"); "USO Recreation Club to Be Opened Tomorrow", *TG*, 19 April 1942, 3 ("electric compression"); "USO Buildings Are Dedicated in Trinidad", *Tropical Topics*, May 1942 (includes photographs of interiors); "USO, 'Grand Central Terminal of Caribbean'", *TNT*, 15 May 1943, 8. In December 1941, *Tropical Topics* published a beautiful perspective drawing of the USO, showing a second courtyard (in addition to the central patio) and tree-lined lawns and median strips in streets surrounding the complex. Existing photographs and written descriptions make it difficult to determine how much of this design was realized. A photograph published by the *Trinidad Guardian* at the time of the opening shows a yard with a low picket

14. Johnson, HTS1, 67–68; "King George V Park for US", *TG*, 21 May 1941, 1; "Lands for US Handed Over", *TG*, 22 May 1941, 9 (quotation).
15. "Future Home of US Boys in Port-of-Spain Goes Here", *TG*, 24 May 1941, 10; "Work on New Camp for American Troops Begins", *TG*, 8 July 1941, 11; "Plan for New US Army Camp at King George V Park", *TG*, 10 July 1941, 7; "Americans at Work", *TG*, 24 July 1941, 9; A. Elwell Reid Jr, "News from the US Bases", *TG*, 10 October 1941, 7 ("noise of the pictures"); "G-5 Jive", *TNT*, 1 January 1942, 17 ("new shrubbery"); "City Council to Ask US Representatives to Discuss Water Contract for Army Camp", *TG*, 26 April 1942, 3; "US to Set Up Radio Station in Trinidad", *TG*, 2 February 1943, 1 ("flown to Trinidad"); "US Radio on Medium Wave Band", *TG*, 3 February 1943, 1, 5; "Headquarters Company Is Versatile Lot", *TNT*, 15 May 1943, 8. Photographs of the St Clair Cantonment are contained in Walsh Construction, *Caribbean Area*, 122–24; and National Archives of the United States, US Army Signal Corps, World War II, Trinidad, Book #1.

 fence (19 April 1942, 3), while a National Archives of the United States photograph, also dated April 1942, shows a chain-link fence and minimal landscaping (US Army Signal Corps, World War II, Trinidad, Book #2, SC 680220).
16. James O. Mann, "Laventille News Meal", *TNT*, 15 December 1942, 3; James O. Mann, "Laventille News Meal", *TNT*, 1 January 1943, 5; Walter Eskridge, "The Rapsey Rapsey-dees", *TNT*, 1 February 1943, 5. On the 99th's service in Trinidad, see Johnson, HTS1, 289; and Annette Palmer, "Black American Soldiers in Trinidad, 1942–44: Wartime Politics in a Colonial Society", *Journal of Imperial and Commonwealth History* 14 (1986): 203–18.
17. "US Asks for Land to Erect USO Building", *TG*, 15 October 1942, 5; "New Colored USO to Open", *TNT*, 1 May 1943, 1.
18. Palmer, "Black American Soldiers in Trinidad", 203–14.
19. Johnson, HTS1, 135, 279, 308; Shoultz, HTS2, 51–55; Walsh Construction, *Caribbean Area*, 48–49. Aerial photographs of Carlsen, Xeres and Exchange Fields are contained in the General Records of the Department of the Navy at the National Archives of the United States.
20. Walsh Construction, *Caribbean Area*, 39–46, 103 (photographs of houses); "Fort Read's New Homes Ready Soon", *Tropical Topics*, October 1941 (accompanied by house plans and elevations); Mary Dwyer, "And So El Mamo Was Born", *TNT*, 5 May 1942, unpaginated. A photograph of the homes and prefabricated sections is also included in Luis Marden, "Americans in the Caribbean", *National Geographic Magazine* 81, no. 6 (June 1942): 727.
21. Johnson, HTS1, 72–73; Walsh Construction, *Caribbean Area*; "Col. Ogden Ordered to Puerto Rico", *TG*, 5 July 1942, 3; "Infantry Theatre at Ft. Read Opened", *TNT*, 22 May 1942, 1 (quotation). For sample photographs of Fort Read, see Walsh Construction, *Caribbean Area*, 101–10; and National Archives of the United States, US Army Signal Corps, World War II, Trinidad, Book #1 and Book #2.
22. "US Official Here to Camouflage Fort Read", *TG*, 18 June 1941, 3.
23. Naval History and Heritage Command (United States), *Building the Navy's Bases in World War II: History of the Bureau of Yards and Docks and the Civil Engineer Corps*

1940–1946, 2:23–31 (available at https://www.history.navy.mil/); "One Year to Build US Navy Base", *TG*, 8 March 1941, 1; "Two Years in Trinidad", *TNT*, 15 May 1943, 1; Morison, *Battle of the Atlantic*, 144–48; Kelshall, *U-Boat War in the Caribbean*, 20–21. The immediacy of the German threat in the Caribbean became clearer to everyone in Trinidad after the night of 18 February 1942, when a U-boat attacked two merchant ships anchored off Port of Spain (see "Two Ships off Trinidad Hit", *New York Times*, 20 February 1942, 1).

24. Naval History and Heritage Command, *Building the Navy's Bases*, 23–31; "US Flag Raised at Naval Base", *TG*, 1 April 1941, 1, 8; "Getting Ready for August 1", *TG*, 2 July 1941, 2 (includes photographs of buildings); "US Navy Builds a 'City' at Chaguaramas", *TG*, 10 August 1941, 4; "'E' Pennant Presentation Ceremony Broadcast to US", *TG*, 14 March 1943, 1–2; Baptiste, *War, Cooperation, and Conflict*, 109–10. A map of facilities in the Carenage Bay and Tucker Valley areas is included in High, *Base Colonies*, 110.

25. Eleanor Roosevelt, "My Day", 18 March 1944, online at George Washington University, http://www.gwu.edu/~erpapers/myday/displaydoc.cfm?_y=1944&_f=md056748. Photographs of Mrs Roosevelt at the African American Seabees camp are contained in the National Archives of the United States, General Records of the Department of the Navy, Box 80-G-624. The US National Archives also holds numerous other photographs of the Chaguaramas base, including aerial images. In addition to its base at Chaguaramas, the navy used the army's Waller Field and Carlsen Field for aviation. At Carlsen the Seabees built a large blimp hangar and various support structures (see Naval History and Heritage Command, *Building the Navy's Bases*, 30, and a nighttime photograph of the illuminated hangar, 1).

26. Johnson, HTS1, 294–96; editorial, *TG*, 20 March 1941, 6; "US Helps Settlers", *TG*, 20 May 1941, 3; "New and Healthier Homes Planned for Evacuees from US Base Sites", *TG*, 21 September 1941, 6 (quotation). A plan of the settlement is included on 6 and photographs on 22.

27. Connor, *Horizons*, 42–50 (quotation, 44).

28. Editorial, *TG*, 17 December 1941, 6; "Trinidad to Launch Big Road Building Projects", *TG*, 17 January 1942, 2; editorial, *TG*, 24 February 1943, 4; Johnson, HTS1, 277–79; Shoultz, HTS2, 50; Walsh Construction, *Caribbean Area*, 31.

29. Naval History and Heritage Command, *Building the Navy's Bases*, 29–30; editorial, *TG*, 5 May 1942, 4; "US Contractors Start Work on $500,000 Maracas Road", *TG*, 21 March 1943, 6; "US Decide on Own Route to Build New Maracas Road", *TG*, 6 May 1943, 1; "The Road to Maracas", *TG*, 24 August 1962, 9.

30. Editorial, *TG*, 16 November 1941, 6; editorial, *TG*, 5 May 1942, 4 ("adequate planning"); editorial, *TG*, 2 August 1942, 8; "Planning Experts' Dream of Maracas about to Come True", *TG*, 7 March 1943, 2; editorial, *TG*, 21 September 1944, 2.

31. Walsh Construction, *Caribbean Area*, 61 (quotation); James C. Shoultz Jr, "History of the Trinidad Sector and Base Command", vol. 5 (United States Army, Caribbean Defense Command, 1947), 94–95 (hereafter HTS5).

32. "City Population 100,585 in 1942", *TG*, 26 August 1943, 2; Anthony, *Port-of-Spain in a World at War*, 61–62; "United States Defence Work Creates Many Problems

for Local Transport Facilities", *TG*, 10 August 1941, 10 (quotations); "Base Workers Free Trains Cancelled", *TG*, 4 October 1941, 1, 5; Johnson, HTS1, 279. In HTS5 (88–106), Captain James Shoultz offers various details on labour relations and working conditions on the bases. Since planters were concerned that American pay rates would draw labourers away from agriculture, the Trinidad government, US military authorities and contractors pursued several efforts to regulate wages. Safety on the bases was also a serious issue. During the first eighteen months of construction on the army bases, there were 29,546 injuries, including fourteen deaths (92). Harvey Neptune notes that construction jobs on the bases attracted not only manual labourers but also clerks, teachers and policemen. He also discusses the Americans' manipulation of wage policies, planters' exaggeration of a labour shortage and the government's easing of immigration restrictions to recruit more labourers (see *Caliban and the Yankees*, 79–92). In *Base Colonies* (107–114), Steven High offers further examination of labour relations in Trinidad and mentions the US military's "decision not to acknowledge the collective bargaining rights of trade unions at the bases" (110). In addition, High cites a navy intelligence report that describes union leader Quintin O'Connor's efforts to organize workers at Chaguaramas (111). In his memoirs, Albert Gomes notes that he collaborated with O'Connor in this activity and says: "We secured a small hut not far from the Base where we held organising meetings regularly" (*Through a Maze of Colour*, 45).

33. Shoultz, HTS5, 22, 130–36 (quotations, 130–31); Wenzel Brown, *Angry Men, Laughing Men: The Caribbean Caldron* (New York: Greenberg, 1947), 245–46; Hugh Marcum, editorial, *TNT*, 1 April 1942, 4. For a general discussion of relations between Americans and local populations in Trinidad and other British Caribbean colonies with US bases, see Annette Palmer, "Rum and Coca Cola: The United States in the British Caribbean 1940–1945", *The Americas* 43 (1987): 441–51. Palmer discusses the Americans' racism and poor treatment of workers on the bases, as well as crimes committed by soldiers, few of whom were tried in local courts. Steven High notes that in March 1941 President Roosevelt "instructed that all officers on duty in base colonies conform to local practice and usage in matters of race" at official events and social functions. In addition, segregated signage was prohibited on the bases. In spite of this official policy, abuse of local people by some Americans remained a problem throughout the war (*Base Colonies*, 101–3). High also suggests that "the epicenter of racial conflict was undoubtedly the main gates of the bases where U.S. soldiers and marines checked the documents and badges of 'native labourers' entering and leaving the leased areas. Many shootings occurred at these crossings" (104).

34. Johnson, HTS1, 301; Robert A. Johnson, "History of the Trinidad Sector and Base Command", vol. 4 (United States Army, Caribbean Defense Command, 1946), 40–52 (hereafter HTS4); Shoultz, HTS5, 132–37; Alfonse Kaufman, letter to the editor, *Tropical Topics*, November 1941; "Respect for Trinidadian Law Must Be Shown", *TNT*, 1 December 1942, 4.

35. "US Units to Participate in Civil Defence Rally Next Week", *TG*, 4 May 1943, 1, 5; "Civil Defence Week Rally Official Programme", *TG*, 9 May 1943, 8; "Huge Crowd

See End of Civil Defence Rally", *TG*, 16 May 1943, 1, 5 (quotation); Shoultz, HTS5, 145.

36. On the challenge of troop morale in Trinidad, see Johnson, HTS1, 282, 317; and Shoultz, HTS2, 17.

37. The Humming Bird, "Talk of Trinidad", *TG*, 28 June 1941, 4; "News from the US Bases", *TG*, 29 June 1941, 4; The Humming Bird, "Talk of Trinidad", *TG*, 1 July 1941, 4 (quotation); A. Elwell Reid Jr, "Around the US Bases", *TG*, 23 July 1942, 8 (quotation); "Flying Showboat", *TNT*, 15 November 1941, 6; Chico Marx, "The First Time I Saw Trinidad", *TNT*, 15 November 1941, 25; Sally Osmon Rowe, "Fort Read Gets Look at Variety Show", *TNT* 1, no. 18 (August 1942), 3.

38. "TBC Follies Tours Bases", *TNT*, 15 April 1942, 1 ("dancing chorus"); "Trinidad Base Command Follies", *TNT*, 5 May 1942, unpaginated ("flying stock company"); "Sally Osman Rowe", *Tropical Topics*, June 1942.

39. Editorial, *TNT*, 1 April 1942, 4; Shoultz, HTS5, 138–48; "USO Club Dance Tomorrow Night", *TG*, 4 June 1942, 5; Neptune, *Caliban and the Yankees*, 158–67.

40. The Humming Bird, "Talk of Trinidad", *TG*, 15 June 1941, 22; "News from U.S. Bases", *TG*, 20 July 1941, 4; "Waller NCO's POS Dance", *TNT* 1, no. 18 (August 1942), 3.

41. *Seamen's Guide to Trinidad* (Port of Spain: Yuille Company, n.d.), quotation on 1. I am grateful to Ray Funk for providing me with a copy of this booklet and of *Victory Calypsoes*, cited below.

42. Shoultz, HTS5, 139–40; Mittelholzer, *With a Carib Eye*, 41–42; "Resident", letter to the editor, *TG*, 26 October 1944, 4; editorial, *TG*, 26 October 1944, 4. A year earlier the *Guardian* had run an editorial attacking recreation clubs at which, it claimed, intoxicated servicemen were being "fleeced by card sharpers and loose women" (*TG*, 5 August 1943, 4). This same year a member of the US military police contributed an article to *TNT* in which he reviewed the work of his colleagues and recalled: "In Port of Spain, Lt. Babb and his men were making nightly visits to every place in town and in San Juan. They became well acquainted, particularly with our mopsey [women] friends. Who does not remember Jean or Olga?" ("Mopsey-Trouble Started Early for Military Police", *TNT*, 15 May 1943, 5). For a 1941 photograph of trams passing the Restaurant Plaza at Green Corner, see Morrison, "Trams and Trolleybuses".

43. Derek Bickerton, *The Murders of Boysie Singh* (London: Arthur Baker, 1962), 45–46, 52–57. Bickerton also describes Singh's wedding on 27 July 1941. Along with a ceremony at Rosary Church, the gangster held a week-long party for nine hundred guests at his house in Woodbrook, with the backyard adorned with orchids, ferns and palm fronds and the top dance band of John "Buddy" Williams hired for two of the nights. Singh even invited some American servicemen who were wandering the streets, having recently arrived at nearby Docksite (48–50).

44. "Voice of the People – That's the Calypso", *TNT*, 1 March 1943, 1–2; "Hits Scored by Calypso Singers", *TG*, 17 January 1943, 5; calypso tent photographs, *TG*, 23 January 1943, 3; Daphne Taylor, "There Is No Carnival But the Calypso Carries On", *TG*, 9 March 1943, 4; "Lent After All Quiet Carnival", *TG*, 10 March 1943, 1 (quotation);

Brown, *Angry Men, Laughing Men*, 254; Quevedo, *Atilla's Kaiso*, 70–75 (quotation, 75); Rohlehr, *Calypso and Society*, 333–56; Donald Hill, *Calypso Calaloo*, 81–84.

45. "News from the US Bases", *TG*, 16 January 1942, 8. Other examples of American commentary on calypso are "And They Call It the Calypso", (*TNT*, 1 February 1942, 8), which includes remarks on calypsoes about servicemen and local women; and "Tin Pan Alley of Trinidad" (*Tropical Topics*, December 1941), a bizarre piece in which Ed Sullivan, "Famous New York Columnist", attempts to paint a picture of Lion, Atilla, Growler and Radio performing on the balcony of a Chinese restaurant in the "quaint city of Port of Spain".

46. Quevedo, *Atilla's Kaiso*, includes the lyrics to "Rum and Coca-Cola" (76–77) and "No Nationality" (140–41). Raymond Quevedo, ed., *Victory Calypsoes* (Port of Spain: Trinidad Publishing, 1944) includes "Pam Palam" (13–14), "Food Distribution" (17), "Save Your Money" (18), "Certain Taxi Driver" (20) and "Scrutinize Their Face" (21). Calypsonians also continued to perform calypso dramas during the war years. Gordon Rohlehr cites one at the House of Lords Tent in 1945 that satirized activity outside the USO on Wrightson Road, with Caresser as the police inspector, Radio as the judge, Lord and Lady Iere as the defendants and Invader as a tout (*Calypso and Society*, 356). While performing for the troops in Trinidad in 1943, American comedian Morey Amsterdam heard Invader's "Rum and Coca-Cola". He subsequently wrote some additional verses and published the song in his own name in New York. Following the Andrews Sisters' 1944 smash hit version, two legal battles over the song's rights occurred in the United States, since Invader's lyrics had been published in a 1943 *Victory Calypsoes* booklet and a similar melody had been published in a 1943 songbook by Trinidadian musician Lionel Belasco. Both Invader and Belasco won their cases, with five servicemen serving as witnesses for Invader. See Rohlehr, *Calypso and Society*, 360–64; and Donald Hill, *Calypso Calaloo*, 234–40.

47. Edric Connor, letter to the editor, *TG*, 5 March 1943; Espinet and Pitts, *Land of Calypso*. For accounts of the 1943 debate in the *Trinidad Guardian* on the origin and significance of calypso, see Gordon Rohlehr and Bridget Brereton, introduction to *Horizons* by Connor, xxviii–xxxi; and Neptune, *Caliban and the Yankees*, 132–36. Neptune also offers a broader analysis of shifting local perspectives on calypso during the war years and of calypsonians' profitable performances for American servicemen (129–57).

48. "Women Asked to Enlist in Local W.V.S.", *TG*, 3 May 1942, 1–2; editorial, *TG*, 28 May 1942, 4; editorial, *TG*, 9 June 1942, 4; "Women Move to Inaugurate Garden Clubs in Trinidad", *TG*, 14 June 1942, 5; "Public Urged to Turn Flower Beds into Kitchen Gardens", *TG*, 17 June 1942, 1–2; editorial, *TG*, 17 June 1942, 4 ("prepared to sacrifice"); "Food Production Depots Distribute Seeds and Plants for Over 1,000 Acres", *TG*, 18 June 1942, 3; "Cultivation of City Squares Suggested", *TG*, 19 June 1942, 1 ("knock down the trees"); "Critical Food Situation for July–October Period Warned", *TG*, 24 June 1942, 1; "Development of W.V.S. in Trinidad Is Traced", *TG*, 16 August 1942, 3 ("good and necessary thing"); Harold Fahey, "1942 Food Acreage Up By 10,000 Over Last Year", *TG*, 16 August 1942, 6; "New W.V.S. Cookery Centre

Opened on Tragarete Road", *TG*, 15 January 1943, 1; Anthony, *Port-of-Spain in a World at War*, 113–16; Singh, *Race and Class Struggles*, 196–202.

49. "House-Finding Problem More Acute as Local American Colony Expands", *TG*, 2 October 1941, 6; "Rent Restriction Ordinance Comes into Operation", *TG*, 10 October 1941, 1, 5; "M.O.H. Stresses Acuteness of the Housing Problem", *TG*, 30 December 1941, 5; editorial, *TG*, 27 October 1942, 4 (includes statistics); "City to Discuss Housing with Government Today", *TG*, 18 December 1942, 2; "City Council to Discuss Housing Situation Today", *TG*, 22 December 1942, 2; editorial, *TG*, 12 February 1943, 4; Singh, *Race and Class Struggles*, 194.

50. "Plans Rushed to Rid City of Ugly John John Slum Spot", *TG*, 28 March 1943, 3; "Workers' Homes to Be Released", *TG*, 13 April 1941, 5; "Before and After", *TG*, 18 May 1941, 3 (includes photographs of downtown slum districts and St James houses); "18 Families, Evacuated from Slum Areas, Sing Praises of New Homes in St. James", *TG*, 7 September 1941, 1, 7 (includes photographs of St James houses); Home, "Transferring British Planning Law", 404.

51. "Colony's Biggest Housing Project Nears Completion at Morvant", *TG*, 18 February 1941, 11; "Families Move into Morvant Township", *TG*, 12 October 1941, 10 ("ever-watchful eyes"); photographs of Morvant, *TG*, 12 October 1941, 22; editorial, *TG*, 14 October 1941, 6 ("first residents"); "Housing Commission Put Up New Type Cottages This Year", *TG*, 11 April 1943, 3 (includes photograph of houses built with hollow clay blocks). For a discussion of the inadequacies of Morvant in terms of rent levels, access to a market and transport, see Cummings, *Barrack-Yard Dwellers*, 152–56. During the war, the Planning and Housing Commission also worked on a housing project near the Mucurapo Cemetery, on land leased from the city council. While the project was proposed for the east side of the cemetery in 1942, by 1943 it had shifted to the west side, where W.H. Watkins and Partners developed plans for middle-income flats in two- and three-storey hollow-tile buildings, arranged around lawns with rows of trees. In 1944 the commission abandoned the scheme in order to focus on other projects. See "Mucurapo Land Transfer for Housing Recommended", *TG*, 29 May 1942, 1; "Housing Commission Erecting Two-Storey Test Building", *TG*, 5 September 1943, 6 (including design plans); and "Mucurapo Housing Plan Abandoned", *TG*, 12 September 1944, 1.

52. Shoultz, HTS2, 4–5, 15, 50–55, 126–32; Shoultz, HTS5, 51; "City Post-War Plans Urged", *TG*, 23 May 1943, 1; editorial, *TG*, 10 October 1944, 4; "20 Acres of City Land Reclaimed", *TG*, 4 October 1944, 5; Anthony, *Port-of-Spain in a World at War*, 167–68, 222–24, 265–67. Reclaimed land in this area (known as "Sea Lots") was eventually used for both commercial buildings and low-income/squatter housing.

53. "Trinidad Man Appointed Architect and City Planner", *TG*, 3 September 1943, 1; "Slum Plan Will Change Use of 20 City Blocks", *TG*, 20 August 1944, 3 (quotation); "New Dwellings for Slum Clearance", *TG*, 8 October 1944, 2. On the postwar flats in eastern downtown, see Cummings, *Barrack-Yard Dwellers*, 157–58, 176.

54. Reinhard W. Sander, "Ralph de Boissière", in *Fifty Caribbean Writers: A Bio-Bibliographical Critical Sourcebook*, ed. Daryl Cumber Dance (Westport, CT: Greenwood, 1986), 151–53; Sander, *From Trinidad*, 304; Nicholas Laughlin, "R.I.P.

Ralph de Boissière, 6 October, 1907–16 February, 2008", *Caribbean Review of Books*, 20 February 2008, http://caribbeanreviewofbooks.com; Sandra Pouchet Paquet, "Samuel Dickson Selvon", in Dance, *Fifty Caribbean Writers*, 439–41; "Samuel Selvon", *The Times* (London), 14 May 1994, 21; V.S. Naipaul, "Prologue to an Autobiography", in *Finding the Center: Two Narratives* (New York: Vintage Books, 1986), 3–72; V.S. Naipaul, *Between Father and Son: Family Letters* (New York: Vintage Books, 2001).

55. For "Wartime Activities", a short story published in 1957, Selvon employs a first-person narrator – a young Indian man from the countryside. In the course of his whirlwind adventures in Port of Spain, the narrator assists a woman from Charlotte Street in hustling tricks on Park Street, obtains a job at Chaguaramas (claiming to be a mechanic), visits the Empire Theatre (where he watches *This Gun for Hire*), meets a pretty girl at the Rock Gardens in the Queen's Park Savannah, gets in a fight near the Royal Theatre, ends up in jail and is relieved when his father takes him back to the country for an arranged marriage. "Wartime Activities" is included in Selvon's *Ways of Sunlight* (Harlow, Essex: Longman Drumbeat, 1979 [1957]), 82–93.
56. Ralph de Boissière, *Rum and Coca-Cola* (London: Allison and Busby, 1984 [1956]). Quotations: "real masters of the island", 121; "white American occupation", 332.
57. Samuel Selvon, *A Brighter Sun* (Harlow, Essex: Longman 2004 [1952]). Quotations: "mixed up good", 78; "live in a mud hut", 109; "keep my hand", 209.
58. V.S. Naipaul, *Miguel Street* (New York: Vintage Books, 1984 [1959]); Naipaul, "Prologue to an Autobiography", 3–19. *Miguel Street* could be classified as a collection of short stories or a novel; Naipaul refers to it as a "book" in his "Prologue". The continuity of the setting, interrelatedness of the characters and growth of the single narrator are all more suggestive of a novel of interlinked chapters than a collection of individual stories.
59. Naipaul, "Prologue to an Autobiography", 5–7, 27, 30.
60. Christie, "Life's Reports: Yankees in Trinidad", 27; "US Seeks No Sovereignty Over WI", *TG*, 12 March 1942, 1; "US Does Not Want to Rule Trinidad: 'Ethnic Potpourri'", *TG*, 25 August 1942, 1, 3; Palmer, "Rum and Coca Cola", 44–51. On early speculation in the British Caribbean about an American takeover, see also W. Adolphe Roberts, "Future of the British Caribbean", *Survey Graphic* 30 (April 1941): 234.

Chapter 7

1. For general discussions of Trinidad and Tobago's politics and economy during the postwar era, see Brereton, *History of Modern Trinidad*; Ryan, *Race and Nationalism*; Ivar Oxaal, *Black Intellectuals and the Dilemmas of Race and Class in Trinidad* (Cambridge, MA: Schenkman, 1982); and Williams, *History of the People*. See also Williams, *Inward Hunger*; Gomes, *Through a Maze of Colour*; and Higgins, *History of Trinidad Oil*. Import and export statistics are included in Henry Dow, ed., *Trinidad and Tobago Year Book, 1952* (Port of Spain: Yuille's Printerie, 1952), 223;

Henry Dow, ed., *Trinidad and Tobago Year Book, 1962–63* (Port of Spain: Yuille's Printerie, 1962), 207; and *Colonial Reports, Trinidad and Tobago, 1956* (London: Her Majesty's Stationery Office, 1959), 2. For insightful analyses of sociocultural conditions in postwar Trinidad, see Braithwaite, *Social Stratification in Trinidad*; and Daniel J. Crowley, "Plural and Differential Acculturation in Trinidad", *American Anthropologist* 59 (1957): 817–24.

2. "Trinidad Prays and Rejoices for Victory", *POSG*, 9 May 1945, 1; "European Victory Sets People Here Rejoicing", *TG*, 9 May 1945, 1, 5; "Church Bells Tell Colony War Is Over", *TG*, 15 August 1945, 1; "Trinidad Gives Peace Noisy Welcome", *TG*, 18 August 1945, 1 (quotation).

3. Oscaret Claude, "Evolution, History and Future of the Steel Band", *TG*, 2 March 1946, 4; Elder, "Color, Music and Conflict", 134; Anthony E. Rouff, *"Authentic" Facts on the Origin of the Steelband* (St Augustine, Trinidad: Bowen's Printery, 1972), 2; Lennox Pierre, "From Dustbins to Classics", Independence Supplement, *TG*, 26 August 1962, 108; Kim Johnson, *From Tin Pan to TASPO: Steelband in Trinidad, 1939–1951* (Kingston: University of the West Indies Press, 2011), 23–36, 52–55, 69; "Decca Officials Laud Trinidad Carnival", *POSG*, 15 February 1940, 7. A clear sense of the sound of an early steelband is provided by the Decca recording "Lion Oh", performed by the calypsonian Lion with a group of metal percussionists called the "West Indian Rhythm Band" (see *West Indian Rhythm*, track 222). For general discussions of the development of steelbands from the 1930s to the post-independence era, see Lloyd Braithwaite, "The Problem of Cultural Integration in Trinidad", *Social and Economic Studies* 3, no. 1 (1954): 82–96; Errol Hill, *Trinidad Carnival*; George "Sonny" Goddard, *Forty Years in the Steelbands: 1939–1979* (London: Karia Press, 1991); Stuempfle, *Steelband Movement*; Shannon Dudley, *Music from Behind the Bridge: Steelband Spirit and Politics in Trinidad and Tobago* (New York: Oxford University Press, 2008); and Johnson, *From Tin Pan to TASPO*. For an extensive collection of steelband photographs and related oral history, see Kim Johnson, *The Illustrated Story of Pan* (Arima, Trinidad: University of Trinidad and Tobago, 2011).

4. See Stuempfle, *Steelband Movement*, 37–44, 95–96; and Johnson, *From Tin Pan to TASPO*, 104–8, 160–66, 254–56.

5. For a detailed account of the lineages, locations and names of early steelbands, as well as biographical profiles of their leading personnel, see Johnson, *From Tin Pan to TASPO*. Along with their participation in tamboo bamboo, some panmen had connections with Yoruba-derived Orisha (Shango) yards and drumming traditions in eastern Port of Spain. In addition, Johnson (83–84, 145–46) notes that Rising Sun's precursor, Belmont United, was based in a yard across from the Rada compound on the Belmont Valley Road. Folklorist Andrew Carr describes this Dahomean-derived compound in detail in "A Rada Community in Trinidad". A diagram shows four residences, shrines for Ogu and Sakpata, a *chapelle* (house of the gods), an open shed for ritual drumming and dancing and a cemetery. No wall or fence surrounded the compound, though there was a variety of fruit trees at the back. Carr also discusses a range of seasonal and non-seasonal ceremonies held by the community.

6. "Steelband Outcome of 'Bamboo-Tamboo'", *TG*, 5 March 1950, 13; Patrick Leigh

Fermor, *The Traveller's Tree: A Journey through the Caribbean Islands* (New York: Harper and Brothers, 1950), 170–71. An additional description of an early panyard structure is offered by Trinidadian writer Errol Hill in the setting for his one-act play *The Ping Pong* (Port of Spain: Department of Extra-Mural Studies, University of the West Indies, 1966 [1955]): "A crude shelter made of bamboo poles and walled around with carat sticks intertwined and coconut branches. The sloping roof is also of the broad coconut or palm fronds. It is about seven feet high with a surface area of approx. 8 by 10 feet, and a dirt floor. This structure is called a 'tent' and is found in the backyard of low-class dwellings in the city. Two adjoining sides of the tent form part of the fence separating this yard from the next-door neighbours'" (7).

7. "Carnival Returns to Trinidad", *TG*, 5 March 1946, 1–2 (quotation, 1); "King Carnival Gives Up Crown After Hectic Two-Day Reign", *TG*, 6 March 1946, 1–2; "All Trinidad Begin Carnival Rejoicing", *TG*, 18 February 1947, 1.

8. For further discussion of steelband performances on the streets during and after the war, see Stuempfle, *Steelband Movement*, 50–61.

9. "Discovery Day Fete Goes with Bang", *TG*, 7 August 1946, 1, 7 (quotation, 1).

10. "More Breaches of the Peace This Year Than in 1946", *TG*, 20 February 1947, 1. For a few examples of coverage of the Casablanca-Invaders feud, see "Steel Bandsman Gets 30 Days'", *TG*, 28 October 1949, 7; "Steelband Leader Charged in Court", *TG*, 11 January 1950, 1; and "Bands Clash: Two Injured", *TG*, 2 February 1950, 1. On violence during the Coronation Carnival, see "Man Killed in Steelband Clash", *TG*, 7 June 1953, 1; "Police Chief Calls Carnival Behaviour Worst Ever", *TG*, 9 June 1953, 2; editorial, *TG*, 9 June 1953, 6; "'Ban the Pan Men,' Says Angry Public", *TG*, 9 June 1953, 7; and "Papineau: June 6 Violence Exaggerated", *TG*, 5 July 1953, 7. The growing number of middle-class steelbands during the 1950s were often referred to as "college boy" bands, owing to the fact that many of their members attended elite secondary schools such as Queen's Royal College and St Mary's College.

11. Disgusted, letter to the editor, *TG*, 16 June 1953, 6; Dawson Rondon, letter to the editor, *TG*, 3 July 1953, 6; Cecil Quesnel, letter to the editor, *TG*, 12 July 1953, 6; Alarmed, letter to the editor, *TG*, 23 June 1953, 6; Claudio Carvalho, letter to the editor, *TG*, 25 June 1953, 6; Son of the Soil, letter to the editor, *TG*, 17 June 1953, 6; Cecil Cameron, letter to the editor, *POSG*, 16 June 1953, 4. For examples of letters defending the steelbands, see issues of the *Trinidad Guardian* on 3, 11, 12 and 22 July 1953. A report on the public forum on the Coronation Carnival appears in "Papineau: June 6 Violence Exaggerated", 7.

12. "Legislature Bans Playing of Noisy Instruments on Streets", *TG*, 8 December 1945, 2.

13. Albert Gomes, "The West Indian Must Decide What Culture Is Best for Him", Behind the Curtain, *TG*, 20 November 1949, 16; Stanley H. Best, "Culture Rests on 'Awareness, Choice'", *TG*, 27 November 1949, 6; Albert Gomes, letter to the editor, *TG*, 4 December 1949, 6. For another example of Gomes's defence of steelbands, see Behind the Curtain, *TG*, 16 June 1946, 4B (he used the pseudonym "Ubiquitous" for his column until the end of the decade). See Gomes's autobiography (*Through a Maze of Colour*, 78–103) for more on his support for steelbandsmen, calypsonians

and Spiritual Baptists – a religious group that combined African- and Protestant-derived spiritual beliefs and was prohibited from 1917 until 1951.

14. "HE Appoints Steel Band Committee", *TG*, 27 November 1949, 1; "New Steel Band Association Meets: First Recital Planned", *TG*, 14 April 1950, 3.

15. "'Limbo' and Bongo Danced During Lecture", *TG*, 1 August 1943, 6 (quotations); Connor, *Horizons*, 52–53; Johnson, *From Tin Pan to TASPO*, 82. Connor repeated his lecture/demonstration in December 1943 at the Prince's Building. For a text of this second presentation, see Connor, *Horizons*, 157–64.

16. Molly Ahye, *Cradle of Caribbean Dance: Beryl McBurnie and the Little Carib Theatre* (Petit Valley, Trinidad: Heritage Cultures, 1983), 2–30, 49–50 (see also a photograph and newspaper clippings in Appendix B). For a description and photographs of McBurnie's dance troupe after the war, see the American photojournalist Earl Leaf's *Isles of Rhythm* (New York: A.S. Barnes and Company, 1948), 174–86.

17. Little Carib Theatre, *Talking Drums*, programme booklet for formal opening of the Little Carib Theatre, 25 November 1948; E.M., "The Little Carib Dance Group", *Caribbean Quarterly* 1, no. 1 (1949): 29–30; Ahye, *Cradle of Caribbean Dance*, 31–33, 49–50.

18. "Steel Band Takes Over from Classical Music – For a Day", *TG*, 7 February 1950, 5; "Steelband Hits New High in Recital with Piano, Vocalist", *POSG*, 30 May 1951, 7. See also "Soprano 'Pan' to Be Played at Recital", *TG*, 13 May 1951, 3.

19. "Dr. Northcote Warns Keen Steelbandsmen Don't Try to Hurry", *TG*, 12 March 1952, 1–2 (quotations, 1). See also "Steelbands for Musical Festival to Be Named", *TG*, 5 March 1952, 7. For more on the formal organization of the steelband movement in the postwar years and indoor concerts, see Stuempfle, *Steelband Movement*, 76–124; and Johnson, *From Tin Pan to TASPO*, 207–59.

20. Williams, *Inward Hunger*, 26–107; Selwyn Ryan, *Eric Williams: The Myth and the Man* (Kingston: University of the West Indies Press, 2009), 11–67.

21. Williams, *Inward Hunger*, 108–17 (quotations, 113, 116); Oxaal, *Black Intellectuals*, 101–5; Ryan, *Eric Williams*, 88–92. For overviews of Williams's activities in Trinidad after 1948 and the formation of the PNM, see also Ryan, *Race and Nationalism*, 105–27; and Brereton, *History of Modern Trinidad*, 233–36.

22. Williams, *Inward Hunger*, 112–32 (quotations, 132); Oxaal, *Black Intellectuals*, 108–10; Ryan, *Eric Williams*, 68–77.

23. Ryan, *Eric Williams*, 79–85 (quotation of lecture, 79); Williams, *Inward Hunger*, 132–36 (quotation, 133); Oxaal, *Black Intellectuals*, 96 (quotation), 113–14.

24. Oxaal, *Black Intellectuals*, 137–52; Ryan, *Eric Williams*, 92–98; Little Carib Theatre, *Talking Drums* (quotation, 6).

25. Eric Williams, "A Movement Is Born", *PNM Weekly*, 18 June 1956, 1, 3; Andrew Carr, "The Balisier: Emblem of the PNM", *PNM Weekly*, 18 June 1956, 1, 3 (quotation, 3); "The PNM and the University of Woodford Square: A Historical Record", *PNM Weekly*, 18 June 1956, 2–3; Ryan, *Eric Williams*, 141.

26. "PNM Presents the Victors", *Trinidad Chronicle*, 28 September 1956, 9; "Crowd Cheers PNM Take-Over", *TG*, 27 October 1956, 1–2; "Williams Pledges: No Victimisation", *TG*, 27 October 1956, 9.

27. Radhica Sookraj, "$2m to Refurbish PNM's Balisier House", *TG*, 25 August 2013, http://www.guardian.co.tt/news/2013-08-25/2m-refurbish-pnm%E2%80%99s-balisier-house.
28. On the 1958 federal election and 1961 Trinidad and Tobago election, see Ryan, *Race and Nationalism*, 183–95, 262–70 (quotations: 192, 267–68). For PNM minister Winston Mahabir's account of his disillusionment with Williams after his 1958 remarks, see *In and Out of Politics* (Trinidad: Inprint Caribbean, 1978), 76–81.
29. "A Foreign Base in Trinidad", *The Times* (London), 1 October 1954, 7. A year earlier, the *New York Times* also reported on the strategic importance of the Chaguaramas base (see Sam Pope Brewer, "US Trinidad Base Guards Caribbean", 12 February 1953, 5). For various discussions of Chaguaramas, see Williams, *History of the People*, 255–78; Williams, *Inward Hunger*, 173–245; Oxaal, *Black Intellectuals*, 128–36; Maurice St Pierre, "The Chaguaramas Affair in Trinidad and Tobago: An Intellectual Reassessment", *Journal of Caribbean History* 40, no. 1 (2006): 92–116; Neptune, *Caliban and the Yankees*, 191–94; Ryan, *Eric Williams*, 185–229; and High, *Base Colonies in the Western Hemisphere*, 175–98. St Pierre examines how Eric Williams used Chaguaramas "to make space for himself and the political independence movement in the political fabric of Trinidad and Tobago, by redefining the base from being a space for the security of the Western Hemisphere to one that was incompatible with the nationalist aspirations of the twin island [sic]" (92). For general discussions of this period and Trinidad's transition to independence, see also Ryan, *Race and Nationalism*; and Brereton, *History of Modern Trinidad*.
30. David Lowenthal, "The West Indies Chooses a Capital", *Geographical Review* 48, no. 3 (1958): 336–64 (quotation, 354); T.S. Simey, "A New Capital for the British West Indies", *Town Planning Review* 28, no. 1 (1957): 63–70.
31. Williams, *Inward Hunger*, 206–11; Ryan, *Eric Williams*, 186–90.
32. On Williams's discontent with Adams and the federation, see Ryan, *Eric Williams*, 190–94. At the time of its launch, the West Indies Federation generated much excitement in Port of Spain and coverage in the press. Princess Margaret, on behalf of the queen, inaugurated the federal parliament at the Red House on 22 April 1958, and a West Indies Festival of the Arts was held during the following week and a half at the Botanic Gardens and several indoor venues. See "Parliament Launched", *TG*, 23 April 1958, 1; Diana Searl, "Festival for a Federation", *New York Times*, 23 March 1958, section II, 19; "West Indies Festival of the Arts", *TG*, 19 April 1958, 10; Adrian Espinet, "Pot-Pourri of Arts Offers Us Look at Ourselves", *TG*, 20 April 1958, 22. On 20 April 1958, the *Trinidad Guardian* ran a sixty-four-page supplement on the federation, with articles about the new body and its constituent units. A different perspective on the city at this moment was provided by the *Evening News* in a series of articles ("Life in the Federal Capital") that began appearing on 15 May 1958. For each instalment, the unnamed writer observed a busy downtown street corner and offered an evocative account of the varied vendors, limers, pedestrians and drivers.
33. "Dr. Evans: No Radiation Hazard", *TG*, 21 January 1960, 1; Mahabir, *In and Out of Politics*, 82–85; "'War for WI Independence Now On' Says Premier", *TG*, 23 March 1960, 10 (quotation).

34. "War for WI Independence Now On", 10 (quotations); "Williams Hits at Weak Federation", *TG*, 22 March 1960, 1. Williams also used the trope of a war between Chaguaramas and Woodford Square during an address at a PNM convention, held shortly before the 21 March meeting (see Williams, *Inward Hunger*, 223). In 1957 the PNM declared 22 April 1960 as West Indian Independence Day, and in late 1958 Williams set the time as 11:00 a.m. (see *Inward Hunger*, 230).

35. "April 22, 1960", *Nation*, 22 April 1960, 1, 8 (quotations on nationalism, 8); "April 22, 1960: We March for Freedom", *Nation*, 22 April 1960, 1 (quotation on discipline); "All Set for 'Freedom March' Today", *TG*, 22 April 1960, 1–2.

36. "Demand for Chag Sent to USA", *TG*, 23 April 1960, 1–2 (quotation, 1); "Constitution Ablaze", *Evening News*, 22 April 1960, 1 (includes photograph of bandstand and crowd in Woodford Square); Williams, *Inward Hunger*, 231–33 (quotations from speech); "The March of Independence", *Nation*, 29 April 1960, 1, 16 (quotation on *Trinidad Guardian*, 1).

37. "Demand for Chag Sent to USA", 1–2 (placards and banners, 1); "The March of Independence", 1, 16. The *Nation* claimed that the demonstration included over thirty-five thousand marchers and bystanders, while Ryan (*Eric Williams*, 196) notes that estimates varied from fifteen to thirty-five thousand. For additional photographs, see *Nation*, 29 April 1960, 19 (including the burning of the *Guardian* and the Women's League marching); and *Nation*, 20 May 1960, 10 (a steelband participating in the march).

38. Williams, *Inward Hunger*, 237–44; Ryan, *Eric Williams*, 219–25. In the latter part of 1962, Williams agreed to $30 million of aid from the United States. In 1966–1967, the Americans evacuated Chaguaramas with the exception of the missile-tracking station and a new navigational station (Williams, *Inward Hunger*, 244). In 1977 there was a ceremony marking the formal end of the US base at Chaguaramas (Ryan, *Eric Williams*, 257).

39. "'Open House' at Chag for Flag Raising", *TG*, 9 February 1961, 1–2; "WI-US Defence Agreement Signed", *TG*, 11 February 1961, 1–2; "WI Contributes to West Defence", *TG*, 11 February 1961, 1–2; "A Memorable Day for the West Indies", *TG*, 13 February 1961, 13.

40. Editorial, *TG*, 24 April 1960, 8. On Macleod's visit to Trinidad, see Ryan, *Eric Williams*, 219–21.

41. "Team of 24 to Lead Independence Fete", *TG*, 24 June 1962, 1–2 ("impress upon everyone", 2); Karl Douglas, "Aim of Independence Body to Inspire Every Citizen", *TG*, 26 August 1962, 11; untitled note on Marguerite Wyke, *TG*, 26 August 1962, 11; "The 'Big Five' Behind Independence Celebrations", *TG*, 28 August 1962, 6 ("on the threshold").

42. "National Flag Ideas Sought", *TG*, 9 June 1962, 1; "Flag, Coat of Arms Approved", *TG*, 15 July 1962, 1–2 (quotation on flag, 2); "National Birds", *TG*, 22 July 1962, 1–2; "3 Changes in Coat of Arms", *TG*, 5 August 1962, 1; Harry Pitts, "The National Anthem Crowns a Fine Career", *TG*, 26 August 1962, 4.

43. "Premier Against an August 31 Carnival", *TG*, 19 August 1962, 1; "Steel Bands to Play at State Ball", *TG*, 5 August 1962, 1–2; "Calypso Finals Tonight", *TG*, 15 August

1962, 1; "Independence Crown to Brynner", *TG*, 16 August 1962, 1; "Indians Plan Show for Independence", *TG*, 19 August 1962, 2 (quotation); "Independence Fever in Trinidad", *TG*, 26 August 1962, 1–2; "Port-of-Spain, San Fernando – A Wonderland of Colour", *TG*, 2 September 1962, 22 (includes photographs of street decorations); "Trinidad Hails Independence with Music", *The Times* (London), 1 September 1962, 5. On 26 August, the *Trinidad Guardian* published a 120-page supplement, with extensive coverage of the country's history and culture, as well as articles on the celebrations themselves. Other independence publications were the government's eight-page pamphlet *What Independence Means to You* (Trinidad: Government Printing Office, 1962), with sections titled "History", "Culture", "Discipline", "Production" and "Tolerance"; and the PNM's 112-page booklet, *This Country of Ours* (Port of Spain: PNM Publishing, 1962), with articles such as "A Scholar Who Founded a Nation", "Our Country and Our People", "A Theory of Government", "The Last Lap to Independence", "Art and Independence", "Theatre and Drama" and "Notes on Architecture". These and other items are contained in "Independence Documents" boxes at the National Archives of Trinidad and Tobago.

44. "Youth Give HRH Rousing Welcome", *TG*, 31 August 1962, 1–2 (quotation, 1); "Williams Tells Youth Rally: No Turning Back", *TG*, 31 August 1962, 20; "Youth Festival at the Oval", *Nation*, 7 September 1962, 13; "Wide Variety of Shows Planned", *TG*, 8 August 1962, 2; "700 Trinidad Artistes for 'Gala Performance' Aug 30", *TG*, 24 August 1962, 1. The Queen's Hall show was repeated on 1 and 4 September.

45. "Trinidad Set for Independence", *TG*, 30 August 1962, 1–2 (quotation, 1); "Trinidad Now Becomes a Nation", *TG*, 31 August 1962, 1–2; "Trinidad Hails Independence with Music", 5; "Up Goes the Black, White, and Red", *Nation*, 2 September 1962, 16. Footage of the flag ceremony and the opening of parliament the next day can be viewed on YouTube as "Trinidad & Tobago Independence 1962" (parts 3 and 4), uploaded by McKelly, 9 May 2013, https://www.youtube.com/watch?v=F0FQY252jso. By this point, the *Trinidad Guardian* had altered its position on the PNM. On the eve of independence, it acknowledged that this was Eric Williams's hour: "He it is who saw the possibilities, who urged his people on to grasp them, and who by incessant labours and dedicated service has brought this country to the gate marked 'sovereignty' through which it will pass at midnight tonight" (editorial, *TG*, 30 August 1962, 12). David Trotman says that after the flag-raising ceremony, there were steelband concerts at the Queen's Park Savannah and Memorial Park and that the bands then led crowds through the streets. See "Acts of Possession and Symbolic Decolonisation in Trinidad and Tobago", *Caribbean Quarterly* 58, no. 1 (2012): 30.

46. "Queen Sends Warm Greetings", *TG*, 2 September 1962, 1–2 (quotations, 1); "HRH Opens New Parliament", *Nation*, 2 September 1962, 1; Paul P. Kennedy, "Trinidad's Chief Calls for Unity", *New York Times*, 1 September 1962, 2; "City Receives the Princess", *Nation*, 2 September 1962, 18.

47. "Industrial Show at Independence", *TG*, 20 July 1962, 14; "Progress Reported for Carnival Exhibition", *TG*, 28 August 1962, 11; "Museum Comes to Life", *TG*, 5 September 1962, 1–2; editorial, *TG*, 12 September 1962, 8 (quotation).

48. Dennis Mahabir, "Trinidad Seen as Diamond of Many Facets", *TG*, 19 August 1962, 12. The ex-mayor was a brother of PNM leader Winston Mahabir.
49. See Gomes, *Through a Maze of Colour* (move to Maraval, 166; burning of effigy, 174; critique of the PNM, 176–78; Federal House, 217). For an example of Gomes's criticism of Williams on the Chaguaramas issue, see "Time to Stop Nonsense Talk About US Bases", *TG*, 2 February 1960, 6.
50. James, *Beyond a Boundary*, 49–71, 225–52 ("every street corner", 238); C.L.R. James, *Party Politics in the West Indies* (San Juan, Trinidad: C.L.R. James, c. 1962), see especially chapters "Dr. E.E. Williams" and "The Middle Classes"; Williams, *Inward Hunger*, 267–68. *Party Politics* appeared first in a shorter version titled *PNM Go Forward*. For reviews of the two editions, see "C.L.R. James Hits PNM Leaders", *TG*, 29 January 1961, 1–2; and Leigh Richardson, "Is C.L.R. James Just a Disappointed Old Man?" *TG*, 15 July 1962, 7. For additional discussions of the James-Williams relationship, see Buhle, *C.L.R. James*, 142–48; and Ryan, *Eric Williams*, 359–67. Ryan suggests that conservative members of the PNM and/or the US government pressured Williams to force the radical James out of the party.
51. V.S. Naipaul, *The Middle Passage* (New York: Vintage Books, 1981 [1962]), 40–85. Naipaul's first visit back to Trinidad occurred in September–October 1956, in the midst of the election and the PNM victory (see Patrick French, *The World Is What It Is: The Authorized Biography of V.S. Naipaul* [New York: Vintage Books, 2008], 163–72). In an article titled "The Disorder of V.S. Naipaul", published in the *Trinidad Guardian* in 1965, C.L.R. James states: "What Vidia said about the West Indies in *Middle Passage* was very true. But what he left out was twice as true and four times as important" (see Gordon Rohlehr, "Intersecting Q.R.C. Lives: James, Williams, Naipaul", in *Transgression, Transition, Transformation: Essays in Caribbean Culture* [San Juan, Trinidad: Lexicon Trinidad, 2007], 216). On communications between Naipaul and James during the 1960s, see French, *The World Is What It Is*, 236–39. Shortly before he returned to Trinidad, Naipaul completed the manuscript for *A House for Mr. Biswas*, his long comic novel modelled on the life of his father. The book chronicles Mr Biswas's experiences, from birth to untimely death, in a succession of houses, with descriptions of architectural features as well as domestic configurations and challenges. At the midpoint of the novel, Mr Biswas leaves central Trinidad for Port of Spain in order to escape his wife's large and suffocating family. Initially he enjoys the thrill of the city and a job writing for a newspaper, but soon he and his family are again sharing accommodation with his troublesome in-laws. Eventually he borrows money and buys a property in St James. Though the house turns out to be full of defects, the Biswas family carries out repairs, grows orchids and plants a garden and a fragrant laburnum tree. Finally, shortly before he dies, Mr Biswas has a place that he can claim as his own. Naipaul's perspective and tone in this novel contrast with those of *The Middle Passage*. Here he draws on family memories from the 1930s and 1940s to construct a largely hopeful account of one man's efforts to create a suitable home and meaningful life. For Naipaul's reflections on the process of writing *A House for Mr. Biswas*, see his foreword to the 1984 edition (New York: Vintage Books, 1984 [1961]).

52. Edward Baugh, introduction to *Selected Poems*, by Derek Walcott (New York: Farrar, Straus and Giroux, 2007), xi–xvii; Bruce King, *Derek Walcott: A Caribbean Life* (New York: Oxford University Press, 2000), 128–46; Derek Walcott, "On Choosing Port of Spain", in *David Frost Introduces Trinidad and Tobago*, ed. Michael Anthony and Andrew Carr (London: André Deutsch, 1975), 14–23. Walcott's *Drums and Colours* was an epic treatment of four centuries of Caribbean history. For a review, see Adrian Espinet, "'Drums and Colours' Seeks to Trace WI Consciousness", *TG*, 27 April 1958, 7.

53. Derek Walcott, "Let's Have the Best in Creative Writing", *TG*, 7 August 1960, 6; Derek Walcott, "Farewell Exhibition One of Staggering Triviality", *TG*, 4 May 1962, 5; Derek Walcott, "Diversity of Techniques Makes for Fine Show", *TG*, 16 May 1962, 5; Derek Walcott, "Painter Chen Tries to Capture Sound", *TG*, 1 July 1962, 4; Derek Walcott, "Local Art Headed in Confident Direction", *TG*, 31 July 1960, 6; Derek Walcott, "Magnificence and Art in the Carnival Spectacle", *TG*, 5 March 1962, 6.

54. V.S. Naipaul, "The Worm in the Bud", in *A Writer's People: Ways of Looking and Feeling* (London: Picador, 2007), 16–17; "Poetry: Enormously Complicated Art", *TG*, 18 June 1962, 3 (quotations); Derek Walcott, *In a Green Night: Poems 1948–1960* (London: Jonathan Cape, 1962); C.L.R. James, "Here's a Poet Who Sees the Real West Indies", *TG*, 6 May 1962, 5; "Little Carib Turns Now to Drama?" *TG*, 6 May 1962, 6; Derek Walcott, "The Prospects of a National Theatre", Independence Supplement, *TG*, 26 August 1962, 105–6; King, *Derek Walcott*, 163–86, 225–26; Baugh, introduction to *Selected Poems*. "Nights in the Gardens of Port of Spain" was first published in *The Spectator* (28 December 1962, 997) and collected in *The Castaway and Other Poems* (London: Jonathan Cape, 1965), 43. For a brilliant review by Walcott in 1984 of a new edition of C.L.R. James's *Beyond a Boundary*, see "C.L.R. James", in *What the Twilight Says: Essays* (New York: Farrar, Straus and Giroux, 1998), 115–20.

55. C.L.R. James, "The Mighty Sparrow", in *Party Politics*, 164–75 (quotation, 173); Gordon Rohlehr, *My Whole Life Is Calypso: Essays on Sparrow* (Tunapuna, Trinidad: Gordon Rohlehr, 2015); *The Mighty Sparrow: First Flight*, notes by Gordon Rohlehr (Smithsonian Folkways SFW CD 40534, 2005, compact disc); Rohlehr, *Calypso and Society*, 527–32; Gordon Rohlehr, *A Scuffling of Islands: Essays on Calypso* (San Juan, Trinidad: Lexicon Trinidad, 2004), 40–42; Louis Regis, *The Political Calypso: True Opposition in Trinidad and Tobago 1962–1987* (Gainesville: University Press of Florida, 1999), 1–9. In 1963 V.S. Naipaul produced two enthusiastic programmes about Sparrow for BBC radio (French, *The World Is What It Is*, 240). For additional discussions of calypso during the independence era, see Crowley, "Toward a Definition of 'Calypso'"; *Calypso Awakening: From the Emory Cook Collection*, notes by Kenneth Bilby and Keith Warner (Smithsonian Folkways Recordings SFW CD 40453, 2000, compact disc); and Jocelyne Guilbault, *Governing Sound: The Cultural Politics of Trinidad's Carnival Music* (Chicago: University of Chicago Press, 2007).

56. Paul P. Kennedy, "Trinidad Calypso Singers Ask, 'Jamaica Why You Run Away?'" *New York Times*, 8 October 1961, 41; Errol Hill, *Trinidad Carnival*, 71; *The Mighty Sparrow*, notes by Rohlehr, 5 ("numerous masks"), 11–14; Rohlehr, *Scuffling of*

Islands, 385 ("calypsos sparkled"). Recordings of "Royal Jail", "May May", "Jean and Dinah" and "Pay as You Earn" are included in *16 Carnival Hits: Mighty Sparrow and Lord Kitchener* (Ice Records 920902, 1992, compact disc). The Miramar Club (site of Sparrow's confrontation) was one of Port of Spain's more raucous night spots. Across from the railway station and close to the docks, it attracted both tourists and locals. An advertisement published a few days before independence noted exotic, limbo and other dances; music and magic acts; and an employment opportunity: "24 Hostesses Wanted.... Must be able to entertain tourists" (Miramar advertisement, *TG*, 27 August 1962, 5). A guidebook from this period says the club featured a balcony from which tourists could watch "girls-of-the-night in many colors". See Sydney Clark, *All the Best in the Caribbean, Including the Bahamas and Bermuda* (New York: Dodd, Mead and Company, 1959), 288.

57. Brunell Jones, "Calypso Tent Opens Tonight", Show-Time, *Evening News*, 5 January 1962, 4; Derek Walcott, "Calypsonians! Danger Lurks in Tin Pan Alley", *TG*, 25 February 1962, 23; "Sparrow Is King", *TG*, 5 March 1962, 1; Carnival advertisement, *TG*, 23 February 1962, 5; Rohlehr, *Scuffling of Islands*, 46–49 (includes excerpts of "Federation" lyrics); "Independence Crown to Brynner", 1. The lyrics of "Model Nation" are available on the Trinidad and Tobago National Library website, accessed 5 November 2017, https://www.nalis.gov.tt/Resources/Subject-Guide/National-Songs#tabposition_25706.

Chapter 8

1. Trinidad and Tobago's population grew from 557,970 in 1946 to 827,957 in 1960. See Dow, *Trinidad and Tobago Year Book, 1962–63*, 145. While the population of Port of Spain proper increased from 92,793 only to 93,930 during this period, the population of its metropolitan area reached 183,662 by 1960. See Goodenough, "Race, Status and Residence", 248, 428.
2. "Trinidad Two for Parley on Town Planning Selected", *TG*, 26 October 1956, 4; "Town and Country Planners Meet in Trinidad", *The Caribbean* 10, no. 5 (December 1956): 137–39, 150; "The Town and Country Planning Exhibition", *The Caribbean* 10, no. 5 (December 1956): 140–41.
3. Peter Bynoe, letter to the editor, *TG*, 30 May 1959, 8; editorial, *TG*, 2 June 1959, 8; editorial, *Trinidad Chronicle*, 9 July 1959, 4.
4. Vernon Khelawan, "Port-of-Spain Needs a Master Plan", *TG*, 31 January 1960, 5; editorial, *TG*, 10 April 1960, 8; "UK Style Towns for Trinidad", *TG*, 30 July 1960, 1–2 (quotation of Williams, 1); "Town, Country Planning Law Passed", *TG*, 30 July 1960, 3 (quotation of bill); Trinidad and Tobago, Lands and Surveys Department, *Sketch Map of Port of Spain* (Trinidad: Lands and Surveys Litho., 1962).
5. "PNM and the Municipalities", *PNM Weekly*, 1 November 1956, 1–2 (quotation, 2); Irwin Merritt, "Era of Discipline and Dignity", in *Golden Jubilee*, by Municipality of Port-of-Spain, 57–58 (see 36–37 for a list of mayors).
6. Merritt, "Era of Discipline and Dignity", 57–58; "$¼m. to Brighten Up PoS", *TG*,

31 October 1961, 2; editorial, *Evening News*, 1 November 1961, 2 (the paper said, "Few things beautify a city more than brightly lit streets"); "$32M Sewerage Scheme Launched", *TG*, 13 June 1962, 1–2; "'Keep Your City Clean' Week On", *TG*, 24 October 1961, 9; John Grimes, "The Drive Is on to Make P-of-S the WI's Most Beautiful City", *Evening News*, 18 June 1958, 6–7 (quotation, 6); "PoS Gets a Botanical Reservoir", *TG*, 6 May 1962, 4.

7. Khelawan, "Port-of-Spain Needs a Master Plan", 5; Valentine Brown, "'Operation Underground", *TG*, 24 September 1961, 3. Joseph Alwin Awon worked as a surveyor in the Trinidad Department of Works and Hydraulics before travelling in 1947 to Britain, where he obtained an architectural degree at the London Polytechnic College, worked with several architectural firms, obtained a diploma in town planning (with a thesis on his proposed Port of Spain civic centre) and was employed as a town-planning officer with the London County Council (see "Architect Coming Home: Staging London Show", *TG*, 12 April 1958, 8).

8. "P-of-S End of Swamp Road", *Evening News*, 30 May 1958, 5; "$3.7m. Highway a Traffic Hazard", *TG*, 10 May 1962, 3; editorial, *Evening News*, 11 May 1962, 4. By 1962 the government was taking action to address water seepage into the Beetham Highway and sinkage, conditions that it had anticipated.

9. "Minister Opens 'Tourist Attraction' Road", *TG*, 4 June 1959, 1–2; "Lady Young Road", *Trinidad Chronicle*, 4 June 1959, 1; Carl Jacobs, "$1½m. Turns Out a Motorist's Dream", *TG*, 5 June 1959, 12. For an indication of the improved access to Port of Spain provided by the Beetham Highway and the Lady Young Road, compare the 1962 *Sketch Map of Port of Spain* with Trinidad and Tobago, Lands and Surveys Department, *Sketch Map of Port of Spain* (Trinidad: Lands and Surveys Department, 1958).

10. For overviews of the demography and residential characteristics of Port of Spain during the postwar era, see Goodenough, "Race, Status and Residence", 291–501; and Ronald Briggs and Dennis Conway, "The Evolution of Urban Ecological Structure: Theory and a Case Study, Port of Spain, Trinidad", *Social Science Quarterly* 55, no. 4 (1975): 871–88.

11. See Watkins, Gray and Partners, "Building in Trinidad", *Architectural Design* 20, no. 9 (1950): 244–47; Newel Lewis, *Ajoupa*, 299–305; and the newspaper articles and advertisements below concerning building products.

12. Gerald Samuel, "New Style Architecture Drives Bestcrete to $1m. Investment", TMA Supplement, *TG*, 13 May 1962, 10 (accompanied by illustrated advertisement), Bestcrete advertisement, Independence Supplement, *TG*, 26 August 1962, 25; Trinidad Clay Products advertisement, *TG*, 1 October 1961, 17; "Caribbean Mosaic Makes the Floor Cleaning Job Easy", TMA Supplement, *TG*, 13 May 1962, 12 (accompanied by advertisement); Ready-Mix Concrete advertisement, *TG*, 11 May 1959, 3; Aluminum Industries advertisement, *TG*, 27 October 1962, 10–11.

13. Trinidad and Tobago, *Report of the Planning and Housing Commission*, 1950, 1954, 1957; editorial, *TG*, 6 September 1956, 8; "Maharaj Glad Notes Exchanged", *TG*, 15 April 1960, 9–11 (this article on a legislative council session includes extended remarks by Gerard Montano on housing issues); "Housing Bill Unanimously

Passed", *TG*, 21 July 1962, 9; "Senate Rushes Through Housing Bill", *TG*, 24 July 1962, 3; editorial, *TG*, 11 January 1961, 8; editorial, *TG*, 7 June 1962, 10 (includes 70 per cent statistic).

14. *Report of the Planning and Housing Commission*, 1950, 1954, 1957; Trinidad and Tobago, *Annual Report of the National Housing Authority, 1963*; John Grimes, "The Planning and Housing Buildings", *TG*, 14 October 1956, 29; "Modern Flats Going Up at Mango Rose", *TG*, 4 September 1962, 16; Cummings, *Barrack-Yard Dwellers*, 157–58, 176. The National Housing Authority report and the 1962 *Guardian* article both include photographs of the nine-storey building at Mango Rose; the authority report also contains examples of floor plans used for its four-storey buildings in the Port of Spain area. A photograph of a three-storey building at an unspecified location in eastern Port of Spain is included in "Trinidad's Progress", *Evening News*, 29 April 1958, 6, with a caption reading, "Buildings like this provide light and air and healthy conditions where at one time people lived in shacks".

15. *Report of the Planning and Housing Commission, 1957*, 4–5; *Annual Report of the National Housing Authority, 1963*, 27; David Renwick, "This Is Morvant", *TG*, 16 March 1958, 4; Lennox King, "450 Families Get Their Own Homes", *Trinidad Chronicle*, 19 May 1958, 5; "Morvant Site for First Public Park", *TG*, 1 April 1960, 14. A Bestcrete advertisement published in the *Trinidad Guardian* on 20 April 1958 (30) includes photographs of a Self-Help house in Morvant under construction with concrete blocks. During this same period, the central government also carried out Aided Self-Help and Rental Mortgage housing projects in other locations around Trinidad.

16. Editorial, *TG*, 24 May 1959, 8; John Grimes, "Shanty Town Sets Example", *TG*, 7 June 1959, 10 (including quotations); John Grimes, "Shanty Towners Not Eager to Start Again", *TG*, 14 June 1959, 5.

17. Editorial, *TG*, 15 July 1960, 8; "Rehabilitation of Shanty Town Starts", *TG*, 14 September 1961, 11; editorial, *Evening News*, 15 September 1961, 2.

18. Mark Raymond, "Modern Trinidad Outlined and the Works of Colin Laird and Anthony Lewis", *Docomomo* 33 (September 2005): 64–70. For additional essays by Raymond on modernism in both residential and public architecture in Trinidad, see "Critical Practice: The Architecture of Trinidad", *Archivos de Arquitectura Antillana* 34 (September 2009): 198–207; and "Architecture, Independence, and Identity in the Commonwealth Caribbean", sx salon (*Small Axe* website), 2013, http://smallaxe.net/wordpress3/discussions/2013/02/11/architecture-independence-and-identity-in-the-commonwealth-caribbean/.

19. Carl Jacobs, "Federation Park! . . . A Show Window for Dreamers", *TG*, 28 April 1958, 3; "Federation Park", *Nation*, 30 March 1962, 3a–4a. Unfortunately, few photographs are available of Federation Park homes during the 1950s, and there has been much renovation and new construction in the neighbourhood since then. As of 2013, however, it was still possible to observe examples of the original designs of Anthony Lewis and Prior, Lourenco and Nothnagel. The firm of Mence and Moore was founded in London, maintained offices in Port of Spain and Bridgetown (Barbados), and carried out extensive work in the Caribbean. See entries for Stanley Mence, Arthur Moore, and Mence and Moore in Smith, *Trinidad: Who, What, Why*, 227, 420.

20. Geoffrey MacLean and Brian Lewis, eds., *Manikin: The Art and Architecture of Anthony C. Lewis* (Port of Spain: acla:works, 2009). For a discussion and illustrations of the Church of the Assumption, see 58–65; for residential projects, see 79–91. In 1950 Anthony Lewis wrote an article titled "Towards a West Indian Architecture" for the journal *Bim* in Barbados. Here he asserted: "Architecture is now gaining momentum, not in the imitation of past styles or of a preconceived new style: its terrific impact is the result of integration between Engineers and Architects aiming to achieve structural honesty and a more down to earth architectural truth, expressing our times, needs, climate and materials" (MacLean and Lewis, *Manikin*, 129). In 1956 Lewis spearheaded the formation of the Trinidad and Tobago Society of Architects (66). For additional comments on Lewis, see Raymond, "Modern Trinidad Outlined", 69.

21. Greig B. Allan, "Virile Trend of National Architecture in Trinidad", *TG*, 10 July 1960, 17; and continuing with five additional articles through 14 August 1960, with the series title "Trinidad's Fine Homes". The instalment on Oswald Chase is "Now the Emphasis Is Put on Style", *TG*, 24 July 1960, 17.

22. Derek Walcott, "Psychological House Like a Clover-Leaf in Concrete", *TG*, 22 May 1960, 5. The fact that Chase built on Nagib Elias Drive suggests that he may have obtained land from Elias in connection with designing his house in St Clair.

23. "Trinidad Seen Headed for Big Post-War Building Boom", *TG*, 5 November 1944, 2; Compton Delph, "3,000 Houses Planned for 'Diego'", *TG*, 10 July 1960, 3; editorial, *TG*, 18 February 1961, 6; John Grimes, "Comeback Cracks Are All There 'By Starlite'", *TG*, 7 October 1956, 26; "Drive-In Cinema to Open Wednesday", *TG*, 21 October 1956, 11.

24. Delph, "3,000 Houses", 3; editorial, *TG*, 10 July 1960, 8; "Premier to Open Housing Project", *TG*, 30 March 1961, 18; "'Greatest Triumph' in Housing", *TG*, 6 April 1961, 2 (quotation); "Giant New Housing Plan for Trinidad", *TG*, 8 April 1961, 8–9. I thank longtime Diego Martin resident Kendall Lewis for information on the previous ownership of the Diamond Road lands.

25. Trinidad and Tobago, *Diamond Road Housing Project, Diego Martin Valley* (Trinidad: Ministry of Housing and Local Government, 1961), 3, exhibits 1–5, and aerial photograph inside front cover; "'Diego' Families Ordered to Quit", *TG*, 30 April 1961, 3.

26. Trinidad and Tobago, *Diamond Road*, 5–9 and exhibits 7–8.

27. Ibid., 10 and exhibit 10. For work on Diamond Road, see "4,000 More Houses by III Planned", *TG*, 3 August 1962, 14.

28. Trinidad and Tobago, *Diamond Road*, 10–11 (quotation, 11) and exhibit 13; Bestcrete advertisement, *TG*, 1 August 1962, 12. Drawings of project houses are included in the planning booklet, as is the floor plan for the Type A house. For a photograph of two model houses (with single- and double-pitched roofs), see "Model Houses", *TG*, 10 October 1961, 14. Though most of the houses in the development have been substantially modified over the years, some (as of 2014) remain fairly close to the original designs.

29. Diamond Road Housing Project advertisement, *TG*, 12 January 1962, 3; "The House of Your Dreams" advertisement, *Nation*, 19 January 1962, 15; "Grand Opening" advertisement, *Nation*, 9 February 1962, 4.
30. "This Is Diamond Vale" advertisement, *TG*, 18 July 1962, 3; "This Is Diamond Vale" advertisement, *TG*, 12 August 1962, 5; Mr and Mrs John Joseph advertisement, *TG*, 8 August 1962, 8; Mr and Mrs Vivian Rivero advertisement, *TG*, 15 August 1962, 12. In 2012, playwright/director Freddie Kissoon reminisced on his move with his wife and two-year-old son to Diamond Vale in 1962. Since prospective buyers were concerned that a concrete roof might collapse, Homes International demonstrated its strength by using a crane to rest a tractor on top of a house on Sapphire Drive. See "50 Years in the Vale", *Trinidad and Tobago Newsday*, 4 August 2012, http://newsday.co.tt/commentary/0,164329.html.
31. *Annual Report of the National Housing Authority, 1963*, 13; "Diamond Road Houses", *Nation*, 25 May 1962, 9; "Homes International Sign Agreement", *TG*, 26 May 1962, 13; *Diamond Road*, 8 and exhibit 8; "Chag Road Likely to Start 1963", *TG*, 15 August 1962, 16; editorial, *TG*, 16 August 1962, 10; editorial, *TG*, 24 March 1960, 8. For an example of commentary after the massive Diego Martin flood of November 1961, see H. Neal Fahey, "Cause of Disaster at Diego Martin", *TG*, 30 November 1961, 8.
32. *Opus: A Review* (December 1960). Articles include Colin Laird, "The Appreciation of Architecture", 8–14 (quotation, 14); Oswald Glean Chase, "Architecture a Cultural Fact", 14–20; John Newel Lewis, "The Architect and Society", 21–25 (see especially 21); Anthony Selman, "The New Shapes of Architecture", 29–37 (quotation, 29); and Anthony Lewis, "Notes on the Practice of Architecture", 38–41 (quotation, 41). In addition, this issue includes Derek Walcott's poem "Castiliane", set in a creole-style hotel near a harbour (29–30).
33. Editorial, *TG*, 14 January 1956, 4; "Traffic Congestion Worsens", *Trinidad Chronicle*, 9 June 1958, 5 (includes photographs); editorial, *TG*, 12 April 1960, 8; "Building Boom on Wrightson Road", *TG*, 30 September 1956, 9; Compton Delph, "PoS Looks to Heavens for Parking Space", *TG*, 30 April 1961, 4; Vernon Khelawan, "A New Deal for the Traveller", *TG*, 27 November 1961, 9. For sample photographs of parking in Marine Square during the postwar era, see "Modern building" (National Archives of the United Kingdom, INF 10-363-4) on Flickr; and "Independence Square" (C-29263) on UWISpace.
34. "Trinidad Honours Greatest Political Champion – Cipriani", *Trinidad Chronicle*, 18 April 1959, 1 ("veteran politician"); editorial, *TG*, 18 April 1959, 6; "'Cipriani Cleared the Way' Says Williams at Statue Unveiling", *Trinidad Chronicle*, 19 April 1959, 1. For a photograph of the Cipriani monument, see "View of Independence Square" (GoldF3_119A) on UWISpace.
35. "Tears as Cipriani Statue Unveiled", *TG*, 19 April 1959, 1–2 (Williams quotations, 1); "A New National Spirit", *Trinidad Chronicle*, 21 April 1959, 7 (La Corbiniere quotation).
36. David Renwick, "Trinidadians Irked about Statue of Capt. Cipriani", *Trinidad Chronicle*, 24 April 1959, 2; Lloyd Cartar, "Art, Beauty Should Unite in Public Places", *TG*, 3 May 1959, 5.

37. Editorial, *TG*, 30 May 1960, 6; "New Name for Marine Square", *TG*, 20 April 1961, 2; "Marine Square Gives in to Independence", *TG*, 21 April 1961, 7; editorial, *TG*, 23 April 1961, 6; editorial, *TG*, 30 May 1961, 8.
38. Gordon Grant advertisement, *TG*, 27 May 1959, 7. For photographs of the Gordon Grant building, see Gordon Grant advertisement, *Trinidad Chronicle*, 27 May 1959, 8; and "Independence Square" (C-29263) on UWISpace. The changing ambience of Marine Square is also captured by Edgar Mittelholzer in his novel *A Morning at the Office*. This narrative of Port of Spain's postwar social order is set in an old two-storey commercial building on Marine Square, with pink-painted brick walls, green iron ornamentation of eaves and windows, and a slate roof. The building is flanked by one of similar age and a modern three-storey concrete structure (London: Heinemann Educational Books, 1974 [1950]), 3.
39. "Salvatori to Erect Six-Storey", *TG*, 12 April 1958, 2; "'How We Built Salvatori's'", *Trinidad Chronicle*, 21 June 1959, 2; Lloyd Cartar, "Salvatori Building Combines Office Space with Penthouses", *TG*, 12 June 1960, 4 (quotations); Williams and Williams Aluminium Sunbreakers advertisement, *TG*, 11 November 1961, 12. Watkins and Partners maintained offices in both England and Trinidad.
40. Brunell Jones, "Penthouse Goes Gay for Anniversary Revels Tonight", Show-Time, *Evening News*, 10 November 1961, 5 (quotation); Brunell Jones, "'Conquerabia' Fails to Click under the Lights", Show-Time, *Evening News*, 14 November 1961, 5.
41. "'Project Skyline' Going Apace in Busy PoS", *TG*, 12 November 1961, 11; MacLean and Lewis, *Manikin*, 68–77 (includes drawings and photographs of the Chase Manhattan Bank). I thank Brian Lewis for additional information on the bank design. As of 2016, the bank building serves as a Kentucky Fried Chicken outlet and is almost unrecognizable. The other Independence Square buildings discussed here still stand, with the exception of the Salvatori Building.
42. "New Town Hall Ends Chapter in City History", *TG*, 27 October 1961, 21; editorial, *TG*, 2 September 1961, 8; "Big Crash at Stone Laying", *TG*, 25 April 1958, 1–2; City of Port of Spain, "New Town Hall Official Opening – Friday, October 27, 1961, Souvenir Brochure", 12–14. The cornerstone ceremony is included in British Pathé film clips titled "Royal Tour of the West Indies (1958)" on YouTube.
43. City of Port of Spain, "New Town Hall Official Opening", cover photograph and 15; "New Town Hall" (GoldF5_97B) and "Town Hall and Civic Centre" (GoldF5_98A) postcards on UWISpace; David Renwick, "Race to Complete New Town Hall", *TG*, 1 May 1961, 16; Compton Delph, "Tiles Used in Town Hall Could Cover Football Field", *TG*, 3 September 1961, 5; "Formal Opening, New Town Hall", *TG*, 28 October 1961, 3. An aerial perspective drawing of the complex appears at 1:20 in "Royal Tour of the West Indies (1958)" on YouTube, uploaded by British Pathé, 13 April 2014, https://www.youtube.com/watch?v=MBCXzeWNlRQ. At present, the new town hall stands with a variety of modifications, including the addition of a third level to the central walkway and east wing of the south block.
44. Judy Raymond, "Carlisle Chang", *Caribbean Beat* 31 (May/June 1998), http://caribbean-beat.com/issue-31/carlisle-chang#axzz3ElEnymCZ; National Carnival Commission of Trinidad and Tobago, "Carlisle Chang", accessed 23 March 2016,

http://www.ncctt.org/50years/index.php/111-heritage-stuff/17927-carlisle-chang; Carlisle Chang, "Painting in Trinidad", in *The Artist in West Indian Society: A Symposium*, ed. Errol Hill (Port of Spain: Department of Extra-Mural Studies, University of the West Indies [1963?]), 25–37. In 1961 Chang created a large mural, *The Inherent Nobility of Man*, for a new terminal building under construction at Piarco Airport. This mural, one of his best-known works, was destroyed in 1979 during another terminal-expansion project (see Raymond, "Carlisle Chang", for a photograph).

45. Carlisle Chang, "Conquerabia", in City of Port of Spain, "New Town Hall Official Opening", 10; Derek Walcott, "'Conquerabia' Mural Decorates Forecourt", *TG*, 3 September 1961, 5.

46. Chang, "Conquerabia", 10 (photograph of mural, 11).

47. "New Town Hall after 4,820 Days", *TG*, 21 October 1961, 1–2; "'Conquerabia' Free Show in Square", *TG*, 22 October 1961, 7; "All Set for Opening of $1.4m. Town Hall Today", *TG*, 27 October 1961, 1; "The Premier Cuts It Short", *TG*, 28 October 1961, 1–2 (quotations, 1); "Pageant Called Off as Square Jammed", *TG*, 28 October 1961, 2; "Patient Crowd Fills Square for 'Conquerabia' Pageant", *TG*, 30 October 1961, 2.

48. Delph, "Tiles Used in Town Hall", 5 (quotation of mayor); editorial, *Evening News*, 4 September 1961, 2; "All Set for Opening of $1.4m. Town Hall Today", 1; editorial, *TG*, 28 October 1961, 8.

49. Mariel Brown, "Queen's Hall: Extended History", 1–4, accessed 28 May 2016, http://queenshalltt.com/about/history/extended-history/; Pam Tait, "Queen's Hall – By the People, For the People", *Trinidad Chronicle*, 19 April 1959, 5.

50. Colin Laird, interviewed by Mark Raymond and Marcos Barinas, "Colin Laird: The Foundation of Modern Architecture in the Caribbean", *Archivos de Arquitectura Antillana* 27 (May 2007): 52–54; Caribbean Icons in Science, Technology and Innovation, NIHERST, "Colin Laird, Architect", accessed 5 November 2017, http://www.niherst.gov.tt/icons-1/tt-icons-2/31-colin-laird.htm. For an overview of Laird's career and interview footage, see the video *Public Spaces: The Architecture of Colin Laird*, produced by Banyan for the Colin Laird Project, 2012, DVD.

51. "Concert Hall Dream", *TG*, 29 March 1958, 8; Tait, "Queen's Hall", 5; Queen's Hall opening advertisement, *TG*, 31 May 1959, 19; Brown, "Queen's Hall", 3; Laird, interviewed by Raymond and Barinas, 57. Objections to locating the hall in King George V Park are referenced in David Renwick, "Concert Hall Start", *TG*, 9 March 1958, 3; "Board of Control for Queen's Hall", *TG*, 2 May 1959, 7; editorial, *TG*, 18 May 1959, 8; and "$370,000 Dream Comes True", *Evening News*, 4 June 1959, 2.

52. The *Random House Dictionary of the English Language* defines a catenary as "the curve assumed approximately by a heavy uniform cord or chain hanging freely from two points".

53. "That Queen's Hall", *Trinidad Chronicle*, 10 May 1959, 7; Dorothy St Aubyn, "The Spirit That Made Queen's Hall", *TG*, 17 May 1959, 7; Queen's Hall opening advertisement, 19 (includes a photograph); Laird, interviewed by Raymond and Barinas, 56–57; "Queen's Hall" (National Archives of the United Kingdom, INF 10-363-2) on Flickr. In addition to these sources, I am grateful to Christopher Laird for providing

me with copies of his father's plans, elevations and a perspective drawing of Queen's Hall, along with sample photographs. Laird used essentially the same design for St Ann's as he had prepared for King George V Park, though he altered the front steps to accommodate the change in terrain (see also Renwick, "Concert Hall Start", 3, on this transfer of the design). During the early 2000s, Queen's Hall underwent a renovation that substantially changed its appearance, though its inverted catenary roof remains.

54. "Board of Control for Queen's Hall", *TG*, 2 May 1959, 7.
55. David Renwick, "It Was Queen's Hall Night", *Trinidad Chronicle*, 5 June 1959, 1; "Queen's Hall Opens New Era", *TG*, 5 June 1959, 1 (quotation of Johnstone); "Queen's Hall Milestone in Cultural Progress", *TG*, 5 June 1959, 8, 10 (quotations of Solomon and Beetham, 8).
56. Queen's Hall opening advertisement, *TG*, 3 June 1959, 5; J.S. Barker, "Queen's Hall: Promising Symbol", *TG*, 6 June 1959, 5; "100-Piece Orchestra to Play in Trinidad", *TG*, 19 June 1959, 5; Wyn Lownie, "US Symphony Orchestra for Trinidad Show", *TG*, 30 May 1959, 5.
57. Diana Searl, "Trinidad to Build a Hilton Hotel", *New York Times*, 25 September 1955, X21; Trinidad and Tobago, "Report on Hotel Development", Council Paper No. 1 of 1959, 3–7; "The Key of Trinidad Tourist Industry", *TG*, 10 June 1962, 18; "Hilton Hotel Fully Staffed", *Nation*, 11 May 1962, 4.
58. Annabel Jane Wharton, *Building the Cold War: Hilton International Hotels and Modern Architecture* (Chicago: University of Chicago Press, 2001), 186–90 ("vision of hotels", 189; "first major", 188). Wharton notes that Edward Durell Stone, with his El Panama Hotel (1951) in Panama City, is commonly credited with introducing a guest-room balcony grid and "a Modern openness to the resort hotel". However, the Caribe Hilton preceded this hotel by two years. On the Caribe Hilton as an economic inspiration for the Trinidad government, see "Report on Hotel Development", 5; and editorial, *TG*, 24 May 1962, 12.
59. "Why the Trinidad Hilton Was Built This Way", Hilton Supplement, *TG*, 10 June 1962, 3; Trinidad Hilton drawings, *TG*, 2 September 1956, 1; "Architect Plans to Marry Air Hostess", Hilton Supplement, *TG*, 10 June 1962, 13; "Hilton Soil Work Costs Cut", *TG*, 5 May 1959, 1; "Lowest Bids Up Hotel Costs", *TG*, 23 May 1959, 1; "IDC Rejects All Hilton Bids", *TG*, 24 May 1959, 1–2; "Hilton Hitch 'Over by Monday'", *TG*, 10 April 1960, 1; Lloyd Cartar, "Socoven Sacked from Hilton Job", *TG*, 6 May 1960, 1–2; "IDC Awards Hilton Job to Cubitts", *TG*, 22 May 1960, 11. During this period, Warner, Burns, Toan and Lunde was already designing university buildings (especially libraries) as well as hotels; both would remain major parts of its practice in later decades. Today the firm is known as WBTL Architects. Bridget Brereton and Primnath Gooptar record that Ranjit Kumar, who directed the expansion of Wrightson Road during 1937–1940, worked on the Hilton project in 1960 as an engineer for Socoven. They suggest that Kumar repeatedly raised design issues that led to work stoppages and eventually to the termination of the relationship between the government and Socoven (see *Ranjit Kumar*, 68).
60. Anthony, *Port-of-Spain in a World at War*, 109–10; "Talk on Shrubs for Hotel:

Hilton", *TG*, 5 March 1958, 7; "Landscape Architect 'Excited over Hilton'", *TG*, 20 March 1960, 7; "There's Beauty in the View", Hilton Supplement, *TG*, 10 June 1962, 14–15.

61. "Welcome to This Upside Down Hotel!" Hilton Supplement, *TG*, 10 June 1962, 2; "Why The Trinidad Hilton Was Built This Way", 3; "'Boucan' Menu Has Rich Local Fare", Hilton Supplement, *TG*, 10 June 1962, 10; "This Cook Never Had a Lesson", Hilton Supplement, *TG*, 10 June 1962, 11; "Hilton Completes Two 'Sample' Guest Rooms", *TG*, 18 June 1961, 14; "Easy to Entertain Friends", Hilton Supplement, *TG*, 10 June 1962, 6. For a brief report on the hotel, including several photographs and a simplified site plan, see "Building for Vacations", *Architectural Forum* 177 (December 1962): 91–93. Numerous postcard images are available in UWISpace under "Trinidad Hilton". In 1969 a north wing of guest rooms, designed by Anthony Lewis, was added to the hotel (see MacLean and Lewis, *Manikin*, 208).
62. "Building for Vacations", 92.
63. "Sybil Quits Teaching to Work on Murals", Hilton Supplement, *TG*, 10 June 1962, 12; Geoffrey MacLean, *Exhibition of Chinese Artists of Trinidad and Tobago* (Trinidad: n.p., 2006); Audley Sue Wing, letter to the editor, *Trinidad and Tobago Newsday*, 23 June 2011, http://newsday.co.tt/letters/0,142741.html.
64. "Carnival and Birds", Hilton Supplement, *TG*, 10 June 1962, 20, 23; "Holder Works on Hilton Mural", *TG*, 7 June 1962, 12; "Frenchman Chosen to Decorate the Hotel", Hilton Supplement, *TG*, 10 June 1962, 18. As of 2014, Atteck's terracottas remain in the Hilton's lobby and Holder's painting is still in the La Boucan room, while Chang's and Morris's Carnival figures have been moved to an extension of the ballroom. Chang's two paintings cannot be seen; artist/writer Christopher Cozier informs me that they remain in their original locations but have been covered with panels. For a photograph of Chang at work on his "Scarlet Ibis" mural, see Raymond, "Carlisle Chang". For a summary of Geoffrey Holder's brilliant career, see Jennifer Dunning and William McDonald, "Geoffrey Holder, Dancer, Actor, Painter and More, Dies at 84", *New York Times*, 6 October 2014, http://www.nytimes.com/2014/10/07/arts/geoffrey-holder-dancer-choreographer-and-man-of-flair-dies-at-84.html?src=xps. On the Hilton's practice of displaying local art at its hotels and the example of the Athens Hilton (opened 1963), see Wharton, *Building the Cold War*, 4–5, 64–65.
65. "$50,000 Ads Plan for Trinidad Hilton", *TG*, 25 January 1962, 14; Trinidad and Tobago Industrial Development Corporation advertisement, Hilton Supplement, *TG*, 10 June 1962, 24; "Carnival Put on at Hilton", *TG*, 15 June 1962, 1–2.
66. "Hilton Set for Big Day", *TG*, 9 June 1962, 12; "Carnival Put on at Hilton", 1–2; Brunell Jones, "Rain-Hit Revue Stuns VIPs at Hilton Opening", *TG*, 16 June 1962, 5; "Hilton Opens with Carnival Last Night", *Nation*, 15 June 1962, 1, 16; Brunell Jones, "Hotel VIPs to See the Best of All", Show-Time, *TG*, 27 May 1962, 16 (quotations). Though the Queen's Hall opening show, *The Happy Wanderer*, was produced by Pat Castagne, it may have been written by Aubrey Adams (see "Queen's Hall Opens New Era", 1). For his Hilton show, Adams depicted the Gaza Strip at a point when it was passing into the realm of nostalgia. On 3 March 1961, the *Trinidad*

Guardian reported that, the previous night, the Reno nightclub "opened its doors for the last time to its bevy of hostesses and waterfront clientele". Since the Flamingo had closed a couple weeks earlier, that left only two clubs on the strip at the time (see "'Gaza Strip' Night Life Heads for Natural Death", *TG*, 3 March 1961, 3).

67. "Hilton Set for Big Day", 12; "Hilton Dedicated in Historic Ceremony", *TG*, 16 June 1962, 1–2; "Hilton Sees Trinidad as the 'World in Little'", *TG*, 16 June 1962, 12 (quotations); "Hilton Opens with Carnival Last Night", 1, 16.

68. On airport improvements, see "Piarco Terminal – Bright New Trinidad Showcase", *TG*, 14 August 1962, 7. While 61,727 passengers arrived at Piarco in 1951, this number had increased to 139,596 by 1960 (see Dow, *Trinidad and Tobago Year Book, 1962–63*, 280). For examples of commentary on the Hilton as an economic engine, see "Hilton Plans for Local Patronage", *TG*, 30 September 1961, 14; "May Opening for Trinidad Hilton Hotel", *TG*, 27 March 1962, 12; editorial, *Evening News*, 7 May 1962, 4; "Hilton Hotel Fully Staffed", 4; editorial, *TG*, 24 May 1962, 12; editorial, *TG*, 14 June 1962, 10; and editorial, *Evening News*, 18 June 1962, 4. See also Diana Searl, "New Hotel Expands Trinidad Tourism", *New York Times*, 10 June 1962, 365. While the Hilton employed primarily local staff, it also reproduced American and Trinidadian racial prejudices. American sociologist Ivar Oxaal attended the Hilton opening and noted white expatriate managers, light-skinned hostesses, darker-skinned waitresses, mainly Indians serving in the Carnival Bar and La Boucan, and generally dark-skinned individuals as bus boys, maids and other lower-level employees (see *Black Intellectuals*, 16).

69. Carl Jacobs, "The Unfinished Hindu Temple", *TG*, 6 November 1961, 12; de Verteuil, *Temples of Trinidad*, 210–17.

70. Jacobs, "The Unfinished Hindu Temple", 12; "$86,000 Hindu Temple Opened", *TG*, 11 March 1962, 12; de Verteuil, *Temples of Trinidad*, 212. De Verteuil notes that, between the early 1970s and early 1990s, various changes were made to the Paschim Kaashi complex, including the expansion of the mandir and the erection of small temples for Shiva, Rama, Hanuman and Kali adjacent to the cultural hall (213–17).

71. Carl Jacobs, "Education with Its Sleeves Rolled Up", *TG*, 18 May 1961, 14; "Technical Education Gets a Big Boost", *TG*, 27 May 1961, 1–2; "Princess Opens $2m. Donaldson Institute", *TG*, 5 September 1962, 2 (quotation); John D. Technical Institute advertisement, *TG*, 5 September 1962, 10 (includes a photograph).

72. "Artist's Impression of Television House", *TG*, 18 March 1962, 2 (includes a perspective view by Watkins and Partners); "Trinidad to Get 1st TV Show November", *TG*, 3 June 1962, 2; "TV: At Last!" TTT Television Supplement, *TG*, 28 October 1962, 2 (quotations); "52 Independence TV Sets for the Public", *TG*, 18 August 1962, 1–2; "TTT Jumps the Gun for Independence", TTT Television Supplement, *TG*, 28 October 1962, 6; television advertisements, TTT Television Supplement, *TG*, 28 October 1962, 13.

Conclusion

1. Clarke, "Kingston: A Creole Colonial City", 1–44 (quotation, 12). This study summarizes and revises Clarke's *Kingston, Jamaica: Urban Development and Social Change, 1692–1962* (Berkeley: University of California Press, 1975).
2. For an overview of the landscape of Kingston and the housing of different social classes during the late nineteenth and early twentieth centuries, see also Brian L. Moore and Michele A. Johnson, "'Tu'n yuh han' mek fashion': Creolizing Material Culture", in *"They Do As They Please": The Jamaican Struggle for Cultural Freedom after Morant Bay* (Kingston: University of the West Indies Press, 2011), 11–27. In another work, Moore and Johnson examine imperial celebrations in Kingston's public spaces – observances that included the same basic symbolic elements employed in Port of Spain during this period. See "The Cult of Monarchy and Empire: Moulding British Colonial Subjects", in *Neither Led nor Driven: Contesting British Cultural Imperialism in Jamaica, 1865–1920* (Kingston: University of the West Indies Press, 2004), 271–310.
3. Diane J. Austin-Broos, "Gay Nights and Kingston Town: Representations of Kingston, Jamaica", in *Postmodern Cities and Spaces*, ed. Sophie Watson and Katherine Gibson (Cambridge, MA: Blackwell, 1995), 149–64 (quotation, 149).
4. Krista A. Thompson, "Diving into the Racial Waters of Beach Space in Jamaica: Tropical Modernity and the Myrtle Bank Hotel's Pool", in *An Eye for the Tropics*, 204–51.
5. Ibid., 247.
6. De Barros, *Order and Place in a Colonial City*.
7. Ibid., 167.
8. Celia Karch, "The Bridgetown Club: Corporate Culture in the City", in Marshall and Welch, *Beyond the Bridge*, 192–222 (quotations, 211–12, 220).
9. David V.C. Browne, "Political Awakening in Bridgetown: The Wickman/O'Neal Years", in Marshall and Welch, *Beyond the Bridge*, 272–88 (quotation, 277).
10. Woodville Marshall, "Clement Payne in the City; Or 'Serious' Times in Bridgetown", in Marshall and Welch, *Beyond the Bridge*, 289–311. For more on Payne's activities in Barbados and the subsequent rebellion, see Hilary Beckles, *A History of Barbados: From Amerindian Settlement to Nation-State* (Cambridge: Cambridge University Press, 1990), 163–68.
11. Thompson, "Developing the Tropics: The Politics of the Picturesque in the Bahamas", in *An Eye for the Tropics*, 92–155 (quotation, 155). For background notes on Nassau, see also Thomas D. Boswell and James E. Biggs, "The Bahamas", in Potter, *Urbanization, Planning and Development*, 252–65.
12. Gail Saunders, "The 1942 Riot in Nassau: A Demand for Change?" in *Bahamian Society after Emancipation* (Kingston: Ian Randle, 2003 [1990]), 151–70; Gail Saunders, "The 1958 General Strike in Nassau: A Landmark in Bahamian Society", in *Bahamian Society after Emancipation*, 189–212.
13. On demographic and settlement change in Trinidad after independence, see Dennis Conway, "Trinidad and Tobago", in Potter, *Urbanization, Planning and*

Development, 49–76. Bridget Brereton notes that by 1965 Pointe-à-Pierre was the largest port in Trinidad, both in tonnage and value of shipments (*History of Modern Trinidad*, 215). For an early report on the merger of the Imperial College of Tropical Agriculture and the University College of the West Indies at St Augustine, see Karl Douglas, "A University Comes to Trinidad", *TG*, 28 August 1960, 5. For synopses of political and economic developments in Trinidad in recent decades, see Mark Wilson, "History (Trinidad and Tobago)", Europa World online (London: Routledge), accessed 25 March 2016, http://www.europaworld.com/entry/tt.hi; and Mark Wilson, "Economy (Trinidad and Tobago)", Europa World online (London: Routledge), accessed 25 March 2016, http://www.europaworld.com/entry/tt.ec.

14. On the 1970 Black Power protests, see Ryan, *Race and Nationalism*; Oxaal, *Black Intellectuals*; and Herman L. Bennett, "The Challenge to the Post-Colonial State: A Case Study of the February Revolution in Trinidad", in *The Modern Caribbean*, ed. Franklin W. Knight and Colin A. Palmer (Chapel Hill: University of North Carolina Press, 1989), 129–46. For an examination of expressions of disillusionment and discontent in poetry during the 1960s and 1970s, see Gordon Rohlehr, "My Strangled City", in *My Strangled City and Other Essays* (Port of Spain: Longman Trinidad, 1991), 168–269. On the 1990 uprising, see Selwyn Ryan, *The Muslimeen Grab for Power: Race, Religion and Revolution in Trinidad and Tobago* (Port of Spain: Inprint Caribbean, 1991).

15. On the Citizens for Conservation and the formation of the National Trust of Trinidad and Tobago, see http://citizensforconservationtt.org/main/index.php/about-us. See also the National Trust of Trinidad and Tobago (Geoffrey MacLean and Vel A. Lewis, editorial directors), *The Built Heritage of Trinidad and Tobago* (Port of Spain: National Trust of Trinidad and Tobago, 2012).

16. Bridget Brereton, "Contesting the Past: Narratives of Trinidad and Tobago History", *New West Indian Guide* 81, nos. 3–4 (2007): 169–96. Brereton also outlines two other historical perspectives: a Tobago narrative that expresses the historical and cultural uniqueness of this small island and marginalization by Trinidad; and an indigeneity narrative that developed during the 1990s and challenges claims of the disappearance of native communities from the island. For additional discussion of Trinidad's Afro-creole and Afrocentric historical narratives, see David V. Trotman, "Performing the History: Contesting Historical Narratives in Trinidad and Tobago", *Canadian Journal of Latin American and Caribbean Studies* 32, no. 63 (2007): 73–109. For an examination of Indo-Trinidadian experience as manifested in visual media (including architecture), see Patricia Mohammed, "The Asian Signature", in *Imaging the Caribbean: Culture and Visual Translation* (Between Towns Road, UK: Macmillan, 2009), 249–88. For an analysis of how Trinidadian concepts of the development of a creole nation have been shaped by ethnic relations and political ideologies, see Aisha Khan, "Good to Think?: Creolization, Optimism, and Agency", *Current Anthropology* 48 (2007): 653–66.

17. David V. Trotman, "Public History, Landmarks and Decolonization in Trinidad", *Journal of Caribbean History* 40, no. 1 (2006): 39–63 (quotations: Columbus Square, 42–43; Lord Harris Square, 43); Trotman, "Acts of Possession", 21–43 (quotation on

place names, 39). A postcolonial landscape modification similar to the erection of the statue of Mahatma Gandhi in 1988 was the renaming of King George V Park as Nelson Mandela Park in 2014. The *Trinidad Guardian* reported that the city council enacted this name change with minimal public consultation and that there were "mixed reactions". See Taureef Mohammed, "King George V Park to Be Renamed for Nelson Mandela", *TG*, 17 July 2014, http://www.guardian.co.tt/news/2014-07-17/king-george-v-park-be-renamed-nelson-mandela.

BIBLIOGRAPHY

Maps (in chronological order)

Goad, Chas. E. *Insurance Plan of Port of Spain, Trinidad*. London: Chas. E. Goad, 1895. Online in the Digital Library of the Caribbean, George A. Smathers Libraries, University of Florida, Gainesville, FL: http://ufdc.ufl.edu/CA02000002.

Girod, J. *Plan of Port of Spain and Suburbs*. Port of Spain: Muir, Marshall and Company, 1912.

Trinidad and Tobago, Lands and Surveys Department. *Port of Spain*. Trinidad: Lands and Surveys Department, 1931.

Trinidad and Tobago, Lands and Surveys Department. *Sketch Map of Port of Spain*. Trinidad: Director of Surveys, c. 1945.

Trinidad and Tobago, Lands and Surveys Department. *Sketch Map of Port of Spain*. Trinidad: Lands and Surveys Department, 1958.

Trinidad and Tobago, Lands and Surveys Department. *Sketch Map of Port of Spain*. Trinidad: Lands and Surveys Litho., 1962.

Photograph Collections

National Archives of Trinidad and Tobago.
National Archives of the United Kingdom.
  Trinidad and Tobago. Online on Flickr: https://www.flickr.com/photos/nationalarchives/sets/72157630713859304/.
National Archives of the United States.
  US Army Signal Corps. World War II. Trinidad. Books #1 and #2.
  General Records of the Department of the Navy. Photograph Boxes.
The Alma Jordan Library, University of the West Indies, St Augustine, Trinidad and Tobago. UWISpace (online repository): http://uwispace.sta.uwi.edu/dspace/.

Government Documents and Local Yearbooks

Trinidad and Tobago

Annual Report of the National Housing Authority, 1963.

Clark, Henry James. *"Iere," The Land of the Humming Bird, Being a Sketch of the Island of Trinidad Specially Written for the Trinidad Court of the World's Fair, Chicago.* Port of Spain: Government Printing Office, 1893.

Collens, James Henry, ed. *Trinidad and Tobago Year Book, 1903.* Port of Spain: Government Printing Office, 1902.

———. *Handbook of Trinidad and Tobago.* Port of Spain: Government Printing Office, 1912.

Diamond Road Housing Project, Diego Martin Valley. Trinidad: Ministry of Housing and Local Government, 1961.

Dow, Henry, ed. *Trinidad and Tobago Year Book, 1952.* Port of Spain: Yuille's Printerie, 1952.

———. *Trinidad and Tobago Year Book, 1962–63.* Port of Spain: Yuille's Printerie, 1962.

"Electrical Systems, Port-of-Spain", Council Paper No. 168. *Trinidad Royal Gazette, July to December 1898*, 2533–42. Port of Spain: Government Printing Office, 1899.

Handbook of Trinidad and Tobago. Port of Spain: Government Printing Office, 1924.

Paget, J. *New Illustrated Guide to Trinidad.* Trinidad: Government Printing Office, 1901.

Report of the Planning and Housing Commission, 1950.

Report of the Planning and Housing Commission, 1954.

Report of the Planning and Housing Commission, 1957.

"Report on Hotel Development". Council Paper No. 1 of 1959. Laid before the Legislative Council on 20 February 1959.

Trinidad Blue Book, 1896. Port of Spain: Government Printing Office, 1897.

Trinidad and Tobago Blue Book, 1901–2. Port of Spain: Government Printing Office, 1902.

Trinidad and Tobago Blue Book, 1935. Trinidad: A.L. Rhodes, MBE, Government Printer, 1936.

What Independence Means to You. Trinidad: Government Printing Office, 1962.

City of Port of Spain

City of Port of Spain. "New Town Hall Official Opening – Friday, October 27, 1961, Souvenir Brochure".

Municipality of Port-of-Spain. *Golden Jubilee of the Restoration, 1914–1964.* Port of Spain: Granderson Brothers, 2003 (1964).

Port of Spain City Council. *City of Port of Spain Silver Jubilee, 1914–1939.* Port of Spain, 1939.

Port of Spain City Council. Minutes. 20 July 1914.

United Kingdom

Colonial Reports, Trinidad and Tobago, 1956. London: Her Majesty's Stationery Office, 1959.
Commission of Enquiry into the Recent Disturbances at Port of Spain, Trinidad. London: His Majesty's Stationery Office, 1903.
Trinidad and Tobago Disturbances 1937, Report of Commission. London: His Majesty's Stationery Office, 1938.

United States

Johnson, Robert A. "History of the Trinidad Sector and Base Command". Vol. 1. United States Army, Caribbean Defense Command, 1945. (HTS1)
———. "History of the Trinidad Sector and Base Command". Vol. 3. United States Army, Caribbean Defense Command, 1946. (HTS3)
———. "History of the Trinidad Sector and Base Command". Vol. 4. United States Army, Caribbean Defense Command, 1946. (HTS4)
Shoultz Jr, James C. "History of the Trinidad Sector and Base Command". Vol. 2. United States Army, Caribbean Defense Command, 1947. (HTS2)
———. "History of the Trinidad Sector and Base Command". Vol. 5. United States Army, Caribbean Defense Command, 1947. (HTS5)
Naval History and Heritage Command. *Building the Navy's Bases in World War II: History of the Bureau of Yards and Docks and the Civil Engineer Corps 1940–1946*, vol. 2. Available at https://www.history.navy.mil/.

Newspapers

Trinidad

Argos
Daily News
Evening News
Labour Leader
Mirror
The People
PNM Weekly, continued as *The Nation*
Port-of-Spain Gazette (*POSG*)
Public Opinion
Trinidad Chronicle
Trinidad Guardian (*TG*)

United States Military in Trinidad

Tropical Topics (unpaginated magazine)
Trinidad News Tips (*TNT*)

Other

New York Times
The Times (London)

Books, Pamphlets and Articles

Abell, H.F. "The West Indies as a Winter Resort". *Westminster Review* 137, no. 1 (January 1892): 277–88.

Abrahams, Roger. *The Man-of-Words in the West Indies: Performance and the Emergence of Creole Culture.* Baltimore: Johns Hopkins University Press, 1983.

Ahye, Molly. *Cradle of Caribbean Dance: Beryl McBurnie and the Little Carib Theatre.* Trinidad: Heritage Cultures, 1983.

AlSayyad, Nezar. "Urbanism and the Dominance Equation: Reflections on Colonialism and National Identity". In *Forms of Dominance: On the Architecture and Urbanism of the Colonial Encounter*, edited by Nezar AlSayyad, 1–26. Aldershot, UK: Avebury, 1992.

Anthony, Michael. *Historic Landmarks of Port of Spain.* Oxford: Macmillan, 2008.

———. *The Making of Port-of-Spain.* Port of Spain: Key Caribbean, 1978.

———. *Port-of-Spain in a World at War, 1939–1945.* Port of Spain: Ministry of Sport, Culture and Youth Affairs, n.d.

———. *Towns and Villages of Trinidad and Tobago.* Marabella, Trinidad: Printmaster, 2001.

Aspinall, Algernon. *The Pocket Guide to the West Indies.* London: Sifton, Praed, 1923.

———. *A Wayfarer in the West Indies.* 2nd ed. London: Methuen, 1930.

Augustus. "Port of Spain". *New York Observer and Chronicle*, 15 August 1895, 193–94.

———. "Trinidad". *New York Observer and Chronicle*, 1 August 1895, 129–30.

Austin-Broos, Diane J. "Gay Nights and Kingston Town: Representations of Kingston, Jamaica". In *Postmodern Cities and Spaces*, edited by Sophie Watson and Katherine Gibson, 149–64. Cambridge, MA: Blackwell, 1995.

Azrieli School of Architecture and Urbanism. *A Tale from the Old Library.* Vol. 2: *An Historical Record of the Public Library on Knox Street.* Ottawa: Azrieli School of Architecture and Urbanism, Carleton University, 2012.

———. *A Tale of Two Houses.* Vol. 1: *An Historical Record of the Boissière and Piccadilly Houses.* Ottawa: Azrieli School of Architecture and Urbanism, Carleton University, 2011.

Baker, Phil. "Arthur Calder-Marshall". In *Oxford Dictionary of National Biography*, edited by H.C.G. Matthew and Brian Harrison, 36:831–33. Oxford: Oxford University Press, 2004.

Baptiste, Fitzroy André. *War, Cooperation, and Conflict: The European Possessions in the Caribbean, 1939–1945.* Westport, CT: Greenwood, 1988.

Baugh, Edward. Introduction to *Selected Poems*, by Derek Walcott, edited by Edward Baugh, xi–xvii. New York: Farrar, Straus and Giroux, 2007.

Bauman, Richard. "Performance". In *A Companion to Folklore*, edited by Regina F. Bendix and Galit Hasan-Rokem, 94–118. Malden, MA: Wiley-Blackwell, 2012.

Beckles, Hilary. *A History of Barbados: From Amerindian Settlement to Nation-State*. Cambridge: Cambridge University Press, 1990.

Belgrave, Joseph. "Reflections on Carnival". In Sander, *From Trinidad*, 40–44.

Bennett, Herman L. "The Challenge to the Post-Colonial State: A Case Study of the February Revolution in Trinidad". In *The Modern Caribbean*, edited by Franklin W. Knight and Colin A. Palmer, 129–46. Chapel Hill: University of North Carolina Press, 1989.

Berthelot, Jack, and Martine Gaumé. *Kaz antiyé jan moun ka rété / Caribbean Popular Dwelling / L'Habitat populaire aux Antilles*. Guadeloupe: Editions Perspectives Créoles [1982?].

Besson, Gérard A. *The History of the ANSA McAL Group of Companies*. Port of Spain: ANSA McAL, 2006.

———. *A Photographic Album of Trinidad at the Turn of the Nineteenth Century*. Port of Spain: Paria, 1985.

Besson, Gérard A., and Bridget Brereton, eds. *The Book of Trinidad*. 3rd ed. Port of Spain: Paria, 1992.

Bickerton, Derek. *The Murders of Boysie Singh*. London: Arthur Baker, 1962.

Bisland, Elizabeth. "Life in an English Government House". *Harper's Bazaar* 28, no. 52 (28 December 1895): 1070.

Bolland, O. Nigel. "Historiography of Decolonization in the Anglophone Caribbean". In *Beyond Fragmentation: Perspectives on Caribbean History*, edited by Juanita De Barros, Audra Diptee and David V. Trotman, 265–96. Princeton, NJ: Markus Wiener, 2006.

Boswell, Thomas D., and James E. Biggs. "The Bahamas". In Potter, *Urbanization, Planning and Development*, 252–84.

Braithwaite, Lloyd. "The Problem of Cultural Integration in Trinidad". *Social and Economic Studies* 3, no. 1 (1954): 82–96.

———. *Social Stratification in Trinidad: A Preliminary Analysis*. Kingston: Institute of Social and Economic Research, University of the West Indies, 1975 (1953).

Brereton, Bridget. "The Birthday of Our Race: A Social History of Emancipation Day in Trinidad, 1833–88". In *Trade, Government and Society in Caribbean History*, edited by B.W. Higman, 69–83. Kingston: Heinemann, 1983.

———. "Contesting the Past: Narratives of Trinidad and Tobago History". *New West Indian Guide* 81, nos. 3–4 (2007): 169–96.

———. "EPOS and Cultural Heritage: Historical Framework", 1–23. Unpublished manuscript for the University of the West Indies, St Augustine, RDIF Project "Leveraging Built and Cultural Heritage for Economic Development in East Port of Spain", 2013.

———. *A History of Modern Trinidad, 1783–1962*. Kingston: Heinemann, 1981.

———. "Jubilees: How Trinidad and Tobago Remembered Victoria's Jubilees, the Jubilee of Emancipation, and the Centenary of British Rule". *Journal of Caribbean History* 46, no. 1 (2012): 1–32.

———. *Race Relations in Colonial Trinidad, 1870–1900*. Cambridge: Cambridge University Press, 1979.

———. "The White Elite of Trinidad, 1838–1950". In *The White Minority in the Caribbean*, edited by Howard Johnson and Karl Watson, 32–70. Kingston: Ian Randle, 1998.

Brereton, Bridget, Rhonda Cobham, Mary Rimmer and Lise Winer. Introduction. In Cobham, *Rupert Gray*, ix–lv.

Brereton, Bridget, and Primnath Gooptar. *Ranjit Kumar (1912–1982): Bridging the East and West*. Trinidad: n.p., 2013.

Brierley, J.N. *Trinidad: Then and Now*. Trinidad: Franklin's Electric Printery, 1912.

Briggs, Ronald, and Dennis Conway. "The Evolution of Urban Ecological Structure: Theory and a Case Study, Port of Spain, Trinidad". *Social Science Quarterly* 55, no. 4 (1975): 871–88.

Broome, Lady. "Colonial Memories". *Cornhill Magazine* 7, no. 38 (August 1899): 157–65.

Brown, Mariel. "Queen's Hall: Extended History", 1–7. Accessed 28 May 2016. http://queenshalltt.com/about/history/extended-history/.

Brown, Wenzell. *Angry Men, Laughing Men: The Caribbean Caldron*. New York: Greenberg, 1947.

Browne, David V.C. "Political Awakening in Bridgetown: The Wickman/O'Neal Years". In Marshall and Welch, *Beyond the Bridge*, 272–88.

Buhle, Paul. *C.L.R. James: The Artist as Revolutionary*. London: Verso, 1988.

"Building for Vacations". *Architectural Forum* 177 (December 1962): 91–93.

Bunnell, Tim. "Urban Landscapes". In *The Wiley-Blackwell Companion to Cultural Geography*, edited by Nuala C. Johnson, Richard H. Schein, and Jamie Winders, 278–89. Chichester, West Sussex: Wiley-Blackwell, 2013.

Burkett, Algernon Albert. *Trinidad: "A Jewel of the West"*. London: Francis and Company Printers, [1914?].

Calder-Marshall, Arthur. *Glory Dead*. London: Michael Joseph, 1939.

Cambridge, Innette. "Audrey Jeffers: Key to Trinidadian Philanthropic and Social Service Heritage". In *Caribbean Heritage*, edited by Basil A. Reid, 175–94. Kingston: University of the West Indies Press, 2012.

Cannadine, David. *Ornamentalism: How the British Saw Their Empire*. Oxford: Oxford University Press, 2001.

Carr, Andrew. "Pierrot Grenade". *Caribbean Quarterly* 4 (1956): 281–87.

———. "A Rada Community in Trinidad". *Caribbean Quarterly* 3 (1953): 35–54.

Chang, Carlisle. "Conquerabia". In City of Port of Spain, "New Town Hall Official Opening – Friday, October 27, 1961, Souvenir Brochure", 10–11.

———. "Painting in Trinidad". In *The Artist in West Indian Society: A Symposium*, edited by Errol Hill, 25–37. Port of Spain: Department of Extra-Mural Studies, University of the West Indies, [1963?].

Chase, Oswald Glean. "Architecture a Cultural Fact". *Opus: A Review* (December 1960): 14–20.

Christie, Trevor L. "Life's Reports: Yankees in Trinidad". *Life* 11, no. 20 (17 November 1941): 16–27.

Citizens' Committee of Port-of-Spain. *Souvenir: Silver Jubilee, Port-of-Spain City Council*. Port of Spain: n.p., 1939.

Clark, Sydney. *All the Best in the Caribbean, Including the Bahamas and Bermuda*. New York: Dodd, Mead and Company, 1959.

Clarke, Colin. "Kingston: A Creole Colonial City (1692–1962)". In *Decolonizing the Colonial City: Urbanization and Stratification in Kingston, Jamaica*, 1–44. Oxford: Oxford University Press, 2006.

———. *Kingston, Jamaica: Urban Development and Social Change, 1692–1962*. Berkeley: University of California Press, 1975.

Cobham, Stephen N. *Rupert Gray: A Tale in Black and White*. Edited by Lise Winer. Kingston: University of the West Indies Press, 2006 (1907).

Collens, James Henry. *A Guide to Trinidad*. 2nd ed. London: E. Stock, 1888.

Connor, Edric. *Horizons: The Life and Times of Edric Connor, 1913–1968*. Kingston: Ian Randle, 2007.

Conway, Dennis. "Trinidad and Tobago". In Potter, *Urbanization, Planning and Development*, 49–76.

Cooper, Frederick. *Colonialism in Question*. Berkeley: University of California Press, 2005.

Cosgrove, Denis. "Geography Is Everywhere: Culture and Symbolism in Human Landscapes". In *Horizons in Human Geography*, edited by Derek Gregory and Rex Walford, 118–35. Totowa, NJ: Barnes and Noble Books, 1989.

———. *Social Formation and Symbolic Landscape*. Madison: University of Wisconsin Press, 1998 (1984).

Cowley, John. *Carnival, Canboulay and Calypso: Traditions in the Making*. Cambridge: Cambridge University Press, 1996.

Craig, Robert M. "Modern Classic in American Architecture". *Grove Art Online. Oxford Art Online*. Oxford University Press. Accessed 8 May 2016. http://www.oxfordartonline.com/subscriber/article/grove/art/T2085956.

Crain, Edward. *Historic Architecture in the Caribbean Islands*. Gainesville: University Press of Florida, 1994.

Cresswell, Tim. "Landscape and the Obliteration of Practice". In *Handbook of Cultural Geography*, edited by Kay Anderson, Mona Domosh, Steve Pile and Nigel Thrift, 269–81. London: Sage, 2003.

Crichlow, F.A. "Carnival, 1891–1941". In Smith, *Trinidad Carnival*, 33–42.

Cross, Malcolm. *Urbanization and Urban Growth in the Caribbean*. Cambridge: Cambridge University Press, 1979.

Crowley, Daniel J. "The Midnight Robbers". *Caribbean Quarterly* 4 (1956): 263–74.

———. "Plural and Differential Acculturation in Trinidad". *American Anthropologist* 59 (1957): 817–24.

———. "Toward a Definition of 'Calypso'". Parts 1 and 2. *Ethnomusicology* 3 (1959): 55–66, 117–24.

———. "The Traditional Masques of Carnival". *Caribbean Quarterly* 4 (1956): 194–223.

Cudjoe, Selwyn R. *Beyond Boundaries: The Intellectual Tradition of Trinidad and Tobago in the Nineteenth Century*. Wellesley, MA: Calaloux, 2003.

Cummings, James. "Barrack-Rooms". In Sander, *From Trinidad*, 240–44.

———. *Barrack-Yard Dwellers*. St Augustine, Trinidad: School of Continuing Studies, University of the West Indies, 2004.

De Barros, Juanita. *Order and Place in a Colonial City: Patterns of Struggle and Resistance in Georgetown, British Guiana, 1889–1924*. Montreal: McGill-Queen's University Press, 2002.

De Boissière, Ralph. *Rum and Coca-Cola*. London: Allison and Busby, 1984 (1956).

De Leon, Rafael. *Calypso from France to Trinidad: 800 Years of History*. Trinidad: n.p., c. 1980s.

De Verteuil, Anthony. *The Corsicans in Trinidad*. Port of Spain: Litho Press, 2005.

———. *The Germans in Trinidad*. Port of Spain: Litho Press, 1994.

———. *Temples of Trinidad*. Port of Spain: Litho Press, 2004.

De Verteuil, Anthony, with Adrian Camps-Campins. *The Great Eight*. Port of Spain: Anthony de Verteuil, 2015.

De Verteuil, Anthony, and Miguel Browne, eds. *St. Mary's College, 1863–1988: 125th Anniversary*. Port of Spain: St Mary's College, 1988.

De Verteuil, Louis A.A. *Trinidad: Its Geography, Natural Resources, Administration, Present Conditions and Prospects*. 2nd ed. London: Cassell and Company, 1884.

Della Dora, Veronica. "Travelling Landscape-Objects". *Progress in Human Geography* 33 (2009): 334–54.

Dudley, Shannon. *Music from Behind the Bridge: Steelband Spirit and Politics in Trinidad and Tobago*. New York: Oxford University Press, 2008.

Duncan, James S. *The City as Text: The Politics of Landscape Interpretation in the Kandyan Kingdom*. Cambridge: Cambridge University Press, 1990.

Duncan, James S. and Nancy Duncan. "(Re)reading the Landscape". *Environment and Planning D: Space and Society* 6 (1988): 117–26.

Edwards, Jay D. "The First Comparative Studies of Caribbean Architecture". *New West Indian Guide* 57, nos. 3–4 (1983): 173–200.

Elder, Jacob D. "Color, Music and Conflict: A Study of Aggression in Trinidad with Reference to the Role of Traditional Music". *Ethnomusicology* 8 (1964): 128–36.

———. "Kalinda: Song of the Battling Troubadours of Trinidad". *Journal of the Folklore Institute* 3 (1966): 192–203.

Eldridge, Michael. "There Goes the Transnational Neighborhood: Calypso Buys a Bungalow". *Callaloo* 25 (2002): 620–38.

E.M. "The Little Carib Dance Group". *Caribbean Quarterly* 1, no. 1 (1949): 29–30.

Espinet, Chas. S., and Harry Pitts. *Land of Calypso: The Origin and Development of Trinidad's Folk Song*. Port of Spain: Trinidad's Commercial Printery, 1944.

French, Patrick. *The World Is What It Is: The Authorized Biography of V.S. Naipaul*. New York: Vintage Books, 2008.

Friess, Daniel A., and Tariq Jazeel. "Unlearning 'Landscape'". *Annals of the American Association of Geographers* 107 (2017): 14–21.

Froude, James Anthony. *The English in the West Indies Or, The Bow of Ulysses*. New York: Charles Scribner's Sons, 1888.

Ghosh, Durba. "Another Set of Imperial Turns?" *American Historical Review* 117 (2012): 772–93.

Gilmore, John. *Glimpses of Our Past: A Social History of the Caribbean in Postcards*. Kingston: Ian Randle, 1995.

Goddard, George "Sonny". *Forty Years in the Steelbands: 1939–1979.* London: Karia Press, 1991.

Gomes, Albert. *Through a Maze of Colour.* Port of Spain: Key Caribbean, 1974.

Goodenough, Suzanne Stephanie. "Race, Status and Ecology in Port of Spain, Trinidad". In *Caribbean Social Relations*, edited by Colin G. Clarke, 17–45. Liverpool: Centre for Latin American Studies, University of Liverpool, 1978.

———. "Race, Status and Residence, Port of Spain, Trinidad: A Study of Social and Residential Differentiation and Change". PhD diss., University of Liverpool, 1976.

Gravette, Andrew. *Architectural Heritage of the Caribbean: An A–Z of Historic Buildings.* Kingston: Ian Randle, 2000.

Guilbault, Jocelyne. *Governing Sound: The Cultural Politics of Trinidad's Carnival Music.* Chicago: University of Chicago Press, 2007.

Harris, Richard. "The Evolution of Urban Housing Policy in the British West Indies, 1929–1960s". In Jaffe, *Caribbean City*, 43–68.

Henderson, George L. "What (Else) We Talk About When We Talk About Landscape". In *Everyday America: Cultural Landscape Studies after J.B. Jackson*, edited by Chris Wilson and Paul Groth, 178–98. Berkeley: University of California Press, 2003.

Henry, Paget and Paul Buhle, eds. *C.L.R. James's Caribbean.* Durham: Duke University Press, 1992.

Herskovits, Melville J., and Frances S. Herskovits. *Trinidad Village.* New York: Octagon Books, 1964 (1947).

Higgins, George E. *A History of Trinidad Oil.* Port of Spain: Trinidad Express Newspapers, 1996.

High, Steven. *Base Colonies in the Western Hemisphere, 1940–1967.* New York: Palgrave Macmillan, 2009.

Higman, B.W. *A Concise History of the Caribbean.* Cambridge: Cambridge University Press, 2011.

Hill, Donald R. *Calypso Calaloo: Early Carnival Music in Trinidad.* Gainesville: University Press of Florida, 1993.

Hill, Errol. *The Ping Pong.* Port of Spain: Department of Extra-Mural Studies, University of the West Indies, 1966 (1955).

———. *The Trinidad Carnival: Mandate for a National Theatre.* Austin: University of Texas Press, 1972.

Hill, Robert T. *Cuba and Porto Rico, with the Other Islands of the West Indies.* New York: The Century Company, 1903.

Home, Robert. *Of Planting and Planning: The Making of British Colonial Cities.* 2nd ed. London: Routledge, 2013.

———. "Transferring British Planning Law to the Colonies: The Case of the 1938 Trinidad Town and Regional Planning Ordinance". *Third World Planning Review* 15, no. 4 (1993): 397–410.

Houk, James T. *Spirit, Blood, and Drums: The Orisha Religion in Trinidad.* Philadelphia: Temple University Press, 1995.

Hutchinson, William F. "The West Indies as a Sanitarium". *Times and Register*, 3 January 1891, 3.

Huxley, Aldous. "Introduction to the 1934 Edition". In Mendes, *Pitch Lake*, 7–8.

Jackson, John Brinckerhoff. *Discovering the Vernacular Landscape*. New Haven: Yale University Press, 1984.

Jackson, T.B., ed. *The Book of Trinidad*. Port of Spain: Muir, Marshall and Company, 1904.

Jacobs, W. Richard. "The Politics of Protest in Trinidad: The Strikes and Disturbances of 1937". *Caribbean Studies* 17, nos. 1–2 (1977): 5–54.

Jaffe, Rivke, ed. *The Caribbean City*. Kingston: Ian Randle, 2008.

James, C.L.R. *Beyond a Boundary*. Durham: Duke University Press, 1993 (1963).

———. *The Life of Captain Cipriani: An Account of British Government in the West Indies*. Nelson, UK: Coulton, 1932.

———. *Minty Alley*. London: New Beacon Books, 1971 (1936).

———. *Party Politics in the West Indies*. San Juan, Trinidad: C.L.R. James, c. 1962.

———. "Triumph". In Sander, *From Trinidad*, 86–103.

James, Preston E. "A Geographic Reconnaissance of Trinidad". *Economic Geography* 3, no. 1 (1927): 87–109.

Johnson, Howard. "The United States and the Establishment of the Anglo-American Caribbean Commission". *Journal of Caribbean History* 19, no. 1 (1984): 26–47.

Johnson, Kim. *Descendants of the Dragon: The Chinese in Trinidad 1806–2006*. Kingston: Ian Randle, 2006.

———. *From Tin Pan to TASPO: Steelband in Trinidad, 1939–1951*. Kingston: University of the West Indies Press, 2011.

———. *The Illustrated Story of Pan*. Arima, Trinidad: University of Trinidad and Tobago, 2011.

Johnson, Nuala C. "Political Landscapes". In *The Wiley-Blackwell Companion to Cultural Geography*, edited by Nuala C. Johnson, Richard H. Schein and Jamie Winders, 173–85. Chichester, West Sussex: Wiley-Blackwell, 2013.

Jones, Charles. *Calypso and Carnival of Long Ago and Today*. Port of Spain: n.p., 1947.

Karch, Celia. "The Bridgetown Club: Corporate Culture in the City". In Marshall and Welch, *Beyond the Bridge*, 192–222.

Kelshall, Gaylord T.M. *The U-Boat War in the Caribbean*. Annapolis, MD: Naval Institute Press, 1994.

Khan, Aisha. "Good to Think?: Creolization, Optimism, and Agency". *Current Anthropology* 48 (2007): 653–66.

———. "Portraits in the Mirror: Nature, Culture and Women's Travel Writing in the Caribbean". *Women's Writing* 10, no. 1 (2003): 93–117.

King, Anthony D. "Colonial Cities: Global Pivots of Change". In *Colonial Cities: Essays on Urbanism in a Colonial Context*, edited by Robert J. Ross and Gerard J. Telkamp, 7–32. Dordrecht, Netherlands: Martinus Nijhoff, 1985.

———. "Writing Colonial Space: A Review Article". *Comparative Studies in Society and History* 37 (1995): 541–54.

King, Bruce. *Derek Walcott: A Caribbean Life*. New York: Oxford University Press, 2000.

Kingsley, Charles. *At Last: A Christmas in the West Indies*. London: Macmillan, 1880 (1871).

Kissoon, Freddie. "50 Years in the Vale". *Trinidad and Tobago Newsday*, 4 August 2012. http://newsday.co.tt/commentary/0,164329.html.

Knight, Franklin W. *The Caribbean: The Genesis of a Fragmented Nationalism*. 3rd ed. New York: Oxford University Press, 2012.

Korom, Frank J. *Hosay Trinidad: Muharram Performances in an Indo-Caribbean Diaspora*. Philadelphia: University of Pennsylvania Press, 2003.

Laird, Colin. "The Appreciation of Architecture". *Opus: A Review* (December 1960): 8–14.

———. "Colin Laird: The Foundation of Modern Architecture in the Caribbean". Interview by Mark Raymond and Marcos Barinas. *Archivos de Arquitectura Antillana* 27 (May 2007): 52–73.

———. "Trinidad Town House". *Caribbean Quarterly* 3, no. 4 (1954): 188–98.

Laughlin, Nicholas. "R.I.P. Ralph de Boissiere, 6 October, 1907–16 February, 2008". *Caribbean Review of Books*, 20 February 2008. http://caribbeanreviewofbooks.com/2008/02/20/r-i-p-ralph-de-boissiere-6-october-1907-16-february-2008/.

Laurence, K.O., ed. "The Trinidad Water Riot of 1903: Reflections of an Eyewitness". *Caribbean Quarterly* 15, no. 4 (1969): 5–22.

Leaf, Earl. *Isles of Rhythm*. New York: A.S. Barnes and Company, 1948.

Leigh Fermor, Patrick. *The Traveller's Tree: A Journey through the Caribbean Islands*. New York: Harper and Brothers, 1950.

Lewis, Anthony. "Notes on the Practice of Architecture". *Opus: A Review* (December 1960): 38–41.

Lewis, Peirce F. "Axioms for Reading the Landscape: Some Guides to the American Scene". In Meinig, *Interpretation of Ordinary Landscapes*, 11–32.

———. *New Orleans: The Making of an Urban Landscape*. 2nd ed. Santa Fe: Center for American Places, 2003.

Little Carib Theatre. *Talking Drums*. Programme for formal opening of the Little Carib Theatre, 25 November 1948.

Liverpool, Hollis "Chalkdust". *From the Horse's Mouth*. Diego Martin, Trinidad: Juba, 2003.

Lorimer, Hayden. "Cultural Geography: The Business of Being 'More-Than-Representational'". *Progress in Human Geography* 29 (2005): 83–94.

Lorimer, Joyce, ed. *Sir Walter Ralegh's Discoverie of Guiana*. London: Ashgate, 2006.

Lowenthal, David. "The West Indies Chooses a Capital". *Geographical Review* 48, no. 3 (1958): 336–64.

Macedo, Lynne. "The Impact of Indian Film in Trinidad". In *Beyond the Blood, the Beach and the Banana: New Perspectives in Caribbean Studies*, edited by Sandra Courtman, 298–311. Kingston: Ian Randle, 2004.

MacLean, Geoffrey. *Exhibition of Chinese Artists of Trinidad and Tobago*. Trinidad: n.p., 2006.

MacLean, Geoffrey, and Brian Lewis, eds. *Manikin: The Art and Architecture of Anthony C. Lewis*. Port of Spain: acla:works, 2009.

Magid, Alvin. *Urban Nationalism. A Study of Political Development in Trinidad*. Gainesville: University of Florida Press, 1988.

Mahabir, Winston. *In and Out of Politics*. Trinidad: Inprint Caribbean, 1978.

Marden, Luis. "Americans in the Caribbean". *National Geographic Magazine* 81, no. 6 (June 1942): 723–58.

Marshall, Woodville. "Clement Payne in the City; Or 'Serious' Times in Bridgetown". In Marshall and Welch, *Beyond the Bridge*, 289–311.

Marshall, Woodville, and Pedro Welch, eds. *Beyond the Bridge: Lectures Commemorating Bridgetown's 375th Anniversary*. St Michael, Barbados: Barbados Museum and Historical

Society and the Department of History and Philosophy, University of the West Indies, Cave Hill, 2005.

Martin, Tony. "Revolutionary Upheaval in Trinidad, 1919: Views from British and American Sources". *Journal of Negro History* 58, no. 3 (1973): 313–26.

Mavrogordato, Olga J. *Voices in the Street*. Port of Spain: Paria, 1996 (1977).

Mc Cree, Roy. "History and Development". In *Behind the Bridge: Poverty, Politics and Patronage in Laventille, Trinidad*, edited by Selwyn Ryan, Roy Mc Cree and Godfrey St Bernard, 33–67. St Augustine, Trinidad: Institute of Social and Economic Research, University of the West Indies, 1997.

Meinig, D.W. "The Beholding Eye: Ten Versions of the Same Scene". In Meinig, *Interpretation of Ordinary Landscapes*, 33–48.

———, ed. *The Interpretation of Ordinary Landscapes: Geographical Essays*. New York: Oxford University Press, 1979.

———. "Symbolic Landscapes: Some Idealizations of American Communities". In Meinig, *Interpretation of Ordinary Landscapes*, 164–92.

Mendes, Alfred. *The Autobiography of Alfred H. Mendes, 1897–1991*. Edited by Michèle Levy. Kingston: University of the West Indies Press, 2002.

———. *Black Fauns*. London: New Beacon Books, 1984 (1935).

———. "Her Chinaman's Way". In Sander, *From Trinidad*, 103–18.

———. *Pitch Lake: A Story from Trinidad*. London: New Beacon Books, 1980 (1934).

———. "Sweetman". In Sander, *From Trinidad*, 118–30.

Merriam, Alan P. "Melville Jean Herskovits, 1895–1963". *American Anthropologist* 66 (1964): 83–109.

Mintz, Sidney W. *Caribbean Transformations*. New York: Columbia University Press, 1989 (1974).

Mitchell, Don. "Cultural Landscapes: Just Landscapes or Landscapes of Justice?" *Progress in Human Geography* 27 (2003): 787–96.

———. "New Axioms for Reading the Landscape: Paying Attention to Political Economy and Social Justice". In *Political Economies of Landscape Change: Places of Integrative Power*, edited by James L. Wescoat Jr and Douglas M. Johnston, 29–50. Dordrecht, Netherlands: Springer, 2008.

Mitchell, Don and Carrie Breitbach. "Landscape: Part I". In *The Wiley-Blackwell Companion to Human Geography*, edited by John A. Agnew and James S. Duncan, 209–20. Chichester, West Sussex: Wiley-Blackwell, 2011.

Mittelholzer, Edgar. *A Morning at the Office*. London: Heinemann Educational Books, 1974 (1950).

———. *With a Carib Eye*. London: Secker and Warburg, 1958.

Mohammed, Asad. "Colonial Influences on Urban Form in the Caribbean, Illustrated by Port of Spain, Trinidad and Tobago". In Jaffe, *Caribbean City*, 24–42.

Mohammed, Patricia. "The Asian Signature". In *Imaging the Caribbean: Culture and Visual Translation*, 249–88. Between Towns Road, UK: Macmillan, 2009.

Moore, Brian L., and Michele A. Johnson. *Neither Led nor Driven: Contesting British Cultural Imperialism in Jamaica, 1865–1920*. Kingston: University of the West Indies Press, 2004.

———. *"They Do as They Please": The Jamaican Struggle for Cultural Freedom after Morant Bay*. Kingston: University of the West Indies Press, 2011.

Morales Padrón, Francisco. *Spanish Trinidad*. Edited and translated by Armando García de la Torre. Kingston: Ian Randle, 2012.

Morison, Samuel Eliot. *The Battle of the Atlantic, September 1939–May 1943 (History of the United States Naval Operations in World War II)*. Vol. 1. Boston: Little, Brown and Company, 1988 (1947).

Morrison, Allen. "The Trams and Trolleybuses of Trinidad and Tobago". Accessed 1 May 2016. http://www.tramz.com/tt/tt.html.

Naipaul, V.S. *Between Father and Son: Family Letters*. New York: Vintage Books, 2001.

———. *A House for Mr. Biswas*. New York: Vintage Books, 1984 (1961).

———. *The Middle Passage*. New York: Vintage Books, 1981 (1962).

———. *Miguel Street*. New York: Vintage Books, 1984 (1959).

———. "Prologue to an Autobiography". In *Finding the Center: Two Narratives*, 3–72. New York: Vintage Books, 1986.

———. "The Worm in the Bud". In *A Writer's People: Ways of Looking and Feeling*. London: Picador, 2007.

National Trust of Trinidad and Tobago (Geoffrey MacLean and Vel A. Lewis, editorial directors). *The Built Heritage of Trinidad and Tobago*. Port of Spain: National Trust of Trinidad and Tobago, 2012.

Neptune, Harvey R. *Caliban and the Yankees: Trinidad and the United States Occupation*. Chapel Hill: University of North Carolina Press, 2007.

Newel Lewis, John. *Ajoupa*. Trinidad: John Newel Lewis, 1983.

———. "The Architect and Society". *Opus: A Review* (December 1960): 21–25.

———. "Trinidad and Tobago, Architecture". In *Dictionary of Art*, edited by Jane Turner, 31:333–35. New York: Grove, 1996.

Newson, Linda A. *Aboriginal and Spanish Colonial Trinidad: A Study in Culture Contact*. London: Academic Press, 1976.

Nobel, Philip. "Who Built Mr. Blandings' Dream House?" In *Architecture and Film*, edited by Mark Lamster, 49–87. New York: Princeton Architectural Press, 2000.

Oakley, Amy. *Behold the West Indies*. New York: D. Appleton-Century Company, 1941.

Ober, Frederick A. *A Guide to the West Indies and Bermudas*. New York: Dodd, Mead and Company, 1908.

———. *Our West Indian Neighbors*. New York: James Pott and Company, 1904.

Oliver, Paul, ed. "Caribbean". In *Encyclopedia of Vernacular Architecture of the World*, 3:1699–725. Cambridge: Cambridge University Press, 1997.

Ottley, Carlton Robert. *The Story of Port of Spain*. St James, Trinidad: Charran Educational, n.d. [1962].

———. *Trinidad Callaloo: Life in Trinidad from 1851–1900*. Diego Martin, Trinidad: Crusoe, 1978.

Oxaal, Ivar. *Black Intellectuals and the Dilemmas of Race and Class in Trinidad*. Cambridge, MA: Schenkman, 1982.

Palmer, Annette. "Black American Soldiers in Trinidad, 1942–44: Wartime Politics in a Colonial Society". *Journal of Imperial and Commonwealth History* 14 (1986): 203–18.

———. "Rum and Coca Cola: The United States in the British Caribbean 1940–1945". *The Americas* 43 (1987): 441–51.

Paquet, Sandra Pouchet. "Samuel Dickson Selvon". In *Fifty Caribbean Writers: A Bio-Bibliographical Critical Sourcebook*, edited by Daryl Cumber Dance, 439–49. Westport, CT: Greenwood, 1986.

Pearse, Andrew. "Carnival in Nineteenth-Century Trinidad". *Caribbean Quarterly* 4 (1956): 175–93.

———, ed. "Mitto Sampson on Calypso Legends of the Nineteenth Century". *Caribbean Quarterly* 4 (1956): 250–62.

Pemberton, Rita. "Water and Related Issues in Nineteenth-Century Trinidad". *Journal of Caribbean History* 40, no. 2 (2006): 235–52.

Potter, Robert B., ed. *Urbanization, Planning and Development in the Caribbean*. London: Mansell, 1989.

Potter, Robert B., David Barker, Dennis Conway and Thomas Klak. "Urban Dynamics and Townscapes". In *The Contemporary Caribbean*, 269–312. New York: Prentice Hall, 2004.

Procope, Bruce. "The Dragon Band or Devil Band". *Caribbean Quarterly* 4 (1956): 275–80.

Punch, Ruskin. "Trinidadian: Indian". In Oliver, *Encyclopedia of Vernacular Architecture of the World*, 1723.

Quevedo, Raymond. *Atilla's Kaiso: A Short History of Trinidad Calypso*. St Augustine, Trinidad: Department of Extra-Mural Studies, University of the West Indies, 1983.

———, ed. *Victory Calypsoes*. Port of Spain: Trinidad Publishing, 1944.

Raymond, Arthur F. "Origins of the Savannah Carnival and the Development of the Down Town Celebrations". In *The Humming Bird Carnival*, edited by Aubrey E. James, 8–10. Trinidad: n.p., 1960.

Raymond, Judy. "Carlisle Chang". *Caribbean Beat* 31 (May/June 1998). http://caribbean-beat.com/issue-31/carlisle-chang#axzz3ElEnymCZ.

———. *The Colour of Shadows: Images of Caribbean Slavery*. Pompano Beach, FL: Caribbean Studies Press, 2016.

Raymond, Mark. "Architecture, Independence, and Identity in the Commonwealth Caribbean". sx salon (*Small Axe* website), 2013. http://smallaxe.net/wordpress3/discussions/2013/02/11/architecture-independence-and-identity-in-the-commonwealth-caribbean/.

———. "Critical Practice: The Architecture of Trinidad". *Archivos de Arquitectura Antillana* 34 (September 2009): 198–207.

———. "Modern Trinidad Outlined and the Works of Colin Laird and Anthony Lewis". *Docomomo* 33 (September 2005): 64–70.

Reddock, Rhoda E. *Elma François: The NWCSA and the Worker's Struggle for Change in the Caribbean*. London: New Beacon Books, 1988.

———. *Women, Labour and Politics in Trinidad and Tobago: A History*. London: Zed Books, 1994.

Regis, Louis. *The Political Calypso: True Opposition in Trinidad and Tobago 1962–1987*. Gainesville: University Press of Florida, 1999.

Rego, Michael. *Queen's Park Hotel, Port of Spain, Trinidad*. West Indies History Booklet No. 2. Wakefield, UK: Michael Rego, 2009.

Roberts, W. Adolphe. "Future of the British Caribbean". *Survey Graphic* 30 (April 1941): 229–34.

Rodriguez, Ivan A., and Margot Ammidown. *From Wilderness to Metropolis: The History and Architecture of Dade County, Florida, 1825–1940*. Miami: Franklin Press, 1982.

Rohlehr, Gordon. *Calypso and Society in Pre-Independence Trinidad*. Port of Spain: Gordon Rohlehr, 1990.

———. "Intersecting Q.R.C. Lives: James, Williams, Naipaul". In *Transgression, Transition, Transformation: Essays in Caribbean Culture*, 199–223. San Juan, Trinidad: Lexicon Trinidad, 2007.

———. "My Strangled City". In *My Strangled City and Other Essays*, 168–269. Port of Spain: Longman Trinidad, 1991.

———. *My Whole Life Is Calypso: Essays on Sparrow*. Tunapuna, Trinidad: Gordon Rohlehr, 2015.

———. *A Scuffling of Islands: Essays on Calypso*. San Juan, Trinidad: Lexicon Trinidad, 2004.

Rohlehr, Gordon, and Bridget Brereton. "Introduction, Horizons: The Autobiography of Edric Connor, 1913–1968". In Connor, *Horizons*, xv–lxi.

Roosevelt, Eleanor. "My Day" (syndicated newspaper column), 18 March 1944. Online at George Washington University. http://www.gwu.edu/~erpapers/myday/displaydoc.cfm?_y=1944&_f=md056748.

Rose, Mitch, and John Wylie. "Animating Landscape". *Environment and Planning D: Space and Society* 24 (2006): 475–79.

———. "Landscape: Part II". In *The Wiley-Blackwell Companion to Human Geography*, edited by John A. Agnew and James S. Duncan, 221–34. Chichester, West Sussex: Wiley-Blackwell, 2011.

Rouff, Anthony E. *"Authentic" Facts on the Origin of the Steelband*. St Augustine, Trinidad: Bowen's Printery, 1972.

Rutter, Owen. *If Crab No Walk: A Traveller in the West Indies*. London: Hutchinson and Company, 1933.

Ryan, Selwyn. *Eric Williams: The Myth and the Man*. Kingston: University of the West Indies Press, 2009.

———. *The Muslimeen Grab for Power: Race, Religion and Revolution in Trinidad and Tobago*. Port of Spain: Inprint Caribbean, 1991.

———. *Race and Nationalism in Trinidad and Tobago: A Study of Decolonization in a Multiracial Society*. Toronto: University of Toronto Press, 1972.

Samaroo, Brinsley. Foreword to *Through a Maze of Colour*, by Albert Gomes, ix–xvi. Port of Spain: Key Caribbean, 1974.

———. "Seeking a Space in the Politics: Muslim Efforts to Join the Political Process in British Guiana and Trinidad in the 20th Century". *Man in India* 93, no. 1 (2013): 201–11.

Samaroo, Brinsley, and Cherita Girvan. "The Trinidad Workingmen's Association and the Origins of Popular Protest in a Crown Colony". *Social and Economic Studies* 21, no. 2 (1972): 205–22.

Sander, Reinhard W., ed. *From Trinidad: An Anthology of Early West Indian Writing*. London: Hodder and Stoughton, 1978.

———. "Ralph de Boissière". In *Fifty Caribbean Writers: A Bio-Bibliographical Critical Sourcebook*, edited by Daryl Cumber Dance, 151–59. Westport, CT: Greenwood, 1986.

———. *The Trinidad Awakening: West Indian Literature of the Nineteen-Thirties*. Westport, CT: Greenwood, 1988.

Saunders, Gail. *Bahamian Society after Emancipation*. Kingston: Ian Randle, 2003 (1990).

Scull, Guy H. "The Merry Carnival of Mi-Carême in Trinidad". *Collier's Weekly* 26 (30 March 1901): 18–19.

Seamen's Guide to Trinidad. Port of Spain: Yuille Company, n.d.

Selman, Anthony. "The New Shapes of Architecture". *Opus: A Review* (December 1960): 29–37.

Selvon, Samuel. *A Brighter Sun*. Harlow, Essex: Longman 2004 (1952).

———. "Wartime Activities". In *Ways of Sunlight*, 82–93. Harlow, Essex: Longman Drumbeat, 1979 (1957).

Simey, T.S. "A New Capital for the British West Indies". *Town Planning Review* 28, no. 1 (1957): 63–70.

Singh, Kelvin. *Race and Class Struggles in a Colonial State: Trinidad 1917–1945*. Kingston: The Press, University of the West Indies, 1994.

Smith, James H., ed. *Trinidad Carnival*. Port of Spain: n.p., 1946.

Smith, Lloyd Sydney. *Trinidad: Who, What, Why*. Port of Spain: n.p., [1950?].

Smith, Victor. "Trinidad". *Chautauquan* 10, no. 4 (January 1890): 450–54.

Stark, James H. *Stark's Guide-Book and History of Trinidad*. Boston: James H. Stark, 1897.

Starr, Ida M.H. *Gardens of the Caribbees: Sketches of a Cruise to the West Indies and the Spanish Main*. Vol. 1. Boston: L.C. Page and Company, 1904.

Stoler, Ann Laura, and Frederick Cooper. "Between Metropole and Colony: Rethinking a Research Agenda". In *Tensions of Empire: Colonial Cultures in a Bourgeois World*, edited by Frederick Cooper and Ann Laura Stoler, 1–56. Berkeley: University of California Press, 1997.

St Pierre, Maurice. "The Chaguaramas Affair in Trinidad and Tobago: An Intellectual Reassessment". *Journal of Caribbean History* 40, no. 1 (2006): 92–116.

Stuempfle, Stephen. *The Steelband Movement: The Forging of a National Art in Trinidad and Tobago*. Philadelphia: University of Pennsylvania Press, 1995.

Sue Wing, Audley. Letter to the editor. *Trinidad and Tobago Newsday*, 23 June 2011. http://newsday.co.tt/letters/0,142741.html.

This Country of Ours. Port of Spain: PNM Publishing, 1962.

Thomas, J.J. *Froudacity: West Indian Fables by James Anthony Froude Explained*. London: New Beacon Books, 1969 (1889).

Thomas, Roy E., ed. *The Trinidad Labour Riots of 1937: Perspectives 50 Years Later*. St Augustine, Trinidad: Extra-Mural Studies Unit, University of the West Indies, 1987.

Thompson, Krista A. *An Eye for the Tropics: Tourism, Photography, and Framing the Caribbean Picturesque*. Durham: Duke University Press, 2006.

"Town and Country Planners Meet in Trinidad". *The Caribbean* 10, no. 5 (December 1956): 137–39, 150.

"The Town and Country Planning Exhibition". *The Caribbean* 10, no. 5 (December 1956): 140–41.

Treves, Frederick. *The Cradle of the Deep: An Account of a Voyage to the West Indies*. London: Smith, Elder, 1908.

"Trinidad Bastion: US Starts Building Base on British Isle". *Life* 10, no. 14 (7 April 1941): 77–81.

Trinidad: The Riviera of the Caribbean. Port of Spain: Trinidad Publishing, 1924.

Trollope, Anthony. *The West Indies and the Spanish Main*. New York: Harper and Brothers, 1860.

Trotman, David V. "Acts of Possession and Symbolic Decolonisation in Trinidad and Tobago". *Caribbean Quarterly* 58, no.1 (2012): 21–43.

———. *Crime in Trinidad: Conflict and Control in a Plantation Society, 1838–1900*. Knoxville: University of Tennessee Press, 1986.

———. "Performing the History: Contesting Historical Narratives in Trinidad and Tobago". *Canadian Journal of Latin American and Caribbean Studies* 32, no. 63 (2007): 73–109.

———. "Public History, Landmarks and Decolonization in Trinidad". *Journal of Caribbean History* 40, no. 1 (2006): 39–63.

———. "Reflections on the Children of Shango: An Essay on a History of Orisa Worship in Trinidad". *Slavery and Abolition* 28, no. 2 (2007): 211–34.

Tuan, Yi-Fu. *Space and Place: The Perspective of Experience*. Minneapolis: University of Minnesota Press, 1977.

———. "Thought and Landscape: The Eye and the Mind's Eye". In Meinig, *Interpretation of Ordinary Landscapes*, 89–102.

Turner, Victor. *The Forest of Symbols: Aspects of Ndembu Ritual*. Ithaca: Cornell University Press, 1967.

Vandercook, John W. *Caribbee Cruise: A Book of the West Indies*. New York: Reynal and Hitchcock, 1938.

Verrill, A. Hyatt. *The Book of the West Indies*. New York: E.P. Dutton and Company, 1917.

———. *West Indies of Today*. New York: Dodd, Mead and Company, 1931.

Vlach, John Michael. "Affecting Architecture of the Yoruba". *African Arts* 10, no. 1 (1976): 48–53, 99.

Walcott, Derek. *The Castaway and Other Poems*. London: Jonathan Cape, 1965.

———. "Castiliane". *Opus: A Review* (December 1960): 29–30.

———. *In a Green Night: Poems 1948–1960*. London: Jonathan Cape, 1962.

———. "On Choosing Port of Spain". In *David Frost Introduces Trinidad and Tobago*, edited by Michael Anthony and Andrew Carr, 14–23. London: André Deutsch, 1975.

———. *What the Twilight Says: Essays*. New York: Farrar, Straus and Giroux, 1998.

Walsh Construction Company. *Caribbean Area, 1941–1943*. N.p.: n.d.

Warner-Lewis, Maureen. *Guinea's Other Suns: The African Dynamic in Trinidad Culture*. Dover, MA: Majority Press, 1991. Reprint, Kingston: University of the West Indies Press, 2015.

Watkins, Gray and Partners. "Building in Trinidad". *Architectural Design* 20, no. 9 (1950): 244–47.

Waugh, Alec. *Hot Countries*. New York: Farrar and Rinehart, 1930.

Wharton, Annabel Jane. *Building the Cold War: Hilton International Hotels and Modern Architecture*. Chicago: University of Chicago Press, 2001.

Wilcox, Ella Wheeler. *Sailing Sunny Seas*. Chicago: W.B. Conkey Company, 1909.

Williams, Eric. *From Columbus to Castro: The History of the Caribbean*. New York: Vintage Books, 1984 (1970).

———. *History of the People of Trinidad and Tobago*. Port of Spain: PNM Publishing, 1962.
———. *Inward Hunger: The Education of a Prime Minister*. London: André Deutsch, 1969.
Wilson, Mark. "Economy (Trinidad and Tobago)". Europa World online. London: Routledge. Accessed 25 March 2016. http://www.europaworld.com/entry/tt.ec.
———. "History (Trinidad and Tobago)". Europa World online. London: Routledge. Accessed 25 March 2016. http://www.europaworld.com/entry/tt.hi.
Wise, K.S. "Conquerabia or Cumacarapo". In Besson, *A Photographic Album of Trinidad*, 1–2.
Wood, Donald. *Trinidad in Transition*. London: Oxford University Press, 1968.
Wyke, Terry, with Harry Cocks. *Public Sculpture of Greater Manchester*. Public Sculpture of Britain, vol. 8. Liverpool: Liverpool University Press, 2004.
Wylie, John. *Landscape*. London: Routledge, 2007.
Yelvington, Kevin A. "The War in Ethiopia and Trinidad, 1935–1936". In *The Colonial Caribbean in Transition: Essays on Postemancipation Social and Cultural History*, edited by Bridget Brereton and Kevin A. Yelvington, 189–225. Kingston: The Press, University of the West Indies, 1999.
Yeoh, Brenda S.A. "Power Relations and the Built Environment in Colonial Cities". In *Contesting Space in Colonial Singapore: Power Relations and the Urban Built Environment*, 1–27. Singapore: NUS Press, 2013 (1996).

Audio and Video Recordings

16 Carnival Hits: Mighty Sparrow and Lord Kitchener. Ice Records 920902, 1992, compact disc.
Calypso Awakening: From the Emory Cook Collection. Notes by Kenneth Bilby and Keith Warner. Smithsonian Folkways Recordings SFW CD 40453, 2000, compact disc.
Calypso Breakaway, 1927–1941. Notes by Dick Spottswood and Keith Warner. Rounder CD 1054, 1990, compact disc.
Calypso Pioneers, 1912–1937. Notes by Dick Spottswood and Donald Hill. Rounder CD 1039, 1989, compact disc.
Calypsos from Trinidad: Politics, Intrigue and Violence in the 1930s. Notes by Dick Spottswood. Arhoolie/Folklyric CD 7004, 1991, compact disc.
The Mighty Sparrow: First Flight. Notes by Gordon Rohlehr. Smithsonian Folkways SFW CD 40534, 2005, compact disc.
Peter Was a Fisherman: The Trinidad Field Recordings of Melville and Frances Herskovits. Vol. 1. Notes by Donald R. Hill, Maureen Warner-Lewis, John Cowley and Lise Winer. Rounder CD 1114, 1998, compact disc.
Public Spaces: The Architecture of Colin Laird. Produced by Banyan for the Colin Laird Project. 2012, DVD.
West Indian Rhythm: Trinidad Calypsos on World and Local Events, Featuring the Censored Recordings, 1938–1940. Reissue produced by Dick Spottswood and Richard Weize; notes by the Classic Calypso Collective (John Cowley, executive editor). Bear Family Records BCD 16623 JM, 2006, ten compact discs with book.

INDEX

Abell, H.F., 50
Achong, Tito, 158–59, 261
Achoy, Ivy, 146, 396n38
Adams, Aubrey, 348
Adams, Grantley, 294, 298
Agostini, Joseph Leon, 73, 74
Alexander's Ragtime Band (steelband), 277
Alladin, M.P., 300, 307
Allan, Greig, 322
Almond Walk. *See* Broadway
Alston Building, 135
American expansionism (summary of), 3–4
American-Trinidadian relations (World War II), 229–30, 234, 241, 248–63, 271–72, 413nn32–33. *See also* United States military bases in Trinidad
Anglo-American Caribbean Commission. *See* Caribbean Commission
Angostura Bitters Factory, 35, 59
architecture: modern, 134, 311, 316–17, 321–22, 329–30; Trinidadian creole/vernacular, 5, 48–49, 86–87. *See also* types of buildings and names of individual buildings
Arthur Brothers and Company, 333, 335, 352
Aspinall, Algernon, 125
Astor Cinema. *See* London Electric Theatre
Atilla the Hun. *See* Quevedo, Raymond
Attale, Chas. H.A., 388n24
Atteck, Sybil, 300, 307, 346–47, 350

Austin-Broos, Diane, 357–58
automobiles. *See* cars
Awon, Joseph Alwin, 314, 427n7

Bahadoorsingh, Jang, 350
Bailey, George, 300, 347
Barataria, 267–69
barrack yards and housing, 85, 88–91, 154–67 passim, 182, 261; as setting for Carnival band and calypso tents, 192, 206
Beacon group, 162, 169–70, 181, 264
Beckles, Aldwyn, 285
Beetham, Edward, 274, 291, 341
Beetham Highway, 315, 319, 320, 331
Belasco, Lionel, 70, 140, 141, 415n46
Belgrave, Joseph, 195
Belmont, 12, 44, 72–73, 80–86 passim, 154, 316
Bisland, Elizabeth, 69
Black Fauns (Mendes), 163, 166–67
Bodu, Ignacio, 191
Borde, Pierre-Gustave-Louis, 60
borough council, 37, 59, 80, 83, 93, 97
Botanic Gardens, 43, 62, 68–70, 339
Bowen, Edward, 88
Brereton, Bridget, 15, 49, 368
Bridgens, Richard, 55, 334
Bridgetown (Barbados), 293–94, 356, 360–62
Brierley, J.N., 59, 83, 380n15
Brighter Sun, A (Selvon), 264, 265, 267–69

457

Brinsley, Herbert G.W., 124, 135–37, 142–43, 151, 333
British colonialism (summary of), 2–3, 7–8
British West Indies Regiment, 100, 101, 119, 130
Broadway, 51
Broome, Lady, 68, 69–70, 84
Brown, George, 49, 52, 66, 74, 86, 87, 88, 367
Brown, Wenzel, 251
Brown, William F., 138–39, 395nn35–36
Browne, David, 360, 361
Brunswick Square, 12, 53–58; as setting for water protests, 98–99. *See also* Woodford Square
Burkett, Algernon Albert, 37, 157
Butler, Uriah, 120–21, 174, 175, 297
Bynoe, Peter, 300, 312, 352

Calder-Marshall, Arthur, 153–54, 178–84
calypso: early development, 193; 1919–1939, 101, 150, 165, 205–14, 216; 1940s–1960s, 257–60, 301, 302, 306, 308–10, 334; tents (characteristics), 205–8. *See also* steelbands
Capildeo, Rudranath, 274, 275, 292–93, 303, 304
Caribbean Architects-Engineers, 232–33, 235, 236, 242, 263
Caribbean Commission, 288–89, 312
Caribe Hilton (San Juan, Puerto Rico), 343–44, 433n58
Carlsen Field, 241, 272, 293, 298, 412n25
Carnival, 92, 188–89, 307; band tents (characteristics), 192–93; downtown versus Savannah controversy, 197–200; early development, 189–97; festive re-creation of the city, 214–16; masquerades (1919–1939), 197–205; masquerades (1940s–1960s), 280, 347–48. *See also* calypso, steelbands
Carr, Andrew, 72, 284, 291, 347
cars (automobiles), 133, 191, 324, 330–31

Cartar, Lloyd, 332
Casablanca (steelband), 278–81 passim, 285–86
Cascade, 80, 81, 82, 134
Castagne, Pat, 301, 341–42
Cathedral of the Immaculate Conception, 13, 48, 51, 93, 94
central city (defined), 44
Chancellor, John, 127, 128, 198
Chang, Carlisle, 300, 336–37, 338, 339, 347, 350
Chase, Oswald Glean, 322–23, 329
Chase Manhattan Bank, 334
Christie, Trevor, 271–72
Churchill-Roosevelt Highway, 246, 248, 268, 315, 349
Cipriani, A.A., 119–21, 149, 150, 157, 158, 170–74 passim, 391n6; on Carnival, 210; on Roxy Cinema, 144; statue of, 296, 297, 331–32
Citizens for Conservation, 367
city council: 1914–1939, 37, 58, 77, 80, 83, 121, 148–49; 1940–1945, 236, 238, 261; 1950–1962, 313–14, 330–32, 339, 351; silver jubilee (1939), 149–51. *See also* housing, town hall, Trinidad War Memorial
city hall. *See* town hall
Clark, Henry James, 40, 64, 68
Clarke, Colin, 356–57
Clifford, Lady, 261
Cobham, Stephen, 42–44, 380n14
Cocorite, 121, 139
Collens, J.H., 64, 85, 96; career of, 379n7; *Guide to Trinidad*, 39–40, 45, 46, 49, 57–61 passim, 68
Colonial Bank, 49
Colonial Hospital, 39, 61–62
colonialism. *See* British colonialism
Columbus Square, 51, 280–81, 369
Connor, Edric, 126, 245, 260, 284
Conquerabia mural (Chang), 336–37
Constantine, Learie, 296, 315
Corbeaux Town, 12, 59

Corlette, H.C., 394n26
coronations. *See* imperial celebrations
Cosgrove, Denis, 4
Coterie of Social Workers, 161–62
Country Club, 203–4, 250
cricket, 41, 63, 67, 164, 306, 370; C.L.R. James and, 66, 163, 164, 305–6
Cummings, James, 155, 399n3
Custom House, 39, 45–46, 92, 133

De Barros, Juanita, 359–60
de Boissière, Jean, 181, 182, 183
de Boissière, R.A.C., 162, 264, 265–67; *Rum and Coca-Cola*, 264, 265–67
de Leon, Raphael (Roaring Lion), 205–13 passim, 258
De Luxe Theatre, 144–45
de Verteuil, L.A.A., 81
Deane, R.E., 148, 149
Deep Water Harbour Scheme, 146–48
Democratic Labour Party, 274, 292, 304, 305, 332, 340, 366
Diamond Vale, 323–29
Diego Martin, 322–24. *See also* Diamond Vale
Discovery Day, 149, 280–81, 369
Docksite, 233, 234, 235, 236–38, 257, 270–71, 352
Donaldson, John S., Technical Institute, 350, 351–52
Douglas, Chieftain, 207, 208, 209
downtown (map of), xii
Dry River (St Ann's River): diversion of, 11; paving of, 148
Duncan, James, 4
Dwyer, Mary, 242

East Dry River, 71–72, 80–86 passim. *See also* John John, Laventille
Eastern Market, 58–59, 148, 151
electric power, 83–85, 148–49
emancipation celebrations, 15, 171–72, 369
Empire Day, 95–96

Empire Theatre, 141
Eskridge, Walter, 240
Espinet, Charles S., 260, 283, 285

factories, 46, 59, 275, 277, 317
Fahey, Harold Neal, 260
Family Hotel (Ice House), 49, 50, 51, 192
Farquhar, M.E., 283–84, 285
Federal House, 294, 305
Federation Park, 294, 321–22
Fernandez, Lionel, 326
fires: 1808, 11; 1895, 52
Fletcher, Murchison, 159, 176, 177, 204
Fort Read, 229, 233, 241–43, 250, 272. *See also* Waller Field
Francisco, Slinger (Mighty Sparrow), 304, 308–10, 334, 370
François, Elma, 173, 174, 183
Frederick Street, 38–39, 52–53, 58, 92, 179
"French Shores", 58, 190, 206–7, 209
Fridal, Austin, 321
friendly societies, 95, 101, 172, 388n24
Froude, James Anthony, 36
Furness Withy and Company, 334, 339

gardens, 41, 42, 85, 87, 125, 322; city beautification projects, 314; "Grow More Food" campaign, 260–61; Trinidad Hilton Hotel, 344–45. *See also* Botanic Gardens, St Clair Experimental Station
"Gaza Strip", 348, 434–35n66
Georgetown (British Guiana), 312, 356, 359–60
Girod, J., 38, 81
Gittens, Rupert, 173, 182–83
Globe Cinema, 135, 141–43, 256, 286
Glory Dead (Calder-Marshall), 178–84
Goad, Chas. E., 38, 52, 80–81, 86, 357
Gokool Meah, 122, 141–42
Gokool, Nur Mohammed, 141–42, 324
Gomes, Albert, 164–65, 183, 274, 275, 285, 304–5, 343; Beacon group, 162, 164–65; on steelbands, 283

Gonzales Place, 121, 157, 158, 159, 276–77, 284
Gordon Grant Building, 333
Government House, 62, 68–70, 93–94, 294, 300, 384n58; as National Museum and Art Gallery, 303
Green Corner, 256–57, 278
Grimes, John, 318, 319–20
Grinnell, Robert, 262, 263

Hahn, Daniel Meinerts, 55, 65–66, 382n35, 383n51
Haji Gokool Meah Masjid, 122
Heap, Desmond, 313
Hell Yard, 277, 279
"Her Chinaman's Way" (Mendes), 166
Herskovits, Melville and Frances, 154, 178, 184–87
Hill, Errol, 207, 302, 419n6
Hill, Robert T., 41
Hilton, Conrad, 343, 347, 348–49
Hilton Hotel. *See* Trinidad Hilton Hotel
Holder, Geoffrey, 347, 350
Holland and Hannen and Cubitts (Trinidad), 344, 352
Holy Trinity Cathedral, 54, 95
Homes International, 324–28
Hosay, 76–77, 122–23, 273, 360, 385–86n70
Hotel de Paris, 49, 50, 202–3, 266, 406n24
hotels, 49–51, 349. *See also* Family Hotel, Hotel de Paris, Macqueripe Hotel, Queen's Park Hotel, Trinidad Hilton Hotel
House for Mr Biswas, A (Naipaul), 424n51
housing, 85–91, 154–61, 182, 261–64, 316–29; Boissière house, 88; Boos house, 87–88; Knowsley, 88; Maraval Road houses, 74; post–World War II elite houses, 321–23. *See also* barrack yards and housing
Huggins, George F., and Company, 135

Hume, C., 144
Humphrey, William P., 144
Hutchinson, William, 50
Huxley, Aldous, 163

Ibrahim, Mohammed, 391–92n9
Ice House. *See* Family Hotel
imperial celebrations, 92–96, 100–101; 1953 Coronation Carnival, 281–82
Imperial College of Tropical Agriculture, 314, 366, 394n26
independence celebrations: committee, 300; events, 299, 301–4; plans, 299–301
Independence Square, 297, 332–34. *See also* Marine Square
Industrial Development Corporation (IDC), 343–48 passim
infrastructure. *See* Dry River, electric power, port, streets, water supply and drainage
Institute for the Blind (as US Army facility), 235, 236
Invader, Lord, 213, 258, 415n46
Invaders (steelband), 278, 281, 285

Jackson, Henry, 56
Jackson, T.B., 66–67
Jacobs, Carl, 315–16, 321
Jama Masjid, 391–92n9
James, C.L.R., 1, 66, 162–65, 288, 304, 305–6; on Derek Walcott, 308; on Mighty Sparrow, 308; *Minty Alley*, 164, 167–69; "Triumph", 165; on V.S. Naipaul, 424n51
James, Preston, 390n2
jamettes, 189–91
Jeffers, Audrey, 161–62, 174
Jerningham, Hubert, 37, 92–93, 405n9
John John, 154, 162, 262, 277
Johnson, Robert A., 231, 235
Johnston, Gaston, 130, 131, 159
Johnstone, May, 286, 338–39, 341
Jones, Brunell, 333

Jones, Charles, 193, 194

Karch, Celia, 360–61
Kaufman, Alfonse, 251–52
Kayanan, A.C., 324
Kent House, 288
King, W.A., 135, 142
King George V Park, 238, 263, 271, 339, 438n17. *See also* St Clair Cantonment
Kingsley, Charles, 13, 178
Kingston (Jamaica), 293, 356–58
Kumar, Ranjit, 147–48, 397–98n46, 433n59

La Corbiniere, C., 331–32
Lady Young Road, 246, 315–16, 319, 345
Laird, Colin, 322, 329–30, 339–40
landscape: concept of, 1–2, 5–7, 16–17, 354–55, 365, 370; scholarship on, 4–5
Lapeyrouse Cemetery, 60
Laventille, 12, 71–72, 80, 85, 135; Orisha yard at, 178, 185–87; US Army base at, 240
Lazare, Emmanuel Mzumbo, 97, 98–99, 198
Leigh Fermor, Patrick, 279
Lewis, Anthony, 263–64, 321–22, 330, 334, 429n20
Lewis, Brian, 334
Lewis, Peirce, 4
Lion, Roaring. *See* de Leon, Raphael
Little Carib Theatre, 285, 291, 302, 308
local empowerment (summary of), 3, 7–8
Lockhart, David, 68
London Electric Theatre, 119, 140–41
Lord Harris Square, 61, 369–70
Lourenco, Ferdinand, 335
L'Ouverture Club, 182–83
Lunde, Frithjof, 344

MacLean, Geoffrey, 334
Macleod, Iain, 298, 299
Macqueripe Hotel, 243, 395n36

Mahabir, Dennis, 304, 313, 331, 335
Mahabir, Winston, 295
Mann, James O., 240
Maracas Bay, 246–47
Maraj, Bhadase, 274, 351
Maraval, 80, 81, 134, 305
Maresse-Smith, Edgar, 37, 97
Marine Square, 48–51, 123–24, 135–36, 315, 330–34; Carnival competitions, 191, 194, 199, 200, 202; early development, 12; statue of A.A. Cipriani, 297, 331–32
Marshall, Woodville, 360, 361–62
Masson, G.H., 89–90, 157
Mavrogordato, Olga, 67
May Day celebrations, 170–71
McBurnie, Beryl, 283, 284–85, 291, 302, 339
Meinig, D.W., 4
Mence and Moore, 321–22, 333, 334, 351, 428n19
Mendes, Alfred, 162–65, 169, 181, 208, 332; *Black Fauns*, 163, 166–67; father's store and house, 51, 61; "Her Chinaman's Way", 166; on Olympic Theatre, 141; *Pitch Lake*, 163, 168–69; "Sweetman", 165–66
Merchants and Planters' Contingent, 130, 162
Metro Cinema. *See* Globe Cinema
Metro-Goldwyn-Mayer (MGM), 141–44 passim
Miguel Street (Naipaul), 265, 269–71
Minshall, Wilson, 125
Minty Alley (James), 164, 167–69
Mittelholzer, Edgar, 181–82, 256–57, 285, 431n38
Montano, Gerard, 317, 320, 324, 325
Morin, Felix, 38–40, 53
Morris, Ken, 307, 347
Morvant, 160, 262–63, 318–19
movie theatre industry, 140–46, 396n38, 397n44. *See also* names of individual theatres

Mucurapo, 10, 80, 121; US Army base and USO No. 2 at, 240–41
Myrtle Bank Hotel (Kingston, Jamaica), 357, 358

Naipaul, V.S., 1, 264–65, 269–71, 304, 306–7; *A House for Mr Biswas*, 424n51; meeting with Derek Walcott, 308; *The Middle Passage*, 306–7; *Miguel Street*, 265, 269–71
Nankivell, Howard, 159, 173, 176, 177
Nassau (Bahamas), 356, 362–64
National Trust of Trinidad and Tobago, 367
Neal and Massy Engineering Company garage, 135
Negro Welfare Cultural and Social Association (NWCSA), 173–74, 175, 183, 264, 361
Neptune, Harvey, 255
New Town, 12, 75, 80, 86, 206, 277
Newbold, John, 97, 98
Newel Lewis, John, 300, 322, 330, 351; on architectural history, 52, 74, 86, 87, 88
nightclubs, 256–57, 309–10, 333–34, 381n26, 426n56, 434–35n66
North Coast Road, 246–47
Northcote, Sidney, 286, 338

Oakley, Amy, 139
Ober, Frederick A., 41
Ogden, David A.D., 232–35 passim, 238
O'Halloran, John, 347, 348
Olympic Theatre, 141, 145
Orisha religion, 178, 184–87, 276, 403n45
Ottley, Carlton, 85, 283
Oxaal, Ivar, 290–91

Paget, J., 40–41, 75
Palmer, Annette, 241, 272
Pan American Airways, 139–40, 362
parks. *See* King George V Park, Queen's Park Savannah

Paschim Kaashi Hindu Mandir, 350–51
Payne, Clement, 183, 361–62
People's Democratic Party, 274. *See also* Democratic Labour Party
People's National Movement (party and government), 274, 287–99, 305–6, 309, 310; town planning and housing projects, 311–13, 317–20, 323–28. *See also* town hall (1961), Queen's Hall, Trinidad Hilton Hotel, John S. Donaldson Technical Institute, Trinidad and Tobago Television House
performances (concept of), 5–6, 92, 215
Peru Village. *See* St James
Phipps, Eric, 314, 315
Piarco Airport, 139, 234, 349, 365
Pierre, Donald, 303, 352
Pitch Lake (Mendes), 163, 168–69
"Plannings, the", 264, 318
Pointer, Joseph, 65
Police Barracks, 56–57
port, 45–47, 146–48, 236–37
Port of Spain: city boundaries, 79–81, 121–22; climate, 374n3; early development, 10–13; population statistics, 44–45, 121, 249, 376n8, 380n16, 426n1; post-independence, 365–71; scholarship on, 15–16; social classes and ethnic groups, 9, 13–14
Portuguese Club, 255–56
Prada, Enrique, 74, 127, 149, 151
Prince's Building, 64–65, 89, 119, 204, 256, 334
Princess Margaret, 335
Princess Royal (Mary), 301, 302, 303, 352
Prior, Alfred, 335
Prior, Lourenco and Nothnagel, 321, 334, 335–36
Procope, Bruce, 194, 200–201
progress (concept of), 8, 367
protests: 1919, 101–4, 390n38; 1933–1937, 172–78, 391n6; march for Chaguaramas, 295–98; Water Riot, 55, 96–100, 388–89n27

public buildings. *See* names of individual buildings
public library, 57, 288
public performances. *See* performances

Queen's Hall, 302, 338–43
Queen's Park Hotel, 66–68, 137–38, 192, 349; 1938 addition, 138–40
Queen's Park Savannah, 17, 41, 42, 43, 62–71, 74; Carnival competitions, 197–200, 203–5, 215; Civil Defence Rally, 252–53; tram service, 85. *See also* imperial celebrations, independence celebrations, protests
Queen's Royal College, 65–66, 164, 288
Queen's Wharf, 45–46, 132
Quevedo, Raymond (Atilla the Hun), 205–13 passim, 258, 259, 407n30

Rada compound (Belmont), 72–73, 418n5
railway. *See* Trinidad Railway
Rapsey (US military base), 240
Ratepayers' Association, 37, 97–99
Raymond, Arthur, 198
Raymond, Mark, 321
Red House, 55–56, 302–3. *See also* Water Riot
Reddock, Rhoda, 173
Reid Jr, A. Elwell, 254, 258
Reinagle, Philip, 48, 54
Renwick, David, 341
representations (concept of), 6
Richards, Alfred, 65, 125, 158, 159, 176, 198
Rienzi, Adrian Cola, 120–21, 231
Rohlehr, Gordon, 309
Roodal, Timothy, 143, 144, 145
Roosevelt, Eleanor, 241, 244–45
Roosevelt, Franklin D., 214, 272
Rosenthal, George, 133, 141
Roslyn, Louis Frederick, 128–29, 393n19
Rowe, Sally Osmon, 254
Roxy Cinema, 144

Royal Gaol, 61
Royal Victoria Institute. *See* Victoria Institute
Rum and Coca-Cola (de Boissière), 264, 265–67
Rupert Gray (Cobham), 42–44, 380n14
Rutter, Owen, 125, 138, 208
Ryan, Selwyn, 120, 290

Sa Gomes, Eduardo, 214
Saint-Gaudens, Homer, 242–43
Salvatori Building, 333–34
Saunders, Gail, 363–64
Scott, T.H., 122, 128, 148, 151, 158, 398n52
Sellier, L.F., 38–39, 64
Selvon, Samuel, 264, 265; *A Brighter Sun*, 264, 265, 267–69; "Wartime Activities", 417n55
Shango religion. *See* Orisha religion
Shanty Town, 319–20
Shoultz Jr, James C., 250–51, 256
Siegert family, 59, 60, 75, 79
Singh, Boysie, 257, 414n43
socio-spatial order (concept of), 2, 6–7, 77, 104–5, 354
Socoven, 344
Solomon, Patrick, 295, 297, 340–41
Sparrow, Mighty. *See* Francisco, Slinger
squares. *See* Brunswick Square, Columbus Square, Independence Square, Lord Harris Square, Marine Square, Victoria Square, Woodford Square
St Ann's, 73–74, 80, 81, 134, 206, 256
St Ann's River. *See* Dry River
St Clair, 38, 74, 80, 81, 82. *See also* St Clair Cantonment
St Clair Cantonment, 238–40, 271
St Clair Experimental Station, 74–75, 121
St James, 76–77, 80, 81, 88, 121–23, 316; government housing project, 262; Paschim Kaashi Hindu Mandir, 350–51
St Joseph, 10, 11
St Joseph's Convent, 61

St Mary's College, 61, 133–34
St Vincent Wharf, 45–46, 51
Stark, James, 52–53, 362
Starr, Ida M.H., 41
steelbands, 276–87, 296, 301, 307, 423n45; panyards (locations and characteristics), 278–79, 419n6
Stewart, James, Associates, 243–47 passim, 250
stores (retail), 13, 48–49, 52–53, 179
streets: cleaning, 83, 164, 176, 314; layout and construction, 44, 80–81, 122, 148; 326. *See also* names of individual roads and highways
Stresau, Frederic, 344–45
"Sweetman" (Mendes), 165–66

Taylor, Edward, 313, 337
Taylor and Gillies, 74, 86, 88
Teachers' Economic and Cultural Association (TECA), 288–91 passim
Teelucksingh, Sarran, 145–46
Television House. *See* Trinidad and Tobago Television House
Teshea, Isabel, 295, 297
Thomas, J.J., 36
Thompson, Krista, 358, 362–63
Toro, Ferrer and Torregrosa, 344
tourism, 50, 124–25, 196, 204–5, 343, 349
Town and Country Planning Ordinance (1960), 313
Town and Regional Planning Ordinance (1938), 124, 160, 312, 392n11
town board (1907–1914), 37, 57, 65, 75, 80
town hall, 57–58; 1961 building, 334–38
town planning, 123–24, 147, 160, 262–64, 311–16, 317–19, 392n11
trams, 84–85, 133, 149, 387n8
Tranquillity neighborhood, 38, 61
Treasury Building, 136–37, 175, 176
Treves, Frederick, 41–42, 72
Trinidad: economy and politics (1880s–1910s), 34–37; economy and politics (1920s–1930s), 117–21; economy and politics (1940s–1960s), 273–75; historical narratives, 368–70; landscapes, 9, 390n2. *See also* American-Trinidadian relations (World War II), United States military bases in Trinidad
Trinidad and Tobago Society of Architects, 312
Trinidad and Tobago Television House, 350, 352–53
Trinidad Art Society, 307, 346
Trinidad Hilton Hotel, 343–50, 435n68
Trinidad Labour Party, 120, 174
Trinidad Music Association, 284, 286, 338
Trinidad Railway, 43, 45, 133, 250; 1924 headquarters building, 132–33
Trinidad Theatre Workshop, 308
Trinidad War Memorial, 127–32, 392–93n17, 393n19
Trinidad Workingman's Association (TWA), 37, 65, 100–103 passim, 119–20, 170–73
Trinity Cathedral. *See* Holy Trinity Cathedral
"Triumph" (James), 165
Trollope, Anthony, 12–13
Trotman, David V., 73–74, 369–70, 403n45
Tuan, Yi-Fu, 4
Tucker, Louis, 143, 396n41
Turnbull, Stewart and Company, 49, 52, 86
Turner, Victor, 375n5

Union Club, 49
United Services Organization (USO): main club, 237–38, 254–58 passim, 410–11n13; USO No. 2, 240–41, 255
United States Engineer Department (USED), 232–36 passim, 251
United States military bases in Trinidad: agreement with Britain, 230–32, 293–94, 298; general characteristics,

229–34, 247–49, 271–72; peak troop strength, 235–36; strategic significance, 230–31. See also Docksite, Carlsen Field, Fort Read, Institute for the Blind, Laventille, Mucurapo, Rapsey, St Clair Cantonment, United States Naval Operating Base, Whitehall
United States Naval Operating Base (Chaguaramas), 229, 243–45, 272, 293–99
United States Navy Construction Battalion ("Seabees"), 243–46, 412n25
University College of the West Indies (St Augustine), 298, 314, 366
University of Woodford Square, 289–93, 295–98
uptown (defined), 60–61
urbanization (Caribbean), 8–9; 356–65

Vandercook, John, 138, 209
VE and VJ Days, 276, 280
Verrill, A. Hyatt, 42, 53, 63, 125
Victoria Institute, 64, 126, 286, 383–84n51
Victoria Square, 38, 59–60

Walcott, Derek, 1, 304, 307–8, 342; on ideal Caribbean city, 9; meeting with V.S. Naipaul, 308; on Oswald Glean Chase house, 323
Walke, Olive, 302, 341, 348
Walker, R.B., 124, 147, 160, 392n11
Waller Field, 242, 293, 298, 412n25
Walsh-Driscoll Construction Company, 232–34, 237, 239, 242, 247, 250, 251
War Memorial. See Trinidad War Memorial
warehouses, 46, 48–49, 51, 133
Warner, Charles, Jr, 344, 346
Warner, Burns, Toan and Lunde, 344
"Wartime Activities" (Selvon), 417n55
Water Riot, 55, 96–100, 388–89n27
water supply and drainage, 81–83, 96–100, 148

Watkins and Partners, 333, 339, 344, 352, 416n51
Waugh, Alec, 137–38
West Indies Federation, 274–75, 292–99 passim, 305, 421n32
West Indies Festival of the Arts, 300, 307
Wharton, Annabel Jane, 343–44
Whitehall: as cultural center, 282, 285–86; as private residence, 74; as US Army headquarters, 234–35
Wilcox, Ella Wheeler, 67
Williams, Eric, 1, 274, 275, 287–93, 305, 370; on A.A. Cipriani, 331–32; Chaguaramas issue and march, 293–99; and C.L.R. James, 288, 305–6; independence celebrations, 301–3; and the Little Carib, 285; and Mighty Sparrow, 309; town hall opening, 337; town planning and housing, 313, 324–25; and V.S. Naipaul, 306
Women's Voluntary Services, 252, 260–61
Woodbrook, 38, 44, 75–76, 80–82 passim, 86, 154, 316; Growler's "History of Woodbrook", 211; high-rise buildings in, 367; loss of sea coast after land reclamation, 147; V.S. Naipaul's *Miguel Street*, 269
Woodford, Ralph, 12, 48, 54, 55, 62, 337
Woodford Square, 55, 337–38, 353, 366, 370; as setting for meetings and protests (1919–1938), 102, 103, 119, 157, 170–74 passim, 183; as setting for PNM meetings, 289–93, 295–98. See also Brunswick Square
Woolford, James, 331
Wrightson, Walsh, 97–98
Wrightson Road, 147–48, 257, 331
WVDI (US military radio station), 239, 252
Wyke, Marguerite, 300

Young, Hubert, 231, 235, 238, 297, 344